In this path-breaking study, Jonathan Scott argues that seventeenth-century English history was shaped by three processes. The first was destructive: that experience of political instability which contemporaries called 'our troubles'. The second was creative: its spectacular intellectual consequence in the English revolution. The third was reconstructive: the long restoration voyage toward safe haven from these terrifying storms.

Driving the troubles were fears and passions animated by European religious and political developments. The result registered the impact upon fragile institutions of powerful beliefs. One feature of this analysis is its relationship of the history of events to that of ideas. Another is its consideration of these processes across the century as a whole. The most important is its restoration of this extraordinary English experience to its European context.

JONATHAN SCOTT is Fellow and Director of Studies in History, Downing College, Cambridge. His previous publications include *Algernon Sidney and the English Republic 1623–1677* (1988) and *Algernon Sidney and the Restoration Crisis 1677–1683* (1991), both published by Cambridge University Press.

England's troubles

*Seventeenth-century English political
instability in European context*

JONATHAN SCOTT

CAMBRIDGE
UNIVERSITY PRESS

PUBLISHED BY THE PRESS SYNDICATE OF THE UNIVERSITY OF CAMBRIDGE
The Pitt Building, Trumpington Street, Cambridge, United Kingdom

CAMBRIDGE UNIVERSITY PRESS
The Edinburgh Building, Cambridge CB2 2RU, UK   http://www.cup.cam.ac.uk
40 West 20th Street, New York, NY 10011–4211, USA   http://www.cup.org
10 Stamford Road, Oakleigh, Melbourne 3166, Australia
Ruiz de Alarcón 13, 28014 Madrid, Spain

First published 2000

Printed in the United Kingdom at the University Press, Cambridge

Typeface 10.5/13.5pt Adobe Minion   *System* QuarkXPress™   [SE]

A catalogue record for this book is available from the British Library

Library of Congress Cataloguing in Publication data
Scott, Jonathan, 1958–
England's troubles : seventeenth-century English political instability
in European context / Jonathan Scott.
p.   cm.
Includes bibliographical references.
ISBN 0 521 41192 0 (hb). – ISBN 0 521 42334 1 (pb)
1. Great Britain – Politics and government – 1603–1714.   2. Great
Britain – Politics and government – 1642–1660.   3. England –
Civilisation – European influences.   4. Great Britain – Foreign
relations – Europe.   5. Europe – Foreign relations – Great Britain.
6. England – Civilisation – 17th century.   I. Title.
DA375.S39   2000
941.06 – dc21   99-38436 CIP

ISBN 0 521 41192 0 hardback
ISBN 0 521 42334 1 paperback

They are the troublers . . . the dividers of unity.

John Milton, *Areopagitica* (1644)[1]

Of any such work as compiling the history of our political troubles I
have no thought whatsoever: they are worthier of silence than of
commemoration.

John Milton to Henry Oldenberg (December 1659)[2]

1 John Milton, *Milton's Areopagitica* [1644], ed. H. B. Cotterill (London 1949), p. 38.
2 In John Milton, *Complete Prose Works*, ed. D. M. Wolfe et al. (8 vols., New Haven 1953–82),
vol. VI, p. xlii.

Contents

Preface

> A writer of history ought, in his writings, to be a foreigner, without country . . . subject to no king, nor caring what any man will like or dislike.
>
> Lucian, *How a history ought to be written*[3]

For Lucian, the imaginative republic of history entailed freedom from subjection, in time and space. All history entails the imagination of experience – of a country – other than our own. A book devoted to the recovery and contextualisation of seventeenth-century English perspectives might usefully begin with an acknowledgement of this author's own.

This study is, first, one product of slightly over a decade spent at the University of Cambridge. My greatest debt in this context is to John Morrill, who has enabled me not only to agree with his conception of our subject, but also to disagree. I am indebted to, and have never taken for granted, the preparedness of Cambridge to take in and reward foreigners, even for asking questions about the story English people tell themselves about their past. Meanwhile it was not in Cambridge that I became a historian. This was the result of an earlier education, incorporating several subjects, at Victoria University of Wellington, New Zealand.

Many of the key influences there – Miles Fairburn, Peter Munz, Lucie Halberstam and Colin Davis – were foreigners in my own country, well accustomed to the imagination of otherness. To them, for better or worse, and despite subsequent training to the contrary, I owe much of my tendency to think generally. My greatest debt in this context is to Colin Davis, who first showed me what history is, while at the same time introducing me to that of seventeenth-century England. Thus more broadly this book is a

---

3 Quoted in Hobbes, *Of the Life and History of Thucydides* (1628), in *Hobbes' Thucydides*, ed. R. B. Schlatter (New Brunswick, N. J. 1975), p. 22.

ix

product of that expatriate condition well known to my wandering fellow New Zealanders.[4] If it is not only about, but also written in, a country other than my own, this situation has had its advantages and disadvantages.

'Fog in the Channel', runs the famous headline, 'continent cut off'. For the student arriving from the other side of the world this perspective upon British maritime geography can be hard to acquire. What has equally affected this author's perspective upon seventeenth-century English history is his failure to encounter it at all before postgraduate level. This book is the general picture that it has been necessary to piece together in the absence of any such inherited account. One disadvantage of this situation has been my own enduring relative ignorance. An advantage, however, has been the making of this construction as an adult, and its exposure to the criticism of colleagues and friends.

A correspondingly powerful influence in the process has been Algernon Sidney (1623–83). The life of a person is not an adequate window on to the life of a century. Yet the most important defence of historical biography at doctoral level is as one of the most effective ways to require students to connect subsections of the discipline now more usually kept apart. The attempt to come to grips with Sidney, to which I was unequal, required attempts to bridge intellectual and political history, the history of England and that of other parts of Europe, ancient and early modern, and the experience of pre- and post-restoration England. These challenges established the intellectual contexts for the present project.

The result is not a history of seventeenth-century England, in the sense that it claims to have comprehended the range of contemporary experience. It is the more limited attempted recovery of three intertwined seventeenth-century processes. These can help us to contextualise, and so to understand, contemporary perceptions that have been easier to ridicule than to explain. Although necessarily selective, this recovery has focused upon those perceptions most important to larger-scale explanation. The reader who warmly applauded the attention paid to the difficulties faced by Charles I, while decrying the equally serious attention given to the views of those who considered his policies dangerous, remained to be persuaded by this method.

The resulting three-part structure, which is analytical first and chronological only second, makes some demands upon the reader. These

4 John Mulgan, *Report on Experience* (Oxford 1947), pp. 1–8.

may be partially compensated for by the recovery of aspects of contemporary explanation the clarity of which has been unnecessarily obscured. It is not the purpose of this book, however, simply to replace one story with another. It is to encourage us, by the recovery of contemporary perspectives, to question our authorities, and ourselves. More specifically this study has three ambitions. The first is to adequately contextualise restoration history. The second is to offer a revised understanding of the English revolution. The third is to recover the European context of the seventeenth-century English experience as a whole.

It is customary to place acknowledgements to one's spouse last. For her support for this project my obligation to Anne comes first. This would have been so even had our daughter not arrived a year before its completion. Thereafter every hour spent on this book was an hour spent by Anne with Sophia (or Sophia's laundry). It is dedicated to her, with gratitude and love. The manuscript of this book was posted to eight colleagues, in five different countries: Glenn Burgess, Colin Davis, Richard Greaves, Mark Kishlansky, John Morrill, John Morrow, Markku Peltonen and John Reeve. Though it had seemed like a good idea at the time, it did eventually dawn upon me that this was an assault upon the profession at large out of proportion to the value of the project. To receive any one of the resulting responses, several of article-quality and length, would have been an enormous privilege. To have received all of them has been humbling.

I am indebted to earlier audiences who did much to shape this argument. The first invitation to speak on this subject came from Ronald Hutton and the second from Jonathan Clark. To Nancy Maguire I owe the memorable opportunity to try again subsequently at Amherst, Massachusetts. I am especially beholden to those students at the University of Cambridge, both undergraduate and graduate, for whom the book was elaborated as a series of lectures between 1994 and 1999. I have learned an enormous amount from the wider community of research students at Cambridge, both under my supervision and otherwise. I have learned as much from friends and colleagues, in particular Patrick Collinson, Adrian Johns, Mike Braddick, Mark Greengrass, Germaine Greer, Quentin Skinner, Mark Goldie, Chris Clark, Istvan Hont, Hans Blom, David Smith and Alan Cromartie.

Since 1991 I have been employed not by the Faculty of History at Cambridge, but by Downing College. It is thus the Masters and Fellows of that beautiful college who have made the writing of this book possible. Within Downing my particular, though not only, debt has been to my history colleagues Paul Millett and Richard Smith, upon whose friendship and generosity I have so relied. The completion of this study was delayed by the writing of another book about my father, my country and my own experience, published in Wellington in 1997.[5] Although the timing of this was inconvenient, there is no convenient time to attempt substantial work outside one's professional field. I wish accordingly to record my profound gratitude to those whose support made possible a project from which I learned so much. In addition to those thanked in that preface, these include Bill Oliver and Peter Munz, the readers for Victoria University of Wellington Press, and Bill Davies, of Cambridge University Press, who bore the delay of *England's Troubles* with admirable but not inexhaustible fortitude. I wish finally to express my deep appreciation to the Humanities Research Board of the British Academy. It was their award of an extra term of leave in 1998–9 that allowed me to bring this to completion.

5 Jonathan Scott, *Harry's Absence: Looking for My Father on the Mountain* (Wellington 1997; Sag Harbor, N.Y. 2000).

Introduction: experience other than our own

Once more I come before the public with a work on the history of a
nation which is not mine by birth.

Leopold von Ranke, *History of England* (1875)[1]

As a foreigner, coming to the history of . . . Spain [from] . . . that of
other West European societies, I was frequently struck by the extent to
which . . . phenomena . . . assumed . . . to be . . . Spanish . . . could be
found [elsewhere].

J. H. Elliott, *National and Comparative History* (1991)[2]

ALL HISTORY RESTS UPON ANALYTICAL ASSUMPTIONS, WHETHER OR NOT THEY ARE MADE EXPLICIT

That the seventeenth-century English political experience was spectacular
and remarkable may not require emphasis, either to historians or to general
readers. A recent account begins accordingly by listing some of its extraordinary features. It then concludes: 'No history can account for such dazzling
achievements. It is perhaps as well to gaze upon so bright a firmament
rather than to try to measure the gaseous compounds of each star.'[3] Thus
did Lord Brooke write in *The Nature of Truth* (1640) of 'leaving the search
for causes to those who are content, with Icarus, to burn their wings at a fire
too hot for them'.[4]

There are few historians, particularly of the seventeenth century, who will

---

1 Leopold von Ranke, *A History of England Principally in the Seventeenth Century* (6 vols.,
Oxford 1875), vol. I, p. v.
2 J. H. Elliott, *National and Comparative History* (Oxford 1991), pp. 19–20.
3 Mark Kishlansky, *A Monarchy Transformed: Britain 1603–1714* (London 1996), p. 5.
4 Lord Brooke, *The Nature of Truth, its Union and Unity with the Soule* (1640), quoted in
William Haller, *The Rise of Puritanism* (New York 1938), p. 335.

1

not respect the prudence of this stance. We cannot account for everything, or anything with finality. Explanation presupposes an informed understanding of what it is we are attempting to explain. Moreover, explanation isn't everything. One of the most important features of history is its capacity to tell a story. History is a story, indeed, not because that is how it occurred, but because that is what historians make of it. History is not the record of past experience, but the imaginative reconstruction of that experience as a story.[5]

One of the most effective ways of telling this is by narrative. Yet still the narrative story is made: it owes its existence to the analytical assumptions which have governed particular selection (of 'events') and therefore general shape. Readers could be forgiven for not always realising this, or its implications, since historians sometimes write as if it were not the case. It is not always necessary, particularly for an introductory audience, for a historian to expose these analytical assumptions. It is necessary, however, that they be capable of exposing and if necessary defending them; that we take this level of responsibility for our imaginative creations. 'The deepest instinct of the human mind', explained F. M. Cornford, 'is to shape the chaotic world and the illimitable stream of events into some intelligible form which it can hold before itself and take in at one survey.'[6] The apparent contrary belief that narrative is capable of constructing itself prior to analysis is a curious feature of recent historiography to which we will return.[7]

This book tells its story by a combination of analysis and narrative, in that order. One purpose of this is to expose its governing assumptions for critical examination. In particular this account makes explicit what are taken to be the central processes at work and the shape they give the story as a whole. The other purpose of this structure is, however, to give priority to the task of explanation. In the old-fashioned words of Samuel Gardiner: 'It seemed to me that it was the duty of a serious inquirer to search into the original cause of great events.'[8]

---

5 Peter Munz, *The Shapes of Time: A New Look at the Philosophy of History* (Middletown, Conn. 1977).

6 F. M. Cornford, *Thucydides Mythhistoricus* (London 1907), p. 249.

7 Conrad Russell, *The Causes of the English Civil War* (Oxford 1990), p. ix: 'My order of researching, and of writing, has been to compose a three-kingdom narrative of events . . . and only then, when I had decided what I needed to explain, to consider *The Causes of the English Civil War*.' The narrative is Russell, *The Fall of the British Monarchies 1637–1642* (Oxford 1991), see p. vii.

8 Quoted in J. H. Hexter, 'The Early Stuarts and Parliament: Old Hat and the *Nouvelle Vague*', *Parliamentary History* 1, 1 (1982), p. 182.

Until recently it was a consequence of revisionism that there were few accounts of the century as a whole.[9] Now what remain relatively rare are such accounts which are explanatory and analytical. This is partly because so much modern 'explanation' has been exposed as teleology. Yet the explanatory analysis pre-dates modernity as the characteristic response of seventeenth-century people themselves to their troubles. When, towards the end of the century, Richard Baxter composed a *Narrative of the most Memorable Passages of his Life and Times*, he explained:

it is my purpose here, not to write a full History of the Calamities and Wars of those Times, but only to remember such Generals with the Reasons and Connexion of Things, as may best make the state of those Times understood by them that knew it not personally themselves.[10]

This study shares Baxter's focus upon 'Generals with the Reasons and Connexion of Things'. The author is correspondingly conscious of what has been left out. In addition, the more general the argument, the greater the scope for particular exception. This book has been written not in the belief that these difficulties may be transcended, but that they are a price well worth paying for a return to the business of large-scale explanatory analysis. Every advance in our specific knowledge makes general analysis more difficult. Yet at the same time it makes it more necessary, for the accumulation of specific 'evidence' is no more important, or interesting, than the questions upon which it is being brought to bear.[11]

A second feature of this book shared with Baxter's is its focus upon contemporary perceptions. This follows from two other presently unfashionable assumptions: that by and large contemporaries understood their situation and knew what they were talking about; and that such perceptions are themselves historical phenomena requiring explanation. Nothing is more ubiquitous in modern histories of the century than the use of the

---

9 The important exception was Barry Coward, *The Stuart Age: England 1603–1714* (2nd edn, London 1994). Now see most recently David Smith, *A History of the Modern British Isles 1603–1707: The Double Crown* (Oxford 1998).

10 Richard Baxter, *Reliquiae Baxterianae: or Mr Richard Baxter's Narrative of the most Memorable Passages of his Life and Times* (London 1696), p. 30.

11 Other recent proponents of this view include David Cannadine, 'British History: Past, Present – and Future?', *Past and Present* 116 (August 1987); Elliott, *National and Comparative History*.

word 'hysteria' to describe contemporary beliefs that were enduringly and widely held.[12] This is not only the case in relation to those religious fears which were the most important motors of the troubles. When Charles I expressed the view from the outset of his reign that there was a conspiracy against the government of monarchy in England, most historians have ascribed this to royal 'paranoia' rather than to the circumstances of his time. This condescension readily communicates itself to students, who explain that the troubles followed from failures both of communication and of understanding. However, that civil war is a tragedy does not necessarily make it an accident.

This book begins from the proposition that we need to take contemporary beliefs seriously. We need to identify them, and then to recover the contexts necessary to explain them. To do this is to discover that it is not contemporaries who have failed to understand their situation but ourselves. This has been partly a result of modern imaginative displacement. It has more specifically reflected our failure to recover the contexts of contemporary perceptions, in time and space. That fear of popery which increased over the seventeenth century is understandable only within the European context of contemporary perceptions: it is modern historians who have been imprisoned by the anachronistic parameters of national historiography. The perception that there was a conspiracy against monarchical government in England was held by every seventeenth-century English monarch, not one. Even the unique utterances of Abiezer Coppe have an explanatory context that transcends centuries, and national boundaries. All of these contexts were understood by contemporaries.

Our starting point is, therefore, in a recognition of the 'otherness' of seventeenth-century England. They did things differently there. Attention will be drawn secondly to the need to understand the century as a whole, and so the restoration period, for instance, not as the beginning of a 'long eighteenth century', but as the second half of the seventeenth century, and a second half peculiarly in the grip of the first. Finally, emphasis will be placed upon the need to understand this subject in its European context, both as

---

12 Jonathan Scott, 'England's Troubles: Exhuming the Popish Plot', in Tim Harris, Paul Seaward and Mark Goldie (eds.), *The Politics of Religion in Restoration England* (Oxford 1990); J. F. Bosher, 'The Franco-Catholic Danger 1660–1715', *History* 79, 255 (February 1994).

the particular English experience of wider European processes, and in terms of England's relationship to other European states.[13]

THE SHAPE OF THE ANALYSIS: THREE PROCESSES

The outline analysis that follows is developed in the next chapter and furnishes the structure of the rest of the book. In it the political and intellectual history of seventeenth-century England is considered as the interaction of three processes. All had European contexts and all connected the first and second halves of the century. The first of these was destructive, the second innovatory or creative, and the third reconstructive.

In the first we are examining the impact upon fragile institutions of powerful beliefs. The three phases of the troubles were those three crises which historians have disparately called the causes of the English civil war, the exclusion crisis and the glorious revolution. In fact all three had similar causes and together they formed a connected sequence of instability. This had a series of contexts, connected to both European processes and events. Early Stuart English political and religious institutions were relatively unreformed and undifferentiated. The polarising pressures to which they were subjected were those associated with the European processes of statebuilding, reformation and counter-reformation. In their most destabilising form these arrived in Stuart England through central Europe in 1618. The troubles by which Charles I's monarchy would be overwhelmed were given their immediate force by the Thirty Years War.

Caroline statebuilding was a response to this context. It was a politically coherent, ideologically focused counter-reformation phenomenon. It was most specifically an attempt to counter the damage done to obedience to monarchy in England by (recently animated, supra-national) reformation religion. It entailed what was the first-attempted seventeenth-century governmental reformation of manners, to which the better-known second, an aspect of the radical reformation of mid-century, was in part a reaction. Those of Charles' opponents who believed that they were engaged in a struggle for the survival of protestantism, not only in Scotland, England

13 John Reeve, 'Britain or Europe? The Context of Early Modern English History: Political and Cultural, Economic and Social, Naval and Military', in Glenn Burgess (ed.), *The New British History* (London 1999).

and Ireland but therefore ultimately in western Europe, may in their own terms have been correct.

The English revolution was an intellectual process, or phenomenon of belief, though with a crucial practical context and some spectacular constitutional as well as literary consequences. Once again it had three phases, each with its European intellectual context: that of civil war radicalism the radical reformation; that of English republicanism predominantly the renaissance; and that of restoration radicalism the refraction of both towards 'the' Enlightenment. Unities within the variety of civil war radicalism allow us to understand it as a single process rather than as a series of discrete groups. Comparable unities are evident within the variety of English republicanism. These hinged upon a moral philosophy of self-government rather than a preoccupation with particular constitutional forms. Finally, since the revolution was not a constitutional phenomenon, but a process of belief, the constitutional restoration of monarchy did not end it. Our examination of restoration radicalism will explain how it responded, and adapted, to institutional reconstruction.

The last, reconstructive process was that of restoration. This again occurred in three phases (1660–5, 1681–5 and 1689–94). It entailed a process of grieving, and of struggle between forgetting and memory. As Robert Fisk observed recently of Beirut, one can, after a brutal civil upheaval, rebuild the capital city. The healing of the mind takes longer. That is why, beneath the shallow surface of restoration institutional history perhaps the most fundamental process at work was a generational one. This erased the troubles only with the passing of that generation too damaged to let them go.

Thus restoration was not a *fait accompli* but an aspiration, quickly inaugurated but tardily and bloodily achieved.[14] The things to which it directed itself included not only institutional reconstruction but the recontainment within those institutions of the ideas, and fears, by which they had previously been destroyed. It aspired, in short, to end both troubles and revolution. The history of the second half of the seventeenth century is that of the struggle between these three processes, in memory and in the present.

14 Jonathan Scott, 'Restoration Process: Or, If This Isn't a Party We're Not Having a Good Time', *Albion* 25, 4 (Winter 1993).

THE CONTEXT OF TIME: CONTINUITY AND CHANGE

Our first context for the reconstruction of contemporary experience and perceptions is that of time. The crucial historiographical concepts at issue are those of continuity and change. Because seventeenth-century English people lived in a traditional, pre-modern society they were a good deal more mindful, and approving, of continuity than of change. This is the reverse of the modern situation, the historiographical prejudices of which are summed up by Lawrence Stone's dictum: 'if history is not concerned with change, it is nothing'.[15]

To the extent that we impose this perspective upon an alien society we will fail to locate that society. The historiographical landscape of the seventeenth century is famously disfigured by the mining damage caused by modern prospectors for change. This does not mean, on the other hand, that there was neither change nor perception of change. On the contrary, spectators of the troubles lived through an astonishing series of experiences that cumulatively left the country much altered. We will be concerned with the limits as well as the extent of that change, for enormous contemporary effort was devoted to such limitation.

Seventeenth-century attitudes to change spanned the range between two extremes. On the one hand there was that hostility to 'innovation' which stood at the heart of the troubles and also informed the restoration process. On the other was that radical demand for change which was the English revolution. Between the two came the perspective of statebuilders like Sir George Downing who understood that fiscal and military modernisation was necessary to maintain the political status quo.[16] These perspectives are to be distinguished from the contemporary *experience* of change, to which they did not necessarily correspond. That those opposed to change in the seventeenth century sometimes introduced it we are reminded by the record both of the Caroline government (1625–40) and of its parliamentary opponents (1640–59). Together the troubles, revolution and restoration processes constituted a brutal and accelerated course of national instruction. Its ultimate consequence was transformation of the national state from European laughing stock to global great power. Over the seventeenth century there transpired a perceived threat, a radical demand and an eventual important experience of

15 Quoted in Cannadine, 'British History', p. 173.
16 Jonathan Scott, 'The Pragmatic Republicanism of Sir George Downing 1623–1683', in Paul Millett (ed.), *Essays on the History of Downing College* (forthcoming).

change within a traditional society anchored by precedent. The resulting strain partly accounts for the political role played in this century by public memory. Each episode of the troubles was crucially informed by public memory. The initial reaction of this society to the mid-century upheaval was to seek refuge in reconstruction and reaction. It was the eventual conclusion of the seventeenth-century learning process that restoration could be made to work only by embracing the limited innovation of statebuilding.

Thus one objective of this study will be to understand seventeenth-century change in the context of continuity. The best way, for instance, of assessing actual differences between the three crises of popery and arbitrary government is within the properly historical context furnished by contemporary perception of their similarities.[17] There will be reason to subject to particular scrutiny in this respect two sorts of modern historiographical claims. One insists that contemporaries thought in one way, and therefore not in another. The second suggests that they were beginning to think in this way in anticipation of ourselves. It will frequently be necessary on the contrary to seek to recover the unity-in-multiplicity of our subject from the modern impulse to categorise and subdivide.[18] This is to rescue from premature subjection to the rules of party politics an age still struggling against this outcome. In the seventeenth century the predominant ambition remained not distinction, but unity-in-variety: harmony in accordance with the government of reason.

THE CONTEXT OF SPACE: NATIONALITY AND MODERNITY

Most modern European historiography has been national historiography. This been not only a consequence, but an arm, of the nation-state. In relation to this, a historian of pre-modern seventeenth-century England needs to consider two questions. One is the appropriate context, or contexts, within which to understand the political experience of the kingdom. The other is the extent to which this story is best understood as focusing upon the development of the nation-state.

---

17 Jonathan Scott, *Algernon Sidney and the English Republic 1623–1677* (Cambridge 1988); Scott, *Algernon Sidney and the Restoration Crisis 1677–1683* (Cambridge 1991).
18 See in particular chs. 10 (pp. 229–46), 13 (pp. 290–316) and 15 (pp. 342–64) below. See also Scott, *Restoration Crisis*, pp. 351–9; Scott, 'Classical Republicanism in Seventeenth-Century England and the Netherlands', in Quentin Skinner and Martin van Gelderen (eds.), *Republicanism and Constitutionalism in Early Modern Europe* (Cambridge, forthcoming).

All historians would accept that the seventeenth century yielded other experiences, and other stories. Most would acknowledge the potential for teleological distortion inherent in the state-evolution approach. The way forward adopted here is, on the one hand, to acknowledge the importance of statebuilding as a seventeenth-century political theme. It is, on the other, to question national assumptions concerning its course, and in particular to challenge the assumption that our understanding of the seventeenth-century political experience needs to be organised around it.

During most of the seventeenth century the English (and, thereafter, British) state had not yet been constructed in its modern form. English contemporaries saw their world, and themselves, in sub- and supra-national as well as national terms. The internationality of contemporary perceptions has been significantly appreciated by historians of ideas.[19] It is histories of events that continue to be rendered almost exclusively in national terms (whether English or British). Yet the major events of the seventeenth century were largely the consequence of contemporary ideas. In no area have the restoration imperatives of statebuilding and forgetting been enforced so completely. It is this pre-modern world of both perception and action which needs to be recovered from a national historiography that has attempted to obliterate it.

One recent study dates the political attempt to inculcate a sense of English national distinctness, complete with 'erroneous national memory', from the Henrician break with Rome.[20] However, the decisive context of British national historiography lies in the long age of military and imperial

---

19 See, for instance, J. H. Salmon, *The French Religious Wars in English Political Thought* (Cambridge 1959); J. G. A. Pocock, *The Machiavellian Moment: Florentine Political Thought and the Atlantic Republican Tradition* (Princeton 1975); Patrick Collinson, *Archbishop Grindal 1519–1583: The Struggle for a Reformed Church* (London 1979); J. C. Davis, *Utopia and the Ideal Society: A Study of English Utopian Writing 1516–1700* (Cambridge 1981); Johann Sommerville, *Politics and Ideology in England 1603–1640* (London 1986); Scott, *English Republic*; Richard Tuck, *Philosophy and Government 1572–1651* (Cambridge 1993); Quentin Skinner, *Reason and Rhetoric in the Philosophy of Hobbes* (Cambridge 1996); Adrian Johns, *The Nature of the Book: Print and Knowledge in the Making* (Chicago 1998).

20 Edwin Jones, *The English Nation: The Great Myth* (Stroud 1998). Until then, Jones explains, England had been 'increasingly and consciously part of continental Europe . . . primarily as part of the Catholic church' (pp. ix, 1). It is not to dispute the reality of this attempt to suggest, as this study does, that Tudor and Stuart governments lacked the capacity to control the minds of their citizens effectively. During the seventeenth century, for instance, when the concept of Christendom remained alive and well, that anti-popery which had, during the later Elizabethan period, served as a unifying political force came to unite English and Scots with 'foreign' protestant subjects against their own rulers.

greatness. It was by these hard means that Britain won its insularity. In pre-modern Europe, where transport was efficient only upon water, the Channel was (as it were) a bridge, not a moat. Two aspects of England's troubles were frequent military incursions, unsuccessful and successful, and a deep and justified accompanying contemporary insecurity. Between the early modern and modern periods these circumstances were reversed. It was only as heir of the subsequent military and political security that Winston Churchill could speak, in a new moment of danger (1940), of 'our long island history . . . and the long continuity of our institutions and our empire':

we shall prove ourselves once again able to defend our island home, to ride out the storm of war, and to outlive the menace of tyranny . . . we shall defend our island, whatever the cost may be, we shall fight on the beaches, we shall fight on the landing grounds.[21]

A few years earlier G. M. Trevelyan had argued that during Elizabeth's reign the 'national or patriotic genius' emancipated itself from 'that obedience to cosmopolitan orders and corporations which had been inculcated by the Catholic church and the feudal obligation'. The Tudors 'abolished or depreciated' everything standing between the individual and the state. Thus, 'In the heat of that struggle English civilization was fused into its modern form, at once insular and oceanic, distinct from the continental civilization of which the Norman Conquest had once made it part.'[22] In fact, during the seventeenth century England's 'beaches' and 'landing grounds' belonged to its invaders, none of whom was effectively opposed. To this extent this national mythology inverted the historical reality.

A few historians of seventeenth-century England have successfully transcended this national historiography. What made David Hume's *History of England* (2 vols., 1754–7) the analytical as well as literary masterpiece it remains was that it found not only its contexts but its subject. That subject was contemporary belief, and destructive religious belief in particular. This was considered across the seventeenth century as a whole and within a European framework. These foci were shared over a century later by Leopold von Ranke. Contemporaneously with Ranke the English historian Samuel

---

21 Angus Calder, *The Myth of the Blitz* (London 1991), pp. 28, 38.
22 G. M. Trevelyan, *History of England* (2nd edn, London 1937), p. 323. This book, like others by the same author, remains a sublime piece of historical writing.

Gardiner had made sense of the Thirty Years War only by positing an imagined state of frustrated German nationhood.[23] Ranke's *History of England,
Principally in the Seventeenth Century* (6 vols., Oxford 1875), by contrast,
correctly emphasised the 'interdependence of the European Dissensions in
Politics and Religion'. More broadly Ranke understood the experience of
England from the standpoint of 'its share in the fortunes and enterprises of
that great community of western nations to which it belongs'.[24]

This was not, as this quote makes clear, because Ranke had any lesser
sense or appreciation than Gardiner of the political life of 'nations'. It was
because he was less inclined to limit his history to that framework. This was
partly because Ranke stood outside the English national historiographical
tradition. It was more particularly because, equipped with his doctrine of
'the primacy of foreign affairs', he had a greater appreciation of the importance of their interrelationship. That this was particularly the case in relation to religion was a matter of importance not only to England but to the
whole of Europe. Just as England's role from the sixteenth century had
'decisively influenced' not only its own history but 'the success of the religious revolution throughout Europe', subsequently it was

against England that the sacerdotal reaction directed its main attack. To withstand
it, the country was forced to ally itself with the kindred elements on the Continent
... the maintenance of Protestantism in Western Europe, on the Continent as well as
Britain, was effected by the united powers of both.[25]

One twentieth-century historian to approach the subject from a similar
perspective has been Hugh Trevor-Roper.[26] Another, with acknowledgement of Ranke, has been John Elliott. 'British history', he has insisted,
'should not be insular history. Our national history has been intimately
connected over many centuries with the history of Europe.' What would be
helpful at present is more emphasis everywhere upon the study of histories
other than our own:[27]

---

23 S. R. Gardiner, *The Thirty Years War 1618–1648* (London 1874), preface: 'Every history, to
     be a history, must have a unity of its own, and here we have no unity of national life.'
24 Ranke, *History of England*, vol. I, p. 280.   25 *Ibid.*, pp. 561, vi–vii.
26 Hugh Trevor-Roper, *Religion, the Reformation and Social Change* (London 1967); Trevor-
     Roper, *Catholics, Anglicans and Puritans: Seventeenth-Century Essays* (London 1989).
     Trevor-Roper's achievement, in this respect, has been to subject the major political events
     of the century to the European perspective of a historian of culture and ideas.
27 Elliott, *National and Comparative History*, p. 15.

While it is true that every society's history is indeed unique, the special concern of historians should be with the . . . nature and extent of that uniqueness . . . [This necessitates] some element of comparison . . . A systematic attempt to set aspects of our national history into a wider, European context is likely to show that some elements or episodes which we tend to regard as uniquely British will prove on inspection to have close continental affinities.[28]

Yet at least one distinguished historian has seen in such European contextualisation an attempt, registering a 'prevailing climate of national defeatism', to 'unmake' a history most appropriately understood as British.[29]

It is important to note that the first of John Pocock's papers developing the 'new British history' was delivered to a New Zealand audience in 1972/3.[30] This was the year when Britain's entry into the European Economic Community wrecked New Zealand's economy and initiated a spurious (that is, politically driven) reconsideration of its historical identity. Pocock's first target in this context was an English historical perspective of such chauvinistic insularity as to be not simply lamentable but risible.[31] From this he made the broader suggestion that, 'having annihilated the commonwealth from the present, the English may be on the point of doing the same to Britain', in history. 'Within very recent memory, the English have been increasingly willing to declare that neither empire or commonwealth ever meant much in their consciousness, and that they were at heart Europeans all the time.' This latter claim was, Pocock remarked, an 'obvious absurdity'.[32] It was from this standpoint that he went on to oppose an imagined European invasion of the 'British' historical space ('Here we reach the point of employing the tendentious and aggressive term "Europe", an expression . . . dynamic, indeterminable and hegemonic') and insisting upon the fundamental distinction of the two ('Scotland is no more English than Britain is European. The fact of a hegemony does not alter the fact of a

28 *Ibid.*, pp. 14, 20, 23–4.
29 J. G. A. Pocock, 'Standing Army and Public Credit: The Institutions of Leviathan', in Dale Hoak and Mordechai Feingold (eds.), *The World of William and Mary: Anglo-Dutch Perspectives on the Revolution of 1688–1689* (Stanford 1996), p. 100; Pocock, 'The Atlantic Archipelago and the War of the Three Kingdoms', in Brendan Bradshaw and John Morrill (eds.), *The British Problem, c. 1534–1707: State Formation in the Atlantic Archipelago* (London 1996), pp. 177–8.
30 J. G. A. Pocock, 'British History: A Plea for a New Subject', *Journal of Modern History* 47 (December 1975), p. 627.
31 A. J. P. Taylor's 'Reply' in the same issue, pp. 625–6 (the correct self-description 'chauvinism' is Taylor's own).   32 *Ibid.*, p. 602.

plurality').[33] Britain, or the 'Atlantic archipelago', lies 'off northwestern Europe', 'partly within and partly without the oceanic limits of the Roman empire and of what is usually called "Europe" in the sense of the latter's successor states', interacting with, but remaining separate from, that 'neighbouring culture complex'.[34]

The territory which would become *England*, of course, lay largely *within* 'the limits of the Roman empire'. When seventeenth-century English people used the term 'Europe', were they doing so 'tendentiously and aggressively'? From the beginning of the century 'Europe' and 'Christendom' were used interchangeably.[35] Throughout the century English ambassadors imagined their work to be of importance to the whole of 'Europe'. In 1663 Louis XIV congratulated Charles II on a Portuguese marriage in the interests of 'all the Kings in Europe'.[36] When in December 1650 Marchamont Nedham wrote: 'Alas poore England! Thou art the Butt that every Statist shoots his Bolt at; but . . . as Justice holds the *Balance* over the world, so dost thou in *Europ*',[37] there is no indication that he was locating 'England' outside the 'Europ' in which it held the balance. He was simply claiming, as English, Scots and Irish people did with more or less plausibility throughout the century, that the outcome of European affairs depended partly upon them. Finally the basis for the apparently proffered distinction between European and imperial/commonwealth identity is not clear. Empire was a European phenomenon.[38]

The British state was an eighteenth-century creation. From 1603 there was a British crown, and an increasingly important Anglo–Scots–Irish subsection of contemporary Europe's turbulent religious politics. We may all applaud the 'new British history' to the extent that it 'denotes the historiography of no single nation but of a problematic and uncompleted experiment in the creation and interaction of several nations'; that it entails 'an

---

33 Pocock, 'Three Kingdoms', p. 173.
34 Pocock, 'The Limits and Divisions of British History: In Search of the Unknown Subject', *American Historical Review* 87, 2 (April 1987), p. 317; Pocock, 'A Plea', pp. 605, 606.
35 J. P. Cooper (ed.), *The New Cambridge Modern History of Europe*, vol. IV, *1609–1658/9* (Cambridge 1970), 'Introduction'.
36 Edward Hyde, Earl of Clarendon, *The Life of Edward Earl of Clarendon . . . Written by Himself*, vol. I (Oxford 1760), p. 352.
37 *Mercurius Politicus*, no. 26, 28 November–5 December 1650, p. 433.
38 Anthony Pagden, *Lords of All the World: Ideologies of Empire in Spain, Britain and France c.1500–c.1800* (New Haven 1995); Nicholas Canny (ed.), *The Oxford History of the British Empire, Volume I: The Origins of Empire: British Overseas Enterprise to the Close of the Seventeenth Century* (Oxford 1998); P. J. Marshall (ed.), *Volume II: The Eighteenth Century* (Oxford 1998).

attempt to overcome Anglocentricity', by its examination of the 'Atlantic archipelago' as a whole;[39] that it is 'highly antinationalist', in its focus upon the interaction of nations and communities rather than regarding 'each star [as] . . . the centre of its universe'.[40] Yet the nature and importance of Anglo–Scots–Irish interaction is difficult to assess outside the European framework of which it was part. Is it not misleading to focus on the relationships of Ireland, Scotland and England, independently of their relationships with France, the Netherlands and Spain?

John Morrill has suggested that 'European' contexts ought to be considered to offer 'a *further* layer of explanation' for events in these islands, 'not an alternative layer, let alone an excuse for ignoring the *British* layer of explanation'.[41] Whether anyone *has* used the 'European context' as 'an excuse for ignoring the British layer' is not clear. One could perhaps more appropriately turn this dictum around and say that it was the British context that offered a 'further layer' within this European state system, 'not an alternative layer, let alone an excuse for ignoring the European layer of explanation'. For of course it is the 'European layer' which *has* been frequently ignored by 'British' contextualists, rather than vice versa. Moreover, surely it was historically the case that the new seventeenth-century dynastic three-kingdom relationship was precisely a 'further layer' added within an established and wider-ranging complex of European relationships that it did not replace?

Glenn Burgess has drawn attention to the place accorded within the 'new British history' to comparative analysis in a European multiple-monarchy context. In this respect 'the new British history has been a comparative European history for much of its existence'.[42] In this case it might be more appropriate to call the history in question 'European'. To this extent the relevant work of Conrad Russell has, for instance, been less 'British' in scope than what John Reeve has called 'Anglo-European'.[43] The general point is that interaction within the 'Atlantic archipelago' is self-evidently important in the seventeenth century. What is not historically defensible, and what cannot help but mislead, is its abstraction from the wider European religious and political complex of which it formed only a part.

---

39 Pocock quoted in Morrill, 'The British Problem, c.1534–1707', in Bradshaw and Morrill, *The British Problem*, p.1; Pocock, 'Three Kingdoms', p. 172.   40 Pocock, 'A Plea', p. 621.

41 John Kerrigan, 'Birth of a Naison', *London Review of Books*, 5 June 1997, p. 16.

42 Glenn Burgess, 'Introduction: The New British History', in Burgess, *The New British History.*   43 *Ibid.*, pp. 5–7.

This is particularly important given the near absence of seventeenth-century British self-perception. The impact of Scotland upon English history between 1637 and 1648, or England upon Scots history between 1698 and 1707, was largely unaccompanied by 'British' sensibility.[44] Even during King William's war for the recovery of Ireland in 1689–91, Tony Claydon has remarked upon the absence of an appeal to a 'British' dimension. English chaplains spoke, as they had throughout the century, of the eternal battle between Europe-wide churches: 'How much the general interest of the Reformed Church and Religion does depend upon the present Juncture I need not tell you.' All political literature accompanying the expedition 'stressed religious, rather than "British" links between William's army and its local supporters.'[45]

Across the century (for instance in the 1620s, 1670s and 1690s) the absorption of English attention by continental affairs contrasts markedly with the relative lack of interest in either Scotland or Ireland.[46] It was the continental conflict of the 1620s, for instance, which first excited the seventeenth-century English craze for printed news.[47] One of the publications that kept this supplied between 1621 and 1625 was the *Weekly Newes*, printed in 'London . . . for *Mercurius Britannicus*'. Drawing upon Dutch material it related news not only from 'Bohemia, Austria, the Palatinate, the Grisons, the Lowe Countries', and everywhere else 'in Europe', or 'Christendome', but from 'East India' and 'the whole World'.[48] During the interregnum the same public appetite was kept supplied by the commonwealth newspaper *Mercurius Politicus* ('Came Traffick enough for *Newsmongers* out of Holland . . . Since the *mad Scabs* have such an *Itch* after *News*,

44 Claydon, 'Problems with the British Problem' (*Parliamentary History*, 16, 2 (1997)), Morrill, 'British Problem', p. 10, Hirst, 'The English Republic and the Meaning of Britain' and Goldie, 'Divergence and Union: Scotland and England 1660–1707', the latter three in Bradshaw and Morrill, *The British Problem*. See also Colin Davis' review of R. A. Mason (ed.), *Scots and Britons: Scottish Political Thought and the Union of 1603* (Cambridge 1994), in *Journal of Ecclesiastical History* 46, 4 (October 1995), p. 746.

45 Tony Claydon, *William III and the Godly Revolution* (Cambridge 1996), pp. 140–2.

46 Claydon, 'Problems with the British Problem'; Reeve, 'Britain or Europe?'

47 Michael Frearson, 'The English Corantos of the 1620s', Ph.D thesis, Cambridge 1994; Richard Cust, 'News and Politics in Early Seventeenth-Century England', *Past and Present* 112 (August 1986); Thomas Cogswell, *The Blessed Revolution: English Politics and the Coming of War* (Cambridge 1989).

48 *A Continuation of the Newes of this Present Weeke*, no. 5, 5 November 1622, p. 9; *The continuation of our Weekly Newes*, no. 17, 14 April 1625.

Ile see they shall not want *Mercury* to cure them').[49] In this the editor Marchamont Nedham reported in detail, weekly, upon the affairs of England, Scotland, Ireland, the United Provinces, Flanders, France, Spain, Scandinavia, the Holy Roman Empire and Italy without categorical distinction or relative weighting of any kind.

Whatever else it may be, therefore, the 'new British history' is not a history of contemporary perceptions. Rather it is, explains John Morrill, an examination of 'the reactions of the various peoples of the islands of Britain and Ireland to the growth of the English state. It was and is a study of state formation and the emergence of new nationalisms.'[50] It is, that is to say, a 'study' of the pre-history of the British, rather than simply English, state. We may prefer this to insular Anglocentricity. But this is 'new' history only in scope, not kind. How it proposes to avoid the teleological distortion characteristic of all such histories, such as were once supported by the 'old' nationalisms, is not explained.

Thus, speaking of Anglo-Scottish marital relationships in the sixteenth century, Morrill observes: 'Each of these was of crucial significance to *the outcome of British history*.' Commenting upon the argument of Hiram Morgan 'that in the sixteenth century the British problem was essentially part of a wider pan-European geopolitical struggle', Morrill continues: 'And yet *what was at stake* was the future constitutional and confessional relationship of the component parts of Britain.'[51] It is only by such teleological selection from what was actually a history of *many* outcomes, with *many* things at stake, that a British history is here constructed. In the story that follows, what has been termed the process of statebuilding is one important theme. What eventually created the British state, however, was not incremental 'British history' but the transformation of English military power. This was, in its second and decisive manifestation, during the 1690s, with all of its far-reaching political consequences, the result most importantly not of Anglo-Scots, or -Irish, but Anglo-Dutch collaboration.

---

49 *Mercurius Politicus*, no. 1, 6–13 June 1650, pp. 27, 33.
50 Morrill, 'Preface', in Bradshaw and Morrill, *The British Problem*, p. vii. Though Pocock has spoken of British history as 'many histories', he has also agreed that it is 'dominated by the attempt to construct a "British" kingdom, state, and nation embracing the archipelago as a whole': Pocock, 'Limits and Divisions', p. 336; Pocock, 'Three Kingdoms', p. 173.
51 Morrill, 'British Problem', p. 23 (my emphasis in both quotations).

HISTORY AND MEMORY

All of these debates, Pocock has rightly pointed out, beg the question of 'our conception of the historian's function'.[52] This in turn hinges upon our view of what history is. This is the most fundamental area in which the assumptions of the following analysis may usefully be made explicit.

In a recent and justified attack upon historiographical pedantry and myopia, David Cannadine explained that historians 'should be the enemies of temporal, territorial and cultural parochialism'. Yet, he went on, in reality they were 'invariably bound' by the perspectives of present time, place and opinion. It was accordingly the then-gloomy British present that made the outlook so bleak for the future of Britain's past.[53] One problem was that 'This country has a weaker sense of national identity now than at any time this century; its self esteem is shattered and eroded.' The difficult task under these circumstances was to put the 'Humpty Dumpty' of a compelling national story 'back together again'. 'Yet', for this purpose, 'as the guardians of the national past, as the keepers of our country's corporate memory, it is precisely in our own time and circumstances that we should be looking for inspiration.' Only this would allow 'the study of history' to once again perform its social function, which was that it 'enhances our self-consciousness, it enables us to see ourselves in perspective, and it helps us towards that greater freedom and understanding which come from self-knowledge'.[54]

Yet are historians 'the guardians of the national past', and the 'keepers' of this 'memory'? Throughout his magnificent tirade it apparently never occurs to Cannadine to ask whether the seventeenth-century history to which he refers is 'British history'; or whether the experience of seventeenth-century English people is best rendered as 'national'. Public memory, which plays a crucial social function in all societies, is also a key subject of this book. It is the rudder which steadies a society across its present and is substantially politically constructed.[55] Should the historian be the 'guardian' of this memory or its challenger, in the service not of power but knowledge? The result of this would be – and surely the actual function of history is – not the 'enhancement of self-consciousness', as if modern self-consciousness really required enhancement, but self-knowledge.

52 Pocock, 'Limits and Divisions', pp. 311–12.
53 Cannadine, 'British History', pp. 169–70.   54 *Ibid.*, pp. 186, 188, 190–1.
55 Marc Ferro, *The Use and Abuse of History: Or How the Past Is Taught* (London 1981).

Memory is that faculty, essential to present self-location, by which we retain some residue of our experience of the past. History is, by contrast, the study, and imaginative recreation, of experience other than our own. This is its principal educative function. Accordingly it enhances self-knowledge not by examination of the self – let alone of an imaginary self elaborated into the past – but by that engagement with the world outside the self which is the only context for genuine self-understanding. As the imagination of otherness history is also *the getting of experience in time*.[56] This view was held by Thomas Hobbes who, at the beginning of England's troubles, translated as a warning that Greek historian with whom he rightly judged 'the faculty of writing history is at the highest':

Look how much a man of understanding might have added to his experience, if he had then lived a beholder of their [the Greeks'] proceedings . . . so much almost might he profit now, by attentive reading of the same . . . The principal and proper work of history being to instruct and enable men by the knowledge of actions past, to bear themselves prudently in the present and providently towards the future: there is not extant any other . . . that doth more fully and naturally perform it [than] . . . Thucydides.[57]

As the imagination of otherness history's negation is the imposition upon that other of ourselves. That this is difficult to avoid, and cannot be avoided entirely, makes no difference to what history is. It is true that historians are affected by the present in which they live and work. This may help them to new, historically valuable perspectives, or it may impede their understanding of the past. It is no excuse, in either case, for refusing to make the imaginative effort in which history consists, and which is necessary to distinguish between present and past. That something is imperfect, as an informed imaginative art, does not make it non-existent, even in this 'scientific' age. Indeed the vital importance of history has never been more obvious; there have been few ages more contemptuous of experience other than their own. If historians wish to agonise about their subject, let it be about this practical failure. The 'hegemony' to be feared is that of modernity.

It is thus the function of history to imaginatively extend our experience

---

56 This social and educative function is discussed in relation to New Zealand by Scott, *Harry's Absence*, in particular chs. 13, 19 and 20.
57 *Hobbes' Thucydides*, ed. Schlatter, pp. xxi, 20; Jonathan Scott, 'The Peace of Silence: Thucydides and the English Civil War', in Miles Fairburn and W. H. Oliver (eds.), *The Certainty of Doubt: Essays in Honour of Peter Munz* (Wellington 1996), pp. 95–9.

beyond the present time and place. In relation to the present subject this is to liberate us from the 'subjected Plaines' of national historiography and modernity.[58] It is difficult to bring home to students living in the 'new global society' the relative parochialism of modern culture. This is true not simply in terms of its relationship to the past. It was Archbishop Abbot who wrote to Sir Thomas Roe in 1617: 'as thinges now stand throughout the whole worlde, there is no place so remote, but that the consideration thereof is mediately or immediately of consequence to our affaires here'.[59]

Genuine history is the only thing standing between cultural self-knowledge and self-absorption. That is why all variants of the 'whig' history of origins are actually not history at all. They are on the contrary contributions to a set of mythologies – whether left, right, national or international – of which the historian should be not the guardian but the scourge. The prize is knowledge: that knowledge which comes from experience of the world.

---

58 The phrase is in Milton's *Paradise Lost* (in *The Poetical Works of John Milton*, ed. H. C. Beeching (Oxford 1922)), bk 12, lines 637–49: see ch. 15 below.

59 Ken Fincham, 'Prelacy and Politics: Archbishop Abbot's Defence of Protestant Orthodoxy', *Historical Research* 61, 144 (1988), p. 50.

1

The shape of the seventeenth century

For of Meridians and Parallels
Man hath weav'd out a net
and this net throwne Upon the Heavens
and now they are his owne.
Loth to goe up the hill, or labour thus
To goe to heaven
we make heaven come to us.

John Donne, 'The First Anniversarie' (1611)[1]

The Channel is no national boundary.

Leopold von Ranke, *History of England* (1875)[2]

INTRODUCTION

How should one structure a large-scale analysis of the seventeenth-century English political experience? Should one do so? Such histories have long been out of fashion. To attempt one is necessarily to step outside one's area of expertise. This is the most complex, the most important and the most violent century of English history. It is equally the most formidable and savage historiographical terrain. Entire historians have disappeared, leaving only a rent garment and the colour of blood in the water to show us where they had been.

One point from which to begin is the identification of those features by which our subject is distinguished, in time and place. In this respect it might be suggested that two things above all make seventeenth-century English

An earlier version of this chapter was published as Scott, 'England's Troubles 1603–1702', in R. Malcolm Smuts (ed.), *The Stuart Court and Europe* (Cambridge 1996), pp. 20–38.
1 In *John Donne: The Complete English Poems*, ed. A. J. Smith (London 1986), p. 278.
2 Ranke, *History of England*, vol. I, p. 5.

history unique. The first is the length and depth of its experience of political instability. The second is its astonishing intellectual fertility. These two features were of course connected. It is this combination which distinguishes the seventeenth century within English history, and the experience of seventeenth-century England within Europe.

This experience of instability I have called, following contemporary usage, England's troubles: 'the late troubles'; 'our lamentable troubles'. It is one aspect of its spectacular intellectual consequence that I will call 'the English revolution'. Despite their uniqueness, these characteristics of English history, both political and intellectual, were a part of, and cannot be understood apart from, the historical experience of Europe. Before we can understand, however, how this body politic came to be torn apart, with such dramatic consequences, we must ourselves put it together again.

THE BROKEN MIRROR

For if we ask what are the most important *historiographical* obstacles to a general account of the seventeenth century in England, we find two: present-centredness and fragmentation. These are intertwined. Together they present us with two problems. One is that our picture of the seventeenth century is broken in pieces, smashed in its frame; how are we to put it together again? The other is that perhaps what is broken is not a picture of the seventeenth century at all. Perhaps it is a mirror, in which we have become accustomed to seeking – and arguing over – an image of ourselves.

By present-centredness I refer to an inability to distinguish imaginatively between the present and the past, between our subject and ourselves. So far as it sets the agenda this prevents us from making contact with the seventeenth century at all. It is one aspect of our modernity impeding the recovery of pre-modernity. It is also an occupational hazard of our discipline. Yet we should also remember that it was present-centredness that provided the basis, in the works of G. M. Trevelyan and Christopher Hill, for the last powerful explanatory analyses of the century as a whole.[3] Anyone who still believes, in these post-revisionist days, that such analyses are possible, indeed essential, will need to show that they can be achieved without the present-centred teleology that these entailed.

---

3 G. M. Trevelyan, *England Under the Stuarts* (London 1904); Christopher Hill, *The Century of Revolution 1603–1714* (London 1969).

Meanwhile the reaction against such teleology has achieved much, but at a price. It has accelerated the tendency already under way, through professional specialisation, towards historiographical fragmentation. Every book now covers less territory, in more pages, than the last. At its worst revisionism has resulted in a fastidious worship of particularity that is arid, self-indulgent and parochial, and that has left us wandering like pilgrims through an explanatory desert. In place of the general explanatory analysis we now have the textbook, which takes its shape passively from chronology, and actively from current historiographical debate. This latter is present-centredness of a different kind.

The problem of fragmentation is as old as the seventeenth century itself, where it took the form of partisanship. It was Richard Baxter who said in the 1670s: 'If other Historians be like some of these Times, their Assertions, whenever they speak of such as they distaste, are to be read as *Hebrew*, backward, and are so far from signifying Truth, that many of them . . . are downright lies.'[4] Such partisanship is still with us, and indeed is taken for granted. It was T. S. Eliot who gave classic status to the cliche that the English civil war has never ended. It has thus for some time been the case that seventeenth-century scholarship is as remarkable for its military as for its historical qualities.[5] 'We are all parties in the same struggle', wrote one veteran recently, 'hoisting and submerging one another in the same turbid stream.'[6]

Yet was the seventeenth-century struggle 'the same' as our own? It is customary to point to these historiographical battles as evidence of the continued vitality of our subject, and so they would be if they were leading us anywhere. In fact, however, under questionable generalship, and through the heat, noise and smoke, the battlefields of the seventeenth century itself are becoming increasingly hard to see under the great piles of bleached bones left by historians murdered by their colleagues. This landscape has become a problem for students, who cannot be expected to bring to it the capacities for separation and reconstruction that it requires. Perhaps we should not, however, confuse this struggle for power with the struggle for knowledge in which we would rather be engaged.

4 Richard Baxter, *Reliquiae Baxterianae*, pt III, p. 187.
5 I do not dissociate myself from this situation: I have been described as the Prince Rupert of the field – a commander no less noted for atrocities committed against civilians than for ending up on the losing side.
6 H. R. Trevor-Roper, Lord Dacre, 'The Continuity of the English Revolution', *Transactions of the Royal Historical Society* 6th ser., 1 (1991), p. 121.

It was John Milton who, during the actual civil war, spoke of Truth as a single (female) form hewed in pieces by a professional (clerical) 'race of wicked deceivers'. This made the task of the revolution 'the closing up of truth to truth'.[7] In the same decade the Leveller William Walwyn lambasted the clergy as

swarmes of locusts . . . making Marchandize of the blessed Word of Truth . . . [who] dress it up in what shape their Art or Rhetorick can devise; and upon pretense of Exposition, raise thousands of doubts and disputes, write millions of books, and preach innumerable sermons, whereby people are divided, and subdivided into Factions, Sects and parties, and whereby the end of the Gospel, which directs [us] only to love, is [lost].[8]

Gerrard Winstanley described this professional triumph of power over knowledge, of form over substance, as 'the husk without the kernall . . . the cloud without rain'.[9] In fact, while we think we are studying the seventeenth century, it may be governing us. We remain in its power and cannot break free. We cannot even tell the difference between it and ourselves for of course its struggle and our own were not, and are not, the same at all.

It is making this *separation* that is our starting point: re-establishing the actual distance between that pre-modern experience and our own. This is a precondition for its imaginative recovery. This means giving the seventeenth century back to itself; it means letting go. Then we may see that we have been watching a pre-national experience from within a national one; that we have been truncating its context in time, as well as space; that what we continue to call 'the causes of the English civil war' relate not only to a series of wars within Britain that were part of a series of wars within Europe, but to the first of three similar crises spanning the century as a whole. Until we re-establish these contexts our answers will be unsatisfactory because our questions are misposed.

One result of this process might be the undomestication of the English revolution. We have made that revolution comfortable by making it familiar, by making it an anticipation of ourselves. But it was not like that at all. It

---

7 *Areopagitica; a Speech of Mr John Milton for the Liberty of Unlicenc'd Printing* (1644), ed. J. C. Suffolk (London 1968), pp. 96, 130.

8 William Walwyn, *The Vanitie of the Present Churches* (1649), in *The Writings of William Walwyn*, ed. J. R. McMichael and B. Taft (Athens, Ga. 1989), p. 270.

9 In Winstanley, *The Works, with an Appendix of Documents Relating to the Digger Movement*, ed. G. H. Sabine (Ithaca 1951), pp. 242, 569.

was pre-modern, frightening and strange. There is brilliance at the heart of it – lightning from a cloud; but it is because we are products of its failure rather than success that its imaginative recovery is not as straightforward as it might seem. If we stopped trying to appropriate it, and allowed it to be what it was again, what was terrifying for contemporaries might recover the power to unsettle us too.

How do we exchange the broken mirror for a preliminary picture? The remainder of this chapter suggests three initial ways forward. The first two concern the contexts of this experience in time and space. The third concerns what we might call the *substance* of this history – what it was made of – and specifically the relationship between events, structures and ideas. This was a period when institutions were fragile, and ideas powerful (the opposite of the present situation). Between 1603 and 1702 England saw its religious and political institutions destroyed by, then reconstructed through, the (European) ideas they were intended to contain. This was terrifying partly because it was unprecedented: let us see what it involved.

TIME: THE UNITY OF THE SEVENTEENTH-CENTURY EXPERIENCE

England's experience of instability has a connected backbone in the three crises of popery and arbitrary government that occurred in 1618–48, 1678–83 and 1688–9. These were the troubles: those 'tragedies and distractions' that had, wrote one contemporary in 1659, '(from the most glorious Nation of Europe) rendred England the most ridiculous nation of the whole world, and made her Natives, once so highly respected in foreign parts, now ashamed to own her'.[10] 'Our Tragedies', wrote another in 1692 (after the third such visitation), 'will scarce find Credit with Posterity, whilst the Ages to come, mistrusting the reports of such enormous villanies, will look upon our unheard-of Vicissitudes, but as the Fancies of Poetry and the Decoration of the Theatres.'[11]

Both the continuity and European context of these observations will have been noted. These three crises were described by contemporaries as being both similar, in their causes, contexts and course, and connected and inter-

---

10 Thomas Dancer, *Metamorphosis Anglorum* [London 1659], pp. 100–1.

11 Sir Roger Manley, *The History of the Rebellions in England, Scotland and Ireland* (1691), quoted in R. MacGillivray, *Restoration Historians and the English Civil War* (The Hague 1974), p. 232.

twined. Yet they have been described by historians, few of whom work upon all three, as if they were different and discrete. They are 'the causes of the English civil war'; 'the exclusion crisis'; and 'the glorious revolution'. These analyses reflect the fragmentation of seventeenth-century historiography, rather than the continuity of seventeenth-century history.[12]

The single most important historiographical dividing line obscuring this continuity has been at the year 1660. What established this were the two greatest quests that have shaped the modern study of the century. It is a condition of modernity that we are crazy about revolution. The restoration period has long been examined for the origins of its so-called (whig) revolution of 1688–9, and of the altered political world it created. This is what established the future-centred agenda of restoration historiography. This has been less concerned with understanding the period in its own terms than with finding the origins of the 'long eighteenth century' in it. The early Stuart period, in turn, has long lain under the shadow of its (mid-century) revolution, and the civil wars from which that emerged. The modern (post-Marxist) assumption both of mid-century revolution, and of revolution as implying discontinuity, has reinforced this division of the century into two halves.

This terminology of revolution also carries with it the assumption of human agency. Another aspect of our modernity is the belief that we make our history. Contemporaries did not, in general, describe their troubles in this way. We hear more about natural phenomena: storm, flood, earthquake and inundation. The sea is high, the air is moving, the ground is shaking:

And when I came, in the Lord's mighty power, with the word of life into the world, the world swelled and made a noise like the great raging waves of the sea. Priests and professors, magistrates and people, were all like a sea, when I came to proclaim the day of the Lord amongst them, and to preach repentance to them.[13]

Seventeenth-century people felt, it may help us to be reminded, that their history lay in the grip of destructive forces larger than themselves and substantially outside their control. This was the mentality of an age more sensible of what Baxter called 'the inexpressable weight of things Eternal'.[14]

The result of the historiographical division at 1660 – a restoration period artificially wedded to its future, and severed from its past – has

12 Scott, *Restoration Crisis*, ch. 1.
13 George Fox, *Journal*, in *George Fox and the Children of Light*, ed. Jonathan Fryer (London 1991), p. 21.   14 Richard Baxter, *Reliquiae Baxterianae*, pt I, p. 3.

been a precise inversion of the historical reality. Restoration people could not predict the future, but they could, and did, remember. It was in vain that one 'wished that the years between 1640 and 60 could be raz'd out of the Book of Time, and the memory of this Age'.[15] For the historical reality was of a period uniquely under the shadow of its past. Like a road accident victim, this generation remained susceptible to both nostalgia on the one hand, and nightmares on the other. The restoration settlement was an act of nostalgia. With the restoration crisis, the second of the three Stuart crises of popery and arbitrary government, the nightmare had come.

After 1660 then, for good and ill, the nation remained a prisoner of memory. That is why these crises were intertwined. For this reason there are *two* seventeenth-century sequences of repetition. One was destructive: the three-phase process of England's troubles. But the other was reconstructive: the three-phase attempt at settlement which followed each: in 1660–5 (the restoration settlement); 1681–5 (the 'loyalist reaction'); and 1689–94 (the 'revolution settlement'). This last was not a revolution at all in the modern sense, but was glorious precisely because it was the successful restoration at last. As the culmination of this restoration process it released the nation from the tyranny of memory, from the need to keep repeating its own past.

Contemporary consciousness of these processes, and of the interrelationship of present events with public memory, is one of their most distinctive features. 'This was the Preludium to the late Rebellion', noted one contemporary, 'loud clamours against popery and arbitrary government.' 'It would be somewhat strange', observed another, 'and without all example in story, that a nation should be twice ruined, twice undone, by the selfsame ways and means.' 'I believe it has hardly ever been known', added a third, 'that any one Humor in one and the same country, has come twice upon the stage by the same Methods in the space of forty years.'[16] What spared the nation from another civil war on this occasion was less any

---

15 *The Character of a Rebellion, and What England May Expect From One* (London 1681); *The Loyal Protestant's Vindication . . . By a Queen Elizabeth Protestant* (London 1681), p. 1.

16 *Fair Warning, or the Burnt Child Dreads the Fire* [London 1680], p. 1; Edward Cooke, *Memorabilia; Or the Most Remarkable Passages and Counsels Collected out of the Several Declarations and Speeches . . . Made by the King* (London 1681), p. 101; *An Essay upon the Change of Manners. Being a second Part of the true Protestant's Appeal to the City and Country* (London 1681), p. 1.

difference between the situations themselves than this contemporary recognition of their similarities. It was certainly to this which the king appealed in his decisive *Declaration* of 1681:

And so we assure Ourself That we shall be Assisted by the Loyalty . . . of all those who consider the Rise and Progress of the late Troubles . . . and desire to protect their Country from a Relapse. And we cannot but remember, that Religion, Liberty and property were all lost and gone when Monarchy was shaken off, and could never be reviv'd till that was restor'd.[17]

But what were popery and arbitrary government? To move from the fact of these sequences of repetition to their causes we must turn from the context of time to that of space.

SPACE: THE EUROPEAN CONTEXT

As observed in the introduction, there is currently a revival of interest in the 'British context' of the English civil wars. What 'British context' principally means is that the territories which later became Britain are being taken to provide an explanatory context for (one part of) the history of seventeenth-century England.

That the events surrounding the crisis and breakdown of Charles I's government involved not only England, but Scotland and Ireland too, has not escaped the attention of any major historian since the seventeenth century itself. Yet the three rebellions of 1637–42 do not constitute a British 'context', but a British crisis, involving three kingdoms, united dynastically, disunited in other ways. The context for this crisis was European. It was the Earl of Clarendon who made the point about contemporary perceptions that events in Edinburgh in 1637–8 took by surprise an English political nation long accustomed to focus its attention upon the continent.[18] Ann Hughes, in her excellent *Causes of the English Civil War*, has remarked that what distinguishes the British rebellions

---

17 Charles II, *His Majesties Declaration to all his Loving Subjects touching the Causes and Reasons that Moved Him to Dissolve the Last Two Parliaments* (London 1681), pp. 4–5.

18 Edward Hyde, Earl of Clarendon, *The History of the Rebellion and Civil Wars in England*, ed. W. D. Macray (6 vols., Oxford 1888), vol. I, pp. 145–6: 'when the whole nation was solicitous to know what passed weekly in Germany and Poland and all other parts of Europe no man ever inquired what was doing in Scotland, nor had that kingdom a place or mention in . . . any gazette'.

from their European counterparts in Portugal, for instance, or Catalonia (both 1640) is their religious character. Yet there is a peculiar chronological literal-mindedness here: as if there can only be a European context if it was precisely contemporaneous.[19]

The immediate context for the collapse of Charles I's monarchy was that broader European upheaval that we call the Thirty Years War. That is why its first major historian, John Rushworth, began his *Historical Collections* chronicling the process not (as he had intended) in 1640, or in 1625, but in 1618.[20] In this year the peace of Europe was shattered by a calvinist rebellion in Bohemia not entirely unlike that twenty years later in Scotland. This occurred within a religiously mixed and unstable multiple monarchy (the Habsburg) not entirely unlike that of Charles I. During the later sixteenth century under Maximilian this had tolerated a politic lack of religious definition not unreminiscent of that of Elizabethan England.[21] But by the early seventeenth century the winds of religious polarisation, and of counter-reformation in particular, were blowing hard. The crisis of 1618–48 threw not only the whole of religiously mixed, half-reformed central and western Europe into conflict, but Britain too, because Britain was part of religiously mixed, half-reformed central and western Europe. It is commonly asserted by students of European history that the thirty-year crisis of the first half of the seventeenth century followed from the unfinished business – in particular religious business – of the sixteenth. This is no less evidently true in England.

The Bohemian rebellion was not the first of its kind. A longer-term view of the impact upon the British kingdoms of this mode of religious politics would begin with that of the Dutch revolt. Meanwhile it is not only the case that from 1618 to 1648/9 developments in England, Scotland and Ireland had this European context, but that they were a part of this single European conflict. When Ferdinand II received the Spanish assistance he asked for against Bohemia he was victorious; when Charles I did not against Scotland he was not. Note that he asked for it, having already added to other provoca-

---

19 See Ann Hughes, *The Causes of the English Civil War* (2nd edn, London 1998), pp. 52–4.

20 John Rushworth, *Historical Collections . . . beginning the Sixteenth Year of King James, Anno 1618. And ending the Fifth Year of King Charls, Anno 1629* (3 vols., London 1659–82), vol. I, preface. Rushworth had intended to begin with the convening of the Long Parliament on 3 November 1640.

21 R. J. W. Evans, *The Making of the Habsburg Monarchy 1550–1700* (Oxford 1979), p. 39, and ch. 1 in general.

tions in Scotland a policy of resumption of church lands at one with its German counter-reformation context. Laudianism was counter-reformation protestantism: it is hardly surprising if the distinction between this and popery appeared too subtle for many of its subjects to grasp. Some of the Scots troops Charles faced in consequence were themselves veterans of the German wars; many English protestants sympathised with them. The last act of the Thirty Years War was not the Peace of Westphalia, or that of Münster, but the execution of Charles I. For what distinguished the *English* experience of this conflict was not its causes – by which we have been so preoccupied – but its consequences. These were not, as in the Habsburg case, a victory for monarchical statebuilding and counter-reformation. In England they were the destruction of monarchy; a first experience of statebuilding (and military strength) under a republic; and that radical reformation we call the English revolution.

Let us remind ourselves now that this was but the first stage of a century-long process through which the principal institutions of English religious and political life were first destroyed, then gradually reconstructed. At every stage of this experience the European context was crucial, and it culminated in a European invasion in 1688–9. Modern British politicians who claim to be defending the state against Europe appear not to understand that the British state was itself a European creation. It was an effect of this intervention, over the years 1689–1714, of which the British kingdoms had been incapable on their own. Every decisive moment in the history of this country has resulted from its participation in, rather than independence of, European history. As Ranke put it, 'the Channel is no national boundary'.[22]

These points are amplified when we turn to the questions of what popery and arbitrary government were.

What one notices first about the seventeenth-century English fear of popery are its range and power: it spanned the century; it crossed all social boundaries; as a solvent of political loyalties it had no rivals. What one should notice next is that it is inexplicable in a purely national context.[23] Within England in the seventeenth century catholics made up a tiny and declining proportion of the population: protestantism was secure, and was becoming more so. It was in Europe that the opposite was the case. Between 1590 and 1690 the geographical reach of protestantism shrank from

22 See n. 2.
23 These themes were explored more fully in my 'Popish Plot'; Bosher, 'Franco-Catholic Danger'.

one-half to one-fifth of the land area of the continent. The seventeenth century in Europe was the century of the victories of the counter-reformation, spearheaded by Spain in the first half of the century and France in the second. It was the century in which protestantism had to fight for its survival. This was the context for fear of popery in England, which found itself thrust into the front line against the European counter-reformation advance.[24]

It was equally the context for domestic political fears. '[Our] liberties have been so invaded', said William Strode in 1628, 'that we are exposed to foreign destruction.' 'These things', echoed Sir Robert Phelips, 'have made God a counsellor to our enemies and a general to their forces. Now fall these things at a time when our religion is almost extirpate in Christendom.'[25] Half a century later in the House of Commons the same perception remained unvanquished: '[We are the last] bulwark of liberty, protestantism, and Christian faith in general, throughout the world . . . the main bank, that hinders the see of Rome from overwhelming all Christian nations with an universal inundation of tyranny and superstition.'[26] '[Everybody knows] that hath the least observed the former times', explained a parliamentarian in 1680,

how . . . ever since the Reformation there hath been a design carried on by priests and Jesuits that came from beyond the seas . . . to subvert the government, and destroy the protestant religion established here in England . . . [There is] An universal design against the protestant party. We see France has fallen upon the protestant party there. The emperor has martyred them in Hungary, and what has been done in Bohemia they say, broke the Prince Elector's heart . . . every session of parliament we are still troubled with popery. In the descent of four kings . . . still the parliaments have been troubled with popery.[27]

The European problem was the counter-reformation advance. One aspect of the domestic problem was English military weakness in the face of it. Thus every episode of the troubles focused upon Stuart governments that had not only done nothing to stem this process but had apparently actually

---

24 Scott, 'Popish Plot'.
25 L. J. Reeve, *Charles I and the Road to Personal Rule* (Cambridge 1989), pp. 25–6.
26 William Bedloe, *A Narrative and Impartial Discovery of the Horrid Popish Plot* (London 1679), p. 2.
27 A. Grey, *Debates of the House of Commons, from the Year 1667 to the Year 1694* (10 vols., London 1763), vol. VIII, p. 328.

allied themselves to it. In each the targets for public rage were not primarily catholic English neighbours but papists at court, foreigners in general and infiltrating Jesuits in particular. To be 'proved' a Jesuit between 1678 and 1680 was fatal.[28]

This brings us to our second rhetorical indicator: arbitrary government. The time scale mentioned above – 'in the descent of four kings' – helps us to date its Elizabethan genesis. Elizabeth had attempted to subordinate religious to political allegiance. In the 1580s, however, under the pressure of European events, a confessional state had developed, defined and defended by European war. At the same time, everywhere in Europe rulers were being forced to respond to a variety of pressures – population increase, price inflation, military revolution – with that complex of measures that we call state centralisation. Elizabeth had woefully neglected this need, and she bequeathed to the Stuarts a motley, contradictory church (catholic in government, more or less calvinist in doctrine) presided over by a weak and declining crown, incapable of defending it abroad. It was the Caroline attempt to repair these defects, executed badly, and late – Charles I was, in James Harrington's memorable words, a king 'as stiff in disputes as the nerve of the monarchy was grown slack' – that contemporaries identified as 'arbitrary government'.[29] It is crucial that they did so within the context of humiliating military failure.

The fundamental function of monarchy was the making of war: this was the bottom line. Its independent basis wrecked by inflation, the Stuart crown was incapable of performing this task. Within the circumstances I have described this had alarming religious as well as political implications. Until 1618 this secret could be kept in the closet like a mad aunt; but throughout the 1620s the whole of Europe could hear Mildred pounding on the door. It was the military ineffectuality and humiliation of the 1620s that established the quite disparate analyses by Charles I and his opponents of what was wrong with British government. For Charles his military dishonour resulted from a fundamental problem of religious and political ungovernability which he associated both with calvinism and with hostility to monarchy. (Since these were the same infections which had apparently sparked the Dutch and Bohemian rebellions it is hardly surprising that he ended up echoing his father's alliance with Spain.) For his opponents these

28 Scott, 'Popish Plot', pp. 119–20.
29 Harrington's analysis of the problem as military at heart is particularly penetrating. See *The Political Works of James Harrington*, ed. J. G. A. Pocock (Cambridge 1977), p. 198.

same humiliations resulted from a government as incompetent as it was popishly affected and arbitrary, and a consequent abandonment of England by God. In short the revisionist view of early Stuart religious and political problems as short-term and relatively superficial is contradicted both by the situation itself and by the contemporary analyses made of it on all hands. Although much to blame, sitting in the front seat of government, for driving like a Ferrari what was actually a Model-T Ford, Charles I and Laud do not constitute an adequate historical explanation for its disintegration on a bend. We need to look not only at the British car (Tudor registration) but also at the European road down which it was being chased. The immediate result of this military incapacity was disaster for European and fear for English protestantism. Since Charles proved incapable of warfare not only in Europe but against his own Scots and English subjects as well, the eventual result was destruction of the monarchy.

With the subsequent restoration of this institution in 1660 came that of Stuart military weakness, and, in time, of England's troubles. That is why all the turning points of Stuart history hinge upon foreign intervention: the importation of kings in 1603, 1660 and 1688–9; their export and indeed reexport in 1648 and 1688; foreign invasion or other humiliation in 1640, 1659, 1667, 1685 and 1688. It is a remarkable thought that the only seventeenth-century English monarch not shunted across the border in either direction was Charles I, executed by his subjects in front of his own banqueting house. It is characteristic of the national historiography – always dressed in black tie even when the history is sleeping rough – that an unsuccessful invasion attempt in 1588 is a famous English victory; a successful one in 1688 is exactly the same thing.

By bridging national boundaries, the Dutch enterprise of 1688–9 made possible the creation of a militarily competent British nation-state. For while the Channel did not wall England off from Europe, or its troubles, it may have from a solution to them. Early modern history shows that state-building only ever succeeded through the urgency of war. The state was created to fund war. In conservative aristocratic societies it took a life-and-death struggle for religious, political or territorial existence to provide the cutting edge necessary for change. In general this meant a land border in common with your enemy. Charles I's withdrawal from the European conflict, a luxury the Channel appeared to allow, may have been his crucial error: there could be no emulation thereafter of Richelieu's achievement. Some progress was made in 1642–59 but was subsequently undone. It was in the 1690s, through integration with the Dutch continental struggle, that Britain acquired a land border at last. The Dutch invasion of 1688, unlike the Scots in 1640, occupied London rather than Newcastle and so proved capable of imposing a settlement.[30] It was thereafter, behind the confidence generated by its European military capabilities, that England's domestic troubles began, though only gradually, to subside.

EVENTS AND IDEAS: THE ENGLISH REVOLUTION

Let us come, finally, to our third explanatory context. This I have called the *substance* of our subject: the relationship between events, structures and ideas. I have already mentioned the fragility of this society's institutional structures, and the power of its ideas. And after the length and depth of its experience of political instability, I have mentioned what I take to be the second defining feature of seventeenth-century English history: its extraordinary intellectual fertility. This embraced science, literature, philosophy and political thought, but here I wish to focus upon those ideas that were a specific consequence of England's troubles; that lay at the vortex of that storm; that followed from the collapse of the country's religious and political institutions. These were English radicalism, and this *was* the English revolution.

Let me repeat: English radicalism, the profoundest intellectual consequence of seventeenth-century instability, *was* the English revolution. This is our last imaginative hurdle: to understand a revolution that was not – although it had spectacular institutional *consequences* – an institutional occurrence at all. This is harder than it might seem, when one aspect of our modernity is to live within the most densely structured and governed social matrix the world has ever seen. It is precisely our modern disposition to look for revolution as a constitutional event that is substantially to blame for the historiographical confusion on this subject. Reputable positions held at the moment include the following:

(1) That there was no English revolution.
(2) That there was, but we don't know when: significant contenders include 1640, 1641, 1649, 1688–9.

---

30 Jonathan Israel (ed.), *The Anglo-Dutch Moment: Essays on the Glorious Revolution and Its World Impact* (Cambridge 1991).

(3) That there was more than one: two, or three, or any other number comprising both major earthquakes and, it may be, small pre- or aftershocks.

(4) That there was an entire century of revolution – one way of getting around the problem of dating.

We are at sea here, because we have been looking in the wrong place. Let me add a fifth position of my own: that there was a revolution, but it is not to when, but what it was that we need to pay prior attention. *What* the English revolution was was belief – radical belief; and this made its mark on time not as an event, but, again, as a process. This was molten, fluid and dangerous, and after the initial eruption of the 1640s it flowed down the blackened and broken mountainside of English political history for some time.

Our modern imagination of revolutions is deeply influenced by Marx. In Russia and China 'revolutionaries' succeeded by taking control of the awesome apparatus of the modern nation-state and using it to transform those societies. When seventeenth-century radicals – Ireton, Cromwell and others – came at last to take such control, the situation could not have been more different. There was no such apparatus. Their attitude to what there was was: what do we do with it? The manipulation of public institutions lay outside the field of radical ambition. Its relationship to them was hostile and negative: transcend and sweep them away as an obstacle to the closer union of man with God; keep them out of the hands of your enemies. In the words of Joshua Sprigge at Whitehall in 1648: 'God will bring forth a New Heaven and a New Earth. In the meane time you're work is to restraine, indeed to restraine the Magistrate from such a power.'[31] That is why *constitutionally* the revolution manifested itself as chaos; an absence; a void. As one royalist poet put it after the regicide:

This crime hath widdowed our whole Nation
voided all Forms, left but privation in
Church and State.[32]

31 Charles H. Firth (ed.), *The Clarke Papers* (4 vols., London 1899–1965), vol. II, p. 87, quoted in J. C. Davis, 'Religion and the Struggle for Freedom in the English Revolution', *Historical Journal* 35, 3 (1992), p. 520.

32 *An Elegie upon King Charles the First, Murthered publikely by His Subjects*, quoted in Peter Malekin, *Liberty and Love: English Literature and Society 1640–1688* (London 1981).

It was of course the inability of the revolution to successfully define itself institutionally during the interregnum that accounted for its *constitutional* failure. Yet since it was not primarily a constitutional occurrence, we should not confuse this history of failure with the history of the revolution itself. How can we turn from these accidental manifestations of the revolution to its substance?

The answer is by turning from so-called political and constitutional history – as if the two were self-evidently equivalent – to the history of radical belief. To see this in its practical and intellectual contexts is to understand both the revolution and its power. In a conservative pre-industrial society the emergence of radical belief on a large scale was a consequence of institutional meltdown. The disappearance of effective religious magistracy from 1640 inaugurated the first phase. The disappearance of monarchy ushered in the second. But radicalism as a process outlived these beginnings and developed its own momentum and history. The radicals themselves were a small minority, yet this phenomenon affected English society as a whole. That this minority were armed and took over the country may help to explain this fact. It is in this sense that the English revolution stands at the heart of the seventeenth-century experience, and held the rest of that experience in its grip.

Understanding the revolution above all means coming to terms with the scale and achievement of the English radical imagination. How could these people have reconfigured themselves so dazzlingly and ambitiously in place and time? How could this process have moved so quickly, and so variously? How could it so often have re-invented the very languages through which it was expressed? One thinks not only of Milton, but of Coppe, Winstanley and others to be reminded that this was a time when history aspired successfully to the condition of poetry. For some, like George Fox, language itself became a form to be transcended: 'I saw that which was without end, and things which cannot be uttered, and of the greatness and infinitude of the love of God, which cannot be expressed by words.'[33] From another perspective William Sancroft spoke after the regicide of 'these enormous crimes, which no words yet in use can reach'.[34]

It is one short step from understanding the fragility of the institutions of

33 Fox, *Journal*, p. 15.
34 Quoted in John Spurr, *The Restoration Church of England 1646–1689* (New Haven 1991), pp. 20–1.

this society to seeing the relative freedom and power of the contemporary imagination in relation to them. God's church was eternal, but the seventeenth-century church was recent, peculiar and, as it turned out, not particularly resilient. Here is John Donne, no radical, talking about the arbitrary human mapping of the sky:

For of Meridians and Parallels
Man hath weav'd out a net
and this net throwne Upon the Heavens
and now they are his owne.
Loth to goe up the hill, or labour thus
To goe to heaven
we make heaven come to us.[35]

Here is the radical Gerrard Winstanley talking about the arbitrary human mapping of the *earth*, by way of imagining away the primary economic institution of his society:

[It is] selfish imagination, arbitrary invention, to enclose parcels of the earth into several divisions and call those enclosures proper or peculiar to oneself . . . [But God is] coming on amain; to break down all your pinfolds and lay all open to the common; the rough ways he will make smooth, and crooked ways straight; and level mountains and valleys.[36]

What these perceptions share is their view of the arbitrariness and triviality of human contrivance in the greatness of God's world. We see the astonishing extent of radical ambition if we follow this imaginative process through the annihilation of inherited institutions to their reconstruction. This culminated in the work of James Harrington who, faced with God's power, couldn't resist plugging himself into the grid. *Oceana* would be immortal, for it had successfully copied the only immortal thing. This was the universe, the perfect handiwork of God. The orbs, galaxies and other astronomical bodies of which Harrington's work is full are actually the heavens. Its author believed he was the first man to scientifically understand, in order to imitate, the creation. Accordingly at the end of *Oceana* the lawgiver Olphaeus Megelator

35 See n. 2.
36 Quoted in Michael McKeon, 'Politics of Discourses and the Rise of the Aesthetic', in K. Sharpe and S. Zwicker (eds.), *Politics of Discourse* (Los Angeles 1987), p. 43.

conceived such a delight within him, as God is [said] to have done, when he finished the creation of the world, and saw his orbs move below him. For in the art of man, being the imitation of nature which is the art of God, there is nothing so like the first call of beautiful order out of chaos . . . as the architecture of a well-ordered commonwealth.[37]

We have seen England's troubles as a shaking of the earth and sky, leading to the collapse of some familiar buildings. We now find its imaginative consequence, the English revolution, spanning the earth and sky. This radical process too had three phases, spanning a much longer period than has usually been understood. While all three connected and overlapped, each had an identifiable English practical and European intellectual context.

The first, civil war radicalism, was a product of the 1640s. This followed from the collapse of religious magistracy and was distinguished by its religious character. Its European context was the radical (non-magisterial) reformation. With the earlier manifestations of this in central and western Europe it shared much, including its millennialism, and its social doctrines of practical christianity.[38] In England, however, the radical reformation outstripped its predecessors, for in England in the 1640s, unlike Germany in the 1520s, the radical army was on the winning side. This was the initial and devastating impulse of the English revolution, and it carried not only English but European history into uncharted waters.

The second phase of radicalism, English republicanism, was a product of the 1650s. This followed most obviously the abolition of monarchy. To it fell the task of attempting to fill this void. The European context to which it turned was the republican thought of the renaissance, and through it that of the ancient world; in the words of Sidney, 'Aristotle . . . Plato, Plutarch, Thucydides, Xenephon, Polybius, and all the ancient Grecians, Italians, and others who asserted the natural freedom of mankind'.[39] For, said Milton, 'the sun, which we want, ripens wits as well as fruits; and as wine and oil are imported to us from abroad, so must ripe understanding and many civil

---

37 Harrington, *Oceana*, in *Political Works*, pp. 229, 341; see Jonathan Scott, 'The Rapture of Motion: James Harrington's Republicanism', in N. Phillipson and Q. Skinner (eds.), *Political Discourse in Early Modern Britain* (Cambridge 1993).

38 See Michael Baylor (ed.), *The Radical Reformation* (Cambridge 1991).

39 Algernon Sidney, *Discourses Concerning Government*, in *Sydney on Government: The Works of Algernon Sydney*, ed. J. Robertson (London 1772), p. 11.

virtues be . . . from foreign writings and examples of best ages; we shall else miscarry'.[40] The result, if it did not secure republicanism in England, became, in several hands, one of the revolution's most significant intellectual and literary legacies.

The final phase of this process was restoration radicalism. This blossomed particularly during the restoration crisis of 1678–83. It drew upon both its religious and classical predecessors; and from this process of historical revisitation, within the broader context of political repetition already described, there emerged in the work of Locke, Sidney and others some of the most influential radical writing of the century.[41] This depicted the revolution itself through the lens of restoration memory. The result became a prism, receiving light from the renaissance and reformation and refracting it towards the Enlightenment.

CONCLUSION

Let us return to the question with which we began: how might we structure a political history of seventeenth-century England? We have the three crises which constitute the troubles. We have the three phases of radicalism that are the revolution that resulted. And we have the three-stage restoration process by which contemporaries struggled to deliver themselves from this situation. One broke the peace and, eventually, the structures of church and state. The second cascaded from this ruptured fabric before it could be repaired. The third saw the painful restitching of a rent garment. I hope we have arrived at this framework by restoring the contemporary experience to its own contexts in time and space. I believe not only that this brings us closer, imaginatively, to seventeenth-century English history. It also enables us better to understand its historical significance. It is by restoring English history to its European context that we can come to see what was actually unique about it. Through its openness, and vulnerability, to both the practical and intellectual forces shaping early modern Europe, the English experience would become a European shaping force in its own right.

---

40 Quoted in Blair Worden, 'Milton and the Tyranny of Heaven', in Gisela Bock, Quentin Skinner and Maurizio Viroli (eds.), *Machiavelli and Republicanism* (Cambridge 1990), pp. 233–4.
41 Scott, *Restoration Crisis*; Scott, 'The Law of War: Grotius, Sidney, Locke and the Political Theory of Rebellion', *History of Political Thought* 13, 4 (Winter 1992).

The principal direct legacy of this experience was intellectual. This would bear fruit not only in Europe but in the United States of America as well. It is hardly surprising that the intellectual impact of the English revolution should ultimately be clearer outside that country than in it. The English reaction to the pain and chaos that brought it into being was, as soon as it safely could be done, to bolt the door against it. From a distance it is this restoration impulse – the impulse of forgetting – that is impressive; we still live in restoration times.

PART I

England's troubles 1618–89:
political instability

The Causes and Motives of seditions are innovation in religion, taxes, alteration of laws and customs, breaking of privileges, general oppression, advancement of unworthy persons . . . and whatsoever in offending people joineth and knitteth them together in a common cause . . . Disputing, excusing, cavilling upon mandates and directions, is a kind of shaking off the yoke, and assay of disobedience . . . Also, as Machiavel noteth well, when princes, that ought to be common parents, make themselves as a party, and lean to a side, that is, as a boat that is overthrown by uneven weight on one side.

Sir Francis Bacon, *Of Seditions and Troubles*[1]

1 *Bacon's Essays*, ed. E. A. Abbott (2 vols., London 1889), vol. I, pp. 47, 49.

2

Taking contemporary belief seriously

Things that love night,
Love not such nights as these: The wrathful skies
Gallow the very wanderers of the darke
And make them keep their Caves: since I was a man
Such sheets of Fire, such bursts of horrid Thunder,
Such groanes of roaring Winde, and Raine, I never
Remember to have heard. Man's Nature cannot carry
Th'affliction, nor the feare.

William Shakespeare, *King Lear*, Act III, scene ii, ll. 38–45[2]

INTRODUCTION: BEHIND THE VEIL OF RESTORATION

To recover England's troubles it is necessary to re-enter an alien mental world. In this respect, as Robert Darnton reminds us: 'the most promising moment in research can be the most puzzling. When we run into something that seems unthinkable to us, we may have hit upon a valid point of entry into an alien mentality.'[3] Our present distance from the perceptions and fears that underlay the troubles is more than simply the effect of the intervening three hundred years. It is politically created: the first and final imperative of restoration was forgetting.

The signs of this are everywhere. They are visible, not least, in English incomprehension in the face of the attitudes sustaining the last theatre of the troubles. That Northern Ireland's conflict has its origins in the seventeenth century is well enough understood. What is less frequently pointed

2 William Shakespeare, *The Tragedie of King Lear*, in *Mr William Shakespeare's Comedies, Histories and Tragedies* (London 1623), p. 296.
3 Quoted in Miles Fairburn, *Nearly out of Heart and Hope: The Puzzle of a Colonial Labourer's Diary* (Auckland 1995), p. 22.

out is that in the seventeenth century those troubles were English. It is then that we find the perceptions and language of that anti-hero Ian Paisley (a protestant enclave under encirclement, 'popery' whooping around the outside) in the mouths of England's heroes: John Pym, Oliver Cromwell, John Milton, the Earl of Shaftesbury, the Prince of Orange. That Ireland remains infected today is a direct consequence of its devastating embroilment in the seventeenth-century English conflict. This was a conflict ultimately resolved, for England at least, not by compromise and negotiation, but by a military power which required the transformation of the English state.

It is the same distance that has rendered so many seventeenth-century English perceptions incomprehensible to modern historians. As we have seen, behind historiographical accusations of irrationality it is not difficult to perceive imaginative distance.[4] Charles I 'appears to have been in the grip of something approaching paranoia whenever he contemplated the question of whether his people were loyal and obedient'.[5] The popish plot fear of 1678 was 'one of the most remarkable outbreaks of mass hysteria in English history'.[6] As our distance from the contexts of contemporary perceptions has increased, so our attempts to substitute for them have become more elaborate. One reviewer of the most recent major study of the first episode of the troubles (1637–42) was moved to ask its author 'why he does not take what men said was happening as the core of his historical analysis'.[7]

It has been a long time since our explanations of the troubles took as their preliminary focus contemporary belief. No participant in the troubles spoke of 'the British problem', or 'the problem of multiple kingdoms'. In his recent analysis Conrad Russell has spoken of 'seven events or non-events'

4 For a suggestion that this situation may be changing, see Alexandra Walsham's '"The Fatall Vesper": Providentialism and Anti-Popery in Late Jacobean London', *Past and Present* 144 (August 1994). As Walsham says (pp. 86–7): 'Far from [being] a set of phobias and irrational beliefs, providentialism, like anti-popery, could on occasion operate as a coherent and unifying force.'

5 Richard Cust, *The Forced Loan and English Politics 1626–1628* (Oxford 1987), p. 88.

6 *Memoirs of Sir John Reresby*, ed. Andrew Browning (Glasgow 1936), quoted in E. Lipson, 'The Elections to the Exclusion Parliaments 1679–1681', *English Historical Review* 28 (1913), p. 74; Geoffrey Holmes, review of J. P. Kenyon, *The Popish Plot* (Harmondsworth 1972), back cover; Kenyon, *Popish Plot*, jacket.

7 Anthony Fletcher, review of Russell, *Causes of the English Civil War, Unrevolutionary England 1603–1643* (London 1990) and *Fall of the British Monarchies*, in *Historical Journal* 36, 1 (1993), pp. 211–16; see also the review article by Blair Worden, 'Conrad Russell's Civil War', *London Review of Books*, 29 August 1991, pp. 13–14.

without which there could have been no civil war.[8] This is in turn the outcome of a longstanding methodological preoccupation. This is the insistence that it is necessary to reconstitute the contemporary narrative before bringing to bear upon it our explanatory questions.[9] The principal consequence of such assumptions is to replace, at two removes (by selection through narrative, and then by secondary analysis), the explanations of contemporaries themselves.

Perhaps there is even a professional imperative at work. If the (misposed) question 'what were the causes of the English civil war?' could be answered, and if the answer, moreover, were relatively straightforward and had been obvious for three hundred and fifty years, the professional implications might be quite serious. We live, accordingly, within a sophisticated historiographical culture, the purpose of which is not to answer questions but to ask them, and to protect them against answers which are offered, violently if necessary.

Yet this is more than a function of modern condescension or professional self-interest. The suggestion that contemporaries didn't understand their situation is as old as the Convention parliament's guilty suggestion to the new king in 1660 that the destruction of his father had followed from 'mistakes, and misunderstandings'.[10] It is an effect, that is to say, of restoration erasure. To recover the troubles it is necessary to step back behind that veil. When we do this we will find that the king was executed deliberately (the alternative being further to expose 'this poore bleeding kingdome' to 'the Tyranny of an enraged and bloud-guilty king').[11] We will discover that there was indeed, throughout the century, a 'popish plot'. We will discover that Charles I's problem was indeed the catastrophic disloyalty of some upon whose support he depended, and who were in this sense 'enemies to all monarchical government' in *practice*.

Our first step in this process of recovery will be the identification of contemporary belief. In relation to the troubles, as later the revolution and restoration,

---

8 Russell, *Causes of the English Civil War*; see also Russell, *Fall of the British Monarchies*.

9 Russell, *Unrevolutionary England*, p. xi.

10 *A Letter to the Kings most Excellent Majesty from The Commons of England* (London, 14 May 1660), p. 2. More recently, Kevin Sharpe and Peter Lake explain ('Introduction', in Lake and Sharpe (eds.), *Culture and Politics in Early Stuart England* (London 1994), p. 2): 'In this [revisionist] interpretative world what was closed to contemporaries was clear to the modern historian.'

11 William Sedgewick, *The Parliament Under the power of the Sword. With a briefe Answer thereunto By some of the Army* (London 1648), p. 7.

we will allow these processes to be defined by those involved. The second step is to recover the contexts, in time and space, within which those contemporary utterances may be understood. The principal imaginative difficulty in this respect, as we will see, is that we are looking at our subject from the wrong side of the decisive restoration of 1689–1714. By a series of measures, including the debarring of catholics from the crown, and the construction of a modern military-fiscal state, that settlement, once it had successfully defended itself by war, began the process of defusing the problems which had governed English politics for more than a century. Without the reality of seventeenth-century religious and political vulnerability, or the fears to which it gave rise, the crises of the century became historically incomprehensible.[12]

POLITICAL INSTABILITY

In the troubles, it has been suggested, we are examining one of the two distinguishing features of seventeenth-century English history. This was both the length, and depth, of its experience of political instability. 'Political stability', wrote J. H. Plumb,

is a comparatively rare phenomenon in the history of human society. When achieved it has seldom lasted. But perhaps one should define political stability: by this I mean the acceptance by society of its political institutions, and of those classes of men or officials who control them. Conspiracy, plot, revolution, and civil war, which have marked the history of most societies of Western Europe in modern times, are obviously the expression of acute instability.[13]

If political stability had indeed been so rare, then our subject here might be little more than England's experience of normality. In fact, however, Plumb's analysis prefaces a more specific study. In this, political stability is the condition perfected by Sir Robert Walpole; its opposite is the condition of England in the seventeenth century:

In the seventeenth century men killed, tortured and executed each other for political beliefs; they sacked towns and brutalised the countryside. They were subjected to conspiracy, plot and invasion. This uncertain political world lasted until 1715, and then began rapidly to vanish. By comparison, the political structure of eighteenth-century England possesses adamantine strength and profound inertia.[14]

12 Scott, 'Popish Plot'.
13 J. H. Plumb, *The Growth of Political Stability in England 1675–1725* (London 1967), p. 12.
14 *Ibid.*, p. 13.

In truth, for most of the century seventeenth-century England did not lack 'the acceptance by society of its political institutions, and of those classes of men or officials who control them'. These institutions and classes were similar in 1620 and in 1720, and similarly accepted: it had been the purpose of restoration to achieve this. They had, however, been enormously strengthened, fiscally and militarily. They had also been internally secured: in 1720 neither established protestantism, parliaments nor monarchy had reason to fear for their own existence. The seventeenth-century problem was not public *acceptance* of those institutions which would at one point be swept away. It was their dysfunctional fragility *in practice*, particularly in the turbulent European circumstances.

Thus, as we will see, there was an institutional *context* for the troubles. There were, similarly, institutional contexts for the revolution (institutional absence) and restoration (institutional reconstruction). It is in turning from contexts to causes that it is necessary to recover contemporary belief. Meanwhile whatever we may think of Plumb's actually very specific understanding of stability, the symptoms of extreme seventeenth-century instability were indeed those mentioned: plot, invasion, conspiracy, crisis, civil war and revolution. During the seventeenth century every serious political disorder that could befall a kingdom did befall England and its Stuart-governed neighbours. Parliamentary crises immobilised English politics in the 1620s, 1640s, 1670s and 1680s. There were successful foreign invasions in 1640 and 1688, and other ineffectively opposed incursions in 1659, 1667 and 1685. There was civil war which, during the period 1640–51, resulted in casualties the extent of which are only now beginning to be understood. If England lost 3.7 per cent of its population between 1640 and 1660 (190,000 people), a greater percentage than in either of the twentieth century's world wars, Scotland may have lost 6 per cent (60,000) and Ireland a chilling 41 per cent (660,000).[15]

Thereafter, between 1660 and 1688 perhaps a thousand people died in England alone for their political or religious beliefs at the hands of a nervous and vengeful restoration judiciary.[16] Torture and execution reached a peak during the same period in Scotland, to be followed by further war in Scotland and Ireland during the 1690s. English casualties, too, ran into the tens of thousands between 1689 and 1713 in wars that may properly be seen as the last phase of the troubles.

15 Charles Carlton, *Going to the Wars: The Experience of the British Civil Wars 1638–1651* (London 1992).   16 Scott, 'Restoration Process', pp. 633–7.

To the extent of these casualties must be added the savagery of the conflicts themselves. There were the massacres of civilians, particularly in
Ireland and Scotland, which killed 10,000–15,000 people during the 1640s
and 1690s. There was the public hanging, drawing and quartering of at least
twenty-four catholics in London between 1678 and 1681, purely on account
of their religion, in the face of unflinching protestations of their innocence,
after show trials fabricated from the publicly funded lies of informers.[17]
Amid the butchery of the Bloody Assizes of 1685, in the course of which
almost 200 men were hanged, drawn and quartered, there was Alice Lisle,
the last woman to be burned alive at the stake in England, for harbouring a
fugitive from the killing fields of Sedgemoor.[18]

None of these atrocities would, in fact, have surprised any French, Dutch
or German person who had lived through their own recent wars of religion.
This was England's deferred experience of a conflict which, in the words of
the French protestant pastor Pierre Vivet, 'is not like other wars, for even the
very poorest man has an interest in it, since we are fighting for freedom of
conscience [la liberté de nos consciences]'. As Locke recorded, religion had in
his time served as 'a perpetual foundation of war and contention: all those
flames that have made such havoc and desolation in Europe, and have not
been quenched but with the blood of so many millions, have been at first
kindled with coals from the altar'.[19] Sir William Temple was one of many
who wrote, in the context of Europe's 'Violent . . . Differences of Religion', of
'The long Civil Wars, at first of France, then of Germany, and lastly of
England'.[20] 'In these late, bad, and worst of times', recorded a pamphlet in
1648,

wherein all the Christian World hath been imbroyl'd with Warre, and all the miseries of Sword, Fire, and Famine; when Nation did rise against Nation, and Realme
against Realme; the *Swede* against the *German* Emperour, the *Pole* against the
Russian, the Spaniard against the French, the Hollander against the Spaniard, and
France in most bloody and cruell Civil war with itselfe. When all those Kingdomes
and Territories were . . . drencht and neer drownd with blood and slaughter, these

17 Scott, 'Popish Plot', pp. 108–9, 126–7.
18 Richard Greaves, *Secrets of the Kingdom: British Radicals from the Popish Plot to the
   Revolution of 1688–1689* (Stanford 1992), p. 293; Robin Clifton, *The Last Popular
   Rebellion: The Western Rising of 1685* (London 1984).
19 Locke, *Two Tracts*, ed. Philip Abrams (Cambridge 1967), pp. 160–1.
20 Sir William Temple, *Observations Upon the United Provinces*, in *The Works of Sir William
   Temple* (2 vols., London 1720), vol. I, pp. 59, 62.

Kingdomes of England, Scotland and Ireland were . . . the onely . . . spectators and lookers on . . . [yet] Warre we would have at any rate or price whatsoever . . . killing and cutting throats, robbing, rifling, plundering . . . spoyling, and ruinating one another (under the fair pretences of Religion and Reformation) with more barbarous inhumanity and cruelty, then could have been committed here by . . . millions of Turkes, Tartars, or Cannibals.[21]

Yet England's seventeenth-century experience was also to take it beyond that of other nations, into revolution. This included the public trial and beheading of the king, an act so far removed from custom and experience as to shock and amaze the whole of Europe. Living through such events, contemporaries resorted to a variety of modes of description. They spoke naturally, and repeatedly, of the awesome power of God. If the regicide had been demanded by God of some, 'while blood defileth the land', so was a response to it by others. 'Now we have nothing left', wrote William Sancroft, 'but to importune God to whom vengeance belongs, that he would show himself forth, and speedily account with these prodigious monsters, or else hasten his coming to judgement.'[22]

Contemporaries spoke equally, alongside God, of the elements: of sea, storm, earthquake and inundation. In his history of 'a War . . . much *more then Civill*', a war contextualised alongside that earlier in the Netherlands, Thomas May apologised for the necessary 'description of Shipwracks, Ruines, and Desolations'.[23] In 1659 Locke wrote to Thomas Westrow: 'O for a Pilot that would steare the tossed ship of this state to the haven of happiness . . . [yet] God is the hand that governs all things, and manages our chaos.' After the restoration he explained that he had lived 'as if in a storm for most of my life', and looked forward to 'the approaches of calm with the greatest joy and satisfaction'.[24] By 1683, however, not only was he to be disappointed, but in exile and in fear for his life. It was accordingly in vain that another contemporary warned 'the great ship of our whole nation' that 'we ought now to be very careful of putting to sea again, that have been so dangerously tost in the storm'.[25] As

21 *Wee have brought our Hogges to a Faire Market* (London 1648), p. 1.
22 Quoted in Spurr, *Restoration Church*, pp. 20–1.
23 Thomas May, *The History of the Parliament of England: which began November the third 1640* (London 1647), preface.
24 *The Correspondence of John Locke*, ed. E. S. de Beer (8 vols., Oxford 1976–89), vol. I, p. 82; W. Spellman, *John Locke* (London 1997).
25 *The Parallel: or, The New Specious Association an old Rebellious Covenant* (London 1682), p. 14.

the quote at the head of this chapter reminds us, seventeenth-century political weather was of that tempestuous kind familiar to the audiences of Shakespeare.[26]

This was the same language with which contemporaries referred to the passions: 'as storms, torrents, tempests. They are winds that put the mind in tumult, sweeping us along like ships in a gale.'[27] It is perhaps no surprise that the dominant contemporary explanation of England's troubles would focus upon religious and political passions. Tumults in the state were prefigured by tumults in the soul. This echoed contemporary explanation in earlier theatres of the troubles, in particular in sixteenth-century France.[28] It was in 1624, the year of England's entry into the European war, that Robert Burton published his famous *Anatomy of Melancholy*. 'Who is not sicke, or ill disposed', its preface asked, 'in whom doth not passion, anger, envy, discontent, fear and sorrow raigne?'[29] Such 'mixte passion' was the result, not only of nerve-wracking contemporary events, but news about them:

I heare new newes every day . . . [of what] these tempestuous times afford . . . of warre, plagues, fires, inundations, massacres, meteors . . . of townes taken, cities besieged in France, Germany, Turkey, Persia, Poland etc. dayly musters and preparations . . . so many men slain . . . shipwrackes, Piracies and Seafights . . . new bookes every day, pamphlets, currantoes, stories, new paradoxes, schisms . . . controversies.[30]

By the restoration period the impact of reading upon the passions had attracted a major scientific literature and body of experimentation.[31]

Finally, contemporaries spoke of the power of belief. When Charles I explained in 1646, 'I have long ago resolved rather to shipwreck my person than either my conscience or my beliefs', he was speaking as a man of his

---

26 For other advice on 'the Safety of the Ship . . . [of] State' in the 'great Storms and rough Seas . . . [of this] Tempestuous Season', see Temple, 'Of Popular Discontents', in *Works*, vol. I, p. 270.

27 Susan James, *Passion and Action: The Emotions in Seventeenth-Century Philosophy* (Oxford 1997).

28 Mark Greengrass, *Governing Passions: The Reformation of the Kingdom in the French Civil Wars 1576–1586* (forthcoming); A. Levi, *French Moralists: The Theory of the Passions* (London 1964).

29 Democritus Junior [Robert Burton], *The Anatomy of Melancholy: What it is* (Oxford 1624), p. 14.   30 *Ibid.*, pp. 3–4.

31 Johns, *Nature of the Book*, ch. 6, 'The Physiology of Reading: Print and the Passions'.

time.[32] He was also providing a characteristic underassessment of the damage involved; the royal person, when finally washed up, would signal a shipwrecked kingdom. Belief was closely linked to, and in the view of some a straightforward function of, the passions. But it was also because belief connected people to the power and authority of God that it was such a formidable force in the seventeenth century. It was affected by events, inside and outside national boundaries, and informed by a rapidly developing print culture. This operated within, and received potency from, a still thriving popular culture of performance and orality.[33] Andrew Marvell, one of the century's most powerful writers, knew of what he spoke when he exclaimed: '*O Printing!* how hast thou disturbed the Peace of Mankind! that Lead, when moulded into Bullets, is not so mortal as when founded into Letters.'[34] William Temple explained: 'the Impressions made upon every man's Belief and Conscience . . . Men may disguise and dissemble, but no man can resist. For Belief is no more in a Man's Power, then his Stature or his Feature.'[35]

If, therefore, 'seventeenth century men killed, tortured and executed each other for political beliefs', that was because belief lay at the heart of the troubles. Every one of the three seventeenth-century processes under examination here focused upon belief, whether as cause (of the troubles), substance (of the revolution) or subject (of restoration recontainment).[36] In the troubles, it has been suggested, we see the destructive effect upon fragile institutions of powerful beliefs. In that fragility we find an institutional context. In those beliefs we will find their cause. Let us look briefly at each in turn.

32 Hence Sir Thomas Wentworth's rule 'which I will never transgress . . . never to . . . contest with a king but when I am constrained thereunto or else make shipwreck of my peace of conscience, which I trust God will ever bless me with, and with courage to preserve it': quoted in Martin Butler, *Theatre and Crisis 1632–1642* (Cambridge 1984).

33 Dagmar Freist, *Governed by Opinion: Politics, Religion and the Dynamics of Communication in Stuart London 1637–1645* (London 1997).

34 Quoted in N. H. Keeble, *The Literary Culture of Nonconformity in Later Seventeenth-Century England* (Athens, Ga. 1987), p. 127.

35 Temple, *Observations*, in *Works*, p. 55.

36 To this extent it is not only the case that our subject is the relationship between political and intellectual history. In the recovery of belief it is necessary to bring to the former some of the methodological self-consciousness of the latter. See Quentin Skinner, 'A Reply to My Critics', in James Tully (ed.), *Meaning and Context: Quentin Skinner and His Critics* (Princeton 1988), pp. 246–59.

PILOT ERROR OR MECHANICAL FAILURE?

As we have seen, modern historians have not been slow to attribute the troubles to contemporary ineptitude, error or misunderstanding. At the moment such explanations fall broadly into two camps. Although these are not mutually exclusive, they are distinct in their implications and best considered in turn. This is the distinction, in seeking to explain the seventeenth-century crash, between mechanical failure and pilot error.

In the aftermath of any disaster the diagnosis favoured by accident inspectors and aircraft makers alike is pilot error. It is the easiest and cheapest, it has no commercial implications, it offers the hope of better things in the future and it is particularly convenient when the pilot is dead. Thus the most important single explanation currently on offer for the collapse of the Caroline monarchy focuses upon the personal and political failures of Charles I.[37] Students readily take to this picture of a king so insecure, incompetent and malevolent as to constitute a complete monarchical self-destruction package. They dwell with fascination upon Charles' supposed personal failings, without ever asking themselves how important these actually were to the practice of contemporary kingship. In an important if limited sense seventeenth-century monarchy was personal government. Yet if monarchy really depended upon the personal qualities of monarchs it would long since have disappeared. The most important personal contributions of any seventeenth-century monarch were dynastic: undisputed succession and the provision of an heir. In these Elizabeth I was the spectacular failure and Charles I the success. The modern inversion of this verdict reinforces the impression that we have not been paying sufficient attention to the contemporary institutional context.[38]

To do this would bring us much more closely into contact with the practical problems Charles I faced. Alongside the vast literature upon the king's supposed personal failings the relative lack of attention paid to the state of early seventeenth-century English monarchy is striking. While this remains

---

37 John Morrill, *Revolt in the Provinces: The English People and the Tragedies of War* (London 1999), ch. 1; David Smith, *Double Crown*; Reeve, *Personal Rule*; Glenn Burgess, *The Politics of the Ancient Constitution* (London 1992); Charles Carlton, *Charles I: The Personal Monarch* (London 1983).

38 Recent exceptions to this generalisation include Kevin Sharpe, *The Personal Rule of Charles I* (New Haven 1992); Mark Kishlansky, 'Charles I: The Man Who Would Be King', paper delivered at Downing College, Cambridge, 28 January 1998.

the case it looks suspiciously as if the appeal of the smoking gun of personality is that it offers the alluring substitution for explanation of blame. It attributes a great deal of (destructive) power to one man in what was an age of limited and declining monarchical power. It pays far too little attention to the continuity of the troubles across the century. In particular it neglects the continuity of relevant religious and political problems across the imaginary dividing lines of 1625 and 1660.

This is not to say in general, however, that the institutional problems of the 1620s have been ignored. This brings us from the verdict of pilot error to that of mechanical failure. Here Conrad Russell has drawn attention in particular to the fiscal insufficiency of parliamentary supply.[39] He has gone on to emphasise the centrality of this problem to the military failures of 1624–9. Drawing upon the work of H. G. Koenigsberger he has attempted to set this in a broader European context, developing an account in the process of the problems of multiple monarchy in this period.[40]

It is not to detract from the crucial importance of this work to suggest some alternative or additional emphases. Russell's European comparisons (France and Spain) may not be as illuminating for the 1620s as Emperor Ferdinand's Habsburg monarchy. This was not only a statebuilding model available to Charles I but also supplies a context that shifts the focus away from the 'problem' of multiple monarchy to that of confessional statebuilding (see chapter 5). Meanwhile an adequate analysis of the institutional context of the troubles requires its extension in time across the whole century.[41] Finally, in a political culture where monarchy and parliaments were interdependent, particularly militarily, it requires as much attention to be given to monarchical as to parliamentary weakness and dysfunction. Intermittently Russell has recognised this, remarking that 'In the middle of the Thirty Years War, it must be an open question how long a monarchy which was unable to fight was able to survive.'[42] Yet in general, in reaction against the previous whig suggestion that parliaments were increasing in

---

39 For Russell the crisis of parliaments was a crisis of financial incapacity: Conrad Russell, 'Parliaments and the English State at the End of the Sixteenth Century', first Trevelyan Lecture, Cambridge, 1995.

40 Russell, 'Monarchies, Wars and Estates in England, France and Spain 1580–1640', in Russell, *Unrevolutionary England*.

41 A need recognised by Russell, who remarks that the necessary 'detailed discussion of the events of James II's reign . . . is beyond the chronological scope of this article': *ibid.*, p. 121.

42 Russell, *Parliaments and English Politics 1621–1629* (Oxford 1979), p. 83.

power and self-confidence, he has directed his attention to a demonstration of their weakness and vulnerability.[43] Parliaments, we are told, were an event, not an institution (in fact they were both). 'Throughout this period England was and remained a monarchy, and even though that monarchy might sometimes call Parliaments, the king remained the only permanent source of power. Any power a Parliament might possess was its power to persuade the king.'[44] This does not explain, of course, how that monarchy came subsequently to be militarily defeated by one of its parliaments, and then abolished.

CONTEXTS AND CAUSES

It is the suggestion of this study that, with these augmentations and re-emphases, what Russell has termed 'functional breakdown', particularly in its fiscal and military dimensions, furnishes a crucial domestic *context* for the troubles. It is an equally central context for that long-term process of statebuilding by which they were eventually brought to an end (chapters 17 and 21). For the troubles' *causes*, however, it is necessary to follow other scholars (including Hirst, Sommerville, Cogswell, Reeve and Cust) who have placed much more emphasis upon the impact of religious and political belief.

It was above all the effect of the European war upon English opinion from 1618 which applied intolerable pressure to an institutional superstructure incapable of making war. It is a crucial argument of Russell's that, contrary to the impression held by earlier historians and by both early Stuart kings, most members of the House of Commons actually opposed war (on financial grounds). Behind the apparent war-fever of 1621 and 1624, orchestrated by Buckingham and a 'war-party' in the Lords, most Commoners were in fact 'isolationist' or 'lukewarm'.[45] Actually, as both primary evidence and recent secondary work makes clear, this interpretation is fundamentally uncon-vincing.[46] The impact made upon English public opinion by the Bohemian crisis and its aftermath was enormous (which is why James, Buckingham and Charles all responded to it, negatively or positively). This was a conflict that involved fundamental English religious and dynastic interests.

---

43 This transformation of historiographical emphasis is traced by Hexter's 'Early Stuarts and Parliament'.   44 Russell, *Unrevolutionary England*, pp. xiii–xiv.

45 Russell, *Parliaments and English Politics*, pp. 78–9.

46 Cogswell, *Blessed Revolution*, pp. 3–35.

Accordingly, in the words of Thomas Cogswell, 'nothing focused public attention so closely and so long as the first decade of the Thirty Years War'.[47]

Thus in 1648, with Charles I facing ruin, Buckingham's own agent Balthazar Gerbier echoed John Rushworth and many others in tracing the troubles back to the impact upon 'the People' of these developments:

To shoe the direct cause of som Jealousies wherewith the People have been tormented even from the beginning of King James' Raigne . . . the first thing which did possesse the People with mistakes was the tenderest, dearest, Important and most powerfull casse that could be in agitation: The preservation of the true Religion . . . And as that was the mayne object whereon the People had fixed their hearts, so were theire Eyes and Eares, Scouts to discover what past abroad: for they conceaved themselves to be secure anough at home . . . the reformed Churches abroad they held as contrescarps and outworkes of the Church of England; And therefore as soone as any of them were threatened, the English did take it as a Cloud which might in time breake uppon them: This gave them apprehentions: Apprehentions raysing passions; Passions Leading to extreames both in action and judgement.[48]

It was these 'Passions' – first religious and then political – that made functional breakdown dangerous to domestic peace. It was by 'Apprehentions raysing passions' and 'Passions Leading to extreames' that failure in war in Europe established the context for rebellion and civil war at home. It was such 'Apprehentions', as we will see, and not military lukewarmness, that accounted for the crucial failure of parliamentary supply in 1625–6, and established the basis thereafter for polarisation and confrontation. It is for this reason that within the *contexts* of institutional fragility – the military vulnerability of the church, parliaments and the crown – we must direct our search for the *causes* of the troubles to the polarisation of belief. What, then, were those 'Apprehentions'? As we will see, they were apprehensions about the vulnerability of those very institutions. The first informed analysts of functional breakdown were contemporaries themselves.[49]

47 *Ibid.*, p. 24; Michael Frearson, 'The English Corantos', ch. 3, 'The Corantos and "Puritan" Opposition to Foreign Policy'. I am very grateful to Dr Frearson for supplying me with a copy of this chapter of his thesis.

48 British Library Add MS 4181, 'The Relation of sr Balthazar Gerbier kyt', 26 June 1648, pp. 7–8.

49 Contrary to the perspective summarised by Sharpe and Lake, 'Introduction', p. 2: 'perhaps the most powerful version of the revisionist case was based on an analysis of the real [*sic*], financial and material, causes of administrative and then political breakdown, causes which were in large part hidden from contemporaries and which their categories of thought were unable fully to comprehend'.

It is in this respect, first, that contemporaries may not have misunderstood their situation: it is we who have failed to understand them. Far from being hysterical or paranoid these anxieties may have been accurate perceptions of the relevant historical circumstances. Thereafter contemporary mistrust and polarisation may have followed not from misunderstanding, but from understanding. Within the context of continuing functional breakdown, civil war (an ideological civil war) may have been made possible only by well-founded and irreconcilable beliefs for which people were ultimately prepared to fight and die.

There is accordingly every reason to take contemporary utterances seriously. The conclusions to which this may lead us include the following:

(1) Parliaments were indeed not increasing in confidence or power, either before 1640, or after 1660. Throughout the period the tenor of parliamentary conduct and rhetoric is deeply defensive. Concern for the survival of parliaments accompanies, and becomes intertwined with, that for protestantism.

(2) That England was a monarchy did not make it a secure or effective one. Royal defensiveness on behalf of the perceived embattled status of kingly power is a no less consistent feature of the period. Here, as in (1) above, defensiveness did not preclude aggression, but it needs to be understood in this context.

(3) Alongside parliamentary anxiety about survival of the reformation, in its European context, we find royal anxiety about the effect of reformation religion on English royal power. The Stuart was the only major monarchy in Europe with predominantly calvinist subjects.

The aspect of these fears about which most has already been said is fear of popery. In the words of Derek Hirst: 'anti-catholicism [was] the one genuine religio-political conviction of ordinary people in the early seventeenth century'.[50] What need to be added to this observation are three things. The first is that this was the case throughout the century. The second is that this conviction hinged upon a perceived threat to protestantism not simply within England, or Britain, but upon the threat to the European reformation.[51] The third is that this opposition to counter-reformation is most accurately understood not simply, or even precisely, as anti-catholicism (thus it was not directed primarily against local catholics) but as anti-

50 Derek Hirst, *The Representative of the People?: Voters and Voting in England Under the Early Stuarts* (Cambridge 1975), pp. 145–6.
51 Scott, 'Popish Plot'; Scott, *Restoration Crisis*, esp. pt I.

popery, where 'the growth of popery' *meant* counter-reformation. In the words of Sir Thomas Meres in the reign of Charles II: 'Our Jealousies of popery, or an arbitrary government, are not from a few inconsiderable papists here, but from the ill example we have from France.'[52] It is because popery meant not just catholicism but anti-protestantism that it could attach itself to Laud's counter-reformation protestantism.[53]

English protestant fear of European popery was above all fear by an encir-cled enclave of invasion. This had its origins in the middle of the sixteenth century when this perspective persuaded William Cecil in favour of military intervention in Scotland to contain the danger through Scotland from catholic France.[54] Thereafter it remained a powerful force throughout the Elizabethan period, intensifying from the later 1570s in the context of the Dutch protestant struggle against Spain.[55] Cecil's fear, in 1569, of 'the invasion of England by the French king ... and the conquest and spoyle of the small flock that are now with all extremity compelled by armes to defend themselves against only the Pope's tyrannous bloody and poysoning persequutors', is an authentic expres-sion of 'the siege mentality of English protestantism' that was the most impor-tant motor of English politics until well into the eighteenth century.[56]

Thereafter, the Elizabethan succession problem helped to consolidate that intertwining of European religious with English dynastic concerns so characteristic also of the succeeding Stuart period. This perception of counter-reformation military danger was entirely justified. It furnishes one context for the increasing turning of English attention to Scotland and Ireland in a search for European confessional military security.[57] It contex-tualises similarly the conviction from the Elizabethan to the Hanoverian period that English and Dutch security were intertwined.[58] Finally this

---

52 Quoted in Kenyon, *Popish Plot*, p. 18.   53 Scott, *Restoration Crisis*, ch. 2.

54 Stephen Alford's 'William Cecil and the British Succession Crisis of the 1560s', Ph.D thesis, St Andrews 1996, subsequently published as *The Early Elizabethan Polity: William Cecil and the British Succession Crisis 1558–1569* (Cambridge 1998), has wider implica-tions some of which are considered in the next chapter. I am very grateful to Dr Alford for supplying me with a copy of his thesis.

55 For a case study in this perspective, see Blair Worden, *The Sound of Virtue: Philip Sidney's Arcadia and Elizabethan Politics* (New Haven 1996).

56 Alford, 'William Cecil', pp. xii, 23.   57 *Ibid.*, pp. 79–81.

58 J. R. Hale (ed.), *The Evolution of British Historiography from Bacon to Namier* (London 1967), p. 102; Longleat Bath MSS, Whitelocke Papers, vol. XIX, ff. 96–7; *The French Intrigues Discovered. With the Methods and Arts to Retrench the Potency of France by Land and Sea* (London 1681), p. 13.

confessional perspective helped to establish the basis for views of the security needs of the state which could and did challenge royal policy.

Less has been said here about the nature (as opposed to the context) of the accompanying seventeenth-century *political* fear of arbitrary government. In its divergent manifestations this identified perceived threats both to parliaments and monarchy. Like the fear of popery these anxieties we will find to be equally accurately anchored in their European and local contexts.

THE STRUGGLE FOR PARLIAMENTS

That members of seventeenth-century parliaments feared for the survival of that institution is not news. Their defensiveness on this score is one of the most consistent features of the period 1603–1702. From the first session of James' reign members of the Commons showed themselves touchy about the protection of parliamentary 'liberties' from perceived royal encroachment. Geoffrey Elton saw this as the normal tone of Elizabethan parliaments, effectively managed by her in a conciliatory way, but sharpened on this occasion by James' hysterically defensive reaction. Members must have contrasted, Elton suggested, Elizabeth's 'golden speech' of 1601 with James' 'general diatribe of abuse and resentment' in 1604.[59] In fact members were also responding to a European context of statebuilding that was eradicating representative assemblies.[60] Thus the ambassador Sir Thomas Roe called the dissolution of 1614 'a dissolution, not just of this, but of all Parliaments'.[61] 'What cause' the Commons had 'to watch over their privileges was manifest to all men. The prerogatives of princes are daily growing; the privileges of subjects are for the most part at an everlasting stand.' They might 'be by good providence and care preserved, but once being lost' were not to be 'recovered but with much disquiet'.[62] 'We are the last monarchy in Christendome', said Sir Robert Phelips famously in 1625, 'that retayne our originall rightes and constitutions.'[63]

59 G. R. Elton, 'A High Road to Civil War?', in C. H. Carter (ed.), *From the Renaissance to the Counter-Reformation* (London 1966), pp. 332–9.
60 H. G. Koenigsberger, 'Dominium Regale or Dominium Politicum et Regale', in his *Politicians and Virtuosi* (London 1986).
61 Quoted in Russell, 'Parliamentary History in Perspective 1604–1629', in his *Unrevolutionary England*, p. 39.
62 Quoted in S. R. Gardiner, *History of England from the Accession of James I to the Outbreak of the Civil War 1603–1642* (10 vols., London 1895), vol. I, p. 182.
63 S. R. Gardiner (ed.), *Debates in the House of Commons in 1625* (London 1873), p. 110.

Thus for several reasons members showed themselves deeply anxious about the delivery to posterity unaltered of 'customs and liberties' entrusted to their care. 'In this first Parliament of the happy reign of your Majesty [King James], the privileges of our House, and therein the liberties and stability of the whole kingdom, hath been more universally and dangerously impugned than ever, as we suppose, since the beginning of Parliaments.'[64] Subsequently Sir Roger Twysden remarked that James was the first monarch in over two hundred years to dissolve parliaments abruptly (in 1614 and 1621) while their business was still incomplete.[65] Sir Benjamin Rudyerd would say in June 1625, 'Certainly (Mr Speaker) the disagreement betwixt the Kinge (who is with God) and his people begun and continued by mutuall distasts in Parliament have been the cause almost of all that wee can call amisse in this state.'[66] Charles I, then, did not create anxiety for parliaments, though he greatly focused and to some extent directed its course.

That the survival of parliaments should quickly have become a central political issue after 1625 is very understandable. By 1626 a king 'bred in parliaments' was talking privately 'of the means used by the Kings of France to rid themselves of parliament'. A specific warning was issued in May: 'Remember that Parliaments are altogether in my power for their calling, sitting and dissolution; therefore, as I find the fruits of them good or evil, they are to continue or not to be.'[67] In 1628, with Rudyerd warning, 'This is the crisis of Parliaments. We shall know by this if Parliaments live or die', the Commons' vote of five subsidies produced the following not very reassuring royal response: 'At the first I liked Parliaments, but since (I know not how) I was grown to a dislike of them. But I am now where I was. I love Parliaments.'[68] By the following year the final parliament of the period had been dissolved in disorder and the country launched upon the unprecedented experiment of personal rule. The contention, once made, that eleven years without parliaments was nothing unusual entirely misses the point. What was new, and made forcefully public in a royal proclamation, was government without parliaments as a matter of policy. Accordingly, in an unusual emotional digression from his narrative, Clarendon recorded:

---

64 Commons, *Apology* (read in the House, 20 June 1604), quoted in Gardiner, *History of England from the Accession of James I*, vol. I, p. 181.

65 Sir Roger Twysden, *Certaine Considerations*, quoted in J. P. Sommerville, 'James I and the Divine Right of Kings: English Politics and Continental Theory', in Linda Levy Peck (ed.), *The Mental World of the Jacobean Court* (Cambridge 1991), p. 55.

66 Gardiner, *Debates in 1625*, pp. 9–10.   67 Reeve, *Personal Rule*, p. 12.   68 *Ibid.*, p. 20.

Parliaments were summoned, and again dissolved: and in the fourth year [it] ... was determined with a profession and declaration that there should be no more assemblies of that nature expected, and all men inhibited ... by proclamation ... upon penalty of censure so much as to speak of a Parliament. And I cannot but let myself lose to say, that no man can shew me a source from whence these waters of bitterness we now taste have more probably flowed, than from this unseasonable, unskilful and precipitate dissolution of Parliaments.[69]

After 1629 the struggle for parliaments became the centrepiece of a broader campaign against arbitrary government (innovatory government against law). The attack on traditional government was a conspiracy like, and linked to, that against protestantism. In the words of parliament's *Protestation* of 3 May 1641: 'there hath been ... and there still are ... endeavours to subvert the fundamental laws of England and Ireland, and to introduce the exercise of an arbitrary and tyrannical government by most pernicious and wicked counsels, practises, plots and conspiracies'.[70] More specifically, recorded Richard Baxter,

One Party said . . . That if Parliaments were once down . . . and Arbitrary Government set up ... we were then all slaves ... that the Subject's Propriety ... and the Being of Parliaments, and that no Laws be made, nor Money's taken from the Subjects, but by the Parliament's Consent, are part of the Constitution ... And ... if thus Parliaments and Propriety were destroyed, the Government was dissolved . . . [and] the King['s] will would be the only law.[71]

Lord Saye and Sele explained in 1646 that the civil war was 'a war made to destroy the Parliament of England – that is, the government of England – in the very root and foundation thereof ... We took up arms to defend the two Houses . . . from being out-raged by a company of ruffians gathered together in the king's house.' If that defence was immediately successful, thereafter 'the two Houses' proved no more capable than the church of weathering the forces unleashed. It owed as much to the arbitrary (military) government of the 1650s as to that of the 1630s that the restoration of the old order did not avoid restoration of parliamentary anxiety.

Parliamentary defensiveness is accordingly a no less remarkable feature of restoration politics. The House of Commons' first serious clash with the king came as early as 1662–3 over an attempted *Declaration of Indulgence*.

69 Hyde (Clarendon), *History of the Rebellion*, vol. I, p. 5.
70 Gardiner (ed.), *The Constitutional Documents of the Puritan Revolution 1625–1660* (Oxford 1979), p. 155.　　71 Richard Baxter, *Reliquiae Baxterianae*, vol. I, pp. 16–17.

While repeating its thanks for 'Your Majesties most Princely and Heroick Professions of relying upon the Affections of Your People, and abhorring all sort of Military and Arbitrary Rule', the House rigidly opposed any royal dispensation from the Act of Uniformity, both because of the continuing 'growth and increase of Popery', and because 'there were Laws of Uniformity . . . in being, which could not be dispensed with, but by Act of Parliament'.[72]

Given Clarendon's mindfulness of the importance of parliamentary government, it is perhaps not surprising that the years after his exile (in 1667) signal the beginning of the descent towards the next crisis. Andrew Marvell's *The Growth of Popery and Arbitrary Government* (1677) and the pamphlet *A Character of Popery and Arbitrary Government* (1679) informed subjects about the ways in which the royal policies of the 1670s amounted to a revived conspiracy to dispense with parliaments.[73] 'I know . . . it is said', said the king in February 1677, 'that I intend the subversion of the religion and government, that I intend to govern by an army and by arbitrary power, [and] to lay aside Parliaments . . . But . . . thos that say it the most . . . are . . . such as would subvert the government themselves and bring it to a commonwealth again.'[74] It was the opinion of members of parliament, however, that 'Now when this great person [the Earl of Danby] is on the point to make parliaments useless, it is treason.'[75]

In its political dimension the subsequent crisis of 1678–83 hinged upon the renewed struggle for parliaments.[76] In the midst of it (1680) Henry Neville looked back over the century as a whole:

Since the parliament of [1614] there has not been one called, (either in that king's reign, or his son's, or since) that has not been dissolved abruptly; whilst the main businesses, and those of most concern to the public, were depending and undecided. And although there has happened in the interim a bloody war, which

---

72 *The Votes and Orders of the Honourable House of Commons Passed February 25, and 26 1662, Upon Reading His Majesties Gracious Declaration and Speech* (London 1662), pp. 7, 9.

73 Andrew Marvell, *An Account of the Growth of Popery and Arbitrary Government in England. More particularly, from the long Prorogation of November 1675* (Amsterdam 1677); Philolaus, *A Character of Popery and Arbitrary Government . . . [and] how [to] prevent the same, by Choosing Good Members to serve in this New Parliament* (London 1679).

74 *Memoirs of Sir John Reresby*, pp. 111–12.

75 Grey, *Debates 1667–1694*, vol. VIII, pp. 348–9, 353, 355, 358.

76 Scott, *Restoration Crisis*, esp. chs. 2–3.

changed the whole order and . . . polity of England; and [then] . . . by his majesty's happy return . . . the old government is alive again: yet it is very visible that this deadly wound is not healed; but that we are to this day tugging with the same diffi- culties . . . which our ancestors did before the year 1640; whilst the King has been forced to apply the same remedy of dissolution to his last parliaments [in 1678 and 1679], that his father used to his four first and king James to his three last.[77]

The same anxiety, and rhetoric, underlay the next crisis of 1688–9, so that invader and domestic participants could unite in defence of a 'free Parliament'. Indeed so continuous were the issues and language, if not the practical circumstances, of these two crises, that Locke's classic polemic against arbitrary government ('When the Prince hinders the Legislature from assembling in its due time, or from acting freely, pursuant to those ends, for which it was constituted . . . the government is dissolved'[78]) could be published after the latter without anyone noticing until recently that it was written during the former.[79]

THE STRUGGLE FOR ROYAL POWER

A no less consistent anxiety across the century concerned the extent and survival of royal power. Given its importance it is remarkable that this has not received more attention. For this omission there appear to be four reasons. The first is that this was a royal anxiety hinging not upon constitu- tional theory (most subjects favoured monarchy in theory) but practice. Monarchs were practitioners and we have only to pay more attention to the extreme difficulty Stuart monarchs experienced in attempting to exercise their prerogatives in practice to begin to take this perception more seriously. When Charles I called some of his subjects 'enemies to all monarchical gov- ernment' he did not mean they were theoretical republicans. He meant that they refused to accept the practical responsibilities of subjection which were essential to the effective exercise of monarchical power.

A second factor shielding us from this reality has been the restoration fiction that the collapse of monarchy followed from specific 'mistakes and misunderstandings' rather than a general structural problem. This has been reinforced by the early Stuart revisionism which insists that we do not read

---

77 Henry Neville, *Plato Redivivus* (1680), in C. Robbins (ed.), *Two English Republican Tracts* (Cambridge 1969), p. 147.

78 *Locke's Two Treatises of Government*, ed. Peter Laslett (2nd edn, Cambridge 1967), p. 427.

79 Scott, *Restoration Crisis*, p. 15; *Locke's Two Treatises*, pp. 25–66.

monarchical weakness back from the moment of its abolition. Finally this situation owes something to the historiography of Tudor statebuilding (did not the Tudors secure not only the monarchy but the modern state?). In fact, as we will see, the Tudors secured only their dynasty, and that only until 1603. In practical terms the monarchy they bequeathed was as dangerously decrepit as its responsibilities were increased: for Stuart anxiety there was every reason.

In James I's defensiveness about his powers on the one hand, and outrageous pronouncements about them on the other ('even by Gods, kings are called Gods'), it is not difficult to see two sides of the same coin. Given his turbulent upbringing in Scotland, and education at the hands of one of Europe's fiercest resistance theorists (George Buchanan), this insecurity on a personal level is readily understandable. If its basis, however, was laid outside the kingdom, it received plenty of reinforcement thereafter in England. It was James who warned Sir Edward Coke against arguing from precedents from the times of weak kings like Richard II and Henry VI when 'the crown was tossed up and down like a tennis ball'.[80] It was James who said that the 1610 parliament's questioning of his right to impositions would leave him with no more power than 'a Doge of Venice'. It was James who, in Star Chamber in 1616, denounced local JPs who 'in every cause that concerns prerogative, give a snatch against monarchy, through their puritanical itching after popularity'.[81] Finally it was James who – most importantly for our purposes – complained bitterly against his first parliament to sit (in 1621) after the outbreak of the European war:

[They left nothing] unattempted in the highest points of sovereignty . . . except the striking of coin . . . [this was] an usurpation that the majesty of a King can by no means endure . . . we cannot with patience endure our subjects to use such anti-monarchical words to us.[82]

Thus if Charles I was 'paranoid' the condition had been hereditary. Charles' perception, from the beginning of his reign, of a vital struggle necessary to protect a royal sovereignty in England which lay under siege in practice was at one with that of his father. What was new were the practical measures which followed under new and extreme military circumstances. It was Charles I who explained to the French ambassador Chateauneuf in

---

80 Sommerville, 'James I and the Divine Right of Kings', p. 63.   81 Ibid., pp. 65, 68.
82 Rushworth, Historical Collections, vol. I, p. 40.

1629 that his problems derived from a parliament 'whose members wished to reduce his power to nothing'. These people were 'puritans', 'republicans' and 'enemies to monarchy'.[83] His *Declaration* of March of that year announcing the beginning of the Personal Rule spoke of the attempts of that House to effect 'innovations (which we will never permit again) . . . to break . . . through all . . . ligaments of government, and to erect an universal over-swaying power to themselves, which belongs only to us'.[84] In the face of the Scots National Covenant a decade later Charles published his opinion that 'the aim of these men is not Religion, as they falsly pretend and publish, but it is to shake all Monarchical Government, and to vilify our Regal Power, justly descended upon us over them'.[85] 'As Concerning the Explanation of their Damnable Covenant', he added, 'I have no more power in Scotland, than as a Duke of Venice, which I will rather dye than suffer', a prediction in which he proved as good as his word.[86]

Once again over the subsequent triumphant restoration of monarchy (1660) there hovered the shadow of its prior actual destruction. Accordingly throughout the restoration period we find the same royal anxiety. On the eve of his return His would-be Majesty was already being warned that 'those who most endeavoured your coming in, desired it upon such terms as that you would have no more power than a Duke of Venice'.[87] As the king put it to parliament in 1662: 'He needed not to tell them, that there was a Republican Party still in the kingdom, which had the Courage still to promise themselves another Revolution.'[88] Thus during the subsequent decade we hear a series of extraordinary but familiar royal pronouncements. When the Commons oppose his pro-French foreign policy Charles tells the French ambassador Courtin that they really want to use war (against France) to reduce him to financial dependence and 'the mere name of a king'. The royal talk of the 1670s is replete with predictions of rebellion, and refusals to change course because (1) his opponents are out to destroy his power and 'take over the government'; and (2) he therefore cannot afford to abandon France as 'the only security he has'. It remains the most probable explanation for these remarkable policies that Charles saw in them a necessary security against his own people. How else are we to explain

83 Reeve, *Personal Rule*, p. 132.   84 Gardiner, *Constitutional Documents*, p. 95.

85 Rushworth, *Historical Collections*, vol. II, p. 830.   86 *Ibid.*, p. 754.

87 Thomas Carte, *Collection of Original Letters and Papers*, 5 April 1660, transcript in Downing College Archive, Box 198.

88 Hyde (Clarendon), *Life of Clarendon*, vol. I, p. 447.

the king's astonishing statement to Louis XIV that he was 'standing up for the interests of France against his whole kingdom'?[89]

It is with weariness that during the subsequent crisis we hear Charles telling Barillon that the alternative to renewed French support of the monarchy is restoration of the republic; that his opponents would leave him no more power than 'a Doge of Venice'.[90] It is with a no less powerful sense of recognition that we hear in the royal proclamation of 1681 of the House of Commons' attempt to 'disable Us', passing resolutions to the effect that anyone advancing money upon 'the Branches of the King's Revenue, arising by Customs, Excise, or Hearth-Money, shall be adjudged to hinder the Sitting of Parliaments'.[91] Thus it is readily understandable that seven years later William of Orange should take a key purpose of his invasion to be the salvation of English monarchy. In his statement to the Earl of Halifax that he had not come over to establish a commonwealth – 'the commonwealth party is the strongest in England and at best they would make him a Doge of Venice' – we see the perspective not of an ignorant foreigner but of a seventeenth-century king of England.

CONCLUSION

The domestic context of England's troubles lay in institutional and particularly military weakness. In the following chapter the principal problem will be identified as that of a decrepit and bankrupt monarchy. The causes of the troubles were those 'Passions' and 'Apprehentions' which under these circumstances could find no effective external military expression and instead turned in upon and polarised the state. This internal polarisation eventually appeared in its military manifestation as war in the three kingdoms.

As we will see, both early major contemporary analysts of the troubles, Thomas Hobbes and James Harrington, focused their attention upon one or both aspects of this picture. These were a militarily decrepit monarchy and dangerous public, in particular parliamentary, passions. Finally it was by their European context, religious, political and military, that from the 1620s to the 1690s these factors were combined to put the English polity under intolerable pressure. The key European processes at work were those of reformation, counter-reformation and statebuilding. Their relationship in England will be our subject hereafter.

89 John Miller, *Charles II: A Study in Kingship* (London 1991), pp. 219–20, 233.
90 Scott, *Restoration Crisis*, pp. 70, 123.
91 Charles II, *His Majesties Declaration* (1681), p. 5.

3

The unreformed polity

I doubt not, but many men, have been contented to see the late troubles in *England*, out of an imitation of the Low Countries; supposing there needed no more to grow rich than to change, as they had done, the forme of their Government . . . And as to Rebellion in particular against Monarchy; one of the most frequent causes of it, is the Reading of the books of Policy, and Histories of the antient Greeks, and Romans.

Thomas Hobbes, Leviathan (1651)[1]

INTRODUCTION: RESTORING THE SENSE OF POSSIBILITY

In the previous chapter we examined two sets of political fears. One was for the continuity, indeed survival, of parliaments. The other was for the efficacy, indeed survival, of royal power. Both existed across the century, and were central to every episode of the troubles.

The first step towards explaining the troubles is to recover the contexts within which these fears may be understood. It is critically important that they were accompanied by religious concerns. Fears for the survival of aspects of the civil polity in England were intertwined with fears for the survival of protestantism and the church. The relationship between these, complicated in itself, was also deeply influenced by events in and outside the kingdom.

Two broad contexts for these perceptions have already been identified. One was religious: the victories of the counter-reformation in Europe. The other was political: the military weakness of the Stuart crown. In the 1620s, as in the 1670s and 1680s, this combination had a devastating effect upon

---

1 Thomas Hobbes, *Leviathan*, ed. Richard Tuck (Cambridge 1991), p. 225.

domestic political peace. The immediate result was that polarisation and conflict on the European continent became polarisation and conflict in England.

That seventeenth-century English religious and political life should prove so permeable was not simply a consequence of European developments. It was equally a product of the absence of development at home. One aspect of this was the half-reformed Elizabethan church. In the European circumstances of 1618–48 this proved a fragile vessel for the safe passage of protestantism. We will return to this subject in the next chapter. The other domestic context was the unreformed civil polity. It is this which is our subject here.

At the beginning of the seventeenth century the English civil polity was relatively unreformed. In 1603 those military, fiscal and administrative developments by which, between 1642 and 1720, the English state would be transformed, had scarcely begun.[2] This is to say that, from the standpoint of early modern statebuilding, a process affecting the whole of central and western Europe in this period, it was also relatively unformed. This may appear an odd claim, since its form was actually precise, complex and ancient. From the constitutional perspective England's troubles were a struggle between domestic antagonists to preserve their understanding of the essence of this form. This struggle was, however, the English experience of a universal European process that was unpredictable in outcome.

Those who described the unreformed polity on the eve of the seventeenth century understood that it contained disparate elements. These existed in a balance, both delicate and durable. Under early modern pressures this balance, if broken, contained more than one possibility. In practice over the course of the century the country would experience both extremes of monarchical absolutism and republicanism. It was James Harrington who described the early Stuart constitution as janus-faced: 'when no Parliament, then absolute Monarchie; when a Parliament, then

2 See part III below, in particular chs. 17 and 21. For an introduction, see Wolfgang Reinhard (ed.), *Power Elites and State Building* (Oxford 1996); Rudolf Braun, 'Taxation, Sociopolitical Structure and Statebuilding: Great Britain and Brandenburg-Prussia', in Charles Tilly (ed.), *The Formation of Nation States in Western Europe* (Princeton 1975); Michael Braddick, *The Nerves of State: Taxation and the Financing of the English State, 1558–1714* (Manchester 1996); John Brewer, *Sinews of Power: War, Money and the English State 1688–1783* (London 1989).

it runnes to a Commonwealth'.[3] This was an analysis with which Thomas Hobbes agreed.

If England in 1603 was indeed a monarchy it was also in European terms a worryingly weak one. This was again a point that attracted the attention of Harrington, who analysed the period 1558–1642 as one without the practical reality of royal power ('*Wherefore the dissolution of this government caused the war, not the war the dissolution of this government*').[4] What enraged Charles I in particular was his inability to translate his understanding of monarchical government into practice. 'You best know', wrote his minister Wentworth to a colleague, 'how much the regal power is become infirm.'[5]

This political weakness, with its immediate military implications, attracted much comment from foreign ambassadors in the 1620s.[6] It was this which made the country so vulnerable to ideological and ultimately military polarisation. The absence of effective statebuilding in the sixteenth century and its initial failure in the seventeenth are therefore crucial contexts for the troubles, which did not subside until this problem was addressed decisively between 1689 and 1714.

This eventual English statebuilding saw the transformation of a weak post-medieval monarchy into a recognisably modern, or early modern, military-fiscal state. Its completion depended upon Dutch intervention; its domestic context was the restoration process described in part III of this volume. In the period before these developments we would be wise to be sensitive to the perceptions of contemporaries who found themselves in an alarming situation. In politics, as in religion, these processes were ones of differentiation. One couldn't be Roman catholic and protestant, though the Church of England did its best (King James was not the only one to describe himself as 'a Catholicke Christian').[7] Similarly everywhere statebuilding strained the relationship of monarchies and estates. Fears for the future of parliaments were voiced in the context of successful monarchical statebuilding (in the Habsburg monarchy, or France) at the expense of representative assemblies. Fears for the future of monarchy should be taken no less seriously in the context of successful statebuilding accomplished (in the Netherlands) by the overthrow of monarchy. To understand contemporary perceptions on the eve of the troubles what is necessary is to recover this sense of possibility.

---

3 *Aubrey's Brief Lives*, ed. O. L. Dick (London 1958), p. 126.
4 James Harrington, *Oceana*, 'The Second Part of the Preliminaries', p. 198.
5 Quoted in Sharpe, *Personal Rule*, p. 135.   6 Cogswell, *Blessed Revolution*, p. 125.
7 W. B. Patterson, *King James VI and I and the Reunion of Christendom* (Cambridge 1997), p. 94.

MEDIEVAL SEVENTEENTH-CENTURY ENGLAND

Was regal power newly decayed in the early seventeenth century? Or was this simply a continuation of the weak monarchy characteristic of late medieval England? The answer to both of these questions may be yes. Writing fifty years ago Margaret Judson found it remarkable that early seventeenth-century English people in possession of a unified state continued to live mentally in the medieval period:

we often wonder whether they were living in the seventeenth century or in the thirteenth. Living in a unified state and confronted with the problem of recognising and accepting the final governmental authority within it, they seem to wander back in their ideas along many byways to the Middle Ages and to employ medieval ideas in the solution to their seventeenth-century problems, ignoring the fact that these older ideas had developed at a time when the state hardly existed and the question of the final authority in its government was not a vital problem.[8]

What made this mentality so mystifying was Judson's assumption of successful Tudor statebuilding.[9] This furnished the background to her entire study. But these modern historiographical assumptions were not shared by contemporaries themselves. The resulting impression is like that made upon John Miller by the equally 'anachronistic' mental religious world of participants in the popish plot crisis of 1678–83 who referred repeatedly to the St Bartholomew's Eve massacres in France in 1572.[10] In fact it is not for historians to tell contemporaries what is anachronistic, but the other way around. The starting point is for historians to question their own assumptions about modernity. It is the assumptions of contemporaries that tell us that as, religiously, the seventeenth century was still the age of reformation so, politically, it was still the medieval period.

Thus English protestants in 1678 spoke of the massacre of St Bartholomew's Eve because their fears were not of local but of European counter-reformation, and French in particular.[11] It is difficult to dismiss this as irrational when the revocation of the Edict of Nantes was to occur only seven years later. It was in this context that the Marquis of Halifax remarked that Titus Oates' story 'must be handled as if it were true, whether it were so or no . . . [though] it were vain to hope it will ever be confessed by

8 M. A. Judson, *The Crisis of the Constitution* (New Brunswick, N.J. 1949), p. 8.
9 *Ibid.*, pp. 1–5.
10 John Miller, *Popery and Politics in England 1660–1688* (Cambridge 1973), pp. 89, 181–2, 188.   11 Scott, 'Popish Plot', p. 133.

those that say still there never was any such thing as the Massacre at Paris or the Gunpowder Treason in England'.[12] Similarly contemporary ignorance of a transformatory process of Tudor statebuilding may strike us as less peculiar now that every aspect of that claimed construct has come to be questioned.

Until recently this had two themes. One was the Tudor reconstruction and strengthening of royal power. The other was the claimed construction in its wake of a 'modern' bureaucratic state. The most influential name associated with this picture was Sir Geoffrey Elton. For Elton accordingly there was nothing wrong with the early Stuart constitutional inheritance which 'tactful and sensible' kingship could not have made successful.[13] This was attested by the outcome, after the 'glorious revolution', when the constitution remained fundamentally unchanged. In fact this later judgement is difficult to sustain. It is not simply that not all fundamental change is constitutional; the constitutional changes of 1689–1701 were important (including the first new coronation oath since 1308).

The full Elton diagnosis of seventeenth-century pilot error focused upon monarchical incompetence combined with in-flight turbulence (including 'Protestantism's fate in Europe').[14] Yet it is equally possible that the fate of protestantism in Europe exposed serious inadequacies of structure. More particularly Elton's account was based upon an understanding of sixteenth-century constitutional developments that is now widely questioned. There was indeed a jurisdictional revolution between 1529 and 1536: the monarch became head of the church as well as the state. Moreover this development carried others in its wake. One was a redistribution of landownership from the church to the laity. Another was the increased importance of parliaments, which would hereafter claim a central role not only in matters of religious and political settlement but (to safeguard these) even concerning the determination of the royal succession. This was one aspect of a broader confessionalisation of politics.[15] All of this contributed to a subsequent fun-

12 Quoted in F. S. Ronalds, *The Attempted Whig Revolution of 1678–1681* (Urbana, Ill. 1937), p. 18.

13 Elton, 'High Road to Civil War?'; Elton, 'The Stuart Century', in Elton, *Studies in Tudor and Stuart Politics and Government*, vol. II (Cambridge 1974).

14 Elton, 'The Stuart Century', p. 188: 'In fact the English situation alone explains nothing: let us not forget the tears of Germany.'

15 Jennifer Loach, *Parliament Under the Tudors* (Oxford 1991), p. 78: 'The Reformation and the changes of the subsequent decades . . . carried out by statutory authority, brought parliament into the centre of religious debate to an unprecedented extent.'

damental political difficulty: the need for a little-altered monarchy to manage greatly altered circumstances. As Jennifer Loach has remarked of Elizabeth's attempts to put this genie back in the bottle: 'The fact that earlier parliaments had legislated on matters they were not allowed even to discuss did not escape the attention of [her] ... critics.'[16]

Such developments, Elton argued, were accompanied by a Tudor revolution in government which laid the basis for the transformation of the medieval royal household into the modern state.[17] This formed part of a more general extension of the power of the crown, in theory and in practice. This was the case domestically, over both nobility and commonalty, particularly by statute;[18] and territorially (over Wales and Ireland). Although it is true that the period 1485–1558 saw gradual governmental administrative reform, the suggestion of such a 'revolution' is now contentious.[19] In particular the fiscal and political benefits of the appropriation of the church were quickly squandered. This left the crown with major new jurisdictional responsibilities without the resources to discharge them. In the words of one Elizabethan historian, 'There was a disjuncture between the expanding claims of the state on its citizens and the necessary machinery for the successful waging of war. It was, to say the least, an unpromising legacy for the future.'[20] In the summary of another: 'the Tudors had never succeeded in putting the crown's finances on a strong long-term basis. Instead, they had lived off occasional windfalls – monastery land, chantries, debasement, bishops' lands ... The crunch was bound to come.'[21]

Most specifically, in the European *religious* context, this left the crown sitting atop an ideological powderkeg deprived of the capacity to fight fire effectively. From 1603 these jurisdictional responsibilities were greatly further augmented by the Union of the Crowns. Thereafter both the monarchies and churches of the three Stuart kingdoms sought to challenge and modify each other. Given that Charles I subsequently faced rebellion, among both the commonalty and nobility, in Ireland and Scotland as well as

---

16 *Ibid.*, p. 154.   17 Elton, *The Tudor Revolution in Government* (Cambridge 1953).

18 Elton, *Policy and Police: The Enforcement of the Reformation* (Cambridge 1972).

19 Christopher Coleman and David Starkey (eds.), *Revolution Reassessed: Revisions in the History of Tudor Government and Administration* (London 1986); Elton, 'Tudor Government', *Historical Journal* 31, 2 (1988), pp. 425–35; Starkey, 'A Reply. Tudor Government: The Facts?', *Historical Journal* 31, 4 (1988), pp. 921–31.

20 W. T. MacCaffrey, *Elizabeth I: War and Politics 1588–1603* (Princeton 1992), p. 69.

21 Loach, *Parliament*, p. 160.

England, few of these imagined Tudor accomplishments now look enduring. This suggestion has been underlined by John Adamson's 'baronial
revolt' thesis concerning the English civil war.[22] It does not follow from this
genuine insight that nothing had changed between the fifteenth century
and the seventeenth. In the words of one parliamentarian chronicler of the
siege of Gloucester in 1643: 'The Action of these times transcends the
Barons Warres, and those tedious discords betweene the houses of *Yorke*
and *Lancaster*, in as much as it is undertaken upon higher Principles, and
carried on to a nobler end, and effects more universall.'[23]

Our subject is the new perceived within the framework of the old. It is in
particular the polarising impact of ideology, most importantly but not
only religious ideology, within a largely unreformed constitution. As is
now well understood, the early Stuart problem was not simply the absence
of long-term Tudor reform. It was the much more specific failure to
respond to the fiscal and other challenges of the second half of the sixteenth century.

By the early Stuart period the real value of royal income had been deci-
mated by inflation. This increased prices fivefold between 1540 and 1640.
Until 1558 there had, at least, been a continuation of the incremental
reform of the medieval period. Under Elizabeth, however, with administrative and political conservatism elaborated to the point of torpor, even this
ended. Revenue at the end of Elizabeth's reign (1601) was 40 per cent less in
real terms than it had been in 1509. The sixteenth-century peak of real royal
income in Edward's reign would not be reached again in England until
1689.[24] One result, particularly during the military struggle against Spain,
was the sale of crown land. During the last five years of Elizabeth's reign
£37,000 of crown land was sold.[25] This was made the basis of political
capital; in the words of Robert Cecil to parliament: 'She selleth her land to
defend us.' As a catastrophic cashing of long-term monarchical assets for
short-term gain this was the equal of Elizabeth's succession 'policy'.
Accordingly the Stuarts inherited a bankrupt polity not simply unreformed, but deprived of the political or cultural context within which it
might conceivably be so.

22 J. S. A. Adamson, 'The Baronial Context of the English Civil War', *Transactions of the Royal
    Historical Society* 5th ser., 40 (1990).
23 Quoted in Nigel Smith, *Literature and Revolution in England 1640–1660* (New Haven
    1994), p. 51.   24 Russell, 'Parliaments and the English State'.
25 Gardiner, *History of England from the Accession of James I*, vol. I, pp. 103, 293.

From 1580, in this sense, England's European religious and political involvements actually further undermined its capacity to respond to its growing military needs. This was another vicious circle which was not decisively reversed until the 1690s. Meanwhile the reign of James I was punctuated by a series of unsuccessful attempts at reform of which the Gunpowder Plot was certainly the most ambitious. It was only one obvious consequence that the crown couldn't afford an effective foreign policy. 'No man gaines by Warre', said James I, 'but he that hath not wherewith to Live in Peace.'[26] 'No man gains by Peace', he might have said more appropriately, 'that hath not wherewith to fight a War.' This was the real epitaph for his failed policy by 1625. In the words of one contemporary, James 'knew butt to well that it was an impossibility to make warre on his particular revenew'.[27]

Thus when the House of Commons in 1604 showed themselves anxious to deliver to posterity the 'customs and liberties' entrusted to their care, this was no more than they had just been promised in a coronation oath unaltered since 1308.[28] One aspect of this inherited constitution was described by Fortescue in the fifteenth century:

Nor can the king there, by himself or by his ministers, impose tallages, subsidies or any other burdens whatever on his subjects, nor change their laws, nor make new ones, without the concession or assent of his whole realm expressed in his parliament.[29]

This system Fortescue called Dominium Politicum et Regale: a constitution which, while monarchical, was also strictly constitutionally circumscribed. The same formula had been used most famously by Aquinas (De regimine principum, bk 4) to describe a monarchy bound by the rule of law, the principle of consent and the object of the public good. It was essential to such a constitution that it was both legal and rational, thus furnishing a middle way between tyranny on the one hand and popularity on the other.[30] Alongside the fact of political subjection, this

---

26 Quoted in Cogswell, *Blessed Revolution*, p. 13.   27 British Library Add MS 4181, f. 23.
28 'Sire, will you grant and preserve, and by your oath confirm to the people of England the laws customs . . . and liberties . . . granted to them by former kings of England . . . and which the community of your realm shall have chosen.' See the discussion in A. L. Brown, *The Governance of Late Medieval England 1272–1461* (London 1989), pp. 12–13.
29 Fortescue, *De Laudibus*, quoted in Brown, *Late Medieval England*, p. 13.
30 Maurizio Viroli, *From Politics to Reason of State: The Acquisition and Transformation of the Language of Politics 1250–1600* (Cambridge 1992), p. 69.

Aristotelian formulation retained space for liberty understood as rational self-government. Even Machiavelli, in the first book of the *Discourses*, retained the distinction between legal or political monarchy on the one hand, and tyranny on the other, before collapsing it at the beginning of book 2.[31]

In England this government was, in the words of one medieval historian, both royal and conciliar at every level. The king had great but not independent power, and the English had a tradition of calling over-mighty kings to account. The most famous examples were Edward II and Richard II, precedents frequently cited not only during the 1640s but in 1688–9.[32] The events of 1688–9 in particular are much more comprehensible within this context than within that of modern revolution. The arrival of a prince with a weak claim to the throne vindicated by a strong army was anything but unprecedented in English history. Since kings had been removed by force on six occasions between 1327 and 1649, 'England hath not wanted examples in this kind.'[33] Following the acceptance of Richard II's 'abdication' by an assembly of the 'estates' in 1399, Henry of Lancaster had explained of the throne: 'God of his grace hath sent me with helpe of my kyn and of my frendes to recover it, the which rewme was in poynt to be undone for defaut of governance and undoyng of the gode laws.'[34] Such occurrences were usually followed by appropriate 'constitutional' proceedings. As in 1689 the assembly of the 'estates' which accepted Richard II's 'abdication' on 30 September 1399 was not a parliament but a gathering of the prelates, lords and commons who had assembled for one.[35] It was the Bishop of Ely who noted in the Lords in 1689 that there had been seven interruptions of the legal line of hereditary succession from William I to Henry VIII.[36] In the Commons Sir Richard Temple made the same point, not only about England but France: 'there have not been seven kings but where the right line has been removed'.[37]

31 Machiavelli, *The Discourses*, ed. Bernard Crick (Harmondsworth 1985), II.2, pp. 275–6.

32 Lois Schwoerer, *The Declaration of Rights, 1689* (Baltimore and London 1981); Scott, *English Republic*, p. 48; *The People's Right Briefly Asserted, Printed for the Information of the Commonality of England, France, and all other Neighbour Nations, that groan under the oppression of Tyrannical Government* (London 1649).

33 Grey, *Debates 1667–1694*, vol. IX, p. 61.

34 Quoted in Brown, *Late Medieval England*, p. 10.   35 *Ibid.*, pp. 8–9.

36 D. L. Jones (ed.), *A Parliamentary History of the Glorious Revolution* (London 1988), p. 266.   37 Grey, *Debates 1667–1694*, vol. IX, p. 61.

RENAISSANCE ENGLAND: A MONARCHICAL REPUBLIC?

Unreformed monarchy, then, was the apex rather than sum of the political nation. Its power depended upon its ability to command the obedience and resources of that broader entity. It was this situation which gave such importance, in relation to allegiance, to contemporary belief, and not simply religious belief. Moreover, embracing all those involved in government both at the centre and in the localities, this political nation traversed a much broader range of social status than we used to think.[38] This was most visible to monarchs themselves in the great city of London, particularly (but not only) in time of parliaments. This was one context for the repeated complaints by all Stuart monarchs about members of the political elite courting 'Popularity'. In addition Patrick Collinson has recently reminded us that alongside the Elizabethan political facts of monarchy, obedience and hierarchy lay a local social reality: a fabric of towns and villages, of self-governing communities, which might even be called quasi-republican.[39] This suggestion has been reinforced by the work of Markku Peltonen, who has examined the extent to which Elizabethan inhabitants, particularly of 'the Citties and cheefe Townes', considered it to be compatible with their duty as subjects to study 'the calling of a Cittizen' in its republican sense.[40]

The practice of collective self-government extended as far up as the Privy Council which found itself, in a moment of crisis, having to think about what it would do if the queen died leaving only the religiously unacceptable Mary Queen of Scots as heir. It is not to anticipate the subsequent actual interregnums of 1649–60 and 1688–9 to point out that one was contemplated, and planned for, in 1585.[41] Nor is it to anticipate the eventual triumph of confessional over dynastic continuity in 1689 to note that Cecil's first attempt to reserve the proclamation of a royal successor to parliament (summoned by the Privy Council acting as a council of regency) had

38 In this respect recent work by Collinson, Peltonen, Cogswell, Cust and others has tended to confirm the thrust of Hirst's *The Representative of the People?*
39 Patrick Collinson, 'The Monarchical Republic of Elizabeth I', *Bulletin of the John Rylands Library* 69 (1987); Collinson, *De Republica Anglorum: Or, History with the Politics Put Back* (Cambridge 1990).
40 Markku Peltonen, 'Citizenship and Republicanism in Elizabethan England', in Skinner and van Gelderen, *Republicanism and Constitutionalism.*
41 Collinson, 'Monarchical Republic'; Collinson, 'The Elizabethan Exclusion Crisis and the Elizabethan Polity', *Proceedings of the British Academy* 84 (1994), pp. 51–92.

occurred during the succession debates of 1563.[42] What is clear is that the capacity of members of the political nation to conceive of themselves as guardians of a religious and political entity separate from the monarch was a feature of succession crises from the 1560s to the 1680s that would eventually prove decisive.

It was with these realities in mind that the Elizabethan Bishop Aylmer explained: 'The Regiment of England is not a mere monarchie . . . as some for lacke of consideration thinke, nor a meer oligarchie, nor democracie, but a rule mixte of all these . . . to be sene in the parliament house.'[43] Sir Thomas Smith, in *De Republica Anglorum*, remarked similarly that the English state was 'a society or common doing of a multitude of free men collected together and united by common accord and covenauntes among themselves as well in peace as in warre'.[44] In a letter to his brother Robert, Sir Philip Sidney asserted that the English government was similar to that of Venice.[45] It was to the same tradition of political thinking that Robert's grandson the republican Algernon Sidney would appeal indignantly a century later, when the word 'commonwealthman' had become a brand of infamy:

[Our ancestors thought] the liberty and welfare of a great nation was of too much importance to be suffered to depend upon the will of one man . . . if a Commonwealth signifies the common good, in which sense it hath in all ages been used . . . and which Bodin puts upon it when he . . . calls [France] a republic, no good man will be ashamed of it . . . It is strange how the word should so change its signification with us in the space of twenty years. All monarchies in the world that are not purely barbarous and tyrannical, have ever been called Commonwealths . . . And in our days, it doth not only belong in Venice, Genoa, Switzerland and the United Provinces . . . but to Germany, Spain, France, Sweden, Poland, and all the kingdoms of Europe.[46]

---

42 John Guy, *Tudor England* (London 1988), p. 270; Alford, 'William Cecil', pp. 35–6.
43 John Aylmer, *An Harborowe for Faithfull and Trewe Subjects* (1559), quoted in Alford, 'William Cecil'.   44 Quoted in Collinson, *De Republica Anglorum*, p. 21.
45 Markku Peltonen, *Classical Humanism and Republicanism in English Political Thought 1570–1640* (Cambridge 1995), p. 47; on the transmission of ideas within the Sidney family, see Blair Worden, 'Classical Republicanism and the Puritan Revolution', in V. Pearl, H. Lloyd-Jones and Worden (eds.), *History and Imagination* (Oxford 1981); Scott, *English Republic*, chs. 2–4.
46 [Algernon Sidney and Sir William Jones], *A Just and Modest Vindication of the Proceedings of the Two Last Parliaments* (1681), in *State Tracts of the Reign of Charles II* (London 1689), vol. IV, Appendix 15, pp. clxviii–clxix. On the authorship of this tract, see Scott, *Restoration Crisis*, ch. 9.

Thus in the Elizabethan period two perspectives could furnish the context for perceptions of the interests of the commonwealth distinct from the crown's perception of its own interests. The first was protestantism, increasingly preoccupied with the military danger first from France through Scotland, and then from Spain through the United Provinces. The second was the humanist perception of the commonwealth as a community charged with civic responsibilities. Moreover, there were in the same period at least two features of the domestic political situation which tended to accentuate these two perspectives and their practical impact.

The first was the long-term effect of Elizabeth's extraordinary refusal 'to abide by the rules of monarchy and select a successor'.[47] This intertwined religious and political insecurities in a way which forced contemporaries to take a view of the nation's interests that was more than simply dynastic. It was partly because when it came to the crunch the realm took precedence over the ruler that citizens were concealed within subjects.[48] The second peculiar feature of Elizabethan politics was the rulership, for almost half a century, of a woman. Markku Peltonen, Stephen Alford and others have all observed some of the ways in which this encouraged the senior political elite to take an independent view.[49]

It was Collinson's conclusion that the Elizabethan realm was, in this respect, 'a republic which happened also to be a monarchy: or vice versa'.[50] If the use of the word republic here sounds improbable, this is to remind us of the historiographical age in which we live. To use it in relation to English politics before 1640 remains almost as treasonable now as it was for Sidney to do so after 1660, and for the same reason. It was part of the restoration political agenda to render English republicanism unthinkable again. This does not mean that it had always been so. It has often been claimed that republicanism was inconceivable in England before 1649. If this were so it would be difficult to explain why every Stuart monarch accused some of his subjects of striving to introduce it (in Venetian form or otherwise). It may be true that it was rarely publicly advocated before the 1640s. That it was entirely conceivable, however, was a consequence both of England's European situation and of its renaissance intellectual culture.

47 Alford, 'William Cecil', abstract.
48 MacCaffrey, *Elizabeth I*; Collinson, 'Elizabethan Exclusion Crisis'.
49 Alford, 'William Cecil'; Peltonen, 'Citizenship and Republicanism'.
50 Collinson, 'Monarchical Republic', p. 407; Collinson, *De Republica Anglorum*, pp. 18–45.

We have needed recent reminders that such a culture did exist between 1540 and 1650: that English humanism did not appear in the Henrician period only to mysteriously disappear until the 1650s.[51] Though humanism did not necessarily mean republicanism, classical and renaissance literature contained within itself a republican history and political imagination.[52] In normal times this needed pose no threat to allegiance to monarchy. To argue from this culture of obedience, however, that to early seventeenth-century people republicanism was inconceivable is to suggest that they were incapable of keeping two ideas in their heads at one time. Their unimpeachable loyalty did not stop some of Elizabeth's subjects considering themselves as citizens, or conceiving of the conquest of Ireland, or the settlement of America, in explicitly republican terms.[53]

Nor, during the gathering military, political and religious crisis of the 1620s, did it stop them bringing these broader imaginative perspectives to bear on the local as well as European situation.[54] This concerned immediate issues not of republic or monarchy, but of public religious and political policy and morality (war versus peace; activism versus passivity; corruption versus virtue; liberty versus slavery). Interpretation of these was capable of being deeply influenced by renaissance perspectives. Even in its mature form English republican thought would hinge not upon external constitutional structures, but upon a partially internalised moral philosophy of self-government. This was Greek in origin, with Roman, christian and contemporary European accretions.[55] This stressed the rational self-

---

51 Peltonen, *Classical Humanism*; David Norbrook, *Poetry and Politics in the English Renaissance* (London 1984); Skinner, *Reason and Rhetoric*, pt I, esp. chs. 1–2. Blair Worden concludes: 'The Humanist foundations on which republicanism would be built were laid before the civil wars, but the building was not begun' (Worden, 'Marchamont Nedham and the Beginnings of English Republicanism, 1649–1656', in David Wootton (ed.), *Republicanism, Liberty and Commercial Society 1649–1776* (Stanford 1994), p. 51).

52 In addition to the items mentioned above, see David Norbrook's superb *Writing the English Republic: Poetry, Rhetoric and Politics 1627–1660* (Cambridge 1999).

53 Peltonen, 'Citizenship and Republicanism'; Peltonen, *Classical Humanism*, ch. 2; Andrew Fitzmaurice, 'Classical Rhetoric and the Literature of Discovery 1570–1630', Ph.D thesis, Cambridge 1996; Fitzmaurice, 'The Civic Solution to the Crisis of English Colonization, 1609–1625', *Historical Journal* 42, 1 (March 1999).

54 Quentin Skinner, 'The Liberty of the Subject', lecture given at Keele University, 12 March 1999.

55 Scott, *English Republic*, ch. 2; Scott, review of Peltonen, *Classical Humanism and Republicanism*, D. Armitage, A. Himy and Q. Skinner (eds.), *Milton and Republicanism* (Cambridge 1995), and Sidney, *Court Maxims*, ed. H. Blom, E. Haitsma Mulier and R. Janse (Cambridge 1996), in *English Historical Review*, September 1997, pp. 951–3.

government not only of city but individual soul. It is precisely because this was at least superficially compatible with public government by monarchy that the work of Peltonen, Worden, Norbrook and others has been able to tell us so much about the intellectual pre-history of English republicanism in the century before the collapse of monarchical constitutional form.[56]

That there was no inevitable tension here is the point being made by Sidney and the others above. When tension arrived, however, from other directions, early Stuart monarchs quickly registered that they did not control their subjects' minds. It was in 1629, following the first serious period of parliamentary turbulence, that Thomas Hobbes published his first analysis of what he took to be a political culture primed for disobedience to monarchy and for war.[57] His subsequent attribution of the troubles to classical education in English universities was part of a flood of contemporary literature analysing their ideological (and especially religious) origins:

And by reading of these Greek, and Latine Authors, men from their childhood have gotten a habit (under a false shew of Liberty,) of favouring tumults, and of licentious controlling the actions of their Soveraigns . . . with the effusion of so much blood; as I think I may truly say, there was never any thing so deerly bought, as these Western parts have bought the learning of the Greek and Latine tongues.'[58]

As we will see, it was its sensitivity to the intellectual (rather than simply practical) challenges it faced that was the most interesting feature of attempted Caroline statebuilding between 1625 and 1640. Thus to suggest that alongside monarchy went a purely monarchical mind-set is to read back into the period before the troubles the process of ideological polarisation that would be their most important consequence. It was again in the aftermath of the parliamentary troubles of the late 1620s that Peter Heylyn attacked what he called 'the . . . *contradiction* . . . of a *free subject*':

should the King be limited within those narrow bounds which you would prescribe him, had you the power; he would in little time be like the antient kings of *Sparta*, in which the *Ephori*, or now Duke of *Venice*, in which the Senate beare the greatest stroke . . . I have before heard of a *free people*, and of *free states*, but never till of late of

56 Worden, 'Beginnings of English Republicanism'; Worden, 'Classical Republicanism'; Worden, *The Sound of Virtue*, esp. pp. 353–4.
57 Hobbes, *Of the Life and History of Thucydides*; Scott, 'Peace of Silence'.
58 Hobbes, *Leviathan*, ed. Tuck, pp. 149–50.

a *free subject*: nor know I any way to create *free subjects*, but by releasing them of all obedience to their princes.[59]

In 1627 Isaac Dorislaus was deprived of his newly established history lectureship at Cambridge for an account of Tacitus that 'placed the right of monarchy in the people's voluntary submission', and '[spoke] in praise of the Dutch rebels against Spain'.[60] That Charles I and his clergy wished to render certain things unthinkable does not mean that they were so. The institutional context for England's troubles was an undifferentiated polity full of ambiguity and possibility. There were at least as many components here to assist as to hinder monarchical statebuilding. When opposition came, however, to the attempted reform of a weak and defensive monarchy, the impediments to obedience were not only of the body but in the mind.

EUROPEAN STATEBUILDING

Far from being peculiar to England, as H. G. Koenigsberger has reminded us, the unreformed inheritance of Dominium Politicum et Regale was the commonest system in Europe. Everywhere between 1500 and 1700 such systems were coming under strain. This was particularly the case, as in France, the Netherlands and England, when disputes over taxation and power were enhanced by religious passions. 'It is not surprising, therefore, that the long-term struggles between monarchies and parliaments tended to escalate to dramatic fights for ultimate power precisely during the . . . century and a half following the Reformation.'[61] The most important practical consequence was the demise of the unreformed polity. Monarchies and representative assemblies found it impossible to live together, leading to the demise of the former (in the Netherlands and Britain) or the latter (in the Habsburg monarchy and France). The intellectual consequences included the partial substitution of the classical politics of reason with a new sceptical reason of state.[62]

---

59 Peter Heylyn, *A Briefe and Moderate Answer, to the seditious and scandalous challenges of Henry Burton* (London 1637), ch. 2, pp. 6, 14–15.
60 Christopher Hill, *Puritanism and Revolution* (London 1958), p. 64.
61 Koenigsberger, 'Dominium Regale or Dominium Politicum et Regale', pp. 17–20.
62 Viroli, *From Politics to Reason of State*; Tuck, *Philosophy and Government*; Geoffrey Baldwin, 'The Self and the State 1580–1660', Ph.D thesis, Cambridge 1998. English republicanism both opposed and partook of this development simultaneously (see below, pp. 290–341).

The practical pressures at work were all European in scope. The most important were three. There was the European population increase, leading to price inflation, between 1500 and 1640. Although this was uneven, and other factors contributed, all governments had to contend with the consequences. This was particularly so in a period when inflation was not understood and demands for more money were likely to be interpreted as evidence of profligacy or something more sinister. The second factor, greatly exacerbating this problem, was the 'military revolution' which increased the size of the largest armies in Europe tenfold between 1500 and 1700. This added to the pressure for money a savage cutting edge: many states had to respond by whatever means were necessary or risk being wiped out.

The third general factor, again reinforcing both of the others, was the religious disintegration of christendom. This fuelled the tendency towards war, both between states and within them. At the same time, in a culture where political was sanctioned by religious authority, it contributed to such conflicts a crucial ideological component. Would-be centralising governments were much more likely to face war; that war was much more likely to be savage; in the worst case it might be against a domestic rebellion sanctioned by religious ideology. Every European ruler had reason to fear this possibility.[63]

What these pressures amounted to was the imperative to statebuilding: to the construction of an effective early modern military-fiscal state. This was the only means to husband the fiscal, political and military resources necessary to survive. 'In an age of inflation, rulers had to increase revenues in the sixteenth and seventeenth centuries simply to stand still. A fivefold increase in revenues in the sixteenth century would still barely keep up with rising living costs.'[64] This exposed the authorities responsible to the dreaded accusation of innovation. The political phrase at the heart of England's troubles – 'arbitrary government' – was just this accusation. Throughout the troubles there was an attempt by both kings and parliamentarians to appropriate the medieval language of conservatism against modern innovation.

63 Koenigsberger, 'Dominium Regale or Dominium Politicum et Regale', pp. 17–20; Koenigsberger, 'The Crisis of the Seventeenth Century: A Farewell?', in Koenigsberger, *Politicians and Virtuosi*, pp. 73–4; W. B. Patterson's *James VI and I* is the case study of a ruler preoccupied by this concern.

64 Richard Bonney, *The European Dynastic States 1494–1660* (Oxford 1991), p. 354.

Everywhere in Europe statebuilders could expect to be opposed by certain groups who, in a locally self-governing society, stood to lose autonomy or power. These included local elites, whether nobilities or the governors of towns. They included the representative assemblies of those elites, concerned about losing their institutional role in government (political, legal, fiscal or all three). They included the victims of increased taxation. They included alienated religious minorities, or even majorities, where the centralising power had assumed a confessional identity. Finally they included alienated regions, or in the case of multiple monarchies even kingdoms.

The struggles unleashed by these processes dominated European politics in the early modern period. All of them were at work in the savage conflicts in France and the Netherlands in the sixteenth century, and the Habsburg and Stuart kingdoms in the seventeenth. During the Dutch 'troubles' Philip II in the Low Countries, like Charles I later, faced a dangerous double adversary. This was a powerful single representative assembly, the States-General, 'of the opinion that important political decisions such as those concerning successions, financial policy, legal issues and foreign affairs should not be taken without their counsel and consent'. In addition this assembly was equipped with a hostile and militant calvinist ideology. By 1559 Philip had, like Charles by 1629, 'decided that the States-General formed a grave threat to royal power and . . . it should not be summoned again'.[65] He had also set about a savage religious persecution. The outcome in both cases showed that in certain circumstances not only could representative assemblies successfully defend themselves but that they could very effectively achieve military-fiscal centralisation in the process. The resulting republican regimes, Dutch and English, would be among the most militarily powerful in Europe, though their security from monarchy would prove fragile.

It is accordingly hardly surprising if within the unreformed English polity both parliamentarians and monarchs found themselves on the defensive. Faced by a crown desperate for money, the House of Commons was deeply suspicious of any threat to its role. Members of the Commons reacted angrily in 1610 when the king spoke 'of France and Spain what they may do'. 'All Kings Christian as well elective as successive', James had asserted on 21 May, 'have power to lay impositions. I myself in Scotland before I came

---

65 *The beginning and cause of the late troubles and calamities* (1571), discussed in Martin van Gelderen (ed.), *The Dutch Revolt* (Cambridge 1993), p. x.

hither, Denmark, Sweden that is but newly successive, France, Spain, all have this power.'[66] 'This speech was so distastfull in some parts therof to the Howse' that a committee was appointed to respond. This drew up a 'petition *de droit*' in defence of 'those liberties and privileges which did anciently belonge to our predecessors serving in parliament'.[67] The king, argued Nicholas Fuller, though 'in truth very wise yet he is a stranger to this government'. Thomas Wentworth quoted Fortescue ('by the law of England no imposition can be made without assent of parliament as in France etc.').[68]

It was the same European context that sustained royal anxieties about the danger to monarchy. James considered the opposition to impositions to be an attempt to make him a 'Doge of Venice . . . No Christians but papists and puritans were ever of that opinion . . . [And as] it is atheism and blasphemy to dispute what God can do . . . so it is presumption and high contempt in a subject to dispute what a king can do or to say that a king cannot do this or that.'[69] As royal attempts to achieve solvency were rebuffed, so too were parliamentary appeals to ally more closely with a United Provinces or Bohemia governed by rebels. In March 1629 Charles' minister Sir Francis Cottington ascribed the refusal to pay tonnage and poundage after the dissolution of parliament to an 'infection' from the United Provinces 'whos kind of government pleaseth us much, and we would fayne be at it'.[70]

What made the forces at work so dangerous was not simply their European scope. It was the way in which they intertwined foreign and domestic affairs and crossed European boundaries. Even in times of peace this could lead to intolerable religious and political pressure. In times of war, however, the result was pressure on the unreformed polity which it might not withstand. The English response to these pressures came relatively late and the reaction was correspondingly severe. As has been well established, the period 1618–48 was a crucial context for statebuilding in several places. What made England relatively unusual in this context, however, was the extent of its unpreparedness. Historians inclined to praise Elizabeth for keeping England out of the religious wars of the sixteenth

---

66 Quoted in Jenny Wormald, 'James VI and I, *Basilikon Doron* and *The Trew Law of Free Monarchies*', in Peck, *Mental World of the Jacobean Court*, p. 37.

67 S. R. Gardiner (ed.), *Parliamentary Debates in 1610* (London 1862), pp. 36–41.

68 Wormald, 'James VI and I', p. 37.

69 Sommerville, 'James I and the Divine Right of Kings', p. 66.

70 State Papers 16/530/36, quoted in Peter Salt, 'Charles I: A Bad King?' I am grateful to Peter Salt for allowing me to read this important unpublished paper.

century must consider to what extent she is responsible for delivering it bound and gagged to those of the seventeenth. What distinguished the early Stuart crown in a European context was its financial, military and political weakness. As the Comte de Tillières observed in 1623, the Stuarts were 'en miserable estate . . . sans argent, sans amis et sans reputation, neantmoins leur gloire et leur vanité leur reste'.[71] For this weakness, recorded Balthazar Gerbier, not only James' 'subjects (zealous without knowledge) did blame him, butt his Neighbours also made Libells of him, and pictured his Majestie with his pocquets drawn out'.[72] This was a context of European mockery to be restored with the monarchy in 1660.

The notion of England as the leader, rather than laggard, in the race to modernity is so engrained in the national historiography (first modern revolution, first parties, first industrial revolution) that the implications of this fact may take some time to strike us. One is that it is the extent of this unpreparedness, with its attendant institutional fragility, that helps to account for the spectacular nature of the subsequent (pre-modern) revolution. Another is that the equally spectacular success of England's later statebuilding, and empire-building, owes a great deal to its deferred timing, with consequent capacity to borrow from the prior European experience, and particularly that of the Dutch.

Unlike the Dutch in 1570, Charles I's English opponents were not facing a foreign absentee. His Scots subjects, however, were, and it was a function even of English opposition rhetoric to portray Charles as foreign, specifically Hispanophile. Other reasons why the process of monarchical statebuilding faced particularly formidable obstacles in England included a powerful, single representative assembly. Over the sixteenth century this had consolidated a role in relation to the political, religious, legal and financial life of the country which had few European rivals. Equally unusually the English nobility paid taxes. The phenomenon of a self-taxing, self-assessing representative assembly posed difficulties to which neither early Stuart monarch was equal.[73] The most remarkable and challenging English peculiarity, however, merits separate treatment. This was the city of London.

71 Quoted in Cogswell, *Blessed Revolution*, p. 125.
72 British Library Add MS 4181, f. 9.
73 Michael Braddick, *Parliamentary Taxation in Seventeenth-Century England: Local Administration and Response* (London 1994); Wolfgang Reinhard, 'Power Elites, State Servants, Ruling Classes, and the Growth of State Power', and Gerald Aylmer, 'Centre and Locality: The Nature of Power Elites', both in Reinhard, *Power Elites and Statebuilding*.

THE BLOODY CITY

London was central to the troubles in more ways than one. It contributed to their causes, furnished their immediate context and above all helped to direct their outcome. In 1644 Milton would exclaim:

Behold now this vast City, a City of refuge, the mansion house of liberty, encompast and surrounded with his protection; the shop of warre hath not there more anvils and hammers waking, to fashion out the plates and instruments of armed Justice in defence of beleagur'd Truth, then there be pens and heads there, sitting by their studious lamps, musing, searching, revolving new notions and ideas wherewith to present, as with their homage and their fealty the approaching Reformation.[74]

Four years later a pamphlet (*A Winter Dream*) examined England's suffering in its European context. After an extensive continental tour, which revealed that such 'fury of the sword' was the common fate of many parts of Europe over the last '30 yeares', the reader was finally brought to 'a large Island', distinguished by a city too big 'to beare any political proportion with that Island'. Before it was a sign: 'Woe be to the bloody City.'[75]

The growth of early modern London was a European phenomenon. In 1500 the biggest towns in Europe – Constantinople and Naples – were both Mediterranean. London, with 35,000 inhabitants, had scarcely a fifth of their population. By 1550 that total was 120,000; by 1700 almost 500,000; and by 1750 London was the largest city not only in Europe but the world.[76] In part this reflected the northwestern drift in the population distribution of Europe's largest towns. Even allowing for this, however, the growth of London was extraordinary: Paris was the capital of a nation of twenty million, London of about four. Moreover of all the super-cities London was the only one which continued to expand throughout the period 1650–1750.[77]

This last feature may have been another consequence of England's late experience of statebuilding. The impact of this expansion was accentuated by the radically uneven pattern of urbanisation in early modern England. The most urbanised areas of Europe remained Italy and the Low Countries. Paris stood at the apex of an ascending complex of major towns. Only in

---

74 John Milton, *Areopagitica*, in *Complete Prose Works*, vol. II, pp. 553–4.
75 *A Winter Dream* (London 1648), pp. 4–5, 11.
76 A. L. Beier and Roger Finlay, *London 1500–1700: The Making of the Metropolis* (London 1986), pp. 1–3, 39.   77 *Ibid.*, pp. 4–5.

England was there not a single other town in the seventeenth century with more than a tiny fraction of the population of its major city. All of these peculiarities contrived to pose an important seventeenth-century question. Could one of Europe's weakest monarchies govern its most prodigious city?

Turbulent London had determined the kingdom's political future even in medieval times.[78] Throughout the early modern period, however, those charged with the government of the city – religiously complex, politically and economically crucial, and with close connections to the continent and the world – all expressed worries about their charge. Elizabeth, James I, Charles I and Cromwell all voiced alarm at the growth of the city, and tried in vain to stem it.[79] 'It is a port, and overmuch populous', recorded Edmund Grindal, 'the Bishop of London is always to be pitied'.[80] James I expressed his dislike of London by spending as much time as possible outside it. He repeatedly ordered his nobility out of the capital where their 'being together and often meeting . . . one revealing their discontents to another and soe in time grow to some head'.[81] Charles and Laud similarly set their faces against its political and religious ungovernability, whether exhibited in celebrations after Buckingham's assassination, or riots against popery.

Discussing Aristotle's *Politics* John Milton drew attention to the process by which the greatest Greek cities, and Athens in particular, had outgrown their kings. Algernon Sidney stated that just as 'All the tumults in the Low Countries began in Antwerp, Ghent, Brussels, and other principal cities', so 'all ours grew from the greatness and strength of London'.[82] Hobbes made the same accusation in *Behemoth* (written 1667–8).[83] Edward Hyde, Earl of Clarendon, allocated similar blame to 'the unruly and mutinous spirit of the city of London, which was the sink of all the ill humor of the kingdom'.[84]

---

78 R. Bird, *The Turbulent London of Richard II* (London 1949); Brown, *Late Medieval England*, p. 153: 'Edward IV . . . could probably not have become king without its support. London's wealth and independence . . . often led it into conflict with the king and its privileges here were confiscated several times and restored only at a price.'

79 Norman G. Brett-James, *The Growth of Stuart London* (London 1935), p. 21. For the mechanisms for maintaining social order in Elizabethan London, see Ian Archer, *The Pursuit of Stability: Social Relations in Elizabethan London* (Cambridge 1991), esp. pp. 259–60.

80 Quoted in Susan Bridgen, *Reformation London* (Oxford 1989), p. 129.

81 Cogswell, *Blessed Revolution*, p. 34.   82 Algernon Sidney, *Court Maxims*, pp. 71–2.

83 MacGillivray, *Restoration Historians*, pp. 71–2.

84 Quoted in Keith Lindley, *Popular Politics and Religion in Civil War London* (London 1997), p. 14.

If it is not the case that London 'caused' the troubles, it would be difficult to overstate the extent to which it made them possible, and influenced their course. Between 1641 and 1642 by the activities of the Common Hall, and then the Common Council, Charles I lost control of the shrievalty, the mayoralty and the city government as a whole.[85] The civil war, made possible by the king's flight from London, was itself a failed military attempt to recover control of the capital. Its temporary outcome was the republican government form of a European city-state. The next visitation of the troubles hinged again upon royal loss of control of a capital electrified by a popish threat. 'This whole work', reported Roger North, of destabilising the monarchy again,

was practicable by one single Operation; which was the gaining . . . a Majority of the Votes of the Common Hall of the City of London . . . For . . . there followed a Succession of factious Lord Mayors, and Sherrifs . . . and (by means of the Sheriffs) the whole nomination of Jurymen . . . this Matter was of that Importance to the Times . . . that Justice cannot be done to its Eminence in History.[86]

It was not until the removal of parliament from London in 1681, and the recovery of control of the city government and judiciary in 1682, that a blood-stained order could be restored. But it did not last for long.

During the final crisis of November–December 1688 the role of the city of London was again crucial. In the same atmosphere of anti-popish rioting, once again the capital slipped out of royal control. This time, however, its governors had learned their lesson. Following the expulsion of the king, the city invited Dutch occupation. It was under the protection of this occupation that, by February 1689, the Convention had established a new settlement. That this erected a form of government in which city and parliament would work in crucial partnership with a Dutch king was another telling, and this time more durable, outcome. In the analysis of Koenigsberger, the successful invasion of 1689 secured a kind of 'parliamentary government' which had existed in the Netherlands since 1579. 'It was not fortuitous that it should have been a Prince of Orange, the representative of the Dutch parliamentary substitute monarchy, who should have become the first truly parliamentary King of England.'[87]

The most important single determinant in each phase of England's

---

85 Valerie Pearl, *London and the Outbreak of the Puritan Revolution* (London 1961), pp. 120–50.   86 Roger North, *Examen* (London 1740), p. 90.

87 Koenigsberger, 'Dominium Regale or Dominium Politicum et Regale', p. 21.

troubles was external intervention (whether Scots, French or Dutch). It is not fanciful, however, to see the government and population of London as the most important *domestic* determinants of the process. All the institutions at the heart of contemporary anxieties – the church, monarchy and parliament – ultimately survived the troubles. That the Stuart succession did not, however, to be replaced by a prince bred up in a republican world of cities, owed a good deal to this most formidable of the challenges English monarchical statebuilding faced.

4

Reformation politics (1): 1618–41

To learn the true causes, the rises and growths of our late Miseries . . . had I not gone so far back as I do, I had not reached the Fundamentals . . . finding those proceedings to have their rise in the year 1618.

John Rushworth, *Historical Collections*[1]

no man less belov'd, no man more generally condemn'd then was the King; from the time that it became his custom to break Parliaments at home, and either wilfully or weakly betray Protestants abroad . . . All men inveigh'd against him.

John Milton, *Eikonoklastes* (1649)[2]

INTRODUCTION: REFORMATION POLITICS

In the foregoing chapters we have sought to understand two sets of political anxieties. These have close parallels to contemporary religious fears. These, too, were for the survival of an insufficiently reformed domestic institution within the context of a European situation fraught with danger.

That the parallel was close is hardly surprising, since religion and politics were intertwined. Elizabethan counsellors managing the war against Spain made no distinction between defending the country's religion and the state. Later John Vicars wrote of a plot 'for the . . . utter subverting of the fundamentall laws and principles on which the religion and government of the kingdom were firmly established'.[3] Sir Walter Erle explained in 1629: 'I dare boldly say, never was there . . . a more near conjunction between matter of

1 Rushworth, *Historical Collections*, vol. I, preface.
2 In *Complete Prose Works*, vol. III, p. 344.
3 John Vicars, *Dagon Demolished* (written 1649, published 1660), quoted in Diana Allan, 'John Vicars', undergraduate dissertation, Cambridge 1995.

Religion and matter of State in any Kingdom in the world than there is in this Kingdom at this day.'[4] Francis Rous echoed the point: 'I desire it may be considered, how the See of Rome doth eat into our Religion, and fret into the banks and walls of it, the laws and statutes of this realm.'[5]

It was not only monarchy and parliaments that were in danger in seventeenth-century Europe, but protestantism. For the fact that in crucial respects, moreover, it was religious passions that drove political ones there were several reasons. One was that, weak though the monarchy may have been, the English protestant church was more recent. It was a product of the still unfolding and embattled reformation. If the national boundaries of politics were therefore permeable and half-formed, those of religion were frailer still. Not all members of the Church of England agreed with one another. All agreed, however, that they were protestants: participants in a European reformation process and identity.[6]

In the most recent major study of early Stuart religious identity Anthony Milton has made two points. One is that recent debates about calvinism and 'arminianism' have tended to overstate the unity of the Jacobean church. Not only did it contain diversity but 'all groupings' within that 'protean' mixture 'were undergoing change and development during this period'. Secondly English religious identity was particularly vulnerable not only to the impact of political developments in general but those involving foreign protestant churches in particular. For it was by means of their relationship to European protestantism, and 'popery', that early Stuart English protestants sought to understand themselves.[7]

We have seen Balthazar Gerbier's statement that as 'The preservation of the true Religion . . . was the mayne object wheron the People had fixed theire hearts, so were theire Eyes and Eares, Scouts to discover what past abroad . . . the reformed Churches abroad they held as contrescarps and outworkes of the Church of England.' Accordingly Gerbier's conclusion concerning the troubles was that

4 W. Notestein and F. H. Relf (eds.), *The Commons Debates for 1629* (Minneapolis 1921), p. 19.
5 Quoted in Robert Zaller, 'The Crisis of European Liberty', in J. H. Hexter (ed.), *Parliament and Liberty from the Reign of Elizabeth to the English Civil War* (Stanford 1992), p. 222.
6 Patrick Collinson, *The Religion of Protestants 1559–1625* (Oxford 1982), p. x; Paul Seaver, *Wallington's World: A Puritan Artisan in Seventeenth-Century London* (Stanford 1985), pp. 143–5.
7 Anthony Milton, *Catholic and Reformed: The Roman and Protestant Churches in English Protestant Thought 1600–1640* (Cambridge 1995), pp. 8–10, 26–7, 531–5.

The apprehension of the People that the reformed Religion would not bee well defended seemes to be the original cause of som mistakes against king James and king Charles. The losse of Wesel proves the [first] Cause . . . The Losse of the Palatinat the second cause . . . [These] proved not only the cause of the prejudiciall opinion of the People, but of the Cooling of theire affections towards theire Souveraigne.[8]

This opinion transcended national boundaries. 'The[se] misunderstandings and exceptions [were] taken both by the People of England and by theire Neighbours of the same Religion with them.' The 'Jealous distrust that [James] would not easily bee moved to arme himself for the Protestants neither in Germanye, nor France' was the cause of 'those dayly Scandalls which both att home and abroade are most Injuriously heapened uppon him'.[9] Thus also the 'Pamphlets and weekly Intelligences', which, from 1620, 'have been multiplied and to[o] greedily receaved by the [English] People', were English-language products of a protestant international centred in the Netherlands.[10] Accordingly the pressure to maintain an Elizabethan pattern of English reformation military intervention was maintained from outside the country as well as inside it. It was this same demand, which found its keenest English institutional audience in the House of Commons, which would still be the focus seventy years later for successful propaganda in Dutch as well as English military interests by the government of William III.[11] In this way that 'Passion', which, in earlier conditions of military dysfunction, had helped to bring about the destruction of the English state, would following later Dutch military intervention underwrite the (re)making of it.

This public apprehension was not a seventeenth-century creation. From their outset Elizabethan politics were infused by confessional anxiety. The dangers of English military indolence in the face of the counter-reformation catholic menace had exercised figures across the political spectrum from William Cecil to Sir Philip Sidney. For much of the reign, indeed, the life of protestantism seemed little more secure than that of the queen herself. 'Upon the international cooperation of Protestantism there depended, its advocates maintained, the survival of England.'[12] This was not a view readily accepted by the queen herself. She

8 British Library Add MS 4181, ff. 12, 52.   9 Ibid., ff. 9, 51.
10 Ibid., f. 5.   11 Claydon, William III; see ch. 21 below.
12 Alford, 'William Cecil'; Worden, The Sound of Virtue, pp. 8–9 and chs. 3–5; Scott, English Republic, ch. 3.

had acceded to direct military intervention in the Netherlands only in 1585 and with the greatest reluctance. In this as in other matters James was her authentic successor.

In Gerbier's analysis a further context for seventeenth-century popular 'misunderstanding' of royal policy was military ignorance. Like 'the People' at large the House of Commons preferred Elizabethan nostalgia to geopolitical reality. Most members never came to grips either with English military incapacity, particularly upon land, or with the strategic difficulty of recovering the landlocked Palatinate. 'Zealous without knowledge', English protestants came wrongly to suspect from their inaction and then their failure the religious fidelity of their kings.

It was thus the fiscal and military decrepitude of the unreformed polity in an age of confessional warfare that furnished the context for the importation into England of central Europe's troubles.[13] In the summary of John Reeve: 'The polarisation of English politics by 1629–30 can be seen as one aspect of the polarisation of international politics under the pressure of war.'[14] It was thus that in 1648 'when the ill effect of these misunderstandings had arrived to such a height that certainne votes passed att Westminster . . . commanding their fellow subjects to make no more addresses unto his Majestie', there remained 'in the Libraries of Curious men their ramaynes certainne scandalous Libells against king James, who the Authors . . . reproche his Conivance towards the Ennemies of those of his own profession in Religion and beleefe'.[15]

Thus the first reason for the devastating impact of religious 'Passions' upon political allegiance was that they struck the state where it was weakest. Government of peace and war was that flower of the royal prerogative which the Stuarts could not afford to exercise effectively. In the 1620s this came to have serious dynastic as well as religious implications. As Mark Kishlansky has pointed out, in seeking to recover the Palatinate Charles I was fighting, until 1630, not only for his own honour but for the patrimony of the heir to the English throne.[16]

The second, of course, was the disastrous fate of European protestantism itself during the counter-reformation century. Throughout a century in which protestantism had to fight for its survival, or perish, the 1620s were

---

13 John Reeve, 'The Politics of War Finance in an Age of Confessional Strife: A Comparative Anglo-European View', *Parergon* n.s., 14, 1 (1996). I am grateful to Dr Reeve for a draft of this article.   14 Reeve, *Personal Rule*, p. 220.   15 British Library Add MS 4181, ff. 3–4.
16 Kishlansky, 'Charles I'.

remembered as the decade of disaster.[17] 'France, Germany, Hungary, Bohemia and the princes of the Low Countries know what rivers of blood flowed from this.'[18]

Conrad Russell has said that within each of the three British kingdoms there were significant minorities who preferred the religion of another to their own. It is to make the point more completely to say that the majority in each kingdom understood their religion (whether protestant or catholic) in more than simply national terms. The Scots and English protestant anxieties that led subjects into rebellious alliance against their king were stimulated initially by the fate of 'foreigners of our religion' in Germany, not Britain. It was the power of confessional identities defined in European terms that made it possible for subjects to put those allegiances ahead of those owed to their own monarch and Archbishop of Canterbury.

The final reason for the political impact of religious fears in England was that political power was religiously sanctioned. Political allegiance was inferior only to the duty of man to God. In the conventional words of James VI and I people owed obedience to their ruler 'as to God's Lieutenant in earth, obeying his commands in all things, except directly against God'.[19] Thus in the aftermath of the religious disintegration of christendom there quickly emerged the first political resistance theories sanctioned by religion.[20] The legitimating power of religion made possible not only rebellion and civil war but its most remarkable English consequence in civil war radicalism.

The struggle for the reformation was thus a European one. England's troubles record the process by which that struggle on the continent became the same struggle within Britain. It was a consequence of the relatively insecure and incomplete state of the early seventeenth-century English reformation that during the 1620s confessional polarisation within Europe could become polarisation within the English church.[21] England's troubles were unusual among Europe's wars of religion for being between, on the

17 Hugh Trevor-Roper, 'Three Foreigners: The Philosophers of the Puritan Revolution', in Trevor-Roper, Social Change, pp. 246–7.
18 Edmund Everard, Discourses of the Present State of the Protestant Princes of Europe (London 1679), pp. 2–4.
19 James, The Trew Law of Free Monarchy, quoted in W. B. Patterson, James VI and I, p. 61.
20 Quentin Skinner, The Foundations of Modern Political Thought (2 vols., Cambridge 1978), vol. II; Martin van Gelderen, The Political Thought of the Dutch Revolt 1555–1590 (Cambridge 1993); J. H. Franklin (ed.), Constitutionalism and Resistance in the Sixteenth Century (New York 1969).
21 Nicholas Tyacke (ed.), England's Long Reformation 1500–1800 (London 1998).

face of it at least, not protestantism and catholicism, but contenders for control of the English reformation. Each claimed to be defending this against those by whom it would be destroyed. Like that to monarchy, allegiance to what subsequently became the restoration 'Anglican church' would be powerfully defined and sharpened by the troubles themselves, and should not be antedated.[22]

THREE DOCUMENTS 1621–41

It has been one aspect of the assault upon the notion of a 'high road to civil war' to posit a discontinuity between 'the political issues of the 1620s, and those of 1640–2'. The latter, Conrad Russell tells us, were 'much more strictly religious'.[23]

That the concerns of the king's English parliamentary opponents in 1640–2 were fundamentally religious is indisputable. We may wish to query the word 'strictly'. Religious and political fears remained closely intertwined, for John Pym as for Charles I. It was, however, religious perceptions that knit together the eruptions in three kingdoms, and it was religious belief that was primarily responsible in England for driving participants in what became the civil war to take sides.[24]

To take an example of this mixture, we might turn to the most famous parliamentary utterance of the crisis. This was the Grand Remonstrance, issued in the aftermath of the Irish Rebellion in late 1641 and presented to the king on December 1st.[25] This exhaustive list of grievances, gaining only a narrow majority in the Commons, established more clearly than anything before it the divisions along which the civil war would be fought.

From it we learn (p. 203) that there is a design for the ruin and destruction of England and Scotland; that the king's own authority has been appropriated to this design; and that its end is 'the advantage and increase of popery'. Its contrivers are 'the Jesuits, and other engineers and factors for Rome'. They have (pp. 204–5) corrupted the Episcopacy and Privy Council:

---

22 John Morrill, 'The Church in England 1642–1649', in Morrill, *The Nature of the English Revolution* (London 1993); Spurr, *Restoration Church*.

23 Russell, *Unrevolutionary England*, p. xvi.

24 Anthony Fletcher, *The Outbreak of the English Civil War* (London 1981); Russell, *Causes of the English Civil War*; John Morrill, 'The Religious Context of the English Civil War', in Morrill, *The Nature of the English Revolution*; Caroline Hibbard, *Charles I and the Popish Plot* (Chapel Hill 1983).   25 Gardiner, *Constitutional Documents*, pp. 202–31.

the government of the church and kingdom. They are responsible for the troubles in, and between, all three kingdoms, culminating in the massacre in Ireland by which the longstanding European design of extirpating prot- estantism by fire and sword has actually been effected.

This 'Jesuited' design (pp. 208–9) has a history stretching back at least to the reign of James I. It is infallibly linked, first, to Spain and friendship with Spain; secondly, to the dissolution of parliaments, and ways of governing without them; and thirdly to (English) military failure abroad. Meanwhile (pp. 214–15) the clergy, assisted by royal authority, have been made instru- ments for the persecution of the godly, in the style of a 'Romish Inquisition'. Those who have done this, and preached up the 'royal prerogative' above 'the religion, laws and liberties of the kingdom' have been the soonest pre- ferred.

The heads of the design were three (pp. 215–16):

I. The government must be set free from all restraint of laws concerning our persons and estates . . . II. There must be a conjunction between Papists and Protestants in doctrine, discipline and ceremonies; only it must not yet be called Popery . . . III. The Puritans, under which name they include all those that desire to preserve the laws and liberties of the Kingdom, and to maintain religion in the power of it, must be either rooted out of the kingdom with force, or driven out with fear.

Finally 'for the effecting of this' design it was an essential preliminary to destroy protestantism in Scotland.

In this document, then, we see two things. The first is that religion, liber- ties and law are held to be intertwined. They are under threat, and must be defended, together. The second is that the *end* of this design is religious: it is the 'jesuitical' (that is, counter-reformation) plot to destroy protestantism.

Let us turn, for purposes of comparison, to two parliamentary utterances of the 1620s. The first is a series of resolutions drawn up by a Commons subcommittee for presentation to the king on 24 February 1629.[26] In these we are told familiarly that there is a dangerous design 'aiming at the subver- sion of all the protestant churches of Christendom'. Evidence for this abounds abroad and at home: protestantism in Germany, France and other places is 'in great part already ruined'; resistance to this has been 'weak'; Scotland is in danger; Ireland is 'almost wholly overspread with Popery, swarming with friars, priests and Jesuits'; in England 'we observe an

26 *Ibid.*, pp. 77–82.

extraordinary growth of Popery' since Elizabeth's time. In short, 'if our religion be suppressed and destroyed abroad, disturbed in Scotland, lost in Ireland, undermined and almost outdared in England, it is manifest that our danger is very great and imminent'.[27]

Bearing in mind this idea of 'our religion . . . abroad' let us turn finally to the third document, issued eight years earlier still, and twenty before the Grand Remonstrance. This was the Commons' Petition and Remonstrance to King James in 1621. It was this which produced the royal outburst quoted in chapter 2 claiming that the Commons had left no aspect of royal sovereignty 'unattempted but the striking of coin'. 'Some fiery spirits', James claimed, had attempted 'to debate publickly of . . . matters far above their reach . . . tending to our high dishonour, and breach of the Prerogative Royal'.[28]

The concerns of the Commons' Petition are familiar. It refers to 'our former petition concerning religion' occasioned by 'the danger of these times'. That danger is occasioned by 'The vigilancy and Ambition of the Pope of Rome . . . The distressed and miserable estate of the professors of true religion in foreign parts . . . The disastrous accidents of your Majesty's children abroad . . . the confederation of popish princes abroad . . . The swarms of Priests and Jesuites, the common Incendiaries of all Christendom, dispersed in all parts of your Kingdom'. The design is 'the subversion of the true Religion'. The solution is to break the Spanish Match; to 'speedily and effectually take your Sword into your hand'; and to secure religion at home by acting on the former petition.[29]

James' sense that this Remonstrance outrageously trespassed upon royal prerogatives – the making of war and peace, and the finding of a spouse for his son – was correct. He was not the first or last English monarch to suffer an assault of this kind. What had driven the Commons to it was not constitutional ambition. It was fear, in the context of European events, for the survival of 'their' religion.

It may be objected that the consideration of a mere three documents, out of their political context, proves nothing. It is to that context that we must now turn. The documents telling this story could easily be multiplied; the Grand Remonstrance was in many respects anticipated, for instance, by the petition drawn up by Pym and Sandys in the first Caroline parliament of 1625:

---

27 *Ibid.*, p. 79.   28 Rushworth, *Historical Collections*, vol. I, p. 40.   29 *Ibid.*, pp. 40–3.

The danger is first in their ends, and in the restlesness of their spirit, for the attaininge of them; they ayminge not only at the utter extirpation of our religion, but also at the possessinge of themselves of the whole power of the State, and . . . if they gayne but a connivencye, they will press for a tolleration, then strive for an equallitye, and lastly aspire to such a superioritye as may worke the extermination both of us and our religion.[30]

It is certainly the case that there was no single viewpoint of the Commons, let alone of parliament as a whole. Yet it has been quite unnecessary to present this as an insuperable barrier to general explanation. It does not follow from the fact that there is no such thing as '*the* Parliamentary attitude to war and liberty' that the attitude of every MP was 'entirely individual, and any true statement which covers them all must be so general as to be meaningless'.[31] Alongside their internal variety parliaments had corporate identities, and contexts. What is necessary, amid the rank undergrowth of secondary interpretation by which student access to this period is inhibited, is to expose some contemporary voices to view.

The first conclusion from these documents is that in terms of contemporary perception of the issues there was *no* fundamental discontinuity between the 1620s and 1640–2. If parliamentary grievances are more purely religious in either period it is in the former. To say this is not to suggest that there was a 'high road to civil war'. It is to make the point that, if it would be difficult to exaggerate the importance of subsequent events like the Scots and Irish rebellions, neither they nor their impact can be explained outside the context of the issues, and passions, ignited during the 1620s.[32]

We have seen, secondly, religious provoking political fears on both sides. Fear for parliaments was connected to, and exacerbated by, fear of popery. Fear for royal power was exacerbated by fear of 'puritanical popularity'. These religious fears, and the pressure they exerted upon domestic politics, were products of the European situation. What connected the period 1618–48 were not only royal and parliamentary perceptions but the events from which they developed, to which we must now turn.

30 Gardiner, *Debates in 1625*, pp. 18–19.
31 Conrad Russell, review of Hexter, *Parliament and Liberty*, in *History* 78 (June 1993), p. 253.
32 Derek Hirst, 'Parliament, Law and War in the 1620s', *Historical Journal* 23, 2 (1980), pp. 455–61.

HABSBURG ATTITUDES

The first cause of the troubles was the development, within the context of weak political structures, not only of ideological polarisation but also of militant religious ideology. This occurred first not in England but central Europe, from where it was imported after the Bohemian rebellion.

The Bohemian rebellion (1618) was a disaster for Jacobean foreign policy. A principled pursuit of peace ('Rex Pacificus') accompanied by confessional bridge-building (by marriage to both protestant and catholic houses) was also the recognition of a pragmatic reality. This is not to say that the beliefs informing James' policy were not genuine. Concerning his aversion to war it was observed that he preferred hunting because the deer did not shoot back.[33] His aversion to confessional politics, the basis for which had been laid in Scotland, connected to his view that the essence of both presbyterianism and Jesuitism lay in antagonism to monarchy.[34] Most of his writing was, accordingly, dedicated to the refutation of protestant and catholic natural law resistance theory. The underlying reality was, however, royal insolvency. Whatever the explanation of members of the Commons for their defensive refusal to address this problem ('to what purpose is it for us to drawe a silver streame out of the contry into the royal cestern if it shall dayly runne out thence by private cocks?'[35]), after the failed parliaments of 1610 and 1614 the king had little domestic incentive to change course. War would require the co-operation of a lower house inclined to trespass upon royal prerogatives; peace did not.

James' first act (1604) was to make peace with Spain. This was accompanied by an alliance with the United Provinces. In 1613, one year after the disastrous death of his eldest son Henry, James sanctioned the marriage of his daughter Elizabeth to Frederick, Elector Palatine, the calvinist prince of the Palatinate on the Rhine. Thereafter his principal foreign policy ambition, deeply unpopular within England, became the marriage of his remaining son and heir Charles to the Spanish Infanta. It was this policy which fell a victim to European events. For James' objectives of peace and bridge-building were being pursued alongside a continental process running in precisely the opposite direction. In the politically unreformed,

---

33 As the Venetian ambassador reported in 1607: the king has 'no inclination to war, nay is opposed to it, a fact that little pleases many of his subjects' (Robert Ashton (ed.), *James I by His Contemporaries* (London 1969), p. 10).

34 W. B. Patterson, *James VI and I.*   35 Gardiner, *Debates in 1610*, p. 15.

religiously mixed Holy Roman Empire, an Elizabethan-style compromise had been in effect from 1550 to 1600. This was, in this case, not a single sanctioned religion but the toleration of limited difference by a complex of political structures too weak to challenge it. By the early seventeenth century, however, this situation was being disturbed by two developments. The first was the arrival of the counter-reformation.

Zealous counter-reformation spirituality was keenly adopted by some German princes for either religious or political reasons, or both. After 1600 counter-reformation religion grew strong alongside Habsburg political weakness, a combination to have its Stuart echo. The second development was the response to this in the form of the Union of German Protestant Princes. This protestant and particularly calvinist front was developed with its headquarters in Heidelberg, capital of the Palatinate. A cornerstone of its strategy in the face of a growing threat was the establishment of links with other protestant powers. The major early coup was the marriage of the Elector Palatine to Elizabeth, daughter of James the king of Great Britain.[36]

In 1618, accordingly, with the Bohemian revolt that would set Europe on fire, one aspect of the Jacobean policy of confessional bridge-building became instead a bridge to convey that fire to England. There had been religious provocation: the destruction of protestant churches at Braunau and Klostergrab. The revolt itself was an uprising by the political elite of an overwhelmingly calvinist kingdom on behalf of their religion and Estates against a zealously catholic Habsburg Prince. Ferdinand II was based (not in Prague, but) in Vienna, birthplace of the Habsburg counter-reformation. The principal kingdoms of this multiple monarchy being Austria, Hungary and Bohemia, this was a serious and direct challenge to Austrian Habsburg power.[37]

That the Bohemian revolt did not end successfully, like its predecessor in the Netherlands or successors in England and Scotland, owed a great deal to the pattern of external intervention. That of Bavaria and Spain, in support of Ferdinand, contrasted with the failure of assistance to the rebels. Elizabethan assistance had eventually been offered to the Dutch, though not immediately. In this case not only was Bohemia's immediate danger greater, but its ties with England were in some ways closer. For the first step by the Bohemian rebels was to invite Frederick, Elector Palatine, to become their prince. Despite James' categorical advice to the

36 Evans, *Making of the Habsburg Monarchy*, pp. 41, 56–7, 63.   37 *Ibid.*, pp. 65–7.

contrary, Frederick accepted. Consequently, within six years of marriage, Elizabeth had become queen of a rebel calvinist European kingdom. As Ferdinand gathered forces to crush the uprising, the plea for military assistance from protestant Europe attracted only a limited local response. The most important such request, to Elizabeth's father, the most important protestant prince, was refused. In the Battle of White Mountain, outside Prague (8 November 1620), the rebels were defeated. Frederick and Elizabeth fled Prague. Bohemia was not only restored to obedience but recatholicised by force; thousands were killed; protestant churches were destroyed and protestant worship banned. Thereafter the Palatinate too was taken and handed over to catholic Bavaria for services rendered. Hereafter as far as possible throughout the Habsburg lands an unambiguous association of religious identity to political allegiance was established. Protestantism, above all calvinism, meant rebellion against princes. Catholicism meant loyalty to monarchy. On the basis of Ferdinand's victories in the 1620s came the successful establishment of the Habsburg monarchy as a zealous counter-reformation confessional state.

The impact of these developments upon England would be immediate and enduring. All sources – parliamentary speeches, pamphlet literature, private manuscripts and the newspapers called corantos – confirm that the political nation was in a ferment about this situation. What unfolded as a decade of disaster for European protestantism entirely overshadowed English high politics and established a body of passionate and informed public opinion.[38] 'What newes?', asked one diary entry. 'Every man askes what newes? Every man's religion is knowne by his newes.'[39] Nor was the news supplied – THE WEEKLIE Newes continued, out of Bohemia, Austria, the Palatinate, the Grisons, the Lowe Countries, and other places – superficial in content.[40] Coverage was detailed, determined not by state borders but by the confessional conflict which was 'the general discourse of Europe'. Approximately 600,000 corantos were published between 1622 and 1632.[41]

38 Cogswell, Blessed Revolution; S. L. Adams, 'Foreign Policy and the Parliaments of 1621 and 1624', in K. Sharpe (ed.), Faction and Parliament (Oxford 1978).

39 Diary of John Rous . . . from 1625 to 1642, ed. M. A. Everett Green (London 1856), p. 45.

40 Cust, 'News and Politics'; Cogswell, Blessed Revolution; A Continuation of the Newes of this Present Weeke, no. 5, 5 November 1622, p. 9; The continuation of our Weekly Newes, no. 17, 14 April 1625.

41 Michael Frearson, 'An Aspect of the Production of the Newsbooks of the 1620s', Cambridge seminar paper, 1993.

In 1632 they were suppressed. But with the revival of the struggle from 1640 printed news recovered with a vengeance. It was partly because participants in the English civil wars associated them with the struggle in Germany that parliamentary newsbooks of the 1640s not only revived the format of the 1620s' corantos but their content. Military news from England and the rest of Europe was mingled.[42] Villages sacked by royalist armies were compared to 'the ruines of Germanie'.[43] The struggle was still for the survival of 'the protestant religion' against 'popery . . . the king of Spaine . . . [and] the Jesuits'.[44]

Thus what Sir Simonds D'Ewes called 'the sad and doleful events of Christendom . . . [Frederick] not being succoured out of England as the Bohemians expected'[45] furnished the context for more than just the parliament of 1621. These events and their continental and British consequences would inform the political struggles of the whole of Charles I's reign. 'We are those', recorded one pamphleteer in 1624, 'upon whom the end of the world has fallen.' In this situation Jacobean inaction appeared culpable. James' response – 'We rather expected you should have given us thanks for the so long maintaining a setled Peace in all our Dominions, wheras all our neighbours about are in miserable combustion of war'[46] – followed by continued negotiations (for a Spanish marriage alliance, and voluntary restoration of the Palatinate) appeared not to be effectively addressing this situation.[47] In the words of his daughter Elizabeth (May 1623): 'my father

42 See, for instance, *The Moderate Intelligencer: Impartially communicating Martial Affaires to the Kingdome of England*, no. 169 (8–15 June 1648), no. 179 (17 August 1648); Joad Raymond (ed.), *Making the News: An Anthology of the Newsbooks of Revolutionary England 1641–1660* (Moreton-in-Marsh 1993), pp. 3, 11–14.

43 *Perfect Occurrences of Parliament*, 13–20 September 1644, pp. 1–2.

44 G. L. V., *British Lightning: or, Suddaine Tumults in England, Scotland, and Ireland, to warne the United Provinces to understand the Dangers and the Causes thereof* (1643), in Sir Walter Scott (ed.), *A Collection of Scarce and Valuable Tracts . . . of the Late Lord Somers* (13 vols., London 1808–15), vol. V, p. 5; see ch. 6 below.

45 *The Autobiography and Correspondence of Sir Simonds D'Ewes*, ed. J. O. Halliwell (London 1845), pp. 136–7.   46 Quoted in Cogswell, *Blessed Revolution*, p. 24.

47 The argument of W. B. Patterson's *James VI and I* that James came close to peacefully resolving the conflict three times between 1622 and 1623 (ch. 9) does not convince. One of the most powerful senses to emerge from this study is of the limited extent to which the king's ecumenical goals were shared, on either side of the Channel; hence the king's conclusion in 1623: 'I awaked as a man out of a dreame . . . the business is nothing advanced neither of the match nor of the palat[inate] for all the long treaties and great p[ro]mises' (p. 346).

will never leave treating, though with it he hath lost us all'.[48] In those of a contemporary pamphleteer:

I can come into no meetinges, but I find the predominant humor to be talking of the wars of Christendome and honour of their country . . . they spare not your Majesties sacred person . . . [but] wish Queen Elizabeth were alive again, who (they say) would never have suffered the enemies of her religion to have unballanced Christendome, as they have done within these few yeares . . . In your Majesties own tavernes, for one healthe that is begun to your selfe, there are ten drunke to the Princes your forraygn children.[49]

In London in particular anti-popery, hatred of Spain, and support for the protestant cause abroad ('what . . . contemporaries assumed to be an ideological consensus')[50] permeated considerably down the social scale. The many apparently providential catholic fatalities when a chapel collapsed at the French ambassador's residence at Blackfriars on 26 October 1623 became an occasion for the public expression of these views.[51] This did little to dislodge Stuart fears about 'puritan popularity'. 'It was made an infallible note of a Puritane', wrote Thomas Scott in 1624,

and so consequently of an ill subject, to speake on the behalfe of the King's children: and a certaine proofe of a good Protestant or a discreete and moderate man, to pleade against them for the Emperour, and the King of Spaine, who are ever linked and interested together in one cause.[52]

It seems unlikely that James shared the Emperor Ferdinand's view after 1618 that calvinism and monarchy were incompatible. It was the case, however, as both James and Charles noted, that those members of parliament most zealously inclined to trample upon monarchical prerogatives, or to render their obedience only upon conditions, were those most exercised

48 Elizabeth of Bohemia to Sir Thomas Roe, The Hague, May 1623, quoted in Michael Strachan, *Sir Thomas Roe: A Life 1581–1644* (Salisbury 1989), p. 160.

49 *Tom Tell-Troath: or a Free Discourse Touching the Manners of the Time* [London 1622?], in Ashton, *James I*, pp. 218–19.

50 Peter Lake, 'Constitutional Consensus and Puritan Opposition in the 1620s: Thomas Scott and the Spanish Match', *Historical Journal* 25, 4 (1982), pp. 806–7.

51 The observation of Walsham in '"The Fatall Vesper"' that what 'metropolitan observers' noted about the English response to this tragedy was 'the striking lack of charity of the common people, indeed their deliberate callousness and cruelty' (pp. 55–6) is reminiscent of the popish plot crisis of 1678–81: Scott, 'Popish Plot'.

52 Thomas Scott, *Vox Regis* (Utrecht 1624), p. 21, quoted in Frearson, 'English Corantos', p. 151.

by the fate of their protestant brethren abroad. Given that those brethren, in Bohemia as earlier in the Netherlands and France, were rebels, the conclusion was not difficult to draw. Charles' first parliament complained about an attempt 'to put a jealousy betwixt the King and his well affected subjects by sayinge ther is a potent prevaylinge faction in the Kingdome . . . calle[d] Puritanes . . . [and that] a Puritan is worse than a Papist'.[53] Charles' subsequent promotion of the author of this libel (Montague) did not set minds at rest.

In fact a growing royal tendency to associate 'puritanism' with disloyalty was a no less direct consequence of the failure of the unreformed polity to respond to the European crisis than the association of 'popery' with arbitrary government. Nor is it surprising, whatever his personal relationship to calvinist doctrine, if James felt that he as well as other monarchs was engaged in a struggle on behalf of monarchy. In every other respect James' relationship to his domestic problems was the opposite of Ferdinand's. Assisted by his allies, Ferdinand secured his position by armed force. James had no armed force. By the last years of his reign he was simply the weak, voluble monarch whose policies the march of European history had consigned to irrelevance. His son was very different. But no aspect of Charles' policies, or the disastrous fate by which they would be overtaken, can be understood outside this context.

Charles' reign was permanently shaped by the practical problems encountered at its inception. In this context, as Glenn Burgess has recently pointed out, it was not primarily what Charles thought or said that was different from his father (though in some respects it was); the difference lay in what he was prepared to do.[54] Within the cage constraining the power, domestic and international, of the Stuart crown, James had made comfortable if slovenly residence. Charles could not help throwing himself against the bars and then, when hurt and angry from many blows, turning upon those inside.

CAROLINE DISHONOUR

The circumstances under which Charles I's reign began were ones of military (following pre-matrimonial) humiliation.[55] Since its entire duration

---

53 Gardiner, *Debates in 1625*, p. 49.   54 Burgess, *Politics of the Ancient Constitution*, esp. ch. 6.
55 Sharpe, *Personal Rule*, emphasises this theme (e.g., pp. 44–5).

was characterised by ever more disastrous renewals of this condition it is no exaggeration to say that this was a shadow from which it never emerged. It is not only during the first five years of Charles I's reign, but the whole of it, that what we see is a militarily weak king fighting for his honour.

This is not to say that Charles was a weak personality. This situation was not a result of personality, though that did, nevertheless, shape his response. It was an effect, first, of the total failure of his two royal predecessors to engage in meaningful fiscal and military reform. The consequences manifested themselves in 1625 not only in royal poverty but also parliamentary military illiteracy (both fiscal and strategic). The second problem was the sheer difficulty of the military objective in view. This was partly a function of geography, and partly of the mismatch in resources between England and its allies and a triumphant Catholic League. The royal income of Castile, alone, was six times that of England in the early seventeenth century.[56]

In the words of one contemporary commentator: 'In plaine termes . . . the Palatinate is very ill seated for us to warre in; it being remote from the sea and surrounded on all sides with our enymies.' In those of another: 'the whole force of his three Kingdomes and all his Allies could not have constrayned the Emperor, the King of Spaine and the Duke of Bavaria to restorre the Palatinat'.[57] In all of these respects the new king Charles must have been deeply galled by the Elizabethan nostalgia that permeated his early parliaments. A member of the first, opining that 'never King found a state so out of order', compared the situation with that under 'that glorious Q[ueen], who with less supplyes defended herself, consumed Spayne, assisted the Low Cuntryes, relieved Fraunce, preserved Ireland'.[58]

Under such circumstances there were two features of Charles' approach that differed sharply from that of his father. The first was his commitment, despite the difficulties, to war. This was visible not only in his role in its initiation, in 1624, but in his all important refusal to retreat from it between 1625 and 1628. The second feature was the new king's concern for, and capacity to feel damage to, his honour. As the Lord Keeper put it at the outset of his first parliament: 'His Majestie puts his fame, his reputation (*which is all he hath of a Kinge*) upon us . . . As soone as he shall be knowne for a valiant Prince, you shall be esteemed a faithfull people.'[59] During the

56 Reeve, 'Politics of War Finance', p. 9.
57 Quoted in Ashton, *James I*, p. 224; British Library Add MS 4181, f. 17.
58 Gardiner, *Debates in 1625*, p. 31 (30 June: the speaker was Sir Robert Phelips).
59 *Ibid.*, p. 2 (my emphasis).

period 1618–25 the crown to which Charles was heir had suffered local and European religious, political and military humiliation. It was not only in London taverns that the country's 'honour' was considered lost. In this sense it was not only the king's 'children in Germany' who had been dispossessed. Moreover Charles' first direct experience as heir of how little his promised crown was now worth was a humiliatingly personal one.

As emphasised by Clarendon, Charles' entry upon the political stage occurred before 1625. The opening scene is easy not to take seriously, since it consisted of the prince's (and Buckingham's) utterly hare-brained expedition to Madrid. It did, however, have deeply serious consequences. After six months of footling delay, punctuated by wall-climbing to catch a glimpse of the Infanta with whom he pathetically imagined himself to be in love, Charles returned home empty-handed. The result was a war finally entered into, against James' better judgement, in prosecution not of religious zeal (though this was a commodity which it harnessed in the Commons) but princely feelings of anger and the desire for revenge. Thereafter it is not fanciful to see Charles' struggle for military honour between 1624 and 1648 as one not only for the reputation but the substance of English monarchy. That is certainly what it became. For what would distinguish Charles as king was a dangerous insistence upon not simply the appearance of monarchy but its substance.

In the first year of Charles' reign, one dishonour was followed by another. The first effort of English arms for a generation, Count Mansfeldt's would-be expedition to the Palatinate of 1624–5, was not simply a failure but a fiasco. This was much more serious, because under the circumstances (of war with Spain, declared 1624) it exposed not only the honour but safety of the kingdom. In this situation the duty of the House of Commons was clear. It was the more so in that, in Charles' view, the Commons had 'engaged . . . [him] in a war, and so were bound to sustain it'; and that this was 'his first request of them'.[60]

We should all therefore be able to imagine the new king's amazement when his first parliament demurred at the request for further major supply. Not content, indeed, with delaying a response, and later responding only inadequately, this Commons additionally failed to confirm to him a traditional aspect of his permanent revenue (tonnage and poundage). Instead it concentrated upon airing its complaints about the strategic and personal

60 *Ibid.*, pp. ix–x, 106–7; Russell, *Parliaments and English Politics*, p. 225.

prosecution of the war; the king's just completed French marriage treaty; and the general state (in particular religious state) of the kingdom. It was not just that the Commons' assumption of a role in these matters trespassed upon most royal powers and prerogatives (the government of war and peace; the arrangement of one's own marriage; the power to appoint ministers; the headship of the church). It appeared to fundamentally confuse the political relationship between subject and sovereign.

In a situation of military emergency, supply was the Commons' political and constitutional *duty*. In a monarchical context, their failure to perform this duty manifested not inability but disobedience. In the formulation of Sir Francis Bacon: 'Disputing, excusing, cavilling upon mandates and directions, is a kind of shaking off of the yoke, and assay of disobedience.'[61] It is hardly surprising, therefore, if in addition to his continuing military problems Charles rapidly concluded that there was a fundamental illness affecting the monarchy at home. His diagnosis was not that there was a constitutional problem. It was that there had developed in England a culture – a disease – of disobedience. The existing monarchical constitution could not function until this had been cured. This was the sense of the king's opinion, reported by the Venetian ambassador three years later, that members of parliament were spearheading a 'popular assault on the very foundation of monarchy'.[62]

It was Charles' initial refusal to withdraw from the conflict in which he had engaged that established the preconditions for what followed. This was a period of further military humiliation and domestic polarisation. It was from this in turn that there emerged the first ambitious attempt at Stuart monarchical statebuilding.

THE FIRST CRISIS OF PARLIAMENTS 1625–9

The 1625 Commons had, of course, reasons for its behaviour. Over the following several years parliamentary anger is as palpable as the king's. To begin with, for the loss of thousands of lives in Mansfeldt's expedition nothing had been attempted, let alone achieved. In contrast to Elizabethan legend, the long-awaited military action against the popish antichrist had been a catastrophic failure. The king now needed more money, but what of

61 Francis Bacon, *Of Seditions and Troubles*, in *Bacon's Essays*, vol. I, p. 47.
62 Cust, *Forced Loan*, p. 87.

that already given, and what guarantees were there that this would be spent any more effectively? This led to the suggestions that royal military strategy had been mistaken; that it had not been the strategy agreed upon in 1624; and that this mistaken strategy had been incompetently executed. All of these were overlaid with invidious Elizabethan comparisons and irrelevant nostalgia (no member explained convincingly how the Palatinate was to be recovered by sea). Once again religious and political anxieties were driving its members to trespass upon royal prerogatives.

This is not to say that these criticisms were devoid of substance. Despite modern apologias, there is little in the record to contradict the contemporary impression that the pre-eminence of the commander in chief, the Duke of Buckingham, owed less to relevant ability than to 'services' in the previous reign considered 'base . . . shameful and vile'.[63] If in place of an effective soldier, feared across Europe, England had as its commander a diamond-encrusted fop, famous in Paris for his dancing, that was a different form of corruption which was dangerous as well as dishonourable. This problem, which led Algernon Sidney, grand-nephew of the military hero Sir Philip, into a whole chapter on the corruption and effeminacy of the modern nobility and its disastrous military consequences, was also given prominence by Clarendon. It offered a golden opportunity for observations to the effect that 'Q Eliz . . . governed by a grave and wise counsell, and never rewarded any man but for desert; and that so sparinglye.'[64]

The Commons was, secondly, alarmed by the unprecedented experience of two large requests for money in succession. The amount was extraordinary (as it needed to be), and it inevitably reactivated insecurities about the future of parliaments:

[Precedents] are not to be neglected; subsidyes have ever come in the last place. It is a prerogative, questionless, for the Kinge to call Parliaments when he pleaseth; our ancestors that could not take that away, set up as a counter-prerogative . . . that they had power to treate of businesses in their owne order.[65]

What the king made of the notion of a 'counter-prerogative' in wartime is not recorded. The House's 'owne order' was to begin by bringing to the government's attention the unprecedented grievances of the commonwealth. 'In Q Eliz tyme ther was never meetinge [of parliament] but to reform greivances.'[66] 'A supplye was propounded; but wee ought rather to consider

---

63 Algernon Sidney, *Court Maxims*, p. 68.   64 Gardiner, *Debates in 1625*, p. 78.
65 *Ibid.*, p. 114.   66 *Ibid.*

how wee may supplye the commonwealth . . . Ther was matter of feare in every part of the state.' 'We have given three subsidyes and three fifteenes to the Q of Bohemia, for which shee is nothing the better. Nothinge hath bene done.'[67]

The most important 'matter of feare' brings us to the third and most important problem. From its inception the 1625 session was overshadowed by alarm about the growth of popery. In a time of plague there still seemed to many members 'more cause to fear the plague of our souls, than our bodies. The best preservative and cure the execution of the laws against Jesuits, etc.'[68] As we have seen, this was in part an effect of the European situation which had been present since 1620. By 1625 it had been accentuated by military failure. It was also, however, drastically augmented by the unpopular marriage treaty with France concluded on the eve of the session. Though the details of the treaty were not published immediately, they were widely rumoured. There could have been few worse times in English history to concede the relaxation of recusancy prosecutions to a foreign catholic power.[69] Not only this, but the treaty entailed the loan to France of ships which were subsequently used against protestant rebels at La Rochelle. This prestigious marriage helped to erase Charles' first humiliation, but at a huge price. Not even a subsequent declaration of war against France, followed by (ineffectual) assistance to the Huguenots, could erase from English protestant memory the alarm caused by these developments or what they appeared to say about the new king's priorities.

All of this helps to account for the 'extreme rage' with which the Commons now renewed what Hume called 'their eternal complaints against the growth of popery . . . [so that] it plainly appears . . . that, of all European nations, the British were, at that time, and till long after, sunk into the lowest and most odious bigotry'.[70] A petition was prepared by Pym and Sandys elaborating the advanced state of the Jesuitical design 'not only [for]

---

67 *Ibid.*, pp. 18–20, 78.
68 Quoted in Russell, *Parliaments and English Politics*, pp. 229–31.
69 See Simon Adams' review of Cogswell's *Blessed Revolution*, in *Parliamentary History* 2, 2 (1992), pp. 302–3.
70 In subsequent editions: 'the most under the influence of that religious spirit, which tends rather to inflame bigotry than encrease peace and . . . charity' (David Hume, *The History of England from the Invasion of Julius Caesar to The Revolution in 1688* (2 vols., 1754–7; 6 vols., Indianapolis 1983), vol. V, pp. 164–5).

the utter extirpation . . . both of us and our religion . . . but also the posses-singe of themselves of the whole power of the State'.[71] Eventually two further subsidies were voted, without fifteenths, and conditional upon an investigation of royal military policy and its execution. All of this helped to secure in Charles' mind the belief that there were in the Commons a group of influential individuals less concerned with doing their duty as subjects than with attempting to dictate royal policy and impose conditions. What was entirely new was the vigour of the royal response.

The Commons' religious concerns were not assuaged by Charles' eleva-tion of its key named 'arminian' (Montague) to a royal chaplaincy. No less remarkable was the king's decision to dissolve the parliament (now adjourned to Oxford) and collect additional funding by the mechanism of Privy Seal loans. It was therefore extremely unfortunate that the immediate outcome – the Cadiz expedition – was another costly fiasco. Accordingly the next parliament met (in 1626) with all the same grievances, considerably sharpened. This was a pattern which we will see repeated during the second crisis of parliaments of 1678–81. The subsequent attempt to impeach Buckingham, as the 'grievance of grievances', and the accessible symbol of royal policy, was as aggressive as the king's preceding actions. In turn it simply deepened the royal perception underlying those. Having betrayed the duty of subjects to support their king adequately in a dangerous war, members of the Commons were now attempting to take over the appoint-ment of government ministers.

However confrontational, Charles' belief that he could not afford to sur-render to such demands is at least understandable. His responses – to undermine parliamentarian strategy by identifying Buckingham's policy as his own; to dissolve the house again, and to resort to a more substantial Forced Loan – all raised the stakes considerably. It was in May 1626 that Charles warned his subjects to 'Remember that Parliaments are altogether in my power for their calling, sitting and dissolution; therefore, as I find the fruits of them good or evil, they are to continue or not to be.'[72] Criticisms of Charles for tactical and political ineptitude miss the point that the king's struggle was not being conducted on a tactical level. Ensuring the next subsidy, vital though it was, was not the most important thing. The war against the enemies of king and kingdom abroad had opened a new front at home.

71 Gardiner, *Debates in 1625*, pp. 18–19.　　72 Reeve, *Personal Rule*, p. 12.

The king was now engaged in a struggle against a treasonous puritan and republican conspiracy for control of the powers he had inherited under God. As he explained to Chateauneuf in August 1629, parliament made war on him rather than on the king of Spain; his problems derived from parliaments some of 'whose members wished to reduce his power to nothing'; and these people were 'puritans', 'enemies of monarchs' and 'republicans'.[73] For his opponents, correspondingly, the reality of a European conspiracy for the destruction of protestantism had been visibly joined within the kingdom by another for the destruction of parliaments and government by law. How else could popery be imposed upon a protestant kingdom except by the destruction of parliaments and the law?

Thus alongside the elaboration of a now clearly anti-puritan ecclesiastical policy the future of parliaments became the major talking point. The Forced Loan was an ominous experiment in this context, with French parallels. In the words of the Earl of Lincoln:

the gaining of a presedent to raise moneyes without law . . . was the overthrow of Parliament and of the freedom that now we injoy in France . . . That which is laboured at is to suppresse Parliament that so great offender might not be called in question, and so they might imposse what burthens they please.[74]

Of the seventy-six refusers the five most famous – those to be the subject of the five knights case – saw their stand as one for the survival of parliaments and the traditional lawful constitution. Charles, in his turn, spoke of the 'notable contempt committed by them against ourself and our government and for stirring up sedition against us . . . to the destruction of the commonwealth'.[75] Thus by the third parliament of this period, in May 1628, all of these grounds for concern had further deepened. The unbroken chain of military disasters had continued, reinforcing opposing analyses of corruption in the state. War against France had joined that against Spain and 3,000 English soldiers had been killed in a fruitless attempt to relieve the Huguenots of La Rochelle. Charles opened the session with a warning that, if he didn't get co-operation, 'I must, according to my conscience, take those courses which God hath put into my hands.'[76]

The Commons' immediate response was to vote five subsidies. This was, however, conditional upon the passage of a Petition of Right drawn up follow-

---

73 *Ibid.*, p. 132.
74 *To all English Freeholders*, 24 January 1627, quoted in Cust, *Forced Loan*, pp. 172–3.
75 Quoted in Reeve, *Personal Rule*, pp. 123–4.   76 *Ibid.*, p. 18.

ing the controversial imprisonment and trial of five who had refused to pay the Forced Loan.[77] For some this was the beginning of that perceived collapse of the law 'into the chaos of a higher power' the corrupting effects of which Clarendon remarkably likened to Thucydides' description of the visitation of the plague upon Athens.[78] The Commons then drew up the Remonstrance, part of which we examined earlier, outlining the grievances of the common-wealth. These focused upon innovations in religion which looked like popery, innovation in government endangering parliament and the laws, and disasters and dangers abroad and at home. 'The conviction', observed John Reeve, 'that the dangers to England were part of a wider European drama was the domi-nant and unifying theme of the remonstrance debate.'[79]

'[Our] liberties have been so invaded', lamented William Strode, 'that we are exposed to a foreign destruction.' 'God has punished us', explained Sir Edward Coke, 'because we have not spoken plainly . . . and until we do so God will not bless us, nor go out with our armies.' 'As religion is decayed', complained Francis Rous, 'so the honour and strength of this nation [is] decayed.' 'Now fall these things', echoed Sir Robert Phelips, 'at a time when our religion is almost extirpate in Christendom.'[80]

By the following year parliaments had been abandoned. In his *Declaration* of March 1629 Charles explained of the Commons:

We are not ignorant how much that House hath of late years endeavoured to extend their privileges, by setting up general committees for religion, for courts of Justice, for trade, and the like . . . they turned the necessities grown by that war, to enforce us to yield to conditions incompatible with monarchy.[81]

In future 'we shall accounyt it presumption for any to prescribe any time for us for Parliaments the calling, continuing and dissolving of which is always in our own power'.[82] Almost three years later the king reported to his Council that

---

77 The findings of John Guy's 'The Origins of the Petition of Right Reconsidered', *Historical Journal* 25, 2 (1982), have now been disputed by Mark Kishlansky, 'Tyranny Denied: Charles I, Attorney General Heath, and the Five Knights Case', *Historical Journal* 42, 1 (March 1999).

78 Hyde (Clarendon), *History of the Rebellion*, vol. I, p. 86: 'For the better support of these extraordinary ways, and to protect [those] . . . employed in them . . . the Council-table and Star-chamber enlarge[d] their jurisdictions to a vast extent, "holding" (as Thucydides said of the Athenians) "for honourable that which pleased, and for just that which profited".'

79 Reeve, *Personal Rule*, p. 26.   80 All quoted *ibid.*, pp. 25–6, 77.

81 Gardiner, *Constitutional Documents*, p. 95.   82 Quoted in Scott, *Restoration Crisis*, p. 73.

by the discourses of many concerning a Parliament he was now offended and his proclamation violated, and therefore wished all men to be wary how they displeased him in that kind, adding further that he would never be urged by necessity or against his will to summon one.[83]

CONCLUSION

What we have observed in this process of polarisation is the development of two ideological interpretations of structural military failure. In one, military failure with disastrous consequences for European protestantism had been occasioned by the corruption of the state by popery and arbitrary government. In the other military failure with disastrous consequences for English monarchy had been occasioned by a corruption of disobedience the religious and political nature of which had been equally clearly exhibited in continental Europe.

Each of these perceptions had a European context and each was anchored in the religious, political and military realities of its time. In his terms Charles could not achieve successful monarchical government, particularly militarily on the European stage, with these parliaments (and therefore this political culture). From the perspective of his opponents, accordingly, parliaments, the laws and their religion were all in real danger, not only in the rest of Europe but at home.

Because he had the prerogative powers first to exit from the European war, and then to govern the meeting of parliaments, the first of these interpretations to underwrite a programme of reform was the king's. In 1640, with renewed religious and military crisis and the forced surrender of that second prerogative, parliament's time would come.

83 Quoted in Reeve, *Personal Rule*, p. 281.

5

Counter-reformation England

[S]uch is the aptness of Christian Preachers to raise Seditions, that oft-times . . . terrible Changes . . . have been occasioned . . . in our times in *Scotland* and *England* . . . And therefore Protestant Kings . . . who own themselves Head of the Church . . . did for their greater safety . . . prohibit all publick Extemporary Sermons and Prayers . . . This *Charles* the First King of England had in part effected by taking away the Sabbath Days Afternoon's Sermons.

Pieter de la Court, The True Interest of Holland (1662)[1]

Could thought be controlled as easily as speech, all governments would rule in safety, and none would be oppressive.

Benedict Spinoza, Tractatus Theologico-Politicus (1670)[2]

CAROLINE STATEBUILDING

One feature of pre-statebuilding England was the relationship between weak institutions and powerful ideas. Alongside weak monarchy, dysfunctional parliaments and a partially reformed church, we have observed the impact of religious and political beliefs animated by the Thirty Years War. This charging of politics with ideology was not simply a feature of the troubles. When statebuilding finally came to Britain it did so within this context.

In its domestic context, the Caroline experiment from 1625 to 1640 was remarkable in two ways. The first was, after seventy years of neglect, its range and ambition. This may have reflected a sense of urgency rather than

---

1 'De Witt and other Great Men in Holland' [Pieter de la Court], *The True Interest and Political Maxims of the Republic of Holland* (London 1702), pp. 406–7.
2 In Benedict de Spinoza, *The Political Works*, ed. A. G. Wernham (Oxford 1958), p. 227.

confidence. It certainly demonstrated the conviction that the time had come to abandon half measures for fundamental reform. A second feature was that it was directed towards the intellectual as much as practical obstacles to effective monarchical government in England. What was necessary was not only the transformation of revenue-raising, and the facing down of opposition, but the re-establishment of obedience to monarchy.

For, as we have seen, the obstacles to royal absolutism in England were cultural as much as institutional. One aspect of these was the humanist intellectual culture, and limited and co-operative government, of the Jacobethan 'monarchical republic'. Another was that reformation religious culture the political consequences of which for obedience to monarchy had been demonstrated on the European stage.

In its European context, Caroline statebuilding had two extraordinary features which require explanation. The first was that this was an attempt at statebuilding in peacetime. Other European examples (whether Dutch, Austrian or French) all suggest that statebuilding only ever succeeded through the urgency of war. The military-fiscal state was created by and for war, and only an appeal to military emergency could persuade domestic elites to submit to the degree of innovation necessary. Charles' determination upon 'new counsels' also emerged from the pressure of war. Thereafter, however, he did not engage in uprecedented innovation to fight a war. He withdrew from a war in order to engage fully in domestic innovation. That subsequently ship money was a temporary fiscal success did not make it politically secure, as its collapse from 1638 showed.[3] It did not escape even obedient contributors that this claim to emergency military funding was unaccompanied by a military emergency. It is possible to say in retrospect that this was a dangerous decision. Yet it reflected a number of features of the English situation.

One was the conclusion from the period 1625–9 that war was impossible without prior reform. Another was the conclusion of a financially exhausted government that reform was impossible without peace.[4] This was in turn informed by geography: withdrawal was a temporary luxury the Channel appeared to allow. Finally this reflected the king's own sense of the struggle he faced. When, in 1626, Clement Coke had opined that it was 'better [to] die by an enemy than suffer at home', Charles had responded: 'Indeed *I* do think it more to my honour to be destroyed by an enemy' than

---

3 Sharpe, *Personal Rule*, pp. 567–83.   4 *Ibid.*, p. 65 (and ch. 2 in general).

by his own subjects.[5] The king's belief that his most dangerous enemies were at home had profoundly important consequences.

Thus abandoning any claim to the loyalty of his subjects against a foreign foe, the king instead made cold (and later actual) war upon a section of his own subjects. The contrast between his amity with Spain and preparedness to co-operate with foreign and local catholics, and his coldness and indeed hostility towards zealous protestant members of his own elite, in England, Ireland and Scotland, caused understandable alarm. Most importantly, the European war did not go away. 'Freedom from actual war', Peter Salt has explained, 'does not mean freedom from the effects of wars going on elsewhere . . . even after peace had been made with Spain in 1630 . . . England was much more influenced by the Thirty Years War than has been supposed . . . the ideological impact of the war was considerable even though English kings were not fighting . . . indeed, it was exacerbated precisely because English kings were not fighting.'[6] Thus ultimately disengagement in one theatre would be followed by engagement in another. When frustrated Anglo-Scots religious passions finally found effective military expression it would be against their own king.

Glenn Burgess has asked: 'Can we plausibly see the British conflicts as *part of* the Thirty Years War, when the British kingdoms were at peace during the 1630s, [and] only involved directly in European warfare in the 1620s'? Even accepting that

European warfare was an important source of both the fears and the military experience of many British people, all of this falls well short of suggesting the British wars were part of the Thirty Years War. It still does not make Europe the crucial contextual framework within which to understand the sequence of events triggered off by the imposition of a new Prayer Book on the Scottish kirk in 1637.[7]

Yet the processes at work in the troubles – statebuilding, reformation and counter-reformation – were all European in scope and understood as such by contemporaries. In this context it is necessary to question the words: 'events *triggered off by* the imposition of a new Prayer Book'. The spectacular Scots eruption of 1637–40 has one context in longer-term developments in the history of Scotland. Like its successor rebellions, however, in Ireland and England, the Scots rebellion also registered the direct ideological impact both of the Thirty Years War, and (within that context) of royal policy.

---

5 Kishlansky, 'Charles I'.   6 Salt, 'Charles I', pp. 11, 13.
7 Glenn Burgess, 'Introduction: The New British History', draft, pp. 21–2.

The second extraordinary feature of Caroline statebuilding in its European context was its confessional identity. That it was confessional in nature was an attempt to support weak institutions by the power of belief. Indeed throughout its history, unsuccessful and then successful, English statebuilding was driven by a confessional agenda (see chapter 17 below). This is because it developed in the context of the troubles. For this reason the counter-reformation agenda of Charles I is no less evident than the reformation ideologies animating the successful statebuilding parliaments of 1642–53 and 1689–1702.

It was not the fact of confessional statebuilding that was unprecedented in European terms. This feature of the Caroline experiment distinguished it from the French, and associated it with the Habsburg model. Charles I was conscious, and envious, of Richelieu's example. Yet French state centralisation was predicated upon the subordination of domestic political and religious concerns to the European military struggle.[8] In both respects Caroline policy was the reverse. It was an irony not lost upon the English population that Gustavus Adolphus' principal ally in the temporary protestant recovery of much of northern and central Germany in the 1630s was catholic France.

The fiscal and political innovation essential to state centralisation placed enormous strain upon domestic obedience. It was central to Richelieu's thinking that any attempt to add to this by acceding, for instance, to *devot* demands to eradicate French protestantism, would be potentially fatal to the whole design. Such plans, to be successful, had to wait (they eventually were, because they did). After seventy years of fiscal, political and military indolence English monarchical reconstruction was never going to be easy. Why, then, did Charles add incalculably to this challenge by engaging in deeply provocative religious reform at the same time?

It is here that we might be tempted to attribute some explanatory weight to the king's 'personality'. In the later words of Lucy Hutchinson: 'he was the most obstinate person in his self-will that ever was, and was so bent upon being an absolute uncontrollable Soveraigne that he was resolv'd either to be such a king or none'.[9] While this may be true, the extent of Caroline ambition is better understood as a reaction to the problems it faced. One explanation for the confessional character of Caroline state-

8 J. H. Elliott, *Richelieu and Olivares* (Cambridge 1984); Bonney, *European Dynastic States*; Robin Briggs, *Early Modern France 1560–1715* (Oxford 1977).

9 Lucy Hutchinson, *Memoirs of the Life of Colonel Hutchinson*, ed. N. H. Keeble (London 1995), p. 68.

building lies in the ideological context from which it emerged during the 1620s. Another point is the limited range of statebuilding resources available in early Stuart England. In this respect Charles may have been attempting to make what was the crown's greatest seventeenth-century political liability (governorship of the church) into its most important asset. The key to statebuilding in England would be the reformation not of institutions, but of 'men and manners'.[10]

As the confessional nature of Caroline statebuilding distinguishes it from the French model, so it associates it with the Habsburg. Throughout the 1620s it was Ferdinand's Habsburg monarchy, not Louis XIII's France, that was the outstanding European example of successful monarchical statebuilding. Although obviously aware of the example, there is no evidence that Charles I consciously took Ferdinand as a model. The parallels between the cases may be explained by shared contexts, both domestic and external. As we have seen, the religious and political polarisation of an unreformed multiple monarchy began in Habsburg central Europe, and transferred itself through the military conflict of the 1620s to Stuart Britain.

It did so, above all, by the political impact of its polarisation of religious allegiance. This was between an anti-catholic protestantism associated with rebellion against princes, and a counter-reformation ceremonialism associated with popery and arbitrary government. Having previously been visible in France, the Netherlands and the Holy Roman Empire, by 1629 this polarisation had come to England. In 1603 a complex tapestry of protestant religious opinion overwhelmingly identified itself with the English church. By the 1630s two extremes had emerged, one opposed to the supra-national threat of popery, the other to that of 'puritanism'. As one contemporary put it: 'King James spoke not so confusedly as if Puritanism were a Religion and all that dislike bishops and ceremonies were of that Religion: and all of that Religion were enemies of Kings.'[11] It was a dangerous situation when the king's own military commander against a protestant Scots rebellion could lament: 'To think well of the Reformed Religion is enough to make the Archbishop one's enemy.'[12]

10 Sharpe, *Personal Rule*, p. 136.
11 Julian Davies, *The Caroline Captivity of the Church* (Oxford 1992), p. 18.
12 Algernon Percy, 10th Earl of Northumberland, 1639, quoted in J. Sears McGee, 'William Laud and the Outward Face of Religion', in R. DeMolen (ed.), *Leaders of the Reformation* (London 1984), p. 318.

Thus it was not in the fact of its confessional nature that Caroline state-building was unique. What was unique was the confessional identity it chose. In counter-reformation catholicism Ferdinand II took one powerful component of the religious culture of his native Austria, and used it to unite the monarchy. It was, moreover, a powerful component of contemporary European religious culture, and that of Austria's dynastic allies. Charles, on the other hand, apparently fixed the fortunes of his political experiment upon a confessional identity that was deeply unpopular even within his own core kingdom, and had no significant body of adherents outside it. It had no such adherents, that is to say, unless we follow contemporaries and count among its allies the powers of catholic Europe.

If it was true that calvinism was incompatible with obedience to monarchy, then Charles I faced vastly greater difficulties than Ferdinand II. For whatever reason, Caroline statebuilding constituted an audacious gamble for exceptionally high stakes. In this lies the immediate context not only of the English civil wars but their result in that extreme confessional reaction, the English revolution. Following the experiment of counter-reformation protestantism would come that of radical reformation.

THE PEACE OF SILENCE

One aspect of that ungovernable political culture upon which Caroline statebuilding set its sights was humanist education. An analysis of the effect of this on contemporary parliamentary behaviour was published in 1629 by Thomas Hobbes.[13] To this earliest entrance on to the public stage Hobbes had been moved by the turbulent parliamentary politics of 1625–8 in general, and what James I had called the 'tribunitial oratory' of members of the House of Commons in particular.[14]

The subject of Hobbes' humanist master-work, his translation of Thucydides' *History of the Peloponnesian War* (1629), was the causes of political instability and war. In relation to the contemporary political situation, however, Hobbes' interest in Thucydides was still more specific. As he claimed in his preface (*Of the Life and History of Thucydides*) 'Truth' being

---

13 Hobbes, *Of the Life and History of Thucydides*; Scott, 'Peace of Silence'.

14 Miriam Reik, *The Golden Lands of Thomas Hobbes* (Detroit 1977), p. 37; Noel Malcolm, 'Hobbes and Spinoza', in J. H. Burns with Mark Goldie (eds.), *The Cambridge History of Political Thought 1450–1700* (Cambridge 1991), p. 531; Johann Sommerville, *Thomas Hobbes: Political Ideas in Historical Context* (London 1992), p. 9.

'the *soul* of history, and *elocution* the body',[15] the ancient historian had two supreme talents for the practice of his craft. One was his masterful treatment of human character 'containing contemplations of those human passions, which either dissembled or not commonly discoursed of, do yet carry the greatest sway with men'.[16] These were of course the same 'Passions', animated by the European war, identified by Gerbier as causing the troubles. The other was his mastery of the rhetoric – the 'deliberative orations' – which by appealing to those passions furnished the 'grounds and motives' for war.[17]

It was accordingly Thucydides' command of deliberative (political) oratory which provided the focus of Hobbes' preface. Thucydides had received his rhetorical training from the master Antiphon, and could accordingly have made a career in politics. That he did not do so followed from his observation of the destructive effects of oratory in the Athenian democracy:

> he least of all liked the democracy. And upon divers occasions he noteth the emulation and contention of the demagogues for reputation and glory of wit: with their crossing of each other's counsels, to the damage of the public; the inconstancy of resolutions, caused by the diversity of ends and power of rhetoric in the orators; and the desperate actions undertaken upon the flattering advice of such as desired to attain, or hold what they had attained, of authority and sway amongst the common people.[18]

In Athens, as apparently in Charles I's parliaments,

> such men only swayed the assemblies, and were esteemed wise and good commonwealth's men, as did put them upon the most dangerous and desperate enterprises. Wheras he that gave them temperate and discreet advice, was thought a coward, or not to understand, or else to malign their power. And no marvel: for much prosperity (to which they had now for many years been accustomed) maketh men in love with themselves; and it is hard for any man to love that counsel which maketh him love himself the less . . . By this means it came to pass amongst the Athenians, who thought they were able to do anything . . . that wicked men and flatterers drove them headlong into those actions that were to ruin them; and good men durst not oppose, or if they did, undid themselves.[19]

---

15 Hobbes, *Of the Life and History of Thucydides*, p. 16.
16 Quoted in David Johnston, *The Rhetoric of Leviathan* (Princeton 1986), p. 5.
17 *Ibid.*, p. 9; Conal Condren, 'On the Rhetorical Foundations of *Leviathan*', *History of Political Thought* 11, 4 (Winter 1990).
18 Hobbes, *Of the Life and History of Thucydides*, p. xxiv.   19 *Ibid.*, pp. 12–13.

One feature of this analysis is its anticipation of that association of Charles I's troubles with the effects of peace and prosperity which would be such a notable feature of royalist explanations after 1660.[20] The other is its apparent identification of Caroline England as an oratorically democratic political culture. At its best, the preface claimed, Periclean Athens was a democracy in form but monarchy in fact. This was an effect of Pericles' personal and rhetorical command. Under the stuttering Charles I England was the reverse. This helps to contextualise one crucial aspect of royal policy from 1629 to 1640: the attempt, not only in relation to parliament, but pulpit and press, to command silence: 'all men inhibited . . . by proclamation . . . upon penalty of censure so much as to speak of a Parliament'.[21]

Following his negative observation of the effect of democratic oratory, Thucydides held himself aloof from politics. Instead he applied his skill to a record of the resulting disaster. Not only did this succeed in conveying the true causes of the conflict. It did so by inviting the reader to imaginatively experience the dangerous passions concerned. As oratory connected with the passions, so Thucydides' recreation of it spoke to same passions in his readers. Hobbes explained, quoting Plutarch: 'Thucydides aimeth always at this; to make his auditor a spectator, and to cast his reader into the same passions that they were in that were beholders.'[22] Hobbes apparently hoped that this imaginative experience of the tragedy which had engulfed Athens would be not only admonitory but cathartic. In 1629 this was offered to an English humanist readership not only to warn against, but substitute for, a similar tragedy in the present. This strategy was not to prove successful. Meanwhile, however, Caroline dramatic culture preoccupied itself with the problem of the passions. Upon his arrival in England in 1636 the papal envoy George Conn attended a new Masque called *The Passions Calm'd.*[23]

According to Clarendon, 'It was now a time of great ease and tranquillity.'[24] 'England in 1637', says Russell, 'did not feel itself to be sitting on a powderkeg.'[25] In the absence of lightning, of course, a powderkeg may feel like a comfortable wooden seat. It is the peace of silence in the 1630s

20 MacGillivray, *Restoration Historians.*
21 Hyde (Clarendon), *History of the Rebellion*, vol. I, p. 5.
22 Quoted in Leo Strauss, *The Political Philosophy of Hobbes* (Chicago 1952), p. 32.
23 Kevin Sharpe, *Criticism and Compliment: The Politics of Literature in the England of Charles I* (Cambridge 1987), chs. 1, 2 and 6; Martin J. Havran, *The Catholics in Caroline England* (Stanford 1962), p. 144.   24 Hyde (Clarendon), *History of the Rebellion*, vol. I, p. 122.
25 Russell, *Fall of the British Monarchies*, p. 1.

which requires that such claims be put in perspective: the enforced silence of parliaments and in relation to parliaments; the control of foreign news and other forms of publication; governmental hostility to anti-popery; the attempt to silence preaching of doctrine in general, and calvinist doctrine in particular. It was the king's express will, wrote Secretary Dorchester in 1629, that 'hereafter none do presume to print or publish any matter of news, relations, histories, or other things in prose or in verse that have reference to matters and affairs of state, without the view, approbation and licence' of the government.[26] These policies had their precursors in the late Jacobean attempt to contain the ideological fallout from the European crisis, albeit for more explicitly ecumenical purposes ('no preacher of what title or denomination soever, shall consciously and without invitation from the text, fall into bitter invectives, and indecent railing speeches against the person of either papists or puritans').[27] Kevin Sharpe has emphasised the difficulty the government experienced in practice attempting to enforce this will. Whatever its success it is not possible to show from the peace of silence that the ideological polarisation set in train during the 1620s did not continue during the 1630s. All that can be shown is that it was not as continuously audible and visible.

Not all contemporaries, anyway, associated peace with health or harmony. The alternative suggestion that unnatural calm might presage a storm, that a nation luxuriating in idleness rather than exercising itself in war might eventually turn in upon itself, appealed to both royalists and parliamentarians.[28] Indeed the association of peace with corruption, in a Europe where the survival of protestantism required the vigorous exercise of arms, had a distinguished Elizabethan ancestry.[29] It was this perception which had returned in the context of Jacobean inaction after 1618, and again following Caroline withdrawal from the European war in 1629–30. Sir Philip Sidney, said Fulke Greville, thought the English 'apt . . . to corrupt with peace'.[30] Meanwhile there were the other associated points made by readers of Machiavelli and Tacitus: that while 'civil war is a disease, tyranny is the death of a state'; that 'a commonwealth whose peace depends upon . . . its subjects' servility may more properly be called a desert'; that such 'peace'

---

26 Sharpe, *Personal Rule*, p. 646.   27 Anthony Milton, *Catholic and Reformed*, p. 59.

28 Nathaniel Bacon, *A Historical and Political Discourse of the Laws and Government of England* (London 1649), p. 2.   29 Worden, *The Sound of Virtue*, pp. 131–2.

30 *Ibid.*, p. 131.

was 'no more to be valued than that which men have in the grave'.[31] As John Milton observed sarcastically in 1649: 'That civil Warr must [have] be[en] the fruits of his seventeen yeares raigning with such a measure of Justice, Peace, Plenty, and Religion, as all Nations either admir'd or envi'd.'[32]

An adequate historical perspective upon the Caroline experiment is difficult to recover from the shadow cast by its later failure. It is necessary to try to do this, for there was nothing inevitable about that failure, which followed from unpredicted external intervention.[33] It is not, however, to suggest that the Scots rebellion was inevitable to return to the point that it was a response to fears of English popery which had their origins in the 1620s.

CAROLINE RELIGIOUS POLICY

The other aspect of the ungovernability of early Stuart England was religious. There was little in the parliamentary politics of 1625–9 to dissuade Charles from the view that this political problem was at root a religious problem. In the summation of Samuel Brooke (Master of Trinity College) in 1630: 'Puritanism [is] the roote of all rebellions and disobedient intractableness in parliaments etc. and all schisme and sauciness in the countrey, nay in the Church itself.'[34]

By 'puritanism' adherents to the Caroline reform programme would appear to have been describing much that had been conventional in early Stuart protestantism. One predominant aspect of Jacobean religious culture had been anti-popery; it was dissenters from this during the 1620s who were most likely to be called 'arminians'.[35] By the 1630s, as the court acquired a distinctly 'Roman Catholic cultural ambience', anti-popery had become instead a sign of 'puritanism'. In this respect Laudianism broke not only with a variety of aspects of the internal self-understanding of the

---

31 Algernon Sidney, *Court Maxims*, p. 22; Algernon Sidney, *Discourses*, in *Sydney on Government*, pp. 132, 224; Spinoza, *Tractatus Politicus*, in *Political Works*, p. 311.

32 John Milton, *Eikonoklastes*, p. 435.

33 Hyde (Clarendon), *History of the Rebellion*, vol. I, pp. 145–6; Sharpe, *Personal Rule*, in particular ch. 12, has suggested that English polarisation and the radicalisation of opposition to Caroline policies occurred as a result of government errors and even bad luck from 1637. This would make the king's own perception of extreme opposition from 1625 difficult to explain.

34 Nicholas Tyacke, *Anti-Calvinists: The Rise of English Arminianism c. 1590–1640* (Oxford 1987), p. 74.   35 Fincham, 'Prelacy and Politics'.

church, but also with its understanding of its relationship with other churches.[36] In the 1625 parliament Richard Montagu's perceived crimes included a reduction of the essential differences between protestantism and popery from forty-eight to seven; the slighting of Calvin, Beza, Perkins, lectures and preaching; and labouring 'to put a jelosy betwixt the King and his well affected subjects by sayinge ther is a potent prevaylinge faction in the Kingdome . . . calle[d] Puritanes . . . and [that] a Puritan is worse than a Papist'.[37] 'Why', wrote Bishop Davenant in 1628, 'that should now be esteemed Puritane doctrine, which those held who have done our church the greatest service in beating down Puritanisme, or why men should be restrained from teaching that doctrine hereafter, which hitherto has been generally and publiquely maintained, wiser men perhaps may but I cannot understand.'[38]

For the purposes of understanding this transformation some of the questions which have informed recent scholarship (what was its focus: doctrine, or discipline?; who was its author: Charles or the Laudian clergy?; which of the resulting polarised extremes spoke for what had been the Jacobean centre ground?) seem of secondary importance, if not misposed.[39] While liturgical in emphasis, in the contemporary religious context Caroline religious policies had powerful doctrinal implications. There is little evidence that the question of the specific authorship of these policies was of importance to contemporaries alongside the facts of their nature and the agreement of the king in implementing them.[40] Finally the notion of 'a' Jacobean *doctrinal* centre ground may be oversimplified.[41]

Whatever the answer to these questions, what is clear is the result of Caroline religious policies. Just over a decade after the Bohemian rebellion, England's fragile protestant unity had been shattered. By the 1630s Caroline religion defined itself increasingly internally, as it had previously externally,

36 Anthony Milton, *Catholic and Reformed*, pp. 61, 530.
37 Gardiner, *Debates in 1625*, pp. 49–50.
38 Tyacke, *Anti-Calvinists*, p. 138 (and ch. 6 in general).
39 Important contributions include P. G. Lake, 'Calvinism and the English Church 1570–1635', *Past and Present* 114 (February 1987); Tyacke, *Anti-Calvinists*; P. White, *Predestination, Policy and Polemic: Conflict and Consensus in the English Church from the Reformation to the Civil War* (Cambridge 1992); Davies, *Caroline Captivity*.
40 Amanda Capern, 'The Caroline Church: James Ussher and the Irish Dimension', *Historical Journal* 39, 1 (1996). The dominant contemporary attribution of these policies to Laud reflects in part the contemporary convention of attributing unpopular policies to ministers.   41 Anthony Milton, *Catholic and Reformed*, Conclusion.

by means of polemical signifiers and boundaries.[42] In this respect at least, modern historians should perhaps resist following the contemporary example. Alongside the vigorously aired differences, for instance, between the interpretations of Nicholas Tyacke and Julian Davies, there is at least as much unexplored basis for agreement.[43] Though they understand it differently, both cast considerable light upon the context of Caroline religious innovation.

Before the last generation of scholarship it would have been unusual to associate the Caroline government with innovation. For whig and Marxist historians alike it was not only conservative but reactionary. As usual, modern revisionism has reversed this picture. The prevalent understanding now is of Caroline political and religious innovation. Far from facing an onslaught from rising parliamentary power and revolutionary puritanism, it was Caroline 'arminianism' which launched an aggressive attack upon the 'calvinist consensus' of the late Elizabethan and Jacobean church.[44]

It is not difficult to see how both these accounts developed, since both may lay claim to a rich seam of contemporary utterance. The accusation of innovation, in both directions, lay at the heart of the contemporary debate. It was royal declarations that accused the Commons of 'innovations', to be laid at the feet of 'puritanism'. In reversing this picture, revisionism had only to take seriously the contrary suggestion that the struggle against innovation was not that against 'puritanism' but 'popery'.

Even so, recent analyses of Caroline innovation offer an important contribution to our understanding. In particular they allow us to understand Caroline religious policy as one aspect of Caroline statebuilding. In relation to this the most striking Caroline innovation may have been not its choice of religious identity, but its insistence upon one religious identity. To set this development in its context entails examining 'the divisions within a Church of England whose ultimate doctrinal and ideological identity was still

---

42 *Ibid.*, p. 541. In this situation of extreme danger, the unity of the non-Laudian church was 'a polemical, not doctrinal unity'.

43 N. Tyacke, 'Anglican Attitudes: Some Recent Writings on English Religious History, from the Reformation to the Civil War', *Journal of British Studies* 35 (April 1996).

44 Nicholas Tyacke, 'Puritanism, Arminianism and Counter-Revolution', in Russell, *Origins of the English Civil War*; Tyacke, *Anti-Calvinists*; Russell, *Causes of the English Civil War*, chs. 3–5. In 'Introduction: Re-thinking the "English Reformation"' in his *England's Long Reformation*, Tyacke attaches the label 'revisionist' to those political historians of the reformation who 'are prone to belittle the power of ideas' in general, and that of 'theology' in particular (p. 1).

unclear, as different groups within the church contended over [how it] . . . was to be understood as both "Catholic and Reformed".[45] In the comparable formulation of Peter Lake, what had been a formal Jacobean 'calvinist consensus' in fact held in tension deep divisions about both worship and doctrine. These included both calvinist and anti-calvinist positions, while enjoining silence, particularly on the latter. This consensus was destroyed by the European war. Thereafter, given the continued governmental commitment to peace, that anti-popery which had supported James' regime until 1618 became a destabilising political force.[46]

In this context seventeenth-century people found 'the fact of political conflict very hard to accept and still harder to explain. In the face of it they resorted to the rhetoric of faction and consensus . . . its use by two parties to a dispute was an indication of deep and irreconcilable differences and bitter party feelings.'[47] Both the accusations of 'puritanism' and 'popery' offered religious diagnoses of political ills with their origins in the sixteenth century. As we have seen, there are reasons (though not predominantly religious ones) for taking seriously this Stuart perception of a newly embattled status for seventeenth-century monarchy. What this royal hostility to puritanism made available after 1618 was patronage of an equivalent clerical perception. This was as mindful of the damage done since the sixteenth century to the authority of the church as to that done to the crown.

The idea was, wrote Henry Parker in 1641: 'to new reforme that Reformation . . . which was begunne by Edw 6. and further matured by Queene Eliz . . . The pretence was, that our Ancestors in the Reformation did depart too farre from Popery, out of favour to Puritanicall Calvin.'[48] It was this alliance of perceptions that came together to underwrite English confessional statebuilding. In the eyes of its architects who – like later those of the restoration process – believed themselves to be engaged in reconstruction, not construction, this was not innovation at all. If the innovations had occurred in the sixteenth century, it is no wonder that 'Laud's supporters came to identify with the medieval Roman Church.'[49]

It has been suggested that to describe Caroline religious policy as 'anti-calvinist' is to mistake its focus, which was not doctrinal but ceremonial. The contemporary term of abuse 'arminian', often no more accurate in this context than 'puritan', has contributed to this confusion. Laud, whose high-

45 Anthony Milton, *Catholic and Reformed*, p. 5.
46 Lake, 'Calvinism and the English Church', pp. 45–7, 51, 70–1.   47 *Ibid.*, p. 69.
48 Anthony Milton, *Catholic and Reformed*, p. 529.   49 *Ibid.*, p. 66.

church clericalism had no more in common with the theology of Arminius than with that of John Pym, did not warm to calvinists on the whole. This was not, however, because he opposed their (or any other) doctrine in particular. It was because they were doctrinal dogmatists. As such, their religion focused upon a matter that was outside the scope of sure human, and particularly lay, knowledge, to the neglect of the fundamentals of piety in practice.[50] Nor, this argument goes, does it make any better sense to call the non-theologically inclined Charles I an 'arminian'. By the re-establishment of ceremonial religion he was attempting to (re-)establish the basis for a sacramental kingship. He was deeply hostile to individual (lay) religious expression of any kind.[51]

This is an important analysis which also pays necessary attention to the political context of Caroline statebuilding. It rightly distinguishes what was in England a predominantly liturgical phenomenon from a Dutch theology that lacked these features. It does not follow from this, however, that the Caroline/Laudian clerical experiment was entirely unaffected by arminian theology. Nor, within a protestant and substantially calvinist culture, does it diminish the doctrinal and broader religious *implications* of such a policy.[52] In its attempted transformation of the practical culture of English piety, as well as in other respects, this policy hit calvinists hardest.

Of all conceivable strands of English religious innovation this was the most provocative. Within the context of a European struggle for reformation against counter-reformation which had already partially been lost, Laudian clericalism, ceremonialism and sacramentalism looked like popery. Were they popery?

It is not difficult to get modern students to see why these policies provoked contemporary fears of popery. What is more difficult, within the existing English story, is to get them to take seriously the possibility that it was popery, that when contemporaries believed that they were witnessing the eradication of English protestantism they were correct. Yet in the absence of fire such a quantity of smoke all blowing in the same direction is very difficult to explain. It is not simply necessary to explain what appeared to be a wholesale resurrection of 'popish' ceremony and religious culture within the church. Why was this accompanied by royal hostility to the protestant

---

50 McGee, 'Outward Face'; Davies, *Caroline Captivity*, p. 303.

51 Davies, *Caroline Captivity*, p. 296.

52 *Ibid.*, p. 315. Julian Davies emphasises that this innovative policy could not but provoke 'an ideological response'.

Netherlands and friendship with Spain? Why did it coincide with the toleration of catholicism (in England and Ireland) and intolerance towards
zealous anti-popery? Why did it coincide with popish activity at court,
including high-profile ministerial conversions to catholicism? Why did the
king accept the residence at court of two papal envoys (Panzani and Conn)?
Why, when the king finally recovered his taste for war, was it against his own
Scots subjects?[53]

COUNTER-REFORMATION ENGLAND

For Charles, as for his opponents, religious and political policies were intertwined. His opponents in the Commons, the judiciary and the wider population were puritans. Puritans were friends to 'popularity', and enemies to
effective government by monarchy. It is not difficult to see why in this
context the government authorised the publication of William Camden's
History of . . . Elizabeth in 1630:

As England was troubled with outward war, so did it travail this year of an inward
schism also (for schism evermore springeth up most rankly in the heat of war). And
certainly never did contumacious impudency, and contumelious malapertness
against ecclesiastical magistrates advance itself more insolently. For when the
Queen (who was *Always the Same*) would not harken to innovators in religion who
would, as she thought, cut the sinews of the ecclesiastical government and her royal
prerogative, some of those who only esteemed the discipline of the church of
Geneva thought there could not be any other means devised to establish the same in
England than by inveighing against the English hierarchy, and raising ill-will among
the people against the bishops and prelates.[54]

In addressing himself to these problems, it has been plausibly argued,
Charles' own focus was not predominantly doctrinal. He was more interested in the reformation of manners than in religious belief. What he
wished to do was radically diminish the role of doctrine and religious
belief of any kind and substitute for them a new culture of conformity and
obedience.[55] Although the monarch could suspend parliaments, changing
thinking in the civil polity was difficult, and in the localities the monarchy

---

53 Hibbard, *Charles I and the Popish Plot*; Havran, *Catholics*, pp. 134–5.
54 William Camden, *The History of . . . Elizabeth* (1630 edn), quoted in Hale, *British Historiography*, p. 115.
55 Davies, *Caroline Captivity*, pp. 296–7; Sharpe, *Personal Rule*, p. 279.

had little direct power. Yet, in his governorship of the church, the monarch had direct control of a clerical hierarchy which penetrated every parish. Moreover weekly worship at parish level played a role in the life of most subjects vastly more significant than that of national politics. In the government of religion lay access not simply to the body but the mind. If religion had, over the past century, been crucial in undermining allegiance to princes, so the adequate harnessing of confessional authority could be crucial to the reconstruction not simply of clerical but of royal power.

In this way 'the interests of state religion . . . infiltrated the sanctuary of true religion'.[56] Small wonder that the bishops became (and remained) despised as the king's creatures. These were those 'bishops addicted to the Roman pontiff . . . who under the couler of Lutheranisme would sett upp such a mase of superstition and Idolatrie in the Church of God as therebie his Roiall Majestie's best and most loiall . . . shall be utterlie ruined'.[57] 'Nor was there anything now wanting', wrote James Harrington later,

unto the destruction of the throne but that the people, not apt to see their own strength, should be put to feel it, when a prince, as stiff in disputes as the nerve of the monarchy was grown slack, received that unhappy encouragement from his clergy which became his utter ruin; while, trusting more unto their logic than the rough philosophy of his parliament, it came to an irreparable breach.[58]

The royal intention to affect manners at the most local level was exhibited in the reissue in every parish of the Jacobean Book of Sports.[59] More important was the direct reform of the culture of worship, and of the church. The focus of Laudian reform was clerical and ceremonial. However the hallmarks of Caroline religious government – distance, deportment, reverence – all preceded Laud's ascendancy, for they were also those of Caroline political government. All were visible within the royal court, household and chapel by 1625.[60] What were the principal features of Caroline religious reform? They included

(1) A change of emphasis from doctrine to ceremony and the sensible 'outward face of religion'.[61]

56 Davies, *Caroline Captivity*, p. 301.
57 Peter Salt, 'Sir Simonds D'Ewes and the Levying of Ship Money, 1635–1640', *Historical Journal* 37, 2 (1984), p. 259.   58 Harrington, *Oceana*, p. 198.
59 Sharpe, *Personal Rule*, p. 355.   60 Davies, *Caroline Captivity*, p. 18.
61 McGee, 'Outward Face'.

(2) Those essentials of the reformation of manners spanning religion and politics: conformity, obedience, order, hierarchy.

(3) The forbidding of theological controversy: enforced peace, and silence.

(4) An attack on the calvinist, and indeed protestant, piety of preaching; an alternative emphasis upon the liturgy, ceremony and the sacramental officiation of the priesthood.

(5) Restoration of the status and power of the clergy (in relation to the laity); an emphasis upon vestments and other outward signs of distinction; an attack upon the whole apparatus of lay control of the church – the lay patronage of a preaching ministry.

(6) Restoration and reorganisation of the physical fabric of the church: repair and beautification; movement of and railing off of the altar; restoration of the sacrament (communion) to the core of worship.

(7) Restoration to the church, and clerical estate, of lands as well as patronage appropriated by the laity since the reformation. This project was being pursued with particular vigour in Scotland, with reason to believe that England would be next.

(8) Uniformity and obedience not only within but also between the three kingdoms; punishment of the disobedient, outspoken and controversial.

(9) Intolerance of anti-popery; relative tolerance of popery, in England and Ireland.[62]

What we see here is not only a remarkable attempt to reshape the English reformation but a wholesale attack upon many central features of it. Small wonder that

At a time when the frontiers of European protestantism were being pushed back, the recatholicisation of Anglicanism under Charles I . . . conversions to popery, and the perceived toleration of recusancy gave the impression that the King and Bishops were conspiring either to return the country to Rome or set up an English popery.[63]

If by 'was this popery?' we mean was it Roman catholic, then the answer is no (though the 'no' is not resounding). There was no re-embracing of the doctrine of transubstantiation; no sacrificing of the royal supremacy for the reunited clerical government of Rome. For short-term political purposes,

---

62 Anthony Milton, *Catholic and Reformed*, pp. 61–72, 84, 529–41; Capern, 'The Caroline Church'; Fincham, 'Prelacy and Politics'.   63 Davies, *Caroline Captivity*, p. 295.

indeed, Charles needed a national church under his control, rather than participation in the reconstruction of catholic christendom. This supplied no guarantees, of course, about the longer-term future. In relation to this, indeed, there were plenty of worrying signs. It was not only Richard Montagu who believed that, after the extraordinary progress of the last ten years, reunion with Rome was now a real possibility. Many Laudians deliberately refrained from attacking Rome's errors, concentrating upon the perceived threat from the anti-ceremonialists.[64] That reunion with the papacy was compatible with effective national control was to be shown in this century by France: there was little to prevent Anglicanism ('our English popery') becoming another version of Gallicanism.

The crucial point, however, concerns what contemporaries meant by popery. By this they referred not specifically to Roman catholicism, least of all to local catholicism, but to that 'restless' counter-reformation design for the extirpation of protestantism. To answer our question, then, it is necessary to ask, as contemporaries did, how much of the English reformation would Caroline/Laudian reforms have left intact? To put it another way, in the context of the Thirty Years War, and at the high point of its European success, had counter-reformation now come to England?

The ambition of Laud in these reforms may be easily understood. Here was an energetic Archbishop of Canterbury seizing a remarkable political opportunity to undo the damage done by the reformation to the church in England. He did not see this as a challenge to protestantism; there is evidence, on the contrary, that he and others considered it essential for the survival of an independent protestant church in the (spiritual, political and military) context of counter-reformation Europe. This was, however, another way in which its counter-reformation context deeply influenced the Laudian project. In the summation of Anthony Milton: 'The emphasis was . . . on the need to sustain an elaborate liturgy and ceremonial sufficient to rival the drawing power of the counter-reformation in order to prevent members of the Church of England defecting to Rome.'[65] In that of Julian Davies: 'the King . . . certainly was attempting to mould the Anglican church into a catholic identity to rival the national Churches of Spain and France'.[66] Meanwhile every one of these policies constituted an attempt to reverse the remoulding of English religious culture as it had occurred since the reformation. This was a project so in tune with the spirit of the times

---

64 Anthony Milton, *Catholic and Reformed*, pp. 61–5.   65 *Ibid.*, p. 82.
66 Davies, *Caroline Captivity*, p. 315.

that it is perfectly appropriate to call it counter-reformation protestant-ism.[67]

Charles' concern was with the damage done by the reformation to obedi-ence to monarchy. Liberation of the church from control by a disobedient laity was essential for its political effectiveness under the control of a king. More importantly, however, Charles' understanding of the English refor-mation itself was deeply suspect. It emphasised the orderly handing over of ecclesiastical jurisdiction from the pope to the crown, free of popular par-ticipation. It neglected the whole spiritual transformation from catholic to protestant worship. 'Popular reformation', Charles said, was 'little better than rebellion'. This has led Julian Davies to conclude that Charles was 'in conscious rebellion against lay and popular protestantism – the very Reformation itself'.[68]

Meanwhile the counter-reformation credentials of Caroline policy were on display elsewhere. The high point of Habsburg counter-reformation ambition had been the infamous Edict of Restitution issued by Ferdinand in 1629. This ordered that all property sequestered by protestant princes or cities since 1552 was to be restored to the Roman catholic church. This measure became the international hallmark of Habsburg confessional absolutism.[69] The only contemporary precedent for such a measure, the Scottish Act of Revocation, had been issued by Charles I three years earlier.[70] This revoked all gifts of both royal and church property made in Scotland since 1540. The king's intention, Allan MacInnes has explained, was to 'equip himself with the constitutional pretext to annexe to the Crown as much of the alienated and dispersed properties and revenues of the pre-Reformation Church as possible'.[71] This would both enrich the crown and

---

67 Thus although he is right to emphasise Laud's desire to distinguish the English project from Rome, Kevin Sharpe's statement that the charge of Laudian 'crypto-Catholicism . . . is . . . completely without foundation' (*Personal Rule*, pp. 285–6) would appear to miss this point.   68 Davies, *Caroline Captivity*, p. 17.

69 Geoffrey Parker, *The Thirty Years War* (London 1987), p. 86; Evans, *Making of the Habsburg Monarchy*.

70 This context was noticed in 1956 by Christopher Hill, who concluded: 'In certain respects the British counter-reformation went even farther back than the continental. The Edict of Restitution resumed all lands secularized since 1552: the Scottish Act of Revocation went back to 1542' (Hill, *Economic Problems of the Church from Archbishop Whitgift to the Long Parliament* (Oxford 1956), pp. 332–7, and p. 337 n. 1).

71 Allan MacInnes, *Charles I and the Making of the Covenanting Movement* (Edinburgh 1991), p. 53.

equip it to reendow (its preferred version of) the church. Nothing before the imposition of the new prayer book in 1637 did Charles' position in Scotland more damage; nothing else so undermined the allegiance of his nobility in particular. It is by no means surprising, in this context, that the first confrontation of these policies should come from Scotland.

In these respects the close relationship between European counter-reformation catholic politics and 'English popery' was in fact blindingly obvious. As Christopher Hill observed in 1956: 'Wherever men looked in the world about them, the signs were ominous . . . all over Europe, the lamps were going out; the counter-reformation was winning back property for the church as well as souls; and Charles I and his government, if not allied to the forces of the counter-reformation, at least appeared to have set themselves identical economic and political objectives.'[72] When contemporaries described Caroline policies as 'popish' they did not necessarily mean Roman catholic. What they meant was that the counter-reformation had come to England. Left unchecked, these policies would eradicate the substance (as opposed to merely outward form) of English protestantism. As John Milton said of the king's complaints against his opponents:

Popular compliance, dissolution of all order and gover[n]ment in the Church, Schisms, Opinions, Undecencies, Confusions, Sacrilegious invasions, contempt of the Clergie and thir Liturgie, Dimunition of Princes: all these complaints are to be read in the Messages and Speeches almost of every Legat from the Pope to those States or Citties which began Reformation . . . Neither was there ever . . . [a] sincere Reformation that hath escap'd these clamours . . . onely instance how he bemoanes *the pulling down of crosses* and other superstitious Monuments, as the effect of *a popular and deceitful Reformation*. How little this savours of a Protestant, is too easily perceav'd.[73]

That we have been slow to take this contemporary perception sufficiently seriously relates to two problems. If one is the parochialism of national history, the other has been an (until recently) inadequate conception of reformation. This had three features. The first was that it insufficiently related the English reformation (and counter-reformation) to those European processes of which they formed a part. The second was that it depicted the English reformation as having been completed in the sixteenth century (in which case counter-reformation could hardly be a danger). The third was

---

72 Hill, *Economic Problems*, p. 337.   73 John Milton, *Eikonoklastes*, pp. 534–5.

that it offered an inadequate account of what reformation was. In the words of F. M. Powicke, 'The one definite thing which can be said about the Reformation in England is that it was an act of State.'[74] This was, as we have seen, Charles I's view. What it omits, however, is the transformation from catholic to reformed belief and religious culture: the substance of the reformation.[75]

In the words of Patrick Collinson: 'we are already removed by a generation or so from those historians who confined the essential history of the English reformation to the thirty years from 1529 to 1559, a manageable three-course meal preceded by a few late medieval aperitifs and rounded off with a small cup of Elizabethan coffee with one or two dissenting digestifs ("Puritanism" and "Recusancy")'.[76] As we now understand, like the English revolution, this reformation was not an act, but a process.[77] It was complex, with political, theological, cultural and social dimensions. It was not only European in scope but long-term. In the early seventeenth century England's reformation was not only not complete. In the absence of effective European arms, and in the context of a subsequent domestic attempt at counter-reformation confessional statebuilding, it was insecure.

CONCLUSION

Thus when participants in the British troubles believed themselves to be fighting for the survival of protestantism not only in their own kingdoms but more generally, they may in their own terms have been correct. Evidence of a threat to the substance of protestantism, on the continent and in Britain, was abundant enough. What future would have remained for reformation religion in general had the 1618–48 conflict been settled by

74 F. M. Powicke, *The Reformation in England* (Oxford 1941), p. 1.
75 Nicholas Tyacke appears to group Julian Davies with 'political' historians of the reformation who 'write out protestantism' and 'belittle the power of ideas' ('Anglican Attitudes', pp. 140–1; 'Introduction', p. 1). This appears to me to confuse Davies' depiction of Caroline perceptions with Davies' own perception. I take it to be Davies' *point* that Charles' hostility to doctrine, individual belief and pulpit-piety *was* an attack on the *substance* of the English reformation.
76 Patrick Collinson, 'Comment on Eamon Duffy's Neale Lecture and the Colloquium', in Tyacke, *England's Long Reformation*, p. 71. Collinson observes that to thus alter our perspective is to exchange event for process: 'to jettison the definite article'.
77 Tyacke, 'Introduction', and Eamon Duffy, 'The Long Reformation: Catholicism, Protestantism and the Multitude', both in Tyacke, *England's Long Reformation*.

France, Spain, Habsburg Austria and Caroline Britain is unclear. Thus the conviction of British protestants that they were living in cataclysmic times is easy to understand. In the famous words of Jeremiah Whittaker (1643): 'These are days of shaking . . . and this shaking is universal; the Palatinate, Bohemia, Germania, Catalonia, Portugal, Ireland, England.'[78]

English reactions to these policies varied. They included significant emigration, to the Netherlands and New England, which would provide an important context for the radical reformation to follow. That the confrontation of these policies became possible within England owed everything to one external event. It owed everything, that is to say, to a familiar military inability to respond to that event adequately. To this, more powerfully than in 1625, the alienation of English protestant opinion made its contribution. In the words of James Harrington, again: 'a monarchy divested of her nobility hath no refuge under heaven but an army . . . Of the king's success with his arms it is not necessary to give any further account, than that they proved as ineffectual as his nobility.'[79]

The British military conflicts of 1638–51 began as a struggle between reformation and counter-reformation. We have observed the processes of polarisation by which this conflict, begun in Bohemia, had transferred itself to Britain. From the resulting successful defence of reformation would emerge a further transformation of belief (the English revolution). In pressing to radical lengths a reversal of the attempted Laudian realignment of the relationship between form and substance, this would come to challenge magisterial religion altogether.

78 Quoted in Geoffrey Parker, *Europe in Crisis 1598–1648* (London 1949), p. 17.
79 Harrington, *Oceana*, p. 198.

6

Reformation politics (2): 1637–60

I shall desire with Castruccio to be buried my face downwards, not to
see or comply in the grave with the universal disorder.

Sir Thomas Roe, 20 June 1644 [1]

God is decreeing to begin some new and great period in his Church,
ev'n to the reforming of Reformation itself.

John Milton [2]

INTRODUCTION

Between 1638 and 1651 there occurred the military culmination of the
first phase of the troubles. In England this became a 'Warre for Defence'
both of 'Religion' and of 'Parliament'.[3] We will not here be discussing its
remarkable product: the English revolution. Our interest is in that
destructive process, with both military and ideological dimensions, which
forms its essential context. The troubles were an attempt to defend traditional institutions – monarchy, parliament and church – against ideological forces by which they were held to be imperilled. How, by 1649 in
England, had they resulted in the destruction of those very institutions?
The answer is that the resulting reformation process, once unleashed,
could not be contained. At every stage its progress was military. When the
successful defence of the reformation, in Scotland, gave way to further reformation and then radical reformation, England moved from rebellion
through civil war to revolution.

---

1 Quoted in Strachan, *Sir Thomas Roe*, p. 278.
2 Quoted in Keeble, *Literary Culture of Nonconformity*, p. 3.
3 *An Advertisement to the whole Kingdome of England* (London 1642), p. 1.

135

DEFENCE OF THE REFORMATION (THE SCOTS REBELLION)

Armed defence of reformation in Britain began in Scotland. It is essential revisionist doctrine that Scots resistance to Caroline religious innovation was as sudden in 1637 as it was unexpected. Thereafter, only when a series of blunders by the king brought the Scots into English politics did they provide the mechanism for the destabilisation of that arena as well.[4]

On the level of short-term narrative this is correct. We have seen Clarendon's observation that events in Edinburgh in 1637–8 took by surprise an English political nation accustomed to focusing its attention upon the continent.[5] The Scots' intervention was crucial both in forcing the king to summon what would become the Long Parliament and in enabling it to deprive him of the capacity to dissolve it. Yet it is absurd *thematically* to treat the Scottish troubles of 1637–40 as if they were unrelated to earlier developments in England.

For the Scots, as for the English, the European military struggle for protestantism underlined the danger from royal policy. The subsequent Scots military achievement had several contexts. One was continued Stuart military weakness, exacerbated by withdrawal from the European conflict from 1629. Another was Scots military strength, crucially assisted by large-scale (private) Scots participation in that conflict during the 1630s. A third was English hostility to royal religious policy, and sympathy with the Scots. As the leader of the king's own army, the Earl of Northumberland, wrote to the Earl of Strafford in July 1638:

The King's Magazines are totally unfurnished of Arms and all sorts of Ammunition; and Commanders we have none ... The People through all England are generally so discontented, by reason of the Multitude of Projects daily imposed upon them ... there is reason to fear that a great Part of them will be readier to join with the Scots, than to draw their Swords in the King's service.[6]

There was the crucial geographic reality that Scotland was the only kingdom with a land border with England. Only Scotland, therefore, could provide the kind of *land-based* military imperative operating for all contemporary continental powers: only through Scotland could England be

---

4 Sharpe, *Personal Rule*, 'Epilogue' (esp. pp. 953–4); Russell, *Fall of the British Monarchies*.
5 Hyde (Clarendon), *History of the Rebellion*, vol. I, pp. 145–6.
6 W. Knowles (ed.), *The Earl of Strafforde's Letters and Dispatches* (2 vols., London 1739), vol. I, p. 186.

reabsorbed into the Thirty Years War. Finally, alongside this geographic context was a historical one. If Scots military intervention helped to save an English reformation imperilled by a Stuart prince in league with its enemies abroad, this was a favour well returned. Eighty years earlier it had been the thinking behind England's intervention in Scotland that, in a menacing European situation, protestantism had to be defended in both countries simultaneously.[7] Exactly the same pattern would manifest itself in Anglo-Dutch relations: English intervention in 1585 would be followed by Dutch in 1688. At no point were England's troubles self-contained.

In other ways, that the confrontation of Caroline religious policy should have begun in Scotland is not surprising. Remote from London, traditionally less passive to rule, Scotland had experienced several decades of increasingly demanding, and decreasingly sensitive, absentee kingship.[8] Most importantly it had in the sixteenth century been transformed by a genuine religious revolution. It had had, that is to say, just that type of reformation – a 'fusion of calvinism and popularity' – to the eradication of which Caroline religious policy was directed.

The danger thus presented by that policy, clear enough even in the more diffuse doctrinal circumstances of England, was unambiguous in Scotland. With it came that of subordination to, perhaps eventually disappearance into, another church and kingdom. As Clarendon put it, 'the kingdom of Scotland generally had been long jealous that by the King's continued absence from them they should by degrees be reduced to be but as a province to England and subject to their laws and government, which it would never submit to'.[9]

As we have seen, these concerns had been underlined, and the political allegiance of the Scots nobility fatally undermined, by the Act of Revocation (1626). This had 'yielded no better fruit than the alienation of the subjectis hartes from ther prince, and layed opin a way to rebellion'. By 1634 'public rumors were . . . equating the progress of the Revocation scheme with the reversal of the Reformation settlement'.[10] The Scots, Clarendon continued, were 'apprehensive of a desire to introduce Popery; their whole religion consisting in an entire detestation of Popery, in believing the Pope to be Antichrist, and hating perfectly the persons of all Papists, and, I doubt, all

---

7 Alford, 'William Cecil', ch. 2.
8 John Morrill (ed.), *The Scottish National Covenant in Its British Context 1637–1651* (London 1990).   9 Hyde (Clarendon), *History of the Rebellion*, vol. I, pp. 113–14.
10 MacInnes, *Covenanting Movement*, pp. 51–2, 91.

others who did not hate them'.[11] The first Scots response to the imposition of Laudian reforms was thus refreshingly to the point. On 23 July 1637, when the new Scots prayer book was read, it was denounced as 'nought but the Mass in English', and those responsible were pelted with excrement by a crowd led by 'various Edinburgh matrons'. Rioting ensued. On 4 August Charles heard of these outrages with 'cold anger' and ordered their suppression. The council in Edinburgh, however, proved unable to control the situation. More rioting followed in October, and throughout the second half of 1637 the organisation took place among resisters that would lead, in February 1638, to the signing of the National Covenant.[12]

In this, responding to the threat of being proceeded against by force, the lay and spiritual leaders of Scotland pledged to defend its reformation – a purer reformation than in any neighbouring country – by arms if necessary. They reiterated the 1581 confession of faith against popery and innovations. They emphasised 'the urgency of an uncompromising Protestant crusade to ward off the unabated threat of the Counter-Reformation', and drew on French and Dutch as well as their own calvinist resistance theory.[13]

There is no space here to recount the curiously drawn-out process which led to the assembly of the Long Parliament in England nearly three years later. Concerning the issues we may observe two documents, one issued in response to the other, in February 1639. The first was *An Information to all good Christians within the Kingdom of England, from the Noblemen, Barons, Burrows, [and] Ministers of Scotland*, which observed that

The work of Reformation now renewed and far advanced in this Kingdom, hath . . . met with all the oppositions which the subtil malice of *Rome*'s Emissaries could plot . . . the arch-enemies of Reformation, have laboured to poison his Majesties sacred Ears with . . . Imputations that we do only pretend Religion, but do intend to shake off the most lawful yoak of Authority, by changing the form of Civil Government . . . whereby we take God to witness, That Religion is the only Subject, Conscience the motive, and Reformation the aim of our Designs, for attaining whereof we have never strayed from the humble and loyal way of petitioning his Majesty for a legal Redress.[14]

The recourse from 'loyal petitioning' to arms came only as a response to the military aggression of 'his Majesty'. This to some extent prefigured the

11 *Ibid.*, pp. 139–40.
12 David Stevenson, *The Scottish Revolution 1637–1644* (London 1973), pp. 58–72.
13 MacInnes, *Covenanting Movement*, pp. 173, 175; Stevenson, *Revolution*, pp. 84–5.
14 Rushworth, *Historical Collections*, vol. I, p. 798.

English parliamentary claims of 1640–2. This was on behalf of that same cause – the lawful self-defence of protestants – which would, mindful of its French, Dutch, Bohemian and Scots ancestry, return also during the next English crisis in 1681–3.[15] To the Scots' *Information* the king responded in a *Proclamation . . . to . . . his Loving Subjects of . . . England.* This asked, anticipating the loyalist literature of 1681–3, if religion were not 'the common Cloak for all Disobedience'?:

the aim of these Men is not Religion, as they falsly pretend and publish, but it is to shake all Monarchical Government, and to vilify Our Regal Power, justly descended upon Us over them: nay . . . in a most cunning and subtil way they have endeavoured to poison the hearts of Our good and loyal Subjects of this Our kingdom, and to seduce them . . . to the like Rebellious Courses with themselves.[16]

Behind this rhetoric what it is necessary to observe is the military reality. On the one side there is glaring royal weakness. It took a year from the decision to crush these disorders by force and the assembly of an army. It was a motley force – paid for, where at all, by loans and anticipations – which achieved little at the Pacification of Berwick (1639).[17] The response to the Scots invasion the following year at Newburn was even less effective, and represented a further European humiliation for Stuart arms.

'The essential clue', wrote John Elliott, 'to the revolutionary situation of the 1640s [in western Europe] is, I suspect, to be found in the determination of governments to exercise fuller control over their states without yet having the administrative means or fiscal resources to ensure obedience.'[18] This determination sprang mainly from the demands of war. David Stevenson, noting the applicability of most of this observation to the Scots situation, commented: 'Charles clearly had such a determination, even though it was not war that led him to it.'[19] As we have seen, however, the origin of the policies to which the Scots rebellion was a response did indeed lie in the demands of (and failure in) the same European war.

On this occasion the fiscal and administrative inadequacy of Stuart military endeavour was exacerbated by the absence of parliaments. Meanwhile the beliefs of many English and Scots troops were closer to each other than either to their king. 'The Tumults in Scotland', wrote Laud, 'hath now

15 Scott, *Restoration Crisis*, ch. 12; and see chs. 8 and 19 below.
16 Rushworth, *Historical Collections*, vol. I, p. 830.
17 Mark Fissel, *The Bishops' Wars: Charles I's Campaigns in Scotland 1638–1640* (Cambridge 1994).   18 Quoted in Stevenson, *Revolution*, pp. 324–5.   19 *Ibid.*

brought that Kingdom in danger. No question, but there is a great Concurrence between them, and the Puritan Party in England.'[20] None of these concerns was eased by the discovery that during 1639, prior to the Pacification, Charles had negotiated with Antrim to bring an army from Ireland, and with Spain to bring Spanish troops from Flanders, in exchange for leave for the Spanish to recruit troops in Ireland.[21] Here was ample reason for that British protestant mentality of counter-reformation encirclement – the besieged protestant fortress menaced by encroaching popery on the continent and in Ireland, and infecting the crown itself – which would be a key feature of every episode of the troubles.

The debacle of 1638–40, however, did not simply follow from English military weakness. It was equally a consequence of the covenanters' strength. Scots religious opinion, like English, had been deeply agitated by the Thirty Years War. Scotland had similarly viewed with alarm the Stuart failure to intervene effectively on the protestant side. Subsequently Scots had gone in large numbers during the 1630s to serve with protestant armies on the continent. 'If the King kept aloof from the wars of Europe . . . many of his subjects did not . . . Perhaps as many as 20,000 of the subjects of Charles I had gone abroad to serve.'[22] In 1637–8, when the front line defending the reformation moved from Germany to Scotland itself, these soldiers came home.

Consequently the Scots covenanting army acquired a backbone of professionals experienced from Dutch and Swedish service. All the artillery officers, gunners and engineers were veterans of the Thirty Years War.[23] Accordingly the supremacy of this army over the English (where inexperience was a major problem at every level) was not simply numerical.[24] Arguably the covenanting movement was second at this time only to the Swedish crown in possessing an experienced national standing army sustained by a centralised government.[25] In this respect it anticipated the English New Model Army by six years. It has suited the English understanding of this debacle, at the time and since, to see it as the failure of a politically

20 *The History of the Troubles and Tryal of William Laud . . . Wrote by Himself, during his Imprisonment in the Tower* (London 1654), p. 55.
21 Russell, *Fall of the British Monarchies*, pp. 79–80.
22 Ian Roy, '"England Turned Germany": The Aftermath of the Civil War in Its European Context', *Transactions of the Royal Historical Society* 5th ser., 28 (1978), p. 130.
23 MacInnes, *Covenanting Movement*, pp. 191–2.
24 Fissel, *Bishops' Wars*, pp. 79–80.   25 MacInnes, *Covenanting Movement*, pp. 191–2.

(and religiously) isolated king.[26] In this respect the illuminating parallel is with 1688–9. This was another Stuart debacle which it has been easiest to blame on James II personally, but which actually hinged upon the humiliation of an ineffectual English army.[27] In both cases the fundamental reality, in the face of a foreign invasion, was not only the collapse of Stuart arms. It was a formidable and experienced protestant European invading force.

Thus with the Scots invasion of 1640 the European military conflict came to England. A catholicising king, associated with Spain and catholic Ireland, found himself divided from his English and Scots protestant subjects. This was one military outcome of the ideological impact made upon the Stuart kingdoms by the Thirty Years War. In the period 1637–40, then, the military struggle between reformation and counter-reformation moved to British soil. That it was not followed by continental European military intervention was a consequence only of the exhaustion of the great powers after more than two decades of war.[28]

Few modern historians have directly connected the 'Thirty Years War' and the subsequent British conflicts of 1637–51. This is partly because nation-state historical parameters begin by distinguishing international from civil wars. Looking at the religious conflicts in France, the Low Countries, the Holy Roman Empire, Scotland, England and Ireland, this was not, however, the primary distinction made by contemporaries. Most of these conflicts combined civil and international dimensions. What distinguished them were the issues at stake. 'God Almightie send a period unto our miserable distractions in England which ells [is like] to be the stage of [similar] warre and rapine', one contemporary had written in the late 1630s.[29] In 1642 the public were warned of *The Manifold Miseries of Civil Warre and Discord in a Kingdome: By the Examples of Germany, France,*

---

26 Thus 'It was the King's maladministration of the institutions at his disposal, rather than structural failure within the institutions themselves, which precipitated failure in a war that was entirely of the King's choosing': Fissel, *Bishops' Wars*, p. 1.

27 John Childs, *The British Army of William III 1689–1702* (Manchester 1987), pp. 4–5.

28 Koenigsberger, 'Crisis of the Seventeenth Century', p. 167.

29 Joseph Hall to Samuel Hartlib [1638?], *Hartlib Papers*, electronic edn, 45/3/43A. Hartlib's correspondence exemplifies this perspective: see for instance 54/63A–64B; 46/14/6A–7B; 46/14/3A–3B; 67/19/1A–2B. In the same context, Nehemiah Wallington recorded that the Scots troubles portended 'nothing but civil wars . . . in the year 1638 I had a book come into my hand of the miserable estate of Germany, wherin as in a glass you may see the mournful face of this our sister nation now drunk with misery': Seaver, *Wallington's World*, pp. 160–1.

Ireland and other places (1642).[30] That the 'troubles' which had begun in Bohemia had subsequently come to England, accompanied by the same 'bloody Tragedies', was something that contemporaries understood very well.[31]

The Scots invasion furnished the context for the English and Irish political crises, and rebellions. It was not, however, identical to the English civil war. It is our next task to understand why the English dimension of the British political crisis had this outcome. In particular, with the Scots occupation of Newcastle and the summoning of the Long Parliament, the court was almost isolated. The majority of the English political elite now also sought confrontation of popery and arbitrary government. How, by 1642, had it become sufficiently divided to fight a civil war?

FURTHER REFORMATION (ENGLISH POLARISATION 1640–6)

What Scots military success made possible was the convening of an English parliament on its own terms. For the first time in relation to this institution, the king was in practical terms almost powerless. The result was a series of concessions which, over the succeeding twelve months, crucially changed the political situation in England.

We have already observed the broad continuity of issues from 1621 to 1642. Members of the Long Parliament, Richard Baxter reported, were united in their opposition to the Caroline 'Reformation of Church and State'. Some, including John Pym, believed that now, as earlier, the most serious problem was the popish conspiracy manifested by 'Innovations in the Church'. For others, including Edward Hyde, the priority was security for parliament itself as central to the ancient political as well as religious government of the kingdom. For most, as we have seen, and as the Personal Rule had demonstrated, the dangers to the two were intertwined. Thus in the Protestation of 3 May 1641 members of the Commons and Lords 'in the presence of Almighty God, promise[d], vow[ed], and protest[ed]'

to maintain and defend, as far as lawfully I may, with my life, power and estate, the true reformed Protestant religion, expressed in the doctrine of the Church of England, against all Popery and Popish innovations within this realm . . . as also the

---

30 Roy, '"England Turned Germany"', n. 1 and pp. 127–31.
31 *The Parliament Scout Communicating His Intelligence to the Kingdome*, no. 23 (24 November–1 December 1643), p. 195.

power and privileges of Parliament; [and] the lawful rights and liberties of the subject.[32]

Pym's perception was of a 'popish and malignant party set upon the destruction of a Protestant State' as one step towards the wider 'extirpation of Protestantism'.[33] Parliaments were then essential insurance against both political and religious dangers. This one began by securing its own existence by successfully demanding temporary royal surrender of the right to dissolve it without its own consent. This suspension of a royal prerogative was striking testimony to the abject practical circumstances in which the king found himself. Charles II's successful resistance of pressure upon the same prerogative, under different military circumstances, would be the key to monarchical survival during the next such crisis of 1678–83.[34]

The short-term security of this parliament was underwritten in practice by collusion with the Scots. Security for the future was provided by the passage of the Triennial Act. Ministerial symbols of popery and arbitrary government were destroyed, most importantly Strafford (executed in May 1641) and Laud (executed 1645). Other royal servants fled or were imprisoned; the prerogative courts were abolished, and various parliamentary attempts were made to dictate political policy and appointments. In most of these areas the king made practical or verbal concessions; by mid-1641 many parliamentarians were satisfied.

For the purpose of safeguarding the ancient constitution, enough, and perhaps more than enough, had been conceded. For the most vociferous opponents of crown policy, nevertheless, a crucial problem remained. Could a humiliated king be trusted to honour any of these concessions for longer than his powerlessness and poverty persisted? For the protection of themselves, therefore, as well as of what they had achieved, parliamentarian hardliners made demands and took actions that exposed them to the charge of arbitrary (innovative) constitutional conduct themselves, in contrast to the recent moderation of the king. This was not a moral failure; it was a consequence of practical circumstances (military, political and ideological) that the constitution was not well equipped to survive. Nor, as we have seen, was this a new development. Since the beginning of the European war the 'passions' of MPs had driven them to encroach upon constitutional royal

---

32 Hyde (Clarendon), *History of the Rebellion*, vol. II, p. 331.
33 Anthony Fletcher, *Outbreak of the English Civil War*, pp. xxi–xxii.
34 Scott, *Restoration Crisis*.

prerogatives. Now that 'the necessities grown by that war' had become more extreme, the same members were simply doing so more successfully.

In this lay parliament's danger, and the origins of a royalist party. John Morrill made the point some time ago that 'There could be no civil war before 1642 because there was no royalist party. The origins of the English civil war are concerned less with the rise of opposition than with the resurgence of loyalism.'[35] In fact the second sentence follows strictly from the first only if we take 'the origins of the English civil war' to be distinct from those of the crisis of three kingdoms of which it was one outcome. It is nevertheless true that the explanation of that outcome is a distinct and important matter in itself.

As we have seen, ideological polarisation had come to England in the 1620s, with the European war. Neither the Personal Rule nor the crisis of 1640–2 did anything to reverse this process. For the *practical* outcome of civil war, however – an outcome which was a tragedy – what was necessary was for the royal perception of parliamentary innovation to become as widely held as that of the innovations of the king. This was one result of the crisis of 1640–2, and of the royal powerlessness and concessions of that period. Within this evening-up of polarised public perceptions the most decisive role was once again played by religion.[36]

By mid-1641 both Houses were divided over the question of religious reform. This was because from the outset there had been a section of the parliamentary opposition to royal policy that was not content merely to sweep away Caroline innovation. It now insisted upon the urgency of completing the half-finished Jacobethan reformation. These were people who had either long desired this or for whom the Caroline experiment had proved a terrifying demonstration of the dangers of a half-reformed church. How could the Church of England have been so nearly delivered to popery in ten years had it not been for ambiguous doctrine and (above all) episcopal government? The earliest statement of this perspective came in the petitions that began arriving at the beginning of the session in November 1640, calling for the abolition of episcopacy and its appendages 'roots and branches'.[37]

---

35 John Morrill, *The Revolt of the Provinces: Conservatives and Radicals in the English Civil War 1630–1650* (London 1976), p. 1.

36 See Morrill, *Nature of the English Revolution*, pt I; Anthony Fletcher, *Outbreak of the English Civil War*.

37 J. P. Kenyon (ed.), *The Stuart Constitution 1603–1688* (Cambridge 1986), pp. 154–7.

This registered also an abandonment of faith in the Elizabethan compromise. This was the culmination of a process which had been in train for more than half a century. As Patrick Collinson has stressed, 'towards 1580' European military developments began to make the *via media* harder to sustain in an 'atmosphere of religious partisanship and ideological commitment'.[38] By 1640 the choice for many now lay between Rome and Geneva: the reformation could not be defended without its completion.

Among those who took this view were the Scots. It was shared by an English parliamentary leadership (including Pym and Brooke) for whom security from the counter-reformation was paramount. In London this alliance was supported, noisily and with force, not only by press and pulpit, but by those crowds given parliamentary licence to demonstrate, present petitions, celebrate the release of protestant political martyrs, intimidate the royal family and the queen in particular, and bar bishops' entry to the House of Lords. In this 'tumultuous petitioning' parliamentary leaders were establishing one practical context for a radical culture that would later turn against them.

The first mass petition of the period was that presented by 10,000 citizens to the king in September 1640 calling for the summoning of a parliament. The presentation of the first root-and-branch petition, accompanied as it was by 1,500 presenters, caused considerable unease in the House. In the debate upon it in early February 1641, during which the practice of mass petitioning was defended by Isaac Pennington and Nathaniel Fiennes, Kenelm Digby spoke for more than himself when he stated that 'no man of judgement . . . will think it fit for a parliament, under a monarchy, to give countenance to irregular, and tumultuous assemblies of people'.[39]

No aspect of the parliamentary cause did more than its 'popularity' to consolidate royalism. Popular belief might have been essential to the reformation, but it was no acceptable engine of early Stuart English politics. One royalist complaint would be that 'the Parliament began the War, by permitting Tumults to deprive the Members of their Liberty, and affront and dishonour the King'.[40] At the end of his life Charles was still drawing attention to the 'Insolency of the Tumults' conjured up by the 'chiefe Damagogues' on the parliamentary side.[41] These tumults said something about the political

---

38 Patrick Collinson, *Godly People* (London 1983), p. 152.
39 Lindley, *Popular Politics*, pp. 4–17 (quote, p. 17).
40 Richard Baxter, *Reliquiae Baxterianae*, p. 35.   41 John Milton, *Eikonoklastes*, ch. 4.

and religious atmosphere in the capital ('He was sometimes prone to think', claimed *Eikon Basilike* (1649), 'that had he call'd this last Parlament to any other place in England, the sad consequences might have been prevented').[42] This was also the parliamentary political culture about which Hobbes had warned now spilling on to the street.

Thus during 1641 those dedicated to the preservation of protestantism and parliaments found themselves driven into two camps. There were those who came to believe that the immediate menace to the Elizabethan constitution in church and state now came from the king's opponents. And there were those for whom political and religious security was anything but complete.

Speeches and sermons detailing the popish danger in 1641 spoke to the same audience that had scoured the city for news in the desperate European situation of 1621. Confirmation of these fears, more terrible than anyone had imagined, shortly arrived. Richard Baxter recorded:

suddenly on October 23 the Irish Rebellion Murdering Two hundred thousand, and Fame threatening their coming into England, cast the Nation into so Great fear of the Papists, as was the Cause (whereever I came) of Mens conceit of the *necessity of defensive Arms* . . . [this] was the main cause that filled the Parliament's Armies: I well remember it cast people into such a fear that England should be used like Ireland, that all over the Countreys, the people oft sate up, and durst not go to Bed, for fear lest the Papists should rise and murder them.[43]

As in 1678 and 1688 the immediate fear was of invasion. In London and along the entire west coast of England protestants armed themselves.[44] The Irish rebellion itself, meanwhile, had been in part motivated by the same context of fear. In the words of Viscount Gormanston:

it was not unknown to your lordship how the Puritan faction of England, since, by the countenance of the Scottish army, they invaded the regall power, have both in their doctrine and practice laid the foundation of the slavery of this country. They teach that the laws of England, if they mention Ireland, are without doubt binding here . . . And what may be expected from such zealous and fiery professors of an adverse religion, but the ruine and extirpation of ours.[45]

---

42 Quoted *ibid.*, p. 396.
43 Richard Baxter, *Against the Revolt to a Foreign Jurisdiction*, quoted in William Lamont, *Richard Baxter and the Millennium* (London 1979), p. 106.
44 *Ibid.*; Anthony Fletcher, *Outbreak of the English Civil War*, p. 137.
45 Conrad Russell, 'The Irish Rebellion of 1641', in Russell, *Unrevolutionary England*, p. 278.

Shortly after the rebellion a parliamentary committee heard that the conspirators 'had good friends in England, the bishops and some privy councillors, and that nothing was done at the Council table in England but it was presently known in Ireland, in Rome and in Spain'.[46] It was at this time that the *Grand Remonstrance* identified as the 'actors and promoters' of this 'malignant and pernicious design':

1. The Jesuited Papists . . . 2. The Bishops, and the corrupt part of the Clergy, who cherish formality and superstition as . . . more probable supports of their own ecclesiastical tyranny . . . 3 Such Councillors and Courtiers as . . . have engaged themselves to further the interests of some foreign princes or states to the prejudice of . . . the State at home.[47]

The Irish rebellion thus catalysed further that process of polarisation which had been in train throughout the English crisis. Throughout the wars that followed – connected theatres of war in England, Scotland and Ireland – parliamentary journals reported the supply by continental 'Papists, through the instigation of Jesuits and Priests amongst them . . . [of] Armes, Ammunition and other supplies . . . to the Rebells . . . in Ireland'.[48] In practical terms the rebellion had two effects. The first was in confirming and hardening parliamentary protestant opinion just when the king's concessions had appeared to be placing it under pressure.[49] The second was in introducing a crucial problem. Who was to control the necessary military force for the rebellion's suppression?

One eventual result, establishing the military basis for a civil war in England, was parliament's unprecedented Militia Ordinance (March 1642). This made arrangements for the gathering of troops under parliamentary authority, bearing in mind that there had been

of late a most dangerous and desperate design upon the House of Commons, which we have just cause to believe to be an effect of the bloody counsels of Papists . . . who have already raised a rebellion in the kingdom of Ireland; and by reason of many discoveries we cannot but fear they will proceed not only to stir up the like rebellion

---

46 Anthony Fletcher, *Outbreak of the English Civil War*, p. 137.
47 Gardiner, *Constitutional Documents*, pp. 206–7; Hyde (Clarendon), *History of the Rebellion*, vol. IV, pp. 424–5.
48 *England's Memorable Accidents*, 3–10 October 1642, p. 37; 15 December 1642, p. 117; *Perfect Occurrences of Parliament*, 22–9 August 1645.
49 Russell, *Causes of the English Civil War*; Anthony Fletcher, *Outbreak of the English Civil War*, p. 46.

and insurrections in this kingdom of England, but also to back them with forces from abroad.[50]

In the same atmosphere was pounded the last nail into the coffin of royal control of London. Since late 1641 the city government had been in the hands of allies of parliament.[51] Since November the city had been making preparations for its self-defence, organising the citizens, fitting chains across the streets, petitioning the king for control of the Tower. Charles' attempt to arrest five members of parliament in early January 1642 (accusing them of 'Treason, as stirring up the Apprentices to tumultuous Petitioning') did little to relieve these fears.[52] Accordingly on 7 January a petition to the king from the mayor, aldermen and common council complained not only of 'the great dangers, fears, and distractions, the city was in, by reason of the prevailing progress of the bloody rebels of Ireland', but

That their fears were exceedingly increased by his majestys late going into the House of Commons, attended by a great multitude of armed men, for the apprehending of divers members of the House . . . [and] That the effects of these fears threatened the utter ruin of the Protestant religion, and the lives and liberties of all his subjects.[53]

The combined effect of the Irish rebellion and this royal attack, reported Clarendon, was 'the Court being reduced to a lower condition, and to more disesteem and neglect than ever it had undergone. All that they had formerly said of plots and conspiracies against Parliament, which had before been laughed at, [was] now thought true and real, and all their fears and Jealousies looked upon as the effects of wisdom and foresight.'[54] Recognising the mood, the king abandoned London.

The city government's alliance with parliament would be the nexus of the subsequent war effort. Parliamentary commentaries constantly monitored threats to its safety ('a Plot on foot to fire the City of London'); the governmental apparatus of the city was crucial to preparations 'for the defence of the City and the Kingdom' ('Warrants are sent by the Lord Mayor of London into every severall Parish of the city, requiring them to assemble all their

50 *An Ordinance of the Lords and Commons in Parliament, for the safety and defence of the kingdom of England and dominion of Wales*, 5 March 1642, in Gardiner, *Constitutional Documents*, p. 245.
51 Pearl, *London and the Outbreak of the Puritan Revolution*, pp. 120–50.
52 Richard Baxter, *Reliquiae Baxterianae*, p. 28.
53 Hyde (Clarendon), *History of the Rebellion*, vol. I, pp. 496–7.   54 *Ibid.*, p. 505.

Inhabitants'); this was indeed the beginning of a kingless period of civic self-government in practice. The city government was assiduously courted by parliamentary leaders. On 24 October 1642

the Lord Mayor of London having convoked a Common Hall of all the Free Citizens into the Guild Hall, there came a Committee of Lords and Commons unto them, where the Earles of Northumberland and Holland, made two pithie and patheticall Speeches unto them, therein expressing to the life, the common miseries and dangers, which this distracted Kingdome now groaneth under, these being finished, Mr Pym did second them with the like.[55]

These accounts emphasised 'no evill intention to the Kinge' himself, but observed that 'they now evidently perceive the Kings Councells and Resolutions tend to the extirpation of our true Religion, by his engagement with the Popish Party, and that he intendeth to expose the wealth of his good people, especially of *London*, to the rapine and spoile of the Cavaliers and Souldiers'.[56] Later the city was condemned for the 'furious and audacious insolence' of thus undertaking to defend itself – these 'Caupon Capon-eaters, Halls and severall Corporations, the main incentive of their pride and rebellion'.[57]

In considering the grounds upon which armed self-defence might be permissible, Baxter recorded that parliamentarians were much confirmed in their stance by 'how far' such writers as Hooker and Bilson 'defend the French, Dutch and German Protestants' wars'. On the political side

They alleged Barclay, Grotius and other Defenders of Monarchy, especially that passage of Grotius *De Jure Belli* where he saith, That if several Persons have a part in the *Summa Potestas* (of which he maketh Legislation a chief Act), each part hath naturally the power of defending its own Interest in the Soveraignty against the other part if they invade it. And he addeth over boldly, That if in such a War they conquer, the conquered party loseth to them his share.[58]

This was *De Jure Belli*, book 1, chapter 4, paragraph 13, for the rest of the century one of the most quoted political sources in England. Between 1681 and 1683 we will find Algernon Sidney and John Locke using the same text

---

55 *England's Memorable Accidents*, 24–31 October 1642, p. 1.   56 *Ibid.*

57 *London's New Recorder: Or, certain Queres to be resolved by the old Recorder, for London's further welfare* (London 1647).

58 Richard Baxter, *Reliquiae Baxterianae*, p. 38. It is possible that Baxter's memory in this matter was affected by the subsequent use of this text during the 1680s (see below, pp. 377–88). I am grateful to John Morrill for this point.

to justify the self-defence of protestants and parliaments. In the Convention of 1689 it was repeatedly deployed in the same cause.[59] Meanwhile the polemical contest between parliament and the king was not solely, or even principally, focused upon justifications of resistance. Rather it involved the competing claims of each to be that institution of state charged with taking action for the public peace and safety in a situation of extreme necessity.[60]

This was necessary self-defence on a larger scale. It was defence of the realm against those dangers animating the troubles, both nationally and internationally. As we will see, radical parliamentary claims in 1681–3 again focused upon the question of that assembly's duty in a situation of religious and political emergency to summon itself and act, even if necessary against the king. It was a short step from here to Henry Parker's claim for parliament, by virtue of its representation of the nation, of that 'arbitrary' or 'absolute' power it denied the king.[61] Reflecting the influence of Bodin, this claim too would be repeated by radical parliamentarians in 1680–1. It was against such pretensions that the Levellers would subsequently direct their campaign.

For most royalists, as for parliamentarians, defence of the church and state were interwined. For some the cause was the defence of a legal polity against tyrannical or plebeian chaos. It was to this Aristotelian centre ground that the king appealed in his *Answer to the Nineteen Propositions* (1642). Orders of Discipline issued to royalist troops in late September of the same year referred to those whose 'Loyalties and Consciences brought them to fight for their Religion, King and Lawes, against trayterous Brownists, Anabaptists and Atheists, who endeavour the destruction of Church and State'.[62]

'We fight', explained a parliamentary journal, 'that we may live and enjoy the protestant religion.'[63] John Dury took parliament to be engaged for defence of the 'Protestant profession from the power of Antichristianity . . . [and] to seeke to unite forrain Churches with us in the same cause'.[64] John

59 Hugo Grotius, *De Jure Belli ac Pacis Libri Tres*, trans. F. W. Kelsey (Oxford 1925), vol. II, (*The Translation Book I*), p. 158; Algernon Sidney, *Discourses*, in *Sydney on Government*, pp. 190, 280, 256; Scott, 'Law of War'.   60 Baldwin, 'The Self and the State', chs. 3–4.
61 Michael Mendle, *Henry Parker and the English Civil War* (Cambridge 1995), pp. 86–8 (for Parker and Bodin, see p. 131).
62 *England's Memorable Accidents*, 26 September–2 October 1642, p. 27.
63 *Perfect Occurrences of Parliament*, 22–9 August 1645.
64 Dury, 'Memo on an English College in Heildeburg [*sic*]' [n.d.], in *Hartlib Papers*, 67/19/1A–2B.

Saltmarsh assured his hearers that 'The warres in the severall States of Christendome, as Germany, Denmark, Italy, Ireland, England etc . . . fall in their severall degrees and orders into the designe of God for his Church, and the ruine of Antichrist.'[65] 'As the King's designe is acted by the Popish party', parliamentary newsbooks drew attention to 'the bloudy massacring in many places in this Kingdom . . . [the] correspondency with Rebels in Ireland . . . the sad tragedies acted in Worcestershire . . . and many Villages looking like the ruines of Germany':

All Nations of Christendome see these things, and yet many here are so blinde that they will not beleeve [them]. A Gentleman of credit who is come from *Spaine*; heard the Jesuits speak there, that they knew well enough that the difference betweene the King and the Parliament was not about Prerogative, or Privileges, or any such thing, but to subdue the Heretickes (meaning Protestants) and to reduce this kingdome to its former state.[66]

Scholars have noted the widespread contemporary association of the British wars with the continental conflict, both in their principles and their bloody practice.[67] For a generation steeped in such news, the barbarity of the Thirty Years War had been fully equalled by the Irish rebellion in particular; 'The German . . . hath now a co-partner in his miseries.'[68] A Dutch pamphlet of 1643, subsequently published in English, agreed:

that star with a tail, seen the year 1618, was a warning...[to] all Christendome, whereupon followed those bloody effects, those horrible wars, lamentable wastings, barbarous destructions of countreys and cities . . . in Germanie. And o that we could yet see the end, the bottom of the cup . . . But the rodd flourisheth still, the destroyer is yet busy . . . [in] Catalonia . . . Portugal . . . Scotland, Ireland, England . . . from the papists . . . the King of Spaine . . . the jesuits . . . now the king's high-way robbers scrabble, spoile, steale, waste, destroy, burne the treasures and riches of England.[69]

---

65 John Saltmarsh, *Dawnings of Light* (1646), quoted in W. Schenck, *The Concern for Social Justice in the Puritan Revolution* (London 1948), p. 86.
66 *Perfect Occurrences of Parliament*, 13–20 September 1644, pp. 1–2.
67 Roy, '"England Turned Germany"'; Barbara Donagan, 'Codes and Conduct in the English Civil War', *Past and Present* 118 (February 1988), pp. 65–71. Roy finds this association to have been well founded in fact; Donagan that English atrocities, though they did occur, were smaller in scale. She acknowledges, however, that this difference disappears if we shift our attention to the Anglo-Irish theatre (pp. 93–4).
68 Donagan, 'Codes and Conduct', pp. 68–71; James Howell, *England's Tears for the present wars* (1644), in Scott, *Somers Tracts*, vol. V, p. 2.
69 G. L. V., *British Lightning*, pp. 3–5.

The embodiment of such conduct on the royalist side was Prince Rupert, third son of Elizabeth of Bohemia and veteran of continental campaigns in 1637–8. According to Thomas May, 'Many towns and villages he plundered, which is to say robbed (for at that time was the word first used in England, being born in Germany when that stately country was so miserably wasted and pillaged by foreign armies) . . . executing some, and hanging servants at their master's doors for not discovering their masters.'[70] In 1642 Rupert's brother, the Elector Palatine, and his mother, felt it necessary to publish a declaration disowning his activities. In 1645 the New Model Army commander Fairfax wrote to the prince himself: 'Let all England judge . . . whether the burning its towns, ruining its cities, and destroying its people be a good requital from a person of your family, which has had the prayers, tears, purses and blood of its parliament and people.'[71]

In 1646, after the loss of over 100,000 lives, the English civil war ended in a parliamentary victory. Yet the potential of the troubles as a destructive process had only partially been demonstrated. By 1649 parliament's own religious and political ambitions lay in ruins. As Charles resisted a peace settlement registering the military outcome, it became the salutary fate of his opponents to be swallowed up by the forces unleashed by their own victory. This was partly a royal achievement. As the king said to the parliamentary commissioners at the Isle of Wight on 28 November 1648: 'My Lords, you cannot but know that, in my fall and ruin, you see your own.'[72]

RADICAL REFORMATION 1646–9

To explain this outcome we must return to the context and cause of the troubles as a whole. That context is the incapacity of failing political structures to resist military pressure. That cause is the impact within this context of polarising belief, in particular religious belief. Between 1646 and 1649 our theme remains, within the context of constitutional deadlock, the deepening of the reformation impulse.

---

70 May, *History of the [Long] Parliament* (London 1854), p. 244; Ronald Hutton, *The Royalist War Effort 1642–1646* (London 1982), pp. 120–42.

71 *The Declaration and Petition of the Prince Palsgrave of the Rhyne, and the Queene his Mother, disclaiming and discountenancing Prince Robert, in all his uncivill actions* (London 1642); *Dictionary of National Biography*, vol. XLIX, p. 411.

72 Quoted in C. V. Wedgwood, *The Trial of Charles I* (London 1966), p. 33.

Neither civil war nor peace were unusual in early modern Europe. What was was the deeply unsettling limbo between the two which prevailed in England for almost three years from the end of the 'great civil war'. This left institutions damaged, but not repaired; governmental authority present but relatively ineffective; and expectations raised, but neither answered nor effectively suppressed. It was the space created by this constitutional hiatus, with war finished, but nothing put in its place, that furnished the context for deepening reformation. During the constitutional deadlock of 1640–2 defence of the reformation had given way to further reformation. So, under these new circumstances, further reformation fell under the sword of radical reformation.

Here the polarisation between presbyterians and independents in 1646–9 mirrored that among parliamentarians earlier. What was at issue was the nature, and future, of the English reformation. Now the forces supporting radical reformation emerged from the same constituencies that had won the civil war: the city of London and the army. The emergence of radicalism as a religious and political force followed from a struggle within the civic environment of London and within the army. Yet these forces also involved ideological transformation, resulting from the experience of war itself. Nowhere is this more evident than in relation to the most shocking constitutional outcome of the troubles: the regicide. This registered the impact, under military circumstances, of one species of radical protestantism.

For this too there was a more specific institutional context and ideological cause. That institution was, of course, the New Model Army. This was a product of the military crisis of 1644–5.[73] The first necessary condition of the regicide was a national institution capable of imposing this outcome upon the country. The ideology was New Model Army providentialism. This was a radical Old Testamentarian protestantism, infused by millennialism shaped by the experience of war. This acquired its substance during the later stages of the first civil war and its deadly shape facing the challenge of the second.[74]

---

73 Mark Kishlansky, *The Rise of the New Model Army* (Cambridge 1979); Ian Gentles, *The New Model Army in England, Ireland and Scotland 1645–1653* (London 1992).

74 Blair Worden, 'Oliver Cromwell and the Sin of Achan', in Derek Beales and Geoffrey Best (eds.), *History, Society and the Churches* (London 1985); Patricia Crawford, 'Charles Stuart, That Man of Blood', *Journal of British Studies* 16, 2 (1977); Leo Solt, *Saints in Arms* (Stanford 1959); David Underdown, *Pride's Purge* (London 1971).

From 1646 the conservative parliamentarian majority ('presbyterians') wished for settlement (on their own terms). This meant a political peace with the king based on the Newcastle Propositions; the settlement of a reformed church based upon the recommendations of the Westminster Assembly; and the partial disbandment of the army and so lowering of taxes. They wished, in short, both to secure the fruits of victory and to respond to the cries of the country for a return to normality.

Impediments to these plans presented themselves from most directions. The first was the king himself, whose would-be defence of the state of monarchy in England simply derived nourishment from the customary adverse circumstances. It was in line with the long-term royal perspective that His Majesty's third answer to the Newcastle Propositions (12 May 1647) resisted the 'divesting himself, and disinheriting his posterity of that right and prerogative which is absolutely necessary to the Kingly office, and so weakening the monarchy in this kingdom that little more than the name and shadow of it will remain'.[75] Meanwhile, radical opposition to the settlement of the church ('independency') existed in London, the army and parliament itself. Reluctant to disband while these matters remained unsettled, the army refused to do so while its professional grievances (arrears of pay, and legal indemnity) remained to be addressed.

The crucial confrontation occurred between March and June 1647, between a panicked presbyterian parliamentary leadership led by Denzil Holles, and an army outraged at being treated as an enemy of state.[76] In response to an army petition against disbandment, parliament's *Declaration* 'published in the name of both Houses highly censur[ed] the said petition ... declaring the petitioners, if they should proceed thereupon, no less than enemies to the state and disturbers of the public peace'.[77] This appeared to overlook the fact that the right to petition was ostensibly one of the liberties for which the war had been fought, in parliament's defence, by the army itself.[78]

---

75 Gardiner, *Constitutional Documents*, p. 314; Sarah Barber, *Regicide and Republicanism: Politics and Ethics in the English Revolution* (Edinburgh 1998), p. 13.

76 The most detailed account is Austin Woolrych, *Soldiers and Statesmen: The General Council of the Army and Its Debates, 1647–1648* (Oxford 1987).

77 'A Solemn Engagement of the Army' (5 June), in A. S. P. Woodhouse (ed.), *Puritanism and Liberty: Being the Army Debates (1647–1649) from the Clarke Manuscripts with Supplementary Documents* (London 1951), p. 401.

78 Kishlansky, *New Model Army*, p. 288; Kishlansky, 'The Army and the Levellers: The Roads to Putney', *Historical Journal* 22, 4 (1979).

One result was a series of declarations of the army's own. These explained, famously, that they were 'not a mere mercenary army, hired to serve any arbitrary power of a state, but called forth and conjured by the several declarations of Parliament to the defence of our own and the people's just rights and liberties'.[79] Another was a developing alliance with radicals in London who had been waging the new struggle against the attempt to reimpose religious uniformity.[80] This hinged upon the accusation that the parliament was now more arbitrary than the king had ever been. In the face of this co-option of their own rhetoric the two Houses were deeply vulnerable.[81]

As ever the important practical reality was the military one. Thus the most important result of this confrontation was the advance on London and (with the ejection of eleven presbyterian leaders from the House of Commons) the first of the series of military interventions in civilian politics by which the constitutional history of the country would be determined until 1660.[82] This was partly in pursuit of military objectives. It was also the armed cutting edge of that struggle against outward bondage – religious, civil, social and legal – that was one of the things by which civil war radicalism was united. The oppressive institutions swept away, however, fell victim not only to this perspective, but to the army's own particular understanding of this struggle.[83]

Statements by New Model members at this time make clear a sense already present of its status as a particular instrument of God. It was against this background that soldiers struggled with the shock of the king's escape from custody and engagement with the Scots (December 1647). The result was a second crisis of three kingdoms, to be followed by a second Scots invasion.[84] For some, including Cromwell and Ireton, Charles' sacrilege in

---

79 *A Representation of the Army* (14 June 1647), in Woodhouse, *Puritanism and Liberty*, p. 404.

80 The most useful collection of primary documents for tracing this alliance is Woodhouse, *Puritanism and Liberty*.

81 These developments are discussed in more detail in ch. 12.

82 Woolrych, *Soldiers and Statesmen*; Kishlansky, *New Model Army*; Gentles, *New Model Army*; Underdown, *Pride's Purge*; Robert Ashton, *Counter-Revolution: The Second Civil War and Its Origins 1646–1648* (London 1994).

83 Kishlansky, 'The Roads to Putney'.

84 John Morrill, 'Three Kingdoms and One Commonwealth?: The Enigma of Mid-Seventeenth-Century Britain and Ireland', in A. Grant and K. Stringer (eds.), *Uniting the Kingdom: The Making of British History* (London 1995), pp. 184–5.

seeking to overturn the judgement of God in the first civil war may in itself have determined them to bring him and all other authors of the ensuing conflict to account. In relation to the king the form this accounting would take (from deposition to death) would have to await the unfolding of a providential rather than fleshly reason.[85] For others, most famously at the New Model officers' prayer meeting at Windsor in late April 1648, the priority was to seek to know the cause of this divine reproof. This resulted in the understanding that the army were being punished for failing to proceed against the blood-guilty delinquent whom God had delivered into their hands in 1646. In both cases the subsequent military contest, in addition to being bitterly angry, was fought for high spiritual stakes.[86] The New Model victory at Preston in August confirmed the return of divine favour, and may have sealed Charles' fate.[87] In the words of Cromwell:

Surely, Sir, this is nothing but the hand of God; and wherever anything in this world is exalted, or exalts itself, God will pull it down; for this is the day wherein He alone will be exalted ... exalt Him, and [do] not hate His people, who are as the apple of His eye, and for whom even Kings shall be reproved.[88]

To bring the king to 'justice' it was necessary to purge the Commons and abolish the Lords. This effectively destroyed parliament as well as the monarchy (a job belatedly completed in 1653). The Purge occurred the day after a panicking parliament at last voted to accept the king's most recent offers as the basis for a peace (those purged were those who so voted). Its timing was a consequence, therefore, not of the fact that a civil peace with the king could not be achieved, but of the fact that it was at last about to occur.

This was a last desperate attempt by those who had begun the war to stitch back together the tattered remnants of the old constitution. With its

85 John Morrill and Philip Baker, 'Oliver Cromwell, the Regicide, and the Sons of Zeruiah', paper given at Downing College, Cambridge, February 1999.

86 See the account by William Allen in Worden, 'Oliver Cromwell'; Gentles, *New Model Army*, pp. 245–59.

87 In January 1648, speaking for the Vote of No Addresses, Ireton had already argued 'that, since the king had ceased to protect his people, they were no longer subject to him and could settle the kingdom without him' (quoted in Gentles, *New Model Army*, p. 237). For his state of mind just prior to the Purge, see *A Remonstrance of His Excellency Thomas Lord Fairfax ... and of the Generall Councell of Officers Held at St Albans the 16 of November 1648* (London 1648).

88 *Oliver Cromwell's Letters and Speeches*, ed. Thomas Carlyle (3 vols., London 1857), vol. I, p. 295.

destruction, one ideological product of the troubles – the imperative of duty to a vengeful Old Testament deity – smashed a hole through the fabric of institutional form. That vast majority who observed the regicide incredulously remained separated from this ideology not only by principle but by the military experience from which it had emerged. It was this journey across the red sea of battle that made sense of the divine demand for retributive sacrifice: blood for blood. 'The black act is done', wrote William Sancroft, 'which all the world wonders at, and which an age cannot expiate. The waters of the ocean we swim in cannot wash out the spots of that blood, than which never any was shed with greater guilt, since the son of God poured out his.'[89]

The regicide was the climax of the first phase of England's troubles. It was the most spectacular institutional consequence of that deepening reformation impulse which was its first major ideological legacy. *A Winter Dream* was one of many pamphlets of late 1648 which again set the ruinous English conflict in its European context. After flying to every part of a contemporary Europe wracked by war – the Empire, the Netherlands, Naples ('never any place suffered more in so short time'), Venice, Spain and France – the dreamer finally landed in England ('a large Island'). It had once, he was told, been uniquely at peace, but not now. There was a saying among foreigners that 'Winter here hath too many tears', but there were not too many now. Now there was

a monstrous kind of wild liberty . . . [and] that which was complained of . . . to draw on our miseries at first, is now . . . in practice . . . *arbitrary rule*, for now Law, Religion, and Allegiance are here arbitrary . . . it was a Northern Nation that brought these cataracts of mischief . . . [along with] a strange race of people sprung up among our selfs, who were confederat with th[em].[90]

Accordingly Charles I's struggle for the substance of monarchy in England had come to this: monarchical absence – 'Which word *King* was once a Monosyllable of some weight in this Ile, but 'tis as little regarded now as the word Pope . . . which was also a mighty Monosyllable once among us'. It used to be a saying that 'the King can do no wrong'; now it was 'the King can receive no wrong'. It was in the same context, however, that George Wither defended 'a Reformation gained, and maintained by the Sword in England':

---

89 Quoted in Spurr, *Restoration Church*, p. 20.   90 *A Winter Dream*, pp. 4–14.

These Objectors themselves would account that man a Papist, or Popishly affected, who should thus reproach the Protestants in *Bohemia, Germany, Switzerland, France*, the *United Provinces*, and *Scotland*, yet did these maintaine their Religion, and gain their Liberties by the Sword, by this the Switzers cantoniz'd themselves, and the Dutch became a Free-state; by this Protestant Religion was defended, and the Presbyterian Government first setled in Scotland.[91]

Contemporary perception of this truth had long informed the troubles. Its confirmation by English experience would give the same perception renewed life throughout the restoration period.

INTERREGNUM

Yet the first step towards reconstruction of the monarchy in England was to be the regicide itself. Charles I contrived to die a martyr to both the monarchy and the church. Meanwhile the revolution never achieved a stable institutional structure to replace those it had destroyed. The historiographical term 'interregnum' signifies this constitutional absence, without giving alternative expression to the positive aspirations, both protestant and republican, by which the revolution was actually shaped.

Constitutional anti-formalism, with its origin in radical protestantism, was one of the characteristic features of the interregnum political experience. William Walwyn had explained that 'as there is no reason why any man should be bound expressly to any one forme . . . so ought the whole nation to be free therein to alter and change the publique form'.[92] It was thus not only Cromwell, thereafter, who was not 'wedded and glewed to forms of government'; who believed that such carnal contrivances were 'dross and dung in relation to Christ'; who would not 'declare . . . either for a monarchical, aristocratical or democratical government: maintaining that any of them might be good in themselves or for us, according as providence should direct us'.[93]

Yet we must not confuse this constitutional instability with the substance of the revolution itself. This took the form of certain moral aspirations, both classical and christian, to be achieved in practice by reformation of

---

91 G[eorge] W[ither], *Respublica Anglicana or the Historie of the Parliament* (London 1650), p. 43.

92 Quoted in J. C. Davis, 'The Levellers and Christianity', in Brian Manning (ed.), *Politics, Religion and the English Civil War* (London 1973), p. 237.

93 Edmund Ludlow, *Memoirs*, quoted in Woolrych, *Soldiers and Statesmen*, p. 329.

manners. Above all, interregnum governments sought to give positive expression to the moral aspirations of radical reformation. These had a republican dimension: an attempt to substitute a moral philosophy of citizenship for one of subjection. More importantly they constituted an attempt to put a substantial christianity of practice in the place of the empty formality of worship, doctrine and ceremony.

This was combined with aggressive protestantism abroad. For the first time since the Elizabethan period, and the last before 1689, England recovered a confessional foreign policy. To a significant extent this was a direct product of the crisis of the 1620s, Cromwell's 'mind' having been 'moulded, fixed and perhaps slightly cracked in [that] grim and lurid furnace'.[94] 'The Power . . . of this republiq', wrote a German correspondent to Cromwell, 'which heretofore and until the beginning of the Warr in Bohemia was the pillar and support of our Empire, is at this time by God lifted upp to so high a degree, that it is the onely comfort and refuge of all oppressed.'[95] England's 'true Interest', wrote Edward Ironside to Samuel Hartlib, which 'wee have ever since the days of Queene Elizabeth declind . . . is to maintayne itself protectrix of the protestant religion with as much zeale as the King of Spayne protects the Catholique'.[96] Protectoral foreign policy was accordingly anti-popish and anti-Spanish. Its positive objective was the composing of 'Jealousies and differences amongst those of the reformed and Protestant Religion', to offer 'a Comon Bulwarke . . . against the bloody Inquisitions . . . force of Armes and all Imaginable Crueltyes' of the counter-reformation design 'so long contended for'.[97] Domestic policy connected protestant liberty of conscience with the quest for 'healing and settling', political and spiritual, which was the internal mirror of this foreign policy.

Thus two things bound together the disparate governments of the interregnum. One was this moral, and in particular religious, aspiration; the other the underlying reality of army power. Thereafter the first episode of England's troubles ended as it began: with invasion from Scotland. That the invading army in late 1659 was not Scots, but an English army under Monck, does not detract from the military reality. As it had taken military intervention to discompose and then destroy the old order, so the same would be necessary to put it back together again.

94 Trevor-Roper, 'Three Foreigners', p. 282.
95 Address to Cromwell by Ludovicus Gustavus de Hohenlohe, January 1657, *Hartlib Papers*, 54/63A–64B, doc. 767.   96 *Ibid.*, 44/6/5A–6B.
97 Downing College Library, Cambridge, Sir George Downing Letter Book 1658, ff. 3–4.

This is not to say that restoration was ever regarded as inevitable, particularly by the would-be king himself. As late as 10 March 1660 it was reported that 'it had been put to the vote in parliament, whether they would be for a monarchy or a commonwealth government; and . . . it was carryed by 20 voyces, that they would be for a commonwealth government'.[98] Nor did it mean that even with that restoration England's troubles were over. To arrest that problem it would be necessary to address its causes, at home and abroad. In that respect, John Milton predicted as early as October 1649:

his sons restorement . . . would be so farr from conducing to our happiness either as a *remedy to the present distempers, or a prevention of the like to come*, that it would inevitably throw us back again into all our past and fulfill'd miseries; would force us to fight over again all our tedious warrs, and put us to another fatal struggling for Libertie and life, more dubious than the former.[99]

98 *A Collection of the State Papers of John Thurloe* (7 vols., London 1742), vol. VII, p. 864.
99 John Milton, *Eikonoklastes*, p. 568.

7

Restoration memory

I know . . . it is said that I intend the subversion of the religion and
government, that I intend to govern by an army and by arbitrary
power, to lay aside Parliaments . . . But . . . thos that say it the most . . .
are . . . such as would subvert the government themselves and bring it
to a commonwealth again.

Charles II to John Reresby, 15 February 1677[1]

All our misfortune arises from the late times. When the King came
home, his ministers knew nothing of the Laws of England, but foreign
Government.

William Sacheverell, 1678[2]

INTRODUCTION

The continuation of the troubles into the restoration period requires us to
address two subjects. One is the continuation, or reappearance, beyond
1660 of the circumstances and fears by which they were sustained. The
other is the initial failure of the restoration process to end them. This
second matter is the subject of chapters 16–17. In relation to the first, two
contexts will be identified. That in space, again, was the European situation. That in time was restoration memory. These were links to the troubles over which restoration governments had little power. Thus it was that
only eighteen years after the return of the monarchy Charles II found
himself facing a crisis universally considered similar to that which had
destroyed his father.[3]

1 *Memoirs of Sir John Reresby*, pp. 111–12.
2 Grey, *Debates 1667–1694*, vol. VII, p. 35, quoted in Mark Knights, *Politics and Opinion in Crisis 1678–1681* (Cambridge 1994), p. 17.   3 Scott, *Restoration Crisis*.

The claim that the troubles did return, and that we must consequently see the period 1660–89 as one of continuing instability, has recently received significant attention.[4] Restoration used to be taken as a given. Subsequent crises and the thought associated with them were considered to be superficial. In fact, initially at least, it was restoration that was superficial. It was also specifically institutional in focus. Since the causes of the troubles, and the substance of the revolution, lay rather in ideas, it is not surprising that this reconstruction of the institutional fabric of the old order did not end them. Instead, it created a new context for them, and so established the basis for that struggle between three processes which determined the shape of restoration history.

Our focus in this study is upon the imaginative reconstruction of religious and political perceptions. Until recently historians have not brought to their perception of restoration politics the preoccupation with a traumatic past which supplied the context for contemporary perceptions. One product of this preoccupation was the attempt to restore traditional structures. The other, however, was the remembered abyss which appeared to beckon should that attempt fail.

TIME: RESTORATION MEMORY

Those who cannot forget the past may be condemned to repeat it. 'The late rebellion need not be remembered since it is impossible it should be forgotten.'[5] Public memory governed restoration politics much more surely than Charles II. It was not, however, only one thing, leading in one direction. It was not much less complex than the embattled past to which it related.

By 'public memory' here is meant something more than the memories of individuals composing this society. By these, needless to say, it was deeply informed. In addition, however, this political culture had suffered a traumatic *collective* experience with which it was necessary to come to terms. The average age of members of the Cavalier Parliament in 1661 was forty-one ('a parliament full of lewd young men chosen by a furious people in spite to the puritans, whose severity had disgusted them').[6] Much of the most insistent modelling of the restoration present upon the past came

---

4 Among the contributors to 'Order and Authority: Creating Party in Restoration England', special issue of *Albion* 25, 4 (1993), this is a suggestion rather amplified than disputed.
5 *The Character of a Rebellion*, p. 5.
6 Sidney, *Discourses*, in *Sydney on Government*, p. 502; Basil D. Henning (ed.), *The House of Commons 1660–1690* (3 vols., London 1983), vol. I, p. 2.

from individuals who could not directly have witnessed the political world of which they spoke. Yet the public memory of that world, and of the events by which it had been destroyed, was everywhere: in the minds of individuals; in families and communities; in the culture of print, which reinforced this society's capacity to transmit collective experience across generations; and in the politicisation of every aspect of restoration life from coffee house and pulpit to the calendar of public holidays.[7]

All societies exhibit some species of collective memory. It has been suggested that 'it is an implicit rule that participants in any social order must presuppose a shared memory. To the extent that their memories of a society's past diverge . . . its members can share neither experiences nor assumptions':

The effect is seen most obviously when communication across generations is impeded by different sets of memories . . . so that, although physically present to one another . . . the different generations may remain mentally and emotionally insulated, the memories of one generation locked irretrievably, as it were, in the brains and bodies of that generation.[8]

This helps to account for two key features of restoration experience. The first is the political power of public memory as a context for present action (and re-enactment). That restoration memory had been politicised registered the impact of unforgettable events.[9] Even in the modern period Jay Winter has recorded a recourse to 'traditional motifs' in the 'search for an appropriate language of loss . . . and . . . mourning' in the aftermath of a major collective tragedy.[10] Though ever present this memory furnished no single prescription. It was, on the contrary, the contested landscape within which the struggle for particular outcomes was conducted. The second feature was the decisive eventual effect upon this situation not simply of present events but of generational change.

The generational context of the first episode of the troubles had been crucial: in particular the impact of the European war upon a generation reared upon Elizabethan and Jacobean anti-popery. So eventually the

---

7 David Cressy, *Bonfires and Bells: National Memory and the Protestant Calendar in Elizabethan and Stuart England* (London 1989), ch. 11; Freist, *Governed by Opinion*, 'Conclusion'; Hannah Smith, 'Images of Charles II', MPhil. thesis, Cambridge 1998; *The Diary of Samuel Pepys*, ed. Robert Latham and William Matthews (11 vols., London 1970).

8 Paul Connerton, *How Societies Remember* (Cambridge 1994), p. 3.

9 Cressy, *Bonfires and Bells*, ch. 11.

10 Jay Winter, *Sites of Memory, Sites of Mourning: The Great War in European Cultural History* (Cambridge 1995), p. 5.

troubles as a whole could subside not only because solutions had been found to longstanding problems, but because the landscape of memory had changed. It was merely one aspect of this situation that as products of the troubles Charles II and James II did a good deal to perpetuate them. If contemporaries believed that the prescription for stability lay in the past, so of course did that for instability. Indeed the restoration settlement, by restoring the old structures, restored many of the old problems as well. At the very least it failed adequately to address them. Thus restoration memory could be drawn upon for constructive and for destructive purposes.[11]

What was the landscape of restoration public memory? The first crisis of popery and arbitrary government, under Charles I, had led the country into an unspeakable series of disasters. Worse still, it had resulted in a more terrible 'popery' (protestant fanaticism) and arbitrary government (high-taxing military rule) than anything imagined under that monarch. As we have seen, the equation of radical protestantism with popery had been a feature of English protestant thinking since the time of Elizabeth and James I. Both threatened to destroy the church and state. By 1660, however, anti-magisterial protestantism had actually done this, perpetrating in the process the regicide defended by the Jesuit Mariana in 1599, and accomplished by Ravaillac in the murder of Henri IV eleven years later.[12] Thus by 1660 English experience had established

That Popery and Phanaticism, are equally dangerous to the Government by Law Established. The Papists, ever since the Reformation, have plotted . . . against this Kingdome . . . but by God's Providence . . . have been always disappointed. The Phanaticks made but one Attempt, and laid aside the Monarchy, Destroyed the Church, and for almost Twenty Yeares, exercised Arbitrary and Tyrannical Government against Law.[13]

All restoration public holidays marked the delivery of the nation from one of these destructive menaces or the other. It was this which accounted for the fact that although

---

11 Scott, *Restoration Crisis*, ch. 1.
12 Juan de Mariana, *De rege et regis institutione* (1599), discussed in Tuck, *Philosophy and Government*, pp. 79–80; hence Bishop Burnet's alarm when in 1683 his friend the Earl of Essex (about to be committed to the Tower for treason) 'brought me Mariana's Book of a Prince' (British Library, Add MS 63,057, Transcript of Burnet's *History of His Own Time*, vol. II, p. 139).
13 *Presentment of the Grand Jury of Ossulston* (1682), quoted in Tim Harris, *London Crowds in the Reign of Charles II* (Cambridge 1987), p. 144.

By the age of Charles II, England's historic deliverances of the Elizabethan and Jacobean period lay beyond the reach of most living memory, yet they continued to influence religious consciousness and political behaviour. Rather than fading with time, such 'mercies' as the triumphs of Queen Elizabeth and the discovery of the Gunpowder Plot remained in view as highly charged points of reference and commentary.[14]

This situation remained in place until well into the eighteenth century, when successful restoration began to permit national forgetting. In the long run these two remembered dangers would be externalised. Within Britain radical reformation would be associated with Scotland, popery with Ireland, the doors to both kept firmly closed by a powerful British state. In the earlier absence of that state, destruction had been ushered into England through Scotland in 1637, and then Ireland in 1641. 'Scotland and Ireland are two Doors, either to let in Good or Mischief upon us.'[15] Thus when England's troubles returned between 1678 and 1683, the old polemical markers of confessional polarisation ('puritan', 'arminian') were replaced by new ones signifying religious banditry in Scotland and Ireland respectively ('whig' and 'tory').[16] Beneath the new labels, signifying recent experience, old fears and dangers remained unaltered.

In this context the political consensus that restored the monarchy in 1660 was both negative and conditional. Loyalty to the institution of monarchy was not conditional but that to the restored Stuart regime was, as 1688–9 would show. It was conditional upon the future protection of the nation, and particularly its ruling elite, from the twin spectres by which it had been terrorised, not once but twice. The shape of the restoration settlement was determined by this fact. The powers of the monarch, of parliament and of the church were debated and settled to this end. In this respect the restoration crisis – the collapse of this negative consensus in the face of the return of popery and arbitrary government – signalled the failure of the settlement

---

14 Cressy, *Bonfires and Bells*, p. 172.

15 *An impartial account of divers remarkable proceedings* [1679], quoted in Kalev P. Peekna, 'British Aspects of English Political Culture 1660–1685', MPhil. thesis, Cambridge 1996, p. 81. It is an argument of this study that English perceptions of Scots and Irish nationality at this time were primarily governed by religion ('We know no difference of Nation but what is expressed by Papist and Protestant', p. 30).

16 *The Character of a Modern Whig* (London 1681); *The Character of a Tory* (London 1681); *The Character of a Good Man, neither Whig or Tory* (London 1681); *The History of Whiggism, or, The Whiggish Plots in the Reign of King Charles the First* (London 1682); Scott, *Restoration Crisis*, pp. 48–9.

itself. One result was a potentially catastrophic repolarisation of belief, which threatened a new civil war. Though temporarily weathered, these problems would not be addressed until the second, successful restoration settlement of 1688–9 and subsequent external war. In the context of this, what remained salvageable of the Elizabethan church and state was at last equipped, by the process of statebuilding, to defend itself in European terms.

Thus documenting the return of the troubles during the restoration period entails recounting the return of the fears by which they were animated. As in earlier chapters we are dealing with three sets of fears. All had survived from the early Stuart period; each had acquired a new dimension between 1640 and 1660. There was the fear of popery, or of 'the growth of popery', which was fear of counter-reformation (or for protestantism). There was the fear of arbitrary government which was above all fear for parliaments (and government by law). And there was the fear for the survival, or at least the effective power, of English monarchy. The first was now also fear of radical reformation. The second was now also fear of standing armies and military rule. The third now pointed to the period 1640–60 in general, and the solemn anniversary of 30 January 1649 in particular, as a reminder of what could happen, and had happened.

In this respect the euphoria of 1660, heartfelt though it was, is misleading as the emblem of a would-be new age. By 1661 Samuel Pepys was already recording: 'In short, I see no content or satisfaccion anywhere in any one sort of people.' By 1667, with 100,000 Londoners dead of plague, much of the city in ashes and a return to the condition of Stuart military failure, the party was over.

SPACE: THE EUROPEAN CONTEXT

What made the British monarchy peculiarly vulnerable to the destabilising impact of European developments was its military weakness. In this respect what would be necessary to end the troubles was successful completion of the process of military-fiscal statebuilding. Herein lay a fundamental problem. For, as we have seen, statebuilding entailed innovation. It was precisely Caroline attempts at statebuilding initiated in the context of a European war that had been identified as popery and arbitrary government. It was subsequent parliamentary fiscal innovation which signalled that arbitrary government was not the exclusive preserve of monarchy. The single overriding purpose of the settlement of 1660–7 was to ensure that these could never return. This meant the resurrection of the unreformed Jacobean polity. This in turn, after an interlude of republican military power, meant a return to vulnerability on an increasingly dangerous European stage.[17]

'This is that', reported ambassador George Downing from the Netherlands in 1661, 'with which continually heer they shune the king and trifle wt can he do he hath no mony.'[18] This was not an opinion which Downing's master Clarendon found it possible to contradict. 'I pray remember the . . . unsettled state of the Crowne', he warned the bellicose Downing in 1661, 'the streights and necessitys we are in for money, the emptiness of all our stores, magazines, etc.'[19] Nor was this impression contradicted by the outcome of the second Anglo-Dutch war, culminating in the unopposed descent upon Chatham in 1667. From this to the 'humiliation' of the English army in November 1688,[20] the restored monarchy's record of military failure was the equal of that of Charles I. This was the most important sense in which, by restoring the old structures, the settlement of 1660–7 restored the old problems. This was the single most important domestic context for the continuation of the troubles. The other, no less important, was the European situation.

From the standpoint of English fears this had become more menacing since the previous reign. In the 1620s those fears had focused upon the traditional enemy, Spain, and its Austrian Habsburg ally. After the restoration the catholic superpower was Louis XIV's France. It was much closer, and more powerful (Louis' standing army of 300,000 in the 1690s was three times the size of the largest armies deployed during the Thirty Years War).[21] It was, by the 1670s, nakedly expansionist. At the same time it became an open force for intolerant confessional absolutism. It is hardly surprising that the English governing elite found this disturbing, even before something remarkable in local policy made it more so.

Restoration politicians, one historian has written, 'were relatively uninterested in foreign politics'.[22] In fact the opposite was the case, in the 1670s, as in the 1620s. Every factor that fed into the subsequent restoration crisis (1678–83) related to this situation. Thus in November 1680 the House of

---

17 Scott, 'Sir George Downing'.   18 Bodleian Library, Clarendon MS, vol. 105, ff. 89, 152.
19 *Ibid.*, vol. 104, f. 8 (30 August 1661).   20 Childs, *British Army*, pp. 4–5.
21 Geoffrey Parker, *The Military Revolution: Military Innovation and the Rise of the West 1500–1800* (Cambridge 1996).   22 J. R. Jones, *The First Whigs* (London 1961), p. 31.

Commons issued a sixteen-page *Address* describing the circumstances in which the kingdom had witnessed the dreaded return of popery and arbitrary government (the 'Attempts of the Popish Party, for many years last past . . . not only within this, but other your Majesties Kingdoms, to introduce the Romish, and utterly to extirpate the true protestant religion').[23] This located it entirely, as Andrew Marvell had three years earlier, in the context of this Anglo-French relationship:[24]

After some time [these Jesuits] . . . became able to influence matters of State and Government . . . the continuance or Prorogation of Parliaments has been accommodated to serve the[ir] purposes . . . Ministers of England were made Instruments . . . to make War upon a Protestant State . . . to advance and augment the dreadful power of the French King . . . [and] When in the next Parliament the house of Commons were prepared to bring to a legal Tryal the principal Conspirators in this Plot, that Parliament was first Prorogued, and then Dissolved. The Interval between the Calling and Sitting of this Parliament was so long, that now they conceive hopes of Covering all their past Crimes, and . . . practising them more effectually.[25]

The popish plot crisis which ignited in these circumstances in 1678 was not created by Titus Oates. It was created by English government policy.

A final destabilising factor in this context was Charles II himself. With the conservative ambitions of his political elite, Charles was out of sympathy in most respects.[26] He was not a lover of tradition or formality, not Anglocentric and not a committed protestant. In the formulation of Sir George Savile, Marquis of Halifax, 'His Wit was better suited to his condition *before* he was restored than *afterwards*.'[27] The dangerous consequences of this situation became manifest after 1667 when the king liberated himself from the political tutelage of Clarendon on the one hand, and the Cavalier Parliament on the other.

Clarendon recorded that Charles had 'in his nature so little reverence or esteem for antiquity, and did in truth so much condemn old orders, forms

---

23 *The Humble Address of the Commons in Parliament Assembled, Presented to His Majesty, Monday 28th day of November 1680* (London 1680), p. 76.

24 Marvell, *Growth of Popery*.   25 *Humble Address of the Commons*, pp. 77–82.

26 The classic study of both in this context is Paul Seaward, *The Cavalier Parliament and the Reconstruction of the Old Regime* (Cambridge 1989).

27 Savile (Halifax), *A Character of Charles II*, in *The Works of George Savile Marquis of Halifax*, ed. Mark N. Brown (3 vols., Oxford 1989), vol. II, p. 498.

and institutions, that the objection of novelty rather advanced than obstructed any proposition'.[28] According to Mulgrave, 'He had so natural an aversion to all formality . . . that he could not . . . act the part of a King for a moment, either at Parliament or Council.' This did not make Charles any less a servant of memory. Halifax tells us: 'He had a very good *Memory* . . . His chain of *Memory* was longer than his chain of *Thought*.'[29] As we will discover, his policies are best understood as a response to what he took to be the dangers to his position demonstrated by the events of mid-century. He was, however, a product of that turbulence, not, like Clarendon, of the preceding period: he had experienced it not as an interruption but as normality.

This is not to say that personality was the key to kingship in the later any more than in the early Stuart period. What was important was the extent to which Charles remained a foreigner not simply to the restoration project but to the country. For the Cavalier Parliament the key to the settlement, as to the troubles, was religion. The intolerant Act of Uniformity and its accompaniments were an attempt to steer both church and state between the twin poperies of counter-reformation and radical reformation. It was extremely unfortunate, then, that Charles, who thought catholicism a Good Thing, Quakerism amusing and toleration both politic and humane, preferred all three to the Church of England. Like his father, Charles liked to emphasise the comparative political loyalty of catholics.[30] His lack of sympathy with the parliamentary religious settlement was alarmingly demonstrated by his attempt to dispense with its provisions, for catholics as well as protestants, as early as 1662.

These attitudes reflected an adult lifetime spent upon the religiously mixed, but predominantly catholic, continent. It is hardly surprising that he emerged a cosmopolitan sceptic, whose priority was to retain rather than use his crown, and who could not take the Church of England's claim to be the only true church seriously. It was Halifax's opinion that Charles lost his 'veneration' for the Church of England in Paris, though he could just as easily have lost it in Cologne or The Hague. 'After the first Year or two he was

---

28 Hyde (Clarendon), *The Continuation of the Life of Edward Earl of Clarendon . . . Written by Himself*, vol. II (Oxford 1760), pp. 195–6.
29 Savile (Halifax), *A Character of Charles II*, in *Works*, vol. II, pp. 497, 499.
30 This was a key theme of the king's account of his escape from Worcester: W. Matthews (ed.), *Charles II's Escape from Worcester* (London 1967), quoted in Hannah Smith, 'Images of Charles II', p. 67.

no more a Protestant.' Modern scholarship has challenged these views but it is highly significant that a senior courtier could hold them.[31]

Thus it was not only James II in 1687, but also Charles II in 1662 and 1672, who attempted to build his security upon the patronage of precisely those heterodox groups excluded by the parliamentary religious settlement. Both were products of exile: in this direct way the first experience of the troubles helped to establish the policy preconditions for the second and third. It was a final consequence of this situation that Charles' mental map of Europe had its centre not in England at all, but France. Charles II was far from the only European prince in this period to be influenced by the spectacle of Paris (as to a lesser extent his father had been by Madrid). Members of his family, including his mother and sister, continued to live there. All of this helps to account for a dependence upon France which deepened rather than receded as the reign progressed, and reached its apogee under the joint government of Louis XIV and the Duchess of Portsmouth.[32] Charles II is no more explicable within a purely English or British context than William III or George I. Until biographers give due weight to this fact, the appropriate metaphor for his reign will remain the story he never tired of telling, of his escape from his own subjects in disguise.[33]

FEAR OF POPERY: 'THE PLOT REVIV'D'

Fear of counter-reformation was a constant in seventeenth-century England. This fear did not depend upon royal policy; what did was the need to keep it at bay. As early as 1663 parliament reminded the king of the growing 'jealousy and apprehension . . . [of] your good Subjects . . . that the Popish Religion may much increase in this Kingdom', and the 'insolencies of Popish Priests and Jesuits, who declare to all the World, they are in expectation of a plentiful harvest here in England'.[34] Part of the reason for this continuing anxiety was the king's attempt to excuse catholics as well as prot-

---

31 Savile (Halifax), *A Character of Charles II*, in *Works*, vol. II, p. 484; Ronald Hutton, 'The Religion of Charles II', in Smuts, *The Stuart Court and Europe*.

32 Nancy Klein Maguire, 'The Duchess of Portsmouth: English Royal Consort and French Politician, 1670–1685', in Smuts, *The Stuart Court and Europe*.

33 Ronald Hutton, *Charles II* (Oxford 1991); Miller, *Charles II*.

34 *The Humble Representation and Petition of the Lords and the Commons concerning Romish Priests and Jesuits* (London 1663), p. 1; Sir Edmund Turner, *The Speech of Sir Edmund Turner KT, Speaker of the House of Commons, to the Kings most Excellent Majesty* (London 1666), p. 3.

estant dissenters from the provisions of the Act of Uniformity in 1662. One of his stated reasons for this was the loyalty those of the 'old religion' had shown to his father. While true, this was not a wise line of appeal. As one of his subjects would put it later: 'As to the papists assisting Charles the first in the late wars . . . they did as much hurt to his Majesty by the scandal they brought to his party, as they did good by their arms. For they were the cause of that war.'[35]

As earlier in the century, the other context for this fear was European. Apprehension of the growing power of France, and of French influence at the English court, significantly pre-dated the formal alliance of 1670.[36] During the Anglo-Dutch war of 1665–7, with France officially on the side of the Dutch, Algernon Sidney wrote not only of the pretensions of Louis XIV to the universal monarchy of Europe but of the secret maxims of the English court, whereby

Union with France and war with Holland is necessary to uphold monarchy in England . . . a strict friendship is to be held with the French that their customs may be introduced and the people by their example brought to beggary and slavery quietly . . . There is nothing so secret in our court, but by the next post it is known at Paris . . . and those are most favoured at court, that conform to the French manners and fashions in all things.[37]

Such apprehensions were partly responsible for the enormous English popularity of the Triple Alliance which ended the Anglo-Dutch War in 1667. By this Sweden, Britain and the Netherlands united to draw a line under French and catholic expansion.[38] The shock may readily be imagined, then, when within a few years of its completion this alliance had been abandoned, replaced by another with France, and that used as the basis for an Anglo-French attack upon, and attempt to annihilate and partition, the United Provinces. This was accompanied (in 1672) by a second attempt to legalise catholic and dissenting worship in England. It was above all these terrifying actions, by which the English king helped to bring 'the protestant Interest in this part of Europe so very near to a final period'[39] that triggered a return of the troubles.

35 *The Popish Plot, Taken from Several Depositions Made before the Parliament* (1678), in Scott, *Somers Tracts*, vol. VIII, p. 59.

36 Steven Pincus, *Protestantism and Patriotism* (Cambridge 1996).

37 Algernon Sidney, *Court Maxims*, pp. 152–6: Scott, *English Republic*, pp. 204–6.

38 'Letters of Sir William Temple', in Temple, *Works*, vol. II.

39 *An Account of the Reasons which induced Charles II . . . to declare War against the States General . . . in 1672* (London 1689), p. 1.

This was the fruit of Charles' own post-Clarendonian freedom to make policy. It was assisted by a group of courtiers favourable to catholicism or dissent. It is a sign of Charles' apparent partial abstraction from reality in this matter that in 1671 he was seriously tempted (against Louis' advice) to tell his nephew the Prince of Orange about these plans for the destruction of his country. He found him, however, to be 'so passionately Dutch and protestant' that he changed his mind.[40] The Treaty of Dover (1670) publicly undertook support for France, and promised to introduce toleration for catholics in England. In the parallel secret treaty Charles promised as soon as possible to publicly declare his own catholicism, and to convert his subjects, using French troops if necessary. If Charles I had plausibly seemed an agent of counter-reformation, Charles II was one.

The most astonishing thing about these developments is that they have not been taken seriously by modern historians. Recent royal biographies have repeated the judgement that Charles was not serious in these undertakings without explaining why therefore he took the huge political risks associated with making them. It is against this background that historians have attributed the inevitable contemporary reaction in the popish plot crisis of the late 1670s ('Nobody can conceive that was not a witness thereof', said Sir John Reresby, 'what a ferment it raised among all ranks and degrees')[41] to 'exceptional ignorance', 'credulity', 'knavery' and 'folly'.[42] It was the invention of 'a group of unscrupulous perjurers led by a psychopath', 'a farrago of stupid and inconsistent fabrications, for which nothing but the public ferment could have obtained credence for a minute'.[43]

This is a mass outbreak not of contemporary hysteria but historiographical amnesia. The story of Titus Oates, that graduate of a continental Jesuit seminary, was a consequence rather than cause of fears which had been gathering momentum for a decade. As they were an early Stuart revival, so Oates would later testify that he had assembled the details of his story from what he had 'read in Sir Hammond L'Estrange's History of Charles the First'.[44] The result was not 'The Popish Plot', but 'The Plot Reviv'd'.[45] What *caused* these fears were those royal foreign and domestic policies which,

40 Stephen Baxter, *William III and the Defense of European Liberty 1650–1702* (New York 1966), p. 59.   41 Quoted in Lipson, 'Elections to the Exclusion Parliaments', p. 74.
42 Scott, 'Popish Plot', pp. 107–8.   43 Kenyon, *Popish Plot*, jacket; *The Popish Plot*, p. 54.
44 *The Popish Plot*, p. 57.
45 *The Plot Reviv'd: or a Memorial of the late and present Popish Plots* (London, April 1680); Scott, 'Popish Plot', pp. 115–20; and Scott, *Restoration Crisis*, pp. 28–38.

throughout the 1670s, gave English protestants every reason for concern. About these royal duplicity provided no reassurance. This was the king who assured his parliament in 1675:

> I know you have heard much of my alliance with France, and I believe it hath been very strangely misrepresented to you, as if there were certain secret articles of dangerous consequence, but . . . I assure you there is no other treaty with France, either before or since, not already printed, which shall not be made known to a committee of this House.[46]

How, then, are these policies to be explained?

FEAR FOR MONARCHY: CHARLES II AND FRANCE

Here again the key contexts appear to have been fear and insecurity, understood in the context of restoration memory. Fear for the monarchy was a constant of seventeenth-century English kingship. How much more reason for it was there, in the mind of a king, once a penniless exile, whose father had been publicly murdered by the people over whom he now reigned?

Here as elsewhere it is possible to be misled by the political theatre of the restoration process. This was its intention: to imply continuity where there had been interruption, and confidence where there was none. None of this accurately conveys the mentality of a king who was astonished to have been called back across the water, and who spent the first year of his reign getting up at four o'clock every morning, determined to use every minute allowed to him. This gave way to a more enduring principle of kingship: survival; a determination 'not to go on his travels again'.[47]

One interpretation of Charles' French alliance entails suggesting that the religious promises in the secret treaty were not serious. They were cynical devices to secure the receipt of annual French pensions, and spoils from the Dutch, for whom (partly on account of their republicanism, partly of the defeat of 1665–7) Charles felt a 'pathological hatred'.[48] It is true that

---

46 Charles II, *His Majesties Gracious Speech to both Houses of Parliament Jan 7 1674 [1675]*, pp. 5–6; Scott, 'Popish Plot'.

47 John Miller, 'The Potential for Absolutism in Later Stuart England', *History* 69 (1984), p. 195.

48 Ronald Hutton, 'The Making of the Secret Treaty of Dover', *Historical Journal* 29, 2 (1986); Hutton, *Charles II*, chs. 10–11; Miller, *Charles II*, p. 194.

France's break from the Netherlands in 1670–2 must have appeared to present a tempting target. It is equally clear from subsequent negotiations that the French subsidies were important to Charles. This seems insufficient to explain, however, not only promises that were extraordinary in themselves, but the decision to prefer the support of a foreign prince to that of the king's own governing elite.

John Miller, while agreeing that Charles' policies were self-interested and erratic, has also spoken of 'what appeared to him sound diplomatic and geopolitical' reasons for the pro-French policy.[49] These embraced the advantages of alliance with Europe's leading military power, and centred immediately upon Britain's share from the planned dismemberment of the Netherlands. While there is again truth in this, there remains much it does not explain. From another point of view, held by many of his subjects, geopolitically the king's policies were insanely irresponsible. The secret treaty was a grand hostage to fortune which tied Charles' hands in relation to France for the rest of the reign. Most important is the king's apparent indifference not only to the probable local reaction to this cynical destruction of a key protestant ally, but to the manifest longer-term dangers of this assistance in the augmentation of French power.

It is against this background that a further line of explanation is necessary. One reason for Charles' indifference to the fears of his subjects may be that he had fears of his own. Recent analyses have emphasised the political insecurity of the court, and of the king in particular, during the decade of the 1670s. That period was punctuated by his talk, in particular to French ambassadors, about the danger of a new rebellion. When he was forced to back down over the accompanying *Declaration of Indulgence* and to pull out of the Dutch war in 1673, he spoke as if he had narrowly escaped a rebellion.[50] When thereafter the Commons became particularly restive over unabated French expansion, he asked Louis why he couldn't give up a town or two to save him from his father's fate, or from being 'chased from his kingdom' again. When the Commons produced an *Address* on 25 May 1677 calling for an alliance with the United Provinces, Charles responded, as his father and grandfather had done, by accusing the lower house of an unprecedented invasion of his prerogative.[51] Most importantly, as anger and alarm mounted during the decade Charles refused to change course because, first,

49 Miller, *Charles II*, p. 233.   50 *Ibid.*, pp. 219–20.
51 Marvell, *Growth of Popery*, pp. 141–8.

his opponents were out to destroy his power and 'take over the government'; and so, secondly, he could not afford to abandon France as 'the only security he has'. This is the only way to make sense of that most remarkable of all royal protestations, to Ruvigny: that Charles 'alone was standing up for France's interests, against his entire kingdom'.[52]

When the restoration crisis came, accordingly, it was what both the king and his brother had been expecting for some time. One of the clauses in the Secret Treaty of Dover about which Charles appears to have been very serious was the promise of French military support for the English monarchy against parliament and people 'should they rise against it'. His response to the crisis when it came was to appeal to Louis to be rescued from it, if not militarily then fiscally, an appeal not initially but eventually heard.[53]

It thus does indeed appear to be the case that behind all other considerations the French alliance was there to provide Charles with security against his own people. In the words of Halifax: 'he did not perhaps think so much of his Subjects as they might wish'.[54] During the breakdown in this relationship in 1678 the king told Barillon that he would refuse no French conditions for support; that he would rather depend on Louis XIV than on his own people.[55] Charles could use his prerogative control of foreign policy to accept either of two dependencies. It was entirely understandable, if equally obviously destructive, in the context of memory of the period 1618–60, if dependence upon France should appear to offer greater security as well as freedom.

In the 1620s we encountered a comparable situation, combining perceived military and religious danger abroad; royal failure to oppose this giving way to alliance with it; popish policies and inclinations at home; and parliamentary protest giving way to government without parliaments. The first result was a weak and defensive king allying with catholic authoritarianism abroad as a response to his perceived inability to rule at home. The second, when the summoning of a new parliament could no longer be avoided, was a major domestic crisis.

Ronald Hutton has argued that the key to Charles' religious preferences was a preoccupation with the security of his power.[56] This suggests that in this respect at least he was no different from his father. This did little to undermine an inclination to catholicism, since, as he explained to a French

---

52 Miller, *Charles II*, p. 244.   53 Scott, *Restoration Crisis*, pp. 70, 123.

54 Savile (Halifax), *A Character of Charles II*, in *Works*, vol. II, p. 493.

55 Knights, *Politics and Opinion*, p. 41.   56 Hutton, 'The Religion of Charles II'.

ambassador, 'no other creed matches so well with the absolute dignity of Kings'.[57] We should accordingly understand the persistent inclination of the Stuart monarchy to catholicism in the context of the dysfunctionally diminished state of seventeenth-century monarchical power. In public it informed at various times either the patronage or persecution of dissent. His reminder to others that his father had died for the Church of England tallies with what we know of the impact upon him of that event. Any suggestion of personal adherence to that church, however, is difficult to square with an apparent preparedness to promise conversion for £160,000.

This suggests that there is no reason to take the explosive religious clauses of the treaty any less seriously than the rest. Whether through political calculation or belief Charles appears to have been personally committed to catholicism. The cause of catholicism in England he understood to be connected to that for liberty of conscience, which he had promised at Breda and to which he was not hostile. His estimate of the political constituency available for this reorientation may have involved an overestimate of the number of dissenters which was common at this time. But it also registered the intense contemporary debate concerning a religious settlement the stability of which we have overestimated.[58] All this appears to supply the context for Charles' statement in 1670 to Ruvigny that 'he too is persuaded that his realm will never be at peace if liberty of conscience is not accorded to all the principal sects, as he himself desires; and . . . he believes that by giving [this liberty] to others, they will not take it ill accordingly when he also takes it for himself'.[59] Both restoration memory and the European context had worked to perpetuate and reinvigorate old fears. During the 1670s these were once again set upon a collision course. The last, but not least important, was fear of arbitrary government.

FEAR FOR PARLIAMENTS: ARBITRARY GOVERNMENT

'Lay popery flat', said Sir Henry Capel in 1680, 'and there is an end to arbitrary government.' With the reappearance of popery could arbitrary government be far behind? On the face of it the belief in the return of arbitrary government in the 1670s may seem surprising, for two reasons. One is that,

---

57 *Ibid.*, p. 230.

58 Gary de Krey, 'Rethinking the Restoration: Dissenting Cases for Conscience 1667–1672', *Historical Journal* 38, 1 (1995).

59 Public Record Office, London, Baschet transcript 31/3, no. 125, 4 August 1670.

unlike in 1629–40, parliaments stayed in being throughout the decade. The other is that parliament did succeed in 1673 in forcing the king to abandon his military and religious experiments. Thereafter a new minister was appointed (Thomas Osborne, Earl of Danby) who made the cultivation of parliaments and intolerant protestantism central to his strategy of reconstruction.[60] Yet in every respect these developments were cosmetic. They signalled no alteration of royal inclinations, or of what had been revealed about them. Indeed they may have increased distrust, partly by providing a public layer of policy through which duplicitous contrary royal manoeuvrings were visible; partly by being directed to the reconstruction of a royal power that was no longer trusted; and above all by failing to disguise after 1673 the ineffectuality of parliaments themselves. In the face of continued French expansion, parliament was desperate for war. This Danby could promise, but could not deliver.

This was the political struggle which dominated the period 1673–8. Fear for parliaments under Charles I had not developed during the absence of parliaments. It had developed during the struggle of 1625–9, marked by dissolutions and prorogations, during which parliament's religious and military objectives had been repeatedly frustrated. Until 1679 Charles did not suspend parliaments themselves, but new parliaments. In their place he created the second 'Long Parliament' of the century, and managed it by adjournments and (particularly) prorogations. By these means, from 1673 to 1678, parliament was kept in being but largely out of session. As pressure began to build, and tempers to fray, attacks followed both on this government by prorogation and on this second Long Parliament.

One pamphlet of 1675, against 'Encroaching Prerogative', both echoed the parliamentary arguments of the first crisis of parliaments, and anticipated those of the next. It insisted that 'Parliaments ought not to be Prorogued, Adjourned, or Dissolved, till all Petitions are heard, and the Aggrievances of the People redressed.' Another insisted that it was against 'the nature of Representatives to be continued for so long a time; and those that choose them, not to be allowed frequent opportunity, of changing [them]'. A third elaborated upon this point by suggesting that all those in the country 'from 21 years of age to 37' had been disenfranchised.[61] This

---

60 Andrew Browning, *Thomas Osborne, Earl of Danby* (3 vols., London 1944–51).

61 *Letter from a Parliamentman to his Friend* (1675), *The Debates or Arguments for Dissolving this Present Parliament* (1676), *The Long Parliament Dissolved* (1676), quoted in Jason Maloy, 'Representation in English Political Thought 1660–1678', MPhil. thesis, Cambridge 1997, pp. 33–5.

argument was broadened by Lord (Denzil) Holles in 1676 into something suspiciously like an attack on the first restoration settlement. 'As this Parliament represented the sickly times, in which they were chosen, when the People of England were in a kind of Delirium or Dotage; so a new Parliament would represent a People restored to their Wits.' This was not likely, however, 'because they never dare call a Parliament to represent the present state of England'.[62]

One result was the *Address* to the king of November 1675 calling for a dissolution of the present parliament. This was viewed as an ominous attempted encroachment upon the royal prerogative and met by a further prorogation of fifteen months. There followed the remarkable attempt, sponsored by Buckingham, Shaftesbury and others, to suggest that the present parliament was actually dissolved anyway.[63] This resulted in the trial of four lords (the others were Salisbury and Wharton) before their House on 15 February 1677 for 'proposinge, Assertinge and maintaininge that this p[arliament] is dissolved'.[64] The eventual political explosion came in late 1678. On 11 December letters were read to the Commons by an ex-ambassador to Paris, Ralph Montagu. These related to secret negotiations conducted between Charles and Louis XIV in May of that year.

The letters were from Charles to Louis, and were signed by both the king and Danby. They reminded Louis of the anti-French fervour which had built up in parliament throughout the decade. They suggested that the king could not keep such feeling, and the parliaments through which it was expressed, bottled up forever on the sort of salary France was paying. If Louis wanted parliaments of that temper further prorogued, he would have to pay something more realistic, something that recognised that it would be years before he could expect to call upon them again. The sum mentioned was six million livres a year for three years.[65]

---

62 Lord Holles, *A Letter to Mons Van B de M—* (1676), quoted in Maloy, 'Representation in English Political Thought', p. 35.
63 J. R. Jones, *Country and Court: England 1658–1714* (London 1978), pp. 191–2.
64 Downing College Library, Cambridge, MS Z.4.17/22: 'Transcripts out of ye Journall books of ye Lords' house'.
65 The letters were subsequently published by order of the House. 'In case the Conditions of Peace shall be accepted, the King expects to have Six Millions of Livres Yearly, for three Years, from the time that this Agreement shall be signed . . . because it will be two, or three years before he can hope to find his Parliament in humor to give him supplies; after having made Peace with France': *An Explanation of the Lord Treasurers Letter to Mr Montague . . . March 25th* (London 1679), p. 4.

Members were stunned. 'I wonder', said one, 'the House sits so silent when they see themselves sold for six millions of livres to the French.' 'After four or five years [when] we have had nothing but Prorogations and Adjournments of the Parliament without doing anything to purpose . . . [and] can get no Bills of Popery passed', the House had now discovered why.[66] 'How clearly', another wrote,

does it now appear as if the old Arts of Adjournments and Prorogations had not been sufficient, it is projected now to let a lease of Parliaments to the French for three years; and 'tis reasonably guest they would have been out of humor to grant supplies when supplies were gotten from others to destroy them; but how after three years the Parliament should be brought in humor, is not to be supposed: 'tis more probable the lease would have been renewed.[67]

This was not only arbitrary government, but delivery of the government to a foreign power. The most important tract to emerge from the ensuing crisis was John Locke's *Two Treatises of Government*, the classic seventeenth-century polemic against arbitrary government. This listed among the four ways by which arbitrary 'Governments are dissolved from within':

Secondly, When the Prince hinders the Legislature from assembling in its due time, or from acting freely, pursuant to those ends, for which it was constituted [and] . . . Fourthly, the delivery also of the People into the subjection of a Foreign Power . . . by the Prince.[68]

The two plots, against protestantism and parliaments, were intertwined. The connection was the king's relationship to France. These letters 'agree . . . with Coleman's Letters . . . This army was raised for a French War, and so many hundred thousand pounds given for that purpose, and yet we had no War! Money given to disband the army, and that not done! The Popish Plot discovered at that time! And all runs parallel.' 'I hope Gentlemen's eyes are now open, by the design on foot to destroy the Government and our Liberties.'[69]

Parliament's initial response was what it had been in 1640: the impeachment of the first minister, amid a widely held belief in his preparedness to use an army to establish the intended popish despotism. 'Now when this

66 Grey, *Debates 1667–1694*, vol. VI, p. 355 (19 December).
67 *An Examination of the Impartial State of the Case of the Earl of Danby* (London 1680).
68 *Locke's Two Treatises*, p. 427; Scott, 'Law of War'.
69 Grey, *Debates 1667–1694*, vol. VI, pp. 348–9.

great person is on the point to make Parliaments useless, it is treason', concluded one member. 'His crime is great', agreed another, 'and tends to the subversion of the nation, and so it is, when the King shall have no Parliaments.' The vote to impeach Danby was carried the same day (19 December).[70] When this forced the king to abandon not only his parliamentary manager but his Long Parliament itself, all the landmarks of customary restoration politics disappeared.

By 1678 contemporaries had detected three signs of arbitrary government. The first was Danby's style of parliamentary management which consisted in part of using secret service money to buy the attendance of loyal supporters ('pensioners') in the House of Commons. The second was the 'standing army' raised (in 1678) for use against France but not used, and not disbanded. This (which both Danby and the Duke of York had indeed discussed using, if necessary, for domestic political purposes) added a Cromwellian dimension to the spectre of arbitrary rule.[71] By 1679, however, Danby had been unseated and the army was eventually disbanded. These two secondary indicators of arbitrary government fell to one side. What remained at the core of the succeeding political crisis was the third: the king's continued attempts to frustrate and manipulate parliaments by prorogations and dissolutions.

CONCLUSION

Thus the restoration crisis was triggered by the coming together of general fears with specific revelations. Moreover the author of those revelations was none other than Louis XIV himself. Having set the agenda of British politics for eight years it was he who now threw it into turmoil. This was partly to punish Charles for his attempts at blackmail, but above all to destroy Danby, who had enraged Louis partly by his anti-French (if empty) military gestures of early 1678, and principally by the Stuart–Orange marriage alliance of November 1677.[72]

All of this was achieved by furnishing Ralph Montagu with the information (and promise of payment) which led to his revelations in the House.[73]

---

70 *Ibid.*, pp. 353, 355, 358.
71 James Dalrymple, *Memoirs of Great Britain and Ireland* (2 vols., London 1773), vol. II, Appendix, p. 143; Scott, *Restoration Crisis*, p. 110.
72 Scott, *Restoration Crisis*, pp. 38–43, 113–20.
73 Public Record Office, London, Baschet transcript 31/3, no. 141, p. 100.

It was as a result of this action, and the withdrawal of French support for three years, that Charles found himself forced into a quite unaccustomed alternative dependence upon a series of parliaments which he could not control. His imperative was to end that dependence and recover French support, before being forced into concessions by which the monarchy would be damaged. That of his opponents was to translate that dependence, while it lasted, into real security for protestantism and parliaments.

Thus the restoration crisis was a struggle for monarchy, protestantism and parliaments; for those very things so recently plucked by restoration from the wreckage of the troubles. It fully revealed the vulnerability of that settlement while old fears remained unburied. The ensuing struggle for monarchy is the subject of chapter 19. Our focus in the next chapter is the second seventeenth-century crisis of protestantism and parliaments.

8

Restoration crisis 1678–83

> Prorogue or Dissolve them before anything be finished, and thus
> Parliaments will be made useless, and this being done, it will not be
> long before they become burdensome, and then away with them for
> good and all.
>
> Henry Booth, *A Speech for the Sitting of Parliament* (1680)[1]

INTRODUCTION: THE UNRAVELLING

The struggle for protestantism and parliaments between 1678 and 1683 took place in many arenas. These included the court (where ministerial rivalries were important), the Houses of Lords and Commons, parliamentary elections, the judiciary, the press, relationships with European ambassadors, the government of the city of London, and its streets and coffee houses. It also therefore took place on several levels. Those which were most visible or have received most attention were not necessarily the most important in determining its outcome.

This upheaval exhibited both a severity and a complexity which have only recently begun to be understood:

He that would give a Punctual and Particular Account of all the Narratives, Discourses, Tryals, Executions, Speeches, Votes, Accusations, Examinations, Commitments, Tumultuous Elections, Petitions, Ryots, Libels, and Seditious Attempts of all Sorts, during the said time, must write a History more Voluminous than Fox or Hollinshead.[2]

This is because it involved an unravelling of the restoration settlement. From the outset this left contemporaries not only confronting dangerous

---

1 Henry Booth, 1st Earl of Warrington, *The Works of Henry late L. Delamer and Earl of Warrington* (London 1694), pp. 123–4; I am grateful to Mark Taylor for this reference.
2 *A Compendious View of the Late Tumults and Troubles* (1685), quoted in Knights, *Politics and Opinion*, p. 2.

problems in the present, but staring back into the abyss of the troubles as memory. It was this fact which eventually ended the crisis. But it did not do so before the question informing restoration had again been put: would the country be governed by a parliamentary dictatorship or a monarchy?

To recover this crisis it is necessary to pay simultaneous attention to ideological continuity and practical fluidity. The principal issues were popery and arbitrary government, in the present and as remembered from the past. If these did not change, stances in relation to them did, in response to a rapidly moving sequence of events. Ideological polarisation was, accordingly, not a permanent state in this crisis (though vestiges of it remained) but a stage within it.

One arena of the resulting upheaval was that of parliamentary politics. As the obstruction of parliaments had been the principal manifestation of arbitrary government, so the royal powers in question remained crucial throughout the crisis. Thus the struggle within parliaments, which reached a climax between November 1680 and January 1681, entailed dissolutions (in 1678, 1679 and 1681), a period of continuous prorogation (September 1679 to October 1680) and the eventual abandonment of parliaments altogether (1681–5).

A second, equally important manifestation of the crisis occurred in print. The refusal of the House of Commons to renew the Licensing Act which expired in 1679 assisted in the breach of restoration controls. The result was a flood of polemical literature rivalling in size and quality that of the 1640s and 1650s.[3] In addition there was considerable overlap in content (including republication). This was partly a consequence of the return of the same issues: the most celebrated exchange occurred between a work written by Sir Robert Filmer in 1628 and opponents who related this defence of arbitrary government to the 1620s.[4] This literature, including published parliamentary and judicial proceedings, newspapers, ballads, pamphlets and books, is our principal source for an understanding of the issues of the crisis. In this arena occurred the struggle for public opinion. By 1680, in the wake of the troubles, had come the re-emergence of radicalism.

3 Betty Behrens, 'The Whig Theory of the Constitution in the Reign of Charles II', *Cambridge Historical Journal* 7 (1941–3); Richard Ashcraft, *Revolutionary Politics and John Locke's Two Treatises of Government* (Princeton 1987); Scott, *Restoration Crisis*; Knights, *Politics and Opinion*.

4 Algernon Sidney, *Discourses*, in *Sydney on Government*, p. 5; *Locke's Two Treatises*, p. 161.

Alongside parliamentary and polemical activity, practical politics took many forms. There were the public demonstrations and processions to commemorate anniversaries like those of the Gunpowder Plot or Elizabeth's accession.[5] There was electioneering for parliaments (in 1679 twice and in 1681). There was petitioning on behalf of them (and for other purposes) which breached the limits laid down by the restoration Act Against Seditious and Tumultuous Petitioning. There was the revival of dissenting protestant religious worship, released from the restoration enforcement of uniformity. There was the continuous activity in coffee houses and taverns.

Finally there were three forces that made contributions of more specific importance. One was the civic politics of London: the election of its officers, and the use of its financial and political power. The second was associated judicial activity, an important focus for political propaganda and (lethal) action. The last was the impact upon the English situation made by external forces. These included not only, most importantly, France, which subsidised the crown's opponents (1678–80) and then the crown (1681–5). It also included another Scots rebellion (1679) and a feared Irish rebellion (1680–1), as well as a planned English rebellion (1681–3).

POPERY AND ARBITRARY GOVERNMENT (JANUARY–JULY 1679)

At the beginning of 1679, as in late 1640, alarm about popery and arbitrary government united the nation. During the first half of 1679 an isolated court had to accept not only a new parliament, but new ministers, a new Great Council, new policies and a series of imprisonments and executions (of 'popish plotters').

The initial focus for the struggle against arbitrary government in this period was Danby. As the accessible face of recent royal policy he came to be seen as the successor to Strafford (and Buckingham) and to deserve their fate. Agitation against Danby and popery dominated the elections of January–February and the proceedings of the resulting parliament.[6]

The plot was, as we have seen, 'The Plot Reviv'd'. England now felt itself to be the last 'bullwark of liberty, protestantism, and Christian faith in general, throughout the world: the main bank, that hinders the see of Rome from overwhelming all Christian nations with an universal inundation of

---

5 Harris, *London Crowds*; Cressy, *Bonfires and Bells*.   6 Scott, *Restoration Crisis*, p. 52.

tyranny and superstition'.[7] London, the major protestant city in Europe, now faced the 'cloud, which has long threatened this land . . . ready to break upon our heads in a storm of ruin and confusion'.[8] This was the last stage of 'the Holy War . . . not only here, but in Christendom: for Popery or Protestantisme must fall'.[9] This was understood to be 'a work . . . so great, and their apprehension so glorious, that the most eminent of the popish clergy in Europe were engaged in it'.[10] 'The design . . . was . . . by fire and sword so perfectly to reduce all his majesty's dominions to the Roman Catholic religion, that . . . [all] protestant[s] . . . should have been extirpated, both root and branch.'[11]

Concern once again focused not on local catholics, who were a known (and small) quantity, but on 'foreigners' in general, and infiltrating 'Jesuits' in particular. 'I have been informed', said the king, 'of a design against my person, by the Jesuits . . . and . . . will take as much care as I can to prevent all manner of practices by that sort of men, and of others too who have been tampering in a high degree with foreigners.'[12] This last remark referred to those opposition conspirators who had helped trigger the crisis by appropriating the crown's own French support: those 'agitators . . . who meddle with matters of state and parliament . . . and carry on their pernicious designs by a most dangerous correspondency with foreign nations'.[13]

Hundreds of tracts appeared describing the 'damnable and pernicious practices of the Jesuits, those pests and incendiaries of all Christendom'; 'those fire-brands of all Europe'; 'the inhuman practices of Jesuits . . . towards protestants at home and abroad'; 'the haughtiness, avarice, and other enormities of that order'; the 'unheard of popish cruelties towards protestants beyond seas'.[14] The purpose of 'that order' was understood to be to 'intermix themselves in temporal affairs, to the disturbance of states and kingdoms';[15] to perpetrate 'rapes and massacres . . . murdered kings,

7 Bedloe, *Narrative and Impartial Discovery*, p. 2.   8 *Humble Address of the Commons.*

9 *A Speech Made by a True Protestant English Gentleman To Incourage the City of London to Petition for the Sitting of the Parliment* [London 1680], p. 2.   10 *The Popish Plot*, p. 1.

11 *Ibid.*, p. 55.

12 Charles II, *His Majesties most Gracious Speech . . . to Parliament* (London, 21 October 1678), p. 4.   13 *Ibid.*, p. 14.

14 *The Popish Wonder, being Truth Confest by Papists* (London 1680); Richard Dugdale, *A Most Serious Expostulation With Severall of my Fellow Citizens* (London 1680), p. 1; *The Narrative of Lawrence Mowbray of Leeds* (London 1680), p. 299.

15 *The Narrative of Robert Bolron . . . Concerning the Late Horrid Popish Plot* (London 1680), p. 9.

poisoning and devestations, tortures, and all the cruel rage that the infernal legions . . . could prompt . . . the barbarous executioners of tyrant Rome, disperse themselves abroad . . . [to] gather in the slain to fill her Babylonish cup with reeking blood from tender hearts'.[16]

Accordingly, many of the catholics who were tried between 1678 and 1680 were executed simply for being 'Jesuits and priests'; 'Jesuits in England'; 'Jesuits, that come from beyond the seas'. In most trials 'proof' of Jesuitism was taken to be proof of participation in the plot. One George Busby was hanged in Derby, for instance, simply for being, by the testimony of locals 'a reputed priest and Jesuit in the neighbour-hood'.[17] This was because the *raison d'être* of being a Jesuit was taken to be participation in the counter-reformation design. The fact of that design, in turn, was not requiring of proof, or susceptible to disproof. Thus all trials began with a lengthy recitation of its history.

This reminded the jury of what 'is not unknown to most persons, nay to every one amongst us, that hath the least observed the former times, how that ever since the reformation there hath been a design carried on by priests and Jesuits, that came from beyond the seas . . . to subvert the government, and destroy the protestant religion established here in England'.[18] This involved the expected characters: the pope, the French king and at least 'four Irish persons';[19] the expected equipment: poison, fire, daggers and the sword;[20] and the expected *dénouement*: an invasion followed by the customary slaughter. All the officers in charge of this invasion 'were French and Irish, and not one English'.[21] It was only following this recitation that the trials turned to the matter of the individual on trial. As the attorney-general Sir William Jones put it at the trial of William Lord Stafford before the House of Lords in 1680: 'My Lords, we have now done with our proofs for the first general head that we opened, which was to make it out, that there was a plot in general. We come now to our partic-ular evidence against this very lord.'[22] There remained only to link the victim with one of the known ingredients of the general design. As John Kenyon demonstrated, the trials were not judicial events at all. They were

16 *An Answer to Blundell the Jesuits Letter* (London 1679).

17 *The Tryal of George Busby* (London 1681).

18 *The Tryals of William Ireland, Thomas Pickering, and John Grove* (London, December 1678), p. 11.　　19 Bedloe, *Narrative and Impartial Discovery*, p. 14.　　20 *Ibid.*, p. 1.

21 *The Popish Plot*, p. 55.

22 *The Tryal of William Viscount Stafford for High Treason* (London 1681), p. 39.

acts of political theatre designed to address, and to that extent assuage, a public concern.[23]

The tone of the House of Commons' pursuit of Danby may be summarised by the remark of Sir Henry Beaumont, that 'If the Treasurer be not suspended in [one] sense, I hope he may be in another.' In fact the king did accept his minister's resignation, and send him to the Tower, where he remained for the rest of the crisis. Thereafter, however, he attempted to protect him with a royal pardon. This the Commons refused to accept. The subsequent search for ways to proceed soon arrived at the method of 'Tryal ... warranted by [the] late precedent ... [of] Lord Strafford's case'. 'Can any man', it was demanded, 'think that the method of Tryal is altered?' This effort was led by men who had actually been involved in Strafford's trial (Serjeant Maynard, Sir Charles Harbord) or witnesses to it as members of the 1641 House (Sir Anthony Irby, Sir Henry Ford). A committee was named to draw up proceedings on this basis, in conjunction with the House of Lords, with which the latter refused to co-operate. A new account of Strafford's trial was published.[24]

Among other manifestations of arbitrary government the standing army, yet to be disbanded, was identified as 'a Limb of Popery, set up by this great Minister'. The navy too was 'one of the branches of the plot. We have a Land-Plot; this is a Sea-Plot.'[25] An erring cleric was compared by Colonel Silius Titus (a key figure in this period) to 'Maynwaring'; in the following session similar references would be made to Laud. The pursuit of arbitrary ministers was extended to Lauderdale, who was the subject of a parliamentary address, though it was observed that the subjects of previous addresses had more often been promoted than removed. This echoed not only Marvell's *Growth of Popery* (1677) (It is 'a Modern Maxime, That no State Minister ought to be punished, but especially upon Parliamentary Applications')[26] but also the Commons debates on the Petition of Right (1628), which had made the same complaint against Sibthorp and Maynwaring ('a parliamentary complaint against a clergyman seemed the surest way to give him a bishopric').[27]

23 Kenyon, *Popish Plot.*
24 Grey, *Debates 1667–1694*, vol. VII, pp. 2, 20–23; *An Impartial Account of the Arraignment, Trial and Condemnation of Thomas Late Earl of Stafford 1641* (London 1679).
25 Grey, *Debates 1667–1694*, vol. VII, pp. 28, 30.　　26 Marvell, *Growth of Popery*, pp. 51–2.
27 Cust, 'News and Politics', p. 86; Derek Hirst, *Authority and Conflict: England 1603–1658* (London 1986), p. 157.

The week-long dispute which began the session, over the appointment of the speaker, followed from the same Commons concern 'not to yield their right' in anything. This was particularly crucial 'Now Popery and foreign fears are upon us! I have ever observed, that Prerogative once gained was never got back again, and our Privileges lost are never restored.' 'I am one of those that have sat here long', observed Mr Garroway, 'and have seen great Miscarriages, Prorogations and Dissolutions . . . I would not give the King offence, but not part with one hair of our right. If you will not stand to it here, you will have a great many things put upon you.' To the fears of renewed prorogation or dissolution such intransigence provoked, reassurance was offered: 'That [Short Parliament] called in 1640 sat but three weeks, and the King repented half an hour after he had dissolved it, and then another was called . . . there is no danger though we are sent away.'[28]

The issue of the succession made its first appearance on 27 April, as the Commons considered the relationship, raised by Coleman's letters, between the plot and the Duke of York. The important intervention came from the Earl of Shaftesbury's client William Russell: 'If we do not do something relating to the Succession, we must resolve . . . to be Papists, or burn.'[29] The result was a motion stating that York's known catholic religion had given the 'greatest encouragement' to the plot, thus naming him in relationship to the religious, as Danby and Lauderdale had been named in relation to the political, plot.

The revival, within this context, of that succession issue by which Elizabeth's reign had been plagued, was highly significant in two ways. It reconnected the troubles with the first period of European counter-reformation danger, in the context of which English and Scots anxieties had similarly focused upon a threatened catholic Stuart succession.[30] Hereafter the succession issue remained part of the history of the troubles, leading to the revival of Oaths of Association (1680, 1691) and culminating in the Act of Succession of 1701. The other special reason for contemporary interest in this issue was that the revival of the House of Commons' claim to be empowered to determine the succession on behalf of the confessionally defined commonwealth struck at the recent constitutional fiction of restoration. In practice the monarchy had been reconstructed by the same powers by which it had been destroyed: the army and parliament. In law,

28 Grey, *Debates 1667–1694*, vol. VII, pp. 407–8, 427.   29 *Ibid.*, p. 137.

30 Alford, 'William Cecil'; Mortimer Levine, *The Early Elizabethan Succession Question 1558–1568* (Stanford 1966); Collinson, 'Elizabethan Exclusion Crisis'.

however, the monarchy had not been destroyed: Charles II owed his restoration to the exercise of its powers solely to the hereditary principle.

The court's response to the exclusion proposal was the remarkable offer of limitations on the powers of a popish successor. This was objected to by the Duke of York himself, as a counter-plot to 'drop the Government more gently into a Commonwealth'.[31] Its patron at court was Halifax, described by Burnet as 'full of commonwealth notions . . . and studied to infuse into some a zeal for a commonwealth . . . he has read the Roman authors much and delights mightily in them'.[32] When, two weeks later, the House debated the succession 'the weightiest speeches . . . were made against the exclusion proposal'.[33] When, ten days after that, an exclusion bill was introduced, it was carried for a further reading (207–128) though a third of the House abstained. We will never know what the outcome of this session would have been had the political situation not then been transformed by a series of dramatic developments. The first was the provocative prorogation of 27 May. This had the effect, as intended, of erasing all the proceedings against the plot, Danby, Lauderdale, the 'Popish Lords' in the Tower and the succession.

Ten days later the political temperature was raised further by an uprising in Scotland. This was a rebellion by local protestants against a 'popish' and 'arbitrary' tyranny which, to judge by its attacks on Lauderdale, must have commanded considerable sympathy in the House. The Scots did nothing to lessen the historical resonance of their action by issuing a *Declaration* calling for the armed defence of the 'True Protestant Religion', and 'the obtaining of a Free and unlimited Parliament . . . in order to the Redressing our aforesaid Grievances, for preventing the Imminent Danger of Popery, and Extirpating of Prelacy from amongst us'.[34] Only a few days earlier Algernon Sidney had written that 'Scotland is every day likely to be in arms . . . and may probably be of as much importance in the troubles that are now likely to fall upon us, as they were in the beginning of the last.'[35]

31 Quoted in J. Clarke, *The Life of James II* (2 vols., London 1816), vol. I, p. 635.
32 British Library Add MS 63,057, vol. II, p. 7.
33 J. R. Jones, *Country and Court*, p. 208.
34 *The Declaration of the Rebels Now in Arms in the West of Scotland* (London 1679). This was followed by reprints of the Solemn League and Covenant, and other Scots declarations of the period 1637–40.
35 Sidney, *Letters of A. Sydney to Henry Savile Ambassador in France*, in *Sydney on Government*, p. 29.

It was therefore crucial that on this occasion Charles succeeded militarily where his father had failed, quashing this revolt without resummoning parliament. He did this despite a public campaign in London pointing out that the Long Parliament had made war against Scotland illegal without parliamentary approval, and demanding the recall of the two Houses. When, thereafter, the still prorogued parliament was dissolved, a new, deeper phase of the English crisis began.

POLARISATION (THE LONG PROROGATION 1679–80)

For although the king immediately called new elections, these simply repeated, with more feeling, the pattern of the last ('the same men being', as Sidney put it, 'something sharpened'[36]). This being the case, Charles had no intention – until its members had come to their senses – of allowing the parliament to meet. The consequence was that key phase in this struggle for parliaments which we may call the long prorogation, and the beginning of the polarisation this would cause. It is from this phase of the crisis that we may date the emergence of the preconditions for the second restoration (1681–5). For the king's confrontational decision to return to government by prorogation had two effects. One was to invite confrontation with, and radicalisation among, his opponents. The other, partly in consequence, was to end the political consensus, by beginning to attract a party to his side.

That the new elections followed exactly the pattern, and issues, of their predecessor, was not accidental. It was a matter of parliamentary policy. Electors were advised:

choose the same Members again that serv'd you faithfully the last time; since in so doing you will take off that fear of Dissolutions, which is of such fatal consequence in a Parliament, as also oblige them to serve you more cheerfully ever after . . . and do not be alarmed or troubled at frequent Prorogations or Dissolutions; since if you persist in the same steady course you have already begun, it will but fall more heavily upon the heads of those, that are the contrivers of the Misunderstandings between his Gracious Majesty, and his most faithful subjects.[37]

As this election pamphlet (*A Character of Popery and Arbitrary Government*) made clear, the fundamental issue remained the same. But dissolutions had now joined prorogations as the devices of arbitrary rule. 'Now in this Government by parliaments there hath been found out ways of

---

36 *Ibid.*, p. 49.   37 Philolaus, *Character of Popery and Arbitrary Government*, p. 5.

corruption and that is when either they sit too long, too seldom, or are too frequently dissolv'd . . . such frequent dissolutions must of necessity ruine us.'[38] Thus when, over the following sixteen months of parliament-less rule, political opinion began to radicalise and divide, it did so over this issue. How far was it permissible to press against this use of the royal prerogative for the meeting of the elected parliament? This was not an abstract matter: the salvation of the nation from popery depended upon it. But this had equally been the case in 1640. It was against this background that there occurred the huge procession in London on 17 November 1679, reputedly attended by 150,000 people, to mark Elizabeth's accession day. This was a period saturated in general – as the 1620s had been, and for the same reason – with Elizabethan nostalgia.[39]

It was around this same issue that the petitioning campaign of 1679–80 developed. Petitioning had been a crucial force in the 1640s. Controls upon 'tumultuous petitioning' had accordingly been a focal aspect of the restoration settlement. Now it was around the petitioning campaign initiated against the long prorogation that the first clear national division developed. This was between petitioners and 'abhorrers' (of those petitions). The petitions demanded 'not merely . . . that Parliament should be allowed to meet in January, but also that it should be permitted to sit until security was obtained for the King's person and the protestant religion'.[40] Without the sitting of parliament, they insisted, popery would come in.[41] The (to parliamentarians) deeply offensive response received from abhorring addresses was 'That petitioning for the sitting of the Parliament was the seed and spawn of Rebellion, and the Principles of 1641'.[42]

The peak period of petitioning was December 1679–January 1680. Petitions came from 'every populous town', and eventually the counties; the city of London petitioned on January 13th.[43] When it was eventually permitted to sit the following October the Commons declared: 'Next to popery,

38 *Ibid.*, p. 8.
39 See for instance Elizabeth I, *The Last Speech and Thanks of Queen Elizabeth of Ever Blessed Memory, to her Last Parliament, after her Delivery from the Popish Plots etc [2 October 1601]* (London 1679).   40 J. R. Jones, *The First Whigs*, pp. 112–13.
41 North, *Examen*, pp. 541–2.
42 Grey, *Debates 1667–1694*, vol. VII, pp. 380, 389–91.
43 North, *Examen*, pp. 541–2; *The Humble Petition of the City of London for the Sitting of this present Parliament Prorogu'd to the Twentieth Instant* (London, 13 January 1680); Mark Knights, 'London's "Monster" Petition of 1680', *Historical Journal* 36, 1 (1993).

this matter of petitioning is the greatest point.' Abhorrers were pursued without mercy, and the resolution passed:

That it is . . . the undoubted Right of Subjects of England, to petition the King for the calling and sitting of Parliaments . . . [and] that to traduce such Petitioning . . . as tumultuous and seditious is to betray the Liberty of the Subject, and contributes to the design of subverting the ancient legal Constitution of this Kingdom, and introducing arbitrary power.[44]

Shaftesbury complained in the Lords that 'The prorogations, the dissolutions, the cutting short of Parliaments, not suffering them to have time or opportunity to look into anything, hath showed what reason we have to have confidence in this court.'[45] The issue was addressed by many pamphlets, among them *Vox Populi: or the People's Claim to their Parliament's Sitting* (1681), with its familiar complaint that 'Their Parliaments [have been] rendered so insignificant by these frequent Prorogations and Dissolutions.'[46] In the short term, however, the petitioning campaign was a failure. The continued suspension of parliamentary politics during 1680 provided the context for the second extraordinary development of this year.

For one immediate effect of it was the relocation of political energies into the civic context of London. This was a fact to which Charles responded in 1681 by the relocation of his last parliament to Oxford (a move customarily associated with outbreaks of the plague). The first sign of the radicalisation of London politics was the shrievalty election of July 1680. The shrievalty had played a crucial role in the pro-parliamentary realignment of London politics in 1641–2. One of the victorious candidates on this occasion was Slingsby Bethel, a notorious interregnum-era republican. 'There were', recorded another contemporary, 'a greate Party in ye Citty for makeing Slingsby Bethell and Mr Cornish Sheriffs, in opposition to Sir Wm Russell, Mr Box and Mr Nicholson three persons of more moderate tempers.'[47]

Despite the plea of Shaftesbury 'not to choose fanatics', Bethel and Cornish won by over a thousand votes. This prompted the remark from his client Lord Russell that 'he was sorry [Bethel] was chosen, for he was as

44 Grey, *Debates 1667–1694*, vol. VII, pp. 368–70.
45 Shaftesbury, *A Speech Made by a Noble Peer of the Realm [in 1680]* (1681), quoted in Ashcraft, *Revolutionary Politics*, p. 132.
46 *Vox Populi: or the People's Claim to their Parliament's Sitting* (London 1681), p. 15.
47 Cambridge University Library, Sel.2.118, marginal note, probably by Ralph Verney, on Philo-Patris, *A Seasonable Address to the . . . City of London* (London 1680).

great a Commonwealthsman as Algernon Sidney'.[48] The French ambassador Barillon reported that

Mr Algernon Sidney is a man of . . . very high designs, which tend to the establishment of a republic. He is in the party of the independents and other sectaries . . .
[who] were masters during the late troubles . . . they are strong in London . . . Mr
Sidney . . . is intimate with Mr [Sir William] Jones, who is a man of the greatest
knowledge in the laws of England . . . and it is through the intrigues of . . . Sidney that
one of the two sheriffs, named Bethel, has been elected.[49]

Sidney and Bethel had been republican co-conspirators in the Netherlands
in 1665–6. Burnet reported:

Bethel was a man of knowledge, and had written a very judicious book of princes;
but as he was a known republican in principle, so he was a sullen and wilful man;
and turned from the ordinary way of a Sheriffs living into the extreme of sordidness,
which was very unacceptable to the body of citizens, and proved a great prejudice to
the party.[50]

Bethel was a student of Dutch economic theory and thrift.[51] This 'sordidness' referred to his own attempted radical reformation of manners. This
took the form of the revival of certain 'ancient laws' limiting the shrievalty's
obligation to entertainment:

and I think no Laws are more properly called wholesome, than those which prohibit
the excess of feasting . . . how great an Enemie this great expence of time, in
Luxurious Eating and Drinking is, to that sober Industry, which is the rise and glory
of a Trading City.[52]

Roger North recorded: 'In the Year 1680, Bethel and Cornish were chosen
Sheriffs. The former used to walk about more like a Corncutter than Sheriff
of London. He kept no House, but lived upon Chops; whence it is prover-
bial, for not feasting, to Bethel the City.'[53]

Bethel's interest in starvation extended beyond the citizenry. The ways in
which the city government was able to influence the national political situation most directly were financial and judicial. Barillon's mention of Sidney's

---

48 B. E. Berry, *Life and Letters of Rachel Wriothesley, Lady Russell* (2 vols., London 1819), vol.
    II, pp. 28–9, 132–4.
49 Public Record Office, London, Baschet transcript, no. 147, pp. 402–3.
50 Gilbert Burnet, *History of my Own Time* (2 vols., Oxford 1823), pp. 242–3.
51 Scott, *English Republic*, ch. 13; Scott, *Restoration Crisis*, pp. 165–7.
52 Slingsby Bethel, *The Vindication of Slingsby Bethel Esq* (London 1681), pp. 5–8.
53 North, *Examen*, p. 93.

relationship both to Bethel and to Sir William Jones gives us a view of the crucial alliance. This was between the city and a similarly radicalised House of Commons, at last permitted to meet in October 1680, in which Jones was to be the most important figure. For behind the public face of politics a financial contest was taking place that would be the actual arbiter of the crisis. It was in relation to this that Jones held the belief, North reported, that 'the Crown must needs, at Length, truckle to the House of Commons . . . this Error being common to the whole Faction with whom he conversed'.[54]

The two most important sources of extra-parliamentary funding in this period were the city of London and the French crown. French funding had now been redirected to the court's opponents.[55] With the city also in hostile hands the crown's financial situation was precarious. Between 1679 and 1680 the king's continued use of his powers of dissolution and prorogation – his capacity, that is to say, to resist what he considered an attempt to establish parliamentary dictatorship – was dependent upon a financial solvency precariously maintained through unaccustomed austerity.

This was accompanied by a vigorous campaign for the restoration of French funding. In June 1679 Charles told Barillon that Louis 'must decide whether he wanted a republic or a monarchy in England. If he did not support the royal authority actively . . . nothing would prevent parliament from taking over control of foreign affairs and everything else.'[56] Barillon's own view was similarly that 'the Affairs of the Crown were low, and just lapsing into the total Arbitrariment of the Commons'.[57] Meanwhile Charles' opponents did everything possible to prevent the restoration of French help. In mid-1680 Sidney warned the French ambassador to the Netherlands, d'Avaux, 'that if the King of England, by the assistance of his Christian Majesty, should be able to do without his parliament, in that case, he would become absolute sovereign; and this would oblige them to make an alliance with the States General'.[58] Meanwhile d'Avaux reported that Sidney had claimed to an associate in the Netherlands

54 *Ibid.*, p. 510.
55 Dalrymple, *Memoirs of Great Britain and Ireland*, vol. II, Appendix; Public Record Office, London, Baschet transcript, nos. 140–56 (1678–83).
56 J. J. Jusserand, *Recueil des instructions données aux ambassadeurs et ministres de France*, vol. XXV, *Angleterre* (Paris 1929), p. 271.   57 North, *Examen*, p. 529.
58 D'Avaux, *Negotiations of Count d'Avaux* (4 vols., London 1756), vol. I, pp. 62–3; Scott, *Restoration Crisis*, ch. 6.

that the Parliament of England would not come to a reconciliation with the King of England, but upon these terms.

(i) That his Brittanic Majesty should renounce all right to prorogue his Parliament by his sole authority; because they pretended this was a power usurped for some years.

(ii) That his Majesty should also give up to Parliament the right of choosing general officers by sea and land.

(iii) And that he should likewise grant them the liberty of naming commissioners for the management of the treasury, and payment of the army.[59]

It is necessary, doubtless, to take this with a grain of salt. It is nevertheless significant, not only because Sidney was a close colleague of Jones, but because he was, with him, the author of the Commons' own *Just and Modest Vindication of the Proceedings of the Two Last Parliaments* (1681).[60] Charles himself certainly believed in the reality of these designs and (as we will see) took particularly seriously the Commons' attempts to 'disable' him financially.

One of the key powers of the shrievalty specifically was the ability to control the selection of London juries. It was, recorded North, 'Bethel and Cornish [who] first broke the Ice; for they took the Business of the setting the Pannels of Jury-men into their own Hands, and [out of those of] the Secondaries':

It will not be strange if, under this Security after it was gained, the Party took Courage and followed their Game full cry, like Hounds in View, without much trouble about Precautions and Evasives; they stuck at nothing. And this Dispensation extended, not only to Means of Defence, but equally offended the adversary . . . for Wo to an Adversary that came to a Trial, upon any Account, under this Reglement of Jury Returns.[61]

Thereafter opponents of the crown were acquitted by *ignoramus* juries; loyalists, in particular catholics or 'abhorrers', were informed upon, tried and where possible executed. The most important victim of this parliament–city judicial alliance was the catholic Lord Stafford, whose trial (in December 1680) was presided over by the attorney general Sir William Jones, and who was conducted to the scaffold by Bethel. The most famous

59 D'Avaux, *Negotiations*, vol. I, pp. 62–3.
60 [Algernon Sidney and Jones], *Just and Modest Vindication*, Appendix 15; Scott, *Restoration Crisis*, ch. 9.   61 North, *Examen*, pp. 94, 90.

such person acquitted was Shaftesbury in 1681, but an earlier and equally well-known case was that of Stephen College, the 'protestant joiner'. (College was later moved to loyalist Oxford and tried and executed there, an early sign of what was to come.) Following this frustration of royal wishes, a loyalist pamphlet parodied a letter from College:

Return my thanks in the lowest and most prostitute manner to Sheriff Bethel (whom next to A[lgernon] S[idney] I esteem as the chief patron of our Cause) for his True Protestant Ignoramus Jury, which so honestly discharg'd their Conscience . . . And thou knowest who teacheth when he holds forth, That for a few to be Perjur'd for the benefit of the Nation, and True Protestancy, is . . . a piece of Service becoming the Godly Party and the favourers of the Good Old Cause.[62]

Radical control of the shrievalty established the first phase of what one contemporary called 'the civil war through the courts'. 'The old civil war had now, as it were, transformed itself into a judicial war: men fought with one another in judicial battle – for what was right troubled neither grand nor petty juries.'[63]

CONFRONTATION (OCTOBER 1680–APRIL 1681)

When, after over a year of prorogation, parliament was finally permitted to meet, the mood in the Commons had greatly hardened. One casualty, as with the shrievalty election, was whatever influence Shaftesbury had possessed over its deliberations. A contemporary reported on 25 November:

My Lord Shaftesbury disowns having anything to do in it[s proceedings], and my Lord Russell. I heard 'twas Montague and the two lawyers Jones and Winnington, who show their profession . . . I fear it will soon appear that those persons who have now most power would leave the King none . . . My Lord Shaftesbury says, he does no more understand the House of Commons than he does the Court. He does lose ground.[64]

The most influential members of the new House were Jones, Francis Winnington, Sir John Maynard and Colonel Silius Titus. Jones, reported Roger North, 'hated Shaftesbury and . . . would not willingly come into the room where he was. His personal virtue and gravity was great, and he could

---

62 *A Letter Written from the Tower by Mr Stephen Colledge . . . to Dick Janeway's wife* (London, July 1681), p. 1.   63 Earl of Anglesey, quoted in Ranke, *History of England*, vol. IV, p. 159.

64 Dorothy Sidney to Henry Sidney, quoted in Julia Cartwright, *Sacharissa* (London 1901), p. 297.

not bear such a flirting wit and libertine as the other was.'[65] Titus, the wittiest speaker in the House, had co-authored (with the 1647 agitator William Sexby) *Killing Noe Murder* (1657), a republican call for the assassination of Cromwell. 'To manage this [republican] design', reported one pamphlet, 'a new set of ministers is contrived . . . Sir W[illiam] J[ones] is to be Lord Chief Justice; Col T[itus] . . . secretary of State.'[66] 'No freedom of debate was left for you', lamented another,

When all was Mov'd and Manag'd by a few
Your leading Maynard Jones and Winnington
as if all wisdom were in them alone
[opponents] . . . urg'd all in vain.
None were of force against the Good Old Cause.[67]

During the first week the Commons turned quickly, via a debate on the king's message, to the two matters of greatest concern. These were the obstructions received in the prosecution of the plot (including the contrivance of a 'Presbyterian Plot . . . or Conspirators in a Meal Tub') and the obstructions received to the sitting of the parliament (including the vindication of the right of petitioning, and the punishment of abhorrers). Five days of animated debate ensued, registering the depth of feeling: 'The King, in his letter to the Convention from Breda, said he looked upon the Parliament as a vital part of the Nation . . . We know the Kings opinion [now].'[68]

The first result was the motion affirming 'the undoubted Right of Subjects of England, to petition the King for the calling and sitting of Parliaments', and denouncing 'this doctrine . . . "That petitioning for the sitting of the parliament is like 1641"'.[69] The second, recommended by Titus, concerned the appropriate procedural response to 'the late interruptions, prorogations etc.'. This was to base the proceedings of this session exactly on the last. As we have seen, this had been the strategy in relation to the elections of September 1679: 'persist in the same steady course . . . choose the same members again'. Titus now argued: 'When the World shall

65 North, *Examen*, quoted in Henry Sidney, *Diary of the Times of Charles II*, ed. R. W. Blencowe (2 vols., London 1843), vol. II, p. 71.

66 *England's Concern in the Case of HRH James Duke of York . . . to be read by all subjects, whether of Royal or Republican Opinions* (1680), in Scott, *Somers Tracts*, vol. VIII, p. 180.

67 *A Dialogue between the Ghosts of the two last Parliaments* (London 1681).

68 Grey, *Debates 1667–1694*, vol. VII, pp. 350–70.   69 *Ibid.*, pp. 368–70, 391–3.

see Parliaments go on where they left off, it will put them by that way of proceeding. Therefore I desire that the Journals of the two last Parliaments may
be inspected.'[70]

Two days later the journals were read. This brought an intervention by
Russell on behalf of the exclusion bill to which Titus responded: 'Pray see in
the journals what that vote was.'[71] The motion was now read and passed
nemine contradicente for the first time. Thereafter every other resolution of
the previous House was read out and passed *nem. con.* The exclusion bill
was therefore passed, and carried to the Lords, when it became attached to
the mainstream of the Commons' strategy for the first time. Its rejection
there, under Halifax's oratory, is well known. In relation to the succession,
division within the Commons had given way to polarisation between the
two Houses.

The overall record of this session shows that the Commons' strategy of
continuity was extremely effective.[72] It was in this context that when the
House was invited by the king to reconsider the exclusion bill it refused (on
7 January). Again Jones and Titus spoke particularly in favour of this
response: 'The thing had been throughly debated and settled, and why we
should withdraw from it, I know not.' The result was a second vote unani-
mously reaffirming the first.[73]

On 28 November the Commons sent the king their *Humble Address* recounting the progress of the plot throughout the decade. This concluded that

even if the subtle [arts] . . . of that Party and Design should yet prevail either to elude
or totally obstruct the faithful Endeavours of Us Your Commons for a happy settlement of this Kingdom, We shall have this remaining comfort, that We have freed
our Selves from the Guilt of that Blood and Desolation which is like to ensue.[74]

In December Charles witnessed, but was powerless to impede, the destruction of Stafford. 'No man that knows anything', explained one MP, 'but
might be large upon the growth of Popery; and I shall show you the progress
the Papists have made, since the dissolution of Parliament . . . When the
good Patriots in the Long Parliament were out-voted in many things, yet
they kept up the Protestant Religion.' 'The springs of all', explained another,
'is from France and Popery, and nothing else. [Yet when we try to mend it, it

---

70 *Ibid.*, pp. 392–3.   71 *Ibid.*, p. 395.   72 Scott, *Restoration Crisis*, pp. 67–8.
73 Grey, *Debates 1667–1694*, vol. VIII, pp. 260, 268–70, 284–5.
74 *Humble Address of the Commons*, p. 85.

is] buzzed around by ill men. Let the king have care of the Parliament; they will pull down the Crown . . . and the actions of 1641 [are] thrown amongst us.'[75]

The plot had, meanwhile, as in 1641, acquired a menacing Irish dimension. The House was informed by the Lords that '[there is a] horrid and treasonable Plot and Conspiracy carried on by those of the Popish Religion of Ireland, for Massacring the English'.[76] It subsequently heard from Colonel Birch how Charles I's toleration of popery had established the context for 'that dismal time . . . in Ireland . . . that bloody Massacre in October 1641'. Maynard asked 'Shall we be led like Ox to the Slaughter? . . . can we believe but they who have so embroiled their hands formerly in Blood, have still the same design?' Sir Henry Capel recounted:

A Parliament met in 1640, and the Massacre was in 41, countenanced by Papists in the Court; and now you have '41 out and explained. It is far from me to justify the Miscarriages of that time to the King's Death; [but] there were provocations on each side.[77]

The final product of this discussion, sponsored by Sir William Jones, was a new Oath of Association, modelled on its Elizabethan predecessor.[78] This undertook to protect protestantism, His Majesty's person and the protestant succession, by force, sanctioned by the House of Commons alone if necessary. Elizabeth's counsellors, observed Jones ruefully, 'took great care to keep out Popery . . . [and] I hope they will do so now; but since they are not of the same disposition now as they were then, I fear it. I wish they were.'[79] He concluded by reminding members not to put their faith in words alone: 'Proclamations have been [made] against Papists, in the late King's time and this, without effect.' 'Ever since King James' time', added another member, 'Popery has been increased when the Parliament was dissolved, and suppressed while they have been sitting.'[80] '[Now the French King is great] wheras in Queen Elizabeth's time, she would not suffer him to set out a cock-boat.'[81]

Following the eventual dissolution of the House (to cries of 'Treason!') on January 9th, a petition was presented to the king by sixteen peers, led by the

75 Grey, *Debates 1667–1694*, vol. VIII, pp. 361–2.   76 *Ibid.*, p. 251.
77 *Ibid.*, pp. 132, 135–6, 140.
78 Collinson, 'Elizabethan Exclusion Crisis'; Scott, *Restoration Crisis*, pp. 71–2.
79 Grey, *Debates 1667–1694*, vol. VIII, p. 135.   80 *Ibid.*, vol. VIII, p. 380.
81 *Ibid.*, vol. VIII, p. 328.

Earl of Essex. This spoke of the terrible 'dangers that threaten the whole Kingdom, from the mischievous and wicked plots of the papists', and 'our unspeakable grief and sorrow [that] the [last] parliament . . . [was again] prorogued and dissolved before it could perfect what was intended for our security'.[82] A *Humble Petition of the City of London* on January 13th expressed its 'extream . . . surprize at the late Prorogation . . . [especially] by reason of the Experience they have had of the great Progress, which the emboldened Conspirators have formerly made in their Designs, during the late frequent Recesses of Parliament'.[83] After the subsequent dissolution at Oxford the next *Humble Petition and Address* from the same source repeated that since

one of the most effectual means the [popish plotters] . . . proposed to accomplish their Designs was by the frequent Adjourning, Proroguing, or Dissolving Your Parliaments We [could not but be] . . . surprized with Astonishment at the untimely Dissolution of Your Late Parliaments, before . . . they could fully pursue the Discovery and Suppression of the said Designs.[84]

Members in January warned that the impasse must be resolved 'or we must come to blood'. Some publicly stated their willingness to defend their religion again by force if there were no other way.[85] Amid scenes of tension remarked upon by many observers, a number of those re-elected to the subsequent parliament arrived in hostile Oxford armed.

The call to Oxford was itself a potent historical symbol of the struggle for monarchy. Once again electors were instructed to choose the same members; the result was a House 'like unto the last'.[86] The Speaker, Sir William Williams, accepted his reappointment on the same basis: 'Apprehending this choice proceeds from the Example you have from your Countries by your own Elections, making the Parliament, as much as in you and them lies, the same with the last; therefore you have the same Speaker.'[87] Once again the same bills were obstinately revived. Once again discussion focused upon the twin menaces of popery and arbitrary government. 'The greatest Arbitrary power that can be used in England, is to cow a Parliament

82 Arthur Capel, Earl of Essex, *The Earl of Essex his Speech . . . [and] Petition* (25 January 1681), in Scott, *Somers Tracts*, vol. III, pp. 282–3, ii.

83 *Humble Petition of the City of London*, p. 8.

84 *The Humble Petition and Address of the . . . Lord Mayor, Aldermen and Commons of the city of London* (London 1681), p. 5   85 Grey, *Debates 1667–1694*, vol. VIII, pp. 264, 404–10.

86 Sidney, *Letters to Henry Savile*, p. 3 (this letter is falsely dated 1678/9).

87 *The Speech of the Hon. William Williams . . . upon the Electing of him Speaker* (London, 21 March 1680).

... Danby ... [and] after him ... new Ministers of State ... shuffle and cut the cards again, and will dissolve and prorogue Parliaments, till they can get one for their turn; and in this condition we are.'[88]

In fact, however, this was to be one of the last parliamentary utterances of the reign. The Oxford parliament was a piece of political theatre orchestrated by the king for public consumption. It advertised his parliamentary persistence, and parliament's intransigence, while meanwhile the outcome of this contest had been decided at the beginning of the year by the restoration of French funding. The strategy of financial strangulation had failed.

It was in December 1680 that Barillon finally lent his support to the king's insistence that the situation had now become so serious that the only alternative to resumed support was the restoration of an English republic. Sidney had, at the same time, been employing a variety of arguments to bring Barillon to 'understand that it is an old error to believe that it is against the interest of France to suffer England to become a Republick'.[89] The ambassador, however, was not convinced. 'I do not think a republic in England would be in the interests of France; one saw by experience how powerful the nation became under such a united government.'[90]

Charles never wavered from his view that this was a struggle for the survival of the English monarchy. It was on this basis that he doggedly resisted the invasion of royal prerogatives, particularly that governing the meeting of parliaments. It was on the basis of this belief, by that time widely shared, that he appealed successfully in his *Declaration* after the Oxford parliament to

all those who consider the Rise and Progress of the late Troubles ... and desire to protect their Country from a Relapse. And we cannot but remember, that Religion, Liberty and property were all lost and gone when Monarchy was shaken off, and could never be reviv'd till that was restor'd.[91]

THE SELF-DEFENCE OF PROTESTANTS 1681–3

The king's *Declaration* was answered by parliament's own *Vindication*, written in part by Sidney and Jones. This Burnet called 'the best writ paper in all that time':[92]

---

88 Grey, *Debates 1667–1694*, vol. VIII, pp. 301, 306, 310.
89 Dalrymple, *Memoirs of Great Britain and Ireland*, Appendix, p. 313; Scott, *Restoration Crisis*, p. 124.   90 Jusserand, *Recueil des instructions*, p. 271.
91 Charles II, *His Majesties Declaration to all his Loving Subjects* (1681), pp. 4–5.
92 Burnet, *History of my Own Time*, vol. I, pp. 276–7.

It is not to be denied, but that our kings have . . . been entrusted with the power of calling and declaring the Dissolutions of Parliaments. But, lest through defect of age, experience, or understanding they should . . . mistake our constitution or by passion [and] private interest . . . be so far misled as not to assemble parliaments, when the public affairs require it; or to declare them dissolved before the ends of their meeting were accomplished: the wisdom of our ancestors had provided by divers statutes, both for the holding of parliaments annually, and that they should not be prorogued or dissolved till all the petitions and bills before them were answered and redressed.[93]

These were parliamentary claims, to be expanded upon by both Sidney and Locke, which took the public debate back towards that of 1642–6. One focus of the polemical exchange between supporters of the king and parliament during the first civil war had been the question of which authority, in a situation of public emergency, had the duty to act for the safety of the kingdom. In parliament's claim that it had this authority, which if necessary it must bear militarily, even against the king himself, we find the anticipation of related claims to be made between 1681 and 1683. In a situation of extreme danger a parliament might even need to summon itself.[94] In the words of Sidney's *Discourses*: if the king

had been drunk, mad, or gained by the enemy, no wise man can think, that formalities were to have been observed. In such cases every man is a magistrate; and he who best knows the danger, and the means of preventing it, has the right of calling the senate or people to an assembly.[95]

In practical terms, although the tide of public opinion had turned, the resolution of the crisis was far from a foregone conclusion in mid-1681. London remained in radical hands and, as the experience of Charles I had shown, a short-term triumph by dissolution was no substitute for victory in the longer contest. Thus, despite the problems facing them in 1681, many of the king's parliamentary opponents may have believed that they had time, and history, on their side. Salvation for protestantism and parliaments appeared to depend upon the hope that government without parliaments could not be more than a short-term expedient. Had matters rested there, the crown's opponents might have weathered this reverse. It was for this

---

93 [Algernon Sidney and Jones], *Just and Modest Vindication*, Appendix 15, p. cxxxiv.
94 Baldwin, 'The Self and the State', ch. 3.
95 Sidney, *Discourses*, in *Sydney on Government*, p. 466.

reason that no such rest was tolerated. What followed was that assault upon 'lives, liberties and estates' which, in the formulations of Locke, Sidney, and other radical protestants, authorised armed self-defence. In formulating these doctrines these writers were indebted to not only the parliamentary, but also the radical, writings of the 1640s. The practical point is, however, that it was in the context of the 'loyalist reaction' that the troubles returned, as they had between 1637 and 1646, to the armed self-defence of protestants.[96]

Serious contemplation of armed self-defence began in 1681. What crystallised words into action, however, as all accounts agreed, was the successful loyalist assault upon the shrievalty on 24 June 1682.[97] 'Now that the law will not defend us, though we be never so innocent', exclaimed William Goodenough, 'some other way is to be thought on.'[98] There is little evidence that any of the designs of 1682–3 posed a major danger to the government. Judicial convictions were secured by testimony that was paid for, or embellished into, various states of 'proof'.[99] This was, however, perfectly sufficient, since as a property of national memory the 'fanatic conspiracy' was no more susceptible to disproof than the popish plot.

Nor is there reason, however, to doubt the reality of some such designs. One, in 1682, centred upon Shaftesbury; another, following the earl's death in Holland (January 1683), upon Sidney. Sidney's design inherited Russell and Monmouth from Shaftesbury's, while bringing in his own friends Essex, Howard and Hampden. This latter group had contacts with those later convicted of the separate 'Rye House Plot'. The most significant shared feature of the first two designs was the planned involvement of Scotland. That which had ended the popery and arbitrary government of Charles I, and delivered him to the attentions of an all-powerful English parliament, was an insurrection in Scotland. Sidney's planned 'war in both kingdoms' hinged upon an insurrection in Scotland, to be led by Monmouth, the royal victor of Bothwell Bridge (1679).[100]

96 Scott, *Restoration Crisis*, ch. 12; Greaves, *Secrets of the Kingdom*, chs. 3–5.
97 British Library Add MS 38,847, 'The Rye House Plot: Robert West's full Confession to the King', pp. 2, 4; Ford, Lord Grey, *The Secret History of the Rye House Plot* (London 1754), pp. 15–17; Dorothy Milne, 'The Results of the Rye House Plot', *Transactions of the Royal Historical Society* 5th ser., 1 (1951), p. 92.
98 Quoted in Greaves, *Secrets of the Kingdom*, p. 249.
99 Scott, *Restoration Crisis*, chs. 12–15.
100 Grey, *Secret History of the Rye House Plot*, pp. 51–3; Scott, *Restoration Crisis*, pp. 273–91.

In 1682 Thomas Walcott showed Robert West a draft manifesto which detailed the attempts of three Stuart kings in succession to introduce popery and arbitrary government, with the result 'that the Government was dissolv'd, and the people at liberty to settle another'.[101] Most conspirators saw their struggle as primarily a religious one. This was the self-defence of protestants, against persecution in general and popery in particular. This was that same European cause which had underlain every aspect of the troubles. 'And no instance', exclaimed John Owen in 1682, 'can be given of any people defending themselves in the Profession of the Protestant Religion by Arms, but where together with their Religion their Enemies did design and endeavour to destroy th[eir] Rights, Liberties and Priviledges.'[102]

In 1682–3, as previously, 'The standing or falling of the Protestant interest in Europe' was understood to 'depend in a great measure upon the event of this undertaking in Britain'.[103] Radical opponents of crown policy saw themselves as European protestants, dependent upon the union of interest between England, the Netherlands and Scotland. This was the case not least for the grand-nephew of Sir Philip Sidney. A few weeks before his trial in 1683 Sidney wrote to his fellow prisoner John Hampden:

Somme say the protestants of Holland, France, or Piedmont were guilty of treason, in bearing arms against their princes, but [this] is ridiculous . . . when it is certaine, they sought noe more than the security of their own lives. Noblemen, Cittyes, Commonaltyes have often taken armes . . . to defend themselves, when they were prosecuted upon the account of religion.[104]

By the end of 1683 Sidney, Russell, Essex and others had perished on the scaffold; Locke and others had fled abroad, primarily to the Netherlands. This exile community was subsequently involved in Monmouth's rebellion, leading to judicial bloodletting on a much larger scale. By 1685, to all appearances, loyalist victory was complete. Yet the troubles were not over, as England was to discover only seven years later when the armed self-defence of protestants was actually effected by a Dutch army.

101 Quoted in Greaves, *Secrets of the Kingdom*, p. 126.   102 *Ibid.*, p. 94.
103 *Ibid.*, p. 282.
104 East Sussex Record Office, Lewes, Glynde Place Archives, no. 794, Sidney to John Hampden, 6 October 1683.

9

Invasion 1688–9

[He] provoked these nations to the last degree . . . not only by invading our civil liberties, but likewise by endeavouring to change the established religion for another . . . yet notwithstanding all his mismanagement, Britain stood in need of a foreign force to save it.

Andrew Fletcher (1698)[1]

INTRODUCTION: THREE PROCESSES

The loyalist reaction that ended the crisis of 1678–83 is the subject of chapter 19. The principal force informing this too was the progress of public memory. The result was, on the face of it at least, that by 1685 the domestic struggle against royal popery and arbitrary government had disappeared. The first elections of the new reign produced the most loyalist parliament of the century.

Thus the return of the troubles only three years later was extraordinary. By the second half of 1688 England faced all its familiar features: a collapse of confidence in and obedience to the government; anti-catholic rioting and 'tumults', particularly in London; a collapse in the enforcement of religious uniformity and of censorship, resulting in the most substantial effusion of printed argument since 1678–83.[2] Jonathan Israel has suggested that, 'far from banishing ideology and philosophizing from the scene, the English revolution of 1688–9 was arguably the most intensely ideological . . . of all major episodes in English history'.[3] In fact it was simply a continuation of that ideological process called the troubles.

1 In *The Political Works of Andrew Fletcher of Saltoun* (London 1737), p. 27.
2 Mark Goldie, 'The Revolution of 1689 and the Structure of Political Argument', *Bulletin of Research in the Humanities* 83 (1980).
3 Israel, 'General Introduction', in Israel, *Anglo-Dutch Moment*, p. 6.

This was only one of the remarkable occurrences of 1688–9. The second was the dramatic intervention within that context of a foreign invasion. As in 1640 this supplied the military challenge that delivered a helpless king to his enraged English subjects. Thereafter, however, the Dutch occupation of London was also the most important practical context for the subsequent political settlement. To this extent the last visitation of the troubles was successfully appropriated by a foreign power. In this connection John Kenyon has rightly remarked upon the extent to which the *initial* English role in this crisis was both passive and reactive.[4]

What the English crisis would have come to without Dutch intervention we will never know. What supplied the framework for its resolution in practice was the alliance between Dutch force and an English religious and political constituency with which it shared a community of interest. In this respect Israel has exaggerated only slightly in saying:

If it is generally true that discussing English history apart from that of Europe, a tendency built into history teaching in English schools and universities, is deplorable and produces major distortion, this is nowhere more the case than with the Revolution of 1688–9 where outside intervention set the ball rolling and decisively shaped much of what ensued.[5]

The events of 1688–9 and their consequences were as complex as they were extraordinary. This complexity results not only from their internationality – of context, cause and outcome – but because from the standpoint of English history they combined several processes. The collapse of Stuart kingship of 1688 which is the subject of this chapter was the last visitation of the troubles. The settlement of 1689 (developed 1689–1701) supplied the third and definitive restoration settlement and will be considered in this context in chapter 20. Finally the military struggle which was the most important outcome (not only from 1689–97, but 1702–13) secured that restoration by furnishing the context for English statebuilding. This will be our subject in chapter 21.

This distinction between three processes, each with their own European contexts and English histories, is an analytical one. In practice the three were intertwined, and never more so than in this period. To address the causes of the troubles was of course to achieve restoration. The fundamental condition of restoration history (1660–1702), it has been suggested, was the relationship of these three processes. It is because of their interrelation-

4 J. P. Kenyon, *The Nobility in the Revolution of 1688* (Hull 1963), pp. 1–5, 9.
5 Israel, 'General Introduction', p. 11.

ship that historians have been able to see this as a period both of 'Revolution', in the sense of decisive change,[6] and of 'a revolution not made, but prevented'.[7] In the words of Sir George Treby, James and his ministers were 'our *true* invaders, that brake the sacred fences of our laws'.[8] To the extent that we can liberate ourselves from the polarities of contemporary opinion we may find that these interpretations are not as incompatible as they have been made to appear. The key to the impact of these events lay in their combination of preservation and change. The key to understanding this is the examination of both troubles and restoration processes in their broader contexts in place and time.

During the first episode of the troubles, the passage from the initial collapse of government support to its reconstruction had taken twenty years (1640–60). During the second it took three (1678–81). On the third occasion the transition from crisis to settlement (1688–9) took less than six months. It will be crucial, however, here and elsewhere, to understand this apparently remarkable achievement within its broader contexts. This not only involved, and drew upon consciousness of, over a century of English struggle. It was itself the outcome of a much longer and bloodier process than conventional chronologies of the 'revolution' might suggest. The 1689 settlement, and the end of England's troubles, was not secured until the completion of its successful defence upon the European stage (1713). This involved an expenditure of English, to say nothing of allied, blood and treasure upon an unprecedented scale.

Thus the subject of this chapter is the final return of the troubles. We do not, however, witness their eclipse, and the new political world which this made possible, until well into the next century.

DOMESTIC CONTEXT

The cause of the return of the troubles in 1687–8 is a familiar one. This was the impact made upon contemporary belief by government religious and political policies in their European context. In this case, given what had

---

6 Schwoerer, *Declaration of Rights, 1689*; Schwoerer, 'Introduction', in Schwoerer, *The Revolution of 1688–1689* (Cambridge 1992).

7 Edmund Burke, *Works* (6 vols., London 1906), vol. III, p. 284, quoted in J. R. Jones, 'James II's Revolution: Royal Policies, 1686–1692', in Schwoerer, *Revolution of 1688–1689*, p. 47.

8 *The Speech of Sir George Treby . . . December the 20th*, quoted in Schwoerer, *Declaration of Rights, 1689*, p. 4.

gone before, those policies were even more remarkable than the Stuart standard. To this extent the purely domestic impetus behind the crisis was
greater than before.

The royal policy context of this crisis was remarkable in another way. For
the first time in the history of the troubles, the root cause of royal policy was
not primarily an attempt to address the perceived weakness of the crown.
Certainly James II was as mindful as any of the Stuarts of past and imagined
present threats to the crown. Yet by 1685 to all appearances the crown was,
fiscally, politically and militarily, stronger than at any previous point in the
century. It is difficult to understand the confessional policies that drew an
exhausted country back into the troubles as an attempt to improve that
strength. It looks more like an attempt to exploit it, and in particular loyalist
opinion further hardened by Monmouth's rebellion, to achieve a confessional objective.[9] Whether that objective was toleration for catholics or
catholic ascendancy is also unclear and perhaps in the long run, in its
counter-reformation context, unimportant.

If this was the case then the king's principal error was to overestimate the
strength of his position. To a significant extent the unparalleled strength of
the monarchy in 1685 was more apparent than real. If it benefited from a
second restoration drawing upon public memory, then the crisis which preceded this had demonstrated that that memory had another face. For more
than one reason it has suited English historians to blame James for single-
handedly destroying an apparently impregnable position. Though his
destructive achievement was indeed remarkable ('Seldom do we find a
precedent of any Prince that laboured, against all the common rule of
policy, so industriously to lose a crown as James II'[10]), the history of the
troubles tells us that his position was far from impregnable.

Fear of popery and arbitrary government had recurred for a century; it
related to a European situation not under English government control.
Moreover to an even greater extent than had been the case in the 1660s, the
restoration of 1681–5 was a reaction. Under its tense and violent surface
lurked real, and recently demonstrated, vulnerability. Fear of popery (and
for parliaments) had not been replaced from 1681, in the sense that it had
ended. It had rather been temporarily eclipsed by another related and
greater concern. To be reminded of its continued potential power we need

9 This is the view of John Miller, *James II* (London 1978).
10 *Quadriennium Jacobi; Or, the History of the Reign of King James II*, quoted in W. Speck,
    Reluctant Revolutionaries (Oxford 1989), p. 117.

to think not of the hunted radical minority of 1683 but the national majority of 1678. In the face of a revived and alarming popish threat – both
domestic and foreign – this earlier situation could and did return.

That its passengers thus had a propensity to rush from one deck to the
other in stormy European seas did not make the English ship of state any
more stable. In this context James' policy accomplishment by 1687 was to
have apparently united both forces by which the restoration process felt
itself to be threatened (fanaticism and popery) against the process itself.
The result was not the loss of the vessel with all hands. It was a mutiny still in
progress when the ship was boarded and commandeered by another vessel
and the captain made to walk the plank.

The threat of popery was, as we have seen, the danger posed by counter-
reformation catholicism to a beleaguered and defensive protestantism. Its
key domestic manifestation from 1686–8 was the royal assault, by means of
the dispensing power, upon the monopoly of legal worship restored in 1662
by parliament to the church. When Charles II had attempted to thus dispense individuals from the provisions of the Act of Uniformity he had upon
two occasions (1662, 1673) been forced by his House of Commons to back
down. By the time of the issuing of the second *Declaration of Indulgence*
(1688), however, parliament had been out of session for over two years,
leaving these measures to be confronted by members of the Anglican clergy.

These policies were accompanied by a remarkably aggressive promotion
of catholics to serve not only in the state and the universities, but also the
army. At the same time catholicism became a highly visible and alarming
presence at court. The king's own devout public catholicism was new. As in
the 1630s this was accompanied by a catholic queen, a papal envoy and catholic conversions among senior ministers. The most powerful minister by
late 1687 was the catholic convert Sunderland; the most notorious, Father
Petre, a Jesuit priest. William Morrice reported Petre's admission to the
Privy Council in November 1687 'in his Jesuits habit, to wit a Long cloak a
cassock and a little band'. Burnet reported: 'Father Petre had gained such an
ascendant that he was considered as the first minister of State.'[11]

Short of erecting billboards on the roadside proclaiming 'Protestantism
in Danger', it is difficult to see what else could have been done to reignite
public fears. Moreover, once again these measures had an immediate
European context which made them still more alarming. French military

---

11 Speck, *Reluctant Revolutionaries*, pp. 68–9.

expansion had continued unimpeded during the 1680s. This was accompanied by a policy of confessional aggression culminating in the revocation of the Edict of Nantes (1685) which created a flood of protestant refugees to England as well as the United Provinces.

Thus James' billeting of catholic cavalry at Gloucester was 'looked upon by some as the commencement of dragooning'.[12] As in 1678–81 there was a widespread fear of French and/or Irish invasion.[13] William Morrice called the return to anti-catholic mob violence in London and elsewhere in late 1688 'the great terror', animated by the 'fear and confident persuasion that they should have their throats cut by the French and by the Papists'.[14] Even the loyalist Countess of Sunderland wrote to Henry Sidney at The Hague on 11 September 1688: 'I love you well, as I do the Prince . . . for think what terrible ruin it must bring on England and the Protestants if the people fail.'[15] Writing on October 7th, John Evelyn recorded the 'hourly expectation of the Prince of Orange's invasion'. The people looked on the Prince 'to be their deliverer from Popish tyranny, praying incessantly for an East wind . . . The apprehension was (and with reason) that his Majesty's forces would neither at land or sea oppose them with that vigour requisite to repel invaders.'[16]

To believe English protestantism not to have been in danger in this period is either to believe France not to have been militarily formidable or England to have been so. It is, that is to say, to allow the English military consequences of the Seven Years War to obscure this aspect of their causes. Since the Elizabethan period, the struggle for English protestant security had been a military one. This had involved the security of Scotland and the United Provinces. It was in the same context that the authors of *A Memorial from the English Protestants, for their Highnesses the Prince and Princess of Orange* (1688) rehearsed the familiar perspectives of '*Protestants of England* . . . intollerably vexed and oppressed by the *Popish* Contrivances and Practices':

We need not remember your Highnesses, that these Attempts and Endeavours, to subvert our Liberty in our Religion and Government, is a part of that general

12 *Ibid.*, p. 161.
13 Miller, *James II*, pp. 128–30; G. H. Jones, 'The Irish Fright of 1688: Real Violent and Imagined Massacre', *Bulletin of the Institute of Historical Research* 55 (1982).
14 Greaves, *Secrets of the Kingdom*, pp. 325–7.
15 Quoted in Henry Sidney, *Diary of the Times of Charles II*, vol. II, p. 276.
16 John Evelyn, *Memoirs*, ed. W. Bray (2 vols., London 1818), vol. I, pp. 614–15.

Design that was formed and concluded on *many years* since in the most *Secret Councils* of the *Popish Princes*, chiefly managed by the *Jesuits*, to root out of all *Europe* the practice of the *protestant Reformed Religion* and the *People's Liberties*.[17]

In line with the present context, however, particular attention was given first to this work of 'Extirpation' in France, accompanied by the familiar '*Torments, Murders*, and all sort of barbarous Cruelty'; and secondly to the earlier 'agreement made between the *French King* and his late *Majesty* of *England*' in 1670 to destroy the United Provinces altogether, 'that they might no more be either a Support, or refuge for the *Protestants*'. Crucial to the frustration of that design had been English parliaments: 'The French King [having] found by experience, that the *Parliaments* had prevailed with our *King*, to break all the measures that they had taken together for the destruction of the *United Provinces*.'[18]

Arbitrary government entailed a threat to parliaments. By 1688 this was very clear not only by the prorogation of the parliament of 1685 but the subsequent manipulations (of persons and boroughs) to secure a compliant parliament in elections scheduled for 27 November 1688. In the course of this process 'approximately two hundred constituencies, returning four hundred out of the five hundred and thirteen MPs, had been subjected to some kind of direct governmental intervention'.[19] A correspondent of the Prince of Orange reported in September 1687: 'In all the King's progress very few of the gentry waited on his majesty . . . Yet the King is still assured that by his power in the corporations he shall have a House of Commons to his liking.'[20]

Arbitrary government was, more generally, government without or contrary to law. Thus James' *Declarations of Indulgence*, by dispensing with the safeguards of the legislative religious settlement, brought all of these threats together. In the words of Justice Powell, summing up before the acquittal of the seven bishops (and his own dismissal) at the end of June 1688:

I can see no difference, nor know of none in law between the King's power to dispense with laws ecclesiastical, and his power to dispense with any other laws whatsoever. If this be once allowed of, there will need no Parliament; all the Legislature

---

17 *A Memorial from the English Protestants, for their Highnesses the Prince and Princess of Orange* (London 1688), p. 6.   18 *Ibid.*, p. 7.

19 J. R. Jones, *The Revolution of 1688 in England* (London 1972), p. 166 (and ch. 6 in general).

20 *Calendar of State Papers Domestic 1687–1689* (1972), p. 66, quoted in Speck, *Reluctant Revolutionaries*, p. 67.

will be in the King, which is a thing worth considering, and I leave the issue to God and your consciences.[21]

Predictably William's subsequent *Declaration* explained that

It is . . . evident to all men, that the publick peace and happiness of any state or kingdom cannot be preserved where the law, liberties and customs, established by the lawful authority in it, are openly transgressed and annulled; more especially, where the alteration of religion is endeavoured, and that a religion, which is contrary to law . . . those counsellors, who have now the chief credit with the King, have overturned the religion, laws and liberties of these Realms, and subjected them . . . to arbitrary government.[22]

The first public disobedience to James' policies came from the Anglican episcopate. This Mark Goldie has called the 'Anglican revolution': passive resistance to the crown offered on Lutheran and natural law grounds. This was resistance both to 'the popish and phanatick commonwealthmen'; to the 'king-killing doctrines of Whigs and Papists'. It was a return, that is to say, to the loyalist moment and dilemma of early 1681: of opposition to the spectre whereby 'all religions would be let in, be they what they will, Ranter, Quaker, and the like, nay even the Roman Catholic religion (as they call it)'. James' own response to the seven bishops' petition against the dispensing power was 'This is a great surprise to me . . . Here are strange words. I did not expect this from you. This is a standard of rebellion.'[23]

Like his father, James had some difficulty distinguishing disobedience from rebellion. Passive disobedience was allowed by every absolutist writer save Sir Robert Filmer. This was particularly the case where a political command contravened the command of God. In such a case those guilty of such disobedience had to accept the earthly punishments prescribed in such a case. It was partly an effect of the impeccable loyalist credentials of his opponents that James' problem was that he could secure no such punishment. In this refusal of the clerical and judicial establishment to do the king's bidding we may detect the first active manifestation of the troubles. The universal outcry against popery and arbitrary government of late 1678

---

21 Quoted in D. L. Jones, *Parliamentary History of the Glorious Revolution*, p. 1.

22 William III [Caspar Fagel], *The Declaration of His Highness . . . for restoring the laws and liberties of England, Scotland, and Ireland* (1688), in Robert Beddard (ed.), *A Kingdom Without a King* (Oxford 1988), p. 125.

23 Quoted in Mark Goldie, 'The Political Thought of the Anglican Revolution', in R. Beddard (ed.), *The Revolutions of 1688* (Oxford 1991), pp. 115–18.

had included future loyalists as well as 'whigs'. Of active domestic resistance before the Dutch invasion, however, there was little sign. In the famous last words of Sunderland in late August: 'I believe there never was in England less thought of a rebellion.'[24] This was not simply because of reluctance to contemplate re-entry into this abyss (some of those least reluctant were to return from Dutch exile with William). It was because between July and November events conspired to make such a desperate act (unassisted) seem unnecessary.

INTERVENTION

It is in one way not surprising that this English context should have been seen by the Dutch as a plausible pretext for intervention. Nor is it surprising that when this intervention occurred the Dutch appealed to the protestant and parliamentary sensibilities informing the troubles ('appearing in arms in the Kingdom of England for preserving the Protestant religion, and for restoring the laws and liberties of England, Scotland and Ireland').[25] In fact, as we will see (in chapter 19), the *causes* of the Dutch invasion lay largely outside England. It was crucial, however, to the *context* of a design the scale and military riskiness of which have recently been emphasised, that the invaders could promise themselves significant domestic support.

The Dutch arrived with a major military force capable if necessary of conquering the kingdom. Yet the military objectives of the invasion could not be achieved by conquest. These lay beyond England, and required its rapid co-operation rather than time- and resource-consuming subjugation. In relation to these strategic objectives William's *Declaration* is informative. For the principal Dutch hopes of English support in their military self-defence lay in the protestant sensibilities of a war-funding House of Commons. These had been on consistent display since the 1620s; their military potential had been demonstrated during the 1640s; and William had personally been watching their frustration by Charles II and James II since 1670.[26] It was these religious and political 'passions' which would be successfully unleashed against France by the settlement of 1689, thus turning the cause of the troubles into the context for their end.

---

24 Quoted in J. P. Kenyon, 'The Earl of Sunderland and the Revolution of 1688', *Cambridge Historical Journal* 11, 3 (1955), p. 281.

25 William III, *The Declaration of His Highness*, pp. 124–5.   26 Stephen Baxter, *William III*.

From 1560, and in particular during the 1580s, many of the English political elite had taken the view that protestantism could not be defended in one
country alone.[27] A key aspect of the resulting Elizabethan military actions
was an English-supported naval invasion of Holland by the then William of
Orange. This is one vantage point from which to understand the moment
one hundred years later when William III would arrive with his own forces,
comprised in part of Scots, English and Huguenot contingents, to invade
England itself.[28] The putative cause was the same: the defence of protestantism, and liberties, embodied by representative institutions, in the face of a
European threat to both. In the words of Sir Edward Seymour in the
Convention on 20 February 1689 'England has done formerly for Holland,
as Holland has now done for England.'[29]

William was forced to this desperate expedient primarily by the immedi-
ate situation in the United Provinces. The decision may also have been
influenced, either in timing or in substance, by the birth in early 1688 of
James' son and heir. More broadly this action was required of the Dutch by
Stuart abandonment of this Elizabethan perspective (see chapter 20). In
January 1688 the States-General had refused James' request to repatriate the
English, Scots and Irish regiments in their service 'presum[ing] to give out',
in the words of d'Albeville, 'that the Protestant Religion is att the Stake'.[30] As
Sir Robert Sawyer explained to the Convention: 'The Protestant Religion
here was interwoven with all the Protestant States of Europe; and that principle justifies the Prince of Orange's coming over, and all that joined with
him; which interest, if it fall, all falls with it.'[31]

One of the broadest contexts within which to understand the events of
1688–9 is that of the general English experience of invasion and conquest.[32]
As we have seen, the country had been vulnerable to military incursions
throughout the seventeenth century and on this occasion foreign intervention resulted in the first successful invasion and occupation of the capital
since 1066. This was certainly the perspective of many contemporaries,

---

27 *A Declaration of the Causes moving the queene of England to give aid to the defence of the Low
   Countries* (October 1584), in Scott, *Somers Tracts*, vol. I, pp. 410–19; W. T. MacCaffrey,
   Queen Elizabeth and the Making of Policy 1572–1588 (Princeton 1981), p. 343.
28 Jonathan Israel and Geoffrey Parker, 'Of Providence and Protestant Winds: The Spanish
   Armada of 1588 and the Dutch Armada of 1688', in Israel, *Anglo-Dutch Moment*, p. 354.
29 Grey, *Debates 1667–1694*, vol. IX, p. 97.
30 Quoted in Greaves, *Secrets of the Kingdom*, p. 320.
31 Grey, *Debates 1667–1694*, vol. IX, pp. 22–3.
32 Koenigsberger, 'Dominium Regale or Dominium Politicum et Regale', p. 21.

including understandably James II himself. In the *London Gazette* the king had broadcast his opinion that William's objective was the 'absolute conquest of these our kingdoms and the utter subduing and subjecting Us and all our people to a foreign power'.[33] On 14 October 1688 Evelyn recorded: 'This day signal for the victory of William the Conqueror near Battel in Sussex. The wind which had been hitherto West was East all this day. Wonderfull expectation of the Dutch fleet. Public prayers order'd to be read in the Churches against invasion.'[34]

The most important previous attempted invasion had occurred a century earlier. Spanish objectives on that occasion – 'to restore England to the Catholic church, and to end English attacks on Spain's interests' – were comparable to those of the Dutch. As the Polish resident in the United Provinces, Moreau, reported on 12 October:

The Dutch are convinced that they will be as fortunate in their plan to attack England as Philip II was unfortunate . . . There are few among them who are unaware of this period of history and who do not know by heart the inscriptions on the medals which were struck at that time.[35]

William's success, according to Jonathan Israel and Geoffrey Parker, was caused by luck with the weather, by strategy (the same as that of William I in 1066) and by naval technology. It was also the result of Dutch wealth and resources: the Spanish had wanted a fleet the size of William's in 1588. The Spanish Armada (130 ships, including 25 warships, and 25,000 men) had been a good deal smaller: even so there is evidence to suggest that had they landed they might have been almost unopposed.[36]

Few historians now subscribe to the one-time national suggestion that the invasion was an altruistic Dutch response to an English invitation (from the 'immortal seven'). Whatever its motivation (to be discussed), its outcome was the result of military facts on the ground. One feature of these was the military strength of the Dutch fleet. With 500 ships (including 53 warships), 40,000 men (including 15,000 soldiers and gunners, 5,000 volunteers, and 19,000 crew) and 500 horses, this armada was by far the greatest naval operation ever mounted in Atlantic waters.[37] The second military fact was the abject collapse of the English army. This had its precedents,

33 *London Gazette*, no. 2397 (5/8 November 1688), quoted *ibid.*, p. 4.
34 Evelyn, *Memoirs*, vol. I, p. 616.
35 Quoted in Israel and Parker, 'Of Providence and Protestant Winds', pp. 335–6.
36 *Ibid.*, pp. 348–57.   37 *Ibid.*, p. 335.

most importantly in 1639–40. James' army was 'disgraced . . . humiliated . . . defeated . . . However much the English generals and senior officers tried to cloud the issue, the naked truth was that their army had been smashed in the field.'[38]

In a recent article discussing the view of Edmund Burke that 'The Revolution of 1688 was obtained by a just war, in the only case in which any war, and much more a civil war, can be just', John Pocock has compared this military failure to an 'Unfought Edgehill . . . in October 1642'.[39] Yet in calling 1688 a civil war Burke surely meant to call attention to the fact that William's was, or became, a decisive military intervention in an English civil conflict. That this parallel is with 1640 rather than 1642 is important in helping us to see what was different about what then occurred. In 1640 the Scots had secured their hold on Newcastle, leaving the king's English opponents to confront him in London. The result had been polarisation, civil war and revolution. In 1688 the Dutch occupied London with the co-operation of the king's opponents. It was this collaboration of external and internal interests which was decisive in the imposition of a settlement. As a result, within five months events had traversed the entire passage from successful invasion (as in 1640) to restoration (1660), missing out most of the bloodshed and revolution between.

The Dutch invasion, then, did not cause the renewed troubles. Rather it exploited them as an ideological and practical context for the achievement of its own military objectives. Plans for the invasion had been underway since April; it was in July that William sought and received an assurance of English support (the so-called invitation). The second factor, crucially affected by these preparations, was the collapse of government policy. In mid- to late September the English government accepted the inevitability of an invasion. On 21 September a *Declaration* debarred catholics from sitting in the Commons and attempted to reassure the Church of England. On 24 September the projected November parliamentary elections were cancelled. At the end of September William issued his *Declaration* at The Hague. In early October James entirely abandoned his policy of toleration and proposed to the Dutch co-operation for the maintenance of the Nijmegen treaty of 1678 against France.[40] All of these concessions were now

38 Childs, *British Army*, pp. 4–5.
39 J. G. A. Pocock, 'The Fourth English Civil War: Dissolution, Desertion, and Alternative Histories in the Glorious Revolution', in Schwoerer, *Revolution of 1688–1689*, pp. 52, 57.
40 J. R. Jones, *Revolution of 1688*, ch. 9.

irrelevant with the course of English history being driven by wider European circumstances.

COLLABORATION

With the Dutch landing on November 5th, public disaffection could become active defection and resistance. This happened far more rapidly than in 1640–2 when it had taken almost three years to turn clandestine Anglo-Scots contacts into an open military alliance. One crucial form of such defection was the desertion of English officers from the army (some directly to William) combined with a widespread reluctance among the soldiers to fight for the destruction of their own religion.[41] A second was the appearance in arms in open support of William of members of the nobility in the midlands and the north. In the formulation characteristic of the troubles, the *Declaration* of the nobility, gentry and commoners of Nottingham explained: 'We count it rebellion to resist a king that governs by law, but . . . to resist [a tyrant] we justly esteem it no rebellion, but a necessary defence.'[42] A third element of more immediate continuity were those English and Scots opponents of the government (including John Locke) who had fled to the Netherlands at the end of the restoration crisis and now returned with the Dutch army.[43]

The events which followed were not peaceful. They not only inaugurated a military struggle in Scotland and Ireland until 1691 which claimed tens of thousands of lives, but thereafter a continuing war with France. Even in England the revolution was not bloodless. 'The estimates of men killed in skirmishes between the two armies at Wincanton and Reading vary but the total figure may have been about fifty.'[44] To this may be added those injured or killed during the weeks of simultaneous anti-catholic rioting in London.

Arguably the most important *domestic* determinant of this episode of the troubles was once again the city of London. It is Robert Beddard who has recently done most to recover this dimension of the crisis. He has in the process ridiculed the suggestion that these events amounted to either a parliamentary triumph or an aristocratic coup. Concerning the first

---

41 Robert Beddard, 'The Unexpected Whig Revolution of 1688', in Beddard, *Revolutions of 1688*, p. 12.   42 Quoted in Greaves, *Secrets of the Kingdom*, p. 344.
43 Ashcraft, *Revolutionary Politics*; Greaves, *Secrets of the Kingdom*.
44 Lionel Glassey, 'Introduction', in Glassey (ed.), *The Reigns of Charles II and James VII and II* (London 1997), p. 6.

('whig') interpretation he has reminded us that the settlement was the work not of a parliament but a 'Convention – a body unknown to the laws of the land'.[45] Concerning the latter it is not only the case that the military actions of William's supporters among the English nobility (Danby, Delamere and others) cannot be shown to have affected the outcome, but also that a crucial subsequent role was to be played by an Assembly of Commoners, summoned by the prince himself. Beddard speaks, therefore, of a dynastic or princely rather than parliamentary 'revolution'.

Two important adjustments are necessary to this view. One is the point, elaborated in chapter 20, that whatever its outcomes the invasion was the work of the Dutch republic, not simply the Prince of Orange, who could not have mounted it on his own. The major insight yielded by the recent work of Jonathan Israel has been an explanation of the circumstances in which there occurred the most important Dutch precondition for the invasion: a political rapprochement between the stadtholder and the States-General.[46] As an act of state the immediate objectives of the invasion were not dynastic. To believe that they were is to misunderstand the expedition from an English perspective, either by confusing its outcome with its causes, or by giving the Dutch political context an inappropriately monarchical cast.[47] Its objectives, in fact, were military. What was necessary was to secure the levers of English military power, the key to which was that House of Commons which would form part of the 'free parliament' to the calling of which the expedition was publicly committed. This was the reason for the summoning of the Assembly of Commoners.

The other necessary adjustment to Beddard's interpretation is the fact that if not 'known to the laws' a Convention was at least known to the country's history. It had been contemplated as early as the 1560s and had served in 1660 as the principal initial constitutional instrument of restoration. As we will see, again in chapter 20, the convention was highly conscious of the problem of its parliamentary authority, particularly in relation to that of 1660. What is necessary, in short, is to set Beddard's local excavation adequately in its larger contexts in space and time: in those of the troubles and of the restoration process.

45 Beddard, *Kingdom Without a King*, p. 65.
46 Israel, 'The Dutch Role in the Glorious Revolution', in Israel, *Anglo-Dutch Moment*.
47 This was a contemporary as well as subsequent error: Sidney, *Letters to Henry Savile*, pp. 50–1; Scott, *Restoration Crisis*, ch. 6.

Within England the Dutch expedition was militarily self-sufficient. To achieve its objectives, however, which included immediate English military assistance to the Netherlands, local co-operation was crucial. Desertions from James' army and declarations for the Dutch were both helpful in the short term, though the subsequent need to reconstruct the English army from scratch was to prove a major drain on Dutch resources.[48] By December the invading army had become an unstoppable military force. In the process, however, it found its most important initial local ally in the city of London.

As early as November anti-catholic rioting in the city had delayed the departure of James' army to the southwest. By November 27th, following the collapse of his military strategy, James was persuaded to negotiate with William by a group of Peers anxious to avoid 'another civil war'.[49] William, too, was willing to negotiate at this stage but events in London outpaced them both. With the capital 'out of control', James, like his father before him, sent his family away and prepared his own escape. His flight on December 11th created an interregnum and may have decided William to take the throne. In the face of spectacular anti-catholic rioting a council of Peers assembled itself between the 11th and 15th of December under Rochester and Halifax to restore order. Roger Morrice recorded, as Richard Baxter had earlier, that once again there was

a universall terrible alarme . . . all over London and Westminster . . . that they should have their throats cut by the French and by the Papists; insomuch that almost all, but soldiers and footmen, kept in their houses, locked and bolted their doors. Luminaries were set up in all windowes in Great Lyncoln's Fields (and in other places) . . . The like . . . fears . . . circulated so generally throughout the Kingdome, that it is in vaine to name particular countyes, but in none was it greater then in Buckinghamshire, Northamptonshire, Leicestershire, and especially Staffordshire, Derbyshire and Nottinghamshire . . . they sate up most of the nights in this weeke, and the universall cry was that their throats should be cut. And . . . that which . . . increased their fears, if that were possible . . . was a universall report, that the disbanded Irish . . . would joyne with the English Papists to cut all their throats.[50]

Meanwhile, as also during both previous crises, there was a revolution in the city government. This took the form of a reversal of the loyalist coup of July

48 Childs, *British Army*, ch. 1; Stephen Baxter, *William III*.
49 Beddard, 'Unexpected Whig Revolution', pp. 12–13.
50 Dr Williams' Library, London, MS Morrice Q, pp. 352, 359, Appendix 13, in Beddard *Kingdom Without a King*.

1682. This was the basis for what Beddard has called an 'astonishing' revival of the whig cause as it had existed during the crisis of 1678–83, a fact 'for too long neglected or denied'.[51] This led to a revival, in turn, of the city–parliamentary axis which had played such a powerful role during that previous crisis. Here too it would play a decisive role in shaping the English political outcome.

From the outset William had courted this constituency, promising in his *Declaration* to restore 'the charter of the antient and famous City of London', and to surrender the Tower to the city. On October 16th James restored the charter.[52] The counter-coup came on December 11th, the day of the king's flight. Ten weeks of sporadic rioting culminated in the confrontation of the loyalist lord mayor Sir John Chapman, who died of a stroke. The result was the whig capture of the city government. On the same day the Recorder, Sir George Treby, made an enthusiastic address to William – 'called by the Voice of the People' – inviting him to enter the city.[53] Jonathan Israel has rightly stressed the crucial importance to the subsequent political settlement of the Dutch military occupation of the city between December and February. Of almost equal importance (as later in the realisation of William's war aims) was the political co-operation of the city and its allies in the Commons. Evelyn reported the prince 'wonderfull serious and silent, and seems to treat all persons alike gravely, and to be very intent on affaires; Holland, Ireland and France calling for his care'.[54]

THE 'OLD CAUSE'

In personnel and objectives the revived cause of 1688–9 exhibited a striking continuity with that of 1680–2. What was now referred to as 'whiggism' was the rather older struggle against popery and arbitrary government. Sidney had written in 1683 of that 'Old Cause . . . with which I am so well satisfied as contentedly to dye for it . . . as I had from my youth endeavoured to uphold the Common rights of mankind, the lawes of this land, and the true Protestant religion, against corrupt principles, arbitrary power, and Popery,

51 Beddard, 'Unexpected Whig Revolution', pp. 18–19.
52 J. R. Jones, *Revolution of 1688*, p. 263.
53 Gary de Krey, 'Revolution *Redivivus*: 1688–1689 and the Radical Tradition in Seventeenth-Century London Politics', in Schwoerer, *Revolution of 1688–1689*, p. 211; de Krey, *A Fractured Society 1688–1715* (Oxford 1985), ch. 1.
54 Evelyn, *Memoirs*, vol. II, pp. 6–7.

I doe now willingly lay down my life for the same'.[55] By late December 1688 Sidney's friends Sir William Waller, Sir Patience Ward, Thomas Papillon, Slingsby Bethel and John Wildman had all returned from the continent (the latter elected both to the Court of Aldermen and to the Commons).[56] Whig city leaders like Treby, Sir Robert Howard and Sir Robert Clayton, 'taught by too sad experience', demanded decisive action against popery and arbitrary government, at home and abroad. Morrice spoke of William's mission 'to retrieve and promote the Reformed interest and religion here and abrode, and to repress the tirany of France'. Loyalists were denounced as 'friends to Popery, and arbitrary Power, who would yet betray the nation into French bondage'.[57]

When in mid-December William acceded to the city's plea that he assume *de facto* government of the kingdom a lord mayor and aldermen who had refused James' earlier plea for physical protection immediately granted a £200,000 loan for 'carrying on the government', and for preparation for 'the defence of the distressed Protestants of Ireland'.[58] On the 16th the fleeing king himself was returned to the capital amid public rejoicing. The following day he agreed to confer 'all the power of war and peace' and ecclesiastical patronage on William for his lifetime. The day after that, however, the king left his capital for the second and last time under escort by a Dutch guard. It was following this expulsion, and on the same day, that William made that triumphant entry into London 'to the loud acclamations of a vast number of people of all sorts and ranks, the bells everywhere ringing', recorded by the Dutch political artist Romeyn de Hooge.[59] James had been deposed and William had taken the crown.[60]

What remained was to give this accomplishment constitutional form. For this purpose the existing Assembly of Peers would not be adequate. At their meeting on December 24th, though 'whigs' argued that there was an interregnum, others were deeply disturbed by the expulsion of the king. Even the Earl of Danby, who had risen for the prince in the north of England, and who returned to London on December 26th, had 'never

55 Algernon Sidney, *The Apology of A. Sydney on the Day of his Death*, in *Sydney on Government*, pp. 27, 29.
56 Beddard, 'Unexpected Whig Revolution', pp. 54–60; Goldie, 'The Roots of True Whiggism 1688–1694', *History of Political Thought* 1, 2 (1980).
57 Beddard, 'Unexpected Whig Revolution', pp. 21, 49.   58 *Ibid.*, p. 71.
59 R. de Hooge, *The Reception of His Highness the Prince of Orange in London (18 December 1688)*, reproduced in Israel, 'General Introduction', fig. 1, p. 1.   60 *Ibid.*, pp. 16–17.

thought that things would have gone so far as to settle the Crown on the Prince of Orange'.[61] This presumably helps to explain William's remarkable action on the 24th in summoning an Assembly of Commoners to meet two days later. This really was a body without historical precedent. Its purpose was 'to advise the best manner how to pursue the ends of his *Declaration*, in calling a free Parliament, for the preservation of the Protestant Religion'.[62]

Most remarkable about this body was its composition. Bypassing entirely James' loyalist parliament of 1685, it was to comprise 'all such persons as had served in any of the Parliaments of King Charles II . . . and the Lord Mayor, Aldermen, and fifty of the Common-Council of the City of London'.[63] Its effect was to precisely recreate the radicalised Commons–city nexus which had been dissolved with the Oxford parliament of 1681. One of its demands had been for the exclusion of James. This, however, had only been part of a wider package of measures for the security for protestantism and of parliaments.

This programme was now reactivated by the summoning of this assembly. It had included the sitting of parliament until its safety had been secured; the punishment of abhorrers and other enemies to parliaments; prosecution of the popish plot, with its Irish and French dimensions; a measure of toleration for protestants for the improved solidarity of that religion against catholicism; and effective action against, rather than alliance with, France. One of the last acts upon which the Commons had been engaged in 1681 was the drawing up of an association for the security of the protestant religion. The first act of the Assembly of Commoners on December 24th was to petition the prince formally to 'take upon him the Administration of public affairs, both Civil and Military', until the ends of his *Declaration* had been secured. The second was to call for that purpose for the summoning of a Convention, to meet on January 22nd. The last was to frame a new association of adherence to the prince, for the security of protestantism, to be signed by all one-time MPs and members of the government of the city of London.[64]

61 W. Cobbett, *The Parliamentary History of England from the Earliest Period to 1803* (36 vols., London 1806–20), vol. VI, p. 847; Thomas, Earl of Ailesbury, *Ailesbury Memoirs* (2 vols., London 1890), vol. II, p. 196.

62 Grey, *Debates 1667–1694*, vol. IX, p. 1; Beddard, 'Unexpected Whig Revolution', p. 25.

63 Grey, *Debates 1667–1694*, vol. IX, p. 1.

64 *Ibid.*; Beddard, 'Unexpected Whig Revolution', p. 52.

To all of these measures William consented. The subsequent elections – held amid continuing fear of popery – produced a Commons more than ready to sacrifice dynastic continuity to confessional security. The Commons of 1680–1 had been dominated by Sir William Jones, Silius Titus, John Maynard, Sir Henry Capel, William Garroway, John Birch and others, under the speakership of Sir William Williams. Jones had died in 1682, but all the others now returned to the new House. There they were assisted not only by radicals like Wildman and Hampden jnr but senior figures in the city: Treby, Howard, Pilkington, Love, Ward and Clayton. All of this ensured the domination of the debates not only by a certain religious and political but also generational perspective. It was in this way that the response to the third visitation of the troubles – and the third opportunity for restoration – built upon the experience of its predecessors. In January 1681 we heard Birch warn how Charles I's toleration of popery had led to 'that dismal time . . . in Ireland . . . that bloody Massacre in October 1641'. Maynard had asked 'Shall we be led like Ox to the Slaughter?'[65] Now, when on the first day of the Convention Sir Richard Temple exclaimed that not only had the country almost been overwhelmed with popery, but 'the King has endeavoured to destroy the Government of the Nation in Parliaments', Maynard responded:

Tis no new project . . . The last Rebellion was by the influence of the Priests and Jesuits, and in 1641 the Protestants were all massacred. They slew 200,000 Protestants, and all that has been done in Ireland . . . would have been done in England . . . There is no Popish Prince in Europe but would [not] destroy all Protestants; as in Spain, France, and Hungary . . . and now they would make Magdalen College a new St Omers.[66]

Ultimately this House would resolve *nem. con.*, exactly as it had on 28 October 1680, to every one of the measures of the previous session, including exclusion: 'That it hath been found by Experience, to be inconsistent with the Safety and Welfare of this Protestant Kingdom, to be governed by a Popish Prince'.[67] The result was the resolution, on February 6th, 'That no Popish successor shall be capable to inherit the Crown of England, and no Papist capable of succeeding to the Crown'.[68] In 1681 such measures had been resisted not only by Charles II but by a House of Lords understandably more sensible of the hereditary principle than was the Commons. In

---

65 Grey, *Debates 1667–1694*, vol. VIII, pp. 132, 135–6, 140.   66 *Ibid.*, vol. IX, p. 12.
67 *Ibid.*, p. 78.   68 *Ibid.*, p. 72.

February 1689, however, with the king absent, London under military occupation, the House under siege by crowds and by five petitions from the city government, opposition in the Lords was overborne.[69]

The fullest statement of the whig agenda was the *Declaration of Rights*, read to William and Mary at the coronation ceremony in the Banqueting Hall on 13 February 1689. This listed thirteen modes of popery and arbitrary government as 'utterly and directly contrary to the knowne Lawes and Statutes . . . of this Realme'. It listed against them thirteen undoubted 'antient rights and Liberties', including that 'Parliaments ought to be held frequently' and that 'Protestants may have Armes for their defence.'[70] Recent historical consideration of this document has been dominated by the question of whether it constituted conditions imposed upon the coronation (the answer appears to be no). In fact its importance is as a written summary of the issues informing not simply the present phase of the struggle but the troubles as a whole. In this sense it was the 'epitome' of more than simply the settlement of 1689. It is true, and important, that this tells us relatively little about its practical context, and in particular about the causes and objectives of the governing invasion. Yet William's preparedness to be publicly associated with this document also tells us something about those local allies with whose help he proposed to achieve these, and with whom in that achievement he did share an interest.

Not the least important aspect of the deferred pursuit of the 'whig' agenda of 1678–83 was the inquiry into the subsequent prosecutions and executions. This began with the arrest, amid scenes of popular tumult, of George Jeffreys on December 12th. It culminated in the posthumous reversal by a Committee of the Lords of the convictions for treason obtained in 1683, including that of Sidney, whose manuscript 'Apology' was supplied to the Committee by his servant Joseph Ducasse.[71] Ultimately it led to a change in the rules governing the use of evidence in trials for treason.[72] By 1696, as in 1679, the acts governing the licensing of the press had also been allowed to lapse.

---

69 De Krey, 'Revolution *Redivivus*', pp. 213–14.
70 Schwoerer, *Declaration of Rights, 1689*, pp. 295–7.
71 *Journal of the House of Lords* (1689), p. 390; Westminster, House of Lords MSS Committee Book, HL vol. IV, 1688–9.
72 Dr Williams' Library, London, MS Morrice Q, pp. 355–6, Appendix 10, in Beddard, *Kingdom Without a King*.

Ultimately the settlement initiated by the Convention would secure in practice the safety not only of protestantism but of parliaments. Yet above all this would be the achievement of that twenty-five years of European warfare which was a fundamental outgrowth of the events described here. Popery and arbitrary government had always needed to be confronted on the European military stage. In this context effective war against France was not simply made possible by the successful Dutch invasion. That invasion was the first act in that war, as we will see.

PART II

The English revolution 1640–89: radical imagination

I saw that which was without end, and things which cannot be uttered, and of the greatness and infinitude of the love of God, which cannot be expressed by words.

George Fox, *Journal*[1]

1 Fox, *Journal*, p. 15.

10

The shape of the English revolution

Clouds they are without water, carried about of winds; trees whose fruit withereth, without fruit, twice dead, plucked up by the roots.

Jude 12

[Y]our word Divinity darkens knowledge; you talk of a body of Divinity, and of Anatomyzing Divinity: O fine language! But when it comes to triall, it is but a husk without the kernall . . . the cloud without rain.

Gerrard Winstanley, The New Law of Righteousnes (1649)[2]

INTRODUCTION: THE ENGLISH REVOLUTION

The English revolution was the most spectacular product of the troubles. English radicalism came to question customary religious, social, legal, economic and political arrangements. It was the terrifying outcome of the troubles that successful struggle against one form of innovation unleashed another. What was for Thomas Edwards the death of reformation, or for William Prynne the death of political liberty, was for the radicals their substantial, rather than simply formal, achievement.

In this respect revolution was the inverse of statebuilding. Both entailed innovation and both were the products of war. One difference between them hinged upon the distinction between reformative and radical innovation. Another concerned their relationship to institutions: English radicalism took as its starting point the absence of those institutions which it was the business of statebuilding to perfect. Finally, therefore, one was a reaction against the other. In the pages to follow we will be studying a reaction

---

2 And *The Law of Freedom in a Platform* (1651), In *Works*, pp. 242, p. 569.

against Laudian formality in the shape of radical anti-formalism. We will find a reaction against counter-reformation monarchical statebuilding in the shape of no monarchy at all.

To begin with we must recover an understanding of this process from the standpoint of those engaged in it. One result will be an analysis of the revolution as a single fluid entity rather than as a series of discrete groups. This is to replace the clerical sectarianisation of radicalism with the perspective of those radicals who saw themselves as united in matters of substance against divisive form. The purpose of freedom from (human) form was unity of godly substance. In the words of Cromwell: 'sure I am, when the Lord shall set up the glory of the Gospel Church, it shall be a gathering of people as out of deep waters, out of the multitude of waters: such are his people, drawn out of the multitudes of the nations and people of this world'.[3]

Three phases of the radical process will here be understood by analysis of their negative and positive objectives. In the case of civil war radicalism these were constituted, on the one hand, by the struggle against outward bondage – religious, political, economic and legal – from which there developed the first political involvements and political theory. They were determined, on the other, by the religious and social agenda of the radical reformation by which (for instance) Levellers, Diggers, Ranters and Quakers were all united. English republicanism did not depart from these objectives but added to them in response to new political circumstances. This it did partly by exploiting the resources of English humanism to lay the basis for what historians have called classical republicanism.[4] This entailed, on the one hand, the struggle against monarchy, not only in the state but in the soul. It involved, on the other, a struggle for the positive moral objective, and benefits, of republican self-government.

Something concerning the revolution's *political* importance has been said in chapter 1. In addition to governing the country for over a decade, conquering Scotland and Ireland, defeating the Dutch and scandalising the rest of Europe, thereafter radicalism kept the seventeenth-century English political memory in its grip. These were, however, among the revolution's incidental consequences. Its substance lay elsewhere.

The special interest of radicalism for intellectual history hinges on the

---

3 Quoted in Colin Davis, 'Cromwell's Religion', in John Morrill (ed.), *Oliver Cromwell and the English Revolution* (London 1990), p. 199.
4 The basis of this tradition of interpretation was laid by Zera Fink's masterly *The Classical Republicans* (Evanston, Ill. 1945).

notion of change. Radicalism was the demand for fundamental change. There are good grounds for distinguishing pre-modern from modern intellectual history around the question of the acceptability and normality of change. In the early seventeenth century almost everybody opposed innovation. By the late eighteenth century even a 'conservative' like Burke could take the inevitability of change for granted. In a pre-modern, traditional society the emergence of a large-scale demand for change was remarkable.[5] Not the least important feature of the resulting revolution was its explicit defence of change.

One aspect of the power of English radicalism was *cultural*. No less striking than the breadth of its imaginative ambition was the quality and vigour of its language. This owes something to its occupation of a cultural space between pre-literacy and literacy.[6] England's was the first experience of Europe's religious troubles to be accompanied by a highly developed culture of the vernacular printed word.[7] London, as the largest protestant city in Europe by 1640, was an island of relatively high literacy within what remained a predominantly oral culture.[8] If the quantity of radical literature owed much to the collapse of effective censorship, its quality, like that of Shakespeare, owed a good deal to its orality. Most of the newspapers of this period, and the 20,000 or so pamphlets, were designed for performance. Not only did they accordingly have a social range well beyond the limits of literacy. Their social context was communal, not individual. A key concern of the radical literature itself was with the practical meaning of 'community' and 'commonwealth'. This was, in its social manifestation, a radical christian concern. Classical republicanism was no less preoccupied with translating into practice, in place of the divisive 'private interest' of monarchy, the reality of a self-governing civic community.

In substance, and within its spiritual context, the focus of English radicalism was upon practical morality. This was the case whether that morality was christian (for charity and equality against pride and covetousness)

---

5 J. C. Davis, 'Radicalism in a Traditional Society: The Evaluation of Radical Thought in the English Commonwealth 1649–1660', *History of Political Thought* 3, 2 (1982).

6 Freist, *Governed by Opinion*; Lindley, *Popular Politics*.

7 Glenn Burgess, 'The Impact on Political Thought: Rhetorics for Troubled Times', in John Morrill (ed.), *The Impact of the English Civil War* (London 1991), p. 67.

8 L. Stone, 'Literacy and Education in England 1600–1900', *Past and Present* 42 (February 1969), pp. 69–129; K. Thomas, 'The Meaning of Literacy in Early Modern England', in G. Baumann (ed.), *The Written Word: Literacy in Transition* (London 1986), pp. 23–50.

or classical (for liberty and virtue against corruption and slavery). Its most ferocious critical attention was accordingly directed towards a traditional society in which these moral values had become empty forms. This territory was investigated over a century earlier by Sir Thomas More from an apparently safe fictive distance.[9] During the period 1640–89, however, assisted by force, or the threat of force, it formed the basis of practical demands.

Although the following chapters will consider the christian, classical and restoration components of the radical process in turn, in practice they overlapped. Much civil war radicalism appealed to christian reason through the medium of humanist sources, and a natural law political language the origin of which was Greek (and Roman).[10] This was true not only of the Levellers but of wilder brethren like Abiezer Coppe whose humanist education at All Souls and Merton Colleges helped to equip him for his later rhetorical anti-intellectualism.[11] It is, meanwhile, the greatest shortcoming of the modern analysis of English classical republicanism that it has failed adequately to explain that religious dimension which was almost as central to the republican as to the civil war phase of the revolution. The origin of this fusion lay in sixteenth-century christian humanism. Its intellectual basis lay in the attempt to harness the moral fruits of that reason which was God's peculiar gift to man. Its practical focus was upon the shared goals of an attempted radical reformation of manners. As a recent historian has remarked:

Christian humanist social theory ... was to dictate the actions of its puritan advocates during the Civil War and Interregnum to such an extent that later historians would come to label it 'puritan' social theory. But let us follow the preachers' example and give credit where it is due. When we do so, we will have to acknowledge puritan social theorists as Christian humanists of the hotter sort.[12]

---

9 Thomas More, *Utopia* (Harmondsworth 1977).

10 Something noticed some time ago by William Haller, *Liberty and Reformation in the Puritan Revolution* (New York 1955), pp. 172–3. For natural law theory, see A. P. d'Entreves, *Natural Law* (2nd edn, London 1970); K. Haakonssen, *Natural Law and Moral Philosophy* (Cambridge 1996); Sommerville, *Politics and Ideology*; Richard Tuck, 'The "Modern" Theory of Natural Law', in A. Pagden (ed.), *The Languages of Politics in Early Modern Europe* (Cambridge 1987).

11 Nicholas McDowell, 'A Ranter Reconsidered: Abiezer Coppe and Civil War Stereotypes', *The Seventeenth Century* 12, 2 (1997).

12 Margo Todd, *Christian Humanism and the Puritan Social Order* (Cambridge 1987), p. 21; see also Scott, *English Republic*, pp. 17–30.

What is finally important about English radicalism is the extent of its moral ambition. There is some difference between a modern culture preoccupied by trivial details about the private lives of its royal family and a seventeenth-century one that not only executed its king and abolished its monarchy but did so as one side product of a more pressing moral end that lay elsewhere. What defined the lives of most seventeenth-century people was not self, or political government, but the government of God. At the heart of the revolution lay an attempt, not just in theory but in practice, to renegotiate the relationship between God's creatures and their creator. That in the longer term the success of this enterprise should have fallen short of expectations is not surprising. What is remarkable is that it should ever have been attempted.

RADICALS, HAVING LAIN DOWN, GETTING UP REFRESHED

That this enterprise was radical, in the sense of cutting to the root of contemporary arrangements, seems clear. It is to this struggle for fundamental change that this study attaches the label 'revolution'. This is to dissent from two recent studies which have sought, for some good reasons, to excise the words 'revolution' and 'radical' from seventeenth-century historiographical vocabulary.[13] This has been partly a reaction against the naive modern politicisation of our subject in which radicals, defined as 'ahead of their time', have been congratulated as anticipatory of ourselves. In particular Conal Condren has argued that the words radical and conservative, which first appear in histories in the nineteenth century, inevitably carry with them the distorting intellectual baggage of modernity.[14] Innovation, almost universally abhorred, was rarely sought, and still less often defended in the seventeenth century. Histories of seventeenth-century radicalism, understood as innovation, are therefore little more than the anachronistic would-be invention of our own origins.

13 J. C. D. Clark, *Revolution and Rebellion: State and Society in England in the Seventeenth and Eighteenth Centuries* (Cambridge 1986); Conal Condren, *The Language of Politics in Seventeenth-Century England* (London 1994), esp. ch. 5, 'Will All the Radicals Please Lie Down, We Can't See the Seventeenth Century'; J. C. Davis' review of Richard Greaves and Robert Zaller (eds.), *A Biographical Dictionary of British Radicals* (3 vols., Brighton 1982), in *Political Science* 37 (1985), p. 172.

14 Condren, *Language of Politics*; Condren, 'Radicals, Moderates and Conservatives in Early Modern Political Thought: A Case of Sandwich Islands Syndrome?', *History of Political Thought* 10, 3 (1989).

It is true that many demands for fundamental changes to contemporary arrangements were packaged in seventeenth-century rhetorics of tradition.[15] The appeal to custom in Leveller Norman Yoke theory (a radicalisation of parliamentary ancient constitutionalism) is one example. Religious reformation was not conceived of as innovation but as the recovery from carnal corruption of a primitive purer state. The basis for the identification of 'radicalism' here is the relationship of demands to *present* religious, social and political circumstances. It is, that is to say, their practical substance, not their rhetorical form.

It is not quite the case, moreover, that a conception of radicalism like that employed here was unknown in the seventeenth century. This combined the linguistic root, meaning fundamental, with the notion of a demand for change. In 1704 Charles Leslie looked back upon 'the root and foundation of all our republican schemes and pretences of rebellion' as 'this supposed radical power in the people, as of erecting a government at the beginning, so to overturn and change it at their pleasure'.[16] Another pamphlet of the same period spoke of 'the great revolutions and changes which have happened in the world'.[17] More importantly, the question of innovation was or became a crucial one during the 1640s. In its statement that it was 'no newes to have all innovations usherd in with the name of Reformation', the bestselling *Eikon Basilike* (1649) made what would remain a staple loyalist accusation for the next 100 years. To it Milton replied, with characteristic vigour: 'sure it is less news to have all reformation censur'd and oppos'd under the name of innovation; by those who being exalted in high place above their merit, fear all change though of things never so ill or so unwisely settl'd'.[18]

Milton had, as early as 1644, defended *religious* change, explaining that this was only bad 'if the Religion which a man changeth be the truth'. If not then '*not* to change Religion is evil'. The adherents of custom 'cry down the industry of free-reasoning, under the term . . . of innovation; as if the womb of teeming Truth were to be clos'd up, if shee . . . bring forth ought, that sorts not with their unchew'd suppositions'.[19] Henry Parker argued likewise that 'if the Parliament and Military Councel doe what they doe without prece-

15 Greaves and Zaller, *Biographical Dictionary*, vol. I, pp. vii–ix.
16 Charles Leslie, *The Wolf Stripped of His Shepherd's Clothing* (1704), p. 59, quoted in J. P. Kenyon, *Revolution Principles: The Politics of Party 1689–1720* (Cambridge 1977), p. 110.
17 *Vox Populi Vox Dei* (1709), in Kenyon, *Revolution Principles*, p. 124.
18 John Milton, *Eikonoklastes*, p. 503.
19 John Milton, *Areopagitica*, quoted in Keeble, *Literary Culture of Nonconformity*, p. 13.

dent, if it appeare their duty, it argues the more wisdom, vertue, and magna-
nimity, that they know themselves able to be a precedent to others'.[20] In fact
Condren's suggestion that defences of innovation were confined to the
'occasional' deployment of rights theory by the Levellers understates the
case.[21] In the stunning words of Richard Overton (1646): 'whatever our
forefathers were, or whatever they did or suffered or were enforced to yield
unto, we are men of the present age and ought to be free'.[22] It is not just that
'rights theory' (natural law theory) was the most important political language linking civil war radicalism with republicanism. The most important
defences of innovation were made, as circumstances demanded, by the new
republican government.

The innovatory nature of the republic was hard to disguise. In the words
of Nedham's *Mercurius Politicus*: 'What if *England* will change yet seven
times more? What is that to Scotland? It being a *Right inherent in every
Nation, to alter their particular Governments, as often as they judge it necessary for the publick weal and safety.*'[23] When, on these grounds, Henry Vane
jnr remarked upon the absurdity of the new commonwealth seal's description of England's 'freedome by God's Blessing *Restored*', its author Henry
Marten defended himself with a story about 'the man that was blind from
his mother's womb whose sight was restored at last'.[24] This was a republican
perception which culminated in the classic defence of political change in
Algernon Sidney's *Discourses Concerning Government* [1681–3].

As there may be some universal rules in physic, architecture, and military discipline,
from which men ought never to depart, so there are some in politics also which
ought always to be observed; and wise legislators, adhering to them only, will be
ready to change all others, as occasion may require, in order to the public good . . .
And I doubt whether it be more brutish to say, we are obliged to continue in the
idolatry of the druids . . . [than that] we are forever bound to continue the government . . . established [by our ancestors].[25]

20 Henry Parker, *The True Portraiture of the Kings of England* (1650), vol. III, pp. 237–8,
   quoted in Norbrook, 'Writing the English Republic', ms. (1997), ch. 6, p. 17.
21 Condren, *Language of Politics*, p. 160.
22 [Richard Overton and William Walwyn], *A remonstrance of many thousand citizens . . . to
   their House of Commons* (1646), in Andrew Sharp (ed.), *Political Ideas of the English Civil
   Wars 1641–1649* (London 1983), pp. 181–2.
23 *Mercurius Politicus*, no. 52, 29 May–5 June 1651, p. 831.
24 *Aubrey's Brief Lives*, p. 194; see Norbrook, *Writing the English Republic*, pp. 195–7.
25 Algernon Sidney, *Discourses*, in *Sydney on Government*, pp. 144, 404; Scott, *Restoration
   Crisis*, pp. 254–7.

Although republicanism was not the first manifestation of radicalism, it was its first manifestation in government. Accordingly its defence of innovation exposed it to the accusation that the innovations concerned had not been radical enough. This complaint was heard throughout the 1650s; it informed James Harrington's criticism of the Rump in *Oceana* (1656), and was expressed in notably Harringtonian language by William Hickman in November 1650:

> hetherto in the chandge of our Government nothing materiall as yet hath bin done, but a takinge of the head of monarchy and placing uppon the body or trunck of it, the name or title of a Commonwealth, a name aplicable to all forms of Government, and contained under the former . . . the onely way to make this a happy Government, is not onely to abolish all things that weare constituted under monarchy . . . But to sett upp a Government in all the parts of it sutable to our republike.[26]

The origins of English radicalism lay, it has been argued, in the deepening of the reformation process. They lay, that is to say, in the transition from defence of the reformation to radical reformation. Although the consequences of this development first came to occupy the central political stage at the end of the first civil war (1646), its origins lay earlier. The warning flag may first be said to have been raised by the transition from rioting against Laud and popery in late 1640 to the demand for the abolition of episcopacy itself. It would be etymologically appropriate, at least, if the origins of radicalism lay with the first root-and-branch bill presented with 15,000 signatures on 11 December 1640. This had helped to pioneer that practice of petitioning to which radical expression would become so indebted. It was one thing for parliament to call upon these forces in the struggle for its own survival. It would be another, when the war was over, to attempt to recover control of them.

CLOUD WITHOUT RAIN

Our discussion of the revolution in chapter 1 focused upon the distinction of intellectual substance from constitutional form. The first phase of the revolution in particular was a struggle to liberate the substance of christian conduct from its imprisonment by carnal form. This set life against death, light against darkness, and knowledge against power. It was a struggle

---

26 John Nickolls jnr (ed.), *Original Letters and Papers of State, Addressed to Oliver Cromwell* (1743), pp. 31ff., quoted in Norbrook, *Writing the English Republic*, pp. 270–1.

against the consequences of sin which, separating us from God, also separated us from one another. To so proceed, however, from that constitutional struggle which was the troubles to the radical belief which was one of its consequences only brings us down through one layer of obscuring cloud. For behind the problematic historical depiction of the revolution there is one of radicalism also. This has its origin precisely in that clerical dismemberment of truth from truth against which we have seen the radicals set themselves.

Here too the problem has been imposed (and obscuring) form. For what have principally been on offer are not descriptions, but representations, of civil war radicalism. Like those of the revolution these have emerged from struggles, both in the seventeenth century and today, not for knowledge of but power over that phenomenon. This is the explanation for something that is otherwise surprising: that in their depiction of radicalism the contemporary 'conservative' heresiographer Thomas Edwards and the modern 'radical' historian Christopher Hill agree.[27] Their agreement stems from the identity of their interest, which has been political.

Hill's major historical achievement has been to establish the existence of English radicalism independently of that constitutional 'revolution' which was actually the troubles. In 1958 he had grumbled that the revolution remained as much of an enigma as it was when R. G. Usher wrote, in 1913. 'No-one has tried to solve it because all assumed it was solved by repeating the Grand Remonstrance.'[28] Yet at the heart of Hill's account of radicalism we find what may be called the sectarianisation of the English revolution. In one book after another, and one chapter after another, radicalism stands arrayed in groups: Baptists, Levellers, Diggers, Quakers, Ranters, Seekers, Fifth Monarchy Men, Muggletonians.[29] This partly reflects Hill's interpretation of the phenomenon through the lens of nonconformity. It partly reflects the organisational exigencies of writing a book. Above all, however, it reflects contemporary labelling, nearly all of it of hostile origin.

---

27 Scott, 'Radicalism and Restoration: The Shape of the Stuart Experience', *Historical Journal* 31, 2 (1988), pt I; J. C. Davis, *Fear Myth and History: The Ranters and the Historians* (Cambridge 1987).
28 Hill, *Puritanism and Revolution*, p. 3.
29 Christopher Hill, *The World Turned Upside Down: Radical Ideas During the English Revolution* (London 1972); Hill, *The Experience of Defeat: Milton and Some Contemporaries* (London 1984).

No achievement, in this respect, compares with the heresiographer Thomas Edwards' *Gangraena*, published in three parts in 1646. *Gangraena*, says Hill, 'is well documented and seems to stand up quite well to examination'.[30] Edwards' extraordinary fulmination offered a full, not to say lurid, depiction of the pestilential heterodoxy overwhelming the contemporary religious scene. This was an unimaginable tragedy to the mapping of which, alongside other contemporary heresiographers, Edwards gave the rest of his life so that imagination at least might become possible.[31]

The historical importance of *Gangraena* derives not from any depiction of contemporary reality – it makes no such claim – but from Edwards' achievement in giving radicalism form. It is in *Gangraena* that we first encounter radicalism as an extraordinary list: Brownists, Beheminists, nudist Adamites, Arians, anabaptists, atheists, antichristians, Antinomians, anarchists. It is odd that historians who have followed him in this have not been more alert to what this process involved, for Edwards was quite open about it.

Edwards was one of those clergy against whom we have heard Milton, Walwyn and Winstanley directing their invective. He was throughout this period engaged in ferocious polemic with London radicals in general and Walwyn in particular. Their complaint was that such men sought to replace the unifying substance of religion with divisive, empty form. For the orthodox, what made this explosion of heresy terrifying was precisely its formlessness and fluidity.

The religious and political necessity was to bring this under control. *Gangraena* was published during that campaign for re-establishment of the national church in 1646 that we will see was the crucial context for the emergence of the Levellers. The necessary preliminary to this process of containment in practice was to effect it in the public mind. Edwards' interest was, therefore, not in describing radicalism as it was for the benefit of future historians. It was in giving radicalism form:

I here give the reader a Synopsis of sectarisme, and have drawn as it were into one table, and do present at one view, the errors and strange opinions scattered up and

---

30 Hill, 'Irreligion in the "Puritan" Revolution', in J. F. McGregor and B. Reay (eds.), *Radical Religion in the English Revolution* (Oxford 1984), p. 206.
31 R. Baillie, *Anabaptisme, the True Fountaine of Independency, Antinomy, Baptisme, Familisme* (1646), and S. Rutherford, *A Survey of the Spiritual Antichrist* (1647), both discussed in R. Birmingham's 'Continental Resonances in Mid-Seventeenth-Century English Radical Religious Ideas', MPhil. thesis, Cambridge 1998, pp. 70–81.

down . . . and have disposed them under certain heads . . . in a methodical way for memories' sake . . . the Reader cannot imagin I found them thus methodized and laid together, but confused and divided, lying far asunder . . . so that to have given them the Reader as I found them, would have been to have brought the Reader into a wildernesse, and to have presented to publike view a rude and undigested Chaos . . . all of which are carefully declined in this following discourse, by joining in one things divided and scattered . . . and by forebearing to lead the Reader thorow Woods and over the mountains, and instead of that, carrying him directly and presently to the bird in the nest.[32]

Nor was this methodisation simply a matter of 'joining in one things divided and scattered'.[33] Each scattered thing had within itself components of the others: 'both the several kinds of sects, and most persons of each kinde, are compounded of many, yea some of all: Anabaptisticall, Antinomian, Manifestarian, Libertine, Socinian, Millenary, Independent, Enthusiasticall, Arminianisme . . . Familisme . . . in one word . . . liberty of conscience, and liberty of preaching'.[34]

Thus to understand what Edwards was seeing, rather than his 'methodisation' of it, we must recover what appeared to him a 'wildernesse', a 'rude and undigested Chaos'. This was that same 'chaos without forme and void' inveighed against by Edmund Calamy in 1644.[35] But how are we to understand the shape of something characterised by its formlessness and fluidity?

Formlessness did not mean shapelessness. In the eye of a storm it is indeed confusing to encounter the absence of familiar scenery. In place of a house, table and chair, there is flying debris. As long as we are looking for what has been lost, what we will see is chaos. When we begin looking, however, at what is there, what we discover is that it has the shape given by its movement.

THE SHAPE OF THE ENGLISH REVOLUTION

'For most godly people in seventeenth-century England', Colin Davis has remarked, 'the issue was the substance of a protestant Christianity . . . of an active living God who could not be confined by or reduced to fleshly forms. The preoccupation with forms, denominations, sectarian identities and labels has for too long obscured this essential truth.'[36] From Edwards we

---

32 Thomas Edwards, *Gangraena* (1646; repr. Exeter 1977), p. 4.   33 *Ibid.*
34 *Ibid.*, pp. 16–17.   35 Tai Liu, *Discord in Zion* (The Hague 1973).
36 J. C. Davis, 'Puritanism and Revolution: Themes, Categories, Methods and Conclusions', *Historical Journal* 34, 2 (1991), p. 490.

have learned that radicalism possessed both a unity and a multiplicity of which the sectarian 'methodisation' is a frank misrepresentation. And we have seen the clergy vilified by the radicals as fomenters of artificial division. It was the clerical power-mongering of form that severed men from unifying christian substance. In his response to *Gangraena*, the witty *A Parable, or Consultation of Physitians upon Master Edwards* (1646), William Walwyn portrayed Edwards, dangerously ill, under the ministration of five healers: Love, Patience, Truth, Hope and Piety. After a traumatic conversion experience the erring minister sat suddenly upright and confessed:

> For matter of outward formes ... [I am now] very reserved. [All religion] is fulfilled in this one word, L O V E ... No man hath been more earnest than I, for compelling all to uniformity ... I now see it to be a work of darkness ... if ever men shall kindly be brought to be of one mind, I see it must be by ... love.[37]

Radicalism had a shape, and there appear to be three keys to its accurate depiction. The first is to recover connection, rather than simply distinction: that unity-in-variety which was essential to the radical enterprise. The second is to understand this variety as fluidity – that is, variety over time, not just in space. It is because radicalism was a thing in motion that it is possible to understand this unity-in-variety as a process. The third is to understand the shape of that process by relation to the rapidly unfolding sequence of extraordinary events to which it was one response.

For the first we must observe, amid its dazzling variety, the concerns the radicals held in common. These were constantly emphasised, for it was the purpose of the abandonment of 'external uniformity' to achieve real 'unity'.[38] This meant unity of heart, 'for love makes men to bee of one mind: and what can bee too strong for men united in love?'[39] It meant unity of spirit, as Cromwell wrote after the capture of Bristol in September 1645: 'Presbyterians, Independents, all had the same spirit of faith and prayer ... they agree here, know no names of difference; pity it should be otherwise anywhere.'[40] All forms of persecution were 'clouds of bondage' to be transcended in the recovery of the single God. This process was to be assisted by liberty of discourse, of preaching and of writing. The result, on earth, would be not uniformity but harmony. As Algernon Sidney explained:

---

37 In Walwyn, *Writings*, pp. 258, 261–2.   38 William Dell, quoted in Solt, *Saints in Arms*, p. 44.
39 Walwyn, *The Power of Love*, in *Writings*, p. 94.
40 Quoted in Barry Coward, *Oliver Cromwell: A Profile* (London 1991), p. 42.

as God by his word gave order and form to . . . the Chaos . . . so he left a pattern unto us by the power of reason the reliques of his Image in us . . . Hereby that variety of nature in individuals is rendrd useful to the beauty of the whole . . . he that would have a State composed of one sort of persons only will appear little wiser than he that wold have a body composd of one element or Musick of one Note.[41]

The unifying agencies at work – reason, spirit and love – were the Creator working inside man. Although perhaps no one else's consideration of this subject attained the majesty of that of Gerrard Winstanley, it was characteristic of its republican no less than reformation stages to scrutinise this terrain with care. In the case of James Harrington we encounter the Creation as a constitutional model.[42]

Our second need is to understand radical multiplicity not simply as variety, let alone division, in space, but as movement in time. John Lilburne was a Leveller, then a Quaker; Lawrence Clarkson an Anglican, Presbyterian, Baptist, Seeker, Digger and Muggletonian in turn. These men were at the heart of the revolution – do we understand it most effectively by considering what divided these groups or what united them? Sectarian groups there certainly were, including some, like the general and particular Baptists, whose existence spanned the whole period. But the majority of the group labels we use – Levellers, Seekers, Diggers, Fifth Monarchy Men, Quakers – in fact describe not simultaneously existing organisations but chronological stages of a single process by which radical expectation mutated in response to a rapidly moving sequence of external events.

'Seekers' were not a group but a process of movement from one of these stages to another. As Cromwell said of his sister Bridget: 'She seeks after that which will satisfy. And thus to be a seeker is to be of the best sect next to a finder.'[43] The end of the civil war ushered in those expectations that we call Levellerism. These were succeeded by True Levelling on the one hand, and providential regicide on the other. From the latter issued both the context for republicanism and the apocalyptic expectations of Fifth Monarchism. Finally in Quakerism we see the turning of radical expectation decisively inward, away from 'carnal' agencies altogether.

The third key to our analysis of the radical process is precise attention to its practical context. The relationship here between events and ideas, and

41 Algernon Sidney, *Court Maxims*, p. 19.   42 Scott, 'Rapture of Motion'.
43 Quoted in Solt, *Saints in Arms*, p. 37.

between radical belief and political and constitutional history, is not simply one way. We need only think of the year 1649 to be reminded of its enormous impact in both directions. In general, however, radicalism was reactive, as may inevitably have been the case in a conservative society. It was as innovative intellectual response to unprecedented practical circumstances, whether negative (the disappearance of traditional institutions) or positive (victorious conduct in war) that radicalism emerged and developed.

The revolution did, then, have a shape. To see it in this way is to recover from a static analysis the vitality of a living thing. In particular it was shaped by two factors. The first was its intellectual content: the reforming agendas of radical reformation and renaissance. The second was the adaptation of those agendas in the face of the opportunities, and problems, posed by the political developments of 1640–89.

INTELLECTUAL AND PRACTICAL CONTEXTS

Caroline statebuilding had set itself against the ungovernable aspects of both reformation and renaissance. Intellectually the revolution was in part a reaction against this audacious attempt to reconstruct both monarchical and clerical power.

Religiously the anti-formalism of English radicalism was an extreme reaction against Caroline and Laudian formality. It had been Laud's ambition to construct a church capable of uniting all men, from high to low. 'No one thing', said William Laud, 'hath made conscientious men more wavering in their own minds or more apt and easy to be drawn away . . . [than the lack of] uniform and decent order in too many churches of this kingdom.'[44] This was, however, a counter-reformation vision of what was necessary to arm the church (and monarchy) against its domestic and European enemies. The radical reformation consequence was a reaction that equated uniformity with divisiveness, not unity; and the outward face of reformation with outward bondage.

Laudian clericalism was the 'husk without the kernall', empty of christian substance. In the words of Abiezer Coppe, echoing Winstanley: 'These are without and . . . would fill their bellies with Husks, the out-sides of Graine . . . they cannot live without Shadows, Signs, Representations; It is death to them, to heare of living upon a pure naked God . . . without the use

44 R. J. Acheson, *Radical Puritans in England 1550–1660* (London 1990), ch. 4.

of externalls.'[45] For 'the heavy judgements [of] God', recorded a hostile observer, 'look no further than . . . Mr Cops . . . he suddenly passed through all forms now in fashion . . . the next brought him into that deep abyss, from whence he vomits out in print to the world, those horrid Blasphemies and impieties'.[46]

The intellectual origins of English republicanism lay additionally in the renaissance humanism of Tudor and early Stuart England. It too, however, was the product of an anti-formal revolution encapsulating an attempted reformation of manners. This was not simply a matter of principle but experience. Republican defences of constitutional change reflected experience of 'the changeablenesse of things'. Writing to a friend in September 1654 Benjamin Worsley (no classical republican) remembered the

wilfullnesse arbitrarinesse Injustice, tyranny, partiality, favour oppression in a king. Yet a Parliament how glorious did we call that Institution . . . [until] wee should experimentally see, that in Parliament may bee selvishnesse, partiality, hight of oppression, unmercifulnesse, folly and weaknesse, both in Counsell, authority and power.

The conclusion was that there was

A cleare and wide difference between the ends of Government and the manner of administration . . . That the ends of Government are alwaies one and necessary. That the media or manner . . . though . . . it should be after some manner, yet not necessary to bee after this or that manner . . . noe Rule, Law or Prescript either in scripture or nature what manner of administration . . . all formes . . . hath manifest Inconveniences.[47]

What mattered more than forms were 'Principles of Government' and 'Persons'. It is thus hardly surprising that the intellectual core of English republicanism too should turn out to be what its protestant authors considered a matter of substance rather than form. This substance was a moral philosophy of self-government. It is because the moral philosophy of city and soul were held to be identical (in everything but scale) that Plato had used one to speak of the other in *The Republic*.[48] It is for the same reason that

---

45 Abiezer Coppe, *Some Sweet Sips, of Some Sprituall Wine* (1649), in Nigel Smith (ed.), *A Collection of Ranter Writings* (London 1983), p. 49.

46 *An Answer to Doctor Chamberlain* (1650), quoted in Birmingham, 'Continental Resonances', p. 81.

47 Benjamin Worsley, 27 September 1654, *Hartlib Papers*, electronic edn, 65/15/1A–4B, doc. 214.

48 Plato, *The Republic*, trans. H. D. P. Lee (Harmondsworth 1959), pp. 100–2.

so much English republican writing addressed not just the commonwealth more generally but the city of the soul.[49]

The revolution was not the inevitable result of either of its intellectual contexts. In practical terms it was the contingent outcome of a military process beginning with parliamentary victory over the king and culminating in parliament's loss of control over its own army. The practical context of the revolution was institutional absence. It was this which created the preconditions for religious and political radicalism in general, and anti-formalism in particular.

Under normal circumstances the discrediting of one set of institutions would have led to their replacement by another. In England, however, a familiar European type of religious struggle became something more remarkable. The first reason for this was the absence of a religious settlement in London between 1640 and 1646. This was a by-product of crisis and civil war. By the completion of the deliberations of the Westminster Assembly (1645), and the cessation of the military struggle making possible some attempt at ecclesiastical reconstruction, a situation had already developed in which this would prove extremely difficult. The subsequent practical context of radicalism was that unique and dangerously prolonged state of unsettlement between war and peace from 1646 to 1648. It was in this absence of effective institutional authority, whether monarchical or parliamentary, that radicalism developed as a public culture.

Radicalism first stepped on to the public stage in 1646 as a challenge to religious petitioning by the presbyterian government of the city.[50] This related, in turn, to another longer-standing development. This was the realisation among some that the same overriding prerogative of public safety that authorised parliament to resist the king might under different circumstances authorise 'the people' to resist their own representatives. In the words of Jeremiah Burroughs in December 1642:

if Parliaments should degenerate and grow tyrannical, what means of safety could there be for such a State? . . . in this case whether a Law of Nature would not allow of standing up to defend our selves, yea to re-assume the power given to them, to discharge them of that power they had, and set up some other, I leave to the light of nature to judge.[51]

49 Scott, review of Peltonen, Armitage and Blom, in *English Historical Review*, pp. 951–3.
50 Murray Tolmie, *The Triumph of the Saints* (Cambridge 1977).
51 *Touching the Fundamental Laws* (February 1643), p. 13, quoted in David Wootton, 'From Rebellion to Revolution: The Crisis of the Winter of 1642/3 and the Origins of Civil War Radicalism', *English Historical Review*, July 1990, p. 663.

Thus although it became a major public presence only in the aftermath of the war, civil war radicalism was a product of the war itself. It took the form, most specifically, of the radical expectations raised by this successful military struggle. We have already seen this of New Model Army providentialism. More generally in 1646 parliament won what it had claimed was a struggle for liberty against popery and arbitrary government. Accordingly many who had been engaged in that struggle began to ask where, and what, that liberty was.

THE POLITICAL THEORY OF THE ENGLISH REVOLUTION

From the standpoint of the history of political ideas the English revolution presents an elusive quarry. This is because radicalism was not, initially, either primarily about politics or primarily theoretical. Our first concern will not, therefore, be with political thought. It will be to understand a phenomenon that was first and foremost religious and social, and pragmatic. That this did, however, make a contribution to political theory of significance followed from the inseparability of politics from these concerns, particularly during a period of disorder.

Thus in particular we will observe the development of two theories, over three phases of the evolution of radicalism. The first may be properly described as an anti-political theory, concerned to circumscribe the exercise of national power. This emerged from the radicalised struggle against arbitrary government of the 1640s. Its intellectual raw material was the juristic language (European natural law theory) that had made possible the first properly political resistance theories during the sixteenth-century wars of religion.[52] Having been used in this way by both protestants and catholics, and opposed accordingly by James I, in the hands of the Levellers in the 1640s this acquired an English vernacular form. It was concerned not simply with resistance to, but the reduction of, public power. It was to this that John Locke and others returned during the restoration crisis in 1681–3. In so doing they furnished a classic statement of one intellectual legacy of the revolution.[53]

The second theoretical legacy was that of English republicanism.

---

[52] Skinner, *Foundations of Modern Political Thought*, vol. II; Salmon, *French Religious Wars*; Sommerville, *Politics and Ideology*.

[53] J. G. A. Pocock, *Virtue, Commerce and History* (Cambridge 1985), p. 226; *Locke's Two Treatises*; Ashcraft, *Revolutionary Politics*; Scott, 'Law of War'.

Following from the practical circumstances of the interregnum this was a theory of and by, rather than against, government. English republicanism, too, survived restoration and played a key role in responding to the (in many respects familiar) political challenges posed by the crisis of 1678–83. The key text in this respect was Algernon Sidney's *Discourses Concerning Government*. In this we find that combination of Aristotelian moral philosophy and Machiavellian military dynamism characteristic of English classical republicanism as a whole.[54]

54 Scott, *English Republic*, ch. 2; Scott, *Restoration Crisis*, chs. 11–12.

11

Radical reformation (1): the power of love

I told them, the Lord had bound me by his righteous law written in my heart, to owe nothing to any man but love.

Thomas Aldam to Margaret Fell (1653)[1]

Now is the time for the compassionate Samaritan to appear . . . for greater love and mercy cannot be amongst men than to take compassion over the helpless and destitute.

Richard Overton (1647)[2]

INTRODUCTION

What were civil war radicals fighting for, and against? It is because of its spectacular effect upon contemporary politics that the answer to the second question has received much more attention than that to the first. The most important aspect of this was the struggle against religious compulsion made by Cromwell a force on the battlefield. To consider this in isolation is again, however, to preoccupy ourselves with form, in the absence of substance. We cannot understand the political struggle against, save in the context of what it was a religious (and social) struggle for.

Thus our concern in this chapter is with the positive aspirations of civil war radicalism. These had theological, spiritual and social dimensions.[3] Our focus here is upon the perceived social duties, and possibilities, of practical christianity. This was the core social agenda of the European radical

---

1 Thomas Aldam to Margaret Fell, York, 3 April 1653, Swarthmore MS 3.43, quoted in Geoffrey Nuttall (ed.), *Early Quaker Letters from the Swarthmore MSS to 1660* (London 1952), p. 89.
2 Richard Overton, *An Appeal from the Commons to the Free People* (1647), in Woodhouse, *Puritanism and Liberty*, p. 331.   3 Birmingham, 'Continental Resonances'.

reformation.[4] As Ralph Cudworth said in a sermon to parliament on 31 March 1647:

if we desire a true Reformation, as we seem to do; Let us begin here in reforming our hearts and lives; in keeping Christ's commandments. All outward Forms and Models of Reformation, though they be never so good in their kind; yet they are of little worth to us, without this inward Reformation of the Heart.[5]

There has been only one study of that social agenda by which (for instance) 'Independents', 'Levellers', 'Diggers', 'Ranters' and 'Quakers' were all united.[6] 'Consider that we may be one in Christ', said John Saltmarsh, 'though we think diversely . . . baptised by one Spirit into oneness and unity.'[7] One way of understanding this quest is as a reaction to the early modern fragmentation of Christendom. Michael Mullett has written of the 'universalist . . . conceptions . . . which characterised religious radicals', and which set them at odds with the fragmentation of aspiration epitomised by national churches (and states).[8] G. H. Williams has portrayed the radical reformation in sixteenth-century Germany as the 'last great effort of the yeomen and burghers of late medieval Christendom to realise the ideal of a universal Christian society'.[9] Within England this was one manifestation of the protestant impulse towards 'universal reformation'. Another, that of the Hartlib circle, which sought to unify both European protestantism and all material and spiritual knowledge, emanated from the same Anglo-central-European context.[10]

To focus upon this pragmatic social agenda is not to argue that in the broadest sense it was apolitical. Even groups like the Quakers who turned away from 'carnal' politics remained intensely interested in power:

4 G. H. Williams, *The Radical Reformation* (London 1962); Baylor, *Radical Reformation*.

5 Quoted in Jon Parkin, 'Trespassing on the Territories of Malmesbury: Richard Cumberland's *De Legibus Naturae*', Ph.D thesis, Cambridge 1995, p. 79.

6 Schenck, *Social Justice*. This brilliant work has a pioneering status in relation to this phase of English radicalism comparable to Fink's *Classical Republicans* (1945) in relation to its successor.   7 Quoted in Schenck, *Social Justice*, p. 86.

8 Michael Mullett, *Radical Religious Movements in Early Modern Europe* (London 1980), p. 5.

9 Williams, *Radical Reformation*, p. 864. Military outcomes were such, concludes Williams, that the movement bore fruit only in the Netherlands and England, anabaptism in the latter coming largely from the former (pp. 778–90, 864–5).

10 Mark Greengrass, Michael Leslie and Timothy Raylor, 'Introduction', in Greengrass, Leslie and Raylor (eds.), *Samuel Hartlib and Universal Reformation: Studies in Intellectual Communication* (Cambridge 1994), pp. 2–3; Trevor-Roper, 'Three Foreigners'.

William Dewsbury was moved to come into these parts . . . sounding the trumpet of the Lord. His testimony was piercing and very powerful, so as the Earth shook before him, the mountain did melt at the Power of the Lord . . . to the renting of many hearts. Oh! it was a glorious day, in which the Lord wonderfully appeared for the bringing down the lofty and high-minded, and exalting that of low degree. Many faces did gather paleness, and the stout-hearted were made to bow and strong oaks to bend before the Lord.[11]

This was empowerment, however, by and through God. It was quite different from Aristotle's *politea*, in which citizens realised their moral potential by participation in the public political community or *polis*.[12] This first phase of the moral trajectory of English radicalism entailed liberty from public institutions rather than through them. Reformation and renaissance radicalism also differed in other ways. Not only were they differently directed: theologically and socially on the one hand; philosophically and politically on the other. In an early modern context there was a major difference in the scale of the challenge each posed. From classical literature there was derived a critique of monarchy and the moral substance of an alternative. In the Bible, with its championship of poverty, humility, equality and peace, there existed a fundamental indictment of every aspect of early modern European society.

Radical reformation social doctrine, with its practical pursuit of equality and community, had 'its firm roots in the gospel'.[13] This was a far more fundamental reaction against Caroline and Laudian hierarchy than anti-formalism. It is a mistake, in this respect, to allow the Levellers' later attempts to dislodge that label to obscure the deeply subversive social implications of their early writings in particular.[14]

RADICAL REFORMATION

The focus of the European radical reformation programme was practical christianity. Informing the struggle against imposed 'ceremonial' worship

---

11 H. Barbour and A. O. Roberts, *Early Quaker Writings 1650–1700* (Grand Rapids, Mich. 1973), p. 58.

12 Sidney defined the word in this sense in the *Court Maxims*, p. 26; Paul Rahe, *Republics Ancient and Modern*, vol. I, *The Ancien Regime in Classical Greece* (Chapel Hill 1994); Maurizio Viroli, 'Machiavelli and the Republican Idea of Politics', in Bock, Skinner and Viroli, *Machiavelli and Republicanism.*   13 Schenck, *Social Justice*, pp. 57–8.

14 Davis, 'Levellers and Christianity'.

was a demand for genuine as opposed to formal 'Christian reformation'. Distinguished from the magisterial reformation, from which it broke free, radical reformation action and doctrine appeared in parts of Switzerland, Austria, Germany, Hungary and the Low Countries during the 1520s.[15] Although it developed in particular circumstances, most importantly the German peasants war (or 'revolution') of 1525, it is possible to see this as a predictable consequence of the delivery to a mass readership of the vernacular Bible. This anxiety was registered by its first translator into English: 'Our holy prelates [say that God's Word] causeth insurrection and teacheth the people to disobey . . . and moveth them to rise against their princes, and to make all common, and to make havoc of other men's goods.'[16] The subsequent development of radical reformation belief paid little heed to national boundaries. It has been argued that one of its principal offshoots, anabaptism, competed within protestant Europe particularly with calvinism, and affected England more than any other country except the Netherlands.[17]

At the heart of this phenomenon lay a highly plausible reading of the social doctrine of the Gospels. Lay pamphleteers in 1523–4 highlighted Christ's social commandments in Matthew 25. Of these, early modern aristocratic societies, with their mass poverty, stratospheric inequality, covetousness, pride and war, offered a remarkably comprehensive contradiction:

We have been regarded as belonging to people, which is distressful, seeing that Christ redeemed and ransomed us with the shedding of his precious blood – there are no exceptions, from shepherds to persons of the highest rank. Therefore it is mandated in the Bible that we are free and want to be free.[18]

The extreme reaction of the German princes – not to say of Luther himself – to the appearance of this message was to this extent understandable. Not all critics of Rome shared Luther's distinction between spiritual and temporal life. The rebels' phrase 'christian reformation' fused what later historians have treated as distinct categories of 'religious reformation, social reform

---

15 See n. 2 above.
16 William Tyndale, *The Obedience of a Christian Man* (1528), quoted in Christopher Hill, *The English Bible and the Seventeenth-Century Revolution* (London 1993), p. 3.
17 Irvin B. Horst, *The Radical Brethren: Anabaptism and the English Reformation to 1558* (Nieuwkoop 1972), pp. 30, 36.
18 *The Ten Articles*, art. 3 (against serfdom), quoted in James Stayer, *The German Peasants War and Anabaptist Community of Goods* (Montreal 1991), p. 52.

and political revolution'.[19] Central to it was the expression of christian belief through social conduct.

True holiness replaced discredited papal 'ceremonial holiness' with practical christianity. Christians should 'provide housing for the poor, giving them food and drink, clothing the naked, caring for the sick, ministering to prisoners and burying the dead'.[20] This stood at the core of a broader account of radical christian social practice. Michael Gaismair (*Landesordnung* (1526)) spoke of a 'wholly Christian order', in which 'all special privileges will be abolished since they are contrary to the Word of God'.[21] *To the Assembly of the Common Peasantry* (May 1525) invoked 'the will and power of God' against 'insolent and arbitrary power'.[22] Hans Hergot (executed by the Duke of Saxony in May 1527) spoke in *On the New Transformation of a Christian Life* (1527) of the Holy Spirit ushering in a new age, in which he would 'remove the tares from the wheat'. All distinctions would be abolished, 'no man will remain in his present estate, for all will enter into one order'.[23] Above all, no one in the new order would say 'That is mine':

Everything will be in common, so that they will eat from one pot, drink from one keg . . . so far as the honour of God and the public welfare require it . . . And the people will all work in common, everyone doing what he does best and what he can, and everything will be in common use.[24]

Thus from the emphasis on practical christianity emerged the most notorious anabaptist doctrine: community of property. In fact this was not a dogma, and in Germany, as later in England, there was no strict dividing line between charitable giving and communal living. From the philosophy of loving your neighbour issued concern for the needy, radical charity and/or the dissolution of private property. The internal objective was liberation from the fleshly snares of selfishness and covetousness. In the later words of James Nayler to George Fox: 'I am here in peace, and joy within, and at rest, though in the midst of the fire . . . to live upon bread and water is [no] bondage to me, within, or without, for it is my liberty . . . to be taken out of all created things is perfect freedom.'[25]

One consequence of this liberation was the freedom to serve God. As another English radical later put it: 'Christian liberty is not . . . an unruly

---

19 Stayer, *Peasants War*, pp. 41–5, 51.   20 *Ibid.*, p. 45.   21 *Ibid.*, p. 57.
22 *Ibid.*, p. 56.   23 *Ibid.*, p. 59.   24 *Ibid.*
25 Nayler to Fox, February 1653, in Nuttall, *Early Quaker Letters*, p. 88.

license . . . but a free gift bestowed upon . . . the faithfull . . . [by which] being delivered from the curse of eternall death, and from the heavy yoake of the ceremonial law . . . [they] beginne willingly to serve God.'[26] Hans Hubmaier explained in 1526:

Concerning community of goods, I have always said that everyone should be concerned about the needs of others, so that the hungry might be fed, the thirsty given to drink, and the naked clothed. For we are not lords of our possessions, but stewards and distributors. There is certainly no-one who says that another's goods may be seized and made common; rather, he would rather give the coat in addition to the shirt.[27]

These were focal concerns of Thomas Muntzer. In his *Manifest Exposure,* and *Highly Provoked Vindication* of 1524, he explained that private property was the outcome of man's distorted relation to others, resulting from the fall. 'All the joys of the body are an obstacle to the working of the Holy Spirit.' In this respect Luther attacked the clerical corruption of religion 'in words, but not in deed . . . It is the greatest abomination on earth that no-one will care for the wants of the needy.'[28]

One group of followers of Muntzer, Hut and the Hutterites, were thus characteristic of radical reformation social thinking in their combination of millennial expectation with radical charity shading into community of property. Williams has emphasised the 'generalised millennialism' informing radical reformation thought, which took many distinct forms.[29] In 1528 an anabaptist in Franconia defended his group against the accusation of demanding community of property: 'We didn't pledge ourselves to anything, beyond helping the poor according to our means . . . The Word of God binds us to love God and our neighbour, and requires that we should help the poor better than others.'[30] Other anabaptists emphasised the apostolic life of community (echoing the insistence of More's Hythloday that *Utopia*, without private property, is 'not merely the best but the only one which can rightly claim the name of a commonwealth').[31] The articles of the Swiss Brethren (1527) laid down:

26 Solt, *Saints in Arms*, p. 44; see also Davis, 'Religion and the Struggle for Freedom'.
27 P. J. Klassen, *The Economics of Anabaptism 1525–1560* (The Hague 1964), p. 32.
28 Quoted in Stayer, *Peasants War*, pp. 108–11.
29 Williams, *Radical Reformation*, pp. 858–9.   30 Baylor, *Radical Reformation* pp. 114–19.
31 Thomas More, *Utopia: The Best State of a Commonwealth and the New Island of Utopia*, ed. E. Surtz (New Haven 1964), p. 146.

Of all the brothers and sisters of this congregation none shall have anything of his own, but rather, as the Christians in the time of the apostles held all in common, and especially stored up a common fund, from which aid can be given to the poor, according as each will have need, and as in the apostles' time permit no brother to be in need.[32]

England's troubles began, as we have seen, as a struggle for reformation, first on the European and then on the local stage. With the collapse of religious and then civil magistracy, civil war radicalism emerged as the radicalisation of that cause. In England, unlike in Germany, the radical army was on the winning side. Consequently the English revolution unleashed in the 1640s became the last and greatest triumph of the European radical reformation.

This context for civil war radicalism was widely recognised by contemporaries. The debacles of the 1520s and then at Münster made this a potent accusation. It was particularly likely to be found in the mouths of those who, having assisted with the parliamentary defence of magisterial reformation, now found it placed in jeopardy. English and Scots protestant heresiographers (Edwards, Rutherford, Baillie) took as their model the attack upon the Strasbourg radicals by Bullinger, Zwingli's successor at Zurich, first translated into English in 1548.[33] Edwards took what comfort he could from Luther:

one of the first preachers and ringleaders of the Anabaptists . . . reproaching Luther, that he . . . favoured only outward things . . . saying that Luther was worse than the Pope himself, promulgating only a carnall Gospel . . . Luther reproved Muncer for his opinion of Liberty and the wayes he went in . . . and . . . all his dayes, both against the Papists and Sectaries, Shwenckfeldians, Antinomians, Anabaptists, notwithstanding all reproaches, went on with courage and rejoycing.[34]

'LEVELLERS': PRACTICAL CHRISTIANITY

One of the first to confront this accusation directly was the 'Leveller' William Walwyn. It was Walwyn's refrain throughout the 1640s that the essence of christianity lay in 'universall love to all mankind without respect of persons, opinions, societies . . . churches or forms of worship':

32 Stayer, *Peasants War*, p. 96.   33 Birmingham, 'Continental Resonances', p. 71.
34 Edwards, *Gangraena*, preface, B3.

Certainley, were we all busied onely in th[is] short necessary truth ... we should soon become practicall Christians; and take more pleasure in Feeding the hungry, Cloathing the naked, visiting and comforting the sicke, releeving the aged, weak and impotent; in delivering of Prisoners, supporting of poor families, or in freeing a Commonwealth from all Tyrants.[35]

Before anything else the Levellers were a petitioning movement.[36] Petitioning was a practical expression of what were for the most part pragmatic concerns. Most of the content of Leveller petitions followed from the application of the doctrine of practical christianity to the economic, religious, legal and social circumstances of the time. *The Petition of March 1647* called for 'some powerfull meanes to keep men, women and children from begging and wickednesse, that this Nation may bee no longer a shame to Christianity therein'.[37] Richard Overton, observing the 'oppressions, exactions and burthens wherewith the people are loaded every where, even till their backs are ready to break', reminded parliament that 'the maine and principall end of their Election and Session ... is for *hearing the cries and groans of the people, redressing and easing their grievances*'.[38] This he called the 'Evangelicall principle of mercy (being of the nearest communication to the nature of God)':

it is not the part of the just and mercifull Freemen of England to behold the Politike Bodie of this Commonwealth fallen amongst thieves ... stript of its precious raiment of freedome and safety, wounded and left grovelling in its blood ... and passe by on the other side like the mercilesse Priest and the Levite: no, now is the time for the compassionate Samaritane to appeare to binde up its wounds, to powre in wine and oyle to engage in the defence and preservation of a distressed miserable people.[39]

This image of 'the compassionate samaritan' had been the focus of the pamphlet of that name in 1644 (probably by Walwyn).[40] Much of Leveller material sought to speak for the powerless and oppressed, tyrannised by unjust and unequal human law, and yet equal in the sight of their Maker, in

---

35 William Walwyn, *The Vanitie of the Present Churches* (1649), in W. Haller and G. Davies (eds.), *The Leveller Tracts 1647–1653* (Gloucester, Mass. 1964), p. 272.

36 A point made by Davis, 'Levellers and Christianity'.

37 Walwyn, *Gold Tried in the Fire, or, The Burnt Petitions Reviv'd* (1647), in *Writings*, p. 285.

38 Richard Overton, *An Appeale From the degenerate Representative* (1647), in D. M. Wolfe (ed.), *Leveller Manifestoes of the Puritan Revolution* (New York 1967), p. 170.

39 *Ibid.*, pp. 179–80.   40 Walwyn, *The Compassionate Samaritane* (1644), in *Writings*, p. 97.

reason and in rights. The living embodiment of this condition became John Lilburne, perpetually 'unjustly imprisoned in New-gate'. Lilburne wrote from his incarceration in October 1645 of the burdens placed upon 'the weake shoulders of the poore . . . [who] are scarcely able to subsist, pay rent, and maintain their families'.[41] Meanwhile

The omnipotent . . . God, creating man . . . in his own Image, (which principally consisted in his reason and understanding) . . . made him Lord over the earth . . . But made him not Lord, or gave him dominion over the individuals of Mankind . . . but ingraved by nature in the soule of Man, this goulden and everlasting principle, to doe to another, as he would have another to do to him.[42]

Lilburne went on to recall man's fall from the perfection of this rational rule by Adam's transgression. Yet the demand for a return to adherence to it in practice, rather than simply form, was a step towards the same christian moral philosophy to be treated by Gerrard Winstanley. In this respect there is reason to doubt Schenck's judgement of Lilburne's later Quakerism, when he wrote of the community of those who 'are to love their enemies, to do good unto their haters', and be 'joined together in mutual love', that 'This tone of Christian love had been entirely absent from Lilburne's earlier writing; he was now a new man.'[43]

Perhaps the most powerful treatment of these themes of christian love and mercy pre-dated the Leveller movement significantly. This was William Walwyn's *The Power of Love* (1643). Walwyn's tract counselled its readers not to 'start' at the names 'Anabaptist . . . Brownist . . . Antinomian':

there is no respect of persons with God . . . he regards neither fine clothes, nor gold rings . . . nor wealth . . . nor any mans birth or calling . . . he regards nothing among his children but love. Consider our saviour saith, he that hath this worlds goods, and seeth his brother lack, how dwelleth the love of God in him? Judge then by this rule who are of God's family; Looke about and you will finde in these woefull dayes thousands of miserable distressed, starved, imprisoned Christians; see how pale and wan they looke: how coldly, raggedly, and unwholesomely they are cloathed; live one weeke with them in their poore houses, lodge as they lodge, eate as they eate,

---

41 John Lilburne, *England's Birth-Right Justified* (October 1645), in Gerald Aylmer (ed.), *The Levellers in the English Revolution* (London 1975), p. 61.
42 Lilburne, *A Postscript to London's Liberty*, p. 71; see also Lilburne, *The Free-man's Freedom Vindicated* (1646), in Woodhouse, *Puritanism and Liberty*, p. 317.
43 Schenck, *Social Justice*, p. 36 (quoting Lilburne, *The Resurrection of John Lilburne* (1656)).

and no oftner, and bee at the same passe to get that wretched food for a sickly wife, and hunger-starved children . . . then walke abroad, and observe the general plenty of all necessaries . . . the gallant bravery of multitudes of men and women abounding in all things that can be imagined . . . Neither will I limit you to observe the inconsiderate people of the world, but the whole body of religious people . . . in the very Churches and upon solemne dayes: view them well, and see whether they have not this worlds goods; their silkes, their beavers, their rings . . . will testifie they have . . . the wants and distresses of the poore will testifie that the love of God they have not.

This was the social doctrine of the radical reformation. What is most remarkable about Walwyn's pamphlet is his bold confrontation of its economic and political implications:

What is here aimed at? (sayes another) would you have all things common? for love seeketh not her owne good, but the good of others. You say very true, it is the Apostle's doctrine: and you may remember the multitude of beleevers had all things common: that was another of their opinions, which many good people are afraid of. But (sayes another) what would you have? would you have no distinction of men, nor no government? feare it not: nor flye the truth because it suites not with your current opinions or courses; on God's name distinguish of men and women too, as you see the love of God abound in them towards their brethren, but no otherwise.[44]

This was before the defensiveness induced in later 'Leveller' pronouncements, in particular the *Second* and *Third Agreements of the People* (1648, 1649), by the accusation of 'levelling'.[45] Walwyn's emphasis upon christianity as conduct was sufficiently extreme to transcend 'outward' boundaries not only of confession but culture. 'And what shall I say?', he famously wrote after reading Montaigne: 'Go to this honest Papist, or to these innocent Cannibals, ye Independent Churches, to learn civility, humanity, simplicity of heart; yea, charity and Christianity.'[46] Montaigne himself he quoted as follows:

If this ray of Divinity [Christian religion] did in any sort touch us, it would everywhere appear: not only [in] our words, but our actions . . . Compare but our manners unto a Turk, or a Pagan, and we must needs yeild unto them . . . All other outward shows, and exteriour appearances, are common to all Religions . . . the peculiar badg of our truth should be virtue.[47]

44 Walwyn, *The Power of Love*, in *Writings*, pp. 79–80.   45 Aylmer, *The Levellers*.
46 Walwyn, *Walwyn's Just Defence Against the Aspersions Cast Upon Him* (1649), in *Writings*, p. 400.   47 *Ibid.*, p. 399.

Gerrard Winstanley spoke similarly of England's 'so-called Christianity ... [we] live worse than heathens'.[48] For the religious and social message at the heart of Winstanley's writing was just the same. 'What is it?', he wrote, 'to walk righteously, or in the sight of Reason? First, when a man lives in all acts of love to his fellow creatures; feeding the hungry; cloathing the naked; relieving the oppressed; seeking the preservation of others as well as himself ... and so doing to them, as he would have them do to him.'[49]

'DIGGERS': WINSTANLEY AND COMMUNITY OF PROPERTY

It is difficult to imagine a more explicit demonstration of christianity as conduct than the most famous radical practical experiment of this period:

this work to make the earth a common treasury was shewed us by voice in trance and out of trance, which words were these:

'Work together, eat bread together, declare this all abroad.' Which voice ... we have declared ... by word of mouth ... by writing ... and we have begun to declare it by action, in digging up the common land and casting in seed, that we may eat our bread together in righteousness.[50]

Bulstrode Whitelocke recorded of the Diggers that their aim was 'to renew the ancient community of enjoying the fruits of the earth, and to distribute the benefit thereof to the poor and needy, and to feed the hungry and clothe the naked'.[51] It was christianity without practice that Winstanley called 'a husk without the kernall'.[52] This was the self-perpetuating mumbo-jumbo of the clergy within which God's liberating word remained imprisoned. In a splendid diatribe he explained:

Let us now examine your divinity ... herein speeches are made not to advance knowledge, but ... to deceive the simple ... he takes upon him to tell you the meaning of other men's words and writing . . . and by thus doing darkens knowledge and wrongs the spirit of the authors who did write and speak those things . . . so, by poring and puzzling himself in it, [a man] loses that wisdom he had, and becomes distracted and mad. And if the passion of joy predominate, then he is merry and

---

48 Winstanley, *Truth Lifting up its Head above Scandals* (16 October 1648), in *Works*, p. 137.
49 *Ibid.*, p. 111.
50 Winstanley and others, *The True Levellers Standard Advanced* (1649), in *Winstanley: The Law of Freedom and Other Writings*, ed. Christopher Hill (London 1973), p. 89.
51 Whitelocke, *Memorials*, vol. III, p. 18, quoted in Hill, *Puritanism and Revolution*, p. 88.
52 Winstanley, *New Law of Righteousnes*, In *Works*, p. 242.

sings and laughs, and is ripe in the expressions of his words . . . but all by imagination. But if the passion of sorrow predominate, then he is heavy and sad, crying out,
He is damned, God hath forsaken him and he must go to hell when he dies, he
cannot make his calling and election sure. And in that distemper many times a man
doth hang, kill or drown himself; so that this divining . . . doctrine . . . is a cheat; for
while men are gazing up to heaven, imagining after a happiness or fearing a hell after
they are dead, their eyes are put out, that they see not what are their birthrights, and
what is to be done by them here on earth while they are living. This is the filthy
dreamer, and the cloud without rain.[53]

This birthright was liberty. This was a gift of God permitting and enjoining moral action in line with his purposes. For Winstanley, however, its
practical implications were immediately more momentous, for in the
present time it held the promise of liberation from 'the curse'. The result of
this would be the restoration of man not only to his Maker, and so to his
fellow man, but to himself:

When this universall law of equity rises up in every man and woman, then none
shall lay claim to any creature, and say *This is mine, and that is yours, This is my work,
that is yours*; but every one shall put to their hands to till the earth, and bring up
cattle, and the blessing of the earth shall be common to all . . . When this restoration
breaks forth in righteous action, the curse then shall be removed from the Creation,
Fire, Water, Earth and Air. And Christ the spreading forth of Righteousnesse, shall
be the onely Saviour.[54]

This combination of 'intense millennial expectation' with a particular vision
of its necessary practical consequences had been equally characteristic of the
writing of the 1520s.[55] For Balthazar Hubmaier, too, 'private property presup-
posed a selfish spirit that was the complete antithesis of love . . . true Christian
love could only result in perfect and complete community of property'.[56]
Winstanley's thought hinged upon the relationship between inward and
outward bondage. The inner bondages were sin: pride, envy, covetousness,
hardness of heart. These, the consequences of separation from God, also separ-

53 Nigel Smith, *Perfection Proclaimed: Language and Literature in English Radical Religion
    1640–1660* (Oxford 1989), p. 233; Winstanley, *The Law of Freedom in a Platform*, in
    Winstanley, pp. 350–3.
54 Winstanley, *The New Law of Righteousnes* (1648), in *Works*, pp. 184, 186.
55 Williams records the 'overwhelming sense of the dawn of the Millennium' characteristic
    of this period (*Radical Reformation*, p. 860).
56 Klassen, *Economics of Anabaptism*, pp. 74–5.

ated us from one another. After the fall man's reason remained trapped within him, 'light shining through flesh . . . darkened by the imagination of flesh':

> When man began to fall out of his Maker, and to leave his joy and rest which he had in the spirit of Righteousnesse, and sought content from creatures and outward objects, then he lost his dominion, and the creature fell out of him, and became enemies and opposers of him, and then rise up mountaines, and valleys, and hils, and all unevenness, both in mans heart and in mans actions. And as the man is become selfish; so are all the beasts and creatures become selfish; and man and beast act like each other, by pushing with their horns of power, and devouring one another to preserve self.[57]

Private property was the extreme manifestation of this selfishness, or covetousness:

> In the beginning of time, the great creator Reason made the earth to be a common treasury, to preserve beasts, birds, fishes and man . . . but not one word was spoken . . . that one branch of mankind should rule over another . . . But selfish imagination . . . working with covetousness, did set up one man to rule over another; and thereby the spirit was killed and man was brought into bondage . . . And the earth . . . was hedged into enclosures by the teachers and rulers, and others were made servants and slaves; and that earth bought and sold.[58]

Until 1651, at least, liberation from this bondage was to be internal, with the rising of the 'Second Adam . . . the New Law of Righteousness Budding Forth in the heart of every man . . . Our spirit waits in quiet and peace upon our Father for deliverance . . . all that I shall say is this; Though the flesh despise you . . . yet wait patiently upon your King, he is coming, he is rising . . . and his glory will fill the earth.' Those so delivered would manifest their transformation in practice, at which time

> the Creation shall become even againe . . . man returning to his Maker, to rest in peace in none but him. The whole Creation shall be governed, preserved and comforted by the one spirit . . . and all bondage, curse and tears shall be done away . . . And they that in these times, will not observe this Rule, to walk righteously in the creation, waiting quietly till Christ come to restore all things, he shall have sorrows, troubles and discontents of heart within, vexing, grudging, rash passions, he shall have no true peace, but be filled with confusion, and be a slave to his lusts.[59]

---

57 Winstanley, *New Law*, in *Works*, p. 156.
58 Winstanley and others, *The True Levellers Standard Advanced*, in *Winstanley*, pp. 77–8.
59 Winstanley, *New Law*, in *Works*, p. 156.

With the digging experiments on St George's Hill in early 1649 this topography of the soul and nature found practical expression. With their eventual failure, however, Winstanley's millennial faith evaporated, to be replaced by an argument for extreme social regulation. Private property must be eradicated before sin; *The Law of Freedom in a Platform* (1651) announced a reversal of Winstanley's understanding of the key relationship:

I speak now in relation between oppressor and the oppressed; the inward bondages I meddle not with in this place, though I am assured that, if it be rightly searched into, the inward bondages of the mind, as covetousness, pride, hypocrisy, envy, sorrow, fears, desperation and madness, are all occasioned by the outward bondage that one sort of people lay upon another.[60]

Among the penalties consequently prescribed for those deemed guilty of imposing such bondage were whipping, slavery and death; in particular, 'If any do buy and sell the earth or fruits thereof . . . they shall both be put to death as traitors to the peace of the commonwealth, because it brings in kingly bondage again.'[61]

'RANTERS': ABIEZER COPPE AND RADICAL CHARITY

We have seen practical christianity manifested, in the writings of the Levellers, as social humanitarianism. We have seen it developed, in the work of Gerrard Winstanley, into the demand for community of property. In one of the most spectacular printed utterances of the revolution we find both of these ideas present, overshadowed by another, which links them: the doctrine of radical charity.

The pamphlet was Abiezer Coppe's *A Fiery Flying Roll* (accompanied by *A Second Fiery Flying Roule*) (January 1650).[62] Like Walwyn's, Coppe's doctrine involves extreme solicitousness towards the poor. As in Winstanley this is underwritten by millennial expectation. Neither the tone nor language, however, is peaceful. It is charged with violence and menace.

For Coppe God resides in the poor: in those who are and have nothing. The *Second Roule* is addressed

---

60 Winstanley, *The Law of Freedom*, in *Winstanley*, p. 296.
61 *Ibid.*, p. 383; J. C. Davis, 'Gerrard Winstanley and the Restoration of True Magistracy', *Past and Present* 70 (February 1976).
62 Republished by the Rota Press at the University of Exeter, 1973. For other works by Coppe, see Nigel Smith, *Collection of Ranter Writings*. For Coppe's thought, see Davis, *Fear Myth and History*, pp. 48–57; McDowell, 'A Ranter Reconsidered'.

To All the Inhabitants of the earth; specially to the rich ones. OR, A sharp sickle, thrust in, to gather the clusters of the vines of the earth, because her grapes are (*now*) fully ripe. And the great, notable, terrible, . . . day of the LORD is come . . . *Howle, rich men, for the miseries that are (just now) coming upon you, the rust of your silver is rising up in judgement against you, burning your flesh like fire . . . And now I am come to recover my corn, my wooll, and my flax, which thou hast . . . detained from me, the Lord God Almighty, in the poor and needy.*[63]

Coppe's tract is full of denunciations: of the rich; of those who fail to take the author seriously ('a terrible wo denounced against those that slight the Roule'); and of the 'well-favoured harlot' or 'holy scripturian whore', by which he means the gathered churches, seen as formalist, hypocritical and devoid of christian conduct. These latter are also Walwyn's target, not only in *The Power of Love*, but most particularly in *The Vanitie of the Present Churches* (1649). By this time the achievement of liberty of conscience had encouraged what both authors saw as a selfish detachment from the demanding practical *substance* of christianity (as if the civil war had been fought only to achieve variety of ceremonial worship). On the other side Coppe champions the poor, the outcast, the destitute, the ugly and deformed ('The Author's strange and lofty carriage towards great ones, and his most lowly carriage towards Beggars, Rogues and Gypseys').[64] The dramatic centrepiece of the *Second Roule* is chapter 3, in which the author relates what he calls 'A strange, yet most true story':

Follow me, who, last Lords day Septem.30.1649. met him in open field, a most strange deformed man, clad with patcht clouts: who looking wishly on me, mine eye pittied him; and my heart, or the day of the Lord, which burned as an oven in me, set my tongue on flame to speak to him, as followeth.

How now friend, art thou poore?
He answered, yea Master very poore.
Whereupon my bowels trembled within me, and quivering fell upon [my] worm-eaten chest . . . that I could not hold a joynt still.
And my great love within me . . . was burning hot toward him; and made . . . [my] mouth . . . again to open: Thus.
Art poor?
Yea, very poor, said he.

Moved by his love to offer charity, Coppe first, however, has to fight 'the strange woman who flattereth with her lips, and is subtill of heart' and

63 Auxilium Patris [Abiezer Coppe], *A Fiery Flying Roll*, with *A Second Fiery Flying Roule* (4 January 1650; repr. Exeter 1973).   64 *Ibid.*, pp. 1, 9.

speaks 'within me'. When her first attempt to moderate what he will give fails she appeals to the full range of possible arguments – selfishness, custom, reason, cliche, narrower social obligation (to his family):

It's a poor wretch, give him two-pence.

But my EXCELLENCY and MAJESTY (in me) scorn'd her words, confounded her language; and kickt her out of his presence.
But immediately the WEL-FAVOURED HARLOT . . . who rose up in me, said:
Its a poor wretch give him 6.d. and that's enough for a Squire or Knight to give one poor body.
Besides . . . hee's worse then an Infidell that provides not for his own Family.
True love begins at home, etc . . .
Have a care of the main chance.
And thus she flattereth with her lips . . . her words being smoother then oile; and her lips dropping as the honey comb.

At this point the struggle going on within Coppe issues into a ludicrous comic interlude. Temporarily won over, he discovers he has only a shilling. He accordingly offers it to the tramp (who has nothing) if he can give him six pence change. 'He answered, I cannot, I have never a penny. Whereupon I said, I would fain have given thee something if thou couldst have changed my money. Then saith he, God blesse you.' Riding away, Coppe is wracked by guilt for having given nothing. Even more absurdly he then returns and asks the tramp to stop at a particular house at the 'next Town' where he will have found change and left the sixpence. In the middle of this performance, however, a cataclysm occurs which radically simplifies the outcome.

But [as God judged me] I, as she, was struck down dead.

And behold the plague of God fell into my pocket; and the rust of my silver rose up in judgement against me, and consumed my flesh as with fire: so that I, and my money perisht with me
I being cast into that lake of fire and brimstone . . .
and the 5. of *James* thundered such an alarm in mine ears, that . . . all the money I had about me to a penny . . . I was fain to cast into the hands of him, whose visage was more marr'd then any mans that ever I saw . . . [and] I rode away from him, being filled with trembling, joy, and amazement, feeling the sparkles of a great glory arising up from under these ashes.[65]

65 *Ibid.*, pp. 4–6.

This struggle is that facing anyone who would be a true christian. It is a struggle between form and substance, carnality and love. Love has no limits; it is not given upon conditions. 'Private' property is not ours. Yet this struggle is of the greatest difficulty, and in this case it is won only by the direct intervention of God. From the millennial destruction of the Coppe of flesh arises somebody transformed, and equipped for battle.

Echoes of this drama abound in radical literature: in the letter, for instance, of Thomas Aldam to Margaret Fell (1654) in which he records that

it came unto me, Wherefore art thou in this room [prison], and the life tramping upon the streets? it was said again, It is because of the money; cast out thy purse, and that thou has laid up in thy chest; and get thee hence . . . and she did open the door . . . and in our freedom we stand.[66]

It is a remarkable irony, highlighted recently by Colin Davis,[67] that it is on the basis of this pamphlet that Coppe has been identified as a 'Ranter'. The Ranters, according to A. L. Morton and Christopher Hill, were a counter-cultural core of the revolution so extreme as to challenge the ('puritan') notion of sin. For the holy, possessed of God, all actions were holy. The apparent evidence for this view is located in chapter 5 (pp. 12–14) where Coppe champions 'base hellish swearing, and cursing' and 'base impudent kisses . . . I'll . . . make thine own child . . . in whom thy soul delighted, lie with a whore – before thine eyes.' It is not necessary to read much further, however, to notice that this is in order to 'confound' the 'plaguy, filthy, nasty holiness', the 'abominable pride, murther, hypocrisie, tyranny and oppression' of 'Papists, Protestants, Presbyterians, Independents, Spirituall Notionists etc. . . . But now me thinks . . . I see a brisk, spruce, neat, self-seeking, fine finiking fellow, (who scornes to be either Papist, Protestant, Presbyterian, Independent, or Anabaptist) . . . who scornes carnall ordinances . . . I mean the Man of Sin.'[68] Coppe has not *abandoned* the notion of sin, but furiously redefined it. It is not the breaking of customary social codes, sexual or otherwise. It is 'plaguy holinesse'. It is the hypocrisy of claiming christianity – particularly a christianity pretending 'superiority to carnal ordinances' – while remaining idle amid a sea of poverty, inequality, oppression and want. It is the continued policing of ceremonial boundaries by those who sought liberty only for themselves. It is the pretended social,

66 Thomas Aldam to Margaret Fell, York, March 1654, Swarthmore MS 3.42, in Nuttall, *Early Quaker Letters*, pp. 105–6.   67 Davis, *Fear Myth and History*.
68 Coppe, *Second Roule*, pp. 13, 15, 17.

spiritual and moral superiority of some of God's creatures to others. How may such moral vermin be compared to the poor, who have nothing?:

> the worst rogue in Newgate, or the arrantest thief or cutpurse [is] farre better then [them] ... Howl, howl, ye nobles, howl honourable, howle ye rich men for the miseries that are coming upon you. For our parts we that hear the APOSTLE preach, will also have all things common; neither will we call anything we have our own ... wee'l eat our bread together in singlenesse of heart ... in equality, in community, and in universall love.[69]

Far from being a rejection of christian moral categories, this is one of the most ferocious christian moral diatribes ever written. Nor is it one from which, in Coppe's subsequent defence of himself from the charge of blasphemy, any retreat was necessary. Against

> prophaneness and wickedness, superstition and formality ... I have thundered more ... then they all. And for my zeal therin, and against finer and subtler pieces of Formality, the coals were first kindled against me ... else all my religion is in vain, I own for dealing bread to the hungry, for cloathing the naked, for the breaking of every yoke, for letting of the oppressed go free ... And as for Community, I own none but the Apostolical ... spoken of in the Scriptures ... I either will or should call nothing that I have mine own.[70]

QUAKERISM: COMMUNITY

The same themes continued to govern the protestant radicalism of the 1650s, in particular Quakerism.[71] For Schenck 'the social radicalism of Quakers before 1660' had been papered over by later denominational historians. Quakerism was itself 'a new Corporate manifestation of Christianity', in particular of christian community, 'at one with a large body of radical opinion during the Puritan revolution'. Quakers shared the earlier hostility to 'buying and selling ... the mark of the Beast'. They were similarly preoccupied with ministering to the fatherless, widowed and poor.[72] In the words

---

69 *Ibid.*, p. 19.

70 *A Remonstrance of the Sincere and Zealous Protestation of Abiezer Coppe Against the Blasphemous and Execrable Opinions recited in the Act of Aug. 10 1650* (1650), in Nigel Smith, *Collection of Ranter Writings*, pp. 120–2. Coppe here makes the point reiterated by Davis: that the yellow-press pamphlets against the 'Ranters' are 'scandalous ... bespattered with Lyes and Forgeries' (p. 122).

71 Scott, 'Radicalism and Restoration', pt I; Barry Reay, *The Quakers and the English Revolution* (London 1985).

72 Schenck, *Social Justice*, pp. 123–8.

of Edward Burrough: 'Every yoake and burden shall be taken off the neck of the poor, true judgement and justice, mercy and truth, peace and righteousness shall be exalted.'[73] George Fox, the father of Quakerism, recorded of his mission:

I was to bring people off from all the world's religions, which are vain, that they might know the pure religion, might visit the fatherless, the widows and the strangers, and keep themselves from the spots of the world. Then there would not be so many beggars, the sight of whom often grieved my heart, as it denoted so much hard-heartedness amongst them that professed the name of Christ.[74]

Quakerism paid particular attention to the aspiration to christian community. Universal, and hostile to national distinction, this expressed itself on a local level not only in care for the poor, weak and sick, but in the involvement of the whole community of 'religious people' in these activities.[75] Fox looked forward to the day when laws would pass away, leaving local communities to resemble the 'Christians in the days of the Apostles . . . Country people would soon decide their business . . . this would be the way to take off oppression . . . to bring the nation [to be] like a garden and free nation.'[76]

REFORMATION OF MANNERS

Among 'Leveller', 'Digger', 'Ranter' and 'Quaker' publications we have observed considerable variety. Yet little of this transcended community of interest in practical christianity. If Harrington's republicanism was, in Pocock's formulation, a 'Machiavellian meditation upon feudalism', the radical reformation in England was a practical meditation upon the moral consequences of the fall.

The notion of christianity as conduct (rather than ceremony) was not of course the exclusive property of the radical reformation. Charity and its related social obligations had been central to medieval piety; the reaction against ceremony had been a driving force behind the reformation as a whole. Moreover the universalist aspirations embedded within radical reformation thought were to some extent common to fragmented christianity as a whole.

---

73 *Ibid.*, p. 121.   74 Fox, *Journal*, p. 22.
75 Mullett, *Radical Religious Movements*, p. 66.
76 Fox, *An Instruction to Judges and Lawyers*, and Fox, *Fifty-nine particulars laid down for regulating things* (1659), quoted in Schenck, *Social Justice*, p. 121.

Thus the doctrine of practical christianity not only united civil war radicals among themselves, but with the broader parliamentarian culture of which they formed a part. It made common cause, for instance, with John Dury, who observed the 'special dutie of Charitie unto all Christians', and sought 'Unity of Spirit' against church government by 'Lordly Prelates', which 'tendeth rather to divide the hearts of Christians one from another'.[77] It overlapped with the concerns of the Hartlib circle, to which Dury belonged, in not only its universalism but above all its pragmatism.[78] Most particularly it belonged to a general mid-century culture of concern about, and publication upon, social problems in general and poverty in particular. This would be recovered and developed during the 1690s in the context of a revived social interest in the reformation of manners.[79]

In *The Poor Man's Advocate* (1649), P. Chamberlen warned: 'The most necessary work of mankind is to provide for the poor . . . And if you provide not for the poor, they will provide for themselves.'[80] Thomas Laurence reminded parliament in the same year: 'God's judgements have been long upon these Nations . . . great bloodshed and burthens have been felt . . . who knoweth but it hath been much for the cause of the poor . . . who stop their ears at the cry of the poor, shall cry themselves.'[81] Readers were directed by *A Poor Man's Friend* (March 1649) to the book of Matthew 25.41: 'God to whom an account must one day be given whether we have fed the hungry, cloathed the naked, visited the sick and imprisoned etc.'[82] Humphrey Barrow reproached hard-hearted christians with that obligation to render 'All that thou hast': 'I was hungry, and ye fed me not.'[83]

77 *Hartlib Papers*, electronic edn, Tract on Church Government, John Dury, 27 December 1641, 68/9/2B; John Dury, 'Concerning the Question Whether it be lawfull to admit Iewes', 68/8/1B.

78 Greengrass, Leslie and Raylor, *Samuel Hartlib and Universal Reformation*; Charles Webster, *The Great Instauration: Science, Medicine and Reform, 1626–1660* (London 1975). Accordingly, Baconian empiricism and seventeenth-century natural philosophy informed both the reformation and renaissance agendas of the revolution (see ch. 14).

79 Dudley Bahlman, *The Moral Revolution of 1688* (New Haven 1957); Craig Rose, 'Providence, Protestant Union and Godly Reformation in the 1690s', *Transactions of the Royal Historical Society* 6th ser., 3 (1993), p. 169.

80 Quoted in Schenck, *Social Justice*, p. 144.

81 Thomas Laurence, *Some Pitty on the Poor* [London n.d.], preface ('To the Parliament').

82 R. B., *The Poor Mans Friend or a Narrative of what progress many worthy Citizens of London have made in that Godly work of providing for the P O O R* (London, 16 March 1649), Epistle.

83 Humphrey Barrow, *The Relief of the Poor, and Advancement of Learning Proposed* (London 1656), p. 1.

Such concerns found expression in parliamentary legislation like the republic's Act for the Relief and Employment of the Poor (1649). Positively and negatively, civil war radicalism fed from the hopes raised by the parliamentary war effort. These aspired to further reformation, and liberty from oppression. Richard Baxter wrote that the fundamental division in England during the 1640s was one of manners, between the profane and godly ('Puritans' and 'Formalists'). It was the union of prelacy with profaneness, and their opposition to the 'Temper of the generality of the Religious Party, [which] was the visible Cause of the overthrow of the King in the Eye of all the understanding World'.[84] In this context radical utterances drew attention to the woeful inadequacy of existing parliamentary measures for the realisation of the moral objectives of the revolution.[85]

It was in the same context that judgements would be made of the revolution's success or failure. Concerning the radical experience as a whole, Christopher Hill, among others, has spoken of 'the experience of defeat'.[86] Yet it seems clear that, in terms of the radical insistence upon practical christianity, the interregnum experience was not of defeat but disillusionment.

It was not that radicals were forever rising up only to be put down. It was that the group upon which successive phases of the process of radical expectation fixed their hopes – the army – actually achieved power, only to disappoint each of them in turn. This became the bitter lesson of the revolution for many radicals – not that 'revolution' could not be achieved, but that when it was so little (with the important negative exception of religious toleration) was achieved with it. In short the victors behaved as their oppressors had before them. As Edward Burrough put it: 'The principle of sincerity . . . of opposing oppression and pressing after reformation [was lost, and many] . . . became self-seekers [and] oppressors even as others before them.'[87] The radicals then were defeated not in the sense that they failed to achieve power. They were defeated by the experience of power-holding itself. George Fox agreed: 'Oh what a seriousness was in the people at the beginning of the wars, yea both small and great . . . oh how is the sincerity choked and smothered and quenched by the fatness of the earth.'[88]

---

84 Richard Baxter, *Reliquiae Baxterianae*, pp. 31–4.
85 R. B., *The Poor Mans Friend*; Barrow, *The Relief of the Poor*; *Act for the Relief and Employment of the Poor* (London 1649).   86 Hill, *Experience of Defeat*.
87 Quoted *ibid.*, p. 150.
88 Quoted *ibid.*, p. 159. Nehemiah Wallington documents the same process of disillusionment, by the 'hardening of their hearts and shutting up of their bowels toward poor creatures that are in misery': Seaver, *Wallington's World*, p. 66.

This was the harsh reality of governing in a pre-industrial society, beset by intractable practical problems and ravaged by war. To many radicals it made the ruling powers of the 1650s even more reprehensible than their predecessors since so much blood and legitimacy had been shed for so little return. The knowing figure at the centre of this tragedy was Oliver Cromwell, who died exhausted by it in 1658.[89]

Thus in contrast to earlier manifestations of the radical reformation, English radicalism was not 'defeated' by any external agency. It was disappointed only in relation to the grandeur of its own moral ambition. Yet this ambition did not disappear. On the contrary, with other aspects of the radical reformation achievement, and restoration notwithstanding, it entered permanently into the culture of English christianity.[90] After 1660 anti-ceremonial, anti-institutional practical christianity lived on. This was true not only within restoration nonconformity, but within a reinvigorated Church of England.[91] Thereafter the movement for reformation of manners which burgeoned during the 1690s was broader than the radical protestantism of mid-century. But it also shared with it several characteristics, and one in particular: the aspiration, by 'removing all Unreasonable Prejudices', to unite all godly protestants. In the words of John Howe, writing in 1698:

To differ about a ceremony or two, or set of words, is but a Tiffle, compar'd with being agreed in absolute devotedness to God, and Christ, and in a design . . . of doing good to all. An Agreement in Substantial Godliness and Christianity, in humility, meekness, self-denial, in singleness of heart, benignity, charity, entire love to sincere Christians . . . universal love to Mankind.[92]

89 Derek Hirst, 'The Lord Protector 1653–1658', in Morrill, *Oliver Cromwell and the English Revolution.*   90 Duffy, 'Long Reformation'.
91 Keeble, *Literary Culture of Nonconformity*; Spurr, *Restoration Church.*
92 Rose, 'Providence', p. 168.

12

Radical reformation (2): outward bondage

[W]here is that liberty so much pretended, so dearly purchased?

John Lilburne, *England's New Chains Discovered* (1649)[1]

There was never yet any prisons or sufferings that I was in, but . . . for the bringing multitudes more *out* of prison.

George Fox[2]

INTRODUCTION: THE LEVELLERS

It is only having examined the positive aspirations of civil war radicalism that we may understand what it was a struggle against. The insistence upon a living christianity of substance, rather than form, was an attempt to realise the government of God, and through it the reality of social community. This entailed the struggle against outward bondage. Effective submission to God required liberty from the carnal oppression of man.

William Walwyn explained: 'If ever men shall kindly be brought to be of one mind . . . it must be by liberty of discourse, and liberty of writing; we must not pretend to more infallible certenty than other men.'[3] This struggle demanded liberty from religious, clerical, political, economic, legal and social oppression. It was this which first drove radicalism into the political arena, and developed civil war radical political theory.

Even here its focus was religious and pragmatic. Leveller pragmatism was expressed in its fundamental identity as a petitioning movement. The primacy of the religious dimension was identified by Thomas Edwards ('In

---

1 John Lilburne, *England's New Chains Discovered* (London 1649), p. 161.
2 Quoted in Geoffrey Nuttall, *Christian Pacifism in History* (Oxford 1958), p. 47.
3 Walwyn, *A Parable*, in *Writings*, p. 260.

one word . . . liberty of conscience, and liberty of preaching')[4] and Richard Baxter ('Liberty of Conscience . . . was the Common Interest in which they did unite').[5] It was this which became the revolution's most important domestic practical achievement. From it, however, developed a demand for liberty from oppression of every kind.

Histories of the Levellers are usually referring to either of two things. The first is that group of writers who came to prominence in 1645–6 in the course of the campaign in London against the reimposition of religious uniformity.[6] The most important were William Walwyn, John Lilburne and Richard Overton. The second is the group who attended the 'Putney Debates' with the Army General Council in October 1647, and argued the case for *The First Agreement of the People*. The most important of these were John Wildman, Colonel Rainsborough and William Petty. Although the cause for which these individuals spoke attained a temporary public following of thousands (in 1648 it even established its own newspaper, *The Moderate*), any notion of a 'Leveller Party' is misleading. Nor was there, initially at least, a Leveller ideology, since the movement drew upon civil war radical belief across the range.[7] As a public phenomenon 'Levellerism' must first be understood as an activity.

The abusive label 'Leveller' was first noted by Richard Overton in July 1647 (and blamed by Richard Baxter in that year upon the army's officers). Later John Lilburne claimed that 'the word Leveller was framed and cast upon all those in the Army (or elsewhere) who are against any kind of Tyranny, whether in King, Parliament, Army, Councel of State etc.'.[8] The movement never established a large-scale organisation of its own. Its leaders were at their most powerful speaking on behalf of constituencies which were not precisely theirs. The most important of these were the

---

4 Edwards, *Gangraena*, p. 17.

5 Richard Baxter, *Reliquiae Baxterianae*, pp. 50–1, 57.

6 J. Frank, *The Levellers* (London 1957); H. Shaw, *The Levellers* (London 1968); Tolmie, *Triumph of the Saints*; David Wootton, 'Leveller Democracy and the Puritan Revolution', in Burns with Goldie, *Cambridge History of Political Thought*; G. Burgess, 'Protestant Polemic: The Leveller Pamphlets', *Parergon* n.s. 11, 2 (December 1993), pp. 45–67.

7 John Morrill has recently challenged the assumption that *The Case of the Army Truly Stated* (1647) contained 'distinctively Leveller ideas' (Morrill, 'The Case of the Armie Truly Re-Stated', draft article, p. 5: I am grateful to Professor Morrill for supplying me with a copy of this article). This may be partly because the closer one looks, the harder 'distinctly Leveller ideas' are to find.

8 Richard Baxter, *Reliquiae Baxterianae*, pp. 53–4; John Lilburne, *The Second Part of England's New-Chaines* (1649), in Haller and Davies, *Leveller Tracts*, p. 1, n. 1.

London gathered churches from 1645, and the army from 1647. They were consequently to be 'betrayed' and 'abandoned' by both in turn. To this extent Leveller power proved illusory: the power that prevailed was that of the army and its religious allies.[9]

Yet in the realm of public belief there is widespread testimony to their prominence as the authors both of petitions and 'Pamphlets, which they abundantly dispersed'.[10] Indeed their political promiscuity makes Leveller utterances more rather than less important. In various ways and at various stages they spoke for the whole radical experience of 1645–9. To assess those utterances it is necessary, first, to look at the range of authorship which differed considerably in style, language and emphasis. It is necessary, secondly, to examine these writings across time, from 1645 to 1649, for they were specific and reactive. It is necessary, finally, to attend to the range of types of utterance. Leveller material came in three forms: petitions, pamphlets and *Agreements of the People* (in 1647, 1648 and 1649). Each had a distinct purpose, and while it is the novel *Agreements* that have attracted the most historical attention the pragmatic reality was the primacy of petitioning.

RHETORIC (AGAINST ARBITRARY GOVERNMENT)

Radicalism was the voice of expectations raised, but not satisfied, by parliament's military victory. That parliament proved so vulnerable to this campaign followed from several factors. Initially it was exposed by its inability to secure a civil settlement; its consequent lack of political authority; and the extreme practical difficulties attending the government of the country in the aftermath of the war. One manifestation of these was the clamour of irreconcilable demands: for religious settlement or liberty; for effective reform or the return of normality; for the satisfaction of military expectations or the reduction of taxation. Alongside these practical difficulties parliament suffered from a deep ideological vulnerability. This followed from its contradiction of every one of its own publicly stated principles in order to win the war.

By 1646 every article of the Petition of Right had been broken. 'The parliamentarian propaganda of 1642 is drenched in the language of civil liberties: of freedom from arbitrary taxation; from arbitrary imprisonment . . .

---

9 Wootton, 'Leveller Democracy', p. 415.
10 Richard Baxter, *Reliquiae Baxterianae*, p. 53.

from the centralizing tendencies of early Stuart monarchy.'[11] In fact the first effective period of English statebuilding, involving sharp centralisation and the development of new forms of taxation, was the accomplishment of parliament in the period 1642–6.[12] This was accompanied by parliamentary claims to absolute or even 'arbitrary' power.[13] Under these circumstances much of the impact of Leveller agitation followed from its effectiveness in using against parliament those weapons it had earlier cultivated in its own support. This meant, rhetorically, a new campaign against arbitrary government. It meant, in practice, petitioning.

John Lilburne was a pioneer of this process. His *England's birth-right justified* (1645) quoted extensively from '*An exact collection of the Parliament's remonstrances, declarations, etc*, published by special order of the House of Commons, 24 March 164[3]'.[14] This spoke of the letter and equity of the law as essential defences against royal tyranny. Lilburne supposed that they would be no less important in defence of the people's 'lives, liberties or estates' against a 'Parliament sitting' as an assembly of their own 'servants':

> Yea, take away the declared, unrepealed law, and where is *meum* and *tuum*, and liberty and property? . . . Therefore doubtless, that man is upon the most solid and firm ground that hath both the letter and equity of a known . . . law on his side, though his practice do cross some pretended privilege of parliament.[15]

Needless to say, no man's practice did this more frequently than Lilburne's own. John Bastwick, a one-time ally, described him calling upon parliament in 1646 with his

> complices, all that Rabble rout, tagragge and bobtaile, that followed him in these his needless and sought for troubles . . . if ever you had . . . heard their confused, hiddious noyses, calling for the liberties of the Subjects, and for the benefit of Magna Charta, and the Petition of Right, and for a publike hearing, you would have thought your self in the very Suburbs of Hell.[16]

---

11 Morrill, 'The Army Revolt of 1647', in Morrill, *Oliver Cromwell and the English Revolution*, p. 307.

12 Braddick, *Parliamentary Taxation*; Braddick, *Nerves of State*; Marjolein 'T Hart, '"The Devil or the Dutch": Holland's Impact on the Financial Revolution in England, 1643–1694', *Parliaments, Estates and Representation* 11, 1 (June 1991).

13 Mendle, *Parker and the English Civil War*, pp. 87–8.

14 Sharp, *Political Ideas of the English Civil Wars*, p. 172.   15 *Ibid.*, pp. 173–4.

16 John Bastwick, one-time Lilburne ally, quoted in Walwyn, *Writings*, p. 22.

The result of this behaviour was early and repeated imprisonment. Building upon his early martyrdom under the lash of Laudian tyranny (1639) Lilburne spent most of the period 1646–9 in prison.[17] This helps to account both for the quantity of his printed polemic and for the proportion of it dealing with contemporary legal process and prison conditions. Accordingly one of the first major collaborative Leveller utterances (1646) made this situation its focal point. This was the

Remonstrance of Many Thousand Citizens, and other Free-Born People of England, To their owne House of Commons. Occasioned through the Illegal and Barbarous Imprisonment of that Famous and Worthy Sufferer for his Countries Freedoms, Lieutenant Col. John Lilburne. Wherin their just Demands, in behalfe of themselves and the whole Kingdome, concerning their Publike Safety, Peace and Freedome, is Express'ed; calling these their Commissioners in Parliament to an Account how they . . . have Discharged their Duties to the Universality of the People, their soveraigne L O R D, from who their Power and strength is derived.[18]

The provocative expression reflected the hand of Overton, soon to join the list of prisoners. But Walwyn was still to be making the same point in *The Bloody Project* (1648):

You saw the Common-wealth enslaved for want of Parliaments, and also by their sudden dissolution, and you rejoyced that this Parliament was not to be dissolved by the King; but did you conceive it would have sat seven yeares to so little purpose, or that it should ever have come to passe, to be esteemed a crime to move for the ending thereof? . . . Was it . . . [that] parliament . . . only might have liberty to oppresse at their pleasure, without any hope of remedy . . . those vast disbursements, and those thousands of lives that have been spent and destroyed in the late war.[19]

In its radicalised form 'arbitrary government' no longer meant simply government without parliament or law, but unrepresentative or oppressive government in general. The question of oppression dominated Leveller petitions. In tune with radical anti-formalism the Leveller focus was upon ends, rather than means; not mechanisms of government, but their effect upon the governed. In time, however, the latter concern compelled

---

17 Pauline Gregg, *Free-Born John: A Biography of John Lilburne* (London 1961).

18 *A Remonstrance of Many Thousand Citizens, and other Free-Born People of England* (1646), in Wolfe, *Leveller Manifestoes*, partially reprinted in Walwyn, *Writings*, pp. 225–6.

19 Walwyn, *The Bloody Project* (1648), in Haller and Davies, *Leveller Tracts*, p. 138.

consideration of the former. As we will see the *Agreements of the People* directed their attention to both.

At the same time the field of application of the accusation of arbitrary government was extended. In the petition of March 1647, for instance, of the thirteen numbered articles, two related to political, three to religious, one to economic, one to social and six to legal oppression.[20] By that of January 1648, for 'Liberties and Freedomes' against 'Oppressors and Tyrants', five articles addressed political, six legal, three economic, one religious and one social aspects of 'our Slavery'.[21] Quentin Skinner has recently located a struggle in this period for liberty understood as freedom from slavery.[22] This was only one component of the English republican understanding of liberty. It was, however, a component already visible in the 1640s.

PRACTICE (PETITIONING)

The primary practical application of this ideology came as petitioning. In the Leveller movement 'tumultuous petitioning' was turned against parliament itself. Indeed the Levellers emerged, initially, as a counter-petitioning movement. The petitions to be countered were those from the presbyterian city of London government calling for the restoration of religious magistracy. This was a plea to which the presbyterian majority in parliament were sympathetic. Even had they not been, this was a constituency upon whom they had been, and remained, dependent.

Neither rhetorically nor in practice, therefore, did Levellerism emerge as a demand for new freedoms. It coalesced in response to a threat to freedoms which had been enjoyed *de facto* for several years. Parliament thus found itself besieged by petitions. Its response, in 1646, as more dangerously the following year, was to establish a public distinction between those petitions which were and were not acceptable. Results in the latter case included not only denunciation and imprisonment, but burning of the offending items by the public hangman. Predictably these further examples of arbitrary government were exploited. In June 1647 Walwyn reprinted *Gold Tried in the Fire; or, The Burnt Petitions Revived.*[23]

---

20 Walwyn, *Gold Tried in the Fire, or The Burnt Petitions Revived*, in *Writings*, pp. 283–5.
21 Wolfe, *Leveller Manifestoes*, pp. 264–71.
22 Quentin Skinner, *Liberty Before Liberalism* (Cambridge 1997).
23 In Walwyn, *Writings*, pp. 275–93.

One response to this treatment was to continue to attract it, drawing attention to the blamelessness of petitioning. The petition of January 1648 explained

That though our Petitions have been burned, and our persons imprisoned, reviled, and abused only for petitioning, yet we cannot despair absolutely of all bowels of compassion in this Honourable House, to an inslaved perishing people. We still nourish some hopes, that you wil at last consider that our estates are expended, the whole trade of the Nation decayed, thousands of families impoverished, and merci-less Famine is entered into our Gates, and therefore we cannot but once more assay to pierce your eares with our dolefull cries for Justice and Freedom.[24]

Another, however, was to appeal over the heads of a deaf representative to the people represented. The principle behind this was explained in one of the most important pamphlets of the period, Overton's *An Appeale from the Degenerate House of Commons to the Representative Body of the People* (1647):

The transgression of our weal by our trustees is an utter forfeiture of their trust, and cessation of their power. Therefore if I prove a forfeiture of the people's trust in the prevalent party at Westminster in Parliament assembled, then an appeale from them to the people is not anti-Parliamentary, anti-magisterial; not *from* that sove-reign power but *to* that sovereign power.[25]

Yet the vulnerability of parliament to petitioning disguised a deeper vul-nerability of the Levellers themselves. Alongside their dependence upon other organisations, whether the army or the gathered churches, petition-ing underlined their dependence upon parliament itself. All the bodies to which the movement looked for redress against arbitrary government were those arbitrary powers themselves. This was one consequence of the relative lack of independent Leveller organisation. It was in turn a practical mani-festation of the campaign against public (civil and clerical) power. To have constructed such an organisation, capable of taking and wielding power, would have exposed the movement to all its own polemical criticisms. This was the anti-formal political dilemma.

Thus the scope of the accusation of arbitrary government was expanded by the Levellers in a second way. It was applied to every institution con-cerned with the public exercise of power. Between 1645 and 1649 it shad-owed the exercise of such power as it was directed in turn against king and

24 Wolfe, *Leveller Manifestoes*, p. 264.   25 In Woodhouse, *Puritanism and Liberty*, p. 327.

clergy, the House of Lords and then the Commons, the army and then the newly erected republic. In the words of Overton, testifying with customary clarity before the republican Council of State in 1649:

> It is all one to me under what name or title soever oppression be exercised, whether under the name of King, Parliament, Council of State . . . for tyranny and oppression is tyranny and oppression . . . and whenever I find it, I shall oppose it, without respect of persons.[26]

In practice this was not simply an appeal against oppression. What it amounted to under early modern conditions was opposition to the exercise of public power. It was in this sense that Leveller practice and theory were as anti-political as its religion was anti-magisterial. This is why, as we will see, the most important Leveller intellectual achievement was the development of a theory supporting the limitation of public power.

Leveller pragmatism was not, of course, uninformed by general principles. On this level there was considerable consistency over time. Thus the petition of 11 September 1648 demanded that government should be solely by the people's representatives (free from 'all pretences of Negative voices . . . in King or Lords'); that such assemblies should be limited in duration and newly elected every year; that 'matters of Religion' should be free 'from the compulsive or restrictive power of any Authoritie upon earth'; that similarly 'future Representatives' should disclaim 'any power of Pressing'; that there should be equality before the law (particularly between Lords and commoners) and the law simplified and rendered into English; that monopolies, enclosures, tithes, imprisonment for debt and oppressive taxation should be abolished; that people should be released from oppression by prerogative courts, parliamentary committees, unnecessary parliamentary ordinances, penal authorities and the government of the city of London; and finally that 'some effectual course' should be found 'to keep people from begging and beggary, in so fruitful a Nation as through God's blessing this is'.[27] The most important beliefs informing these demands were in popular sovereignty, in liberty (from oppression) and in equality (or 'equity'). All were extrapolations from that practical christianity examined in the previous chapter, and here too the Leveller position involved a radicalisation of parliamentary claims.

26 John Sanderson, *'But the People's Creatures': The Philosophical Basis of the English Civil War* (Manchester 1989), p. 102.   27 Wolfe, *Leveller Manifestoes*, pp. 287–9.

These three principles came together in a statement like that of John Wildman at Putney that 'Every person hath as cleere a right to elect his representatives as the greatest person in England. I conceive that's the undeniable maxim of government, that all government is in the free consent of the people.'[28] In general, however, Leveller polemic emphasised the particular rather than general and ends rather than means. We may better understand this by looking at the first and most famous Leveller constitutional proposal, *An Agreement of the People* (1647).[29] This in turn requires some preliminary attention to its political context.

THE PUTNEY DEBATES

Both for its content and its apparent practical purpose the first *Agreement* is a striking document. Additionally, it is famous for the key role it played on the second day of the so-called Putney Debates of late October and early November 1647. These record the debate between Leveller spokesmen and army officers at the high point of their 1647 alliance against the arbitrary government of parliament.[30]

The modern book most responsible for focusing our attention upon these was C. B. MacPherson's *The Political Theory of Possessive Individualism*. This used day two of the debates, dominated by an argument about the electoral franchise, to say that the Levellers understood political freedom to entail economic self-sufficiency. Those 'free-born Englishmen' on behalf of whose rights they struggled excluded those in receipt not only of alms but also of wages: anyone economically dependent.[31] Since MacPherson's book discussion of the Levellers has been dominated by the question of their view of franchise.[32] This is unfortunate both because they didn't have such a view, corporately held, and because this is precisely why their opponents made this subject the focal point for discussion.

---

28 Firth, *The Clarke Papers*, vol. I, p. 318, quoted in Morrill, 'Case of the Armie', p. 14.
29 *An Agreement of the People, for a firme and present Peace, upon grounds of Common-Right* (1647), in Wolfe, *Leveller Manifestoes*, pp. 226–30.
30 Firth, *The Clarke Papers*; Woodhouse, *Puritanism and Liberty*.
31 C. B. MacPherson, *The Political Theory of Possessive Individualism: Hobbes to Locke* (Oxford 1962).
32 J. C. Davis, 'The Levellers and Democracy', *Past and Present* 40 (July 1968); Keith Thomas, 'The Levellers and the Franchise', in G. E. Aylmer (ed.), *The Interregnum: The Quest for Settlement 1646–1660* (London 1972); Iain Hampsher-Monk, 'Putney, Property, and Professor MacPherson', *Political Studies* 24 (1976), pp. 397–422.

Democracy is a political preoccupation of the modern west. It therefore comes naturally to twentieth-century historians who wish to argue about how 'radical' the Levellers were to do so by holding them up for measurement against the slide rule of the franchise. In fact the test of that radicalism would be their attitude to change, not to the franchise. This was a crucial contemporary issue and day one, not two, of the debate at Putney was dominated by it (October 28th). This discussion hinged upon the question of the extent to which the army could consider itself free from adherence to its previously published engagements.[33] When the question of the franchise was put the following day no two Leveller answers were the same. This was because it had never occurred to them.[34] Thus the resulting historiography is a less adequate introduction to Leveller thought than to the things about which they had not thought.[35]

The debates at Putney church were the unintended outgrowth of a regular meeting of the army's own Council of Officers. Their context has been greatly clarified by Mark Kishlansky and Austin Woolrych. To Kishlansky we owe the recovery of the distinction between Leveller and army causes.[36] This has intruded into our hazy modern admiration of radical belief a much-needed dose of military reality. To this Woolrych has added by focusing our attention upon the preoccupation of the army's officers with unity. This not only informs everything said at Putney by Cromwell and Ireton but explains why the discussions were held in the first place.[37]

From 1646 those agitating for a presbyterian national church settlement referred to opposition both among the London gathered churches and in the New Model. Yet until the collision over army disbandment in April and May 1647 these were potential allies pursuing separate courses. In one crucial respect, indeed, their trajectories were opposed. As John Morrill has explained, the embattled parliamentary authority could not simultaneously address the demand by the Levellers for an end to arbitrary government and that by the army for arrears of pay.[38]

---

33 Woodhouse, *Puritanism and Liberty*, pp. 1–37.   34 *Ibid.*, pp. 38–94.

35 For a recent summary and verdict, see Wootton, 'Leveller Democracy', pp. 429–33.

36 Kishlansky, *New Model Army*; Kishlansky, 'The Roads to Putney'.

37 Woolrych, *Soldiers and Statesmen*; Woolrych, 'Putney Revisited', in S. Roberts (ed.), *Politics and People in Revolutionary England* (London 1986).

38 Morrill, 'Army Revolt', pt IV.

In early 1647 the Levellers were pamphleteers and petitioners of the state; the army its employees. It was parliament's proposals for disbandment which, in March 1647, turned the New Model into a petitioner too. It petitioned on behalf not of general religious or political principles but its professional grievances: above all that there should be no disbandment before attention had been given to arrears of pay and the issue of legal indemnity.[39] It is not surprising that faced by extreme political and financial problems parliament should have had difficulty attending to these grievances. What was fatal was its overreaction to their presentation.

The resulting *Declaration* 'published in the name of both Houses highly censur[ed] the said petition . . . declaring the petitioners, if they should proceed thereupon, no less than enemies to the state and disturbers of the public peace'.[40] Reflecting panic at the possibility of resistance to disbandment, this denunciation nevertheless overlooked two things. One was that package of liberties (including that of petitioning) on behalf of which parliament had encouraged others to hazard their lives in its defence. The other was the army's responsibility for the subsequent victory.

The resulting indignation provided much of the motive force behind the series of army responses in May and June. These took the form of internal organisation and commitment to the objective of resisting disbandment until the growing list of grievances had been addressed:[41]

We shall cheerfully and readily disband when thereunto required by the parliament . . . having first such satisfaction . . . in relation to our grievances and desires heretofore presented, and such security that we ourselves, when disbanded and in the condition of private men, or other the freeborn people of England (to whom the consequence of our case doth equally extend), shall not remain subject to the like oppression, injury, or abuse.[42]

This was accompanied by a series of declarations putting the army's case in increasingly general political terms. These claimed that 'Parliament hath declared it no resistance of magistracy to side with the just principles of law, nature and nations.' They spoke of 'the proceedings of our ancestors of famous memory, to the purchasing of such rights and liberties as they have enjoyed through the price of their blood':

---

39 Kishlansky, *New Model Army*; Kishlansky, 'The Roads to Putney'; Morrill, 'Army Revolt'.
40 'A Solemn Engagement of the Army' (5 June), in Woodhouse, *Puritanism and Liberty*, p. 401.   41 Woolrych, *Soldiers and Statesmen*.
42 Woodhouse, *Puritanism and Liberty*, p. 402.

Especially considering that we were not a mere mercenary army, hired to serve any arbitrary power of a state, but called forth and conjured by the several declarations of Parliament to the defence of our own and the people's just rights and liberties.[43]

It is not surprising that in this context army and Leveller spokesmen found common cause. Between May and September, culminating in the army's march on London and the expulsion from the Commons of eleven presby- terian leaders, there is plenty of evidence of Leveller input to New Model agitation.[44]

Until October nothing about this process threatened control of the army by its own officers. The grievances of the rank and file were expressed through a structure of 'agitators' erected under their supervision. What caused alarm, however, in October, was not only the circulation of a new document without approval of the General Council and in competition with the army's own *Heads of Proposals* (August 1647). This was *The Case of the Armie Truly Stated* (15 October) usually said to have been written at least in part by John Wildman.[45] Even more troubling was the appearance among the rank and file of 'Agents' distinct from the agitators and operating outside officer control.[46]

This appeared to pose a threat to the unity upon which the army's very sur- vival depended. This was the background to the decision to call that meeting of the General Council of Officers which became the Putney Debates. To this the authors of *The Case* were invited – 'as there is no hope of accommodation or union, except we receive the counsels . . . of them that come to us'[47] – expo- sure being the essential preliminary to recovered control. It is for this reason that the first day of discussion on 28 October focused on the question of the army's previous engagements. Having observed that 'this paper [*The Case*] does contain in it very great alterations to the very government of the kingdom, alterations from that government that it hath been under, I believe I may almost say, since it was a nation', Cromwell continued:

How do we know if, whilst we are disputing these things, another company of men shall [not] gather together, and put out a paper as plausible perhaps as this? . . . And

43 'A Representation of the Army' (14 June), *ibid.*, p. 404.
44 Richard Baxter, *Reliquiae Baxterianae*, pp. 53–4; Gentles, *New Model Army*, pp. 200–14; Woolrych, *Soldiers and Statesmen*.
45 Morrill, 'Case of the Armie', challenges the attribution to Wildman.
46 Woolrych, *Soldiers and Statesmen*.
47 Woodhouse, *Puritanism and Liberty*, p. 31 (the speaker is Cromwell).

if so, what do you think the consequence of that would be ... Would it not be utter confusion? ... But first of all there is the question what obligations lie upon us and how far we are engaged ... we have in the time of our danger issued out declarations; we have been required by the Parliament, because our declarations were general, to declare particularly what we meant ... and God does expect from men the performance of every honest obligation.[48]

While the strategic purpose of this speech is obvious enough, there is also no more important discussion of the issues surrounding radicalism itself. The Leveller response was that they felt bound by justice rather than precedent. Their attempt to recover the initiative the following day by introducing without warning a new document (*An Agreement of the People, for a firme and present Peace, upon grounds of Common-Right*) might have been more successful against a lesser opponent. Caught temporarily off guard, however, Henry Ireton proved terrifying on the rebound.

THE FIRST *AGREEMENT OF THE PEOPLE* (1647)

In his response to the *Agreement*, Ireton displayed the tactical sensibilities of any talented military commander. Behind this vague talk about justice and freedom there was an absence of the practical planning upon which success in battle depended. This is ironic in view of our understanding of the Levellers as pragmatic. They were indeed precise about the manifestations of outward bondage they would have removed. It was in relation, however, not to the effect of government upon the governed but to the mechanisms of government themselves that their utterances had yet to transcend the level of general principle.

Thus after reading the *Agreement* as a whole, and then again the first article, Ireton's response was

The exception that lies in it is this. It is said, they are to be distributed according to the number of inhabitants: 'The people of England' etc. And this doth make me think that the meaning is, that every man that is an inhabitant is to be equally considered, and to have an equal voice in the election of those representers.[49]

To this the response ranged from Petty's 'all inhabitants that have not lost their birthright should have an equal voice in elections' to Rainsborough's famous 'the poorest he that is in England hath a life to live, as the greatest

---

48 *Ibid.*, p. 9.   49 *Ibid.*, p. 52.

he'.[50] In a debate called to restore army unity, Ireton achieved the objective of destroying the unity of his opponents. The route to understanding Leveller objectives is not to follow the charge subsequently mounted against these scattering remnants. It is to look at the document itself.

The preamble and postscript reminded readers of the 'late labours and hazards' run in defence of 'our just freedom'. In speaking 'not only [of] the examples of our Ancestors, whose bloud was often spent in vain for the recovery of their Freedomes', but also of 'our own wofull experience', it offered a direct challenge to the army's strategy of continued negotiation with the king: 'having long expected, and dearly earned the establishment of these certain rules of Government [we] are yet made to depend for the settlement of our Peace and Freedome, upon him that intended our bondage, and brought a cruell Warre upon us'.[51] The body of the document, however, came in two sections, numbered respectively with Roman (I–IV) and Arabic (1–5) numerals. The common concern of both was the limitation of political power.

The first section addressed the issues of limitation of duration, and accountability. Power might only be exercised by assemblies of the people's representatives. These needed to be made more representative by electoral reform; to be limited in time to two years; and remained inferior in power to those 'who chose them'. The second section exempted a series of key matters from the jurisdiction of government altogether. These included pre-eminently 'matters of Religion, and the wayes of Gods Worship'; but also 'the matter of impresting and constraining any of us to serve in the warres'; indemnity for acts committed during wartime; and equality before the law.[52] All of these amounted to the removal from the jurisdiction of human government those matters which belonged only to the government of God.

Richard Tuck has suggested that the primary interest of 'Lilburne and his followers' was 'in the principle of [parliamentary] election and representation' rather than with 'fundamental limitations on *any* Parliament's capacities'. It was, that is to say, in the first rather than the second part of the *Agreement*. According to Tuck, indeed, Lilburne believed 'in the supremacy of Parliament, provided it was truly representative and properly elected'.[53] In fact, however, there seems to be more evidence to suggest that Lilburne,

---

50 *Ibid.*, pp. 53, 83.
51 *An Agreement of the People* (1647), in Wolfe, *Leveller Manifestoes*, p. 228.
52 *Ibid.*, pp. 227–8.   53 Tuck, *Philosophy and Government*, p. 243.

like other Levellers, believed in the supremacy of the people (to say nothing of God, history, nature and the law) over their representatives. Almost all Leveller writing was directed to the curtailment, rather than construction of parliamentary power. The section of the *Agreement* on accountability – on the people as authors, rather than subjects, of power – was in service of this objective.

In this radicalised conception of popular sovereignty the Levellers were once again using against parliament an adapted version of one of its own arguments. The popular authorship of political power had been claimed by parliament in its struggle against the king. The Levellers agreed that the only legitimate government lay in the people's representatives. In authorising those representatives to act on their behalf the people did not, however, transfer to them that political power which remained in themselves. On the contrary they chose them to exercise it by representation: a commission that could be revoked at any time.

If this was the theoretical position informing the first section of the *Agreement*, that informing the second was more important. This was a radicalised version of another parliamentary language: natural law theory. The most articulate exponent of this, as of the radical theory of popular sovereignty, was Richard Overton. It built upon a conception of God-given reason common to civil war radicalism and republicanism. In the words of Rainsborough at Putney: 'I do think that the main cause why Almighty God gave men reason . . . was that they should make use of that reason, and that they should improve it for that end and purpose that God gave it them.'[54]

LEVELLER POLITICAL THEORY

In several works written between 1628 and 1652, Sir Robert Filmer attacked three ways of speaking about politics which supported what he called 'the whole Fabrick of this vast Engine of Popular sedition'.[55] The first was ancient constitutionalism, which Filmer associated with Sir Edward Coke and claims for the antiquity of parliaments.[56] The second was natural law

---

54 Woodhouse, *Puritanism and Liberty*, p. 55.
55 Filmer, *Patriarcha* (London 1680), p. 4; on the dating of Filmer's work, see Tuck, 'A New Date for Filmer's *Patriarcha*', *Historical Journal* 29, 1 (1986); Filmer, *Patriarcha and Other Writings*, ed. Johann Sommerville (Cambridge 1991), p. viii.
56 Filmer, *Patriarcha and Other Writings*, pp. 89–92.

theory, which he associated with Suarez, Bellarmine and Grotius.[57] The third was classical republicanism, which he associated with the bloody politics of ancient Athens and Rome, and their defender Machiavelli.[58] The radical potential of the latter would be demonstrated after the regicide. Leveller political theory principally entailed a radicalisation of the first two languages, and indeed some tension between them.

Another way of saying this is that Leveller demands were underpinned by appeals first to history, and then to reason. The most famous purveyor of Leveller ancient constitutionalism was John Lilburne. In 1645 William Walwyn attempted to bring Lilburne to see the limitations of such appeals to precedent. The people's freedom needed a securer basis than Magna Charta ('a mess of pottage'): not that which was oldest, but best. Here as elsewhere Lilburne was adapting parliamentary rhetoric. The *Petition of Right* and the ancient rights of freeborn Englishmen could be appealed to not only in defence of parliament, but also against it.

The most famous manifestation of Leveller ancient constitutionalism – Norman Yoke theory – adapted parliamentarian claims to the point of inverting them. Early Stuart defenders of the antiquity of parliaments and the common law had denied that a Norman conquest had occurred, insisting that William had submitted himself to govern by the English law.[59] This argument was repeated during the interregnum by John Milton (against Salmasius), and during the restoration period by William Penn and Algernon Sidney. The Levellers, however, while similarly seeking conformity to an imagined state of Anglo-Saxon freedom and good government, argued that present English government and law derived from a state of Norman bondage introduced in 1066. In this way a conservative argument was inverted to the service of change.

Walwyn and Overton agreed about the moral and intellectual limitations of ancient constitutionalism. It was the two collaboratively who, after repeating this argument about Norman slavery, made the most striking attempt of the period to liberate the radical cause from appeals to precedent altogether:

The history of our forefathers since they were conquered by the Normans doth manifest that this nation hath been held in bondage . . . But . . . then ye [parliament]

---

57 *Ibid.*, pp. 5–22, 64–5, 208–34.   58 *Ibid.*, pp. 24–31, 134, 288.

59 J. G. A. Pocock, *The Ancient Constitution and the Feudal Law: A Reissue with Retrospect* (Cambridge 1987), pp. 52–5; Burgess, *Politics of the Ancient Constitution*, pp. 82–5.

were chosen to work our deliverance and to estate us in natural and just liberty agreeable to reason and common equity. For whatever our forefathers were, or whatever they did or suffered or were enforced to yield unto, we are men of the present age and ought to be free from all kind of exorbitancies, molestations or arbitrary power.[60]

This was to open the only direct route to the realisation of radical objectives anchored in a relationship not to time but God. Precisely for this reason, however, Lilburne's rhetoric, like his person, enjoyed a popularity and public impact beyond comparison with the others. It combined the attraction of an appeal to English chauvinism with that of one to custom. The resulting public currency was not to be emulated by the universalist ambition of Overton's concept of limited self-propriety or Walwyn's insistence upon the moral superiority of Montaigne's cannibals.

That is why, at his trial in 1649, Lilburne's stand had not changed at all. He sought the protection of 'the Laws and Liberties . . . of every free-born Englishman . . . which by my birth-right and inheritance is due unto me'. He explained that his accusers

come to ensnare and entrap me with unknown niceties and formalities that are locked up in the French and Latin tongue . . . it is not fair play according to the Law of England, plainly in English expressed in the Petition of Right, and other good old statutes of the land.

He explained to his 'honest jury and fellow citizens' that they had 'in them alone the judicial power of the law', calling his judges 'but cyphers to pronounce' the sentence. When he added that the latter were 'the Norman Conqueror's intruders . . . The People with a loud voice cried Amen, Amen, and gave an extraordinary great hum.'[61] The defendant was acquitted.

In terms of public impact, therefore, Leveller ancient constitutionalism remained important. In intellectual terms, however, Leveller claims became principally dependent upon a radical natural law theory. Developed from Aquinas' christianisation of Aristotle, natural law theory was the dominant early modern christian political language. In the train of the wars unleashed by the reformation it had been used by both catholics and protestants to

---

60 [Overton and Walwyn], *A remonstrance of many thousand citizens*, in Sharp, *Political Ideas*, pp. 181–2.

61 *The Triall of Lieutenant Collonel John Lilburne* (1649), p. 4, quoted in Annabel Patterson, *Early Modern Liberalism* (Cambridge 1997), pp. 115–16.

justify resistance.[62] James I directed his polemic principally against catholic natural law theorists, though similar language had been used for the same purpose by his own protestant tutor Buchanan. Thereafter Filmer, while equally emphasising the catholic origins of the theory, also attacked Buchanan and denounced its most important recent reworking by the Dutch protestant Hugo Grotius.[63]

From 1640 the language of England's troubles also was dominated by natural law theory in general and Grotius in particular. They stood at the core of parliamentary justifications of resistance by the laws of necessary self-defence. If the common law had furnished the language of the early Stuart pacified polity, it was natural law theory which spoke to the condition of the troubles.[64] This was because it provided a general moral authority above that of human law. With it, the emphasis of polemical appeals shifted from historical and scriptural particularity to reason.

Accordingly Overton's *Appeale from the Degenerate House of Commons* (1647) turned parliament's earlier appeals to the people into the basis of an appeal to them against it. 'It is a firme Law and radicall principle in Nature', Overton reminded his readers,

engraven in the tables of the heart by the finger of God in creation for every living moving thing . . . to defend, preserve . . . and deliver it selfe from all things hurtfull [and] destructive . . . to the utmost of its power: Therefore from hence is conveyed to all men . . . an undoubted principle of reason, by all rationall and just wayes and meanes . . . to save, defend and deliver himselfe from all oppression, violence and cruelty whatsoever . . . to deny [this], is to [overturn] the law of nature, yea, and of Religion too.[65]

'[U]pon this *Principle*', he continued,

the *Netherlanders* made a . . . defence and resistance against the King of *Spaine* . . . for the recovery of their just rights and freedomes; and upon the same *point* rose the *Scotch* up in Armes, and entred this Kingdome . . . and were justified for that very act by this present Parliament. Yea, and even this Parliament upon the same principle,

62 Franklin, *Constitutionalism and Resistance*; Skinner, *Foundations of Modern Political Thought*, vol. II, ch. 9; Martin van Gelderen, 'The Machiavellian Moment and the Dutch Revolt', in Bock, Skinner and Viroli, *Machiavelli and Republicanism*, pp. 221–2.

63 In Filmer, *Patriarcha and Other Writings*.

64 Glenn Burgess, *Absolute Monarchy and the Stuart Constitution* (New Haven 1996), pp. 161–4; Scott, 'Restoration Process', pp. 633–7.

65 Overton, *Appeale From the degenerate Representative*, in Wolfe, *Leveller Manifestoes*, pp. 159–60.

tooke up Armes against the King. And now (*right worthy patriots of the Army*) you your selves upon the *same principle*, for *recovery of common right* and *freedome*, have entered upon this your present honourable and *Solemne Engagement*, against the oppressing party at *Westminster* . . . and tell them in the fifth pag. of your Declaration, *That the Parliament hath declared it no resistance of Magristracie to side with the just principles and law of nature and nations, being that law upon which you have assisted them.*[66]

Overton understood this 'Principle' not simply as a defence of rights. We had a 'duty to [our] own safety and being' grounded in that to their author, God. It was by consideration of this relationship to man's creator that Overton would make natural law theory more than simply a double-edged justification of resistance. For the theoretical basis not for self-defence against illegitimate power, but the radical limitation of all political power, we need to turn to his *An Arrow against All Tyrants* (1646).

This pamphlet put forward Overton's doctrine of limited self-propriety. This claimed not only that

To every individual in nature is given an individual property in nature not to be invaded and usurped by any. For everyone . . . hath a self-propriety else could he not be himself . . . [and] it is nature's instinct to preserve itself from all things hurtful and obnoxious . . . from this fountain or root all just human powers take their original . . . as we are delivered of God by the hand of nature into this world . . . with a natural innate freedom and propriety . . . no second may partake [of this] but by deputation, commission, and free consent from him whose natural right and freedom it is.[67]

As the law of nature forbade invasion of the freedom and property of others so it equally forbade us to abuse ourselves. This was because this self-propriety was in fact limited, our persons belonging absolutely only to our creator, not to ourselves. And from this limited self-propriety followed the limited power of all governments. 'For as by nature no man may abuse, beat, torment or afflict himself, so by nature no man may give that power to another . . . for no more can be communicated . . . [to] the general than is included in the particulars whereof the general is compounded.'[68]

Pre-Grotian natural law theorists like Suarez had distinguished between natural rights and property. Private property ownership was not possible

66 *Ibid.*, pp. 160–1.
67 Overton, *An Arrow against All Tyrants* (1646), in Sharp, *Political Ideas*, pp. 177–8.
68 *Ibid.*, p. 179.

without civil law and so it was one of the principal reasons for leaving the state of nature and establishing civil society to make private property ownership possible. It was Grotius who first insisted that not only our liberties and persons but also the private property necessary to sustain them were held in nature, not only in civil society. According to Grotius, therefore, we entered civil society not to acquire private property but to better secure that which we already owned.

For Grotius, however, this natural right to property (including property in one's person) was absolute. Henry Parker agreed: every man 'has an absolute power over himself'.[69] Accordingly should people decide in a state of nature that the only way to protect their lives was to sacrifice their liberties they were perfectly entitled to erect a despotism. Constitutions specified the extent of civil power in any particular polity.[70]

Overton agreed with Grotius that property was a natural rather than civil construct. Because, however, for Overton this natural property right (and self-propriety) was limited (property was held in trust from God, the actual owner of nature), the erection of a legitimate despotism was impossible. For that reason all 'tyranny, oppression and cruelty whatsoever and in whomsoever is in itself unnatural, illegal, yea, absolutely anti-magisterial'.[71]

Thus the most important contribution of civil war radicalism to political theory followed from a characteristic emphasis not only upon rights but duties: the limits of our liberty and property under the government of God. The Leveller objective remained liberty not as an end but rather a means to the appropriate relationship to God. A vestige of this perspective would remain within English republicanism. It was in an attempt to put these assumptions into practice that the *Agreements of the People* abstracted from human governmental authority those areas immediately subject to the government of God.

One other, broader natural law theory assumption underpinned the *Agreements of the People*. This was that the civil war of 1642–6 had dissolved the old fabric of civil government. It was because England had returned to a state of nature that it became possible and necessary to erect a new constitutional fabric. *The Agreement of the People* (1647) was to be that constitution,

69 Mendle, *Parker and the English Civil War*, p. 88 (for Parker and Grotius, see pp. 131–2).
70 Richard Tuck, *Natural Rights Theories* (Cambridge 1979); Burns with Goldie, *Cambridge History of Political Thought*, ch. 17; Tuck, *Philosophy and Government*, ch. 5 (e.g., p. 173).
71 Overton, *Arrow against All Tyrants*, in Sharp, *Political Ideas*, p. 179.

signed by every political person submitting themselves to it. It was this assumption which was attacked by Ireton when he said:

The Law of God doth not give me property, nor the Law of Nature, but property is of human constitution. Constitution founds property . . . If you will take away that, and set up, as a thing paramount, whatever a man may claim by the Law of Nature . . . where then remains property?[72]

Contrary to Richard Tuck's understanding of him as a student of Grotius, this would appear to indicate that Ireton's position was orthodox and pre-Grotian.[73]

THE LIMITS OF POLITICAL THEORY 1648–9

The climax of the struggle against outward bondage came in the abolition of the church, monarchy and House of Lords. This was secured without theoretical assistance. It was also secured against the wishes of 'the people', Levellers included, by the power of the sword placed by God in certain hands.

This, too, was a matter of duty. There was the duty to God to cleanse the land of innocent blood. The alternative was (as the bloody events of 1648 had shown) the continuation of those wars for ever. What more pragmatic ideology was there than providentialism: the interpretation of God's actions in the world? This is not to say that the army did not, even before the event, attempt to defend its actions in theoretical terms. The most important such document was Ireton's *Remonstrance of His Excellency Thomas Lord Fairfax . . . and of the Generall Councell of Officers Held at St Albans the 16 of November 1648*. That this had any practical bearing upon the outcome is, however, to be doubted. Nor is this to deny that the regicide was defended with some vigour, not least in Milton's *The Tenure of Kings and Magistrates* (1649). It is necessary, however, to distinguish the causes of this action from its retrospective justification.

In political terms at least, the first phase of the revolution, no less than the second, would end in failure. For liberty from outward bondage, whether parliamentary or monarchical, no less than for the practical government of God, the people of England remain waiting.

72 Woodhouse, *Puritanism and Liberty*, pp. 69, 60.
73 Tuck, *Philosophy and Government*, p. 246.

13

Radical renaissance (1): after monarchy

> Hobbes indeed doth scurrilously deride Cicero, Plato and Aristotle, *caeterosque Romanae & Graecae anarchiae fautores*. But 'tis strange that this anarchy . . . that can have no strength and regular action, should overthrow all the monarchies that came within their reach . . . I desire it may be considered whether it were an easy work to conquer Switzerland: Whether the Hollanders are of greater strength since the recovery of their liberty, or when they groaned under the yoke of Spain: And lastly, whether the entire conquest of Scotland and Ireland, the victories obtained against the Hollanders when they were in the height of their power, and the reputation to which England did rise in less than five years after 1648, be good marks of the instability, disorder and weakness of free nations?
>
> Algernon Sidney, *Discourses Concerning Government*[1]

INTRODUCTION

Much modern historical discussion of the English revolution has been governed by attempts to appropriate it. As revolutions are considered the harbingers of modernity, no revolutionary entrails have been inspected more fastidiously than the English.[2] One consequence is the elision of a historical 'other' into an anticipation of ourselves. The other is sectarianisation: the intrusion of the modern need to categorise and subdivide.

To this generalisation the historiography of English republicanism, despite its quality, is no exception. Over the last generation the concepts of republicanism in general, and classical republicanism in par-

---

1 Sidney, *Discourses Concerning Government*, ed. T. West (Indianapolis 1990), pp. 49, 143–4.
2 For a recent study of one aspect of this phenomenon, see Alastair MacLachlan, *The Rise and Fall of Revolutionary England: An Essay on the Fabrication of Seventeenth-Century History* (London 1996).

ticular, have enjoyed a spectacular rise to prominence. Informing this has been a specific debate about 'the ideological origins of the American revolution'.[3] A recent article assures us that 'a wide variety of pamphleteers in the 1650s understood that it was possible to be modern'.[4]

To the extent that this literature does not engage with contemporary belief it need not detain us here. What must is the shape given by these struggles to even the best work. The principal antagonists in this respect have been 'classical republicanism' (held to be ancient) and 'liberalism' (held to be modern). English republicanism, we have been told, owes either everything to classical republicanism, however understood (Pocock, Skinner), or little or nothing (Rahe). Another aspect of this analysis has been the linguistic definition of schools of political thought for the purposes of distinction between them. This is most importantly between a (classical) language of virtue and a (liberal) one of rights. This would have made little sense to most English republicans, who combined the two languages (classical republicanism and natural law theory) among others.[5] Nor would it have impressed John Adams, who praised 'what are called revolution principles. They are the principles of Aristotle and Plato, of Livy and Cicero, and Sydney, Harrington and Locke. The principles of nature and eternal reason. The principles on which the whole government over us, now stands.'[6]

The moral philosophy of English republicanism did indeed hinge upon 'eternal principles of nature and reason' which, though christian in application, were Greek in origin. We should perhaps therefore not be surprised that the analyses of Pocock, Skinner and Rahe among others have all identified genuine features of the republican intellectual landscape, while inaccurately claiming to offer a complete map.

3 Bernard Bailyn, *The Ideological Origins of the American Revolution* (Cambridge, Mass. 1971).
4 Steven Pincus, 'Neither Machiavellian Moment nor Possessive Individualism: Commercial Society and the Defenders of the English Commonwealth', *American Historical Review*, June 1998, p. 736.
5 In 'Neither Machiavellian Moment nor Possessive Individualism', Steven Pincus correctly notes that contemporaries did not think in terms of these modern political polarities. This raises the question of why his article directs its analysis to them. An example of the resulting confusion is the (mistaken) *political* suggestion that 'Pocock's ideological targets are scholars of the left of the political center' (p. 710).
6 Quoted in Annabel Patterson, *Early Modern Liberalism*, p. 279.

Pocock is right to have perceived the existence of an English classical republicanism. This is correctly understood as entailing an Aristotelian moral philosophy of self-government transmitted through the renaissance. This 'articulated the positive conception of liberty . . . a style of thought . . . in which . . . the development of the individual towards self-fulfillment is possible only when [he] . . . acts as a citizen . . . [in] a conscious and autonomous decision-taking political community'.[7] What Pocock did not perceive is that the writer he took to be the exemplar of this mode of thought was the one English republican who had apparently departed from it. It is not the case that James Harrington in particular was 'a classical republican, and England's premier civic humanist and Machiavellian'.[8] This does not, however, destroy Pocock's general thesis. Far from being the exemplar of English republicanism Harrington is the exception to most of the generalisations that can be made about it. It has long been customary to define English republicanism by reference to Harrington, the study of whom preceded study of it. What is urgently necessary for an understanding of both is a restoration of the necessary relationship of part to whole.[9]

Paul Rahe has correctly observed that one of the informing forces behind Harrington's science of peace is not classical republicanism but Hobbesian natural philosophy.[10] In Harrington's work classical republican language is used 'to camouflage what is . . . a new typology grounded on a material rather than a moral foundation'.[11] Yet Rahe too has unwisely taken Harrington to stand for English republicanism as a whole. His discussion of the seventeenth century, by focusing upon Hobbes and Harrington, fails to notice (as the quote at the head of this chapter illustrates) that simultaneously in the hands of Milton, Nedham, Sidney and others, those against whom Hobbes railed – 'all the Philosophers, Plato, Aristotle, Cicero, Seneca, Plutarch, and the rest of the maintainers of the Greek and Roman Anarchies' – were furnishing the basis for a genuine and warlike English

---

7 Pocock, *Virtue, Commerce and History*, p. 40; Hans Baron, *The Crisis of the Early Italian Renaissance*, discussed in Pocock, *Politics, Language and Time: Essays on Political Thought and Theory* (New York 1971), p. 85.

8 Pocock, 'Historical Introduction', in Harrington, *Political Works*, p. 15.

9 Scott, 'Rapture of Motion', pp. 140–1.

10 Rahe, *Republics Ancient and Modern*, vol. I, *The Ancien Regime in Classical Greece*, and vol. II, *New Modes and Orders in Early Modern Political Thought*, p. 180.

11 Rahe, *New Modes and Orders*, p. 181; Scott, 'Rapture of Motion'.

classical republicanism.[12] Accordingly, for instance, Rahe's general observation (true only of Harrington) that the pursuit of institutional security at the expense of virtue entailed abandonment of the ancient stress on education would have surprised Marchamont Nedham, who wrote in *Mercurius Politicus* in 1652 of the 'essentially necessary rule . . . That Children should bee educated and instructed in the Principles of Freedom', quoting Aristotle, Plutarch, Isocrates and Machiavelli in support.[13]

Similarly the recent analysis by Quentin Skinner is not inaccurate but incomplete.[14] The recovery of a neo-Roman dimension of the republican understanding of liberty is not contextualised alongside its other dimensions (Greek, neo-Stoic, christian humanist and even, in the case of Harrington, Hobbesian). Thus Skinner has helped to explain why English republican writers paid such close attention to Livy as well as to Machiavelli. It is equally true, however, that the accounts of 'free states' given by Milton, Nedham and Sidney were deeply indebted to Greek sources in general and to Aristotle in particular. Of this Sidney was typical when he spoke of 'Aristotle . . . Plato, Plutarch, Thucydides, Xenophon, Polybius and all the ancient Grecians, Italians and others who asserted the natural freedom of mankind'.[15] Thus it is a mistake to associate Aristotle primarily with scholasticism and thereby distinguish him from republicanism.[16] Aristotle was the most ubiquitous renaissance classical source and there is a republican Aristotle. It is because Aristotle was a key source for English humanist moral philosophy that Hobbes aimed his criticism particularly in this direction. This point has been made by other scholars of seventeenth-century humanism: 'it is time that we took seriously the eclecticism of seventeenth-century thinkers; it was quite possible to be an Aristotelian and a humanist

12 Quoted by Rahe in 'Antiquity Surpassed: The Repudiation of Classical Republicanism', in Wootton, *Republicanism, Liberty, and Commercial Society*; see the review of Wootton by Scott in *Parliamentary History* 16, 2 (1997), pp. 243–6.

13 *Mercurius Politicus*, no. 104, 27 May–3 June 1652, p. 1.

14 Skinner, *Liberty Before Liberalism*.

15 Sidney, *Discourses*, in *Sydney on Government*, p. 11. More broadly Sidney's invocation on p. 55 of 'Plato, Aristotle, Cicero and the best human authors' exhibits a classical republican allegiance entirely in line with that originally established by Nedham and Milton and perfectly compatible with his identification of Grotius' *De Jure Belli ac Pacis* as the most important modern political text (Scott, *English Republic*, pp. 19 and 14–30). Plato and Aristotle were, of course, key sources for Cicero himself.

16 See for instance Skinner, 'The Republican Ideal of Political Liberty', in Bock, Skinner and Viroli, *Machiavelli and Republicanism*, p. 302.

at the same time. False dichotomies between scholasticism and humanism, scholasticism and Ramism fail to do justice to the complexity of early modern intellectual method.'[17] In this preference for synthesis over distinction – in particular of the intellectual heritages of ancient, medieval and early modern – we return to a characteristic feature of seventeenth-century thought.[18]

Thus English republicanism was larger and less categorically discriminate than any particular existing historiographical interpretation. More generally no historical subject can be adequately contextualised by an inquiry after modern origins. We will understand the revolution in general, and republicanism in particular, when our question is not 'of what were they the cause?', but 'of what were they the consequence?' English republicanism was one aspect of the English revolution. That revolution was one intellectual consequence of the troubles.

REPUBLICAN PRINCIPLES

Republicanism drew upon the intellectual resources not only of English humanism but also of civil war radicalism. The second phase of English radicalism was not a complete break with the first.[19] Rather it registers the response of the radical process to a dramatic change in practical circumstances.

Civil war radicalism, it has been suggested, had a distinct moral, intellectual and linguistic identity. Its moral impulse was christian; its intellectual ambition lay in the achievement of a (negative) liberty from 'arbitrary' religious and political government. It sought above all the liberation of the soul from carnal oppression that it might adequately serve its maker. Its principal intellectual instruments in this struggle were the languages of history and natural law. While crucially adding to, English republicanism

---

17 Todd, *Christian Humanism*, p. 70, quoted in John Coffey, *Politics, Religion and the British Revolutions: The Mind of Samuel Rutherford* (Cambridge 1997), p. 69. Coffey notes that Rutherford's education in Edinburgh in the 1620s was dominated by Aristotle (the humanist rather than scholastic Aristotle, read in Greek), Cicero and the Roman poets, and Buchanan (pp. 66–7). By the Hartlib circle we see pragmatic eclecticism elevated to the status of a methodology.

18 James, *Passion and Action*, pp. 18–25.

19 Aspects of the relationship between civil war radicalism and English republicanism are explored by Worden, 'Beginnings of English Republicanism'; and Nigel Smith, 'Popular Republicanism in the 1650s', in Armitage, Himy and Skinner, *Milton and Republicanism*.

also incorporated, most of these features. Most English republicanism combined the languages of classical republicanism, natural law theory and ancient constitutionalism. These latter were now adapted to specifically republican purposes, accompanied by republican analyses of the Old Testament. English republicans shared the radical hostility to clerical religious compulsion in general, and (to a lesser degree) to a national church in particular.

Republicanism also shared civil war radicalism's emphasis upon practice. The linguistic origin of the word republican is Roman; the origin of the practice of citizenship, Greek. Similarly, as we have seen, anti-formalism was common to civil war radicalism and republicanism.[20] No English republican was more religious than Henry Vane, none less so than Marchamont Nedham, but on this they agreed. 'It is not so much the form of the administration as the thing administered, wherein the good or evil of government doth consist . . . God did not universally . . . tye all the world to one form of government.'[21] 'Government . . . depending upon future Contingents . . . must be alterable according to Circumstances and Accidents . . . no certain Form can be prescribed at all times.'[22] Milton and Sidney similarly displayed what Martin Dzelzainis has called 'a high degree of indifference . . . to constitutional forms'.[23] This has led historians whose conception of republicanism is informed by the constitutionalist Harrington to question their republican status. For John Pocock it is not clear what was specifically republican about Sidney ('one is not persuaded that he spent much time considering how a kingless form of government might be given institutional form').[24] Similarly, for Blair Worden, Milton's 'claims as a political thinker are limited' by the fact that he was 'more interested in the spirit of a constitution than its form'.[25] By 'the spirit of a constitution' would appear to be meant those moral

---

20 J. C. Davis, 'Against Formality: One Aspect of the English Revolution', *Transactions of the Royal Historical Society* 6th ser., 3 (1993); Davis, 'Cromwell's Religion'.

21 Quoted in Scott, *English Republic*, p. 108.

22 *Mercurius Politicus*, no. 354, 19–26 March 1657, p. 7675; Scott, *English Republic*, pp. 110–12; Scott, 'The English Republican Imagination', in J. S. Morrill (ed.), *Revolution and Restoration: England in the 1650s* (London 1992), pp. 40–5; Scott, 'Rapture of Motion', pp. 144–7; Harrington, *Political Works*, pp. 34–7.

23 Dzelzainis, 'Milton's Classical Republicanism', in Armitage, Himy and Skinner, *Milton and Republicanism*, pp. 19–20; Scott, *English Republic*, chs. 2, 6 and 12; Scott, *Restoration Crisis*, chs. 10–11.

24 J. G. A. Pocock, 'England's Cato: The Virtues and Fortunes of Algernon Sidney', *Historical Journal* 37, 4 (1994), pp. 917, 918, 921, 935.

25 Worden, 'Beginnings of English Republicanism', pp. 56–8.

principles – classical and christian – of which most English republicanism was actually composed. Why these merit any lower place in the history of ideas than constitutional forms is not clear.

The interregnum challenge lay not in liberation from, but reconceptualisation of, government. The republican result was movement beyond the Leveller reaction against subjection, to a christian humanist politics of citizenship. This envisioned not freedom from government but through it. The moral philosophy informing this vision was Greek in origin, with Roman and christian accretions. It posited self-government as the only means to human moral fulfilment.[26]

This development registered one aspect of the new practical circumstances to which republicanism was a response. This was the fact that it was largely the creation of members of the new government. By this means in particular the nature of English republican ideology was deeply influenced by the practical experience of republicanism.[27] Our excavation of this ideology will again proceed in two stages. The positive end was that virtue which was the product of rational self-government.[28] This was a question not only of politics but manners: the government both of city and soul. Our prior focus, however, is upon the negative precondition of liberty understood as self-government. This was liberty from monarchy: in Sidney's phrase, the absence of 'dependence upon the will of another . . . if there be no other law in a kingdom than the will of a prince, there is no such thing as liberty'.[29] This was a specifically republican continuation of the preceding struggle against arbitrary government. This is to dissent from the argument of those historians who have taken liberty from monarchy as constituting not only a sufficient, but 'the strictest' understanding of republicanism.[30] In fact, as in

---

26 Hobbes, *Leviathan*, ed. Tuck, pp. 149–50; Quentin Skinner, 'Thomas Hobbes on the Proper Signification of Liberty', *Transactions of the Royal Historical Society* 5th ser., 40 (1990).

27 Scott, 'Republican Imagination'; Scott, 'Rapture of Motion', pp. 142–6.

28 Skinner, *Liberty Before Liberalism*, criticises as misconceived the view that 'individual freedom . . . can in some sense be *equated* with virtue or the right of political participation' (p. 74, n. 38). It certainly cannot be equated with virtue, which was the end to which this liberty was the means. It was, however, in this Aristotelian formulation, equated with participation, which was the positive aspect of a liberty consisting also in independence from monarchy (see ch. 14).

29 Sidney, *Discourses*, in *Sydney on Government*, p. 348.

30 Skinner, *Liberty Before Liberalism*; Skinner, 'The State', in Terence Ball, James Farr and Russell Hanson (eds.), *Political Innovation and Conceptual Change* (Cambridge 1989), p. 114.

civil war radicalism, it was a negative means to the all-important positive moral (and religious) end.

The practical context of English republicanism was the military destruction of monarchy. This had a profound impact upon political practice and thought not only during the interregnum, but subsequently. That republicanism had in this sense been a reality was the key aspect of national experience and memory which the restoration process set itself to erase.

Yet this monarchical absence was never secure. It was one thing to abolish the institution of monarchy, but how could the idea be abolished from the English public mind? There it sat enthroned not only by all the social and political structures of the time, but by time itself. In a traditional society the regicide was the most unpopular act of the century. It was this struggle for hearts and minds, including those of members of the new government itself, which was the first republican challenge.

Then there was the fact that the military struggle against monarchy did not end in 1649. Throughout its life the first republican government (the 'Rump Parliament') was preoccupied by the struggle to secure itself against the would-be Charles II. Thirdly there was the monarchy which remained present, and evolved, in the republic's midst. This was given constitutional form by the Protectorate – increasingly traditional government by 'a single person' between 1654 and 1659. Even the Rump, however, was not immune from republican criticism for its structural and moral inadequacies. Monarchy was not simply a matter of constitutions but of manners. Its moral essence was 'self-interest', an accusation wielded against every interregnum regime. For most republicans the prospects for lasting political change depended upon moral change. The final challenge was restoration of the monarchy.

English republicanism evolved in response to these challenges. At its core the republican experience spanned thirty-five years (1649–83): that is, a single generation. For it was the product of one group, bound by a common experience. For all its variety, all the branches of English republican ideology issued from this one trunk rooted in the practical experience of republicanism.

We may divide its development into five stages. It was the centrality of political practice that made the first (1649–53) the most important. Here the pioneers were Nedham and Milton, who established themes that would never be outgrown. In the second, in opposition to the Protectorate, republicanism extended its range. This now spanned the considerable distance from Harrington to Vane. And this marriage of political adversity with intellectual diversity remained characteristic. It was evident in 1659, as republicanism stared its own failure in the face. It persisted as the restored monarchy was assailed from continental exile by Ludlow and Sidney. And we see it in the last stage of English republican activity in London from 1680 to 1683. One last time the capital became a republican bastion: even a sheriff, Slingsby Bethel, published something. It took a further wave of exiles and executions to bring this chapter of English history to a close.

This was not the end for republican ideology. This displayed a prodigious capacity for posthumous (and international) reinvention.[31] But it was the end of the practical experience by which it had been sustained. Milton and Nedham had been employed by the republican Council of State. Their achievement was built upon by a series of members of that Council. In stages two and three (1656, 1659) there was the republican leader Henry Vane. In four to five, there was Vane's close friend and protege Algernon Sidney. Joining Sidney in the latter was another Council member and Sidney's own second cousin Henry Neville. All of these senior republican politicians were patrons of other writers (Vane of Sidney and Stubbe, Sidney of Bethel, Neville of Harrington) as well as authors in their own right. These factors help to account for the thematic consistency of English republicanism, equal to that of civil war radicalism. Thus at the far end of the republican chronology Sidney and Neville remained securely within this tradition. At its core sat the same Aristotelian natural law theory, the same Ciceronian rhetoric of liberty, and the same Livian and Machiavellian militarism that lay at the heart of the Rump's own ideology. Both men borrowed the Anglo-Saxon ancient constitutionalism ('the Gothic Polity') adapted by Milton from Tacitus (*Germania*, *Agricola*) and Hotman (*Francogallia*). Neville became the translator of Machiavelli's works.

The durability of this early ideology also owed something to the high profile – national and international – of the propaganda organs through which it was disseminated. Milton's polemic became famous; *Mercurius* 'flew every week to all parts of the nation . . . tis incredible what influence it

31 Caroline Robbins, *The Eighteenth-Century Commonwealthsman* (Cambridge, Mass. 1959); Pocock, *Machiavellian Moment*; Scott, *English Republic*, ch. 1.

had'.[32] Above all it reflected some salient characteristics of the republic's own political life.

THE CASE AGAINST MONARCHY IN PRINCIPLE: TYRANNY AND SLAVERY

In military terms, monarchical absence preceded the regicide. Thus the origins of English anti-monarchism may be discerned in that Leveller polemic of 1646 against those instruments of 'slavery' and 'bondage . . . amongst whom we always esteemed Kings the chiefest':

> The continual oppressors of the nation have been Kings, which is so evident that you cannot deny it; and ye yourselves have told the King . . . 'that his whole sixteen years' reign was one continued act of breach of the law' . . . And yet [you continue to act] as if it were impossible for any nation to be happy without a King.[33]

Another pamphlet of the same year spoke of 'the endeavour of Kings and their Counsells, time out of minde . . . to intrench upon the People's Liberties by usurped Prerogatives . . . and a Liberty of doing things above, and contrary to Law'.[34] By 1648 the standard-bearers of anti-monarchism had become the army. Ireton's *Humble Remonstrance of his Excellency the Lord General Fairfax* (16 November 1648) anticipated that interest theory which would become fundamental to English anti-monarchism throughout the interregnum and restoration period. This spoke of the irreconcilable 'Opposition' between 'Principles of Public Interest' and the 'Principles of Prerogative and particular Interest' of a king. 'Those Contraries God hath . . . so separated viz. of Principles . . . of Liberty, with Principles of Tyranny . . . of Zeal and the Power of Godliness, with Principles of Formality and Superstition . . . we might say indeed, of Light with Darkness, of Good with Evil.'[35]

One aspect of this argument was religious. The triumph over monarchy was located in the 'contrariety of principles there is between God and the Devil'. In the words of Henry Vane, the foundation of monarchy lay in 'that great idol . . . self interest', the product of the fall. This was 'a frame of spirit

---

32 Wood, cited in the introduction to John Milton's *Complete Prose Works*, vol. IV, pp. 53–6.
33 [Overton and Walwyn], *A remonstrance of many thousand citizens*, in Sharp, *Political Ideas*, p. 182.
34 *The Interest of England Maintained* (London 1646), p. 3.
35 [Henry Ireton], *The Humble Remonstrance of his Excellency the Lord General Fairfax* (London, 16 November 1648), p. 187.

in direct contrareity to Christs . . . serving to promote and advance the great . . . interest of the Devill in the world'.[36] It was also the case that the subjection attaching to monarchy belonged properly only to God. Thus the abolition of monarchy in 1649 was the highpoint of the struggle for liberation from carnal political oppression. As Sidney put it: 'God had deliver'd us from slavery, and shewd us that he would be our King.'[37] In the words of Henry Burton: 'The church is a spirituall Kingdom, whose onely King is Christ, and not man, it is a spirituall Republick [over which] . . . no man, nor power on earth, hath a kingly power.'[38]

Another feature of this argument was a collapsing of the Aristotelian distinction between monarchy and tyranny. In both the Dutch and English cases this came to form a theoretical basis of anti-monarchism. Aristotelian monarchy had been government of the one in the interests of the governed; tyranny in the interest of the governor only. Pieter de la Court misleadingly referred to this section of Aristotle's *Politics* in support of the quite distinct contention that all government by one person was self-interested, and that therefore this interest was invariably opposite to that of the political community.[39] The most famous actual author of this opinion was Machiavelli. The relevant passage of the *Discourses*, which had maintained the distinction until this point, suddenly used the words 'prince' and 'tyrant' interchangeably:

it is beyond question that it is only in republics that the common good is looked to properly . . . The opposite happens where there is a prince; for what he does in his own interests usually harms the city, and what is done in the interests of the city harms him. Consequently, as soon as tyranny replaces self-government [the city] ceases to make progress and to grow in power and wealth: more often than not, nay always, what happens is that it declines.[40]

It was this Machiavellian innovation which furnished the basis of that interest argument essential to English and Dutch anti-monarchism: that

---

36 Sir Henry Vane jnr, *The Retired Man's Meditations* (London 1655), 'To the Reader', and p. 3.

37 Sidney, *Court Maxims*, quoted in Scott, *English Republic*, p. 186.

38 Henry Burton, *A Vindication of Churches, commonly called Independent* (London 1644), pp. 5–6.

39 'De Witt' [de la Court], *True Interest*, p. 6; the references are to Aristotle, *The Politics* (ed. Stephen Everson (Cambridge 1988)), bk 5, ch. 11, and bk 7, ch. 11.

40 Machiavelli, *Discourses*, II.2, pp. 275–6. Until this point the book maintains the usual distinction between legal political monarchy and tyranny.

the self-government of a free people was public interest government; that that of a single person was private interest government; and that the two were irreconcilably opposed.[41] John Hall spoke accordingly of the 'contrariety and antipathy' of interest between monarch and people, 'we seeing People languish when their Princes are fullest'.[42] Sidney's *Court Maxims*, written in the Netherlands in 1665, and drawing upon both these Dutch and English contexts, would become the most systematic treatment of this claim.[43] Yet it was clearly visible as early as 1650 in the work of de la Court's English equivalent, Marchamont Nedham, whose own pioneering compilation of the 'Maxims' of a free state had enjoyed a similar context of official patronage a decade earlier on the other side of the Channel. Classical example is mined in general by Nedham, and Aristotle in particular. Yet for his anti-monarchism Machiavelli was the authority, and so 'there is no difference between king and tyrant'.[44] One reason for these parallels was a similarity of practical circumstances. In both cases new republics were defending themselves against a still present and dangerous (Stuart or Orange) 'monarchical interest'.

Yet on a theoretical level at least this equation of monarchy with tyranny was not maintained consistently. In line with their indebtedness to Greek sources in general, and Plato and Aristotle in particular, both Milton and Sidney reiterated the Aristotelian distinction between lawful monarchy and tyranny. In his *Defence of the English People* (1651) Milton doubted that there ever was 'any one person besides Salmasius of so slavish a spirit as to assert the outrageous enormities of tyrants to be the rights of kings'.[45] Sidney claimed in the *Discourses* that 'absolute monarchy . . . is all I dispute against, professing much veneration for that which is mixed, regulated by law, and directed to the public good'. Earlier Sidney's *Court Maxims*, confessing that 'I dare not say all monarchy is absolutely unlawful', had then followed Aristotle in explaining that its only just bases in nature were either where a people lacked the rational capacity to rule themselves (and so were 'slaves by nature') or where one man had an overwhelming pre-eminence of

---

41 'De Witt' [de la Court], *True Interest*, pp. 2–14; Scott, *English Republic*, ch. 13.

42 John Hall, *The Grounds and Reasons of Monarchy Considered* (London 1651), pp. 40–1.

43 Scott, *English Republic*, chs. 12–13.

44 *Ibid.*, pp. 208–9; Marchamont Nedham, *The Case of the Commonwealth of England Stated*, ed. Philip Knachel (Charlottesville 1969), p. 127.

45 John Milton, *A Defence of the People of England* (24 February 1651), in *The Prose Works of J. Milton*, ed. J. A. St John (5 vols., London 1848–53), vol. I, p. 31.

virtue above all others.[46] Milton's *Defence* agreed: it was not that monarchy was universally unlawful, but rather that it was 'not fitting or decent, that any man should be a king, that does not far excel all his subjects'.[47]

Some historians have written as if this adherence to Aristotle in theory mitigated the anti-monarchism of these writers in practice. It is true that both Milton and Sidney praised the Polybian doctrine of the mixed constitution (combining the Aristotelian one, few and many), which contained a monarchical element. Like constitutionalism in general, however, this doctrine was fundamentally important only to Harrington, and even he altered its application. Although both Sidney and Milton mention it approvingly, its importance to their thought (Sidney's *Maxims* makes no mention of it) has been considerably exaggerated.[48] The hardline Nedham was hostile to the mixed constitution, praising Athens, a pure democracy, as 'the only pattern of a free state, fit for all the world to follow'.[49] Most importantly it is necessary to distinguish between the monarchical element in a mixed constitution, and monarchy proper. In *practice* both Milton's and Sidney's anti-monarchism was unqualified.

While claiming in one place that absolute monarchy is all he disputed against, the half million words of Sidney's *Discourses* in general are directed against the 'government of princes'. The same is true of the *Court Maxims* which, for all the obeisance to the appropriate Aristotelian distinctions, is directed not against absolute monarchy but against monarchy:

If it be said, these and other nations, after [being] wearied with civil dissensions, have sought monarchy as their port for rest, I answer, few or none of them have sought monarchy as their rest, but have fallen or been driven into it as a ship upon a rock. We may as well conclude death better than life because all men doing what they can to preserve life do yet end in death. That free states by divisions fall often into monarchy only shows monarchy to be a state of death unto life, and as death is the greatest evil that can befall a person monarchy is the worst evil that can befall a nation.[50]

46 Sidney, *Discourses*, in *Sydney on Government*, p. 106; Sidney, *Court Maxims*, p. 193, and Fifteenth Dialogue in general.

47 John Milton, *Defence of the People of England*, in *Prose Works*, pp. 53–4.

48 Dzelzainis, 'Milton's Classical Republicanism', p. 8; Sidney, *Court Maxims*.

49 This interpretation of Nedham differs from that of Worden in 'Beginnings of English Republicanism', pp. 67–8.

50 Sidney, *Court Maxims*, p. 20. Concerning the unlikely event, mentioned by Aristotle, of one man having more reason and virtue than an entire nation, Sir William Temple, coming across this repeated in Sidney's *Discourses*, called it the key to the whole book. 'For I, who knew him well, can assure you he looked upon himself as that very man.'

Elsewhere Milton tells us that 'the name of Kings has ever been hateful to free peoples', and Sidney agrees: 'the name of King' was never known to free peoples 'but as the object of their hatred'.[51] The explanation for these apparent anomalies is simply that the Aristotelian theoretical distinctions were not held to apply in the contemporary case. These writers were political practitioners; their polemic must be related to its practical circumstances.

It meant nothing *in practice* for Milton and Sidney to concede the Aristotelian circumstances for natural monarchy when these were known not to apply. There were two aspects of these circumstances which were crucial in this case. The first concerned the moral preconditions for English citizenship: the reality of the English rational capacity for self-government, and the absence of any one man who 'excelled all his subjects'. As Sidney put it: 'monarchy is itself an irrational, evil government, unless over those who are naturally beasts and slaves'.[52] Milton explained:

But where men are equals, *as in all governments very many are*, they ought to have an equal interest in the government, and hold it by turns. But that all men should be slaves to one that is their equal, or (as it happens most commonly) far inferiour to them, and very often a fool, who can so much as entertain such a thought without indignation?[53]

The first practical reality then was English freedom, predicated upon moral fitness (and thus need) for freedom. The second concerned contemporary kingship. It again meant little to observe Aristotle's theoretical distinction between monarchy and tyranny when this was held in contemporary practice no longer to apply. It was the observable reality of seventeenth-century European kingship that contemporary kings had in practice turned once-legal monarchies into tyrannies.

It was indeed a key purpose of the English republican use of Aristotle to make this point. Monarchy had been abolished in England not only because it was inappropriate for a rational, equal people but also because monarchy had itself disappeared into the abyss of tyranny. This claim, which was fundamental to almost all English republican writing, was an attack upon monarchical statebuilding. This had both local and wider application. It

---

51 Quoted in Worden, 'Republicanism and the Restoration 1660–1683', in Wootton, *Republicanism, Liberty and Commercial Society*, p. 161.
52 Sidney, *Court Maxims*, p. 65.
53 John Milton, *Defence of the People of England*, in *Prose Works*, pp. 53–4.

was the charge, first, against Charles I that he had attempted to turn a once-legal (unreformed) monarchy into a 'downright tyranny'. It was for liberation from this that the military struggle of the 1640s had been fought. 'What reason for waging war', asked John Milton, 'is more just than to drive off slavery?':

> Do you not remember . . . that the Romans had a most flourishing and glorious republic after the banishment of the kings? Could it happen that you forgot the Dutch? Their republic, after the expulsion of the king of Spain, after wars that were lengthy but successfully waged, bravely and gloriously obtained its liberty.[54]

Milton underwrote this analysis by a reading of Greek history, attributed to Aristotle's *Politics* (book 3), whereby Greek kingship, initially deriving from matchless virtue, and degenerating into tyranny, had been thrown off by a growing and more civilised people.[55] Above all, however, it was contextualised by the contemporary European historical analysis of the gothic polity, partly imported from France. By this Milton, Sidney and others explained – as had been explained the previous century by 'Hottoman's Franco-Gallia' and the *History* of Philip de Comines – how, ever since the reign of Louis XI of France, the once legal 'gothic polities' of central and western Europe had been turned by their princes into 'absolute monarchies' or tyrannies.[56] Under Nedham's editorship, *Mercurius Politicus* took a close interest in other European struggles, particularly that in Bordeaux, 'for a restauration of the Liberty of their Country'.[57] Milton's *Second Defence* (1654) began, and Harrington's *Oceana* (1656) ended, with a call for the liberation of the whole of Europe.[58] It was in this context that Admiral Blake remarked in 1651 that 'monarchy is a kind of government the world is weary of', and predicted that within ten years it would disappear from France and Spain.[59]

As in the case of Leveller Norman Yoke theory, this account of the gothic polity was also a development of early Stuart ancient constitutionalist arguments against arbitrary government. Now, however, what was necessary to

---

54 John Milton, *A Defence of the English People*, in *Political Writings*, ed. Martin Dzelzainis (Cambridge 1991), pp. 88, 155.

55 John Milton, *The Readie and Easye Way* (2nd edn, 1660), ed. Howard Erskine-Hill and Graham Storey (Cambridge 1983), p. 221.

56 John Milton, *Defence of the English People*, in *Political Writings*, p. 164; Salmon, *French Religious Wars*, pp. 160–70.   57 *Mercurius Politicus*, no. 1, 6–13 June 1650, p. 10.

58 John Milton, *Second Defence* (30 May 1654), in *Prose Works*, p. 217; Harrington, *Oceana*, p. 323.   59 Wootton, 'Leveller Democracy', p. 421.

achieve the restoration of legal government was liberation from monarchy altogether. In both Milton and Sidney's case, as in that of the Levellers, this historical analysis was equipped with an account of Anglo-Saxon liberty. In addition, mindful of his Percy ancestry, Sidney conjured up a militarily splendid 'Plantagenet age' in which a vigorous nobility had successfully restrained the pretensions of their princes.[60]

It might be thought that such polemic against modern absolute monarchy and slavery needed only to aim at the restoration of legal kingship. Blair Worden is one who has written that this gothic monarchy was held by these writers to 'remain the legitimate system of the seventeenth century'.[61] It is true that aspects of this analysis were adapted in this direction after the restoration. Yet again such an interpretation does not do justice to the republican reading of the contemporary situation. There is nothing in the writings of Milton, Sidney, Nedham, Hall and others to suggest that they thought restoration of limited monarchy desirable. For the government of a free people even legal monarchy was a fatally flawed system, hostile to virtue and productive of corruption ('Kings naturally fall into pride, lust and covetousness').[62] Above all monarchy denied rational people the God-given capacity, and therefore right, to govern themselves. 'Man is by nature a rational creature. Everything, therefore, that is irrational, is contrary to man's nature.'[63]

There was, in addition, the question of whether such a restoration was historically possible. Harrington's was the most famous negative answer, at least in the present state of 'the balance of dominion in the foundation'. Nor, equally, did Sidney believe this possible. 'The balance by which it [the legal monarchy] subsisted was broken; and it is as impossible to restore it, as for most of those who at this day go under the name of noblemen, to perform the duties required from the antient nobility of England.'[64] This is why what Sidney's opposition to 'absolute monarchy' entailed in practice was opposition to monarchy altogether. Like other Europeans the seventeenth-century English had now to choose between tyranny and a republic.

60 Sidney, *Court Maxims*, pp. 71–80.   61 Worden, 'Republicanism and the Restoration', p. 162.
62 Sidney, *Court Maxims*, p. 194.   63 *Ibid.*, p. 35.
64 Harrington, *Oceana*, pp. 163–4; Sidney, *Discourses*, in *Sydney on Government*, p. 464. Sidney may have taken this opinion from Harrington, directly or indirectly. Lucy Hutchinson (*Memoirs of Colonel Hutchinson*, ed. J. Hutchinson (repr. London 1965), pp. 55–62) similarly followed the contemporary pattern of absorbing *Oceana*'s historical theory while ignoring its constitutional core ('The Model of the Commonwealth'): David Norbrook, 'Lucy Hutchinson and the Historiography of the English Revolution', paper given at Keele, 13 March 1999.

THE CASE AGAINST MONARCHY IN PRACTICE: LIVY,
MACHIAVELLI AND WAR

So far we have examined anti-monarchism as a development of the polemic against arbitrary government. This entailed a reaction against monarchical statebuilding. A further aspect, however, of the republican case against monarchy followed from the republic's own political and military achievement. This owed its impact to republican statebuilding.

Alongside the ancient moralists (Plato, Aristotle, Sallust, Cicero and others), the only other source of comparable importance to English republicanism was Machiavelli. This is in some ways surprising, particularly in the aftermath of a religious revolution. Machiavelli's *Discourses* had, in praise of ancient Rome, mounted a savage attack upon the political influence of christianity. He had additionally dispensed with classical political morality, substituting for ancient rational virtue a new *virtù* of his own.

These were, as we will see, departures in which most English republicans did not follow him.[65] In other respects, however, Machiavelli regarded himself as, and was, not only faithful to, but (in James Harrington's words) 'the only politician that hath gone about to retrieve',[66] ancient republicanism. It was the purpose of his break with classical and christian political morality to restore, under extreme contemporary conditions, key elements of classical republican political practice. Foremost among these was the primacy of active citizenship, and of war. Machiavelli's indispensability to English republicanism followed not only from this aspect of his relationship to the classical republican tradition. It followed from the special applicability of this teaching to English political circumstances.

One aspect of this was Machiavelli's insistence upon the inescapability of change: 'Since . . . all human affairs are ever in a state of flux and cannot stand still, either there will be improvement or decline.'[67] By 1649 such an assumption made good sense to any observer of the English revolution.

---

65 See ch. 14. This is to disagree with Worden ('Beginnings of English Republicanism', pp. 57–8, 70) who describes Milton, Nedham and Harrington as sharing Machiavelli's understanding of civic virtue. The morality thus described, setting austerity, frugality and activity against luxury, effeminacy and sloth was common to most ancient moralists from Plato onwards and does not encapsulate Machiavelli's shocking new conception of *virtù*. As we will see, even the keenest English Machiavellian – Sidney – defended the Aristotelian understanding of civic virtue against Machiavelli himself.

66 Harrington, *Oceana*, p. 161.   67 Machiavelli, *Discourses*, I.6, p. 123.

Nedham took to the republican stage pointing at Fortune's wheel: there is 'a perpetual rotation of all things'.[68] Accordingly 'When a people have ingaged themselves in an alteration of Government, and confirm'd it by a compleat Conquest over the Family that formerly was invested, it is in their Power to dispose of the Government in such a Form as shal best please themselves.'[69] Sidney improved upon the Machiavellian insight that political change was unavoidable, insisting that it was essential:

To affirm otherwise . . . is no less than to . . . render the understanding given to men utterly useless . . . whatever we enjoy, beyond the misery in which our barbarous ancestors lived, is due only to the liberty of correcting what was amiss in their practice, or inventing that which they did not know . . . if [therefore] it be lawful for us, by use of that understanding, to build houses, ships and forts, better than our ancestors . . . to invent printing . . . why have we not the same right in matters of government, upon which all others do most absolutely depend?[70]

The other even more important aspect of Machiavelli's teaching in relation to English republican experience was his related insistence upon the primacy of arms. In a world where 'all human affairs are ever in a state of flux and cannot stand still', arms were the necessary cutting edge of change. Thus Sidney summed up book 1, chapter 7, of Machiavelli's *Discourses* when he wrote

that government is evidently the best, which, not relying upon what it does at first enjoy, seeks to increase the number, strength and Riches of the people . . . If it do not grow, it must pine and perish; for in this world nothing is permanent; that which does not grow better will grow worse . . . [and] When a people multiplies, as they will always do in a good climate under a good government, such an enlargement of their territory, as is necessary for their subsistence, can only be acquired by war . . . that government is best which best prepares for war.[71]

It was Machiavelli's purpose in *The Discourses* to analyse the relationship between Rome's liberty and its expansion. The resulting accomplishment was to treat republican liberty not as an end, but as the means to this military end, and so to seek to imitate not the stability of Venice, but the expansion of Rome. Like Machiavelli, Nedham and Sidney both criticised Venice. Nedham rejected it as a 'tyranny' not worthy of the name of a republic;[72]

68 Nedham, *Case of the Commonwealth*, p. 7.
69 *Mercurius Politicus*, no. 35, 6 February 1651, p. 567.
70 Sidney, *Discourses*, in *Sydney on Government*, pp. 304–5.   71 *Ibid.*, pp. 178–9.
72 Worden, 'Beginnings of English Republicanism', pp. 67–8.

Sidney remarked that 'the over-inclination of the Venetians to peace is a mortal error in their constitution'. Sidney named Machiavelli as the source for his picture of a modern Italy where 'the thin half-starved inhabitants of walls supported by ivy fear neither popular tumults nor foreign alarms; and their sleep is only interrupted by hunger . . . or the howling of wolves'. 'Such peace is no more to be commended, than that which men have in the grave':

> It is ill, that men should kill one another in seditions, tumults and wars; but it is worse, to bring nations to such misery, weakness and baseness, as to have neither strength nor courage to contend for anything; to have nothing left worth defending, and to give the name of peace to desolation.[73]

There was indeed, then, a Machiavellian moment in England. As a whole English republicanism both faced, and embraced, its instability in time. In Nedham and Sidney in particular it had two distinguished Machiavellians who understood and supported every hard decision taken before them by the master. The most important of these was the choice of vigour, of armed force and of the 'tumults' they would bring, at the expense of longevity and stability.

As the heirs of the regicide the Rump Parliament faced universal hostility not only within the British kingdoms but across Europe.[74] The republic's first two ambassadors to the continent – Anthony Ascham in Spain and Isaac Dorislaus in the Netherlands – were both murdered. One MP committed suicide on the first anniversary of the regicide; another fell into depression and died the following month; a third wrote that he was 'full of melancholy and apprehensions of death'. In April 1650 Henry Vane wrote that they were

> now in a far worse state than ever yet they had been; that all the world was and would be their enemies; that their own army and General [Fairfax] were not to be trusted; that the whole kingdom would rise and cut their throats upon the first occasion; and that they knew not any place to go unto to be safe.[75]

It was to explain this situation that Nedham made one of his earliest public references to Machiavelli, who

> compares such as have been educated under a monarchy or tyranny to those beasts which have been caged or cooped up all their lives in a den . . . and if they be let loose,

73 Sidney, *Discourses*, in *Sydney on Government*, pp. 132, 224.
74 Blair Worden, *The Rump Parliament* (Cambridge 1975).
75 Worden, 'The Politics of Marvell's Horation Ode', *Historical Journal* 27, 3 (1984), p. 152.

they will return in again because they know not how to value or use their liberty. So strong an impression is made . . . by education and custom from the cradle.[76]

Milton deployed Aristotle at the same time to make a similar point, that if

after such a fair deliverance . . . with so much fortitude and valour shown against a Tyrant . . . people should seek a King . . . [they] would shew themselves to be by nature slaves, and arrant beasts; not fit for that liberty which they cri'd out and bel-low'd for, but fitter to be led back again into thir old servitude, like . . . clamouring and fighting brutes . . . that know not how to use or possess the liberty which they fought for.[77]

The sense of oppression felt by the regime followed equally from the practical problems it faced. Its priority had to be self-defence against its enemies abroad, particularly in Ireland and Scotland. But it equally faced government of a nation shattered by war, and still oppressed by high taxa-tion: 1649 was a year of harvest failure and actual starvation. These chal-lenges were addressed by an improvised governmental apparatus with no precedent in English history (in Harrington's words: 'this under an old name was a new thing').[78]

It is only against this background that we may understand both the scale of the accomplishments of 1651–3 and their impact upon those responsible for them. Their context was that of the troubles: Stuart military failure. The civil war, and accompanying parliamentary centralisation of government, had dragged England in one decade through its first successful experience of military revolution and statebuilding. The first government to inherit this new-found power was the English republic. By 1654 not only had Ireland and Scotland been conquered, and incorporated, for the first time in English history: Charles II had been defeated, and so had the mightiest naval power in Europe (the Dutch).

The result for some of those at the helm of the ship of state was republi-can self-belief. This is why almost all the themes of republican ideology emanate from the Rump period. This registered the transformation not only of the republic's internal situation, but of its European status. Few involved in this experience ever forgot it, or what it appeared to say about the potential of republican power. Not only could government without monarchy survive in England: in a few short years it had stood the record of

76 Nedham, *Case of the Commonwealth*, pp. 111–12.
77 John Milton, *Eikonoklastes*, p. 581.   78 Harrington, *Oceana*, p. 205.

Stuart military negligence on its head. By 1653 Milton was speaking of the birth of a 'new Rome in the West'. 'We never bid fairer', remembered Thomas Scot in 1659, 'for being masters of the whole world.'[79]

It was under the influence of this transformation that, between 1651 and 1653, there emerged what we now know as English classical republicanism. The nation had witnessed the result of government based upon merit, rather than birth. 'When Van Tromp set upon [the English admiral] Blake in Folkestone Bay', reminisced Algernon Sidney,

the parliament had not above thirteen ships against threescore . . . to oppose the best captain in the world . . . But such was the . . . wisdom and integrity of those who sat at the helm, and their diligence in choosing men for their merit was blessed with such success, that in two years our fleets grew to be as famous as our land-armies; the reputation and power of our nation rose to a greater height, than when we possessed the better half of France . . . [and] all the states, kings, and potentates of Europe, most respectfully, not to say submissively, sought our friendship.[80]

In *A Defence of the English People* (1651) Milton astonished Europe with the force of his account, from Plato, Aristotle, Cicero and Livy, of the irresistible benefits of liberty. Most important were the series of editorials in *Mercurius Politicus* which, from 1650 to 1653, began to address themselves to the ideological potential of this situation. It was in the editorial pages of the republic's official newspaper that Marchamont Nedham compiled England's first militaristic classical republican ideology.[81]

This achievement followed from Nedham's earlier defensive observation concerning the 'impression made by education and custom from the cradle'. Now with the republic apparently winning the struggle for its survival, Nedham's attention turned to a more ambitious objective. This was to change the nature of education and custom in England. Republicanism would not be secure until a new political generation had been raised, educated in the history and precepts of liberty. An 'Error in Policy', explained *Mercurius*, 'which ought especially to be taken notice of, and prevented in a Free State, hath been *a keeping of the People ignorant of those wayes and meanes that are essentially necessary for the preservation of their Liberty.*'[82] It

79 Thomas Burton, *Burton's Diary*, ed. J. T. Rutt (4 vols., London 1828), vol. III, p. 112.
80 Sidney, *Discourses*, in *Sydney on Government*, pp. 240–1.
81 The following discussion of this theme does not pretend to be a complete account of Nedham's thought or his (in part, critical) view of the Rump. For the latter, see Worden, 'Beginnings of English Republicanism'.
82 *Mercurius Politicus*, no. 101, 6–13 May 1652, p. 1.

was to attend to this need, in a nation entirely youthful in relation to it, that week by week *Mercurius* served up a classical republican education 'in sippets'.

Its themes may be summarised as those of manners and arms. For the first Nedham drew upon the Greeks and Romans, and renaissance Italians, to stress both the necessity and benefits of republican self-government. Liberty, he explained, citing Cicero, suited the rational nature of mankind. 'Men have liberty to make use of that Reason and understanding God hath given them . . . to choose their own Governours.' He contrasted the rational and manly public virtues which naturally attended such a system with the private vices, the corruption and the slavish lusts adhering to monarchy and its principle of 'Birth and Inheritance . . . [which] must needs be the most irrational and brutish in the world'.[83] Moreover, people who made their own laws were far more ready to obey them than the arbitrary will and interest of a single person.

Secondly Nedham drew upon Aristotle, Livy and above all Machiavelli to emphasise the essential relationship between liberty and arms. The English republic's military achievements illuminated Machiavelli's observation that 'experience shows that cities have never increased either in dominion or wealth, unless they have been independent'.[84] The superiority of republics and free states to monarchies and tyrannies in war, Nedham explained, derived from the fact that they were 'more tender of the Publique . . . than of particular interests'. Athens had showed the effects of this, but especially 'the Romans arrived at such a height as was beyond all imagination'.[85] 'When Rome was in its pure estate, virtue begat a desire of liberty, and this desire begat in them an extraordinary courage and resolution to defend it; which three walked a long time hand in hand together . . . the ancient virtue which purchased their liberty and an empire over the world.'[86]

On 11 August 1651 a correspondent wrote to Benjamin Worsley that he was 'of opinion . . . [and] have long bin with Mr Hobbs, that the reading of such bookes as Livy's History has bin a rub in the way of the advancement of the Interest of . . . Monarchs'.[87] Roman education, Nedham explained, was

---

83 *Ibid.*, no. 87, 3–10 February 1652, pp. 1381–3.
84 Machiavelli, *Discourses*, II.2, p. 275.
85 *Mercurius Politicus*, no. 68, 18–25 September 1651, pp. 1077–9.
86 Nedham, *Case of the Commonwealth*, p. 113.
87 William Rand to Benjamin Worsley, Hartlib Papers, 62/21/2A, quoted in Norbrook, *Writing the Republic*, pp. 282–3.

careful to maintain in the people 'an irreconcilable enmity to Kings'.[88] It was similarly necessary for the English republic 'That the People be continually trained up in the exercise of Arms; and the Militia lodged only in the People's hands'.[89] This relationship between liberty and greatness had been demonstrated by 'our own Nation; whose high achievements may match any of the Ancients'.[90] Sidney would later spectacularly elaborate this claim:

> The same order that made men valiant and industrious in the service of their country in the first ages, would have the same effect if it were now in being. Men would have the same love to the public as the Spartans and Romans had, if there was the same reason for it. We need no other proof of this, than what we have seen in our own country where, in a few years, good discipline, and a just encouragement given to those who did well, produced more examples of pure, complete, incorruptible and invinceable virtue, than Rome or Greece could ever boast; or if more be wanting, they may easily be found among the Switzers, Hollanders and others; but it is not necessary to light a candle to the sun.[91]

It was thus the republic's military conquests that did most to establish the case against monarchy in England in practice. They did this by reversing the condition of military failure that had been a context of the troubles. This had an impact upon English and European opinion which would greatly outlast the republic itself. It was the ex-republican ambassador George Downing who complained following the restoration 'to the Lords States of Holland, telling them to their faces that he observed that he was not received with the respect and observance now, that he was when he came from that Traitor and Rebell Cromwell'.[92] It was Downing who wrote disconsolately from the Netherlands:

> I would to God . . . something [were] done . . . for the augmentation of his Majesties Revenue . . . nothing being more certaine, then that . . . his Majesty cannot keepe . . . neither honour nor interest with his neighbours . . . unlesse his Majesty have a much greater Revenue.[93]

Downing had been intimately involved with the republic's conquests as scoutmaster-general of the English army in Scotland. Beneath his subse-

---

88 *Mercurius Politicus*, no. 70, 2–9 October 1651, p. 1109.

89 *Ibid.*, no. 103, 20–7 May 1652, p. 1. This should be read as a criticism of the military monopoly enjoyed at that time by the professional New Model Army.

90 *Ibid.*, no. 85, 18–25 January 1652, pp. 1349–52.

91 Sidney, *Discourses*, in *Sydney on Government*, p. 184.

92 Pepys, *Diary*, vol. III, 12 March 1662, p. 45.   93 *Ibid.*, 2 March 1662, p. 37.

quent royalist disguise we hear the residue of this experience in his emotional reaction to the rumour that the restored king would be selling the military acquisition of Dunkirk:

I confesse that I am such a doting foole in this point that I had rather . . . let his Majesty have . . . ye litle I have in the world . . . then that he should want where withall to maintaine this place: England was never considerable, I meane to say considerable indeed since it wanted a footing on this side ye water . . . and if this footing be lost, I doubt whether ye youngest that is now alive will ever see England have any other . . . should [France] . . . thus go about to take [this] away . . . God almighty would punish them for it, and they would find their is now alive, that old brave English blood and spirit that hath shewed itselfe on this side ye water in former ages.[94]

THE CASE AGAINST MONARCHY IN HISTORY

The most substantial historical analysis of the collapse of the English monarchy came in James Harrington's *Oceana* (1656). This was also the most important contemporary historical analysis of the troubles. Its theory of 'the balance of dominion' became a talking point from 1656; it played a prominent role in republican debates in Richard Cromwell's parliament in 1659, and from November 1659 to February 1660 the smartest talking shop in London (the Rota Club) took as its subject Harrington's theories more generally.[95]

The basis of this theory was a material analysis of political power. In Harrington's account the failure of the English monarchy was a material rather than a moral phenomenon. Harrington distinguished the 'Principles of Government' into two categories: 'Empire' and 'Authority'. These entailed respectively the 'goods of fortune' and 'the goods of the mind'. 'The goods of fortune' was the term employed by Aristotle's *Nichomachean Ethics* to denote the non-moral human goods.[96] For Harrington the disposition of 'Empire' was determined by 'the balance of dominion in the foundation'. The resulting disposition of moral authority was regulated by the 'superstructure'.[97]

---

94 British Library, Egerton MS 2538, Letters of Sir George Downing, f. 35 (28 February 1662).
95 *Aubrey's Brief Lives*, p. 125; Fink, *Classical Republicans*, pp. 87–9.
96 J. M. Cooper, 'Aristotle and the Goods of Fortune', *Philosophical Review* 94 (1985), p. 97.
97 James Harrington, 'The Preliminaries, showing the Principles of Government', in *Political Works*, pp. 161–87.

Harrington's historical account rested upon his analysis of the balance of dominion in the foundation. By 'dominion' he meant material property, in particular but not only land. Harrington's famous theory was that in any state the stable potential political arrangements of the superstructure were circumscribed by the disposition of property in the foundation. They were determined, to be specific, by the 'balance' of dominion, by which Harrington meant the owners in any state of more than 50 per cent of the property. During the early sixteenth century the 'balance' of dominion in England had passed out of the hands of 'the few' (capable of supporting a weak monarchy) into those of 'the many'. Given the resulting 'popular balance', the only possible stable constitutional structure in England now was popular.

Not every aspect of this analysis was new. In *Mercurius Politicus* Nedham had referred to the 'policy of Harry the 8, who when he disposed of the Revenues of the Abbies' followed the example of Brutus in distributing 'the Royal Revenues among the people'.[98] When the pamphlet *A Copy of a Letter from an Officer in Ireland* used the same historical account in early 1656 its author was accused of stealing from the still-unpublished *Oceana*.[99] Harrington himself claimed that his doctrine of the balance had been anticipated by Aristotle ('You have Aristotle full of it in divers places, especially where he says that immoderate wealth ... [is] where one man or a few have greater possessions than the . . . frame of the commonwealth will bear').[100] In his depiction of the English monarchy which had existed Harrington also drew upon the established republican notion of the 'gothic polity'. Characteristically, however, he radically changed its character. Whereas for Milton and Sidney this had involved an appropriately limited and militarily vigorous monarchy, for Harrington the 'gothic balance' was an inherently flawed form of government. With the balance divided between king and nobility, it was inherently unstable. What were for Milton and Sidney conditions favourable to liberty were for Harrington inimical to stability:

By which means this government, being indeed the masterpiece of modern prudence, hath been cried up to the skies as the only invention whereby at once to

---

98 *Mercurius Politicus*, no. 101, 6–13 May 1652, pp. 1586–7.
99 Pocock, 'Introduction', in Harrington, *Political Works*, pp. 10–12; Scott, *English Republic*, pp. 115–16.
100 Harrington, *Oceana*, p. 166; see M. Downs, *James Harrington* (Boston 1977), pp. 24–6.

maintain the sovereignty of a prince and the liberty of the people, whereas indeed it hath been no other than a wrestling match.[101]

This was by no means Harrington's only departure from republican orthodoxy. His analysis was as potent a criticism of existing republican as of prior monarchical arrangements. Alone of the major republican authors, Harrington was not himself involved in the republican cause. In *Oceana* Harrington offered to Cromwell, its destroyer, a savage criticism of the political credentials of the Rump. His description of it as an oligarchy, like that of Athens, or the thirty tyrants of the same, as described by Thucydides, was comfortably in line with Cromwell's self-serving (and probably inaccurate) account of the reasons for its dissolution.[102]

Hardly less significantly, what personal involvement Harrington had had in England's troubles had been on the other (royalist) side. As an intimate friend of the captured Charles I he 'passionately loved his Majestie', and contracted 'so great a griefe' at his death that 'never any thing did goe so neer to him'.[103] Among the subsequent features of *Oceana* remarkable within the republican canon were a denial of the right of political resistance (shared with Hobbes),[104] and an insistence upon the right of defeated royalists to full citizenship, which embroiled him in controversy with other republicans including Nedham, Stubbe and Vane.[105] At the same time he was attacked by royalists for dabbling in republican theory and betraying an impeccably loyal background.[106]

Harrington's one personal link with the republican experience was through his friend Henry Neville. It was Neville who persuaded him to stop writing bad poetry and turn to political thought. Subsequently Hobbes claimed of *Oceana* that Neville 'had a finger in that pye' and (as Aubrey remarked) ''tis like enough'. Neville was also rumoured to be the author of

---

101 Harrington, *Oceana*, p. 196.

102 *Ibid.*, pp. 205–6; Blair Worden, 'James Harrington and "The Commonwealth of Oceana" 1656', in Wootton, *Republicanism, Liberty and Commercial Society*; Worden, *Rump Parliament*.   103 *Aubrey's Brief Lives*, p. 124.

104 Perez Zagorin, *A History of Political Thought in the English Revolution* (London 1954), p. 140.

105 Henry Stubbe, *An Essay in Defence of the Good Old Cause* (London 1659), written under Vane's patronage; J. C. Davis, 'Pocock's Harrington: Grace, Nature and Art in the Classical Republicanism of James Harrington', *Historical Journal* 24, 3 (1981).

106 J. Lesley, *A Slap on the Snout of the Republican Swine*, quoted in Downs, *Harrington*, pp. 40–1.

A Copy of a Letter (1656) already mentioned.[107] When *Oceana* was published, Samuel Hartlib noted in his 'Ephemerides': 'Oceana a Polit[ical] Book about all Governm[en]ts written by Mr Harrington. Mr Nevil the witt commends it as one of the best books written in that kind.'[108]

All of this helps us to understand why Harrington's book was not primarily a polemic against monarchy.[109] It was, instead, an attempt to understand its collapse. It was more broadly an attempt to analyse the causes of the troubles in order to end them. It was accordingly not Harrington's primary purpose to establish the basis for liberty: that had been established. It was his purpose, under those circumstances, to establish the basis for stability. This involved understanding the causes of the troubles in both their material and moral dimensions. Materially what was necessary to end them was to identify the present balance; to erect upon it a superstructure appropriate to that known foundation; and by means of an 'agrarian law' to fix it in place. Morally what was necessary, for Harrington as for Hobbes, was to equip that superstructure to neutralise the destructive effects of those 'Passions' which had caused the troubles. Whereas for others the moral philosophy of republicanism hinged upon harnessing the fruits of God-given reason (virtue), for Harrington it hinged upon containing the destructive consequences of the passions.

Thus from different perspectives both major interregnum analyses of the troubles shared a view of their causes. These were the 'Passions' aroused by the Thirty Years War within an unreformed monarchy too weak either to give vent to them abroad or to contain them at home. It is as an analysis of the causes of political instability that Harrington's 'Preliminaries' take their place as the first major contemporary history of the troubles.

107 *Aubrey's Brief Lives*, pp. 124–5; 'The Publisher to the Reader', in Neville, *Plato Redivivus*, p. 68. A copy of the *Letter* in Cambridge University Library features a contemporary attribution to Neville.

108 Samuel Hartlib, 'Ephemerides' (1656), transcript, p. 65, Hartlib Papers, University of Sheffield.

109 As we will see, Harrington does mount a moral case against monarchy. This is, however, secondary and conditional. It is the fundamental Harringtonian principle that the superstructure is determined not by moral fitness but by the material circumstances of the foundation.

14

Radical renaissance (2): republican moral philosophy and the politics of settlement

Children should bee educated and instructed in the Principles of Freedom.

Marchamont Nedham, in Mercurius Politicus (1652)[1]

The spirit of the people is no wise to be trusted with their liberty, but by stated laws or orders; so the trust is not in the spirit of the people, but in the frame of those orders.

James Harrington, Oceana (1656)[2]

THE REPUBLICAN POLITICS OF VIRTUE

In general English republicanism defined itself in relation not to constitutional structures but moral principles. These were what Sidney called those

universal rules . . . from which men ought never to depart . . . and wise legislators, adhering to them only, will be ready to change all others, as occasion may require, in order to the public good. This we may learn from Moses, who laying the foundation of the law . . . in that justice, charity and truth, which having its root in God is subject to no change, left them the liberty of [ordering all other things] . . . as best pleased themselves.[3]

These were like those principles of which Nedham spoke when he explained in *Mercurius Politicus* that 'Children should bee educated . . . in the Principles of Freedom'; Milton when he praised 'fortitude and love of

---

1 *Mercurius Politicus*, no. 104, 27 May–3 June 1652, p. 1.
2 Harrington, *Oceana*, p. 737.
3 Sidney, *Discourses*, in *Sydney on Government*, pp. 144, 404; Scott, *Restoration Crisis*, pp. 254–7.

freedom . . . wisdom . . . valour, justice [and] constancy';[4] and Vane when he wrote to Harrington to 'join . . . in witness with you . . . unto those principles of common right and freedom, that must be provided for in whatsoever frame of government it be'.[5] These constituted the moral philosophy of English republicanism; that is to say, the positive moral good republicanism proposed to itself.

This was what Sidney and others called 'the end of all civil government'. It was by their ends (in relation to which means were flexible) that governments were to be judged good or evil. It was in relation to the same ends that Locke and Sidney would later develop their justifications of resistance. Resistance was justified against governments that came to contradict 'the ends of their own institution'. 'Why should . . . kings not be deposed, if they set up an interest in their own persons inconsistent with the publick good, for the promoting of which they were erected?'[6]

In the positive moral end of self-government we also see the republican aspect of that proposed reformation of manners which was the general positive objective of the English revolution. English republican moral philosophy has rightly been called classical republicanism in that it owed a particular debt to the moral philosophy of Greek antiquity. Civic activity – the life of the *polis* – was the only means to achieve man's *telos*, or end: the life of virtue. The precondition for this achievement was reason.

This was Aristotle's adaptation of the moral philosophy of 'his master Plato' (the phrase is Sidney's). Plato's primary interest had been in the moral knowledge accruing from the rational self-government of the soul.[7] This idea in relation to the individual remained important in English republicanism. It was Aristotle's most important innovation, however, to speak of the moral necessity of public citizenship, a theme subsequently amplified by Cicero. This stood at the heart of what Maurizio Viroli has called 'the republican idea of politics' in renaissance Italy. It equally stood at the heart of English republicanism.[8] English republicanism was, therefore,

---

4 John Milton, *Eikonoklastes*, pp. 344, 346.

5 Quoted in Margaret Judson, *The Political Thought of Sir Henry Vane the Younger* (Philadelphia 1969), p. 21.

6 Sidney, *Discourses*, ed. West, pp. 53, 226, 392; *Locke's Two Treatises*, pp. 418, 430–1.

7 This is to read Plato's *Republic* as a discussion of the city that is within us: Plato, *The Republic*, bk IX (in *The Portable Plato*, ed. Scott Buchanan (Harmondsworth 1976), pp. 656–7).

8 Viroli, 'Machiavelli and the Republican Idea of Politics'; Viroli, *From Politics to Reason of State*; Scott, 'Classical Republicanism'.

a moral conception of politics as self-government, both of the self and of the *polis*. It was indebted to Plato and Aristotle, Sallust and Cicero, Livy and Machiavelli for its understanding of the essential relationship of liberty to virtue.

This humanist vision of politics was compatible with a christian rationality. Christian morality preoccupied itself primarily not with reason and virtue but sin. As a christianisation of Aristotle, however, natural law theory emphasised the moral importance of reason as a fragment of the divine nature in fallen man. In the words of William Ball in 1646: 'Reason is Queen-Regent of Humane Affaires; by the sight whereof men discern to walk in the prudent paths of Morality and Policy . . . And albeit that this interior light . . . is . . . darkened by the fall of our first Parent, yet doth the Eternall Light ever communicate to Mankind sufficiency of Reason . . . for worldly things.'[9] It is because most English republicanism was rational christian humanism that the application to it of the modern distinction between the political languages of virtue and of natural rights has been misconceived.[10] Most republicans combined the two in pursuit of a practical as well as moral objective. As monarchy was a denial of the God-given right of rational creatures to govern themselves, so self-government was the only means to the moral fruits of God-given rationality.[11]

In Sidney's words: 'Virtue is the dictate of reason, or the remains of divine light, by which men are made benevolent and beneficial to each other.'[12] Because the 'light of nature and reason in man . . . ha[d] its beginning in God', there was no contradiction between the teachings of 'Plato and other great masters of human reason' on the one hand and 'Scripture . . . the reason of the father' on the other. The 'Essence of the Law . . . consists solely in the justice of it . . . For the understanding of this Law we should not need to study Littleton and Coke but Plato, Aristotle and others . . . [and] above all the Scripture . . . being the dictate of God's own spirit':[13]

Magistrates ought so to exercise their power, as that under them we may live in all godliness and honesty, says the apostle. The like is said by all philosophers who deserve to be hearkened to. Aristotle says the end of civil society is *vita beata secundum virtutem*, Socrates and Plato say the perfection of action and contemplation,

9 William Ball, *The Rule of a Free-Born People* (London 1646), p. 1.
10 Scott, 'Classical Republicanism'.
11 For the christian humanist moral philosophy of Algernon Sidney's ancestor Sir Philip, see Worden, *The Sound of Virtue*, ch. 2.
12 Sidney, *Discourses*, in *Sydney on Government*, p. 229.   13 Sidney, *Court Maxims*, pp. 127–9.

others the attaining of justice in order to arrive at that perfection in action and contemplation . . . We may truly say that all rational men without the law, and all inspired men under the old law and new, have agreed in showing this to be the end of government. Whatever decree therefore is contrary to the law of God and light of nature, is consequently unjust and evil, and so cannot be law.[14]

Milton agreed: 'if any law or custom be contrary to the law of God, of nature, or of reason, it ought to be looked upon as null and void'.[15] The nineteenth-century reader William Gladstone underlined and added an exclamation mark to Sidney's later formulation in the *Discourses*: 'That which is not just is not law, and that which is not law ought not to be obeyed.'[16] For Milton nothing was more fundamental to the republican enterprise than the rational conformity of 'the laws of God and man'. His *Second Defence* (1654) accordingly lavishly praised both God and the 'Greeks and Romans . . . under whom tyrants were not beheld with a superstitious reverence'.[17]

For an understanding of the moral fruits of reason, Milton, like Nedham and Sidney, made particular use of Plato and Aristotle with their Roman followers ('Aristotle and Cicero . . . are . . . as credible authors as any we have').[18] The virtues enumerated by the English republicans were both Greek and Roman, in particular wisdom, pre-eminent among the Greeks. This wisdom entailed moral knowledge in general, including ultimately that of God, source of 'all that is good'. 'Nothing is more agreeable to the order of nature', wrote Milton, 'or more for the interest of mankind, than that the less should yield to the greater, not in numbers, but in wisdom and virtue.'[19]

It was a key feature of this intended revolution of manners that nothing was more fundamental to public liberty than private government of the self. As Plato and Aristotle had explained, the prerequisite for liberty was the rational capacity for virtue. In Milton's words, it was a violation of justice and nature that one who 'is incapable of governing himself, should . . . be committed to the government of another'. This was that 'real and substantial liberty; which is rather to be sought from within than from without; and whose existence depends . . . on sobriety of conduct and

---

14 *Ibid.*, p. 127.   15 John Milton, *Defence of the People of England*, in *Prose Works*, p. 169.
16 British Library, Additional MS 44,729, ff. 19–20.
17 John Milton, *Second Defence*, in *Prose Works*, p. 217.
18 John Milton, *Defence of the People of England*, in *Prose Works*, pp. 31–3; for Milton's Platonism, see Haller, *Rise of Puritanism*, p. 348; for Sidney's, see Scott, *English Republic*, chs. 2, 11; the best account of Milton's politics of virtue is Dzelzainis, 'Milton's Classical Republicanism'.   19 John Milton, *Second Defence*, in *Prose Works*, p. 265.

integrity of life'.[20] Concerning the interdependence of private and public liberty, John Dury explained that 'all the rest are slaves to their proper passions, lusts, opposite interests, but he that is subject to the law of Liberty doing all by a rule, is truely free, and none but he'.[21]

Sidney pointed out more forcefully that the mechanism by which the interests of private and public self-government were intertwined was the law:

The fancy of . . . man . . . always fluctuates, and every passion that arises in his mind . . . disorders him. The good of a people ought to be established upon a surer basis. For this reason, the law is established, which no passion can disturb. It is void of desire and fear, lust and anger. It is . . . written reason, retaining some measure of the divine perfection. It does not enjoin that which pleases a weak, frail man; but commands that which is good, and punishes evil in all, whether rich or poor, high or low.[22]

It was by this means that the function of government was not simply the negative restraint of sin. It was the rational advancement of the good of mankind. In this lay the nub of Sidney's later argument with Sir Robert Filmer:[23]

The Grecians, among others who followed the light of reason, knew no other original title to the government of a nation than that wisdom, valour, and justice, which was beneficial to the people . . . [For] if governments . . . are instituted by men according to their own inclinations, they do therein seek their own good . . . [and] such only deserved to be called good men, who endeavoured to be good to mankind . . . And inasmuch as that good consists in a felicity of estate, and perfection of person, they highly valued such as had endeavoured to make men better, wiser, and happier. This they understood to be the end for which men entered into societies.[24]

Thus the advancement of 'good men', and of 'the good of mankind', was the positive moral objective of the republican experiment. This was that 'public good' opposed by all republicans to 'the private interest of a king'. With its link through reason to the source of all goodness, God, this 'seem[s] so far to concern all mankind, that, besides the influence upon our future life, [it] may be said to comprehend all that in this world deserves to be cared for':

20 *Ibid.*, pp. 258, 299.
21 John Dury, *Considerations concerning the present Engagement* (1649), p. 12, quoted in Baldwin, 'The Self and the State', p. 178.   22 Sidney, *Discourses*, ed. West, pp. 400–1.
23 Scott, *Restoration Crisis*, ch. 10.   24 Sidney, *Discourses*, in *Sydney on Government*, p. 37.

The misery of man proceeds from his being separated from God; his separation is wrought by corruption; his restitution therefore to felicity and integrity, can only be brought about by his reunion to the good from which he is fallen . . . In all his laws and politics . . . Plato looks upon this as the only worthy object of man's desire . . . If Plato therefore deserve credit . . . [no man can] perform the part of a good magistrate, unless he have the knowledge of God, or bring a people to justice, unless he bring them to the knowledge of God, who is the root of all justice and goodness.[25]

The republican experiment thus appeared vital to its participants in practice because government was a key means for the attainment of this moral good. It was not only that, as Nedham and Milton insisted, 'the only school of virtue is liberty', while 'monarchy is the receptacle of all vice'.[26] The challenge in this respect was, explained Sir Henry Vane, 'to show how the depraved, corrupted and self-interested will of man, in the great body, which we call the people, being once left to its own free motion, shall be prevailed with to espouse their true public interest'.[27]

'The weakness in which we are born', explained Sidney,

renders us unable to attain good of ourselves; we want help in all things, especially in the greatest. The fierce barbarity of a loose multitude, bound by no law, and regulated by no discipline, is wholly repugnant to [this good] . . . The first step toward the cure of this pestilent evil, is for many to join into one body, that every one may be protected by the united force of all. [The next is that] . . . the various talents that men possess, must by good discipline be rendered useful to the whole, as the meanest piece of wood or stone, being placed by a wise architect, conduces to the beauty of the most glorious building . . . [Men] are rough pieces of timber or stone, which it is necessary to cleave, saw or cut; this is the work of a skilful builder, and he only is capable of erecting a good fabric, who is so. Magistrates are political architects.[28]

When the republic tasted greatness, it was at the moral consequences of this recovered architecture of liberty that English republicans believed they were looking. Thus previously, too, 'The Roman virtue was the effect of their good laws and discipline. The world could not resist just and wise laws, exact discipline, and admirable virtue.'[29] As Sidney had summarised Plato

---

25 *Ibid.*, pp. 63–4.   26 John Milton, *Second Defence*, in *Prose Works*, p. 294.

27 Vane, *A Needful Corrective*, quoted in Judson, *Vane the Younger*, p. 39.

28 Sidney, *Discourses*, in *Sydney on Government*, p. 64.

29 Sidney, *Court Maxims*, pp. 140–1.

in the *Court Maxims*, 'when things are in this right order there is a perpetual increase in all that is good'.[30] 'This is not accidental, but according to the rules given to nature by God . . . As a man begets a man, and a beast a beast, that society of men which constitutes a government upon the foundation of justice, virtue, and the common good, will always have men to promote those ends; and that which intends the advancement of one man's desires and vanity, will abound in them that foment them.'[31]

This christian humanist politics of virtue was sufficiently important even to be defended by Sidney against Machiavelli himself. No modern word, he said, has been 'more abused than that of policy or politic':

The mistake will be discovered by the etymology of it. *Polis* signifies a city, and *politeia* is nothing but the art of . . . governing cities or civil societies . . . that men in them may live happily. We need seek no other definition of a happy human life in relation to this world than that set down by Aristotle as the end of civil societies . . . (Aristotle *Politics* bk III). For as there is no happiness without liberty, and no man more a slave than he that is overmastered by vicious passions, there is neither liberty, nor happiness, where there is not virtue . . . By this you may see whether the name of policy be fitly given to that wicked malicious craft, exercised with perfidy and cruelty, accompanied with all manner of lust and vice, directly and irreconcilably contrary to virtue and piety, honesty and humanity, which is taught by Machiavel and others.[32]

This was of course the Machiavelli of *The Prince* rather than *The Discourses*. These words are nevertheless all the more remarkable in issuing from the pen of one of the republican Machiavelli's most perceptive English disciples. It was a consequence of the military experience of the republic (1649–53) that to these Aristotelian moral assumptions about citizenship became connected Machiavelli's teaching about change and war. It was this combination which characterised English republicanism as a whole.

It was in relation to this moral end that constitutional particulars were held to be adaptable. In the formulation of Skinner, 'What the republicans take themselves to be describing is any set of constitutional arrangements under which it might justifiably be claimed that the res (the government) genuinely . . . promotes the good of the publica (community as a whole).'[33] As Collinson put it: 'It was characteristic of humanist political

---

30 Scott, *English Republic,* p. 197.   31 Sidney, *Discourses,* in *Sydney on Government,* p. 236.
32 Sidney, *Court Maxims,* p. 24.   33 Skinner, 'Republican Ideal', p. 302.

thought . . . to be concerned less with the fabric of institutions than with "the spirit and outlook of the men who run them".[34] 'Wise and prudent men', explained Milton, 'are to consider what is profitable and fit for a people in general [only]; for it is very certain that the same sort of government is not equally convenient for all nations, nor for the same nation at all times.'[35] It was in pursuit of this moral end that Sidney insisted that '[I]t is the fundamental right of every nation to be governed by such laws, in such a manner, by such persons, as they think most conducing to their own good.'[36] Similarly Henry Stubbe explained that 'The reason why God did not universally by his law tye all the world to one forme of Government, is, because the difference of persons, times, places, neighbours, etc, may make one forme best to one people, and at one time and place, that is worst to another.'[37]

HARRINGTON'S SCIENCE OF PEACE

If James Harrington was the exception to this rule about constitutional specificity this was one consequence of an equally distinct moral philosophy. As Harrington's principal end was the achievement not of virtue but of stability, so his means to this end was not the harnessing of the moral fruits of rationality but the constitutional containment of the passions. The fundamental moral objective of *Oceana* was peace. This ambition was shared by that other interregnum masterpiece of attempted settlement, Hobbes' *Leviathan* (1651), to which *Oceana* was deeply indebted.[38]

It was not the purpose of *Oceana's* 'orders' to mould the moral character of its citizens but to substitute for that character, on a public level. 'The spirit of the people is no wise to be trusted with their liberty, but by stated laws or orders; so the trust is not in the spirit of the people, but in the frame of those orders.'[39] Accordingly Harrington's achievement did not depend upon the moral quality of civic participation: 'It is not possible for the people, if they can but draw the balls, though they understand nothing at all of the ballot, to

---

34 Collinson, 'Elizabethan Exclusion Crisis', p. 61, quoting Skinner, *Foundations of Modern Political Thought*, vol. I, p. 46.   35 John Milton, *Defence*, in *Prose Works*, p. 79.

36 Sidney, *Discourses*, in *Sydney on Government*, p. 462.

37 Stubbe, *Essay in Defence*, p. 22.

38 Scott, 'Rapture of Motion'; Scott, 'Peace of Silence'; Rahe, *New Modes and Orders*; Arihiro Fukuda, *Sovereignty and the Sword: Harrington, Hobbes, and Mixed Government in the English Civil Wars* (Oxford 1997).

39 Harrington, *A Discourse upon this Saying*, in *Political Works*, p. 737.

be out.'[40] The foremost purpose of those orders was not to render the people free, but the commonwealth stable. It was the primary purpose of any constitutional architecture not to achieve virtue, but to give stable constitutional expression to the balance of property in the foundation.

In pursuit of these ends, behind the fashionable form of classical republican language what we find in *Oceana* is a work of Hobbesian moral philosophy.[41] This is why none of the key terms – liberty, virtue, balance, interest – has the conventional classical or contemporary meanings. All describe the disposition, or motion, of material property ('dominion') or of a 'people' whom Harrington calls 'the materials of the Commonwealth'.[42] This does not mean that Harrington's thought is uninformed by humanist sources. To understand Harrington, as Hobbes, it is necessary to consider the relationship between humanism and natural philosophy.[43] What it does mean is that it is no truer of Harrington than of any other seventeenth-century republican that he is writing in one language, on behalf of one conception of politics, to the exclusion of all others.

At first glance it is not surprising that Harrington has been taken to be the exemplar of English classical republicanism. *Oceana* (1656) asserts the superiority of commonwealths ('ancient prudence') over monarchies ('modern prudence'). It aligns itself with Machiavelli ('the only politician that hath gone about to retrieve' ancient prudence) against Hobbes ('that Leviathan ... who ... goes about to destroy' it).[44] Moreover behind Machiavelli Harrington invokes the whole lineage of the classical republican tradition: Plato, Aristotle, Cicero, Livy, Tacitus, Guicciardini, Gianotti and others. In terms that would have made sense to Aristotle, Machiavelli and Rousseau, he describes ancient prudence as government according to 'laws and not men'.[45]

---

40 Harrington, *Oceana*, pp. 320, 222.   41 *Ibid.*   42 Scott, 'Rapture of Motion'.
43 Scott, 'Peace of Silence'; Skinner, *Reason and Rhetoric*.
44 Harrington, *Oceana*, p. 161.
45 *Ibid.* The striking recent analysis of this aspect of *Oceana* is Fukuda, *Sovereignty and the Sword*. It is not to dispute the analytical power of that study to say that its attempt to *equate* Harrington's understanding of ancient prudence with Polybius' doctrine appears to have little textual warrant. Harrington makes relatively little use of Polybius; the First Part of the 'Preliminaries' discusses many other things; the one-sentence summary on the first page calls ancient prudence 'the government of laws and not men'. This understanding of constitutional government is Aristotelian in origin and is what Fortescue meant by 'politicum'. Thus when Harrington repeated the formula in *The Prerogative of Popular Government* (in *Political Works*, p. 401), he did so with acknowledgement of Aristotle and Livy and when Sidney made the same idea central to the *Discourses* he illustrated it with a quotation from book 3 of Aristotle's *Politics*: 'Lex est mens sine affectu, & quasi Deus (*Discourses*, ed. West, p. 288). Fukuda's concern to align Harrington with Polybius against Fortescue appears to this extent to be misconceived.

In addition *Oceana* has a clear relationship to the English republican intellectual context already described. One of *Oceana's* two 'fundamental laws', rotation of office, was a hobby-horse of Nedham's *Mercurius Politicus*. It was also a feature of the republican Council of State's own political practice.[46] The concerns underlying the other, the agrarian law, had also been adumbrated in this period. Milton had used Cicero's *De lege agraria* in his *Defence of the English People* (1651).[47] Nedham, in one three-issue run of *Mercurius* (6–27 May 1652) had insisted upon three essentials of republican policy that lie at the heart of *Oceana*: that a free state must 'limit . . . the wealth' of its citizens, and particularly its senators, 'that none of them grow over rich'; that it must limit their term of office 'that the affairs of the commonwealth [not] be made subservient . . . to a few persons'; and 'that the people be continually trained up in the exercise of arms'.[48]

All of these doctrines form part of what was a wholesale adoption by Harrington of the sources and range of the early English republican tradition. In addition to classical republican language this included aspects of interest and natural law theory, and of republican-adapted ancient constitutionalism (the history of the 'gothic polity'). This establishes one of the intellectual contexts in relation to which he must be understood. What it does not do is establish his relationship to it. To understand this it is necessary to examine the use to which these republican borrowings (and others) were put.

This requires that careful relationship of a text to its intellectual and linguistic contexts which has been enjoined by John Pocock and Quentin Skinner. It was by establishing these contexts in relation to Machiavelli, for instance, that Skinner established that Machiavelli was using a conventional word (*virtù*) in a highly unconventional way.[49] Machiavelli was appropriating a traditional language precisely in order to challenge it by saying something new; the same is true of Hobbes' use of natural law theory. We have observed the appropriation by the Levellers of both major parliamentary political languages for the purpose of demanding something new. It is therefore not surprising that we should find Harrington's appropriation of classical republican language to be a superficial guide to his purposes in doing so.

Harrington's non-participation in republican politics was important

---

46 Scott, *English Republic*, pp. 36, 100.
47 John Milton, *Defence*, in *Complete Prose Works*, vol. IV, pp. 485–6.
48 *Mercurius Politicus*, nos. 101–3, pp. 1586–7, 1594.
49 Skinner, *Foundations of Modern Political Thought*, vol. I, ch. 5; Skinner, *Machiavelli* (Oxford 1981); Skinner, 'A Reply to My Critics', pp. 252–5.

partly because several of the distinguishing features of English republican theory derived from its close relationship to practice. One was that stress upon contingency and flexibility shared with Machiavelli. This is the same contingency that has been eradicated from Harrington's system. It was important, secondly, because he himself laid great emphasis upon it: 'Some have [said] that I, being a private man, had been ... mad ... to meddle with politics; what had a private man to do with government? My Lord, there is not any public person, not any magistrate, that has written in politics worth a button.'[50] We will shortly have reason to question the nature of political participation in *Oceana* itself. Vickie Sullivan has recently reiterated the point that the view that Harrington's 'dominant purpose is the release of personal virtue through civic participation' is hard to square with his statements about what Oceanic participation actually involves.[51]

John Pocock has attempted to contrast Harrington the republican with Spinoza the juristic philosopher. 'Harrington ... did not belong to the new philosophy ... and he [was] not engaged in trying to construct a deductive model of human nature and the natural world.' In fact, however, as we will see, Harrington was indeed a natural philosopher whose debt to Hobbes was much greater than Spinoza's own. 'Policy is an art', he explained, and 'Art is the observation or imitation of nature.' While Spinoza commended Machiavelli and ridiculed philosophical detachment from political practice, Harrington defended it.[52]

It is one consequence of Harrington's objective of stability that the domestic orders of *Oceana* are modelled not upon those of Rome but of Venice. Concerning the relationship between these, Machiavelli is accused of 'Saddling the wrong horse'.[53] In *Oceana* as a whole Harrington believed he had combined internal Venetian constitutional immortality with a Machiavellian republic for external expansion.[54] This was what Machiavelli

---

50 Spinoza, *Tractatus Politicus*, in *Political Works*, pp. 261–3; *The Examination of James Harrington*, in *Political Works*, p. 858.

51 Vickie Sullivan, 'The Civic Humanist Portrait of Machiavelli's English Successors', *History of Political Thought* 15 (Spring 1994), pp. 86–7.

52 J. G. A. Pocock, 'Spinoza and Harrington: An Exercise in Comparison', *Bijdragen en Mededelingen Betreffende de Geschiedenis der Nederlanden* 102, 3 (1987), p. 439; Scott, 'Classical Republicanism'.   53 Harrington, *Oceana*, p. 277.

54 Harrington organised *Oceana* for foreign war, having carefully separated foreign and domestic government. Here, too, however, the ultimate object was peace, gifted to a war-ravaged Europe by the establishment of a universal empire. 'A commonwealth is a minister of God upon earth ... for which cause ... the orders last rehearsed are buds of empire, such as ... may spread the arms of your commonwealth like an holy asylum unto the distressed world, and give the earth her Sabbath of years or rest from her labours, under the shadow of your wings': *ibid.*, p. 323.

had said was impossible: it was necessary to choose. A second peculiarity of *Oceana* was its utopian form and the extreme particularity of its orders. For it is partly through a constitutional order that is perfect that Harrington seeks England's exit from the troubles. Here again Harrington disagreed with Machiavelli:

'If a commonwealth' saith he 'were so happy as to be provided often with men that, when she is swerving from her principles, should reduce her unto her institution, she would be immortal.' But a commonwealth . . . swerveth not from her principles, but by and through her institution . . . a commonwealth that is rightly instituted can never swerve . . . wherefore it is apparent . . . Machiavel understood not a commonwealth as to the whole piece.[55]

Harrington's separation from his predecessors on this point owed everything to his natural philosophy. Natural philosophers followed Bacon's search for 'the pure knowledge of nature', the handiwork of God. Oceana's claims to 'immortality' rest not upon the flawed moral make-up of its citizens but the relation of its constitution ('Art') to Harrington's understanding of nature. According to Sidney: 'Nothing can or ought to be permanent but that which is perfect. And perfection is in God only, not in the things he has created.' According to Harrington, however: 'A man is sinful yet the world is perfect, so may the citizens be sinful, and yet the commonwealth be perfect.'[56]

In the application of this natural philosophy Harrington drew upon not only the languages of the republican tradition but also Hobbes' languages both of art and nature and of prudence. For Hobbes prudence was a derivation from experience: it was 'a Presumption of the Future, contracted from Experience of time past'. To Harrington's division of 'Experience of time past' into 'ancient and modern prudence' we will return. In addition *Oceana* is full of astronomical language – 'rotation', 'orbs', 'galaxies' – which needs to be explained. Meanwhile the meaning of familiar words has also changed. For Polybius 'balance' had meant a stabilising balance within the three-part mixed constitution composed of the one, few and many. In *Oceana* 'balance' has a new meaning relating not to the superstructure but the foundation. This is because the stabilising feature in Harrington's system is not constitutional but material: it is the foundation of property upon which the whole superstructure will rest. This was part of the whole-

---

55 *Ibid.*, pp. 321–2.   56 *Ibid.*, p. 320; Sidney, *Discourses*, in *Sydney on Government*, p. 406.

sale creation of a jargon. Alongside 'foundation', 'superstructure' and 'authority', Property became 'dominion', power 'Empire', and history 'prudence'. This feature of *Oceana* was related to, and as usual in competition with, that definition of terms which is such a prominent feature of Hobbes' *Leviathan*. This was a necessary feature of that art which followed from the accurate observation of nature. Thus Milton and Sidney's free 'gothic polity' became Harrington's flawed 'gothic balance'. 'Virtue' was still the moral achievement of political action in line with the public rather than private interest. What had changed entirely was the means of arriving at it.

For Aristotle this had been a consequence of rational political choice and action, individual and collective. It consisted in the voluntary placing by the citizen of the public ahead of private interest. In Sidney's formulation: 'the chief and necessary duty of a governor is to divest himself of those interests and passions which sway with men intent on their private interests, so as to apply himself wholly to promote the public welfare'.[57] For Harrington the action that would achieve this result was not that of individuals but of the constitution. It is not Oceana's citizens, but its orders, which secure that computation of 'right reason' which Harrington calls the 'common right, law of nature, or interest of the whole'.[58] This is what Harrington meant in saying that his government is an 'empire of laws and not of men.' For Aristotle this was to say that it was through the laws that men expressed their rational selves collectively. For Harrington, however, the common interest is secured by orders operating independently of the moral condition of 'the people', in which rational action is irrelevant, and in the making of which they have no part.

HARRINGTON'S NATURAL PHILOSOPHY: MATERIAL IN MOTION

Harrington's most important contemporary critic, Matthew Wren, first made the point: 'though Mr Harrington professes a great Enmity to Mr Hobs in his politiques, underhand notwithstanding he . . . does silently swallow down such Notions as Mr Hobs hath chewed for him'.[59] To this Harrington replied candidly: 'It is true that I have opposed the politics of

---

57 Sidney, *Court Maxims*, pp. 137–8.   58 Harrington, *Oceana*, pp. 171–2.
59 Matthew Wren, *Considerations upon Mr Harrington's Oceana* (London 1657), p. 41.

Mr Hobbes, *to show him what he taught me* . . . I firmly believe that Mr Hobbes . . . will in future ages be accounted, the best writer at this day in the world.'[60]

Though often quoted, this statement has not been taken seriously by historians. While the similarity of Hobbes' and Harrington's ecclesiology has been noted, until recently no equally close relationship between their political thought has been discerned.[61] This is, not least, because the first part of *Oceana*'s Preliminaries is a point-by-point refutation of *Leviathan*; and because the connection has not been obvious between what Pocock saw as 'the theorist of absolute sovereignty and the theorist of participatory virtue'.[62] In fact the sovereignty of *Oceana*'s laws is no less absolute than that of *Leviathan*, and participatory virtue no more evident. How then does it help us to explain *Oceana* if we accept literally the claim of its author that he wrote it, opposing *Leviathan* in the process, to show Hobbes what he had taught him?

The sharpness of Harrington's dispute with Hobbes followed from their shared objective. It was, that is to say, the squabbling of intellectual rivals, and siblings. That objective was settlement and peace. What Harrington took from Hobbes was his understanding of the basis upon which this had to be achieved. This was an adequate understanding of nature. Hobbes said: 'Nature is by the Art of Man . . . so imitated, that it can make an Artificial Animal . . . For by Art is created the great Leviathan called Commonwealth . . . which is but an artificial man.'[63] In Harrington's words: 'The ways of nature require peace. The ways of peace require obedience unto laws. Laws in England . . . must [now] be popular laws; and the sum of popular laws must amount unto a commonwealth.'[64]

Both Perez Zagorin and Felix Raab discerned in *Oceana* a Hobbesian search for universal laws of nature, tethered however by a Machiavellian historical empiricism governing their recovery. This did not, then, interfere with their perception of Harrington as a Machiavellian and a humanist. For Harrington (said Zagorin) the principles of politics must 'come from

60 Harrington, *Prerogative*, in *Political Works*, p. 423 (my emphasis).
61 Pocock, 'Introduction', in Harrington, *Political Works*; Mark Goldie, 'The Civil Religion of James Harrington', in A. Pagden (ed.), *The Languages of Political Theory in Early Modern Europe* (Cambridge 1988).   62 Pocock, *Machiavellian Moment*, p. 397.
63 Hobbes, *Leviathan*, ed. Tuck, p. 9.
64 Harrington, *The Art of Lawgiving*, in *Political Works*, p. 660.

history, and history alone'.[65] Yet this is not actually what Harrington said. According to Harrington: 'Policy is an art. Art is the observation or imitation of nature . . . by observation of the face of nature a politician limns his commonwealth.'[66] Therefore 'No man can be a politician except he be first a Historian *or a Traveller.*' Except he be, that is, an observer of nature, either in 'what has bin' or 'what is'.[67] Lycurgus became a supreme politician in Sparta without any knowledge of history: 'Lycurgus, by being [only] a Traveller, became a legislator, but in times when prudence was another thing.' In the ancient world, prudence (the political observation of nature) was recorded in what is, not only (as in the gothic world) in what had been.

For Harrington, then, history was indeed Hobbesian prudence. 'Experience of time past' was one kind of experience of the world. Although (in the words of Hobbes) it 'concludeth nothing universally', it could be used to recover, and demonstrate, principles which were otherwise derived (from nature). Nor, similarly, could unaided experimental (as opposed to historical) empiricism give true knowledge. But, like prudence, experimental demonstration could reveal to the world the universal principles inherent in nature. In this connection both Harrington and Hobbes admired the anatomist Harvey. His demonstration, from the dissection of particular bodies, of the universal principle of the circulation of the blood, accorded perfectly with the metaphysical assumptions of both men.[68]

One of Harrington's disagreements with Hobbes was that to reject, as *Leviathan* did, the prudence (experience) of the ancients, on the grounds that 'the Greeks and Romans . . . derived [politics] not from the principles of nature but . . . the [particular] practice of their own commonwealths', was 'as if a man should tell famous Harvey that he transcribed the circulation of the blood not out of the principles of nature, but out of the anatomy of this or that body'.[69] In other words Harrington thought that the ancients had perceived the principles of nature; Hobbes did not.

Thus the actual function of Harrington's famous history in the Second Preliminary is the illustration of a universal principle (of nature). Its local purpose is to explain the collapse of the old regime. Its analytical focus is upon that most destabilising aspect of monarchical weakness: the failure of royal arms. Here Hobbes is congratulated for grasping (unlike Machiavelli)

65 Felix Raab, *The English Face of Machiavelli* (London 1964), ch. 6; Zagorin, *Political Thought*, ch. 11.   66 Harrington, *Oceana*, p. 417.
67 *Ibid.* (my emphasis); Raab, *Machiavelli*, pp. 193, 249.
68 Hobbes, *Leviathan*, ed. Tuck, pp. 48, 53.   69 Harrington, *Oceana*, pp. 162, 178.

the material basis of government. 'But Leviathan, though he seems to skew at antiquity, following his furious master Carneades, hath caught hold of the public sword, unto which he reduceth all manner and matter of government.'[70] What he has failed to do is follow this principle far enough, in seeing that the sword itself has a material foundation. The result is the first of Harrington's two 'great discoveries', the 'balance of dominion . . . as ancient in nature as herself, and yet as new in art as my writings'[71]. This says that all government ('empire') has a material foundation. Left unattended this will in due course alter (exhibit motion), causing instability. In the possibility of fixing it, by artifice, lies one key to permanent peace.

What Hobbes 'taught' Harrington was what nature was. Nature was material in (linear) motion. That motion was perpetual unless arrested or diverted by motion from another direction: 'When a thing is in motion, it will eternally be in motion, unless somewhat els stay it.'[72] Hobbes' famous picture of the 'naturall condition of mankind' as a state of 'war of all against all' expressed this ballistic vision. The most politically important motions were the passions, '*Voluntary Motions*' or species of 'Endeavour'. 'This Endeavour, when it is toward something which causes it, is called APPETITE, or DESIRE . . . And when . . . fromward something . . . AVERSION'. All passions were aspects of desire or aversion and upon them depended moral judgements.[73]

It was in line with this analysis of nature that Hobbes redefined liberty as 'the absence of all the impediments to action [voluntary motion] that are not contained in the nature and intrinsical quality of the agent'.[74] The first step towards peace came with the surrender of that 'Liberty . . . of doing any thing' which Hobbes called 'The RIGHT OF NATURE'.[75] Members of the commonwealth accepted some collective restraint on their motion (peace, secured by the public sword) in exchange for protection from the prospect of its end (death).

For Harrington, too, nature was material in perpetual motion. 'In the institution or building of a commonwealth, the first work is no other than fitting and distributing the materials. The materials of the commonwealth

70 *Ibid.*, pp. 165, 174.   71 Harrington, *Prerogative*, in *Political Works*, p. 411.

72 Hobbes, *Leviathan*, ed. C. B. MacPherson (London 1984), p. 87.

73 Hobbes, *Leviathan*, ed. Tuck, pp. 37–46.

74 Hobbes, *Of Liberty and Necessity: A Treatise* (1654), in *The English Works of Thomas Hobbes*, ed. Sir William Molesworth, vol. VI (London 1840), pp. 273–4.

75 Hobbes, *Leviathan*, ed. Tuck, p. 91.

are the people.' The 'form of the commonwealth is motion'. The most important thing about which Harrington disagreed with Hobbes was the shape of this form. It followed from Harrington's analysis of *Oceana*'s balance of dominion that this would have to be not monarchical but 'popular'. 'In motion consisteth life . . . [and] the motion of a Commonwealth will never be current, unless it be circular.'[76] This was partly because peace was not to be had on any other basis:

now . . . all we can do is but to make a virtue of necessity, we are disputing whether we should have peace or war. For peace you cannot have without some government, nor any without the proper balance; wherefore, if you will not fix this which you have, the rest is blood.[77]

Harrington's first reason for insisting upon a commonwealth was thus not that it was intrinsically superior, but that the existing 'popular balance' in England made it necessary for settlement. In this respect, as with every other republican, his anti-monarchism was not absolute, but conditional upon the (in this case material) practical circumstances. Nevertheless, like others, and subject to these circumstances, Harrington gave his reasons for believing monarchy a 'less perfect' form of government in general; and these related not to the foundation but the superstructure.

Here, as elsewhere, behind the classical moral language, *Oceana*'s public virtue hinged in practice not upon moral civic action, but upon a single constitutional mechanism. This was the second of his 'great discoveries': the superstructural twin of the balance of dominion in the foundation. Here again the image was a material one. 'That which great philosophers are disputing upon in vain is brought into light by two silly girls: even the whole mystery of a commonwealth, which lies only in dividing and choosing.'[78] If one girl divides a cake, explained Harrington, and the other chooses, the shares will always be equal. This disposition of equal shares is right reason, or 'the interest of the whole'. Crucially this outcome depended upon the assumption of self-interested behaviour by both parties: should anything else occur the mechanism would break down.

Thus the 'reason' of *Oceana*, like its virtue, is constitutional, not individual. This is because Harrington shared Hobbes' assumption that all political behaviour was self-interested. The faculty to be contended with was not

---

76 Harrington, *Oceana*, pp. 212, 248. See Scott, 'Rapture of Motion', pp. 160–1.
77 Harrington, *Oceana*, p. 241.   78 *Ibid.*, p. 172.

reason but the passions (motion). Machiavelli agreed, but had attempted to harness the passions in the creation of *virtù*. He had, most famously, praised the 'tumults' of republican Rome. It was Machiavelli's opinion, explained Harrington, that to 'cut off the occasion of her tumults, she must have cut off the means of her increase'. It was Harrington's purpose to abolish tumults, not only for the present but for all time. Thus here too Harrington was driven to found 'a commonwealth against the judgement of Machiavel ... the greatest artist in the modern world gives sentence against [it] ... notwithstanding the judgement of Machiavel, [however] your commonwealth is safe and sound'.[79]

HARRINGTON'S MORAL PHILOSOPHY: THE PEACE OF SILENCE (REVISITED)

Although accordingly different in every detail, the orders of *Oceana* are, following *Leviathan*, a constitutional mechanism not for harnessing the moral fruits of rationality but for containing the destructive potential of the passions. This was the lesson from the 1620s when public religious 'Passions' had resulted in the fatal polarisation of the domestic polity. Hobbes' own analysis of the causes of instability and war had focused upon rhetoric and the passions. By *Leviathan* (1651) Hobbes had turned a philosophic analysis of the problems Thucydides had identified – rhetoric, the passions and war – into the basis of a prescription for peace.[80] Harrington's republican rethinking of the political application of this moral philosophy was to some extent reminiscent of Spinoza, for whom, too, the key to practical politics was the constitutional management of the passions:

Since men ... are led more by passion than by reason ... it is necessary to organise the state so that all its members, rulers as well as ruled, do what the common welfare requires whether they wish to or not; that is to say, live in accordance with the precept of reason, either spontaneously or through force or necessity ... this only happens when the administration is so arranged that nothing ... is wholly entrusted to ... any man.[81]

However, to a greater extent than either Harrington or Hobbes, Spinoza had transcended the traditional ethics associated with the passions. In

---

79 Quoted in Sullivan, 'Civic Humanist Portrait', pp. 82–3. By contrast, in the *Discourses*, Sidney defended the Roman republican tumults as the means by which the state responded to the need for change (in *Works*, ed. West, p. 50).

80 Scott, 'Peace of Silence'.   81 Spinoza, *Tractatus Politicus*, in *Political Works*, p. 315.

nature they were not vices, he emphasised, but properties, to be understood rather than denounced.[82] Nor, therefore, were the passions particularly associated with self-interest. On the contrary the distinction between passion and reason was precisely that between ineffective and informed pursuit of self-interest. For Harrington, however, the moral distinction between passion and reason was crucial. Passion was associated with self-interest and reason with the public interest. The uninhibited indulgence of the passions was inimical to peace. Thus the second reason for Harrington's championship of a republican superstructure over monarchy was his belief in the superiority of his elaborate 'orders' (to those of Hobbes) for controlling the passions (motion):

sovereign power . . . is a necessary but a formidable creature . . . tell us whether our rivers do not enjoy a more secure and fruitful reign within their proper banks, than if it were lawful for them, in ravishing our harvests, to spill themselves? . . . The virtue of the loadstone is not impaired or limited, but receiveth strength and nourishment, by being bound in iron.[83]

This was a government which no member of this divided nation could 'have the interest, or having the interest can have the power to disturb it with sedition'.[84] This was achieved partly by the subdivision of political functions, and by other mechanisms like rotation. It was achieved partly by the depersonalised voting system itself. ('Men are naturally subject unto all kinds of passion . . . the Venetian boxes be the most sovereign of all remedies against this.'[85]) As we should expect, however, from a student not only of Hobbes, but of Hobbes' reading of Thucydides, no aspect of this was more fundamental than the government of oratory.[86]

In *Oceana*, as in *Leviathan*, the rhetoric permitted is that of the author. In 'The Model of the Commonwealth', Harrington's public 'Orator' 'speaks' Oceana's orders. Like the rhetoric of *Leviathan*, this is the voice of authorial reason. *Oceana*'s 'Orators' are charged with 'informing the people of the reason' of those orders. It is necessary, in this respect, to perpetrate a crucial

82 *Ibid.*, p. 265.   83 Harrington, *Oceana*, pp. 229–30.   84 *Ibid.*, p. 179.
85 *Ibid.*, p. 244.
86 For a fuller analysis of the Thucydidean background, see Scott, 'Peace of Silence'. I am grateful to Professor Gary Remer for allowing me to see a manuscript of his 'James Harrington's New Deliberative Rhetoric: Reflection of an Anticlassical Republicanism', forthcoming in the *History of Political Thought*.

deception. This is to support the claim that Oceana has 'popular' (as opposed to monarchical) government. For this purpose the authorial voice of reason must pose as that of 'the people' themselves. 'This free-born nation is herself King People... Is it grave Lacedaemon... which appears to chide me that I teach the people to talk?'[87]

It is thus only during an initial spurious constitutional procedure that the 'people' themselves may speak:

> all parties (being indemnified by proclomation of the Archon) were invited to dispute their interests . . . to the council of the prytans, who (having a guard of a matter of two or three hundred men, lest the heat of the dispute might break the peace) had the right of moderators . . . This . . . made the people (who were neither safely to be admitted unto, nor conveniently to be excluded from the framing of their commonwealth) verily believe when it came forth that it was no other than that whereof they themselves had been the makers.[88]

Following this deception Oceana's citizens promise that they will 'well and truly observe . . . the orders and customs of this commonwealth *which the people have chosen*'.[89] One of these is

> *the twenty second order* . . . they will neither introduce, cause nor to their power suffer debate to be introduced into any popular assembly of this government, but to their utmost be aiding and assisting to seize and deliver any person or persons in that way offending and striking at the root of the commonwealth unto the council of war.[90]

Harrington's model for what follows is Venice, 'the great council [of which] never speaks a word . . . [it] is of all others the most quiet, so the most equal commonwealth'.[91] There follows the intervention of the significantly named Epimonus de Garrula, who, steeped in the rhetorical culture of the English parliament – that precise problem identified by Hobbes' preface to Thucydides – protests that such a 'dumb show' is inconsistent with the name of a commonwealth ('For a council, and not a word spoken in it, is a contradiction'). John Pocock has described this intervention on behalf of 'the free exercise of the personality which utopias habitually eliminate' as suggesting that 'Harrington is . . . himself aware of the case for it.'[92] It is

87 Harrington, *Oceana*, p. 229.
88 *Ibid.*, pp. 208–9. Like much else in *Oceana*, this deception has a Platonic flavour.
89 *Ibid.*, p. 277.   90 *Ibid.*, p. 267.   91 *Ibid.*, p. 276.
92 John Pocock, 'A Discourse of Sovereignty: Observations on the Work in Progress', in Phillipson and Skinner, *Political Discourse in Early Modern Britain*, p. 405.

surely more to the point to explain that Garrula's case is laughed aside. After a good deal of sport his opinions are refuted and the orders he has opposed are promulgated.[93]

Oceana does permit debate in the senate. As other parts of the rational person of the state are carefully distinguished, so this is separated from the popular arena of political choice. The alternative, Harrington tells us, is 'the people . . . making themselves as much an anarchy as those of Athens'. In relation to which,

give me my orders, and see if I have not trashed your demagogues . . . what convenience is there for debate in a crowd, where there is nothing but jostling, treading upon one another and stirring of blood . . . Nor shall any commonwealth where the people . . . is talkative ever see half the days of one of these, but being carried away by vainglorious men . . . swim down the sink; as did Athens, the most prating of those dames, when that same ranting fellow Alcibiades fell on demagoguing for the Sicilian war.[94]

Deceived concerning the authorship of their orders, Oceana's people are not in any classical sense free. Not least important among all the transformations of meaning in *Oceana* concerned the republican concept of liberty. Negatively, the liberty secured by Oceana's constitution consisted in freedom from government by the passions. Thus 'if the liberty of a man consist in the empire of his reason, the absence whereof would betray him into the bondage of his passions; then the liberty of a commonwealth consisteth in the empire of her laws, the absence whereof would betray her into the lusts of tyrants'.[95] Positively, this same freedom had its basis in Hobbes' material natural philosophy. Aristotelian liberty had meant individual and therefore collective rational self-government. The most important contemporary attack upon this understanding came from Hobbes, who both ridiculed and replaced it.[96]

93 Harrington, *Oceana*, p. 244.   94 *Ibid.*, pp. 266, 268.   95 *Ibid.*, p. 170.

96 Skinner, 'Hobbes on the Proper Signification of Liberty', pp. 140–1; Hobbes, *Leviathan*, ed. Tuck, p. 149: 'The Libertie, whereof there is so frequent, and honourable mention, in the Histories, and Philosophy of the Antient Greeks, and Romans . . . is not the Libertie of Particular men; but the Libertie of the Common-wealth: which is the same with that, which every man should have, if there were no Civil laws, nor Common-wealth at all. And the effects of it also be the same. For as among masterlesse men, there is perpetuall war, of every man against his neighbour . . . So in States, and Common-wealths not dependent on one another . . . they live in the condition of a perpetuall war.'

Hobbes' own treatment of liberty was, by contrast, properly informed by an understanding of nature. Accordingly liberty became not collective civic participation, but the absence of constraints upon action (motion). This 'liberty' pertained only to the last stage of a chain of necessary causes, all action ('voluntary motion') being in fact necessitated:

of *voluntary* actions the *will* is the *necessary* cause, and [as] . . . the *will* is also *caused* by other things whereof it disposeth not, it followeth, that *voluntary* actions have all of them *necessary* causes, and therefore are necessitated . . . [therefore] I conceive *liberty* to be rightly defined in this manner: Liberty is the absence of all the impediments to action that are not contained in the nature and intrinsical quality of the agent.[97]

Harrington's view of this explicitly anti-Aristotelian formulation is therefore crucial:

[Mr Hobbs'] treatises of liberty and necessity . . . are the greatest new lights, and those which I have follow'd, and shall follow . . . as is admirably observed by Mr Hobbs . . . [the] will is *caus'd*, and being caused is *necessitated*.[98]

We should accordingly not be surprised to hear Harrington describing individual civic participation in terms not of liberty and virtue, but of motion, causation and necessity:

at Rome I saw [a cage] which represented a kitchen . . . the cooks were all cats and kitlings, set in such frames, so tied and ordered, that the poor creatures could make no motion to get loose, but the same caused one to turn the spit, another to bake the meat, a third to skim the pot and a fourth to make green sauce. If the frame of your commonwealth be not such as *causeth* everyone to perform his certain function as *necessarily* as this . . . it is not right.[99]

---

97 Hobbes, *Of Liberty and Necessity*, pp. 273–4.
98 Quentin Skinner has suggested (at the European Science Foundation workshop on republicanism at Göttingen in April 1996) that Harrington may here have been agreeing with Hobbes' metaphysics of liberty without accepting his political definition. This would involve assuming both that the metaphysics did not determine the politics (which was Hobbes' view) and that Harrington was vocal about the agreement while remaining silent about the disagreement. It is the argument here that *Oceana* is explicable only *as* an alternative working through of the political implications of Hobbes' metaphysics.
99 Harrington, *A Discourse upon this Saying*, in *Political Works*, p. 744; Davis, 'Pocock's Harrington'.

THE RAPTURE OF MOTION

It is only in relation to the idea of liberty as 'the absence of impediments to action [motion]' that it becomes possible to understand Harrington's claim to have delivered to the people of *Oceana* not only their security but their freedom. By its own metaphysical criteria *Leviathan* was crude. It could produce peace from a ballistic world only by restraining motion. The liberty left to *Leviathan*'s subjects was that motion allowable by the 'silence of the laws'. Harrington believed he had transcended this need. In a world of material in perpetual motion peace was to be achieved not by the artificial restraint of motion, but by its perpetual guidance along a grid of civic ritual. All danger of collision was thereby removed. 'Why should not this government be much rather capable of duration and steadiness by a motion?'[100] As Wren disgustedly observed: 'this libration is of the same nature with a perpetual motion in the mechanics'.[101]

Like Hobbes, Harrington achieved this by erecting an artificial copy of the natural art of God. This was an imitation, however, not simply of 'that Rationall and most excellent worke of Nature, man', but of the created universe as a whole.[102] Nature was a universe the planets and stars of which (Harrington's 'orbs' and 'galaxies') moved in perpetual circular motion. By so copying nature's perfection Harrington believed he had harnessed for politics its very immortality. *Oceana* is full of the excitement produced by this extraordinary ambition. This culminates (in 'the Corollary') in an exultant paraphrase of *Leviathan*'s own famous opening paragraph. Passionately admiring his own creation, Harrington's lawgiver

conceived such a delight within him, as God is described by Plato to have done, when he finished the creation of the world, and saw his orbs move below him. For in the art of man, being the imitation of nature which is the art of God, there is nothing so like the first call of beautiful order out of chaos and confusion as the architecture of a well ordered commonwealth. Wherefore Lycurgus, seeing . . . that his orders were good, fell into deep contemplation how he might render them . . . unalterable and immortal.[103]

---

100 Harrington, *Oceana*, p. 212.
101 Wren, *Considerations*, p. 67, quoted in Harrington, *Prerogative*, in *Political Works*, p. 430.
102 Hobbes, *Leviathan*, ed. Tuck, p. 9.   103 Harrington, *Oceana*, p. 341.

Thus *Oceana*'s concerns are *Leviathan*'s: material and motion; 'the matter and forme of a Commonwealth'.[104] Oceana has a material foundation (the balance), further motion in which is prevented by the agrarian law. The superstructure has its own material balancing principle (dividing and choosing) and its own mechanism for motion (rotation). It is in imitation of the heavens that 'the motions of Oceana are spherical'. Order by order, the 'materials' of *Oceana* are pitched into perpetual circulation, 'the parishes annually pour themselves into hundreds, the hundreds into tribes, the tribes into galaxies'.[105] Like *Leviathan*'s 'Artificial Man' this is also a giant imitation of Harvey's human body: 'so the parliament is the heart which, consisting in two ventricles, the one greater and replenished with a grosser store, the other less and full of a purer, sucketh in and gusheth forth the life blood of *Oceana* by a perpetual circulation'.[106] Perfectly constructed, it followed from the teaching of Hobbes that such a commonwealth

should be immortal, seeing the people, being the materials, never dies, and the form, which is motion, must without opposition be endless. The bowl which is thrown from your hand, if there be no rub, no impediment, shall never cease; for which cause the glorious luminaries that are the bowls of God were once thrown forever.[107]

Thus when Olphaeus Megelator, having 'cast the great orbs of this commonwealth into ... perpetual revolution ... observed the rapture of [their] motion ... without any manner of obstruction or interfering, but as it had been naturally', he saw his work was done. He 'abdicated the magistracy of Archon'.[108] Thereafter, even the author's own rhetoric may die: 'And the orators ... having at their return assisted the Archon in putting the senate and the people or prerogative into motion, they abdicated the magistracy both of orators and legislators.'[109]

CONCLUSION

One manifestation of English republican moral philosophy spoke of the moral triumph over monarchy, the other of its material collapse. One directed its attention to the moral fruits of that victory, through the harnessing of human reason. The other directed its attention to the material

---

104 *A System of Politics*, in Harrington, *Political Works*, pp. 834–54.
105 Harrington, *Oceana*, p. 245.   106 *Ibid.*, p. 287.   107 *Ibid.*, p. 229.
108 *Ibid.*, p. 342.   109 *Ibid.*, p. 340.

and moral causes of the troubles, with a view to their cure. In the process English republicanism spanned the distance from Aristotelian moral to Hobbesian natural philosophy. It participated in both Machiavellian militarism and the interregnum quest for peace. Within the latter, Hobbes' system could have served as a basis for reconstruction of the old order. Harrington's starting point, however, was the insistence that it could not successfully be restored.

15

Radical restoration (1): 'the subjected Plaine'

In either hand the hastning Angel caught
Our lingring Parents, and to th' Eastern Gate
Led them direct, and down the Cliff as fast
To the subjected Plaine; then disappeer'd.
They looking back, all th' Eastern side beheld
Of Paradise, so late thir happie seat,
Wav'd over by that flaming Brand, the Gate
With dreadful Faces throng'd and fierie Armes:
Som natural tears they drop'd, but wip'd them soon;
The World was all before them, where to chose
Thir place of rest, and Providence thir guide;
They hand in hand with wandring steps and slow,
Through *Eden* took thir solitarie way.

John Milton, *Paradise Lost*[1]

INTRODUCTION

Milton's image in *Paradise Lost* of 'the subjected Plaine' reflects the influence of Jean Bodin. In *Six Books of the Commonwealth* (1576) Bodin had analysed the variety of European government in relation to three climatic zones (torrid, temperate and frigid). In addition, governments reflected topography, itself a determinant of climate. Thus mountainous, topographically turbulent Switzerland would never be amenable territory for monarchy. Similarly within Italy republicanism had flourished in the Tuscan hills; monarchy on the Lombard plain.[2]

---

1 John Milton, *Paradise Lost*, bk 12, lines 637–49, pp. 447–8.
2 Jean Bodin, *Six Bookes of a Commonweale*, a facsimile reprint of the English translation of 1606, ed. K. D. McRae (Cambridge, Mass. 1962), 'The Fift Booke', pp. 545–636.

Like other contemporary republican writing, Milton's reflected these theories, and Aristotle's anticipation of them.[3] Thus it was natural that leaving the self-government of Paradise Adam and Eve should descend to the subjected Plaine. We may contrast this republican topography with that of Winstanley, the purpose of whose God was to make 'crooked ways straight; and level mountains and valleys, and all unevenness, both in man's heart and in his actions'.[4] This was the difference between the christian morality of equality and the classical commitment to virtue. Monarchy was a violation of nature precisely because it denied political expression to inequality of virtue:

Justice is that virtue which ought to be the perpetual director of all our actions in the world . . . The fundamental maxim of it is to give that which is equal unto equals. It is a furious violation of this rule to set up one family that is naturally or rationally not different from others in such dominion over others as to arrogate unto themselves the privilege of being unaccountable to any man . . . he that pretends preference before another must show he has the advantage in that very thing which is in question.[5]

Another of Bodin's *Six Books* had been devoted to 'Changes and Revolutions in Governments'. For republicans like Milton and Sidney the return of monarchy in 1660 was the settlement over the landscape of featureless low grey cloud. This was devastating. But there was no reason to believe it more permanent than those regimes it had succeeded.

That English radicalism survived the restoration is not news to historians. Several of the masterpieces of the revolution belong to the period 1660–88. These include, in verse, Milton's *Paradise Lost*, a reinvestigation (but not recantation) of English republican moral philosophy. They include, in prose, Bunyan's *Pilgrim's Progress*, a classic account of the radical reformation moral journey under restoration circumstances. They include Sidney's *Discourses Concerning Government*, and John Locke's *Two Treatises of Government*. From these and other restoration works Enlightenment Europe and America derived much of their understanding of the ideology of the revolution as a whole.

3 Aristotle, *The Politics*, bk 8; Nedham and Sidney, like Milton, make substantial use of Bodin: Nedham, *Case of the Commonwealth*, pp. 11, 32, 85, 101, 106, 107; Scott, *English Republic*, pp. 19, 55.   4 Quoted in McKeon, 'Politics of Discourses', p. 43.
5 Sidney, *Court Maxims*, pp. 33–4.

Monarchical reconstruction could no more instantly change contemporary thinking than the abolition of monarchy had. As the Earl of Halifax put it:

the Liberty of the late times gave men so much light, and diffused it so universally amongst the people, that they are not now to be dealt with, as they might have been in an Age of lesse inquiry . . . [It is no longer possible for] good resolute Nonsense backt with Authority . . . [to] prevaile . . . [The people] are become so good Judges of what they heare, that the Clergie ought to be very wary before they goe about to impose upon their understandings, which are grown lesse humble then they were in former times.[6]

As Charles I had found, the restoration of institutional controls over public utterances and publication were not adequate mechanisms for the government of belief. This perception, not shared by senior clerics, may help to explain the king's several attempts to abandon this central aspect of the restoration religious enterprise. The king's friend Sir William Petty was not the only one to believe that such an attempt was fundamentally misconceived. It was not only that 'no man can believe what he himself pleases: and to force men to say they believe, what they do not, is vain, absurd, and without honour to God', but

if one-fourth of the people were heterodox, and . . . if that whole quarter should (by miracle) be removed; that, within a small time, one-fourth of the remainder would again become heterodox, some way or other: it being natural for men to differ in opinion in matters above Sense and Reason.[7]

Meanwhile public memory had many faces, and among them was radical memory.

The revolution was ideological rather than institutional in focus. Accordingly the reconstruction of the institutional fabric of the old order did not end it. Instead it created a new context for it, and one which would in many respects prove a stimulus. It reinvigorated the struggle against outward bondage. Religiously, radicalism was equipped not only to survive, but develop through, the experience of persecution. The republic's collapse, no less than its earlier success, was something for which an explanation was required. Most works of restoration radicalism offer testimony to these stimuli.

6 Savile (Halifax), *The Character of a Trimmer*, in *Works*, vol. I, pp. 206–7.
7 Sir William Petty, *Political Arithmetic* (1690), in G. A. Aitken, *Later Stuart Tracts* (London 1903), p. 21.

This is not to understate the bloody struggle to which restoration exposed radicals in practice. Of this, the ordeal undergone by Bunyan's Faithful (who is beaten, whipped, stabbed and burned at the stake) is the most famous contemporary allegory.[8] Here, as earlier, radical utterances were primarily responses to this struggle going on in practice. This was true even for the exile Edmund Ludlow who, in being deprived 'of my country', and 'throw[n] ... off the Publique Theater', had been made 'for the future a spectator of the Bloody Tragedie'.[9] The settlement of 1660–5 attempted to smash radicalism by force. After the re-establishment of church and monarchy, religious dissenters were ejected and imprisoned; the regicides and other republicans executed or murdered. Many fled abroad. It became treason to speak ill of the king in person or in print. Censorship was reimposed. The Act Against Tumultuous Petitioning banned petitions with more than twenty signatures or ten presenters.

Yet by 1679, as we have seen, all of these measures had failed. In the wake of the revived troubles London once again became a radical bastion. By the end of the 'restoration period', in 1689, between 600 and 800 people had perished in prison or on the scaffold for their religious or political beliefs; the country had been invaded; and London lay under military occupation.[10] Restoration did not, therefore, achieve the recovery of an imagined early Stuart religious and political 'normality'. In place of the picture we once had of relative calm after the mid-century storm, the period is now depicted as lurching from one crisis to another, with every aspect of its religious and political 'settlement' in dispute.[11]

INSTITUTIONAL RESTORATION: CHURCH, MONARCHY, PARLIAMENT

Radical religious belief, already directed away from carnal institutions, was deprived by the religious settlement of that of which it had least need. At the same time it was introduced to a new dimension of christianity: 'Bearing the

---

8 John Bunyan, *The Pilgrim's Progress* (1st pub. London 1678); Richard Greaves, '"Let Truth be Free": John Bunyan and the Restoration Crisis of 1667–1673', *Albion* 28, 4 (Winter 1996), pp. 604–5.

9 Bodleian Library, Oxford, MS Eng. hist c. 487, Edmund Ludlow, 'A Voyce from the Watchtower', f. 363.

10 Scott, 'Restoration Process', p. 637.

11 *Ibid.*, pp. 622–7; see the articles in the same issue by Richard Greaves ('Great Scott!: The Restoration in Turmoil, or, Restoration Crises and the Emergence of Party'); and Gary de Krey ('The First Restoration Crisis: Conscience and Coercion in London, 1667–1673'; and 'Party Lines: A Reply', *Albion* 25, 4 (Winter 1993)).

Cross, Persecution, Self-Denial'.[12] Meanwhile the practical effectiveness of the settlement was limited by its narrowness; by the unevenness of its enforcement; and by its vulnerability to destabilisation from sectors of the political establishment including the king. Far from being accepted as final, the religious 'settlement' of 1662–5 was subject to almost continuous pressure.[13]

Republicanism was forged in the shadow of monarchy, and restoration simply underlined this practical and moral challenge. At least since Zera Fink's *Classical Republicans* (1945) the period has been identified as producing some of the most important English republican writing.[14] 'When the honeymoon between the king and his subjects was over, much was again to be heard of the notions of classical republicanism, and they were once more to become an issue in English politics.'[15] Recent work has emphasised the permanent impact made by the republican experiment across the restoration period.[16] Throughout the period republicanism remained a presence not only in memory, but also in the neighbouring United Provinces, and in England. During the Anglo-Dutch war of 1665–7 the Dutch war effort was supported by English republican exiles. During the subsequent crisis of 1678–83 the crown found its policies undermined by an alliance of English and Dutch republicans, opportunistically supported by France.[17]

Like nonconformity, republicanism was also to some extent internally equipped for survival. As we have seen, it hinged upon a partially internalised moral philosophy of self-government. It aspired, that is to say, to the government not only of the country but of the self. It remained the case, as Sidney put it, quoting Seneca, that 'the kingdom ... [of] a wise or good man ... is only over himself'.[18] A retreat from the political struggle has been discerned in Milton's related evocation of

---

12 Keeble, *Literary Culture of Nonconformity*, p. 23.

13 De Krey, 'Rethinking the Restoration'; de Krey, 'First Restoration Crisis'.

14 Fink's view was accepted by Caroline Robbins (*Eighteenth-Century Commonwealthsman* (1959)). It was expanded upon by John Pocock, who also identified the phenomenon of neo-Harringtonianism: Pocock, *Machiavellian Moment*; Harrington, *Political Works*, ed. Pocock; Pocock, *Virtue, Commerce and History*, ch. 1. In his *French Religious Wars*, John Salmon recognised the fragility of the 1660 settlement: 'all the conflicts of the preceding age were implicit in the new settlement ... The position of Charles II was not unlike that of Catherine de Medici before the onset of the Religious Wars. The balance of the constitution was far from clear and religious hostilities threatened its uneasy equilibrium' (p. 123). See also J. Walker, 'The Republican Party in England from the Restoration to the Revolution', Ph.D thesis, Manchester 1930.   15 Fink, *Classical Republicans*, p. 123.

16 For reviews of some of these items, see Pocock, 'England's Cato'; Scott, review of Wootton, pp. 243–6; Scott, review of Peltonen, Armitage and Blom, pp. 951–3.

17 Scott, *Restoration Crisis*, ch. 6.   18 Sidney, *Court Maxims*, p. 31.

the summe
Of wisdom; hope no higher, though all the Starrs
All secrets of the deep, all Nature's works,
Or works of God in Heav'n, Air, Earth, or Sea,
And all the rule, one Empire; onely add
Deeds to thy knowledge answerable, add Faith,
Add Vertue, Patience, Temperance, add Love,
By name to come call'd Charitie, the soul
Of all the rest: then wilt thou not be loath
To leave this Paradise, but shalt possess
A Paradise within thee, happier far.[19]

But this seems misconceived. It was, in practical terms, the struggle which had retreated from Milton, not vice versa. Republicanism was always a precarious moral experiment in the context of a fallen world. Against this background, its practical failure was matter for investigation and reflection. Meanwhile what is summarised in the passage above is the moral substance of the revolution. This internal struggle had not been alternative, but essential, to the political. With the occasion for the latter temporarily removed the former was more important than ever. Thus as David Norbrook rightly stresses, accounts of *Paradise Lost* which have seen it as a retreat from politics falsify 'the epic's speech act, turning it from an affirmation into an abandonment of his earlier republican principles'.[20] The poem was in fact (according to Aubrey) almost half complete when Milton's republican beliefs were restated with passion in *Readie and Easye Way* (1660). The politics of the poem are indeed complicated, nor is it reducible to its politics. Yet the founding tragedy of man's fall from moral perfection was both cause and context of his latest fall from freedom. It was this which made 'vain the blood of so many thousand valiant Englishmen, who left us in this libertie, bought with their lives'.[21] Milton's exploration of this context no more signifies political acquiescence in these circumstances than moral acquiescence in the consequences of sin.

---

19 John Milton, *Paradise Lost*, p. 446.

20 Worden, 'Milton and the Tyranny of Heaven'; Armand Himy, '*Paradise Lost* as a Republican "Tractatus Theologico-Politicus"', in Armitage, Himy and Skinner, *Milton and Republicanism*; Norbrook, *Writing the English Republic*, ch. 10.

21 John Milton, *Readie and Easye Way*, in *Complete Prose Works*, vol. VII, pp. 358–9. Compare Sidney, *Court Maxims*, pp. 197–8: 'God had delivered us from slavery and showed us that he would be our king; and we recall from exile one of that detested race as if the war which destroyed so many thousands of men had been only to drive him into foreign countries, where, if possible, he might learn more vicious and wicked customs than what had been taught him by his father and the histories of his family.'

In this context reconstruction of monarchy was explicable, as tragic but unsurprising public moral failure. This was the central terrain of both Milton's *Paradise Lost* [1658–66] and Sidney's *Court Maxims* [1665–6]. This did nothing to undermine the nobility of the republican experiment in principle, whatever its practical mistakes. On the contrary the moral tenor of restoration political life, in particular at court, furnished plenty of subsequent material for the republican case, as the work of Sidney would show. Indeed, after several years of restoration public life, morally sordid and militarily incompetent, the republic came to appear to some more heroic in retrospect.

Nor, finally, did the restoration of parliament end the political struggle against outward bondage. In her *Declaration of Rights, 1689* Lois Schwoerer described whigs who were 'radical in the sense that they were on the left hand side of the essential issue of the seventeenth century – whether King or parliament should exercise sovereignty'.[22] Whether the century had such a central issue may be left to one side (either the left hand or the right). What is clear is that the survival of parliament was the issue of the troubles, not the revolution. Much civil war radicalism had been directed against the arbitrary government of parliament itself. This was a mode of thought well equipped to confront a settlement to which parliament's contribution was a good deal more oppressive than that of the king.

During his trial the regicide Thomas Harrison claimed that that act had been done not only 'in the name of the *Parliament of England*' but 'by a Parliament of England . . . There are Cases alike to this, you know, in King Richard the Second's Time, wherein some Question had been of what had been done by a *Parliament*, and what followed upon it, I need not urge it.' To this Denzil Holles responded with understandable outrage: 'You do very well know, that this horrid, detestable Act, which you Committed, could never be perfected by you, till you had broken the Parliament.' At this point Harrison retreated to that God whose cause parliament had once owned, but who was 'no Respector of persons' or of institutions. 'I would have abhorred to have brought him to Account: had not the blood of English-men, that had been shed' established that necessity.[23]

22 Schwoerer, *Declaration of Rights, 1689*, p. 286.
23 *An Exact and most Impartial Accompt of the Indictment, Arraignment, Trial, and Judgement (according to Law) of Twenty nine Regicides* (London 1660), pp. 49–51.

Yet sixteen years later in a different House Holles would himself be calling the parliamentary authority of the restoration settlement into question. 'This [Cavalier] Parliament represented the sickly times, in which they were chosen, when the People of England were in a kind of Delirium or Dotage.'[24] It had by this time become customary for dissenters like William Penn to question oppressive parliamentary religious legislation created in defiance of the ancient constitution and of the natural rights of those electors to whose authority that body remained subject.[25] During the mid-1660s republican exiles Edmund Ludlow and Algernon Sidney made savage attacks on the assumed religious authority both of church and state ('No religion is to be suffered but what is established by Authority of Parliament'). As during the tyrannical reign of Henry VIII this had involved the idolatrous grafting of 'a temporall head on [to] a spiritual body . . . the head of a filthy devouring fish' on to the 'body of a beautiful woman . . . the pure and undefiled spouse of Christ'.[26]

As in the 1640s no radicals attacked the *idea* of representative government in principle. In the formulation of John Wildman: 'that's the undeniable maxim of government: that all government is in the free consent of the people';[27] and of his friend Sidney 'it is the fundamental right of every nation to be governed by such laws, in such manner, and by such persons, as they think most conducing to their own good'.[28] As earlier, however, a radical commitment to popular sovereignty in principle was no obstacle to the struggle against parliamentary oppression in practice. In the words of Sidney, again (in the *Discourses*):

Many people knew not what they did when they annulled the triennial act; voted the militia to be in the King; gave him the excise, customs and chimney money; made the act for corporations, by which the greatest part of the nation was brought under the power of the worst men in it, drunk or sober passed the five mile act and that for uniformity in the church . . . [this] emboldened the court to think of making parliament to be the instrument of our slavery, which had in all ages been the firmest pillar of our liberty . . . [Yet] how great soever the danger of [trusting in parliament] may be, it is less than to put all into the hands of one man, and his ministers. The hazard of being ruined by those who must perish with us is not so much to be

---

24 Holles, *Letter.*   25 William Penn, *England's Present Interest* (London 1675).

26 Sidney, *Court Maxims*, pp. 82, 86; Edmund Ludlow, *A Voyce From the Watchtower*, ed. A. B. Worden (London 1978), p. 7; Scott, *English Republic*, p. 200.

27 Maurice Ashley, *John Wildman: Plotter and Postmaster* (London 1947), p. 30.

28 Sidney, *Discourses*, in *Sydney on Government*, p. 462.

feared, as by one who may enrich and strengthen himself by our destruction . . . it were to be wished, that our security were more certain; but this being, under God, the best anchor we have, it deserves to be preserved with all care, till one of a more unquestionable strength is framed by the consent of the nation.[29]

HISTORIOGRAPHY

The wholesale historiographical recovery of restoration radicalism is relatively recent. Until recently the restoration crisis, for instance, was explained in terms of personalities rather than ideas, and its political thought was dismissed as derivative and second-rate.[30] In the words of Gary de Krey, 'To political ideas [such historians] devoted selective attention, dismissing "radical" or "revolutionary" ideas in particular as without influence, or as without sincere proponents, or as epiphenomena arising from the anachronistic semantics of certain historians.'[31] This picture is now undergoing a reversal. In the summary of Richard Greaves: 'In the mid-1980s historians began a major re-evaluation of the restoration era. Among the principal themes are the period's unsettledness, the continuing impact of the radical tenets that had been manifested so forcefully in the mid-century upheavals, the significance of religion and ideology.'[32] The crisis of 1678–83 is now understood as an ideological watershed, giving rise to not only the largest outpouring of pamphlet and newspaper literature since the 1640s but some of the masterpieces of seventeenth-century political writing, including that of John Locke.[33]

An aspect of the earlier picture had been the notion of a decline in the centrality of religious belief and enthusiasm. This was one aspect of the retrospective creation of a 'long eighteenth century'. Specifically it read back into the troubled later seventeenth-century religious sensibilities fundamentally altered by the new-found military security of eighteenth-

---

29 *Ibid.*, p. 503.
30 J. R. Jones, *The First Whigs*; Scott, *Restoration Crisis*, chs. 1–3, and pp. 14–15 in particular.
31 Gary de Krey, 'The London Whigs and the Exclusion Crisis Reconsidered', in A. L. Beier, David Cannadine and James Rosenheim (eds.), *The First Modern Society* (Cambridge 1989), p. 458.   32 Greaves, '"Let Truth Be Free"', p. 587.
33 Tim Harris, *London Crowds*; Scott, *Restoration Crisis*; Knights, *Politics and Opinion*; Greaves, *Secrets of the Kingdom*; Mark Goldie, 'Restoration Political Thought', in Glassey, *Reigns of Charles II and James VII and II*; *Locke's Two Treatises*; Ashcraft, *Revolutionary Politics*; John Marshall, *John Locke: Resistance, Religion and Responsibility* (London 1994).

century protestantism. The process of falsification involved has recently been dramatically illustrated by new manuscript discoveries. One is the genuine manuscript of Edmund Ludlow's *Memoirs* which has revealed, behind the fabrication by John Toland, shorn of its religious enthusiasm for an eighteenth-century readership, the deeply religiously engaged original.[34] Another is Algernon Sidney's *Court Maxims* [1665–6], similarly a product of continental exile. Equally saturated with biblical and spiritual imagery, this is a savage attack on every aspect of restoration and an appeal for military resistance to it.[35]

These were part of a protestant literature of exile (in the Netherlands, Germany and Switzerland) that was of profound importance to restoration radicalism. The restoration exiles saw themselves as heirs to their Marian predecessors, committed to the survival of protestantism through another period of reaction. Engagement with the United Provinces, and with the relationship of politics, religion and trade, was to some extent characteristic of restoration radicalism as a whole. It is a principal achievement of Richard Greaves' trilogy to show how restoration radicalism remained preoccupied, as Elizabethan subjects had been, with the self-defence of protestantism within the beleaguered triangle of England, Scotland and the Netherlands.[36]

The most important recent attempt to revive the argument for restoration secularisation has come from Steven Pincus. Its tactical preliminary is to attribute to the present author a purely confessional view of the seventeenth century. 'Against this view', writes Pincus, 'I will maintain that the English in the Restoration period . . . participated actively in a European debate . . . about universal monarchy, not about true religion.'[37] In fact, as will be clear to readers of *Algernon Sidney and the Restoration Crisis*, or even just the phrase 'popery *and* arbitrary government', this polarity is a recently coined historiographical fiction.[38] What is apparently envisaged is a society

34 Ludlow, *Voyce*, ed. Worden.   35 Sidney, *Court Maxims*; Scott, *English Republic*, chs. 11–13.

36 Richard Greaves, *Deliver Us from Evil: The Radical Underground in Britain, 1660–1663* (Oxford 1986); Greaves, *Enemies Under His Feet: Radicals and Nonconformists in Britain, 1664–1667* (Stanford 1990); Greaves, *Secrets of the Kingdom*.

37 Steven Pincus, 'The English Debate over Universal Monarchy', in J. Robertson (ed.), *A Union for Empire: Political Thought and the British Union of 1707* (Cambridge 1995), pp. 37–8.

38 Scott, *Restoration Crisis*, ch. 2, treats the perceptions of popery and arbitrary government as intertwined ('arbitrary government was considered a necessary means to, and thereby an indicator of, the European design to introduce popery', p. 33). In it less space is given to popery (pp. 28–32) than to arbitrary government (pp. 32–8).

incapable of keeping two ideas in its head simultaneously. Thus, Pincus tells us, 'The rhetoric of balance of power is necessarily incompatible with a confessional foreign policy'; 'The centre [*sic*] of later seventeenth-century political discussion was captured by those who understood the world in national *rather than* religious terms'; 'James, it becomes clear, lost his crown not because of his religious belief, but because he had forsaken the national interest.'[39] It is perhaps unnecessary to point out that for every Steven Pincus there are hundreds of contemporaries on record as saying that James' religious belief had everything to do with the loss of his crown.[40]

Taking restoration evidence as a whole, indeed, the purpose of these arguments is initially very difficult to see. Throughout the period contemporaries expressed their anxieties, and advanced their analyses, in both confessional and political terms. In 1689 an *Address* of a Committee of the Commons referred to 'the Mischiefs brought upon Christendom in late Years by the *French* King, who . . . has, by Fraud and Force, endeavoured to subject it to an Arbitrary and Universal Monarchy'.[41] The following year another pamphlet explained 'the melancholy present Condition of . . . the whole Protestant Interest . . . in Europe' by means of the kind of bipolar confessional historical analysis which had been deployed throughout the century.[42] Recent work has simply confirmed a role played by religious alongside political rhetoric between 1688 and 1697 as central as that during the preceding military and political struggles against popery and arbitrary government.[43]

If we wish really to know whether 'the rhetoric of balance of power' was 'necessarily incompatible with a confessional foreign policy', we need only to consult one of Pincus' own key sources, Algernon Sidney's *Court Maxims* [1665–6]. According to Sidney, 'he that would have a State composed of one sort of persons only will appear little wiser than he that would have a body

---

39 Pincus, 'Universal Monarchy', pp. 59, 61 (my emphasis).

40 Glenn Burgess, 'Scottish or British?: Politics and Political Thought in Scotland, c. 1500–1707', *Historical Journal* 41, 2 (1998), p. 589.

41 *An Address agreed upon at the Committee for the French War, and read in the House of Commons, April the 19th, 1689* (1689), in *The Harleian Miscellany: or, a Collection of Scarce, Curious, and Entertaining Pamphlets and Tracts*, vol. I (London 1744), p. 52.

42 *The Present Case of England, and the Protestant Interest* (1690), in *Harleian Miscellany*, vol. I, p. 32.

43 Bruce Lenman, 'English Thought in the Era of the Revolution' (see also the editors' 'Introduction'), in Hoak and Feingold, *World of William and Mary*, pp. 137–43 and 6–8 respectively; Claydon, *William III*, pp. 3–5 and *passim*; Rose, 'Providence'.

composed of one element or Musick of one Note'.[44] Discussing this treatise Pincus again claims, first, that Sidney's critique of Caroline foreign policy has hitherto been presented only in confessional terms;[45] and secondly that this is the reverse of the truth. 'Clearly Algernon Sidney understood foreign policy in terms of opposition to universal monarchy *not* in terms of "uniting the Protestant cause of Europe".'[46] Again readers turning to the text will find extended religious *and* political analyses of the European balance of power. There is the confessional struggle for the 'publick good [and] advancement of the cause of Christ in the world, and diminishing the power of antichrist', a struggle rooted in 'the irreconcilable contrariety that is between God and the devil'.[47] And there is the struggle against 'Universall Monarchy', a struggle presently anchored in the 'perpetual contrariety between the interest of France and Spain'.[48] Both have been fully acknowledged in existing secondary discussion.[49]

This must naturally lead us to inquire after the purpose of these arguments. The answer appears to involve the identification of a process of secularisation that will underwrite a larger argument for change. If so, there is considerable irony about the choice of fear of a universal monarchy as a medium for the identification of change. As Sidney himself pointed out, this had been a theme of European politics since at least 'the dissolution of the Roman empire'.[50] It had been employed by Sidney's father and grandfather; it had a history which was ancient, medieval, early modern and modern; and its variants continue to dominate European politics to this day. Pincus' argument (in which fear of Spain, of the republican Netherlands and of France is all fear of 'universal monarchy') catches this quality of changelessness very well.

What was new in the early modern period, on the contrary, was precisely that rupture within Christendom which gave rise to the religious perceptions which Pincus appears to regard as old hat. It was religion, as we have seen, that gave rise to radicalism. There is arguably no aspect of the

---

44 Sidney, *Court Maxims*, p. 19.
45 This is not the case: Scott, *English Republic*, pp. 204–6, 207–21.
46 Pincus, 'Universal Monarchy', nn. 80 and 100 (my emphasis).
47 Sidney, *Court Maxims*, p. 178; Sidney's confessional analysis of European interest is in the Thirteenth Dialogue (pp. 177–82) and of domestic interest in the Eighth Dialogue (pp. 87–112). The tract as a whole is saturated with religious argumentation and imagery.
48 *Ibid.*, p. 155; Sidney's discussion of universal monarchy occurs primarily in the Eleventh Dialogue.   49 Scott, *English Republic*, pp. 204–6.   50 Sidney, *Court Maxims*, p. 155.

European history of this period more genuinely responsible for ushering in the modern than the reformation, counter-reformation and their consequences. More generally, contemporaries had no difficulty combining religious with political perceptions, continuity with change.

Restoration radicals regarded themselves as the heirs of the 'old cause'. In 1659 Henry Stubbe reminded his readers that 'L I B E R T Y , civill, and spirituall, were the good old cause'.[51] Gary de Krey has sought to distinguish, in this context, between 'a radical ideology' and 'a republican creed'. The latter is seen as too narrow, reading 'too much of the mind of Sidney into the minds of his London allies'. The former is broader, finding its base in 'the dissenting posture in London . . . premised upon the notion of an individual accountability to God, in conscience, that took precedence over the ecclesiastical claims of the magistrate and that defied the political agenda of the persecuting state'. According to de Krey, 'The good old cause was very much alive in the [city] corporation in the 1680s . . . understood as radically libertarian rather than dogmatically republican.'[52]

In fact republicanism was not an alternative to radicalism, but one species of it. Why de Krey believes it to have been particularly narrow or 'dogmatic' is not clear. Nor is the meaning of 'libertarian', unless, as seems likely, it means liberty from oppression in general, and from that of conscience in particular. If so then all republicans shared these objectives, believing them unattainable without liberty from monarchy. This was the revolution's centre ground. As he explained repeatedly, Sidney saw his cause as fundamentally religious. This was not only because 'The Power of Princes [could] not be fully established unless they had a power over consciences.'[53] It was because his republicanism was a struggle for good, understood in religious terms.

Thus the seed-bed of restoration radicalism in general was the reignited struggle for liberty of conscience against reimposed outward bondage. Many participants in this struggle were not explicitly republican. Since explicit republican utterance was not encouraged in restoration circumstances, its precise extent is difficult to gauge. Certainly the period is replete with private denunciations of the restored monarchy in general, or Charles II and James II in particular. At the same time its published literature is deeply informed by appeals for civil or spiritual liberty to which monarchy

---

51 Stubbe, *Essay in Defence*, p. 22.
52 De Krey, 'First Restoration Crisis', pp. 579–80; de Krey, 'London Whigs', p. 482.
53 Sidney, *Court Maxims*, pp. 41, 43.

was at best irrelevant. Even the Earl of Halifax, who wrote that, abstractly speaking, a republic was the best form of government, was described by Burnet as addicted to 'ye Roman authors' and 'full of commonwealth notions', and by the Duke of York as 'a man yt [that] in his heart hated all kingly government'.[54]

In his study of restoration radicalism Richard Greaves explained that he had 'not equated radicals with all Protestant nonconformists, but have instead limited the term "radical" to those who espoused active disobedi-ence to the law, particularly . . . such activities as rebellion, assassination, the publication of allegedly seditious literature, and the use of violence to prevent legally constituted authorities from enforcing the law'.[55] He also defended the use of the term radical as preferable to ideologically loaded contemporary terms like 'phanatick'. The latter at least reminds us that our subject had a history of its own. A product of the past, radicalism sought its own restoration: in the words of Francis North: 'for overturning all, and restoring their fancyed commonwealth'.[56]

There does, however, appear to be a problem with Greaves' definition. This is that it concedes the force of the word 'phanatick' by understanding radicalism in relation to sedition and violence rather than liberty. By focus-ing upon effect rather than cause, this definition may not identify its sub-stance. Violent individuals in conflict with the state for whatever reason might become by this definition radical. Quakers, on the other hand, who had eschewed such conflict but remained true to their beliefs, would not. Thus it is necessary to return to the suggestion that radicalism is the demand for fundamental change. Its appearance on a large scale, challeng-ing traditional arrangements, was the product of remarkable circumstances from the 1640s. Restoration radicalism was the persistence and adaptation of these beliefs in the new circumstances of 1660–89.

RESTORATION DEFENCES OF CHANGE

It is not surprising that change should have been an issue during the resto-ration period, with its struggles for and against reconstruction of the old order. Restoration was a conscious experiment in historical reconstruction. One consequence was the return of much restoration political polemic to

---

54 British Library Add MS 63,057, vol. II, p. 7; Savile (Halifax), *A Rough Draught of a New Modell at Sea*, in *Works*, vol. I, pp. 302–3.   55 Greaves, *Enemies Under His Feet*, p. viii.
56 Quoted *ibid.*

the terrain of the ancient constitution.[57] In the 1640s and 1650s two forms of radical ancient constitutionalism came to our attention. The first was Norman Yoke theory, an attempt to harness the weight of historical prescription to the cause of present change. The second was Harrington's remarkable debunking of the myth of the ancient constitution itself. In his hands the 'gothic balance' became the flawed 'gothic polity'. It was the collapse of this inferior 'modern prudence' which explained the necessity of present political change.

It is against this background that John Pocock has drawn attention to the phenomenon of 'neo-Harringtonianism'. This was an adaptation of Harrington's historical analysis to restoration political circumstances.[58] The form this took, however (Pocock's Caroline examples are the *Letter from a Person of Quality to His Friend in the Country* (1675) and Henry Neville's *Plato Redivivus* (1680)), appears in the former case at least to register as much alteration as continuity.

The thrust of the *Letter* is to say (as Harrington did) that a monarchy can be supported only by a nobility or an army.[59] It is not, however, either to attack the monarchy or to suggest that it is doomed or obsolete. Its purpose is to appeal to the king for greater political attention to the role of the nobility, an objective perfectly in line with the suggested authorship of the Earl of Shaftesbury, a recently fired courtier. In a letter to the Earl of Carlisle of 3 February 1675 Shaftesbury explained: 'I hope it shall never be thought unfit for any number of Lords to give the Kinge privately their opinions when askd when in the former dayes through all the northerne kingdomes nothinge of great moment was acted by their Kinges without the advice of the most considerable and active of the nobility.'[60] This was the theory of the gothic polity current elsewhere in Europe and used, as we have seen, by Milton and Sidney, among others. Its use here, however, is not radical politically, since it is not arguing for republican or other fundamental change. Nor is it so historically, since it is not arguing alongside Harrington and Sidney that historical change has occurred that is irreversible. Finally, since it was from this

57 Pocock, *Ancient Constitution and the Feudal Law*.
58 Pocock, *Machiavellian Moment*, ch. 12; Pocock, 'Introduction', in Harrington, *Political Works*, ch. 7. For a criticism of Pocock's analysis, see Michael Zuckert, *Natural Rights and the New Republicanism* (Princeton 1994), pp. 170–81.
59 *A Letter from a Person of Quality to His Friend in the Country* (London 1675).
60 Downing College Library, Cambridge MS Z.4.17/16, 'Transcript of my Ld Shaftsburyes Letter to ye Ea. of Carlisle. Feb 3d 1674 [1675]'.

aristocratic idealisation of the gothic polity that Harrington had radically departed, it is not clear in what sense this historical analysis was Harringtonian.

What we see in Shaftesbury's *Letter* is the co-option of an aspect of Harrington's analytical terminology, independently of its historical substance. It is a testimony to Harrington's late interregnum impact that this was fairly common in the restoration period. One example is William Penn, who defined government properly speaking as 'a just and equal Constitution, where Laws rule, not the Wills or Power of Men', and insisted upon the notion of 'governing on a ballance', in particular religiously.[61] Similarly Harringtonian influence of a broad kind has been detected in Shaftesbury and Locke's *Fundamental Constitutions of Carolina* (1669). This Shaftesbury described as having established 'a sort of republic'.[62]

No such terminology necessarily carried with it the substance of Harrington's conclusion that irreversible change made monarchy in England untenable. In fact it was the rhetorical strategy of Shaftesbury's *Letter* to direct the accusation of innovation against the government, and Danby's Test Act (1673) in particular. The arguments of the *Letter* belong, alongside Marvell's *Growth of Popery* (1677), to the literature denoting that revival of the troubles which would culminate in the crisis of 1678–83. This would be a crucial context for restoration radicalism. It did not in itself, however, contribute to it.

Elsewhere Harrington's conclusions were influential in the restoration period. In 1663 the Earl of Peterborough accepted that the gothic polity had been destroyed, though not that the result would necessarily be determined by a 'popular balance': 'These old notions, of mix'd Governments, priviledges, and conditions, have ... beene put out of the essence of things ... and the consequence of all undertakings, can noe more bee, but monarky, or a commonwealth.'[63] The most important intervention of Harringtonian substance in the political debate of the 1670s came as Pocock has suggested in

61 Penn, *Works*, vol. I, p. 674; vol. II, p. 482.
62 Robert Bliss, *Revolution and Empire: English Politics and the American Colonies in the Seventeenth Century* (Manchester 1990), pp. 210–17; Haley, *Shaftesbury*, pp. 242–8; Robert Weir, 'Shaftesbury's Darling': British Settlement in the Carolinas at the Close of the Seventeenth Century', in Canny, *The Origins of Empire*, pp. 381–2.
63 Public Record Office, London, State Papers 21/81/94. I am grateful to Paul Seaward for this reference. See also Lucy Hutchinson, *Memoirs of Colonel Hutchinson* (1965), pp. 59–60.

Henry Neville's *Plato Redivivus* (1680). This set the present 'illness, and distemper' of the English body politic in both its historical and European contexts.

The historical context was that of the troubles: a century of disorder which offered evidence of the disease but had failed to furnish a cure. The disease was that the political superstructure, in particular the power of the monarchy, did not reflect the economic and social circumstances of the foundation. Neville attributed the domestic plot to establish popery to a clergy who had little justification remaining for their powers in the absence of an abandonment of protestantism. He attributed the project of absolutism – the completion of which could be seen in neighbouring France – to a doomed attempt by the king of a disordered polity to find some remedy for this condition. In fact the remedy could come only from the king's voluntary attention to the people's grievances.

The result of this would be some constitutional amendment, including the abandonment of the key royal prerogative of summoning and dissolving parliaments, and its replacement by annual parliaments. The alternative was that 'the polity of England, must die of this disease', collapsing into renewed civil war or falling 'to the lot of some foreign power'.[64] *Plato Redivivus* was relatively faithful to the substance of Harrington's analysis. To this extent the tract, politically and historically, was republican, though Neville was prepared for his republic to have a limited king, like Sparta or Venice. This was the king's own correct interpretation of his argument.

Finally, as we have seen, although his account of English history was different, Sidney accepted Harrington's conclusions. The gothic polity, and with it limited monarchy, had irreversibly disappeared. The instrument of its destruction had been the modern court, which had destroyed the nobility. This was the same process alluded to by Shaftesbury, but in Sidney's view, as in Harrington's, it was long since complete:

The balance by which it subsisted was broken; and it is as impossible to restore it, as it is for most of them who at this day go under the name of noblemen, to perform the duties required from the antient nobility of England . . . This [feudal] dependence being lost, the lords have only more money . . . but no command of men; and can therefore neither protect the weak, nor curb the insolent. By this means all things have been brought into the hands of the king, and the commoners; and there is nothing to cement them, and to maintain the union . . . [And if the monarchy has]

---

64 Neville, *Plato Redivivus*, p. 175.

by that means increased a party which never was, and I think, never can be, united to the court, they are to answer for the consequences, and if they perish, their destruction is from themselves.[65]

Harrington had developed his historical analysis to explain change in the past, not to champion it for the future. It was his purpose to analyse that instability which had brought tragedy, and to end it. Sidney, however, not only shared Machiavelli's view that some instability was inevitable and necessary. He constructed an argument for the importance of continuing change.

This was indeed a defence of progress. It did not entail, and should not be confused with, a modern belief in its inevitability.[66] For Sidney whether there would be moral and material progress depended entirely upon a state's government. 'It is absurd to impute this to the change of times; for time changes nothing; and nothing was changed in those times, but the government, and that changed all things.'[67] Under a good government, however, thriving upon virtue rather than vice, such progress might be continuous. In the previous chapter we saw Harrington reproving Machiavelli for believing that change was inevitable ('a commonwealth . . . swerveth not from her principles, but by and through her institution . . . a commonwealth that is rightly instituted can never swerve'). By 1681–3 Sidney was correcting Machiavelli for not taking *enough* account of change:

[N]othing can or ought to be permanent but that which is perfect, and perfection is in God only, not in the things he has created . . . Some men observing this, have proposed a necessity of reducing every state, once in an age or two, to the integrity of its first principle; but they ought to have examined, whether that principle be good or evil, or so good that nothing can be added to it, which none ever was; and this being so, those who will admit of no change would render errors perpetual, and deprive . . . mankind of the benefits of wisdom, industry, experience, and the right use of reason.[68]

We thus find at the centre of the confrontation between Filmer's *Patriarcha* and its opponents in 1680–3 a sharp struggle over the status of historical prescription. On either side this superseded properly historical

65 Sidney, *Discourses,* in *Sydney on Government,* p. 464.
66 An understanding of this point resolves the contradiction perceived in Sidney's thought by J. Connif, 'Reason and History in Early Whig Thought: The Case of Algernon Sidney', *Journal of the History of Ideas* 43, 3 (1982).
67 Sidney, *Discourses,* in *Sydney on Government,* p. 236.   68 *Ibid.,* p. 406.

claims altogether, between the suggestion that God created the only legitimate form of government when he created the first man, and that he created the only basis for government and its improvement when he invested man with reason. Locke, who took the latter view, and whose whole argument is about the relationship of rational creatures to their creator, did not offer a historical analysis at all.

Thus, as seventeenth-century writers increasingly accepted change, political argument expanded its independence from the historical domain. This was one of the least expected outcomes of the troubles, that century-long struggle against religious and political innovation. It helped to consolidate that wider outcome whereby restoration itself would not succeed until it had incorporated to a limited degree the same conclusions.

LAW AND WAR

In the adaptation of the intellectual legacy of the revolution to restoration circumstances, two other themes would be particularly important. The first of these was law. Restoration was the restoration of government by law: of that 'government by law established' which had been undermined by a king and then obliterated by a republic.[69] This law was, in turn, the crucial stabilising link with custom. Glenn Burgess has reconstructed the political discourse of the early Stuart 'pacified polity'.[70] Most political was legal discourse and its practitioners assumed that all necessary political boundaries and remedies existed within the law. This was the common law, and Coke was an archetypal spokesman for this view of politics, which the events of 1627–59 consigned to the dustbin.

During the troubles the common law was overwhelmed by the different (and European) legal language of natural law. This asserted natural rights (and constraints) which stood above particular codes of positive law. This language had accompanied the earlier troubles in both France and the Netherlands and it was as its modern master that Grotius would prove indispensable in England from Selden to Locke.[71]

---

69 Scott, 'Restoration Process', p. 633.
70 Burgess, *Absolute Monarchy and the Stuart Constitution*, pp. 160–4.
71 Scott, 'Law of War'; Skinner, *Foundations of Modern Political Thought*, vol. II; Tuck, *Natural Rights Theories*; Tuck, *Philosophy and Government*; Sommerville, *Politics and Ideology*.

The first stage of restoration was an attempt to reconstruct the legally bounded pacified polity. That this failed – at least in the short term – is hardly surprising. In the restoration period it became clear that the law was, as Hobbes had insisted, but a paper scabbard for the sword. Magistracy became an instrument not simply for 'pacification' but revenge. Now protestant dissenters came to experience that legal fusion of religious dissent with political sedition which had faced catholics since Elizabethan times.

Opposition to restoration religious persecution resulted, from the early 1670s, in trials. The most famous was that of the Quakers William Penn and William Mead (1670) which resulted in an acquittal. This produced a trial transcript – reprinted nine times in four months – which appealed to the law of nature and to the 'fundamental' against the positive law. For 'to take away the LIBERTY and PROPERTY of any (which are natural Rights) . . . [is] breaking the Law of *nature*'.[72] That religious coercion was provided for by parliamentary statute was no defence. Laws directed to particular occasions were 'superficial' rather than 'fundamental', and parliament erred when it adopted laws that 'crossed' the fundamental liberties preserved in Magna Charta. The likely consequences were depicted in stark terms: 'Where Liberty and Property are destroyed, there must alwayes be a state of force and war, which . . . will be esteemed intolerable by the *Invaded*, who will no longer remain subject.'[73]

Most of this weaponry had already been wielded by the Levellers and others, against earlier parliamentary oppression. Penn's work is also notable for an emphasis upon the accountability of parliamentary representatives that is characteristic of that period. What is most striking, however, about these arguments, is their specific anticipation of Locke, who would develop the classic defence of 'the Right of War' in the face of invaded rights. As Richard Ashcraft has shown, many components of Locke's language and argument were common parlance amid the London radical community in 1679–83.[74] But they also had longer-term origins. Grotius had shown in *The Law of War and Peace* (1625) that, whereas positive law might govern societies in a settled state of peace, it was in time of war that it was necessary to understand the law of nature, which was also the law of war.[75] In the words of

72 De Krey, 'First Restoration Crisis', p. 572.
73 [Thomas Rudyard and William Penn], *The Peoples Antient and Just Liberties*, quoted with commentary *ibid.*, p. 573.   74 Ashcraft, *Revolutionary Politics*, ch. 5.
75 Scott, 'Law of War'; Grotius, *De Jure Belli ac Pacis Libri Tres*, vol. II (*The Translation Book I*), e.g., p. 33.

Locke: 'Force, or a declared design of force . . . where there is no common Superior on Earth to appeal to . . . is *the State of War* . . . 'tis the want of such an appeal gives a Man the Right of War . . . against an *aggressor*.'[76]

Thus the second additional theme of restoration radicalism was war. We have already observed two attitudes to this within mid-century republicanism: Roman and Venetian. Within restoration radicalism these maintained their prominence, and altered their emphasis, for several reasons. One was that this was a period living under the shadow of the civil war. As instability returned, particularly during the 1670s, this was the governing memory. Moreover, as the crisis of 1678–83 deepened, over the same issues as in 1637–42, this was a practical choice that had to be faced. When in 1680 Neville published his *Plato Redivivus*, calling for a radical reduction of monarchical power, he made equally clear his opinion that the civil war had been a tragedy a repetition of which could not under any circumstances be justified. In the famous words of Marvell the cause was 'too good to have been fought for'.[77] When, three years later, however, Sidney was tried for treason, one witness for the prosecution was a manuscript voicing the opposite opinion. As Machiavelli had said, 'if civil war was a disease, tyranny is the death of a state'. Thus 'If the laws of God and men are therefore of no effect, when the magistracy is left at liberty to break them, and if the lusts of those, who are too strong for the tribunals of justice, cannot otherwise be restrained, than by seditions, tumult and war, those seditions, tumults and wars, are justified by the laws of God and man.'[78] Little wonder that in the opinion of Lord Chief Justice George Jeffreys, Sidney's manuscript contained

all the malice revenge and treason, that mankind can be guilty of . . . there is not a line in the book scarce but what is treason . . . [and] Gentlemen [of the jury] I must tell you, I think I ought more than ordinarily to press this upon you, because, I know, the misfortune of the late unhappy rebellion, and the bringing of the late blessed king to the scaffold, was first begun by such kind of principles.[79]

In this aspect of restoration radicalism we see the reapplication of Machiavellian and Grotian insights drawn from the primacy of European war to the case of civil conflict within a country.[80]

76 *Locke's Two Treatises*, p. 298.
77 Marvell, *The Rehearsal Transpros'd*, quoted in John Wallace, *Destiny His Choice: The Loyalism of Andrew Marvell* (Cambridge 1980), p. 202.
78 Wallace, *Destiny His Choice*, p. 188.
79 *The Tryal of Algernon Sydney*, in *Sydney on Government*, p. 58.   80 Scott, 'Law of War'.

The fundamental restoration reality was that the war was not over. It was in the trials against religious dissenters, as we have seen, that we find defendants claiming politico-judicial rights of resistance that were actually rights of war. These became the basis of both Locke's and Sidney's resistance theories. Meanwhile the crisis of 1678–83 produced not simply rumination on the civil war, but its actual return through the courts. In the two great waves of treason trials of 1678–80 and 1680–3, against 'popery' and 'fanaticism' respectively, 'the old civil war transformed itself into a judicial war: men fought with one another in judicial battle – for what was right troubled neither grand nor petty juries'.[81] This furnished the practical context for Locke's and Sidney's writings.

THE OLD CAUSE

Within restoration radicalism we find all the principal political languages of the revolution. These included interest theory, natural law language, classical republicanism and ancient constitutionalism. During the restoration crisis in particular we see the gravitation of all of these languages towards the centre ground. This is because that crisis itself took the form of an extended rumination upon the past. As previously this revolution was a radicalisation of the parliamentary cause. The insistence upon liberty of conscience, and upon a religion of conduct, was a radicalisation of the reformation struggle against popery. The insistence upon political liberty was a radicalisation of the struggle against arbitrary government. These liberties, 'civil and spiritual', were the 'old cause'. It is thus not surprising that this cause enjoyed its most spectacular revival with the return of the troubles in 1678–83.

It is the principal purpose of the following chapter to examine this revival in its political and intellectual contexts. This will help to contextualise Sidney's *Discourses Concerning Government*, and Locke's *Two Treatises of Government*.[82] The focus of both of these works was upon civil liberty. Both furnished radical versions of the arguments against arbitrary government which were animating the crisis in general. This is not to say, however, that either was less concerned with liberty of conscience. Both furnished substantial arguments on behalf of this elsewhere (Sidney's *Court Maxims* and

81 Earl of Anglesey, quoted in Ranke, *History of England*, vol. IV, p. 159.
82 The evidence for the comparable dating of Locke's and Sidney's works is discussed in Scott, 'Law of War'.

Locke's *Letter Concerning Toleration*). Both made clear their practical affiliation with those 'people of God in England', the renewed persecution of whom was a crucial context for their works.

The focus on civil liberty owed something to the polemical context: the task of answering Sir Robert Filmer. It owed most, however, to a belief that spiritual was part of civil oppression. As popery and arbitrary government the two went hand in hand. In the *Apology . . . in the Day of his Death* [1683], Sidney opined:

I dye in the faith that . . . God will in his mercy speedily visit his afflicted people . . . and am soe much the more confident he will doe it, in that his cause, and his people is more concerned now then it was in former time. The lust of one man and his favourites was then only to be set up in the exercise of arbitrary power over persons and [e?]states; but now, the tyranny over consciences is principally affected, and the civill powers are stretched unto this exorbitant height, for the establishment of popery.[83]

Under Charles I protestantism had been endangered for the augmentation of civil power. Under Charles II the project of arbitrary government was approaching completion for the establishment of popery.

---

83 Sidney, *Apology*, pp. 30–1.

16

Radical restoration (2): the old cause

And when the Protestants of the Low-Countries were so grievously oppressed by the power of Spain . . . why should they not make use of all the means that God had put into their hands for their deliverance? . . . by resisting they laid the foundation of a most glorious and happy Commonwealth, that hath been, since its first beginning, the strongest pillar of the Protestant Cause now in the world.

Algernon Sidney, *Discourses Concerning Government* (1683)[1]

INTRODUCTION

Throughout the restoration period, as earlier, the struggles against religious and political oppression were intertwined. The period 1662–72 was dominated by the imposition of, and then struggle against, the parliamentary religious settlement. This culminated in what Gary de Krey and others have called 'the first restoration crisis' 1667–73.[2] Its precursor was the crisis of 1667 giving rise to a new phase of politics which culminated in an attempt by the king himself to unhinge the religious settlement.

The accompanying debate took its force from these practical issues. At the same time it had a polemical focus in Samuel Parker's defence of the religious settlement (*Discourse of Ecclesiastical Polity* (1669)) which played a role comparable to that of Filmer in the later crisis. Radical opposition to the restoration settlement before 1667 necessarily took a more muted form. The persistence of domestic plotting and seditious utterance in this period has been documented by Richard Greaves. This was accompanied by the activities of a republican community in exile, particularly during the Anglo-Dutch war (1665–7).[3]

---

1 This passage, probably taken from the *Discourses*, ch. 2, section 32, was read at the *Tryal of Algernon Sidney*, pp. 24–5.
2 De Krey, 'Rethinking the Restoration'; de Krey, 'First Restoration Crisis'.
3 Greaves, *Deliver Us from Evil*; Greaves, *Enemies Under His Feet*; Scott, *English Republic*, chs. 11–13.

The most important remains from the assault upon restoration from exile are Ludlow's *Voyce from the Watchtower* and Sidney's *Court Maxims*. The two authors disagreed about the scope for practical action against England in this period, in alliance with the Dutch. Ludlow held the Dutch responsible for the kidnapping and subsequent execution of the regicides Okey, Corbet and Barkstead in 1662. He was suspicious of them as 'those who preferr their Trade, before the honr of God and Christ'.[4] Nor was it clear to him that the time for such action had yet arrived:

I cannot promise my selfe a blessing from ye Lord upon [such] undertakings . . . till I observe a greater spirit of meekness and condecension amongst us then yet I doe . . . but when ye Lord hath humbled a people and fitted them for himselfe, making them willing to be abased for him he will certeinly lift them up, and bring them to honour.[5]

Meanwhile, however, Ludlow took comfort from the 'Unanimous witness' of the regicides; of 'those who had an hand in yt eminent act of Justice upon ye Late Tyrant in England'. He reaffirmed his alignment with

Those of the palamt and Army who minded ye welfare of ye publique Interest; and regarded ye Blood yt had bin shedd both of their friends and Enemies . . . [and] Looked upon it as their duty to hearken unto this and other Loud Voyces of ye Lords Providences, so to bring the Author of so much blood ye King to Justice, as a tyrant, Traytor, Murder[er], and Enemy to the Commonwealth of England.[6]

Above all Ludlow took comfort in the ultimate victory promised to 'those who are good, even when they seeme . . . to be most miserable'. In this respect

The Lords day is coming . . . the wicked are like Spunges whom God fills, that he may squeeze, Like Leeches that shall vomit their blood . . . Cain, Pharaoh, the Evil Kings of Israel and Judah, Baltazar, Zenacherib, Herod, Pylate, and those monsters of mankind Tiberius, Nero, Caligula, their sinfull dayes of pleasure had an end . . . yet is their end miserable, because its a beginning of Hell wch shall never have End.[7]

Ludlow and Sidney agreed about what their fellow exile Nicholas Lockier called 'the few yeares past of our Egiptian slavery'.[8] Both men rejected the

---

4 Scott, *English Republic*, pp. 174–5.
5 Bodleian Library, Oxford, MS Eng. hist c. 487, ff. 1057, 1082.   6 *Ibid.*, f. 29.
7 *Ibid.*, f. 323.   8 *Ibid.*, f. 1115.

reimposition of the government of religion by the civil power, whether prince or parliament, a usurpation they traced to that 'monster of mankinde' Henry VIII.[9] 'Hence grew the necessity of acknowledging the power of the civil magistrate in spiritual things, ridiculously setting a temporal head upon a spiritual body.'[10] Both inveighed equally against the re-establishment of monarchy, 'that government which God had laid in the dust', with its corrupt supports, the lawyers and the clergy.

Ludlow and Sidney reserved particular venom for the treatment being meted out in England to religious dissenters. 'Those bishops', said Sidney,

who lately altered the Common Prayer Book . . . should have said, the goodly and sacred fellowship of tyrants praise thee; the glorious army of thieves, murderers and blasphemers that uphold them magnify thee; the holy assembly of proud and cruel bishops, corrupt lawyers, false witnesses, and mercenary judges who persecute and endeavour to destroy thy church and people throughout the world, adorning the gates and towers of the city with the mangled limbs of thy choicest servants, to gratify the lusts and uphold the interest of their two masters, the king and the devil, do acknowledge thee.[11]

Sidney's furious tract, like Ludlow's never published in his lifetime, was both the widest-ranging and hardest-hitting early attack on the restoration process. It attacked not only the king, courtiers, bishops ('teachers of lies, workers of iniquity, persecutors of saints, apes of Rome')[12] and lawyers, but also every aspect of government strategy and policy, domestic and foreign. Above all it attacked the insanity of restoration as public choice. This was a result of moral failure; of wickedness and vice; above all of ignorance. This signalled the failure of the republican educational project; of the attempt to instil the public preference for substance over appearance; for virtue instead of vice; to equip a people for self-governing rationality. Restoration had entailed the public rejection of political adulthood. 'Burnt children dread the fire, but we more childish than children, tho oft scorch'd and burnt, do agen cast ourselves into the fire, like moths and gnats, delighting in the flame that consumes us.'[13]

These claims were infused with biblical imagery and Platonic epistemology. Both Sidney and Ludlow likened the English people to 'the stiffnecked people of Israel' who had, in the book of Samuel, insisted upon a king. Both

9 Ludlow, *Voyce*, ed. Worden, p. 7; Sidney, *Court Maxims*, p. 100.
10 Sidney, *Court Maxims*, p. 95.   11 *Ibid.*, p. 44.   12 *Ibid.*, p. 94.   13 *Ibid.*, p. 197.

observed 'their folly and madness in choosing a seeming good, instead of a reall one, and catching at shaddows and neglecting of ye substance'.[14] 'He is not happy', argued Sidney, 'that has what he desires, but desires what is good and enjoys it. For we very often desire things that are evil and hurtful to ourselves . . . The people of England, deceived by the fraud of the courtiers and the priests, grew to that height of madness as to seek servitude rather than liberty.' When, however, 'they . . . discover their misery and folly in the emptiness of that enjoyment which they thought would make them happy . . . nothing is more reasonable than that they should repent of their choice *and endeavour to unmake what they have made*'.[15] Thereafter Sidney's polemic against the 'maxims' of the restored monarchy drew upon English and Dutch republican interest theory. Monarchy was private interest government. Republicanism was government in the public interest. The two systems were thus founded in principles between which there was an 'irreconcilable contrariety'. This contrariety of interests – between public and private, republic and monarchy, God and the devil – Sidney called 'the principle [*sic*] comprehension of all civill and morall things'. It determined the fate of the state as a whole between progress and decline.[16]

Public interest government, and the 'political perfection of Liberty, security and happiness', resulted in a situation whereby 'understanding advanceth in the discovery and knowledge of truth through the rectitude of the will . . . Where things are in this right order, there is a perpetual advance in all that is good.'[17] As Plato said in the *Republic*: 'the State, if once started well, moves with accumulating force like a wheel. For good nurture and education implant good constitutions, and these constitutions taking root in good education improve more and more.'[18] Private interest government, on the contrary,

leaves an easy entrance for corruption in the administration as the will wch is not guided by a right understanding is easily overcome with the allurement of vice, or deceits of the Devil . . . This corruption of the law perpetually adds to ye evill of the administration. Thus these two plagues, if suffered to continue still feed one another, till the body that was strong healthy and beautiful becomes a carcass full of ulcers, boils, and putrid sores.[19]

---

14 Bodleian Library, Oxford, MS Eng. hist c. 487, f. 326.   15 Sidney, *Court Maxims*, pp. 4–7.
16 Scott, *English Republic*, p. 197.   17 *Ibid.*
18 Plato, *Republic*, bk 4, in *Portable Plato*, ed. Buchanan, p. 419.
19 Sidney, *Court Maxims*, p. 132 (I have made minor alterations to this published transcription from the manuscript in the Warwickshire Record Office MS CR1886).

Thus the interest of monarchy could be secured only at the expense of the public interest. The result was a people languishing in weakness, baseness and poverty. 'All people grow proud when Numerous and rich . . . the least injury putts them into a fury; But if poor weak, miserable and few they'l be humble and obedient.' That is how England, in a few years, had fallen from its 'flourishing state' under the Commonwealth, to become 'one of the most miserable nations at home and . . . despicable abroad'.[20] Sidney's attack on the 'tyranny over consciences' found its origin in the same 'contrariety of principles' with the same root:

Tyrants and priests ever agree together against God and his anointed, as pagan idolators and Turks do. And the fanatics or true Christians follow the examples also of their forerunners, the prophets, apostles, and all the saints from the beginning of the world; continuing in faith, prayer, and exercise of the gifts God has given them, fearing nothing but sin . . . Here are Augustine's two cities of God and the world, or of God and the devil, still in uniform, fixed, constant opposition to each other . . . The one vainly boasts and triumphs in a momentary perishing power, the other is steadfastly fixed upon the rock of Israel.[21]

The English church was now engaging in Roman persecution having by the break with Rome divested itself of the requisite theological authority:

If our prelates follow the steps of Rome in this as in many other things, they must prove infallibility in themselves, in the king, in the parliament . . . if there be no infallibility, none can have the confidence to defend that church or impose its doctrine upon others; every man having a rational and natural right of disputing what is uncertain, and of not receiving it till convinced that it's a certain truth.[22]

Since belief was not 'an act of the will' it could not be compelled; nor was compelled worship 'acceptable to God'. Meanwhile 'I shall take my liberty to differ from them when I see them apt to fall into the lowest path of sin and darkness, as well as I, wanting light and therefore subject to the same errors I am.'[23]

Sidney's most urgent response to the persecution of this period, and purpose in writing the *Court Maxims*, was to oppose the renunciation of that force which offered the only means of self-defence. 'At this day we find none to espouse these opinions but our Quakers, some few anabaptists in Holland and Germany, and some of the Socinians in Poland. It is most generally

---

20 Sidney, *Court Maxims*, pp. 71–80.   21 *Ibid.*, p. 106.   22 *Ibid.*, p. 107.
23 *Ibid.*, pp. 98, 108.

known all christian churches have rejected the opinion of those that thought no use of the sword lawful, having made use of it against such princes and their ministers as have governed contrary to law.'[24] This was a harsh condition of the world. Renunciation of force was not possible while the bishops themselves behaved like 'most savage wolves'. The bishops 'preach patience that people may submit to their tyranny, as the thief persuades the traveller to go unarmed that he may safely rob and kill him . . . No impudence is greater than that of those who preach doctrine so contrary to their practice.' Like much else in the *Court Maxims* Sidney's treatment of this theme was deeply influenced by the experience of attempted Caroline counter-reformation:

Who will endure that bishops, the greatest incendiaries in the whole world, should now preach the highest meekness? They who said it was better all the streets in England and Scotland should run with blood than the power of the clergy be diminished, say now, it is better England should be dispeopled, the best men in the nation banished and destroyed, than that their lusts should be resisted.[25]

Christian pacifism under these circumstances made society ungovernable: it was 'disallowing the use of force, without which innocency could not be protected, nor society maintain'd'. To wield the sword of justice was fundamentally necessary 'on behalf of the innocent; on behalf of the oppressed'. That is why even Grotius, though a 'gentle spirited man', considered resistance to authority justified in cases 'of the extremest injury'; because such a transgressor 'breaks the comon pact by which humane society is established . . . [and in doing so] renders himself a delinquent'. 'Whence I infer that, no man having a just power over my conscience, whoever offers violence to it, or to me for it, injures me in what is most dear unto me, [and] gives me a right in self-defence of repelling the injury.' The authority of Grotius on this point was seconded by that of Livy.[26] This imperative was so important that in an imperfect world it might even entail 'the hard necessity of sinning against God':

Those that by violence are brought to the hard necessity of sinning against God or suffering their families to be ruined and persons perpetually imprisoned, banished or murdered, may seem enough to justify those who by force seek to repel such violence.[27]

Sidney's tract is thus the most substantial early construction of the case for armed self-defence against restoration, particularly in its religious man-

24 *Ibid.*, pp. 101–3.   25 *Ibid.*, p. 103.   26 *Ibid.*, pp. 101–2.   27 *Ibid.*, p. 102.

ifestation. As such it anticipates much of the basis of Sidney's and Locke's later classic justifications of resistance, written in the context of the reimposition of religious persecution from 1681 to 1683.[28] The option of force was particularly important to Sidney because the restored monarchy 'so well remember[s] the temper of [our subjects'] swords, we avoid all disputes that are determin'd that way'.[29]

1667–72

Other works echoed these themes. Among them are Slingsby Bethel's *The World's Mistake in Oliver Cromwell* (1668) and *The Present Interest of England Stated* (1671) (republished in expanded form as *The Interest of Princes and States* (1680)). These echoes are not surprising since Bethel had been associated with the Rump Parliament; had shared Dutch exile with Sidney in the mid-1660s; and was later elected sheriff of London with his support in 1680. Bethel's tracts (which, unlike Sidney's, were published) do not engage in overt denunciation of the restored monarchy. *The World's Mistake* does, however, associate itself with 'the Long Parliament' and its policies in attacking the man who had destroyed them.[30] Moreover, like the *Maxims*, it champions as the European model of civil, religious and economic government that 'Republick' called the United Provinces.

One of Bethel's concerns was to argue for liberty of conscience, and to attack religious persecution as contrary to the 'Interest' of nations.[31] Like Sidney, Bethel is deeply concerned about the 'Protestant Interest' in Europe, and details assaults upon it, particularly the Irish massacre of 1641.[32] The principal focus of Bethel's work was to apply to English politics an analysis of national 'Interest' imported from Dutch republicanism. 'The prosperity, or adversity, if not the life and death of a state, is bound up in the observing or neglecting its Interest.' The 'principal interest' of England, like that of the United Provinces, 'is Trade'. Like the Dutch republican Pieter de la Court, both Bethel and Sidney agreed that this national 'Interest' had two dimensions – domestic and foreign – and each is treated separately.[33]

---

28 Scott, 'Law of War'.   29 Scott, *English Republic*, p. 195.
30 Slingsby Bethel, *The World's Mistake in Oliver Cromwell* (London 1668), p. 2.
31 Bethel, *The Interest of Princes and States* (London 1680), pp. 18–36.
32 *Ibid.*, pp. 18–19, 42–4; Sidney, *Court Maxims*, p. 178.
33 'De Witt' [de la Court], *True Interest*. The first edition of this tract was published in the Netherlands in 1662; the second in 1664. See Scott, *English Republic*, ch. 12.

Like Sidney, Bethel repeatedly praises Dutch political management. Against restoration politics in England both championed Dutch policies concerning trade, politics and religion. Bethel explained in 1680 that his writings were 'the result of observations made by the Author long ago, in the time of his Travels, and writ some years hence'.[34] The specific purpose of his *Present Interest* (1671) was to make a pro-Dutch intervention in the debate over religious and foreign policy in that period. As England's domestic interest lay in religious and political liberty, so its interest abroad lay in 'firm peace and amity with the Netherlands'. Indeed among all

Countries having observed their Manners, and read their Disputes, and Transactions with other Nations . . . in the generality of their Morals, they are a reproach to som Nations . . . [and] I cannot think their Trade or Wealth . . . to be a good or honest foundation for a quarrel; for their commerce [is] . . . alone the effect of Industry, and Ingenuity.[35]

Bethel was one of many putting the case for liberty of conscience in the period 1667–72.[36] Others included Charles Wolseley, Nicholas Lockier, John Humfrey and William Penn. Penn's tracts shared with Bethel and Sidney the prominence of interest language. He called 'Civil Interest the foundation of Government'; insisted upon the importance of a 'united Protestant interest'; and upon that of 'governing on a ballance, as near as possible, of the severall Religious interests'.[37] Like them he insisted upon the importance not only of liberty of conscience, but of liberty in general. Like them he pointed for the outstanding example of the success of 'a United Civil Interest' to the government of the United Provinces.[38]

As we have seen, Penn was important for waging this struggle not only in print but in practice (in the courts). The result was an insistence not only upon that 'Liberty and Property' which Penn called our 'Natural and Civil Rights'. It was an invocation of that natural right of resistance to the 'invasion' of these properties. This was the same doctrine invoked by Sidney in the *Court Maxims*. It was also the same right of resistance that Locke would come to call the Right of War. Sidney was himself adopting an argument

34 Bethel, *Interest of Princes and States*, preface.
35 Bethel, *The Present Interest of England Stated* (London 1671), p. 33.
36 De Krey, 'Rethinking the Restoration'.
37 Penn, *One Project for the Good of England* (1679), in *Works*, vol. I, p. 482; Penn, *England's Present Interest Considered* (1675), in *Works*, vol. I, p. 674.
38 Penn, *England's Present Interest*, in *Works*, vol. I, pp. 684–6.

already used by the Leveller Richard Overton in 1646–7. From 1678 to 1680 Penn and Sidney were close friends and political allies. The person who introduced them was the Rotterdam Quaker Benjamin Furly, host to the exiled Sidney in 1664–5 and the exiled Locke in 1683–7.[39]

For all of these writers the most important embattled liberty and property was conscience. In 1675 Penn defined that property for the protection of which government was founded as a 'Right of Estate, and Liberty of Person: That is to say, I am no Man's Bond-man, and what I possess is Absolutely Mine Own'.[40] In 1677 Marvell wrote that 'men ought to enjoy the same Propriety and Protection in their Consciences which they have in their Lives, Liberties, and Estates'.[41] In a pamphlet written by Penn in support of an election campaign by Sidney in 1679 he defined property as the 'Right and Title to your own Lives, Liberties and Estates' in relation to which 'every man is a sort of little Soveraign to himself'.[42] By the time Locke wrote the *Two Treatises* this terminology had become commonplace in the London radical community.[43]

One aspect of this radical vernacular was to speak, as both Locke and Sidney did, of a situation in which governments acted 'contrary to the ends of their own institution'. This authorised armed resistance, in Locke's case by dissolving the government, in Sidney's by nullifying its political authority. Another feature of this language was to speak of justified self-defence against 'invasion'. The context in which this language moved to the forefront of radical speech was the reimposition of religious persecution in 1681–3. The early works of Sidney and Penn (among others) remind us, however, that this language was older than the crisis of 1678–83. It had appeared during the first restoration persecution and attempts to resist it. Its actual origin lay in the struggle against the attempted reimposition of religious uniformity of 1646–7.

---

39 Scott, *Restoration Crisis*, pp. 128–34; Scott, *English Republic*, pp. 218–21; Maurice Cranston, *John Locke* (New York 1979); Rosalie Colie, 'John Locke in the Republic of Letters', in E. H. Kosman, *Britain and the Netherlands* (London 1960), vol. I, pp. 111–29.
40 Penn, *England's Present Interest*, in *Works*, vol. I, p. 677.
41 Marvell, *Growth of Popery*, p. 33.
42 Philanglus [William Penn], *England's Great Interest in the Choice of This New Parliament* (London 1679), p. 2.
43 Ashcraft, *Revolutionary Politics*, ch. 5; Tim Harris, '"Lives, Liberties and Estates": Rhetorics of Liberty in the Reign of Charles II', in Harris, Seaward and Goldie, *Politics of Religion*.

1672–80

One effect of the king's own attempt to unhinge the religious settlement in 1672 was to encourage opposition to it. Throughout the period 1673–8, therefore, in his attempt to reconstruct the policies of restoration, the king's chief minister Danby faced vigorous opposition. This spanned the social spectrum from London nonconformity to the House of Lords (Lords Buckingham, Shaftesbury, Halifax and Holles in particular).

This in turn was only one aspect of a wider opposition to Danby's policies, and so to the original restoration settlement. This opposed the arbitrary government of both church and state. It opposed, specifically, what Marvell called 'the growth of popery and arbitrary government'. This return of the troubles furnished the context for the revival of radical activity and writing during the 1670s.

In place of the arbitrary government of church and state Danby's opponents demanded parliamentary politics (a role for both Commons and Lords); the dissolution of the present foetid and reactionary 'Long Parliament'; a protestant anti-French foreign policy; and toleration for protestant dissenters. The focus for religious grievance was Danby's Test Act of 1673. Shaftesbury's *Letter from a Person of Quality* (1675) detected in this a whiff of the papal doctrine of infallibility. To require people to 'swear never to alter' the existing political or religious settlement rather suggested that it was perfect: the creation of 'God itself'. The Test's design was to make 'a distinct party' of the high churchman and cavalier, for a return to the discredited persecution of the Clarendon Code. Worse still, the Test signalled a return to the policies of Charles I: divine right monarchy offered by the bishops in return for divine right episcopacy. In this respect the Test was the vehicle for innovation. Its 'design was to declare us first into another Government more Absolute, and Arbitrary, then the Oath of Allegiance, or old Law knew, and then make us swear to it'. To this extent the 'distinct party' being revived was in fact a 'new Partie' whose 'standard [was] not yet set up'.[44]

This accusation of innovation was crucial. It was of course a characteristic of the troubles. It was also to determine the terms in which the issues during the subsequent crisis would be argued. Thus it was that Shaftesbury's client Locke, and Sidney, would both seize upon the resusci-

---

44 *Letter from a Person of Quality*, pp. 1, 20, 26, 32; Greaves, *Enemies Under His Feet*, p. 230.

tated Sir Robert Filmer as the spokesman for a new-fangled design of arbitrary innovation. 'In this last age', wrote Locke, 'a generation of men has sprung up among us, who would flatter princes with an Opinion, that they have a Divine Right to absolute Power, let the Laws by which they are constituted, and are to govern, and the conditions under which they enter upon their authority be what they will.'[45] This was a design against the unreformed polity, its powers carefully circumscribed by law. Like Filmer's work this design (of clerically assisted absolutism) was a revival from the early Stuart period.

Neville made the same point and Marvell agreed. There had 'lately sprung up' a design to convert 'the nations religion to popery' and its legal constitution to 'downright tyranny'. The return of this polemic against arbitrary innovation could be read by moderate persons as a defence of the restoration settlement. It was being used here in practice as an instrument against it, and particularly its religious clauses. Finally, as we have seen, it could furnish the context for a republican reading of the experience of the troubles: of modern monarchy as inevitably and inherently illegal and tyrannical.

It was in the context of this campaign against Danby that Shaftesbury made the historical claims discussed in the previous chapter. These inquired after the

> pains taken by the Court to debase, and bring low the House of Peers, if a Military Government be not intended by some. For the Power of a Peerage, and a Standing-Army are like two Buckets, the proportion that one goes down, the other exactly goes up.[46]

This was a formulation repeated in other pamphlets in the same year.[47] Shaftesbury's concern was to argue for an essential role for the nobility in relation to the monarchy as in 'all the Northern nations'. In making this accusation he was associating the Stuart monarchy with what was generally understood to be the Europe-wide process of its destruction.[48] It was in the late 1670s that John Hampden jnr, a republican conspirator in 1683, met the historian Mezeray in Paris and was told that France had once enjoyed the same free institutions as England, before losing them to the

---

45 *Locke's Two Treatises*, p. 160.   46 *Letter from a Person of Quality*, p. 34.
47 For instance *Two Seasonable Discourses Concerning This Present Parliament* (1675), attributed by Richard Greaves to Shaftesbury (*Enemies Under His Feet*, p. 230).
48 Salmon, *French Religious Wars*, chs. 7 and 8, esp. pp. 160–2.

encroachments of its kings. 'Think nothing, he said, too dear to maintain these precious advantages; venture your life, your estates, and all you have rather than submit to the miserable condition to which you see us reduced.' 'These words', recorded Hampden, 'made an impression on me which nothing can efface.'[49]

What Shaftesbury was not doing was accepting that that process of destruction had passed the point of no return. Neville's *Plato Redivivus* was by contrast relatively faithful to the historical substance of Harrington's analysis. What had altered since Harrington were the political circumstances of composition. Neville was asking Charles to surrender some of his powers, as Harrington had earlier asked Cromwell. Yet he was doing so within the context of a re-established monarchy, not a purported (if not actual) republic. Thus when Neville's 'English Gentleman' was accused of 'nibbling at . . . a commonwealth', he replied not to the effect that a commonwealth would be undesirable but that he 'abhor[red] the thoughts of wishing . . . any such thing, *during the circumstances we are now in*: that is, under oaths of obedience to a lawful king'.[50]

One cannot imagine Sidney taking such a conciliatory line. Yet Neville's qualification was crucial, for in relation to it a good deal would have changed by the following year. The last parliament of the reign had been abandoned, Charles had recovered his relationship with France, and the most severe religious persecution of the period had begun. It was in this situation that Sidney and Locke faced the much harder possibility of a king whose actions were contrary to law, and to whom such oaths might no longer be binding. The king had after all taken oaths himself, and entered upon his reign under conditions. Thus Sidney detailed the measures necessary 'against an usurping tyrant, or the perfidiousness of a lawfully created magistrate, who adds the crimes of ingratitude and treachery to usurpation [of powers contrary to his institution]'.[51] Locke, having spoken of the 'Laws by which they are constituted, and are to govern, and the conditions under which they enter upon their authority', went on to suggest that in such a case the subject might have to choose between allegiance to the king and to the laws. '*Oaths of Allegiance* . . . are taken . . . [but] *Allegiance* . . . is nothing but an *Obedience according to Law*.' Sidney repeated: 'oaths of allegiance

49 *A Collection of State Tracts published during the Reign of King William III* (London 1706), vol. II, p. 313; *Dictionary of National Biography*, vol. XXV, pp. 262–3.

50 Neville, *Plato Redivivus*, p. 173.   51 Sidney, *Discourses*, in *Sydney on Government*, pp. 193–4.

[may be taken] . . . but Allegiance signifies no more (as the words 'ad legem' declare) than such an obedience as the law requires'.[52]

Neville had referred to the desperate circumstances recently experienced in England, a repetition of which he was attempting to avoid:

Wherever any two coordinate powers do differ, and there be no power on earth to reconcile them . . . they will, in fact, fall together by the ears. What can be done in this case justly, look into . . . Machiavel, and Grotius; who in his book *De Jure Belli ac Pacis*, treated of such matters long before our wars . . . [but] I will not rest myself in so slippery a place.[53]

'Controversies among those', Grotius had written, 'not held together by a common bond of municipal law are related either to times of war or times of peace . . . we set out to treat the law of war.'[54] As we have seen, reference to the resulting formulation had been a feature of the Long Parliament's own justification of its resistance to Charles I. The key text was *De Jure Belli*, bk 1, ch. 4, para. 13, a key source for Sidney's *Discourses*.[55] For it was in exactly these circumstances, and this 'slippery place', that Locke and Sidney would produce what were to become the classic seventeenth-century English resistance theories. In doing so they drew upon the intellectual contexts of all three phases of the revolution. In Locke's *Two Treatises* we find a version of Richard Overton's theory of limited self-propriety, the principal adaptation made by civil war radicalism to European natural law theory. In Sidney's *Discourses* we find the fullest statements of both the Machiavellianism and the christian–Greek moral philosophy characteristic of English republicanism. In both cases these appear within the context of a defence of resistance indebted to Grotius, among others. In this way the restoration crisis acted as a prism through which both the principal issues and languages of the revolution were given a new form by immediate practical needs.

THE LAW OF WAR 1681–3

Locke's and Sidney's objectives in writing the *Two Treatises* and the *Discourses* were both polemical and practical. They wished to refute Sir Robert Filmer's *Patriarcha*, and to justify resistance. That both authors shared the common ground of Grotian natural law theory is partly

---

52 *Locke's Two Treatises*, II, para. 151; Sidney, *Discourses*, in *Sydney on Government*, p. 458.
53 Neville, *Plato Redivivus*, pp. 148–9.   54 Grotius, *De Jure Belli ac Pacis*, vol. II, p. 33.
55 Sidney, *Discourses*, in *Sydney on Government*, pp. 190, 280, 256.

explicable on polemical grounds. Filmer had written to attack that doctrine of 'the natural freedom of mankind' and Grotius' *De Jure Belli* in particular. Tyrell's *Patriarcha Non Monarcha* shows an even greater preoccupation with the defence of Grotius against Filmer.[56] For Locke and Sidney, however, the refutation of Filmer was the preliminary to a practical end. This was to relay the basis for that very 'Popular sedition' Filmer had written to uproot.

It is coincidences between Locke's and Sidney's answers to Filmer which have hitherto attracted the attention of scholars. Some of these are explained by Filmer's own text, as when both men quote against him his admission that even '*Hayward, Blackward, Barclay and others*, that have bravely *vindicated the Rights of Kings in most Points . . . admitted the Natural Liberty and Equality of Mankind.*'[57] Much more important, however, is a broader identity of polemical approach. Both men identify Filmer as a modern ideological innovator who has destroyed political peace. 'In this last age', writes Locke, 'a generation of men has sprung up . . . As if they had designed to make War upon all Government.' Filmer, repeats Sidney, 'seems to denounce war against mankind, endeavouring to overthrow the principle in which God created us'.[58]

Both then go on to identify this 'generation of men' identically. They are those who believe that, in Locke's words, 'all Government is absolute Monarchy'; in Sidney's, that 'there is but one government in the world'.[59] According to Sidney, 'no-one had impudence enough . . . to publish [such] doctrines . . . till these times. The production of Laud, Manwaring, Sibthorp, Hobbes, Filmer, and Heylin, seems to have been reserved . . . to complete the shame and misery of our age and country.'[60] Locke agreed: 'By whom this Doctrine came at first to be broach'd, and brought in fashion

---

56 Filmer, *Patriarcha*, p. 4; Philalethes [James Tyrell], *Patriarcha Non Monarcha* (London 1681), pp. 10, 18–19, 20, 97–126. Filmer's attack on Grotius, though part of the Cambridge ms. of *Patriarcha* published in 1949 by Peter Laslett, was not contained in the 1680 edition. It had, however, been published as 'Observations upon H. Grotius, *De Jure Belli ac Pacis*', in Filmer, *Observations concerning the Originall of Government* (London 1652), republished as *Reflections concerning the Originall of Government* (London 1679). Locke's work responds to the publications both of 1679 and 1680.

57 *Locke's Two Treatises*, I, para. 4; Sidney, *Discourses*, in *Sydney on Government*, p. 55.

58 *Locke's Two Treatises*, I, para. 3; Sidney, *Discourses*, in *Sydney on Government*, p. 3.

59 *Locke's Two Treatises*, I, para. 2; Sidney, *Discourses*, in *Sydney on Government*, p. 1.

60 Sidney, *Discourses*, in *Sydney on Government*, pp. 4–5.

amongst us, and what sad Effects it gave rise to, I leave to *Historians* to relate, or to the Memory of those who were Contemporaries with *Sibthorp* and *Manwaring* to recollect.'[61]

What was contained within these observations was a threat. It was the threat of repetition of the English civil war. Filmer's ideology was a declaration of war, associated with those held responsible for creating the conditions for the last war. This same threat had in fact been made earlier in the same year (1681) by another pamphlet: *A Just and Modest Vindication of the Proceedings of the Two Last Parliaments*. Replying to Charles II's *Declaration*, justifying the dissolution of his two last parliaments, the *Vindication* had observed, menacingly:

The first Declaration of this sort which ever I met with, being that which was published in 1628 [1629] . . . was so far from answering the ends of its coming out, that it filled the whole Kingdom with jealousies, and was one of the first sad causes of the ensuing unhappy war.[62]

Richard Ashcraft has identified this tract as the most important forerunner of certain features of Locke's resistance argument.[63] Ashcraft, however, believed that the *Vindication* was written by Robert Ferguson, like Locke a client of the Earl of Shaftesbury. In fact it was written, as Burnet tells us, by Algernon Sidney, with his friend the attorney general Sir William Jones.[64] As a partnership of war and law Sidney and Jones are difficult to improve upon.

For opponents of crown policy, the principal political issue after April 1681 was the indefinite suspension of parliaments. The obstruction of parliaments had been the major political issue throughout this crisis, as under Charles I. By 1683 Sidney was attempting to organise a repetition of the events of the year 1640. This would have seen a Scots rebellion forcing the summoning of parliament upon a popish and arbitrary monarch.[65] This was part of a projected 'war in both kingdoms', in relation to which Colonel Sidney

---

61 *Locke's Two Treatises*, pp. 160–1.
62 [Algernon Sidney and Jones], *Just and Modest Vindication*, Appendix 15, p. cxxxvi. See Scott, *Restoration Crisis*, pp. 186–7, and ch. 9 in general.
63 Ashcraft, *Revolutionary Politics*, pp. 317–18.
64 British Library Add MS 63,057, vol. II, p. 116; Burnet, *History of my Own Time*, vol. II, p. 276; Scott, *Restoration Crisis*, pp. 186–7.   65 Scott, *Restoration Crisis*, chs. 10, 12.

looked upon a rising in Scotland to be of infinite advantage and security to us, both as it would give a diversion, and be a place of retreat for us if we met with ill success in England; that the oppressions there were so grievous, that (as he was inform'd) the hearts of all the common people were set upon an insurrection to shake off their yokes . . . [and] he thought we must tell the world how the King had broken the laws and his own oath; and secure the settlement of the kingdom to a parliament, which if we were successful would know how to provide for the safety of ourselves and the people.[66]

As late as 28 December 1682 a correspondent of the Earl of Carlisle reported the execution of Scots captives from Bothwell Bridge who, offered their lives if they would say 'God blesse the King', refused and were hanged.[67] Meanwhile if suspension of parliaments was the major issue, it was not the most pressing practical problem. It was the loyalist reaction, both political and religious, that forced the crown's opponents into armed self-defence. Specifically it was the loss of the London shrievalty that lay at the heart of the practical emergency of mid-1682. It was in this context that Locke and Sidney penned their justifications of resistance. For it was by this event that the judicial powers of the politicised shrievalty were wrested back for use against its opponents by the crown.

This involved the overturning by force of a legitimate vote, taken by over a thousand people. A riot ensued, during which the ejected sheriff Slingsby Bethel and his patron Sidney were both arrested for incitement.[68] The agent of this coup was the loyalist lord mayor, Sir John Moore, who followed his instructions in claiming the right to impose new sheriffs. Bethel later claimed:

Sir John More . . . overthrew all the Rights of the City relating to the Choice of offi-cers, and thereby laid us open to a Deluge of Misery and Blood . . . the Right of Electing Sheriffs belongs to the Freemen, so our Ancestors have been in nothing more careful than that all Elections should be managed with Freedom, without Fraud [or] force . . . [The Mayor's crime is great to] make the King lose the love and confidence of five parts in six of the whole City . . . [and] to engage the King in a visible Contest with a Great People, in a point that they will not part with, and

---

66 Grey, *Secret History of the Rye House Plot*, pp. 51–3, 55.

67 British Library, Sloane MS 2723, f. 6. The victims defended their 1679 action as 'noe rebel-lion but that wch they were in conscience obliged to . . . calling his Majesty a Tyrant and a Usurper'.

68 *An Impartial Account of the Proceedings of the Common Hall of the City of London at Guildhal* (London, 24 June 1682); Scott, *Restoration Crisis*, pp. 272–4.

which his Majesty cannot wrest from them, without declining from the course of the Law, which both his Justice and his Oath oblige him against.[69]

Locke subsequently listed as the first three of the four principal ways by which governments are dissolved from within:

when [the] . . . Prince sets up his own Arbitrary will in place of the Laws . . . declared by the Legislative . . . when the Prince hinders the Legislative from assembling in its due time, or from acting freely . . . [and] When by the Arbitrary Power of the Prince, the Electors, or ways of Election are altered, without the Consent, and contrary to the common Interest of the people.[70]

Scholars have largely assumed that this last point at least is a reference added later to events under James II. But if we follow the participants in this crisis, in attributing as much importance to civic as to national politics, its context in 1682 seems clear. The final cause of political dissolution, explained Locke, was when the prince violently 'invade[s] the Property of the Subject . . . to make [himself] . . . Arbitrary disposer of the Lives, Liberties or Fortunes of the People'.[71] What defence could there be now that the laws themselves had become instruments of political vengeance?

The king having informed Barillon that he would have to 'cutt off a few heads' to restore order, a series of executions followed.[72] Over the following eighteen months not a single radical tried was acquitted or pardoned. The relevance of Grotius in this situation is not difficult to see. With the king's 'Arbitrary will in place of the Law' there was not only no tribunal of municipal law binding the king to his opponents. Those tribunals themselves had been turned into instruments of war. With the civil war being refought through the courts there was no law in England now but the law of war.

This became the condition of England when, in Locke's words, echoing the interest theory of Sidney's *Court Maxims*, 'flattery prevailed with weak Princes to make use of [their] power for private ends . . . and not for the publick good . . . as if the Prince had a separate Interest from the good of the Community . . . [this] tend[s] . . . to set up one part, or Party, with a distinction from . . . the rest'. Sidney's claim in the *Court Maxims*, however, had been one not only of distinction but 'irreconcilable contrariety'. The *Discourses* accordingly echoes Locke with its own emphasis: 'when a magistrate . . . sets up an interest . . . in himself, repugnant to the good of the

69 [Slingsby Bethel], *The Right of Chusing Sheriffs* (London 1689), pp. 2–3.
70 *Locke's Two Treatises*, II, paras. 214–16.   71 *Ibid.*, para. 221.
72 Ranke, *History of England*, vol. IV, p. 188.

public, for which he is made to be what he is . . . These contrary ends certainly divide the nation into parties . . . and this creates a most irreconcilable
enmity.'[73] A more specific problem was that of the monarch failing to
summon, or, in Locke's words, 'using . . . force to hinder the *meeting . . . of the
Legislative,* when the Original Constitution, or the publick Exigencies
require it . . . [This introduces] a state of War with the People, who have a
right to *reinstate* their *Legislative in the Exercise* of their Power.'[74] Sidney
repeated:

> Kings may call parliaments, if there be occasion, at times when the law does not
> exact it; they are placed as sentinels, and ought vigilantly to observe the motions of
> the enemy . . . but if the sentinel fall asleep, neglect his duty, or maliciously endea-
> vour to betray the city, those who are concerned may make use of all other means . . .
> to preserve themselves.[75]

Both men made it clear that the rights of war which applied internationally also applied domestically. Says Locke:

> That *Subjects,* or *Foreigners* attempting by force on the Properties of any
> People, may be *resisted* with force, is agreed on all hands. But that *Magistrates*
> doing the same thing, may be *resisted,* hath of late been denied . . . Wheras their
> Offence . . . is greater . . . as being ungrateful, for the [power] . . . they have by
> the Law.[76]

Sidney repeats:

> [as the sword of war was given by God] to protect the people against the violence of
> foreigners . . . [so] the sword of justice is put into the[ir] hands for protection
> against internal injury . . . The people think it the greatest of crimes to convert that
> power to their hurt which was instituted for their good . . . [and] that the injustice is
> aggravated by ingratitude.[77]

Yet the difference between Locke and Sidney in all these points becomes
clear through a further coincidence of language. 'Nor let anyone think', says
Locke, 'that this lays a perpetual foundation for Disorder: for this operates
not, till the Inconvenience is so great, that the Majority feel it . . . and find a
necessity to have it amended.' 'If it be said', echoes Sidney, 'that this may
sometimes cause disorders, I acknowledge it; but no human condition

---

73 Sidney, *Discourses,* in *Sydney on Government,* pp. 188, 379–80; *Locke's Two Treatises,* II,
    paras. 162–3.   74 *Locke's Two Treatises,* II, para. 155.
75 Sidney, *Discourses,* in *Sydney on Government,* p. 466.   76 *Locke's Two Treatises,* II, para. 231.
77 Sidney, *Discourses,* ed. West, p. 219.

being perfect, such a one is to be chosen, which carries with it the most tolerable inconveniences.'[78]

THE POLITICAL THEORY OF REBELLION

Throughout these texts the two men were putting the same arguments to the service of what were actually opposite political instincts. One involved the inflection of Grotius towards the querulous Puffendorf; the other towards the warlike Machiavelli. Locke was not, like Sidney, a 'Christian soldier', but a lifetime advocate of peace. For him, accordingly, just war and the Right of War, however presently necessary, were antithetical to the normal functioning of political society. If the intrusion of royal force made peace impossible, the Right of War which resulted was not a fact of political relations but a consequence of their dissolution. That is why, although Locke shared with Sidney Grotius' preoccupation with war as an instrument of justice, unlike him he followed Puffendorf in carefully restricting its scope.

According to Puffendorf, 'the Right of War, which always attends all Men in the State of Nature, is taken from private persons in Commonwealths . . . and Civil States . . . no private subject hath a Right of War'. Grotius, by contrast, had opposed the view that 'since the establishment of public tribunals, all rights to private war cease'. They 'still hold good . . . where judicial procedure ceases to be available . . . or where those . . . administering the law refuse to take cognizance'.[79] This was Sidney's view. But for Locke, as for Puffendorf, this 'Right' was applicable only in a state of nature, where there was no 'common establish'd Law and Judicature to appeal to'. In this case what Locke called his 'strange doctrine' of the 'Executive Power of the Law of Nature' gave people a 'Right of War'. '[F]orce . . . where there is no common Superior on Earth to appeal to . . . is the State of War . . . 'tis the want of such an appeal gives a man the Right of War . . . against an *agressor*.'[80]

For Locke, then, the right to resist was not a political but a natural right. It arose only after the dissolution of government, and responsibility for this desperate state of affairs rested securely with the monarch. Governments

---

78 *Locke's Two Treatises*, II, para. 224; Sidney, *Discourses*, in *Sydney on Government*, p. 461.
79 Samuel von Puffendorf, *The Law of Nature and Nations* (London 1749), bk 8, ch. 6, 'Of the Right of War', para. 8; Grotius, *De Jure Belli*, bk 1, ch. 3, para. 2.
80 *Locke's Two Treatises*, II, para. 19.

existed for the protection of their subjects' property (life, liberty, estate). By invading this they contradicted the end of their own institution and so dissolved themselves. It was following this dissolution that ex-subjects, returned to the state of nature, found themselves with a Right of War against their ex-governors. It was therefore arbitrary governors who, by invading their subjects' property, laid 'a Foundation for perpetual Disorder . . . Tumult, Sedition and Rebellion'. Specifically they 'introduce[d] a state of War' where previously there had been peace. It was therefore such *monarchs* who were '*Rebels . . . Rebellare* [being] . . . to bring back again [a] state of War'.[81]

Thus rhetorically, at least, the effect of Locke's polemic was not to justify rebellion. It was to redirect the odium of it on to the government. Nor was it to justify resistance to government as such. Rather, governments dissolved themselves, exposing those responsible to the law of war. Accordingly Locke's resistance theory hinged entirely upon, and his *Second Treatise* was constructed to culminate in, its final chapter, 'Of the Dissolution of Government'. In describing the circumstances in which governments came to be dissolved 'from within' this described the circumstances pertaining in England in 1678–83 in general, and 1681–3 in particular.

It was for this reason that at the core of Locke's political theory there was, and had to be, an account of the *limits* of government power. His argument depended not upon people's rights against their government but upon the universal limits of what any government could do. Thus Locke did not say, as Grotius had, that the rights of resistance of any people against their government depended upon what type of government it was. Against absolute government there might be no right of resistance. For Locke people had no right to resist any government. But nor was any absolute government legitimate. Absolute or arbitrary governments were contradictions in terms. Government was established for the protection of property and a government that contradicted this end was not a government at all.

There was only one radical theory already available that had directed itself to the *limitation* of government power. This was that developed by the Levellers between 1646 and 1649 to extract certain areas of human life from the purview of civil authority. Informing this was the theory of limited self-propriety most clearly articulated by Richard Overton. This said, correcting Grotius, that our property in our persons was not held absolutely. That is why it could not be surrendered absolutely to any civil government. Rather it was

81 *Ibid.*, para. 226.

held in trust from God, whose creatures we were; and by the prior government of whom (particularly over conscience) civil powers remained limited.

That at the heart of Locke's theory we find exactly this argument does not necessarily mean that he read the Levellers. This was the radical natural law theory vernacular of the English revolution which had survived, in London in particular, to inform the next visitation of the troubles. For Locke too no government could deploy absolute powers over property because they were not man's to give. Man's property in his life, liberty and estate was limited by, and subject to, the larger property rights of God. As 'Every one . . . is *bound to preserve himself*' (in Overton's words: 'no man may abuse, torment or beat himself') and nothing 'may Authorise us to destroy one another', so the governments we make are restricted to the 'Peace and *Preservation of all Mankind*':

> For Men being all the Workmanship of one Omnipotent, and infinitely wise Maker; All the Servants of one Sovereign Master, sent into the World by his order and about his business, they are his Property, whose Workmanship they are, made to last during his, not one anothers Pleasure.[82]

Sidney's contextualisation of the Right of War, though closely related to Locke's, was at the same time crucially different. His statement about the need to accept that level of disorder which carried with it 'the most tolerable inconveniences' came not from Puffendorf but from Machiavelli.[83] Similarly, when Sidney made exactly the same etymological point as Locke about the meaning of 'rebellion', his purpose was not to redirect the odium of it on to the government. It was to offer the seventeenth century's only explicit defence of rebellion, both word and thing:

> [R]ebellion is not always evil. That this may appear, it will not be amiss to consider the word . . . [which] is taken from the Latin 'rebellare', which signifies no more than to renew a war . . . Rebellion, being [thus] nothing but a renewed war . . . of itself is neither good or evil, more than any other war; but is just or unjust, according to the cause or manner of it.[84]

---

82 *Ibid.*, paras. 6–7; James Tully, *A Discourse on Property* (London 1980).
83 Machiavelli, *The Discourses*, p. 121: 'So in all human affairs one notices . . . that it is impossible to remove one inconvenience without another emerging . . . Hence in all discussions one should consider [only] which alternative involves fewer inconveniences.'
84 Sidney, *Discourses*, in *Sydney on Government*, pp. 457–60; Scott, *Restoration Crisis*, pp. 260–2. In 1652 Sidney's father the Earl of Leicester had recorded in his commonplace book: 'though Livy use the word Rebellare, that seems to be the makin warr again; rather than to imply subjection . . . Rebellare is used frequently in Livy [in this sense]' (Kent Archives Office, Maidstone, De Lisle MS, U1475 Z1/9, loose pages, fourth item, f. 2).

No less remarkably, Sidney went on to justify the very 'seditions, tumults and wars' from which Locke had just dissociated himself. The provocation was not lessened by his insertion of the word 'civil' before 'wars'. 'It is vain to seek a government in all points free from civil wars, tumults and sedition: that is a blessing denied to this life, and reserved to complete the felicity of the next.' What must be asked, therefore, is not whether they ought to occur, but whether they are just or unjust:

> It may seem strange to some [compare Locke's description of his Right of War as a 'strange doctrine'] that I mention tumults, seditions and wars upon just occasions; but I can find no reason to retract the term . . . the law that forbids injuries were of no use, if no penalty, might be inflicted on those who do not obey it . . . If injustice therefore be evil, and injuries forbidden, they are also to be punished . . . The ways of punishing injuries are judicial or extrajudicial. Judicial proceedings are of force against those who submit to the law . . . [and] all are just, when he will not . . . If the laws of God and men are therefore of no effect, when the magistracy is left at liberty to break them, and if the lusts of those, who are too strong for the tribunals of justice, cannot otherwise be restrained . . . [then] extrajudicial proceedings, by sedition, tumult or war, *must take place*.[85]

This notion of just war drew not only upon Grotius, but also perhaps upon Buchanan, whose *De Jure Regni apud Scotos* was published in English in 1680. For Buchanan, too,

> if a king do those things which are directly for the dissolution of society, for the continuance whereof he was created, how do we call him? A Tyrant . . . Now a Tyrant hath not only no just authority over a people, but is also their enemy . . . Is there not a just and Lawfull war with an enemy for grievous and intolerable injuries . . . It is forrsooth a just war . . . and . . . Lawfull not only for the whole people to kill that enemy, but for every one of them.[86]

It is thus not altogether surprising that in 1683 Sidney's manuscript would be used to convict its author of 'conspiring and compassing the death of the king'.[87]

For Sidney war did not result from the dissolution, and so absence, of political relations. It stood at the heart of them. It was that essential without which the dissolution of political society would result. This was not simply the case

85 Sidney, *Discourses*, in *Sydney on Government*, pp. 187, 188, 193–4; Scott, *Restoration Crisis*, pp. 238–41.

86 George Buchanan, *De Jure Regni apud Scotos*, trans. 'Philalethes' (London 1680), p. 127; J. H. M. Salmon, *Renaissance and Revolt* (Cambridge 1987), pp. 142–3.

87 Scott, *Restoration Crisis*, p. 325 and chs. 13–14 in general.

internally, whereby it was 'madness to abandon the use of force . . . without which innocency cannot be protected, nor society maintain'd'. Externally, too, 'That government is best that best prepares for war.' This was Sidney's lesson not only from England's troubles but from those of early modern Europe.

Everywhere that protestantism and liberty had survived this had been the consequence of success in arms. Everywhere that protestant arms had failed they had been wiped out. This was the lesson from France, Bohemia and the Netherlands. This was the struggle in which his great-uncle Sir Philip Sidney had given his life. It was also the English struggle in which Algernon had risked his, and which was not yet over. The danger from popery and arbitrary government in England had never been greater.

It is thus no surprise to find Sidney's *Discourses* praising successful Dutch war against these scourges, as Milton's *Defence* had in 1651. 'By resisting they laid the foundation of a most glorious and happy Commonwealth, that hath been, since its first beginning, the strongest pillar of the Protestant Cause now in the world.' This had equally been the military lesson of the English republican experience. Sidney's *Discourses* accordingly produced the most strident evocations of all of the republic's might in arms. It was the centrality which he gave to arms as well as change that accounted for the extent of the *Discourses'* exploitation of Machiavelli.[88] Its other most important feature was the most complete exposition of English republican moral philosophy.[89]

CONCLUSION

Indeed, protestantism and parliaments would need to be rescued in England only a few years later by European, and specifically Dutch, arms. By the end of 1683 Sidney had been executed and Locke was in exile. Following the publication of their works the following decade (1690, 1698), however, these would become among the most influential products of the revolution. By the middle of the following century both Montesquieu and Rousseau could wonder why two such masters had devoted so much time and trouble to answering the now obsolete Filmer.[90]

---

88 In particular, *Discourses,* in *Sydney on Government,* ch. 2, sections 14–30.
89 Scott, *English Republic,* ch. 10.
90 P. Karsten, *Patriot Heroes in England and America* (Madison 1978), pp. 215–16; R. Shackleton, 'Montesquieu and Machiavelli: A Reappraisal', *Comparative Literature Studies* 1, 1 (1964), pp. 8–10; Rousseau, *Political Writings,* ed. C. E. Vaughan (2 vols., Oxford 1962), vol. I, p. 240, vol. II, pp. 205–6.

The greatest intellectual impact of the English revolution occurred in eighteenth-century America and continental Europe (above all the Netherlands, Germany and France).[91] This was exerted partly on behalf of the principles of limitation of government, and of resistance to tyranny; and partly by the christianised moral philosophy of republican self-government. It was exerted partly, particularly in America, by the notion that such liberties must be armed.

This is not to say that the English revolution was without a powerful legacy within England itself. During the eighteenth century the notion that 'God has left it to every nation . . . as their fundamental right, to be governed in such a manner, by such persons, and such laws . . . as they may judge to be best for them . . . became a truism.'[92] Republican and other radical arguments returned with the troubles in 1688 ('the delivery of the people from slavery . . . can never be done radically and effectually but upon this advantage . . . it is better that a king cease, than that a whole nation should perish'),[93] and they survived thereafter to inform criticism of the new politics and state evolving from 1689.

What did end, however, after 1688, was the experience of the troubles by which radicalism had been sustained. This was that radicalism of practice, given its initial context by institutional absence, and its second layer by the experience of (republican) government itself. Between 1660 and 1689 these intellectual legacies struggled to mould, and where possible reverse, the restoration process. The lasting effect of the successful Dutch invasion, however, was to secure and shape restoration.

Thereafter the struggle against popery and arbitrary government would be external, not internal. This replacement of domestic disorder by foreign war replaced the context for revolution with that for statebuilding. English radicalism was anti-formal and anti-institutional in focus. The triumph of restoration was to this extent a triumph over the revolution itself.

Yet the first stage of successful statebuilding in England had itself been a parliamentary and then republican achievement. Thereafter the completion of this process between 1689 and 1720 would draw decisively upon this parliamentary, rather than monarchical, experience. It is to this restoration process that we must now turn.

91 Scott, *English Republic*, ch. 1, esp. pp. 5–6.
92 J. C. D. Clark, *English Society 1688–1832* (Cambridge 1986), p. 176.
93 *Now is the Time: A Scheme for a Commonwealth*, and *Good Advice before it be too late*, in Scott, *Somers Tracts*, vol. X, pp. 197–202.

PART III

Restoration 1660–1702: reconstruction and statebuilding

For Our Restoration . . . [and] That the memory of what is passed may be buried to the World . . . We . . . do not desire a further effusion of precious Christian blood, but to have [our Subjects] . . . peace and security founded upon that which can only support it; an Unity of affections amongst ourselves, an equal Administration of Justice to Men, restoring *Parliaments* to a full capacity of providing for all that is amiss, and the Laws of the Land to their due veneration.

Charles II, *Preface to the Declaration of Breda* (1 May 1660)[1]

1 Charles II, *Preface to the Declaration of Breda*, in *Two Letters from His Majesty. The One To the Speaker of the Commons Assembled in Parliament. The other to His Excellencie The Lord Generall Monck . . . Read in the House of Commons assembled in Parliament, Tuesday May 1 1660* (London 1660), pp. 9–10.

17

Restoration process

De witt sayth that the King is little to be considered for he is not yett
setled and ... he hath no mony.

Downing to Lord Chancellor Clarendon, 4 October 1661[2]

make no doubt, but that his Majesty will ... in a short time be considered in Europe as he ought to be . . . . God be thanked England is
England, and his Ma[jes]ty hath a Parliament who will not suffer him
to want what is fitting for his honour and the defence of his subjects.

Downing to Secretary Nicholas, 18 April–2 May 1662[3]

RESTORATION AND STATEBUILDING

Restoration was not an experience peculiar to seventeenth-century
England. Such a process, not only of reconstruction but of memory and
mourning, is necessary wherever a profound upheaval has occurred.[4]
Restoration of monarchy in England in 1660 was part of a much more complicated and long-lasting process. This had many contemporary parallels in
central Europe in the aftermath of the Thirty Years War. Peter Dickson was
accordingly right to contextualise his study of *The Financial Revolution in
England* within a general period of European 'administrative and economic
reconstruction' following the 'war clouds of the terrible middle decades of
the seventeenth century'.[5]

As in England, continental reconstruction had a pre-history, stretching
back to the period before 1648. While institutional in focus, this attempt by

---

2 Bodleian Library, Oxford, Clarendon MS, vol. 105, f. 89.
3 British Library, London, Egerton MS 2538, ff. 57, 61.
4 Winter, *Sites of Memory, Sites of Mourning*.
5 P. G. M. Dickson, *The Financial Revolution in England 1688–1756* (London 1967), p. 3.

shattered contemporaneous societies to reconstruct the basis of their order, their peace and their moorings in time was far from simply an institutional matter.[6] In this context, what struck Ranke about England by the end of the troubles was not what Trevelyan had called its precocious liberation from 'feudal' and 'cosmopolitan' orders but, on the contrary, its success in preserving the institutional remnants of the old order: 'nowhere have more of the institutions of the Middle Ages been retained than in England'.[7] In Ranke's analysis the medieval institutions of both crown and parliament had been strengthened by the religious changes of the sixteenth century. In the religious wars of the seventeenth, both would be swept away. Yet the instinct in 1660, as in 1689, and one eventually made good, would be to 'seek safety in a return to the old and approved historic forms'. This would be a process with crucial Dutch components as well as contemporary German parallels.[8]

Again our first task is to recover some understanding of restoration from the perspective of those engaged in it. The imaginative difficulty this poses is in this case a function not of distance but of proximity. We still live in restoration times. The institutional legacy of the restoration process, successfully modernised between 1689 and 1714, still governs English public life. In relation to no aspect of the seventeenth-century experience, accordingly, is it more difficult for those at its end to recover the perspective of those before it began.

In retrospect restoration seems to have been inevitable. For contemporaries, on the contrary, it was a miracle. For Dryden and others Charles II was 'David' because his return was so extraordinary that it could not be contextualised in secular time.[9] For this reason in 1660, as in 1689, providentialism was a no less important context for contemporary perceptions of restoration than it had been for the prior caesura of the regicide. As John Evelyn put it: 'It was the Lord's doing, et mirabile in oculis nostris: for such a Restauration was never seene in the mention of any history, ancient or modern, since the returne of the Babylonian captivity.'[10]

---

6 For parallel experiences in the Habsburg monarchy, Bavaria, Saxony and Brandenburg-Prussia, see F. L. Carsten (ed.), *The New Cambridge Modern History*, vol. V, *The Ascendancy of France* (Cambridge 1961), pp. 452–547; C. W. Ingrao, *The Habsburg Monarchy 1618–1815* (Cambridge 1994), pp. 58–64; Braun, 'Taxation, Sociopolitical Structure and Statebuilding'.   7 Ranke, *History of England*, vol. I, p. vi.   8 *Ibid.*, pp. vi–viii.   9 Hannah Smith, 'Images of Charles II', ch. 4.
10 *The Diary of John Evelyn*, ed. Esmond de Beer (Oxford 1955), p. 244.

We are inclined, accordingly, to overestimate in retrospect restoration's stability and finality. No contemporary made this mistake. In May 1661 Pepys was still pondering 'the greatness of this late turne and what people will do tomorrow against what they all, through profit or fear, did promise and practise this day'.[11] Later the same year, the 'Ship' of restoration having 'put forth to Sea' and His Majesty having 'undertake[n] to be their Steersman', the Speaker of the Commons offered 'In case a Storm doth arise' to 'trim and lore the sails . . . watch aloft the decks [and] work at the Pump'.[12] We speak as if the British monarchy were ancient, yet it is a seventeenth-century reconstruction. If monarchy could be abolished once it could happen again. As the king put it to parliament in 1662: 'He needed not to tell them, that there was a Republican Party still in the kingdom, which had the Courage still to promise themselves another Revolution.'[13]

The final achievement of restoration was national forgetting. It was only with the gradual disappearance of the troubles in practice that they could begin to disappear from the public mind. One consequence of that 'process of erasure' has been the consignment to oblivion of key aspects of the national experience.[14] One of these was of participation in Europe's religious wars and that religious anxiety by which this was sustained.[15] Another was of the consequences of this in radical reformation and English republicanism. These were in turn the contexts of restoration as contemporaries experienced it.

Before the triumph of forgetting a principal problem with which restoration had to contend was the power of public memory. Writing in 1661, for instance, of the difficulty the king faced in establishing a just settlement for Ireland, Clarendon recorded that 'the Memory of the Beginning of the Rebellion in Ireland . . . the most barbarous . . . that any Christians have been engaged in in any Age . . . was as fresh and as odious to the whole People of England as it had been the first Year'.[16] The transformation of public memory would be a work of time: both further experience and generational change. Meanwhile, however, attempts to legislate forgetfulness were a feature of restoration from its inception.

11 Pepys, *Diary*, vol. II, 28 May 1661, p. 109.
12 *The Speeches of Sir Edward Turner KT, Before the King, Lords and Commons* (London, 10 May 1661), p. 30.   13 Hyde (Clarendon), *Life of Clarendon*, vol. I, p. 447.
14 Norbrook, *Writing the English Republic*, Introduction ('Acts of Oblivion and Republican Speech-Acts'); Derek Hirst, 'Locating the 1650s in England's Seventeenth Century', *History* 81, 3 (1996).   15 Scott, 'Popish Plot'.
16 Hyde (Clarendon), *Life of Clarendon*, vol. I, pp. 380, 389.

One aspect of this was the pretence that the monarchy had never been interrupted. Constitutionally restoration was not that of monarchy but of the king to the exercise of a 'Crown and Dignity' that had never legally been abolished.[17] This was one aspect of the broader 'statute of 12 Car. II, c. 11 declaring the events of 1641–60 to be a constitutional nullity'.[18] The centre-piece of this enterprise was 'the happy Act of Indemnity and Oblivion'. This, His Majesty said, 'was the principal Corner-Stone that supported that excellent Building' of restoration as a whole.[19] Passing this bill was the central, but also ironically the most divisive, legislative achievement of the Convention. Members were reminded by Clarendon in September 1660 of the severe penalties specified

if any person or persons, within the space of three years next ensuing, shall presume malitiously to call, or alledge, or object against any other person or persons any name or names, or other words of reproach, any way leading to revive the memory of the late differences, or the occasion thereof.

Such 'Envy and Malice . . . by any sharp memory of what hath been . . . is but to rebel against the Person of the King, against the known Law of the Land, this blessed Act of Oblivion.'[20] 'And this Warmth of his Majesty upon this Subject', the chancellor later recorded, 'was not then more than needed: For . . . there were great Combinations entred into, not to confirm the Act.'[21] Under considerable pressure it was confirmed. The spirit informing it was not, however, to govern the initial settlement, particularly after the election of the Cavalier Parliament in 1661. Even at the end of the century 'call[ing] any other person . . . names, or other words of reproach, any way leading to revive the memory of the late differences', was to be of the essence of the new party politics. In the words of a weary observer in 1715: 'Political Papers serve to keep the Fire still burning, like the Vestals of old, never to be extinguish'd . . . We are continually charging one another with Crimes that we were never guilty of . . . Why, Gentlemen, must we have all this Noise about Forty-One? Why so many Repetitions?'[22]

17 *The Earl of Manchester's Speech to His Majesty* (London 1660), p. 1.
18 Hirst, 'Locating the 1650s'.
19 Hyde (Clarendon), *Life of Clarendon*, vol. I, p. 360.
20 Charles II, *His Majesties Most Gracious Speech, Together with the Lord Chancellors* (London, 13 September 1660), pp. 11–12.
21 Hyde (Clarendon), *Life of Clarendon*, vol. I, p. 360.
22 *An Attempt Towards a Coalition of English Protestants* (London 1715), pp. 21, 24–5. I am grateful to Geoff Kemp for this reference.

It is accordingly necessary to penetrate beyond the constitutional surface of restoration not only because it was superficial but also because it was deliberately misleading. It was precisely the purpose of the reconstruction of institutional form – the notion of a governing arch, superior to time – to obscure the facts both of fragility and of truncation. In August 1661 Clarendon reminded the overzealous ambassador to the United Provinces:

> I pray remember the streights and necessitys we are in for money, the emptiness of all our stores and magazines, etc, when all these shall be replenished, how easy it will be to fall out with any we have a mind to, in the meane time I think we should anger as few as possible.[23]

In truth this government would never find the realisation of its military ambitions 'easy'. In 1689 the need for complete English military reconstruction would have to be faced again, by an invading power.[24] Without Dutch intervention restoration in England would not have been completed when it was, or in the form which it took. It might instead have entailed the eclipse of parliaments, or of monarchy.[25]

At the broadest level, therefore, successful restoration required successful statebuilding. This was the greatest tension within the process, for the two were not only not identical but in some sense opposite. It was the Caroline attempt at statebuilding that initiated the troubles. The impulse of restoration, on the other hand, was not merely conservative but nostalgic. It was to banish popery and arbitrary government by 'restor[ing] the Nation to all that it hath lost'. During the first phase of the process we may see this tension exemplified by the struggle between Clarendon and Downing, masters of restoration and statebuilding respectively. The former sought 'to restore rather than reform'; the latter to attend to the government's fiscal and military weakness by Dutch-inspired administrative innovation.[26]

To the extent to which it was completely successful, indeed, nostalgic restoration reconstructed the domestic contexts for the troubles. It

---

23 Bodleian Library, Oxford, MS Clarendon, vol. 104, f. 8 (30 August 1661).
24 Childs, *British Army*, pp. 4–5; Stephen Baxter, *William III*, p. 381.
25 Brewer, *Sinews of Power*.
26 Robert Bliss, *Revolution and Empire*, p. 166; Scott, 'Sir George Downing'; Henry Roseveare, 'Prejudice and Policy: Sir George Downing as Parliamentary Entrepreneur', in D. C. Coleman and Peter Mathias (eds.), *Enterprise and History: Essays in Honour of Charles Wilson* (Cambridge 1986); Charles Wilson, *Profit and Power: A Study of England and the Dutch Wars* (London 1957).

reconstructed that unreformed polity which had proved so vulnerable to European destabilisation and domestic fears. In the longer term restoration was a learning process in the course of which, to conserve, it proved necessary to adapt.[27] This achievement was made possible by external intervention; by the luxury of a second attempt at settlement (1689–1701); and by a developing capacity to draw upon experience rather than simply be governed by it. The result was an eventual transition from reaction to complex settlement. Meanwhile in the short term the reconstruction of the old regime bound the country painfully to its troubled immediate past.

This was the understandable reaction of a conservative pre-modern society which had just received an overwhelming demonstration of the destructiveness of innovation. How natural was it that 'the Quiet and Happiness of their Countrey' should be sought 'in the Restauration both of King, Peers and People, to their Just, Antient and Fundamental Rights'?[28] Under the circumstances, indeed, the immediate reaction could have been far more savage, and more complete. That it drew a line under the country's immediate capacity for recovery, however, quickly became evident. The first sign was the government's failure, despite unprecedented financial support, in the second Anglo-Dutch war. This had been an act not only of economic but ideological aggression.[29] Having confronted the demons of the past at home, sectarianism and republicanism were now confronted on the European stage. The resulting disaster, coinciding with the great plague and fire, and culminating in the humiliation at Chatham, had by 1667 produced a crisis of confidence from which the government never entirely recovered.

In the analysis which follows, therefore, we will be looking at the processes both of reconstruction (restoration) and of construction (statebuilding), and the relationship between them. This is to recognise that the deeper ambition of restoration was not simply to recover what had been lost, institutionally, but also that half-remembered state of civil peace and unity for which the unreformed polity had once offered adequate protection. One feature of this analysis is, accordingly, to draw attention to the protracted

---

27 Dickson, *Financial Revolution*; Henry Roseveare, *The Financial Revolution 1660–1760* (London 1991).

28 Charles II, *His Majesties Gracious Speech to the House of Peers, The 27th of July 1660, Concerning the speedy passing of the Bill of Indemnity and Oblivion* (London 1660), p. 3.

29 Pincus, *Protestantism and Patriotism*.

nature of this process. Another is to emphasise the operation of its objectives on many levels: institutional, legal, ideological, social and emotional. Before this, however, it is necessary to attend to the history both of statebuilding and of restoration before 1660.

THE PRE-HISTORY OF ENGLISH STATEBUILDING

Our last sighting of this subject came with the failed confessional statebuilding of Charles I. Although this had religious and political contexts, the failure concerned was a military one. This 'degradation of the English military' between 1610 and 1640, according to one historian, had crucial consequences not only within the Stuart kingdoms and on the continent, but in the American colonies.[30]

A consequence of the subsequent civil wars, however, was a dramatic reversal of that decline of English arms. This was the work not of the monarchy but of parliament's New Model Army. This development was accompanied, and made possible, by the fiscal and political innovations crucial for statebuilding to succeed. This was the accomplishment of the Long Parliament and its republican successors. Although this recovery of arms proved temporary, and although some of these deeply unpopular reforms were reversed in 1660, many were not. More than any other aspect of the first restoration settlement, the fiscal re-establishment of the monarchy was built upon interregnum foundations. In the longer term it is particularly significant that the decisive developments of 1689–1713, which built upon this foundation, were again the work, in similar military circumstances, of a protestant parliamentary regime.

The early Stuart problem, as we have seen, had been fiscal poverty and so military impotence. Even in peacetime the decay of the real income of the royal demesne had made it difficult for the king to 'live of his own'. In war, this made him entirely financially dependent upon the House of Commons, which constituted a royal problem in its own right. The political aspect of this problem was that it undercut in practice that royal government of war and peace which was fundamental to the constitution. This was particularly important in circumstances of ideological polarisation. Meanwhile before 1640, in relation to the cost of contemporary warfare, the structures of

---

30 Stephen Saunders Webb, *The Governors-General: The English Army and the Definition of the Empire 1569–1681* (Chapel Hill 1979), pp. 440–1.

parliamentary taxation were as 'fatally flawed' as the income from the royal demesne.[31]

The authority on the fiscal aspect of English statebuilding is Michael Braddick.[32] Looking at the century as a whole Braddick has drawn attention to three developments. The first, drawing upon the analysis of Schumpeter, is the transition from a demesne to a tax state. Over the century, the inadequate royal demesne disappeared to be replaced, as early as 1660, by a royal income funded entirely by parliamentary taxation. A parallel development was the transformation of that taxation: the replacement of the decrepit first fifteenths and tenths, and subsidies, with new forms of direct taxation (monthly assessment, land tax) and indirect (excise).[33] The third key accomplishment was the development, in relation to that taxation, of a system of public credit. The result of all of these processes was the transformation not only of expenditure, particularly in time of war, but of permanent state (royal) revenue. In 1605 this was under £1 million; in 1660 under £2 million; in 1705 it was almost £10 million; and by 1763 there was public expenditure of £20 million and a national debt of £103 million.[34]

Braddick has rightly insisted that the state is a social as well as a fiscal and military construct. 'Although there was clearly a military-fiscal state, there was also a state with other purposes whose activities are not revealed by an analysis of exchequer spending.' Still, he agrees with what John Brewer has appropriately emphasised: that the principal engine for these transformations as a whole was war.[35] This may make it misleading to generalise about these developments over the century as a whole as if they were incremental and continuous. In the context of this study the retrospective conclusion that 'The early modern English state had evolved very successfully in the period 1558–1714' would appear to give new meaning to the words 'evolved' and 'successfully'.[36] This is reminiscent of Mark Kishlansky's inclusion in the list of the achievements of 'The Stuarts' the foundation of the Bank of England in 1694 and the Bank of Scotland in 1695.[37] The foundation of these banks – notoriously republican institutions objected against as such in 1695 as in 1665 (see below, pp. 415–16, 486) – was in fact made

31 Braddick, *Nerves of State*, p. 91.   32 *Ibid.*; Braddick, *Parliamentary Taxation*.
33 Braddick, *Nerves of State*, pp. 91–103.
34 *Ibid.*, pp. 6–34; Roseveare, *Financial Revolution*, pp. 2–3; Brewer, *Sinews of Power*, p. 38.
35 Braddick, *Nerves of State*, pp. 34, 29–33.   36 *Ibid.*, p. 199.
37 Kishlansky, *Monarchy Transformed*, p. 1: 'The Stuarts inaugurated nearly every element of modern commerce and finance.' It is true that there was a Stuart on the throne until late 1695 but her contribution to the development of public credit remains to be established.

possible by the military ejection of the Stuarts by a Dutch army. The 'evolution' of this state during the seventeenth century occurred not as the result of its 'success' but in the context of its collapse, and from the consequent expenditure of blood and steel. This was indeed survival of the fittest: evolutionary nature red in tooth and claw.

Thus hardly less important than the overall transformation are the specific political circumstances in which this was achieved. By far the greater part of the development occurred only after 1688. The pre-history of this crucial last stage occurred in two phases: first during the 1640s (in particular) and 1650s; and secondly during the restoration period in general and the Anglo-Dutch War of 1665–7 in particular. These accomplishments did not match in scale the military, political and fiscal transformations of 1689–1714. But they were important preliminaries that not only formed part of the longer-term context of those transformations but also help to inform us about the political circumstances in which they were capable of taking place.

The first of these was its foundation in war. In the words of Charles Tilly: 'war is the characteristic condition, and armed force the characteristic instrument, of the state system'.[38] Common to all the periods when English statebuilding was successful was the combination of parliamentary revenue-raising and war. Before 1660 it was the Irish, Scots and Dutch who found themselves on the receiving end of a military-fiscal state capacity transformed by the English civil wars.[39] This was not a Stuart or even a monarchical achievement. It was a consequence of the military destruction of the Stuart monarchy and a principal practical context for the development of English republican ideology. Thus the first successful ideology of English statebuilding was republican: '[Men] are rough pieces of timber or stone, which it is necessary to cleave, saw, or cut . . . Magistrates are political architects.'[40] Accordingly the construction of the English military-fiscal state in the 1690s drew heavily upon republican experience, both Dutch and English.

Even under the restored monarchy, the further development of effective fiscal state practice depended upon the lessening of the element of monarchical control, and was opposed by Clarendon for that reason.[41] Thus a

---

38 Tilly, 'Reflections on the History of European State-Making', in Tilly, *Formation of Nation States*, p. 52.   39 Scott, *English Republic*, pp. 103–5.

40 Sidney, *Discourses*, in *Sydney on Government*, p. 64; Scott, *Restoration Crisis*, pp. 220–8.

41 Hyde (Clarendon), *Life of Clarendon*, vol. II, pp. 190–215; Braddick, *Nerves of State*, pp. 40–1.

second feature of the practical political context of English statebuilding is that it was parliamentary in nature. It was not simply that all such developments occurred in the context of war, but that they were the accomplishment in wartime of parliamentary political authority. That authority could be effectively republican (1642–59) or monarchical (1665–7, 1689–1714): the presence or absence of monarchy was not decisive. This is why statebuilding was achieved by the development of parliamentary taxation, not of the royal demesne.

The third feature of this political context was the most important. In his analysis of the process Braddick pays important attention to the state's capacity to harness social as well as fiscal resources.[42] No less important, however, was its exploitation of ideological resources. It is in this respect above all that we cannot understand the history of English statebuilding without seeing it as a product of the troubles. England's seventeenth-century wars, whether civil (1640s) or international (1624–9, 1665–7, 1689–1713), were ideological. They were wars against popery and arbitrary government.[43] It did not matter, from this point of view, whether the embodiment of those threats was Charles I, his son 'Charles Stuart' (Nedham's 'that young Pretender'), James II or Louis XIV.[44] The earlier struggle had been at the expense of monarchy; the later co-opted it. In either case a crucial force behind the processes of fiscal and military innovation was that same power of public, and specifically parliamentary, belief which had caused the troubles. One aspect of this, as we have seen, was parliament's struggle for its own survival. Another was the struggle for the survival of European protestantism.

In this sense the modern English state was a product of, as well as a structure for ending, its religious wars. Those same beliefs and fears which in circumstances of military and political weakness resulted in state paralysis (1620s and 1670s) were equally responsible in other contexts for the construction of the state. The transformation of the English into the British state in the 1650s, and more decisively in the early eighteenth century, was

---

42 Braddick, *Nerves of State*, p. 197.

43 The Anglo-Dutch War of 1665–7 is not an exception to this generalisation. Steven Pincus (*Protestantism and Patriotism*) has correctly pointed out that this was an ideological struggle against a religious and political antitype: fanaticism and republicanism were the loyalist versions of popery and arbitrary government. What does not follow from this is the further assertion that therefore 'commercial competition' was 'not' a factor in the war (p. 198). See, on the contrary, Wilson, *Profit and Power*; Jonathan Israel, 'England, the Dutch Republic and Europe in the Seventeenth Century', *Historical Journal* 40, 4 (1997), pp. 1119–20.   44 *Mercurius Politicus*, no. 51, 22–9 May 1651, p. 815.

again a product of these ideological, and particularly religious, concerns. A result in practice of military developments and consequent political dominance, control of Scotland and Ireland helped to secure the English state against future (counter-reformation and radical reformation) destabilisation. Ultimately this entailed a transformation not simply of institutions but of self-perception. As Linda Colley has shown, war against France (on behalf of protestantism, and of the reformed state) even had a capacity to persuade English, Welsh and Scots to see themselves as British.[45]

Emphasis is accordingly placed, in chapter 21, on the successful efforts made by the Anglo-Dutch government of the 1690s to harness for military purposes the known resources of parliamentary religious and political ideology.[46] Such an approach also helps us to answer perhaps the key question about the process of English statebuilding as a whole. How did the war against popery and arbitrary government of 1689–1713 succeed in unlocking parliamentary fiscal resources where that of 1624–9 had failed? The answer hinges upon more than one factor, and it is here that the parliamentary experience of 1642–9 was important and perhaps crucial. None, however, was more important than the difference in domestic religious and political circumstances which meant that from 1689 monarch and parliament could unite in a military struggle exploiting the same beliefs by which previously they had been divided.

The last general feature of the process of English statebuilding was its co-option of Dutch fiscal, administrative and military practice. The most important of these developments, from 1689, will be discussed in chapter 21. Before then Pym's introduction of the excise in 1643 followed the example of the United Provinces, where it was the main tax.[47] Brandenburg-Prussia was to do the same, continuing thereafter, like England, to develop the tax further between 1660 and 1688.[48] Although the scope of this unpopular tax was temporarily narrowed in England in 1660, the key advocate of its retention and subsequent development was the ambassador to the United Provinces Sir George Downing.[49] Thereafter

45 Linda Colley, *Britons: Forging the Nation 1707–1837* (New Haven 1992).
46 Claydon, *William III*.   47 'T Hart, '"The Devil or the Dutch"', pp. 43–4.
48 Carsten, *Ascendancy of France*, pp. 452–547; Braun, 'Taxation, Sociopolitical Structure and Statebuilding'.
49 Braddick, *Parliamentary Taxation*, pp. 168, 180–1; Braddick, *Nerves of State*, pp. 98–101; Henry Roseveare, *The Treasury 1660–1870: The Foundations of Control* (London 1973), pp. 23–5.

Downing's construction, in the Additional Aid Bill of 1665, of a new parliamentary mechanism for public credit, combined with his modernisation of both Exchequer and Treasury, was directly inspired by Dutch example.[50] In general Downing's remarkable contribution to the process of English statebuilding was driven by both his English and Dutch republican experience.[51]

These and other borrowings reflected in part the closeness, and complexity, of seventeenth-century England's relationship with the United Provinces. They reflected the fact that the English and Dutch troubles were intertwined. It is not clear whether the survival in either country of protestant government by representative assemblies could have been secured without the military involvement of the other. It was the invasion of 1688 and the subsequent Anglo-Dutch military and political relationship which set the seal on the fact that in that experience England would follow the Dutch rather than the French model.[52] This is not to say, as the foregoing discussion has made clear, that the process was not informed at least as deeply by England's own experience.

Thus when monarchy was restored in 1660 the process of statebuilding was already under way. Restoration interrupted but did not end it. It was not simply that it 'adopted and acclimatized' the 'revolutionary financial innovations of the period of Civil War and Interregnum'. Thus 'the devices of excise and monthly assessment' were to become 'permanent elements in the English tax system', alongside further restoration innovations like chimney money (1662) and poll taxes.[53] One of the greatest mid-century alterations, following the abolition of royal fiscal feudal revenues (wardship, monopolies, purveyance) with the king's consent in 1641, had been the destruction and sale of the royal demesne. The first restoration financial settlement resurrected the medieval aspiration that the king should live 'of his own'; that is, that there should be a permanent financial settlement (this was abandoned in 1689). It made no attempt, however, to resurrect the dispersed demesne itself; henceforth its place would be supplied by regular parliamentary taxation. This was calculated to meet estimated royal needs (the estimate of 1660 was based on the Protectorate income of 1658).

50 'T Hart, '"The Devil or the Dutch"', pp. 49–50; Roseveare, 'Prejudice and Policy'; Scott, 'Sir George Downing'.   51 Scott, 'Sir George Downing'.
52 William Speck, 'Britain and the Dutch Republic', in Karel Davids and Jan Lucassen (eds.), *A Miracle Mirrored: The Dutch Republic in European Perspective* (Cambridge 1995).
53 C. D. Chandaman, *The English Public Revenue 1660–1688* (Oxford 1975), p. 1; Braddick, *Nerves of State*, pp. 102–3.

Thus in relation to the once genuinely independent royal estates and incomes – however inadequate they had been – the mid-century abolition of monarchy was not reversed. Again to the consternation of Clarendon – the guardian not of statebuilding but of restoration – Charles II showed a continuing willingness to sacrifice aspects of that independence for improvements in income in practice. In the context of the military needs of the 1690s this was a process which William III took much further.

Indeed restoration politics never entirely realised in practice the theory that for the purposes of ordinary revenue the king should live 'of his own'. Chandaman has called the gradual 'undermining of this concept . . . the most important constitutional development of Charles' reign'.[54] Alongside these elements of financial continuity with the interregnum went many other aspects of fiscal, political and bureaucratic management.[55] Yet in other respects restoration set itself against statebuilding, as against parliamentary and republican innovation in general. It was fundamental to the restoration project that in form, if not always in substance, what was reconstructed was the old (unreformed) regime.

With this came the dismantling of the military government of the interregnum and the reduction of peacetime military expenditure; the reduction of actual levels of taxation and the return of self-government to the localities, in England if not in Scotland; and the eventual unwelcome return of international military impotence. This was signalled not only by military failure against the Dutch in both 1667 and 1673, but the subsequent relationship of subservience to France. It was in vain that Downing warned from the Netherlands that it was 'not [enough] to say what moneyes were sufficient for England in former times, for then England's revenue though small, yet held proportion with the revenues of neighbouring Princes and States about them, and that must be the rule now, or England is undone'.[56] In August 1661 he repeated that 'unless a great addition be made to the King my Master his revenue . . . he cannot be considerable either at home or abroad . . . the case is quite otherwise now than formerly'.[57] From 1670, however, rather than submit to the parliamentary

---

54 Chandaman, *Public Revenue*, p. 279.
55 G. E. Aylmer, *The State's Servants: The Civil Service of the English Republic 1649–1660* (London 1973), ch. 5 and Conclusion.   56 Quoted in Firth, *Clarke Papers*, vol. III, p. 178.
57 Bodleian Library, Clarendon MSS, vol. 104, ff. 252–4 (6 August 1661).

dictation of religious and foreign policy the crown accepted French dictation of it.[58]

This is not to say that, even militarily, the mid-century experience had no
impact on restoration government. In the view of one historian, indeed,
'armed prerogative, an authoritarian politics developed during the civil
wars, the royal exile, and the Interregnum' continued to inform restoration
governmental practice.[59] In particular the return of the troubles during the
1670s underlined the impossibility of a complete return to civilian government without arms. At the same time, as Chandaman has shown, royal
poverty was eased during the 1680s by a buoyant customs revenue as well as
by the effect of the recent crisis on parliamentary supply. The result, under
James II, was a military establishment rising from 25,000 to almost 40,000
men. Yet in the ensuing crisis, facing a foreign invasion and riven by religious
disunity and political disaffection, this force would prove no more effective
than the army of Charles I against the Scots in 1639–40. There is no better
illustration of the importance to effective statebuilding of public belief.

THE PRE-HISTORY OF RESTORATION

Like statebuilding, restoration too had a history before 1660. We may chart
the progress of the attempt to restore what the troubles had destroyed
throughout the interregnum. Though in relation to the church and monarchy Cromwell 'would not build Jericho again', he was in other respects a
spokesman for this impulse. It was consequently within the context of
'healing and settling' that constitutional restoration made as much progress
as it did between 1649 and 1659. Until the election of the Cavalier
Parliament this set the tone for His Majesty's restoration itself. What
Cromwell said to his second parliament, quoting Isaiah 53.12, Charles
might have said to either of his: 'And if God should bless you in this work . . .
the generations to come will bless us. You shall be the "repairers of breaches,
and the restorers of paths to dwell in".'[60] Thus it was not only in fiscal and
administrative terms that the agenda of restoration was partly established
by the interregnum.

---

58 Stephen Baxter, *William III*, p. 174: 'The Stuarts paid a high price for their pensions . . .
    Barillon complained [in 1681] that Charles had no right to permit William's visit without
    the authorisation of Louis XIV. This was apparently not an impertinence but a statement
    of fact. Certainly Charles was ordered by the French to withdraw his ambassadors from
    northern Europe.'
59 Webb, *Governors-General*, p. 3; Braddick, *Nerves of State*, pp. 29–33.
60 *Oliver Cromwell's Letters and Speeches*, vol. III, p. 325.

The other reason for the interregnum drift back towards established forms was the poverty of the radical constitutional imagination. The regicide was perpetrated not as the means to some constitutional end. The fulfilment of this religious duty left a gaping constitutional void. Yet the regicide was the climax, rather than beginning, of a process of institutional destruction. To this extent the yearning for restoration manifested itself well before 1649.

Much civil war radicalism was itself expressed in the reformation rhetoric of restorationism.[61] We find one aspect of the pre-history of the first restoration settlement in that 'passive strength of Anglican survivalism' chronicled by John Morrill for the 1640s and John Spurr for the 1650s.[62] We find another, of course, in the persistence of royalism in the period 1646–59. We find a third in that continuing popular devotion to the ancient forms broken by army intervention between 1647 and 1659. These were the traditional allegiances – implacably opposed to innovation in church and state – that had informed the troubles. When restoration came, initially at least, it would be the work of parliamentarians as well as royalists.

In this context the first attempted restoration settlements were the attempts to agree terms for peace with the still-living Charles I. Charles reported characteristically, if emptily, from Carisbrooke Castle on 26 November 1647 upon 'the continuance of our Resolutions to improve every occasion for the satisfaction of all chief Interests, that so a happy Peace may be settled in our Dominions'.[63] After earlier efforts in 1643, 1644, 1646 and 1647 the most significant opportunity was the near-agreement on the Isle of Wight in November–December 1648. It was the most significant both because this was the first occasion upon which the king made real concessions and because on December 5 the House of Commons voted for the first time to accept the king's offers as a sufficient basis for the making of a peace. These events were accompanied by an outpouring of published projects for 'the admirable fullnesse, of the restauration and satisfaction of all Interests'.[64] As David Underdown put it: 'the Commons . . . had in fact voted for a restoration, eleven years too early'.[65]

61 Birmingham, 'Continental Resonances'.
62 Morrill, 'Church in England', p. 150; Spurr, *Restoration Church*, ch. 1.
63 British Library, Egerton MS 2618, f. 21.
64 *The Presbyterian's Prophecie, concerning the King, Parliament, City, Army and Kingdome* (London 1648), p. 1; William Sedgewick, *The Spiritual Madman, Or A Prophesie* (London 1648).   65 Underdown, *Pride's Purge*, p. 139.

In 1660 there would be an attempt by parliamentary peers (Northumberland, Saye and others) to return to the terms of this treaty as the basis for restoration. On 26 March Charles was advised that 'the conditions (if any) questionless will be hard, and I believe much after the nature of those sent your father at the Isle of Wight'. At the same time he was warned: 'You may remember, twas once the generall opinion that the army would restore your father ... I mention this, that too hasty a belief be not given to faire pretences, but still to provide for the worst.'[66] As late as 1679 (during discussions of the proposal for limitations upon the powers of any popish successor) there was the suggestion by a royal minister that their omission from the first restoration settlement as it had occurred had been a lost opportunity.[67] The immediate consequence of the Commons vote of December 1648 was Pride's Purge. The subsequent military intervention of April 1653 to dissolve the Rump may be seen as another attempt to forestall restoration.[68]

Until 1660 the only body standing in the way of restoration in practical terms continued to be the army. This makes more striking the drift throughout this period towards monarchical form.[69] Moreover, the fluidity of the constitutional history of this decade to some extent belies the continuity of local administration.[70] A constitutional milestone was the Instrument of Government (December 1653). In founding the Protectorate this created what was in effect an elective monarchy, with half a parliament and constitutionally protected non-traditional religious freedoms. Thereafter the *Humble Petition and Advice* (1657) oversaw a return to traditional kingship in all but name. 'Wheras in December 1653 [Cromwell] had worn "a plain black suit and cloak" ... he now donned "a robe of purple velvet lined with ermine" and carried a golden sceptre.'[71]

An 'Other House' was restored to parliament; a 'Privy Council' was introduced; and the following year the Protectorate became hereditary. These developments were opposed by republicans, both civilian and military, and sponsored by new courtiers like Downing, who said in parliament on 19 January 1657 'I cannot propound a better expedient for the preservation

---

66 'Heads of Advice to King Charles II', in Thurloe, *Collection*, vol. VII, pp. 872–3.
67 Ian Ward, 'The English Peerage 1648–1660', Ph.D thesis, Cambridge 1989; Sir William Coventry, in Grey, *Debates 1667–1694*, vol. VII, pp. 245–57.
68 Worden, *Rump Parliament*, pp. 363–75.
69 David Smith, 'The Struggle for New Constitutional and Institutional Forms', in Morrill, *Revolution and Restoration*.
70 Stephen Roberts, *Recovery and Restoration in an English County: Devon Local Administration 1646–1670* (Exeter 1985), Conclusion.
71 David Smith, 'Constitutional Forms', p. 27.

both of his highness and the people than by establishing the government upon the old and tried foundation.'[72] It was possible that the success of this enterprise might have given restoration enduring Cromwellian form. Yet standing against this outcome was the continuing hostility not only of republicans but of much of the royalist, Anglican and 'presbyterian' establishment. Above all, in the hands of Oliver's successor, it did not have the support of the army.

Of all these restoration tendencies that in religion was least pronounced. Parliamentary Blasphemy Acts in 1651 and 1657, and the Cromwellian edifice of triers and ejectors may all be taken as hesitant steps back along the road of religious formality. At their centre, however, the revolution's commitment to liberty of conscience for peaceable and godly protestants remained secure and fundamental. The delayed assault on this would be the fundamental challenge of restoration itself, and arguably its greatest failure. Accordingly when contemporaries spoke of the 'anarchy' following the collapse of Richard's Protectorate they did not simply mean constitutional anarchy. They were referring also, and perhaps principally, to that 'Münsterian anarchy' of religion which had its most spectacular manifestation in the Quakers and to the protection of which Henry Vane's Committee of Safety (October 1659–January 1660) was specifically committed.

It was in relation to this, above all, that by the coming in of the king 'God ha[d] been pleased by a miracle of mercy to dissipate this confusion and chaos.'[73] In terms of political history the unravelling of 1659–60 was not in fact anarchical. It simply repeated, at greater speed, the developments of 1640–56 in reverse. In May 1659 Richard Cromwell's Protectorate was peeled back to reveal the Rump still lurking beneath. In January 1660 the Rump was restored by military power for a second time. Shortly afterwards it was required by the same means to readmit those members 'secluded' in 1648. This restored Long Parliament then voted to dissolve itself and called for the election of a Convention in May. It was this Convention which began the reconstruction of the parliamentary unity lost in 1641. Its first act was to call back the monarchy. Neither the parliamentary nor monarchical veneer of restoration (in 1660 as in 1689) altered the fact that it was an accomplishment of military power. The military unhinging of civilian political normality had begun with a Scots

72 Sir Charles Firth, 'Downing, Sir George', *Dictionary of National Biography*, vol. XV, p. 1304.   73 Quoted in Spurr, *Restoration Church*, p. 29.

invasion in 1640. With Monck's march south in 1659–60 it would end the same way.

The resulting combination of military intervention, occupation of London and the calling of a Convention became the pattern for restoration not only in 1660 but in 1689. Like William on the latter occasion, Monck took care not only to send troops loyal to the previous administration out of the city, but then also to back his own appeal to 'Parliamentary Authority' with overwhelming force:

upon Mature deliberation we have thought it our duty as to continue the usual Guards for the safety of your sitting, so for the present to draw the rest of the Forces under our Command into the City, that we may have a better opportunity to compose spirits and beget a good understanding in that great City, formerly renowned for their resolute adhering to Parliamentary Authority.[74]

The opportunity for restoration came, in short, only with that conquest of the capital which had eluded Charles I.

RESTORATION OBJECTIVES

The subsequent restoration process had four objectives. Its first ambition was the institutional reconstruction of the old regime. Restoration of monarchy in 1660 was accompanied by that of parliament, including the House of Lords (the first genuine parliament was called in 1661); of the Privy Council, though not the prerogative courts; of the episcopal Church of England accompanied by an Act of Uniformity (1662). Episcopacy was also reimposed upon Scotland.

Its second objective was ideological containment. Ideological controls attempted to put the lid back on both the revolution and the troubles. Spearheading this effort in religion were those measures punishing religious dissent, particularly in towns (including London). These included the Conventicle Act (passed in May 1664; renewed 1670), the Corporation Act and the Five Mile Act.[75] Politically there was a parallel attempt to re-establish the boundaries of acceptable political belief and expression, including published expression. Licensing of the press was reimposed, amid a widespread understanding of the role played in the preceding

---

74 G. Monck, *A Letter from His Excellencie the Lord General Monck, And the Officers under his Command, To The Parliament* (London, 11 February 1659), p. 4.
75 Greaves, *Enemies Under His Feet*, p. 129.

upheaval by uncontrolled publication. The Act for the Preservation of the King, mindful that 'the late troubles did in very great measure proceed from a multitude of seditious sermons, pamphlets and speeches daily printed and published' imposed capital penalties upon anyone 'incit[ing] or stir[ring] up the people to hatred or dislike of the person of his Majesty or the established government'.[76] The Act Against Tumultuous Petitioning banned all petitions with more than twenty signatures or ten presenters.

The third aspect of restoration and the fabric of the whole was restoration of government by law. Arbitrary government – which had come in two waves from 1625–40 and 1642–60 – was government contrary to law. In seeking to rescue the nation from this spectre restoration law had two faces. One was as the re-establishment of that link with custom, and security for liberty and property, which were held to be the essence of the old regime. The other was as the cutting edge of the struggle against those forces by which this had been overwhelmed. In the words of Gilbert Sheldon, the first restored Archbishop of Canterbury:

Tis only a resolute execution of the law that must cure this disease, all other remedies serve and will increase it; and its necessary that they who will not be governed as men by reason and persuasions should be governed as beasts by power and force, all other courses will be ineffectual, ever have been so, ever will be.[77]

There was a short-term tension here in relation to the longer-term objectives of unity and peace. Division into parties, to say nothing of internal conflict and civil war, were diseases of the body politic in a society which did not believe, as some modern societies do, in institutionalised division. Accordingly Charles II's *Declaration at Breda* (1660) had continued Cromwell's emphasis on healing and settling,

that these wounds which have so many years together been kept bleeding, may be bound up . . . desiring and ordaining that henceforward all Notes of discord, separation and difference of Parties, be utterly abolished among all our Subjects, whom we invite and conjure to a perfect union among themselves, under our Protection.[78]

---

76 Keeble, *Literary Culture of Nonconformity*, p. 29.
77 Quoted in Spurr, *Restoration Church*, p. 47.
78 Charles II, *King Charls II His Declaration To all His Loving Subjects . . . Dated from his Court at Breda in Holland The 4/14 of Aprill 1660* (London 1660), pp. 1–2.

Both radical protestantism and republicanism had pursued, but not realised, their own agendas for unity of substance. Now the restoration prescription sought a unified body politic under one king and one church. If it
did not believe in institutionalised division it did believe in the treatment of
disease by purgation or amputation. The savage treatment of religious and
political dissent by law engaged in the short-term exacerbation of division
for its expected long-term cure. This was a practical prescription which did
not command unified support within the government. By 1663 the king's
own, different strategy had been temporarily overborne by his Cavalier
Parliament.

Finally restoration sought the security of these achievements, and above
all of institutional reconstruction, for the future. 'We well foresaw', said the
king, 'that the great violation which the Lawes of the Land had for so many
years sustained, had filled the hearts of the People, with a terrible
Apprehension of Insecurity.'[79] No test would be sterner than the eradication of these fears. The short-term response would be the attempted 'burial
. . . of what is passed' by the Act of Indemnity and Oblivion. For the king it
was because this was crucial 'in extinguishing this Fear, which keeps the
hearts of men awake', that the act was the only 'solid Foundation of that
Peace, Happiness, and Security I hope and pray for'.[80] In the long term,
however, such institutionalised forgetting would be no substitute for the
real security achieved by European military action.

Any suggestion of a smooth progress along the learning curve between
1660 and 1702 would be misleading. The period as a whole saw a fragile and
unstable situation in which most of the religious and political issues of
1618–60 remained alive. Most immediately the events of 1660–5 constituted a reaction: narrow, ideological and temporary. The initial 'restoration' administration itself was not restored but brand new, and young too.
Indeed this regime, centred upon two one-time exiles corrupted by foreign
manners and foreign religion, was to prove almost as narrowly based, as
politically off-balance and religiously destabilising as its interregnum predecessors. For this reason it was to meet a similarly ignominious fate in
rejection in 1688. This was, however, to create the opportunity for another
attempt at the sort of moderately conservative Clarendonian settlement
that had eluded the nation in 1660.

79 Charles II, *His Majesties Gracious Message To the House of Commons* (London, 20 June
     1660), p. 5.
80 Charles II, *His Majesties Gracious Speech to the House of Peers, The 27th of July 1660*, pp. 2, 4.

By sharply restricting, rather than extending, the provisions for liberty of conscience in operation at the time of its occurrence; by establishing satisfactory guarantees against further innovation from the throne; and by centring itself around a known conservative protestant, the anti-republican, anti-French prince of Orange, this settlement (1689–1701), once it had successfully defended itself by war (1689–1713), successfully established the basis for a government which truly expressed the fundamental conservatism, intolerance and anti-catholicism that were the bases of English parliamentary policy. Moreover, it did so without the reactionary overkill which had helped to destabilise the 1660 attempt; without, that is, the alienation of a significant part of the elite whose acquiescence had made it possible in the first place. In 1689 loyalists, however uncomfortable, were kept aboard, not thrown over the side as the presbyterians (and all other non-Anglicans) had been in 1662.

Consequently it was only after 1720, not 1660, that religion ceased to be the major destabilising factor in English politics. It was only at the turn of the century that the ruling elite in England recovered the level of political if not ideological unity that it had lost between 1640 and 1642. It was only after 1689, not 1660, that England began its 'growth of stability', dominated by the cohesion of, and deference to, a recovered, enriched and unchallenged nobility. Finally it was in 1689, not 1660, that republicans in England and in the Netherlands finally saw their hopes dashed. With Dutch assistance the 'glorious revolution' saw the final victory of England's conservative parliamentary elite over the non-parliamentary debris – monarchical as well as republican, catholic as well as protestant – remaining from the experience of the troubles.

Restoration was, then, not a *fait accompli* but an aspiration, quickly inaugurated but tardily and bloodily achieved. The things to which it directed itself included not only institutional reconstruction but the recontainment within those institutions of the ideas, and fears, by which they had previously been destroyed. Although this struggle was continuous we will observe three principal phases to have occurred after successive episodes of the troubles, in 1660–5, 1681–5 and 1689–94.

18

First restoration 1660–78

> You cannot but remember with what universal joy did all parties
> amongst us, even as one man, receive the King at his return . . . But
> behold! how soon our growing hopes were blasted, and all hands at
> work to hinder any settlement either in Church or State.
>
> *The Present Great Interest both of King and People* (1680)[1]

INTRODUCTION

The subject of this chapter is the first phase of restoration, from its establishment to near unravelling. This analysis falls naturally into three phases.
The first (1660–7) is the period of reconstruction ending with the fall of
Clarendon.[2] During the second (1667–73) the most important minister was
Arlington, but the guiding spirit was the king. The result was a series of
reversals of policy, particularly in foreign affairs and religion. These laid the
basis for the descent, from 1670, from the first phase of restoration to the
second full-scale crisis of popery and arbitrary government.

The third period (1673–8) spans that descent, from the parliamentary
confrontation of royal policy (1672–3) to the crisis that followed. A crisis
followed because in fact in this period royal policies did not change. Those
policies were considered an attack upon the fundamentals of the restored
state: protestantism and parliaments. They were considered thus by
members of the Cavalier Parliament, whose prescription for restoration
had always differed from that of the king. Between 1662 and 1667 parliament had triumphed. What the king attempted to recover, between 1667

---

1 *The Present Great Interest both of King and People* (1680), in Scott, *Somers Tracts*, vol. IX,
 p. 116.
2 Clayton Roberts, 'The Impeachment of the Earl of Clarendon', *Cambridge Historical
 Journal* 13, 1 (1957); Colin Lee, 'Charles II and the Destruction of the Earl of Clarendon',
 paper delivered at Cambridge, 10 November 1993; Seaward, *Reconstruction*.

and 1673, was an aspect of his own original agenda for peace and settlement.

What undid the first phase of restoration was, therefore, not only the return of popery and arbitrary government at home and abroad. It was division within the governing elite about the practical prescription for restoration, particularly in relation to religion. Danby's purpose was to arrest the slide into crisis by reasserting the values and policies of the Cavalier Parliament. We thus see in this period the attempted revival of intolerant high Anglicanism at home and monarchical protestantism abroad.

INSTITUTIONAL RECONSTRUCTION (1): MONARCHY

It was restoration of monarchy that provoked rejoicing in the streets and that became one of the process's most enduring achievements. It was also the key to the whole, not only institutionally (being necessary both to parliaments and the church) but also more generally, in bending the royal 'Heart . . . to all means for the Restoring of this Nation to their Freedom and Happiness'.[3] The constitutional form of the monarchy restored was that amended with Charles I's reluctant consent in 1641. This meant the preservation of key royal prerogatives, though not of the prerogative courts. The most important of these were the government of war and peace, and of parliaments (summoning, prorogation and dissolution). Similarly restored were government of the church and control of the militia, and of political and religious appointments.

It was in relation to the financial settlement that this appearance of constitutional restoration disguised the greatest changes. 'The royal prerogative . . . could be reassumed virtually intact, but the royal revenue, which had inevitably been caught up in the financial operations of the republican state, had been profoundly changed in the process.'[4] One aspect of the ensuing settlement was the restoration to the crown of a permanent annual revenue (£1,200,000) in relation to which it was expected to live 'of its own'. More significant, however, were the changes in the sources of this income, which was no longer the crown's 'own' in this respect. No attempt was made to undo the dissolution of the remaining royal demesne, including the abolition of fiscal feudal revenues. Instead their place was supplied by

3 Charles II, *His Majesties Gracious Answer to The Earl of Manchester's Speech* (London, 29 May 1660), p. 2.   4 Chandaman, *Public Revenue*, p. 196.

parliamentary taxation, including the new and hated (because efficient) forms of assessment, and excise, to be supplemented by others (in particular the hearth tax, 1662). One result was a slight improvement upon the woefully inadequate revenue of the early Stuart crown.

In this context political histories that speak of the financial inadequacy of the restoration settlement are identifying a general feature of seventeenth-century English monarchy rather than the specific character of a revenue which was, on paper at least, over twice that of James I (£500,000 in 1625) and more than that of Charles I even after the politically ruinous expedient of ship money (£1,000,000 in 1639).[5] To this extent the restoration financial settlement took a clear if short step in the direction of necessary reform. What it did not do, however, was take any such step boldly enough to endanger that state of mutual dependence (between Commons and crown) essential to the unreformed polity. It was thus no accident that weak monarchy remained a problem essential to the destabilising political developments after 1667. It was Gilbert Burnet who wrote that Clarendon, that devotee of constitutional balance, 'had no mind to out the king of the necessity of having recourse to parliament'. Similarly James II, would-be state-builder of an incautious kind, would write after his expulsion from the country that Clarendon had been

faulty, in not getting all of the destructive laws, in the long rebel parliament of Charles I, repealed; which, most were of opinion, might have been done, and such a revenue settled on the crown, as would have supported the monarchy, and not exposed it to the dangers it has since run.[6]

It was essential to the same perspective, however, that Clarendon was equally concerned to prevent further parliamentary encroachment upon remaining royal financial independence. This was the burden of his vociferous opposition to George Downing's Dutch-inspired credit experiment which culminated in the Additional Aid Act (1665). The reform embodied by the Act for the Additional Aid has rightly been called 'the most important financial experiment of the period'. By its 'technique of raising credit upon Orders, registered and repayable in course . . . an entirely new credit structure was erected'. Although this began as an emergency wartime measure – during a war Downing was widely credited with having started – the

5 *Ibid.*, pp. 262–72 (270 in particular).
6 Burnet, *History of my Own Time*, vol. I, p. 278; James MacPherson, *Original Papers* (2 vols., London 1775), vol. I, p. 17, quoted in Seaward, *Reconstruction*, p. 16.

principle of appropriation concerned was regularised and applied to the ordinary revenue from 1667, with Downing as secretary to the Treasury commissioners and later a commissioner himself.[7]

That this development was the brainchild of Downing is confirmed not only by Clarendon but Pepys, to whom the Maestro proselytised ceaselessly upon the subject over two years.[8] It had been introduced under the same circumstances of parliamentary war-mongering (1665–7) that had accompanied every other stage of successful seventeenth-century statebuilding. Although that process would achieve decisive success only between 1689 and 1714, the importance of these reforms to its pre-history would be difficult to overstate. For they applied to English state finances for the first time the two features that would be fundamental to its success. The first was 'the acquisition by the Commons of the power of appropriating its supplies, the first significant limitation of the financial freedom of the action of the executive'. Although this 'was in origin merely a by-product of Downing's Order experiment' of 1665, it became the basis of the subsequent transformation of the military-fiscal state.[9] The other was that it did this by incorporating Dutch credit facilities and management techniques into English state financial management for the first time. Here too it anticipated the core developments of the subsequent financial revolution in the 1690s with the creation of the Bank of England.[10]

It did these things in 1665 despite the fact that the United Provinces was a republic and England a monarchy. In so doing it strengthened the state by reducing monarchical power. In its novelty, in its diminution of royal autonomy and worst of all in its support by the king himself, this struck at everything the chancellor took to be essential to restoration:

> Downing . . . told them . . . by making the Payment with Interest so certain and fixed, that . . . it should be out of any Man's Power to cause any Money that should be lent To-morrow to be paid before that which was lent Yesterday . . . he would make [the] Exchequer (which was now Bankrupt and without any Credit) the best and the greatest Bank in Europe . . . and all Nations would sooner send their Money into [it] . . . than into *Amsterdam* or *Genoa* or *Venice*. And it cannot be enough wondered at, that this Intoxication prevailed so far that no Argument would be heard against it . . . without weighing that the Security for Monies so deposited in Banks is the

---

7 Chandaman, *Public Revenue*, pp. 216–17.

8 Pepys, *Diary*, vol. VI, 1665, pp. 292, 322, 327, 330, 334; vol. VII, 1666, pp. 9, 23, 87, 124; vol. VIII, 1667, pp. 131–2, 397–8, 407.   9 Chandaman, *Public Revenue*, p. 278.

10 Roseveare, *Treasury 1660–1870*; Dickson, *Financial Revolution*; see ch. 21 below.

Republick itself, which must expire before that Security can fail; which can never be depended on in a Monarchy, where the Monarch's sole word can cancel all those formal Provisions . . . upon that and the like Acts of Parliament.

It was in this context that Clarendon complained that Charles had 'in his nature so little reverence or esteem for antiquity, and did in truth so much condemn old orders, forms and institutions, that the objection of novelty rather advanced than obstructed any proposition'. The passion with which he was driven to express himself on this subject, not least to Downing himself in the king's presence, permanently damaged Clarendon's relationship with his master. Yet the royal financial necessities outweighed other considerations, 'so without any more Opposition, which was not grateful to the king, that Act passed the House of Commons'.[11]

Hard on the heels of the additional aid came the reform of the Treasury, not only its government (put into commission) but its management, administration and record keeping. In the words of the modern historian of the Treasury in this period:

it was the Lord Chancellor . . . who had to bear the initial shock of the king's uncounselled decision – a decision which, although taken amid the debts and disasters of the second Dutch war, was not a hasty one. Evidently Charles and his brother had been pondering the merits of Cromwellian administration which they knew to have been, characteristically, government by committee, and had decided that they preferred this republican style of managerial control to the courtly deference of some superannuated peer.[12]

In certain contexts, in short, the reconstruction of form was no substitute for effective substance. In the chancellor's defeat over this issue we accordingly catch an early glimpse of the limits of restoration. They were underlined by his subsequent fall, to be replaced by ministerial enemies from the next generation, including Coventry, Arlington and Buckingham.

In other respects the impression of a return to the unreformed Jacobean monarchy was assisted rather than undermined by the new king's personality. This bore a much greater similarity to that of his grandfather than his father. This may have related to similar circumstances of insecurity preceding their accession to the throne. One result was a certain limitation of political ambition – the ambition to have (and keep) rather than use the crown.

---

11 Hyde (Clarendon), *Life of Clarendon*, vol. II, pp. 195–6.
12 Roseveare, *Treasury 1660–1870*, p. 20.

This was allied to a brittle sensitivity to threatened impingements upon its power. Connected to this were tolerant/ecumenical instincts towards those elements of religious diversity not seen to pose a political threat. As in James' reign, these objectives were pursued amid an atmosphere of heedless moral licence. We find a commentary upon this in Reresby and in Pepys. In another confrontation, predictive of the chancellor's fall, Clarendon told the king in early 1667 that his 'Excess of Pleasures . . . had already lost very much of the Affection and Reverence the Nation had for him'.[13]

Nor, elsewhere, was the constitutional form of the settlement a better guide to its substance. The legal fiction that the reign began with the moment of regicide in 1649 could not eradicate several problematic realities. One was memory of that act, which presided over the culture as well as politics of the 1660s.[14] Another was the practical fact that restoration was the accomplishment not of heredity, but of that same armed force which had been responsible for its demise. As Charles put it in a letter to Monck in 1660: 'Wee shall alwaies . . . acknowledge them to be the great Instruments of restoring Us to the Nation, and the Nation to Us.'[15] Republicanism had collapsed, despite at one point looking unassailable (militarily in particular). Monarchy might collapse too. At the end of September the final meeting of the Convention heard of the first 'seditious [design] . . . to attempt the change of the present Government, and to erect the Republick'.[16]

This contemporary understanding helps to explain the palpable government, and especially royal, anxiety on this score that continued throughout the reign. This was particularly so at times of military vulnerability like 1667, a disaster contrasting so obviously with earlier republican military success. Such circumstances help to explain why, in addition to the execution of the regicides, including three kidnapped from the Netherlands in 1662,[17] the government attempted to murder other republican exiles, and

13 Hyde (Clarendon), *Life of Clarendon*, vol. II, pp. 262–3 (and 258); *Memoirs of Sir John Reresby*, p. 35.
14 Nancy Maguire, *Regicide and Restoration: English Tragicomedy 1660–1671* (Cambridge 1992).
15 Charles II, *His Majesties Letter to His Excellency The Lord General Monck* (London, 24 May 1660), pp. 2–3.
16 Charles II, *His Majesties Gracious Speech Together with the Lord Chancellors . . . on Saturday the 29th day of September 1660* (London 1660), pp. 10–11.
17 *The Speeches, Discourses and Prayers, of Colonel John Barkstead, Col. John Okey, and Mr Miles Corbet, Upon the 19th of April, being the Day of their suffering at Tyburn. Together with an Account of the Occasion and Manner of their Taking in Holland* (London 1662).

executed the most dangerous of them who remained or returned (Sir Henry Vane in 1662, Algernon Sidney in 1683). Both restoration Anglo-Dutch wars were crucially animated by 'hatred to a commonwealth'.[18] On the second occasion this became an attempt to destroy the United Provinces altogether, against which parliament rebelled on confessional grounds.

INSTITUTIONAL RECONSTRUCTION (2): PARLIAMENTS

Thus even the restoration of monarchy was felt, with reason, to be fragile. The same was true of that of parliaments. We should not be blinded to this by the essential rhetorical appeal throughout the early restoration process to parliamentary authority. The claim to have been acting on behalf of parliaments had been a feature of all the military interventions of the period 1647–60 (the regicide included). In the words of the republican veteran Sir Arthur Haselrig to Monck in April 1660, 'I have alwayes acted with the authorety of parlmt and never against it.'[19] This meant, of course, the cause of parliaments as currently understood. Thus Monck himself declared in February 1660, having restored the Rump for the second time, that 'the ground of our undertaking was not only the return . . . [of] the parliament . . . to your Trust, but also the Vindication of the Liberties of the People . . . and encouragement of the godly and faithfull therein'.[20] The enemies of this cause were the members of that 'Illegal and Tirannical Committee of Safety', assisted by 'the treachery of some Officers of the Army', whose recent intervention had 'struck at the Root of *English Parliaments*'.[21] The 'speedy filling up of the House' was an augmentation of parliamentary authority; so was the Convention which followed; and so above all (and finally) was restoration of the king.

Accordingly both king and Monck addressed the Convention, with appropriate formality, as a parliament. Throughout the initial phase of restoration Charles exhibited a positively Clarendonian rhetorical tenderness towards parliamentary anxieties. The *Declaration of Breda* emphasised the king's willingness to 'consent to any Act or Acts of Parliament' for the settlement of religion, disputes over land titles and arrears of army pay.[22] A speech on 1 May 1660 struck a worryingly familiar Stuart note:

18 Charles Davenant, *An Essay Upon the Ballance of Power* (1701), in *The Political and Commercial Works of . . . Charles D'Avenant*, ed. Sir C. Whitworth (5 vols., London 1771), vol. III, p. 309.   19 British Library, Egerton MS 2618, f. 71.
20 Monck, *Letter*, p. 1.   21 *Ibid.*, p. 2.   22 Charles II, *King Charls II His Declaration*, pp. 4–5.

We do assure you upon Our Royal word, that none of our Predecessors have had a greater esteem of Parliaments, then We have, in our judgement, as well as from our obligation; We do beleeve them to be so vital a part of the constitution of the Kingdom, and so necessary for the Government of it, that We well know, neither Prince, nor people can be . . . happy without them; and therefore you may be confident, that we shall always look upon their Councels as the best We can receive, and shall be as tender of their Privileges, and as carefull to preserve and protect them, as of that which is most neer to Ourself, and necessary for Our own preservation.[23]

The truth to which these reassurances spoke was that restoration owed no more to parliaments than it did to heredity. As the destruction of parliament had preceded, so its full reinstitution succeeded, that of monarchy. The first 'full, free and legal Parliament' was in fact called in 1661 (in the further somewhat confused formulation of the Speaker, Sir Edward Turner: 'That was Your Parliament by Adoption, but this is Yours by Birth-right; this Parliament is Free-born').[24] In the words of the king, in 1660:

as . . . Parliaments [are] most necessary for the Government of the Kingdom, so we are most confident, that you beleeve, and find that the preservation of the King's Authority is as necessary for the preservation of Parliaments; and that it is not the name, but the right constitution of them, which can prepare, and apply proper remedies for those Evils, which are grievous to the People, and which can thereby establish their peace and security. And therefore we have not the least doubt, but that you will be as tender in, and as jealous of any thing that may infringe Our Honour, or impaire Our Authority, as of your own Liberty and Property, which is best preserved, by preserving the other.[25]

This was precisely the point to which the king would return in that *Declaration* of 1681 which became the focal point of the 'second restauration'. It was the obvious lesson of the revolution that the security of monarchy, parliament and the church were interdependent. Yet these uncontentious principles did little to address the problem (soon also to be restored) of contentious royal practice. The first example of this would come with the king's attempt to hijack the religious settlement with a *Declaration of Indulgence* in 1662.[26] Subsequently anxiety concerning the

23 *Two Letters from His Majesty*, p. 4.
24 *The Speeches of Sir Edward Turner* (May 1661), p. 39; *The Speech of Sr Edward Turner* (London, 20 December 1661), p. 3.   25 In *Two Letters from His Majesty*, p. 4.
26 Charles II, *His Majesties Declaration to All His loving Subjects* (London, 26 December 1662).

'liberties' and security of parliaments would again become one of the most prominent features of the reign. Requesting the repeal of the Triennial Act, in 1664, which had indeed been a notable invasion of the royal prerogative, Charles again declared that 'never king was so much beholden to parliaments as I have been, nor do I think the crown can ever be happy without frequent parliaments'.[27] Charles I had said much the same thing in 1625, one year before threatening to dispense with them altogether.

INSTITUTIONAL RECONSTRUCTION (3): THE CHURCH

In many ways the most remarkable institutional reconstruction of this period – a phoenix rising from the ashes of both popery and sectarianism – was the church. It was remarkable partly for its unexpectedness, the settlement of 1662–5 following the failure of attempts both at comprehension, and to secure the promised 'liberty for tender consciences'.[28] It was also a notably bloody-minded triumph of religious and political will over more general circumstances. These circumstances were, on the one hand, historical. Since 1625 England had experienced attempts by its own governments to eradicate first protestantism and then the episcopal church. By 1660 the religious situation was so confused that it would have taken remarkable prescience to predict the emergence within a few years of a situation whereby episcopal protestantism should once again be declared the only true and legal form of worship.

The same circumstances were, on the other hand, more general. What had given England's domestic troubles force was their relationship to broader trends affecting western Europe in the seventeenth century. One was monarchical absolutism associated with counter-reformation catholicism. Another was parliamentary protestant rebellion against princes. In continuing to seek a way between these two extremes, restoration religious reconstruction continued to face the same European enemies. Thus the first European war of the new regime pitted itself against both. Enthusiastically backed by the Cavalier Parliament (had Charles I received the same level of funding (£2 million) in 1625 things might have been different) the conflict of 1665–7 was primarily motivated by hostility to fanatical protestantism and republicanism (embodied by the Netherlands), but also to catholicism and absolutism (in 1666 France joined the war on the Dutch side).

27 *Parliamentary History* 4, 291, quoted in Seaward, *Reconstruction*, p. 19.
28 I. Green, *The Re-establishment of the Church of England* (London 1978); John Spurr, 'Religion in Restoration England', in Glassey, *Reigns of Charles II and James VII and II*.

The religious settlement registered the notable triumph of some domestic constituencies over others. It was a triumph for parliamentary loyalism and Anglicanism. Those excluded included not only protestant 'fanatics' and catholics but also moderate parliamentarians ('presbyterians') who had been crucial in bringing restoration about. They included, finally, and not least, the king himself. In this respect two features of the king's *Declaration of Breda* were found to be in conflict: the declaration (not promise) of 'a liberty to tender consciences'; and the consigning of details of the religious settlement to the 'mature Deliberation' of parliament. Yet the royal will was made clear, looking towards that 'Act of Parliament . . . for the full granting that indulgence' which never came.[29] Nor was this a matter of secondary importance. Charles' speeches from 1660 to 1662 were preoccupied by the need to honour the promise made at Breda. It was because for the king this was a matter not only of honour and conscience, but of security, that when parliamentary co-operation was not forthcoming he attempted to secure it alone (in *Declarations of Indulgence* in 1662 and 1672).[30] For parliament in turn these attempts provoked the gravest fears not only of popery but also of arbitrary government.

The dissent of the governor of the church himself established limits to the effectiveness of the parliamentary religious settlement. This is not to say that the king was indifferent to the theoretical political benefits of persecution and uniformity.[31] Yet if ecclesiastical reconstruction was the most remarkable and uncompromising restoration achievement, so in terms of its objectives it was also the least successful. This was not only because of the very large spectrum of belief left outside the settlement, as important a force in restoration religious life still in 1689 as it had been in 1660.[32] It was also because enforcement of the legislation was wildly uneven both in the localities and across time.

Nor were these consequences of division within the government simply religious failures. Religious settlement was fundamental to settlement in general. If the years from 1667 to 1689 showed anything it was that opposition to the religious settlement had the capacity to unhinge political peace. The purpose of this parliamentary resurrection of magisterial protestantism

29 Charles II, *His Majesties Declaration* (26 December 1662).
30 This is clear in both *His Majesties Declaration* (26 December 1662) and Charles' account of the reasons for his further attempt in 1672 (see below, pp. 424–5, 429).
31 Hutton, 'The Religion of Charles II'.
32 O. Grell, J. Israel and N. Tyacke (eds.), *From Persecution to Toleration: The Glorious Revolution and Religion in England* (London 1991).

was of course the reconstruction of a shattered confessional state. As this had been an Elizabethan creation so its restoration now deployed Elizabethan legislative sanctions against papist and radical protestant alike.

IDEOLOGY

This brings us to the second ambition of restoration: ideological containment. We have already observed the limited mechanisms at the disposal of any seventeenth-century government for the control of information and belief. Clarendon complained continually about the 'Infinite Scandals' against the government which were 'scattered amongst the people'.[33] In early 1667 the king raised with his chancellor the coffee house problem: the 'Calumnies and Scandals . . . so much seditious Prattle in the Impunity of those Houses'. Clarendon advised their suppression, but the king accepted the contrary view of Sir William Coventry that this was neither possible nor wise.[34] The same relative impotence attended those public fears and memories which would in due course reignite the troubles. Like their early Stuart predecessors, restoration contemporaries were 'mad for news', both domestic and foreign. This was particularly the case during periods of European tension or war. In 1667 a London newspaper reported, as other publications had in 1621–5:

> You could not come into a tavern, alehouse, tippling or coffee-house, or sit at dinner . . . [without] men, women and children of every rank to the very lowest, raving out their ill-digested humor which they call'd opinion, sparing neither law nor gospel, as if they would have as many governors as people.[35]

Religious enforcement did, under certain circumstances, produce political quiescence. Yet this posture was strategic; it did not signify a change in belief. Accordingly when controls were relaxed (as between 1678 and 1681) religious dissent became once again powerfully associated with political sedition. The same was true of recovered controls on public spoken and written expression. It is true that to some extent these had a permanent impact upon the range of what was said. Yet again the collapse of such controls, as with the refusal of the Commons to renew the Licensing Act in 1679, resulted in an avalanche of religious and political literature reminiscent of that of the 1640s.

---

33 Hyde (Clarendon), *Life of Clarendon*, vol. II, p. 1 (1664).   34 *Ibid.*, pp. 260–1.
35 *The Mercury*, 1–5 August 1667, quoted in Pincus, *Protestantism and Patriotism*, p. 276.

LAW

We come thirdly, then, to the restoration of government by law. A scrupulous attention to the forms of law was one of the hallmarks of the first phase of reconstruction. This owed a good deal to the pre-eminence of Clarendon, who had exclaimed in the Long Parliament in 1640, of the recent judgements concerning ship money in particular,

[What] greater instance of a sick and languishing Commonwealth . . . when the judges themselves have been delinquents! Tis no marvell that an irregular arbitrary power, like a torrent, hath broke in upon us, when our banks and bulwarks, the Laws, were in the custody of such persons.[36]

Clarendon's analysis of the rebellion remained that its most potent cause had been the inroads made by Charles I's court upon government by parliaments and the law.[37] Now the key to reconstruction was that 'reverence and obedience may be paid to the fundamental Lawes of the Land . . . and that Justice may be equally and impartially administered to all men'.[38] As Paul Seaward explains: 'In 1661 he contrasted the government's observance of rule and custom, of due process and the formalities of law with the illegality and exorbitance of the interregnum regimes; the lightness of the monarchy's burden with their weight; the correctness of procedure and the gravity of debate in privy council with their conspiratorial caballing.'[39] It was essential that the lawyers, by their 'civil, upright and generous proceedings', and the judges, by their 'grave deportment . . . and strict administration of justice to all men', should increase confidence in the law, disposing men to 'such reverence of the laws, and such an estimation of the persons who justly execute those laws, that they may look upon those who could pervert the laws at home, as enemies of the same magnitude, as those who would invade the country from abroad'.[40]

The king may have found Clarendon's insistence upon legal procedure as wearisome as his moralising. Certainly this emphasis upon legal form only partially obscured the new context in which law enforcement operated in the aftermath of a civil war. As the Earl of Newcastle put the alternative view to Charles in 1660: 'it is with an army, not with lawyers, that the sovereign

36 R. W. Harris, *Clarendon and the English Revolution* (London 1983), p. 67.
37 Hyde (Clarendon), *History of the Rebellion*, vol. I, p. 86.
38 Charles II, *Two Letters from His Majesty*, p. 6.   39 Seaward, *Reconstruction*, p. 19.
40 Clarendon MSS 73, f. 93, quoted in Seaward, *Reconstruction*, p. 19.

controls multitudes'.[41] A feature of the initial restoration settlement was its relative mercy. The king spoke of the 'universal Joy for his Restoration without Blood, and with the Indemnity of so many hundred Thousands who had deserved to suffer the utmost Punishments'.[42] As the emotion behind this utterance suggested, however, the potential for blood was there, and ultimately it was realised, against more than simply the regicides. Alongside this fact there was the readiness of the king, and others around him, to attempt circumvention of the law for religious or political purposes. For rescue of the settlement from the ensuing crisis a conspicuous return would be made to the rhetoric of law alongside the fact of force.

UNITY AND PEACE

The settlement's broader objectives of unity and peace were a work of time. In the words of His Majesty: 'We must not think that God Almighty hath wrought the Miracle to that degree, that a Nation, so miserably divided for so many Years, is so soon, and entirely United in their Affections and Endeavours as were to be wished.'[43] Such progress as had been achieved, however, Charles attributed in 1661, 'next to the miraculous blessing of God . . . to the happy Act of Indemnity and Oblivion . . . that creates kindness in us to each other . . . our joynt and common security'.[44] Yet in relation to the vital area of religion the failure of toleration constituted a rejection of the king's own chosen method of healing and settling. As such it offered (in his stated opinion) a threat to the kingdom's security for the future.[45] The failure of comprehension constituted a victory not for healing but for its enemy, revenge. Clarendon made this point in parliament with some force:

It is a Consideration that must make every religious heart to bleed, to see Religion, which should be the strongest obligation and ciment of affection . . . made now by the perverse wranglings of passionate and froward men, the ground of all animosity, hatred, malice and revenge: And this unruly and unmanly passion . . . too frequently transports those who are in the right, as well as those who are in the wrong . . . How would . . . the Primitive Christians look upon our sharp and virulent Contentions . . . and the bloody Wars that have proceeded from th[em] . . . whilest

---

41 Newcastle's *Advice*, quoted in Webb, *Governors-General*, p. 446.
42 Hyde (Clarendon), *Life of Clarendon*, vol. I, p. 390.
43 Charles II, *His Majesties Gracious Message*, p. 4.
44 Charles II, *His Majesties Gracious Speech To The Lords and Commons* (8 May 1661), p. 2.
45 Charles II, *His Majesties Declaration* (26 December 1662), pp. 2–3.

every one pretended to all the Marks which are to attend upon the true Church, except onely that which is inseperable from it, *Charity to one another*.[46]

The resulting persistence of domestic religious division, combined with European developments, helped to keep political division alive. The outcome, during subsequent visitations of the troubles, was renewed ideological polarisation.

SECURITY FOR THE FUTURE

The final restoration objective was security for the future. This meant security for the traditional constitution in church and state from two dangers presiding securely over public memory. The first was royal absolutism in league with counter-reformation catholicism; the second republicanism in league with 'Amsterdam religion'.

There is little evidence of a feeling of security in the face of either threat in the period under consideration. The years 1660–5 were replete with news – true and false – of 'fanatic' plots. This was linked with hostility to the 'fanatic's' allies, the republican Dutch. The Dutch were 'vermin antimonarchical', largely to blame for England's own rebellion, in 'teaching subjects to depose their princes', and in establishing 'a precedent for the shedding of that royal blood which to this day calls to heaven for vengeance'.[47] Neither the growing power of France nor the king's attempt in 1662 to secure legal worship for catholics assuaged parliament's concern that popery 'may much increase in this kingdom'. 'As to that most pernicious and injurious Scandal', said the *Declaration* of 1662, 'so artificially spread and fomented, of Our Favour to Papists . . . it is but a repetition of the same detestable Arts, by which all the late calamities have been brought upon this Kingdom in the time of Our Royal Father of Blessed Memory.'[48] In flatly rejecting this attempt to secure an indulgence, 'His Majesties most Dutiful and Loyal Subjects . . . in Parliament' returned 'the humble thanks of this house . . . to his Majesty for his gracious Invitation to this house to prepare some Laws against the growth and progress of popery'.[49] Ultimately the key to this security was military. This helps to account for the devastating impact of the Dutch raid on the Medway in 1667.

---

46 *Ibid.*, pp. 17–18.   47 Quoted in Pincus, *Protestantism and Patriotism*, p. 307.
48 Charles II, *His Majesties Declaration* (26 December 1662), p. 9.
49 *The Votes and Orders*, p. 3.

Even before this came the worst visitation of plague in London's history, killing a quarter of the population, followed by a still more spectacular fire. After the fire, described by Clarendon as 'the highest calamity this nation hath ever felt', what national confidence and optimism had existed evaporated.[50] After the devastating emotional impact of these events there followed military humiliation. The Dutch fleet was guided unopposed into the mouth of the Thames by English republican exiles. There it burned undefended ships and towed away the royal flagship. 'The dismay that is upon us all in the business of the kingdom and navy at this day', wrote Pepys, 'is not to be expressed, nobody knowing which way to turn themselves.'[51] 'There is a general consternation and wonder', wrote Jeremy Bentham, 'that we were in no readiness to receive the enemy . . . how strangely were all our counselors lulled into a dead sleep of security that nothing less than so mortal a blow and irreperable loss should awaken them.'[52] 'The terror that the city of London was possessed with', wrote Sidney later, 'when a few Dutch ships came to Chatham, shews that no numbers of men, tho naturally valiant, are able to defend themselves, unless they be well arm'd, disciplin'd and conducted.'[53]

It was by this sequence of disasters that restoration England was thrown into its first political crisis. Its context was that same atmosphere of insecurity and alarm to which the nation would return still more profoundly in 1678. This all but ended the first stage of restoration reconstruction. This was an experiment which had been denied the favour, and indeed attracted the punishment, of God. It remained exposed to its enemies at home and abroad. And those charged with its completion and defence had, despite vast disbursements by parliament for the war, proved incapable of the task.

One symptom of the crisis was renewed fear for monarchy. 'The government is hated and the people desire a change', reported the Venetian ambassador. '[M]ost people I meet with', recorded Pepys, believe 'that we shall fall into a commonwealth in a few years, whether we will or no; for the charge of a monarchy is such as the kingdom cannot be brought to bear willingly'.[54] Another was revived fear of absolutism and popery. 'Our gentry help on the cry of Popery', complained John Beale; 'we are apparently and irrevocably back to 42.' It was 'not only whispered but publicly discoursed [among] the

---

50 Pincus, *Protestantism and Patriotism*, pp. 346–7.   51 Pepys, *Diary*, vol. VIII, p. 268.
52 Quoted in Pincus, *Protestantism and Patriotism*, pp. 417–18.
53 Sidney, *Discourses*, in *Sydney on Government*, p. 209.
54 Pepys, *Diary*, vol. VIII, pp. 390–1; Pincus, *Protestantism and Patriotism*, p. 420.

ignorant common people that the king is a Papist and intends to set up the Popish religion.'[55] The country had already suffered an invasion by the republican Dutch. Now characteristically this fear of popery expressed itself as expectation of invasion and massacre by the French. 'People make nothing of talking treason in the streets openly', Pepys complained, 'as, that we are bought and sold and governed by Papists and that we are betrayed by people about the king and shall be delivered up to the French.'[56]

It was in relation to this need of security for the future that the first phase of restoration fell furthest short of its ambitions. The government had not, by 1667, succeeded in allaying public anxiety about any aspect of the reconstructed constitution. It was in 1667 that people began to reminisce admiringly about 'Oliver's time'. This was sufficiently the case, indeed, to induce Slingsby Bethel to publish an attack on Cromwell to prevent the 'defrauding', through this 'idolatrous' adoration of one man, 'of the Long parliament of that which is due to them'.[57] Throughout the century this vulnerability had provided the context for the troubles. In the following two decades these fears would worsen.

THE UNRAVELLING 1667–78

One feature of the political crisis of 1667 was one of the bitterest parliamentary sessions of the reign. Paul Seaward, Steven Pincus and others have shown how serious, and ideologically charged, the parliamentary crisis of this year was. One consequence was the exile of Clarendon, a convenient if wholly inappropriate scapegoat. Another was the Anglo-Dutch peace (1667), a scrap of presentational respectability snatched from the jaws of disaster. This led, the following year, to the Triple Alliance, negotiated by Sir William Temple, for the security of protestant powers (the United Provinces, the British kingdoms and Sweden) in the face of the rising ambition of France.[58] Fear of popery and France had now eclipsed that hatred of fanatical republicanism which had fuelled the discredited war. This was the process that would reverse itself in 1681, in the face of the reappearance of domestic religious and political radicalism. As in that year, one of these

---

55 Quoted in Pincus, *Protestantism and Patriotism*, pp. 421–2.
56 Pepys, *Diary*, vol. VIII, pp. 269–70; Scott, 'Popish Plot'.
57 Bethel, *The World's Mistake*, p. 2.
58 For the context of the negotiation, see 'Letters of Sir William Temple', in Temple, *Works*, vol. II.

fears did not replace the other. Entirely compatible, both continued to exist, one simply supplanting its sibling in the dominant role. Consequently Temple's treaty was enormously popular. It was the first step taken after this crisis to address the continuing problem of national religious and political vulnerability.

The third outcome of this crisis was therefore more important still, and laid the basis for the turbulence of the following decade. This was the freeing of the king from Clarendonian tutelage. There followed a ministerial revolution and alterations of policy. Cavalier Anglicanism discredited, new ministers included both patrons of dissent (Ashley, Buckingham) and catholics (Clifford).[59] This also signalled a generational break with those whose conservatism followed from direct experience of the early Stuart breakdown. The king's experimentation with policy he put to work first and foremost in European affairs. It was on the basis of a spectacular realignment of European relationships that an attempt then followed to realign domestic religious and political policy.

This was nothing less than an attempt to renegotiate the restoration process, and was to lead to an appropriately extreme parliamentary reaction. For Charles had also been affected by the disasters of 1665–7. He felt, more keenly than most, the vulnerability which they signalled. The monarchy had been restored for less than the preceding time of republican rule, the military success of which (against the Dutch in particular) had contrasted so glaringly with his own. Throughout that period he had endured humiliating and penniless exile. Now some of that humiliation had returned.

In chapter 7 we asked what could account for the alterations of foreign and domestic policy between 1670 and 1672. The answer was the king's own sense of political vulnerability. The principal manifestation of this insecurity, shared by his heir James, was a belief that restoration was insecure, and that many of his people (inside parliament and outside) were simply awaiting an opportunity to rise against him.

Thus the Treaty of Dover, which replaced the Triple Alliance in 1670, was to address Charles' anxiety in a number of ways. One strategy was to associate his regime with the most powerful monarchy in Europe, including the promise of French military aid in the event of a domestic uprising. Another involved the secret promise to embrace that religion everywhere associated

---

59 Maurice Lee, *The Cabal* (London 1965).

with powerful monarchy in Europe. A third was the plan for the military destruction and dismemberment of the United Provinces (with the religious, political and territorial benefits to the crown which would follow). A fourth was the promise of regular French financial payments. Finally this realignment provided a context for the proposal to tolerate both catholicism and dissenting protestantism. Aside from expressing Charles' own religious wishes, and his original strategy for settlement, there was also in this policy an element of political appeasement. It is worth noting in this connection the advice given to Charles from one source in 1660 to

insist upon a tolleration for all, as well Roman-catholiques as others . . . There is not any thing you can doe will be of more advantage than this; for thereby you will secure yourself against the Presbiterians and sectarys, by equally poising them with others of contrary judgements; for you may doubt, that the Presbyterians and sectarys will at length fall to their first principalls againe, and endeavour to make you at best but a duke of Venice.[60]

That the king found a number of ministers to speak for this agenda is not at all surprising. It is a reminder of the distance the nation remained from the cavalier vision of religious and political uniformity. As a retreat from parliamentary government both of politics and religion the king's policies constituted not only an assault upon the first restoration settlement. They amounted to a return to something like the foreign and religious policies of the Rump Parliament.

This realignment announced itself in practice in 1672, with the Declaration of War on the Netherlands accompanied by the *Declaration of Indulgence*. The latter attracted the support of many who had been campaigning for a revision of the first religious settlement. Some of these, however, like Andrew Marvell, later expressed alarm at the prerogative means employed to effect religious changes which were in themselves highly desirable. Marvell lamented that the 'Quintessence of arbitrary malice' (the Conventicle Act, renewed in 1670) should have been restrainable only by 'a Piece of absolute universal Tyranny'.[61] Of others, like the Earl of Shaftesbury, instrumental in the parliamentary presentation of these policies in 1672–3, it would later be pointed out by the House of Commons that they appeared to have been prepared to buy the relief of dissent with the safety of European protestantism (and parliaments).

60 Thurloe, *Collection*, vol. VII, p. 873.   61 Wallace, *Destiny His Choice*, pp. 189–90.

Amid angry scenes in the Commons, the government was forced to withdraw the indulgence and then to withdraw from the war. The United
Provinces would survive, thanks to the cutting of the dykes around
Holland. The crisis created by the French invasion did, however, lead to the
murder of the Dutch Pensionary de Witt, and the re-establishment of
William of Orange as stadtholder. This constituted the accidental achievement of a longstanding royalist foreign policy objective. Now there was an
acceptable non-republican focus for a pro-Dutch pan-protestant foreign
policy.

The royal retreat of 1673 helped to contain the damage done by this
policy realignment. However the king had glaringly advertised his own
religious and political preferences. The attempt to champion the causes of
catholicism and dissent against the Act of Uniformity indicated more than
simply disaffection from the restoration religious settlement. It indicated
dissent from the principle of government by parliamentary legislation. This
had been combined with an alliance with the European embodiment of
popish absolutism. From the crisis point of 1667, therefore, the fortunes of
restoration had sunk still lower. For the process had discovered a major
destabilising element in its own king. Far worse, this 'element' was in league
with the country's principal religious, political and military enemy. As
the shadow of popery and arbitrary government lengthened throughout the rest of the decade, the architects of the first restoration settlement
faced the destruction of everything they had worked for.

The government's response was twofold. The public policy was that of
Thomas Osborne, Earl of Danby, a Yorkshireman and protege of Arlington
appointed treasurer in 1673.[62] Danby understood the fears that had been
aroused, particularly in the House of Commons, and set out to assuage them.
The first matter to be dealt with was religion. This was a question not only of
returning to but reinforcing the battered religious settlement and its vision of
a confessional state. This was done domestically by the passage, in 1673, of the
Test Act, barring both catholics and protestant dissenters from holding public
office. This had the unfortunate early effect of exposing the heir to the throne
as a catholic. And it was done on the European stage by distancing the
country from France and seeking a return to the protestant strategy of Anglo-
Dutch military containment. This latter policy culminated in the marriage
treaty of November 1677 between Mary Stuart and William of Orange.

---

62 Browning, *Thomas Osborne, Earl of Danby*.

Danby's other concern was to address the fear of arbitrary government. This meant a return to respect for the customary forms of law combined with specific cultivation of parliament. This cultivation was achieved partly by attention to parliamentary opinion and grievances. It was achieved by the appearance of consultation and the provision of information. And it was achieved by the presentation of popular policies. By all of these methods Danby began the process of reconstructing a loyal and enthusiastic parliamentary constituency for the crown. Amid all of these efforts, however, he had one special problem. The overwhelming concern of the Commons from 1673 to 1678 was what it had been from 1621 to 1629. This was the popish menace, in the European military ascendant. As French expansion continued unimpeded, the passion for war against France reached fever pitch. This Danby could promise (going so far, in January 1678, as to transport 20,000 English troops to Flanders) but could not deliver.[63]

The government could not deliver war with France because alongside Danby's policy was that of the king. This entailed the secret continuation of the relationship with France initiated in 1670. If the origins of that policy lay in monarchical insecurity, Charles' insecurity was not likely to have been moderated by the parliamentary reaction of 1673. It may be that, in the Secret Treaty of Dover, Charles had already delivered a hostage to fortune which made impossible English military action against France. That Louis XIV could, if necessary, have used exposure of the terms of the treaty to throw domestic English politics into turmoil is suggested by the effect of his subsequent exposure of the lesser agreement of May 1678 (see chapter 7).

Throughout this period Charles was receiving secret annual payments in exchange for allowing French expansion to continue unimpeded. This frustration of parliament's anxiety for war he achieved by frequent prorogations. The full title of Marvell's tract drawing attention to this situation was *An Account of the Growth of Popery and Arbitrary Government in England. More particularly, from the long Prorogation of November 1675* (1677). This particular prorogation had been the king's response to the *Address* of the House of Commons in that month calling for the Cavalier Parliament to be dissolved.

---

63 Kenyon, *Popish Plot*, p. 41; K. D. H. Haley, *The First Earl of Shaftesbury* (Oxford 1968), p. 437.

Throughout this period Danby's domestic opponents were not only those cavaliers who wanted the substance rather than simply the appearance of an anti-French policy. They were also those sympathetic to protestant dissent who opposed the original narrow religious settlement and wanted it renegotiated. In this they had been encouraged by the king's *Declaration*. This group were incensed by the Test Act and hostile to the attempt to rebuild the Anglican–cavalier consensus. They were strong in London, including the city government, where the combination of religious dissent with anti-French protestant internationalism acquired an increasingly high profile during the 1670s. They included ex-ministers like Shaftesbury and Buckingham, as well as the three most important ministers to replace Danby in 1679: Halifax, Sunderland and Essex. All of these Peers, and their allies, like the presbyterian Lord Holles, stood for a tolerant parliamentary protestantism at odds with the policies both of Danby and the king. It was this constituency in the Lords and Commons that led the campaign to have the Cavalier Parliament dissolved and another elected. It was from this that the most famous tracts of the period emerged. One explained:

It is the first time in the World that ever it was thought adviseable, after fifteen years of the highest Peace, Quiet, and Obedience, that ever was in any Countrey, that there should be a *pretence* taken up, and a reviving of former miscarriages, especially after so many Promises and Declarations, as well as Acts of Oblivion, and so much merit of the Offending party, in being the Instruments of the King's Happy Return, besides the putting so vast a number of the King's Subjects in utter despair of having their crimes ever forgotten.[64]

The other enemy to which Danby found himself exposed by the king's duplicity was Louis XIV. By early 1678, following the Stuart–Orange marriage alliance, the French ambassador Barillon had been instructed to engineer the fall of the lord treasurer. This he did by paying a member of the Commons to reveal the details of Charles' secret negotiations for an increased pension the previous May.[65] These negotiations, which Danby had opposed, were to end his career, in this reign at least.

This was not only the result of the necessary convention of holding ministers responsible for the policies of their king (the actual signatures on the

---

64 *Letter from a Person of Quality*, p. 33.
65 *Explanation of the Lord Treasurers Letter*, p. 4; Grey, *Debates 1667–1694*, vol. IV, p. 355 (19 December); *Examination of the Case of the Earl of Danby*.

bottom of the letters belonged to Charles). Montagu's revelations showed Danby's policies to have been a sham. Their real purpose, it appeared, had been to reconstruct and augment the power of a royal master who could not be trusted to use it. It was thus that in December 1678 Danby was impeached – like Strafford before him – as the accessible embodiment of popery and arbitrary government. Charles' response, as we have seen, was to dissolve the Cavalier Parliament. With this action the process of unravelling was completed.

During the upheaval which followed every aspect of the restoration settlement was called into question. The achievements of 1660–5 were imperilled first by popery and arbitrary government and then additionally by fanaticism and republicanism. It was from this trial that there emerged another phoenix conjured from the ashes of public memory. This was North's 'second Restauration'.

19

'Second Restauration' 1679–85

Why am I forc'd, like Heav'n, against my mind,
To make examples of another kind?
Must I at length the Sword of Justice draw?
Oh curs'd Effects of necessary Law!
   ... Th' Almighty nodding gave consent;
And Peals of Thunder shook the Firmament ...
Once more the God-like *David* was Restor'd,
And willing Nations knew their Lawfull Lord.

John Dryden, *Absalom and Achitophel* (1682)[1]

INTRODUCTION

By 1679 the first phase of restoration had collapsed. This was a consequence of the suspicion, followed by the revelation, that the king had been auctioning the state's religion and government to a foreign power. Although the church and parliaments remained in existence they appeared to be in danger. Although the monarchy remained in existence it was the monarch himself who appeared to be placing it in peril. Over the next few years the consequences of this collapse included the end of peace (leading to civil war through the courts); the end of unity (leading to ideological polarisation); and the return not only of the troubles but of revolution. All of this served as a reminder of the initial superficiality of the restoration process itself.

The resulting reliving of the troubles, and revolution, had its context in the relationship between present events and public memory. The same context furnished the immediate outcome of the crisis in what Roger North called 'a second Restauration'.[2] The second phase of restoration was accord-

---

1 Dryden, *Absalom and Achitophel* (5th edn, rev., London 1682), pp. 30–1.
2 Quoted in Knights, *Politics and Opinion*, p. 5.

ingly, like its predecessor, a reaction. As such it repeated, with emphasis, most of the essential features of its predecessor. It was to be correspondingly short-lived.

LOYALIST REACTION: '41 AGAIN

Charles and James Stuart both believed that the restoration crisis was a struggle for English monarchy. The second restoration recorded the process by which this belief came to be held by the nation at large. This involved the eclipse of the general preoccupation with the revived menace to protestantism and parliaments with the perception that ''41 [was] here again'.

The loyalist rallying cry ''41 again' had two meanings. It registered first the perception of a radical and intransigent opposition to the crown which now posed a greater immediate danger of popery and arbitrary government than the popish plot before it. In addition it registered the fact of political polarisation and a resulting belief in the proximity of civil war. The prehistory of these perceptions, which reached their climax in 1681, may be traced from late 1679. It is not surprising that their first sparks were visible in the abhorring addresses of late 1679–early 1680. These, and the petitions to which they responded, marked the beginning of a phase of radicalisation of the crisis, and of polarisation.

The context for this had been created by the king's own provocative use of his powers of prorogation, rendering parliamentary politics impossible. The result was the development of extra-parliamentary politics, particularly in London. This stimulated public memories of the same during the period 1640–2: 'The humor of the citty', reported John Verney, is 'the same as it was 40 years ago'.[3] It equally drew attention to the fact that restoration legal controls upon such activities were being flouted.

In relation to the major issues, Charles had by this time made a series of publicly advertised concessions. These included the delivery of plot victims to execution; the removal of catholic Peers (and Danby) to the Tower; the formation of a new extended Council; and the disbandment of much of the army.[4] What he would not do was surrender crucial royal prerogatives – the government of foreign policy, the church and parliaments

---

3 Quoted in Mark Knights, 'Politics and Opinion During the Exclusion Crisis 1678–1681', DPhil. thesis, Oxford 1989, p. 18.

4 See for instance Charles II, *His Majesty's Gracious Speech* (London, March 1679), pp. 3–4, which listed them.

themselves – the absence of which would render him a 'Doge of Venice'. Nor would he, in the context of this struggle with the Commons, compromise the hereditary basis of the monarchy. To do this would be to abandon the constitutional fiction embodied in the restoration settlement in favour of the fact that his enthronement had been the work of a kingless Convention.

The king's initial prorogation of the first parliament in May 1679 had been caused by 'fear of revolt'. He had refused at this time to take Danby's advice that he issue a *Declaration* comparing the Commons' conduct with that of 1641. His first concern was always with control of London. He had been deeply concerned when in late 1678 the city authorities had insisted on fixing chains across the streets. In September 1679 he described the city as 'rotten ripe for rebellion'.[5]

It is thus notable that in the public development of this perception the king himself took a lead. This he did both by personally confronting petitioners and by encouraging, and setting the tone for, abhorring replies. Responding to the presentation of a petition in January the king demanded: 'What do you take me to be and what do you take yourselves to be? I admire gentlemen of your estates should animate people to mutiny and rebellion . . . You come from a company of loose and disaffected people who would fain set us in troubles.'[6] More succinctly he demanded of the interregnum veteran Henry Mildmay, presenting a petition from Kent, 'Sir, do you remember 1641?', to which he received the reply, 'Your Highness, I remember sixty.'[7] Accordingly the response of the abhorring addresses, presented by figures like Sir George Jeffreys and Justice Withins who would be prominent in the coming reaction, was not only 'That petitioning for the sitting of the Parliament is like 1641', but that it was 'intended to bring his Majesty to the block, as his Father was brought'.[8]

Though this was far from the universal opinion by early 1680, a public theme had been established. As opposition to the court subsequently radicalised there was a stream of evidence for it. The next was the radical election to the London shrievalty in July 1680. The Duke of York remarked: 'This looks as if London would set up for a Commonwealth.'[9] Secretary Leoline Jenkins wrote, hopefully:

5 Miller, *Charles II*, pp. 290, 311–12, 319.   6 Quoted *ibid.*, p. 329.
7 Ronalds, *Attempted Whig Revolution*, p. 79.   8 North, *Examen*, p. 542.
9 James II, 'Life of James II 1660–1698, Written by Himself', in J. MacPherson (ed.), *Original Papers* (2 vols., London 1775), vol. I, p. 112.

The losing of the day in the election of the new Sheriffs in London is, it must be confessed, a disreputation to the loyal party . . . but the Sheriffs can do the Government no great harm that can be forseen . . . The country gentlemen have an indignation at the proceedings of the city, and do look upon their election as a parallel line drawn to that of 1641–2.[10]

The election did indeed cause a public sensation. It was in the view of Roger North the crucial episode in the revival of that 'Party . . . which raged against the Person and Government of King Charles II . . . It was a fresh Growth out of the *Caput mortuum* of that which actually destroyed king Charles I, and through many odd Incidents of his Son's Reign acquired a Strength almost at Par with that of the Government.'[11] Witnesses to Bethel's victory were warned that they now had genuine cause to fear another

Rebellion . . . [and] the [English] know upon experience that they shall all then be rifled of their Plate, Pewter, and Brass, their Pigsties and Henroosts robb'd, and their Daughters ravisht . . . And as our late unnatural Wars begat such Taxes and Impositions, as England never heard of before, so another like War will revive the same.[12]

Jenkins opined in September 1680: 'the Danger is from the Wealthy dissenters that pretend the fear of Popery, but under that pretense drive at the change of Government into a Commonwealth'.[13]

This emerging loyalist perspective had two most important components. One was an emphasis upon the element of repetition, both to connect with public memory and to make the point that experience must serve as a warning. 'It would be somewhat strange, and without all example in story, that a nation should be twice ruined, twice undone, by the self-same ways and means.'[14] The second point is that the popish plot had now been joined by another. Its methods and objectives were identical: 'The papists would destroy our Church and State; so would the Common-Wealthsmen: The Papists would set up Popery and absolute Monarchy; the other an Amsterdam Religion and Arbitrary Government . . . the Plot is the same carried on by different Parties.'[15] Those seeking to draw attention to the Commonwealth plot could appeal to a public memory still more recent and

---

10 Henry Sidney, *Diary*, vol. II, p. 87.   11 North, *Examen*, p. 16.
12 *Goodman Country: To His Worship the City of London* (London 1680), p. 3.
13 Quoted in Greaves, *Secrets of the Kingdom*, p. 13.
14 *Fair Warning*, p. 1; Cooke, *Memorabilia*, p. 101; *Essay upon the Change of Manners*, p. 1.
15 *Advice to the Men of Shaftesbury* (London 1681), p. 4.

painful than its predecessor. 'Have they (in 1641)', asked Roger l'Estrange, 'not actually once before overthrown the Monarchy, set up Arbitrary Power, trampled under the foot our Magna Charta, Liberty, Property, Lives and Religion, murdered their lawful Prince, banished his son?' 'The Wrack of the Crown in the King your Father's time', wrote the Duke of Ormonde to Charles himself, 'is fresh in the memory of many of us; and the rocks and shelves he was lost upon (tho' they were hid to him) are so very visible to us, that if we avoid them not, we shall perish rather derided than pitied.'[16]

From 1680 these parallel plots competed in the marketplace of public belief. In this respect the politics of opinion, and of memory, proved more fluid than in 1640–2. In early 1679 public opinion, preoccupied with the popish plot, was overwhelmingly pro-parliamentary and anti-court. By mid-1681, however, this position had substantially reversed itself.[17] By this time the dominant public concern had become the visible revival of the 'old Cause'.

Principally responsible for this, building upon the extra-parliamentary politics of 1679–80, were the parliamentary sessions of 1680–1. These provided a crucial public exhibition of disobedient intransigence in contrast to apparent royal flexibility. This was understood in the context of the radicalisation of London; of the House of Commons leadership, and of the alliance between the two. It was Colonel Titus who said, two days before the dissolution in January: 'mankind cannot consist together without a supreme Power . . . and that in our Government is the Legislative'.[18] There was the aggressive use, in partnership with the city, of the Commons' judicial and financial powers. There was the inflammatory Oath of Association, accompanied by talk of war. Speaking of this Dryden remarked (in January 1681):

You would fain be nibbling at a parallel betwixt this Association, and that in the time of Queen Elizabeth. But there is this small difference between them, that the ends of one are directly opposite to the other: one with the Queen's approbation . . . the other without either the consent, or knowledge of the King, against whose Authority it is manifestly designed.[19]

16 Duke of Ormonde to Charles II, 27 May 1681, quoted in K. Feiling, *A History of the Tory Party 1640–1714* (Oxford 1924), p. 181.
17 This does not mean, needless to say, that opposition to the court had ceased by the latter date. As we have seen, it continued, in writing and action, until 1683 (and thereafter in exile): see Scott, 'Restoration Process', pp. 627–8.
18 Grey, *Debates 1667–1694*, vol. VIII, p. 278.
19 Dryden, *The Medall: A Satyre against Sedition* (London 1682), Epistle to the Whigs.

Above all there was the refusal not only to compromise with the crown, but to accept its right to determine the being of parliaments themselves. All of this 'added up', in the words of John Miller, 'to a comprehensive assault upon the royal prerogative'.[20]

'THE GOOD OLD CAUSE REVIV'D'

It was an assault, most specifically, on that prerogative which had been equally central to the political struggles of 1621–40. 'If', wrote one indignant 'well-wisher to the King',

it be the undoubted Prerogative of the King to Call, Adjourn, Prorogue, and Dissolve Parliaments at his will and Pleasure; it is a high impudence in any Subject, or Assembly of men, to take upon them to Advise him (unasked) how and when to execute his Power.[21]

This echoed Charles I's *Proclamation* of 1629: 'the late abuse having driven us out of that course we shall accouynt it presumption for any to prescribe any time unto us for Parliaments the calling continuing and dissolving of which is always in our own power'.[22] Behind such rhetoric the crucial practical breakthrough for Charles II had been the resumption of his relationship with France. It was this which enabled the king to repeat his father's action of 1629, amid comparable scenes of uncontrollable parliamentary behaviour, in turning away from parliaments altogether and publishing an explanation to the people.

His Majesties Declaration to all his Loving Subjects (1681) was a masterful appeal to public memory. It developed the deepening public feeling that parliamentary behaviour itself had become arbitrary.[23] This included 'Arbitrary Orders made, for taking Persons into Custody, for matters that had no Relation to privileges of Parliament, and strange illegal Votes, declaring divers eminent persons to be enemies to the State, without process of Law, or hearing their defence, or having any proofs made against them'.[24] It also included the attempt to 'disable Us' financially, passing

---

20 Miller, *Charles II*, p. 341.
21 *Reasons Offered by a Well-Wisher to the King and Kingdom* (London 1681).
22 James Larkin and Paul Hughes (eds.), *Stuart Royal Proclamations* (2 vols., Oxford 1973–83), vol. II, pp. 223–6.   23 Knights, *Politics and Opinion*, pp. 307–11.
24 *A Dialogue at Oxford* (London 1681) (this pamphlet is here paraphrasing the *Declaration*), p. 15.

resolutions to the effect that anyone advancing money upon 'the Branches of the King's Revenue, arising by Customs, Excise, or Hearth-Money, shall be adjudged to hinder the Sitting of Parliaments'.[25] Thus the *Declaration* culminated in the assurance

That we shall be Assisted by the Loyalty . . . of all those who consider the Rise and Progress of the late Troubles . . . And we cannot but remember, that Religion, Liberty and property were all lost and gone when Monarchy was shaken off, and could never be reviv'd till that was restor'd.[26]

This appeal became the focus for the subsequent deluge of loyal addresses (and accompanying pamphlets). This was the loyalist equivalent of the parliamentary petitioning campaign of 1679–80. During the rest of the year loyalists made dominant use of the press; in the words of Roger l'Estrange's *Observator:* "'Tis the press has made 'em mad and the press must set 'em right again.'[27]

Predictably the dominant theme of loyalist addresses and publications in this year (and after) was the parallel between this and previous anti-monarchical plots. In the succinct motto of one author, quoted from Ecclesiastes: 'That which hath been is now, And that which is to be, hath already been':[28]

I desire you only to peruse the Records of 40 and 41 . . . it is just as if the old Game was playing over again: 1. In their seditious and factious Pamphlets, thereby endeavouring to render the present Government odious to the People. 2. Their aspersing and calumniating the Ministers of State, as being Popishly affected. 3. Their Whisperings at Coffee-Houses . . . of the fears and apprehensions they have of an Arbitrary Government; these seem exactly to be Ushers on to the Good old Cause.[29]

Cross-historical document comparison became a favourite genre of loyalist publication.[30] This was not simply to warn of past consequences but to assert an explicit connection between the two plots. Since 1678 the wheel of

25 Charles II, *His Majesties Declaration to all his Loving Subjects* (1681), p. 5.
26 *Ibid.*, pp. 4–5.   27 Quoted in Miller, *Charles II*, p. 347.
28 Ecclesiastes 3.5, quoted in *History of Whiggism*.
29 *A Letter to a Friend in the Country, Touching the Present Fears and Jealousie of the Nation* (London, 29 February 1680 [1681]), p. 1.
30 *The Parallel; A Letter to a Noble Peer [Essex] about his late Speech and Petition* (London 1681); *The Two Associations. One Subscribed by CLVI Members of the House of Commons In the Year 1643. The other seized in the Closet of the Earl of Shaftsbury* (London 1681); Theophilus Rationalis, *Multum in Parvo aut Vox Veritatis: Wherein the . . . Transactions of . . . Parliament Ad 1640, 1641. As also 1680, 1681. are most faithfully and impartially Examined, Collected, and Compared* (London 1681).

restoration memory had thus turned full circle. 'The [popish] Plot reviv'd' had become 'The Good Old Cause reviv'd'. As Dryden wrote, in *Absalom and Achitophel* (1682):

The Good Old Cause reviv'd, a Plot requires
Plots, true or false, are necessary things,
To raise up Commonwealths, and ruine kings . . .
The thrifty Sanhedrin [parliament] shall keep him poor:
and every Sheckle which he can receive;
shall cost a Limb of his Prerogative.[31]

Although in political competition, beliefs in the popish and republican plots were not mutually exclusive. This is because the historical experiences informing them were consecutive, and real. Passage from one to the other simply registered in belief and memory the actual national experience. That is why, by 1681, belief in the republican plot had come to overshadow, rather than replace, its predecessor. It is notable how relatively little loyalist material questioned the existence of the popish plot. Thus Dryden's 'Plots, true or false' were not invented but 'improv'd', and 'turn'd . . . to ruine Church and State'.[32] 'The Outcry was then [in 1641]', explained one pamphlet 'as great upon *Presumption*, as now upon *Proof*; and Popish Plot, Popish Army, Popish Council, Popish Prelat, was the burden of all their Oaths, and Covenants.'[33] 'All honest men', explained another, still

believe in the Popish Plot. But it would be more vigorously prosecuted if Commonwealth Protestants did not endeavour so visibly to make a hand of it . . . and, having got a real Popish Plot, resolve to make that do the same feat, which, before they did under the bare pretence of one: viz the Alteration and ruin of the government both in church and State.[34]

A third elaborated:

Was not a Pretended Conspiracy of the Papists, a Prologue to those sad Catastrophes? Was there not as full a cry then as there is now against Arbitrary Government? . . . Indeed the difference is that the late sad Times were ushered in by a pretended Popish Plot, and the present by a hellish true and real one . . . but its neck being broken, I know not why it should be allowed to be made use of for the carrying on of the same Designs as brought us so lately into Ruin and Destruction, and made

31 Dryden, *Absalom*, p. 12.　　32 *Ibid.*, pp. 27–8.　　33 *The Parallel*, p. 9.
34 *The True Protestant's Appeal to the City and Country* (London 1681), pp. 2–4.

us groan under the heaviest Yoak, and Arbitrary Government, *that ever any Nation was oppressed with.*[35]

This movement from one end of this spectrum of memory to the other did not necessarily entail a shift in belief. Belief in the popish and fanatic plots was more often connected than distinct: fanaticism *was* popery. This was true for the substantial middle ground who supported the restored monarchy, parliament, church and rule of law. It was on the basis of this common ground that Bishop Fell wrote to Richard Newdigate after the dissolution at Oxford:

We both aim at the same thing though we differ in the methods of procuring them. The preservation of the Protestant religion, and established government, is our common care, but . . . you imagine the nation can only be preserved by letting in all dissenters into your church; and on the other side, we are most firmly persuaded that your proceedings must draw after them the alteration of government, and popery: toleration being certainly destructive of our reformed religion, whether procured by a Lord Clifford, or a popular pretence to the uniting of Protestants . . . We remember very well the time, when blood and rapine put on the mark of godliness and reformation; and we lost our king, our liberty and property and religion . . . As it then appeared that we poor cavaliers were Protestants, though scandalled with the names of malignants and papists; so I hope we shall still continue: and be as willing to suffer and die for our religion, as others are to talk of it.[36]

It was this transition of public opinion which established the context for the 'second Restauration'. By swimming across an ocean of remembered misery the country found its way back to the haven of 1660. This return, however, would have a sharp cutting edge. As Fell's letter reminds us, there was no unanimity of public opinion in 1681. Gilbert Burnet, who referred to what was to follow as 'that fury', reported that, 'In their cups, the old valour and the swaggerings of the cavaliers seemed to be revived.'[37]

The loyalist reaction of 1681–5 followed closely the first phase of restoration of 1660–5. There was a recovery of government control over 'seditious' publication and political activity. There were the recovery and deepening of controls over municipal corporations, 'the seminaries of all separation in Church and State'.[38] Above all there was a reapplication of the religious con-

---

35 *Essay upon the Change of Manners*, p. 1.   36 Quoted in Spurr, *Restoration Church*, p. 80.
37 Burnet, *History of my Own Time*, vol. I, pp. 276–7.

trols specified in the Act of Uniformity. In practice, however, in its immediate political circumstances this renewed would-be 'pacification' bore many of the hallmarks of war.

'THE SWORD OF JUSTICE'

As previously the public face of restoration was the law. The accusation of the king's *Declaration* had been that the last two parliaments had behaved 'without any Order or Process of Law ... We requir'd of Them to make the Laws of the Land their Rule, as We did.' Concerning this use of the sword of justice, the situation had however, by 1681, considerably intensified. For, as we have seen, a feature of the crisis had been just such a political use of the law by the government's opponents. The result was the militarisation of justice, for the purpose of refighting the 'civil war through the courts'.[39] All the catholics executed between 1678 and 1681 (including Lord Stafford in 1680 and Archbishop Plunket of Ireland in 1681) and all of the 'fanatics' executed in 1683 were convicted of treason against the state. The cutting edge of the second restoration was victory in this second civil war.

Like the measures of 1660–5 this savagery contained an element not only of reaction but also of revenge against enemies who had unwisely disported themselves behind temporary barriers of political and judicial protection. 'Tis now', wrote a contemporary after the dissolution at Oxford, 'come to a civil war not with the sword but law and if the King cannot make the judges speak for him he will be beaten out of the field.'[40] In *Absalom and Achitophel* Dryden had Charles speaking as David:

Why am I forc'd, like Heav'n, against my mind,
To make Examples of another kind?
Must I at length the Sword of Justice draw?
Oh Cursed Effects of necessary Law!
How ill my Fear they by my Mercy scan,
Beware the fury of a Patient Man.
Law they require, let Law then shew her Face;
They could not be content to look on Grace ...
Th' Almighty nodding gave consent;

38 Miller, *Charles II*, p. 321.
39 Earl of Anglesey, quoted in Ranke, *History of England*, vol. IV, p. 159; Scott, 'Law of War',
   p. 575.   40 Quoted in Miller, *Charles II*, p. 347.

And Peals of Thunder shook the Firmament . . .
Once more the God-like *David* was Restor'd,
And willing Nations knew their Lawfull Lord.[41]

Before the sword of loyalist 'justice' could be unsheathed, however, it was necessary to recover control of London. The occasion was the annual election to the shrievalty on 24 June 1682. When in 'the Great Hall . . . In which there were Assembled . . . Three or Four Thousand People . . . [the radical candidates] Papilion and Duboii were chose by the Majority abundantly', they were 'put aside' by a loyal lord mayor imposed by the court.[42] Sir John Moore insisted instead upon the exercise of his claimed ancient right to nominate holders of the shrievalty. Contemporaries reported 'the outragious Tumults in the city'. 'This is the Model of Forty One exactly: those Times began with like Brawls in the City.' Sidney's *Discourses*, partly written in this year, justified 'tumults' under extraordinary political circumstances.[43]

What made loss of control of London juries so ominous were the offensive political uses to which those institutions had recently been put. It was of these that Bethel was thinking when he spoke of now being 'laid . . . open to a Deluge of Misery and Blood'.[44] It is accordingly hardly coincidental that it was after 'The Office of Sherriff was taken out of the hands of the Faction' that 'That Winter there was a bloody Conspiracy formed.'[45] Whatever its practical basis the 'fanatic plot' of 1683 was also, and most importantly, a loyalist legal construction.

During late 1682 and 1683 insurrection was certainly discussed in both England and Scotland.[46] Treasonable talk had, however, been a consistent feature of the crisis. What created the specific plots (most colourfully the 'Rye House Plot') was above all the capacity of the government to create them. The evidence in both cases pointed to activities which were organisa-

41 Dryden, *Absalom*, p. 30; see Philip Harth, *Pen for a Party: Dryden's Tory Propaganda in Its Contexts* (Princeton 1993), ch. 3. Harth's study is properly concerned with appeals to public opinion understood as phases of a process (p. ix).

42 Cambridge University Library Sel.2.118, *An Impartial Account of the Proceedings of the Common Hall of the City of London at Guildhal* (London, 24 June 1682), marginalia by Ralph Verney.   43 Sidney, *Discourses*, in *Sydney on Government*, pp. 193–4.

44 [Bethel], *The Right of Chusing Sheriffs*, pp. 2–3.

45 *Reflections upon some passages of Mr Le Clerc's Life of John Locke* (London 1711), p. 690.

46 Recent treatments include Ashcraft, *Revolutionary Politics*, ch. 7; Scott, *Restoration Crisis*, ch. 12; and Greaves, *Secrets of the Kingdom*, chs. 3–5.

tionally well short of posing a danger and which indeed rarely went beyond words. There was, on these occasions, no cellar full of gunpowder or its equivalent. This did not mean that there had been no general danger to the government. As judicial phenomena the plots were foci for, and ways of expressing, the public belief that such a danger was real.

Specifically what created the plots were three things. The most important was a climate of public belief, both in 1678–80 and in 1681–3, with a genuine grounding in the events of the period. The second was the political opportunity and means to permit prosecution. This entailed the receiving, and in some cases publication, of testimony whether by the House of Commons or the court. This both furnished the means and focused the political concerns in the context of which prosecutions could take place. An early sign of events to come was the crown's co-option of star witnesses to the popish plot – John Smith, Stephen Dugdale and Edward Turberville – to testify at the trials, first of Stephen College and then of the Earl of Shaftesbury (both in 1681).[47] Though the prosecution of College (conducted in Oxford) was successful, that of Shaftesbury was not, and could not be expected to be so until the recovery of control of London juries. Thus the final requirement for the plot as a judicial phenomenon was the compliant legal apparatus necessary to give this will lethal expression. With the control of London juries now in opposing political hands, it did not take much foresight to know what lay in store.

THE FANATIC PLOT

The first step was for the general loyalist rhetoric about the 'Good Old Cause Reviv'd' to give way to the specific 'discovery' of a plot. The terms in which this was then described mirrored precisely those of its popish predecessor. There was a 'Most Horrid and Bloody Plot' by 'phanaticks' to kill the king, destroy the church and establish arbitrary government against law.[48] This was a natural outgrowth of the radicalisation of London politics and of parliamentary conduct in 1680–1. This fanaticism was the same, whether protestant or catholic. Dryden was not the only one in 1682 to equate fanatical whiggery with the catholic Holy League during the French wars of

47 Harth, *Pen for a Party*, pp. 139–43.
48 *A True and Just Account of a Most Horrid and Bloody Plot conspired against His Most Sacred Majesty* (London 1683).

religion: a jesuit cause responsible for the assassination of two kings.[49] William Dugdale explained: 'The Holy League in *France* is so exact a Pattern of ours in England, as we have just reason enough to conceive, that the Contrivers of this Rebellion, did borrow the Plott from thence.'[50] In the words of Dryden's *Prologue to the Duke of Guise* (November 1682):

Our Play's a Parallel: The Holy League
Begot our Cov'nant: Guisards got the Whigg:
Whate'er our hot-brain'd Sheriffs did advance,
Was, like our Fashions, first produced in France.[51]

For the purpose of gathering 'evidence' concerning the fanatic plot, the government's sponsored witnesses gave very general attention to the situation in London over the last several years. One John Fitzgerald, for instance, reported

sev[era]ll treasonable expressions he . . . heard from Coll: Englesby, Major Wildman, Coll Sydney and others . . . Coll Henry Englishby . . . said in my company and the Quakers that, notwithstanding the last Parliament at Westminster was prorogued and dissolved and all the other discouragement England met with from their King . . . England will be England still and ever and Englishmen will lose their lives and fortunes, before they lost their properties and liberties . . . Much after the same manner have I heard Major Wildman, Col Sidnie and others speak treasonable expressions, as I shall more amply declare.[52]

As with the popish plot, government efforts to gather 'information' paid almost as much attention to its long- as its short-term history. John Wildman, Henry Ingoldsby and Algernon Sidney had all been prominent during the 1640s and 1650s as Levellers and republicans respectively; those arrested and tried featured a heavy preponderance of members of republican families and/or one-time members of the New Model Army. The informant who particularly set the ball rolling was Josiah Keeling, a minor conspirator and acquaintance of Rumsey and West, who visited Whitehall on 12 June. Warrants were issued for the arrest of West and Rumsey on 20 June, Sidney on 25 June, Russell on 26 June, Wildman on 28 June, Aaron Smith on 5 July, John

49 *The Parallel*, p. 27.
50 William Dugdale, *A Short View of the Late Troubles in England* (London 1681), ch. 47 (pp. 600–50).
51 Dryden, *Prologue to the Duke of Guise* (London 1682), p. 1.
52 Public Record Office, London, State Papers 44 nos. 81–2; *Calendar of State Papers Domestic*, July–December 1682, pp. 65–6.

Hampden on 9 July and the Earl of Essex on 10 July.[53] Henry Ingoldsby and Lord William Howard were also arrested; Monmouth went into hiding; and other more seasoned conspirators, including Ferguson, Armstrong, Nelthorp and Wade, succeeded in fleeing the country.[54]

Prominent among those trying the resulting cases were leading 'abhorrers' like George Jeffreys and Justice Withins. When they came, the trials themselves were modelled precisely upon those which had preceded them. They began, that is to say, with a recitation of what every 'Englishman does believe, that for several years past a design was laid . . . and public libels spread abroad, to persuade the people that the king was introducing arbitrary power . . . [and that] the king was a papist'. This became 'a design of raising and making a rebellion' by 'open force' or the 'assassination of the king'.[55] It was only having reviewed this 'general evidence' that the trial turned to whatever testimony might be available to connect the defendant to this design. The most famous victim of 1683, Algernon Sidney, vigorously protested against this proceeding, as well he might, having seen it in operation many times. When he explained that its effect was not to examine the truth of the indictment, but to 'prepossess . . . the jury', George Jeffreys had a devastating reply:

Mr Sydney, you remember in all the trials about the late popish plot, how there was first a general account given of the plot in Coleman's trial, and so in Plunket's, and others; I do not doubt but you remember it. And Sir William Jones, against whose judgement, I believe, you will not object, was attorney at that time.[56]

During the trial of Plunket, indeed, the defendant had issued a warning to all those who might in future face 'such witnesses as these that come against me'. Sidney's own trial, in turn, became notorious, partly because of the lengths to which the government proved capable of going to secure a conviction, but principally because Sidney fought it as the historical and political struggle it was. No one knew better than this close associate of Bethel what odds he faced. These included the 'all possible care taken, to give us such . . . Judges . . . as have neither understanding nor honesty'. 'You knowe', he wrote to his fellow prisoner John Hampden in the Tower,

53 Milne, 'Rye House Plot', p. 122; *Calendar of State Papers Domestic*, January–June 1683, p. 385.
54 Howard's examination, Public Record Office, London, State Papers 29 no. 428, p. 33.
55 *Tryal of Algernon Sydney*, quoted in Scott, *Restoration Crisis*, pp. 322–3.
56 *Tryal of Algernon Sydney*, pp. 12–16.

what advances have bin of Late made towards that good work . . . [We] may consider wheather . . . the [crown's] Judgement against the Citty Charter doth not abolish the sheriffs chosen by it, and . . . soe wheather wee may not plead against the validity of their new commission.[57]

No one knew better the crucial role that would be played by the new sheriffs. This led Sidney to object with particular strenuousness to his jury. After the trial he recorded with fine imperiousness in his *Apology*:

I thought that my birth, education, and life, might have deserved a jury of the principal knights and gentlemen that were freeholders in Middlesex . . . but I found that all rules of decency . . . and humanity had bin neglected, as well as thoes of lawe; the bailifes had not bin suffered to summon such of the freeholders . . . as seemed most fit for such a service; but receaved orders to summon by name such as Graham and Burton had, with the under-sheriff, agreed upon . . . Upon examination I found, that they had not only put in very many that were not freeholders, but picked up a rabble of men of the meanest callings, ruined fortunes, lost reputation, and hardly endowed with such understanding, as is required for a jury in a nisi prius court for a business of five pounds.[58]

In a famous subsequent scene, considerably amplified by Burnet, the sheriffs visited Sidney on 4 December 1683 to give him notice of his execution. Sidney recounted to another visitor shortly afterwards how 'he had locked them in and told them he laid his blood at their doors'.[59]

Thus the theatre of the courtroom played to a political audience. Public attendance at the trials was high, and printed accounts, authorised and otherwise, did a brisk trade. As with the popish plot trials the veracity – or even plausibility – of witnesses' 'revelations' was immaterial. The procedures functioned as a response to public concern. The harvest of their victims – subject, below the level of nobility, to the same barbaric procedures prescribed for treason suffered by the popish plotters, and the regicides before them – was approximately equivalent in number.

In addition, of course, the trials exploited this public concern for practical purposes. One was to rid the kingdom of individuals whose hostility to

---

57 East Sussex Record Office, Lewes, Glynde Place Archives, no. 794, Letter 1, p. 1.

58 Sidney, *Apology*, p. 9. Significantly, Sidney's objections to the jurors were omitted from the printed *Tryal*. The fullest account is in N. Luttrell, *A Brief Historical Relation of State Affairs* (Oxford 1857), p. 289.

59 *Historical Manuscripts Commission report, House of Lords MSS 13th Rep 17.3*, p. 51; British Library Add MSS 63,057, vol. II, pp. 157–8; Scott, *Restoration Crisis*, p. 342.

the restored structures of church and state had just once again been made manifest. Another was revenge, against persons who had used real anti-governmental power ruthlessly. Finally it was the political function of these prosecutions not only to make a public display of governmental power but also to redescribe the boundary between the permissible and the proscribed. It followed from this that the trials themselves paid as much attention to ideas and words as actions. In the words of Jeffreys at the trial of John Hampden (1684):

When once people come to believe that the raising of Tumults, and making seditions . . . is a legal way to obtain their ends . . . what will they not do under that pretence, That all they do is according to Law? They think it is lawful to resist and oppose the Government, and the Old Cause is a Good Cause to this day.[60]

Like the restoration process as a whole, therefore, the trials of 1683 were about the containment not only of action but also of belief.

As in 1660–2 the formula was exemplary violence against a few. The victims in this case included several of high social status (one earl, the brother of another and the son of a third). Some effort was expended in extracting confessions of guilt upon the scaffold, with more success than in the case of the popish plotters but also some famous failures. Sidney's defiant *Last Paper*, published first in the Netherlands and then in London, caused a sensation and attracted many replies.[61] His 'trial', according to Burnet, 'being universally cried out on, as a piece of most enormous injustice' produced the last of this series of executions.[62] That of Hampden the following February failed to substantiate the initial charge of treason, a fact attributed by Dorothy Milne to the public backlash caused by Sidney's trial.[63]

'SECOND RESTAURATION'

These judicial procedures were among many measures proceeding simultaneously until the end of the reign and establishing the context for the next. There was the second abhorrence movement of 1682, a resuscitation of the first (of 1680) and a continuation of the loyal addresses of 1681. This took as its focus the Commons' Association, the aim of which was, according to the

60 *The Tryal of John Hambden 6 February 1684* (London 1684), p. 48.
61 Scott, *Restoration Crisis*, pp. 342–7.   62 Burnet, *History of my Own Time*, p. 398.
63 Milne, 'Rye House Plot', p. 182.

city of Norwich, 'to Destroy both Your Majesty and Monarchy it self, by Levying War upon no other Authority, but the Arbitrary Orders of a Disaffect, though Dissolv'd part of Parliament'.[64] In 1682 and 1683 sermons were published that had been delivered to the now loyal 'Lord Mayor, Aldermen and Citizens of London . . . on the Anniversary Fast [30 January] for the most Execrable Murder of K. Charles the first ROYAL MARTYR'.[65] These set the immediate crisis in the context of the troubles as a whole, dwelling upon the extent to which 'the contagion of the Popish principles of Rebellion [hath] over-run these Protestant Kingdoms', and laying out the doctrines in question for inspection in the manner of Edwards' *Gangraena*. They included the beliefs

That the Parliament without the King was supream power of this Nation . . . That it was lawful to take up defensive arms . . . That . . . the late Rebellion . . . was the cause of God . . . [and] That all People, the *English* in particular, have a right to choose their own Government . . . One would surely think there needed no other Argument amongst us against Rebellion or Sedition . . . than the bare rememberance of what this Nation hath already suffered by them; especially . . . in this present Age, when the memory of it is fresh, and the Scars still remain . . . Ye have yourselves seen the horrid Consequences of Republican Principles, unbridled Liberty, popular Reformation.[66]

Thereafter there was the sequel to the *Declaration* of 1681 in the publication on 28 July 1683 of *His Majesties Declaration to all His Loving Subjects, concerning the Treasonable Conspiracy against his Sacred Person and Government, Lately Discovered.* This was, like its predecessor, 'Appointed to be Read in all Churches and Chappels in This Kingdom'. In addition to furnishing details of the conspiracy, and of His Majesty's lucky escape, this appointed 'the Ninth day of *September* next, to be observed as a day of Thanksgiving in all Churches and Chappels within this our Kingdom'.[67]

---

64 Quoted in Harth, *Pen for a Party*, p. 152.
65 George Hickes, *A Sermon Preached before the Lord Mayor, Aldermen and Citizens . . . at Bow-Church on the 30th of January 1681/2* (London); John March, *The False Prophet Unmaskt, or the Wolfe Stript of his* SHEEPS-CLOTHING, *in a Sermon* (London 1683).
66 Hickes, *Sermon*, Dedication and pp. 21–2; March, *The False Prophet*, p. 10.
67 Charles II, *His Majesties Declaration to all His Loving Subjects, concerning the Treasonable Conspiracy against his Sacred Person and Government, Lately Discovered* (London, 28 July 1683), pp. 222–3.

These measures were accompanied by exact attention, in the war for public opinion, to the importance of the press. Measures were taken to recover control of the press through the system of licensing; to suppress seditious opinion wherever possible, and answer it where not; and to give the widest possible circulation to loyalist utterances. All of these measures were accompanied by more important practical efforts. One was the successful campaign for the surrender, and where appropriate amendment, of municipal charters not simply in London (surrendered early 1683) but throughout the kingdom. This was an intensification of that aspect of restoration which had made its first mark with the Corporation Act of 1665. It is not surprising, therefore, that this was accompanied by an uncompromising reapplication of the religious controls at the centre of the first settlement.

This signalled, in one respect, the effective establishment of that union of interest between crown and Church of England which had been assumed but never actually secured by that settlement. Underlying this was not only the recent renewed demonstration of the connection between religious 'fanaticism' and political sedition. There was what the king felt to be the ruthless exploitation of his earlier mercy by his enemies. The prosecution of dissent between 1681 and 1685 bore a resemblance to the prosecution of the fanatic plot in more than simply its exploitation of public anxiety. It employed the same apparatus of informers and judiciary, and its harvest of victims was infinitely larger.[68] When they spoke of that 'invasion' of 'lives, liberties and estates' against which armed resistance was justified, John Locke and others were referring most broadly to this religious persecution.[69]

All of this helps us to understand that atmosphere of great apparent public calm in which (we are told by Reresby and others) James II eventually acceded to the throne in 1685. The frightening events of 1678–81 had established a reunion of that alliance of loyalist gentry, Anglican church and crown which had underlain the first restoration. This situation was assisted by improved royal income from the customs revenue, followed by a first parliament for James the generosity of which followed partly from the further warning of Monmouth's rebellion. All of this has encouraged some historians to assert that James II inherited a stronger crown than any of his

---

68 Mark Goldie, 'The Hilton Gang and the Purge of London in the 1680s', in Howard Nenner (ed.), *Politics and the Political Imagination in Later Stuart Britain* (Rochester, N.Y. 1997).

69 Tim Harris, '"Lives, Liberties and Estates"'.

Stuart predecessors. Yet if the situation in 1685 looked like that peace and unity which was the fundamental objective of restoration, this may have been no less misleading than the peace of silence of the 1630s.

Since 1678 the nation had been reminded not only of the undesirability of the alternatives to monarchy, but of the fragility of restoration. This was not a country in command of its own destiny, but one being tossed from one wave to another of its turbulent past and present. The true fragility of the restoration process is one necessary context for understanding the rapidity of its subsequent dissipation. By the second half of 1688, support for James had evaporated and the troubles had returned.

How could any monarch have thrown away such a strong hand in such a short time? To understand the answer we need to be reminded of what the dangers were in the face of which the restoration process was fragile. The first was the threat to church and state from arbitrary monarchy in league with counter-reformation. The second was the threat to church and state from arbitrary republicanism in league with the radical reformation ('Amsterdam religion'). The remarkable achievement of James II was to unite them both.

James' principal political assets were a deeply loyalist parliament and church, and the vanquishing of the 'whigs' of 1679–81 who had so frightened his father. His principal ambition was to secure freedom of worship for catholics. When the former constituencies would not permit the latter ambition James turned to the dissenters. This was a route pioneered by Charles II in 1672, resulting in sufficient uproar to cause a retreat. Religiously this was to attempt to unite protestant and catholic dissenter behind the common cause of liberty. Politically it was to unite both the spectres by which restoration felt itself to be threatened against the process itself.

Above all it was to unite them against the loyalist/church/monarchy alliance by which that process had been sustained. Unlike Charles, moreover, James was not one to back down. The *Declarations of Indulgence* of 1687 and 1688, and the legal and political actions by which they were accompanied, combined catholicism, 'fanaticism' and arbitrary (anti-parliamentary) royal prerogative. By late 1688 James was facing resistance not only from revived radical whiggism, but from loyalist gentry and previously ultraloyal churchmen.

William's invasion did not cause, but exploited, the third visitation of the troubles. What caused it, as the others, was royal policy in church and state. The Dutch invasion may have completed, or rather simply demonstrated,

James' loss of control. Most importantly, however, it was an agency for restoration. Its avowed purpose was the salvation of protestantism and parliaments from royal popery and arbitrary government. Its actual purpose was the rescue of the political functions of monarchy, and the fiscal powers of the House of Commons, that they might be put to use in Dutch interests in the continental military theatre. It is to the achievement of this objective, under astonishing circumstances of urgency and danger, that we must now turn.

20

Third restoration 1688–94

Because King Charles II was called home by the Convention, and nothing settled, you found the consequence. Charles II was a young man, in the strength of his youth, and, you know, how much Money was given him, and what became of it?

Sir William Williams (January 1689)[1]

In the great joy of the King's Return, the Parliament overshot themselves so much, and to redress a few Grievances they got so much Money, that they could live without you.

Mr Sacheverell (January 1689)[2]

INTRODUCTION

In chapter 9 we examined the third visitation of the troubles. It was the European context that furnished, in the Dutch invasion, the most important means for the successful confrontation of popery and arbitrary government. By driving out the king, creating an interregnum and presiding militarily over the subsequent constitutional settlement, the invading army exercised considerable control over the final outcome. It was the English historical context, however, that furnished not only the local persons and beliefs but also the experience and constitutional instruments necessary to deliver this outcome quickly and peacefully. For these purposes the most important were the government of the city of London; the unprecedented contrivance of the Assembly of Commoners which met at St James' from 24 December; and the Convention, of both Lords and Commoners, which met from 22 January 1689.

1 Grey, *Debates 1667–1694*, vol. IX, 1688–9, p. 30.   2 *Ibid.*, p. 33.

It is the purpose of this chapter to understand the third and decisive phase of restoration in the same contexts. The principal European instrument of restoration was, once again, the Dutch invasion. Initially this deepened the troubles, in the sense that it completed the collapse of governmental authority. Almost immediately, however, it set about its intended business. This was, from disorder, the rapid reconstruction, and strategic rearrangement, of order; from the danger of republicanism the securing of monarchy; and from the danger of civil war the securing of the fiscal, political and military instruments necessary for war on the European stage.[3]

Restoration drew upon those same passions which had animated the troubles. Most members of the English elite opposed innovation in church and state, whether from 'popery and arbitrary government' or 'Amsterdam religion' and republicanism. What gave each of these fears different force at different times was the passage of external events. The key context for the first episode of the troubles had been the disasters suffered by protestantism in the Thirty Years War. By 1688 a lengthy process of French expansion had resulted in an equally urgent situation. From the 1670s English politics had been deeply affected by this, which also furnished the context for Dutch intervention in 1688. As Jonathan Israel has reminded us, the Nine Years War did not begin with British participation in May 1689. The Dutch invasion of England was an act in that war, which had in effect begun a year earlier.

The same context was crucial to the restoration process. Successful restoration required statebuilding, which depended upon the context of European war. During the 1620s, as we have seen, the Thirty Years War provoked both the fears behind the troubles and the first seventeenth-century attempt at statebuilding. It was only in the 1690s, however, that fear of popery and arbitrary government became itself a decisive force *for* statebuilding, rather than against it.

Thus if William's *Declaration* spoke to the concerns animating the troubles it also spoke the language of restoration. It was *The Declaration of His Highness . . . for restoring the laws and liberties of England, Scotland, and Ireland.* The entire accent of the document, read to the Assembly of Peers on

---

3 John Dunn argues that all pre-twentieth-century 'revolutions' ended in restoration: Dunn, 'Revolution', in Ball, Farr and Hanson, *Political Innovation and Conceptual Change*, pp. 338, 345–6.

21 December, was upon the recovery and preservation of 'law, liberties and customs' which had been 'openly transgressed and anulled'.[4] It promised the restoration not only of a protestant supremacy protected by law, and of 'a free and legal parliament', but of all the recently transgressed legal rights and liberties (including those of the Fellows of Magdalen College) and the recently surrendered town and borough charters.[5]

The *Declaration* was written by Caspar Fagel, 'the leading figure in the States of Holland', and translated into English by Gilbert Burnet.[6] Jonathan Israel has called it not only the 'manifesto' but in some sense the very 'essence' of the 'revolution', unlike the *Declaration of Rights* which was simply a (non-binding) means of legitimating its ends.[7] Yet he has also showed that as a propaganda document for local consumption it is far from encapsulating an explanation of the invasion. For this we must turn to the Dutch situation.

DUTCH REASONS

The European context of the Dutch invasion was first explored in detail by John Carswell's *Descent on England*.[8] Israel's recent work has altered our understanding of it in two ways. The first is by examining not the European context of an English, but the English consequence of a European, situation. The second has been by situating the invasion within the context of the history of the United Provinces.[9] This latter adjustment is important, not only because the invasion was a product of Dutch internal politics. Its most important effect is to remove the spotlight solely from William and cast it instead upon the European policy of the Dutch state.

It has suited the English story to regard William's intervention as personal and dynastic. Only from this perspective could a foreign incursion become an agency for the continuation of local history. Even in the seventeenth century the English were inclined, wrongly, to regard William as a quasi-monarch. As Algernon Sidney complained to the French ambassador in 1679: 'Sir William [Temple], who was taken for the oracle of those parts,

4 William III, *The Declaration of His Highness*, pp. 124–5.   5 *Ibid.*, pp. 125–49.
6 See the discussion by Israel, 'General Introduction', p. 13.   7 *Ibid.*, pp. 13–25.
8 John Carswell, *The Descent on England: A Study of the English Revolution of 1688 and Its European Background* (London 1969).
9 Jonathan Israel, *The Dutch Republic: Its Rise, Greatness, and Fall 1477–1806* (Oxford 1995), pp. 841–53.

assured them that there was no such thing as a party in Holland inclined to oppose the prince of Orange; that all was submitted unto his authority, and united.'[10] The truth was that William did not govern Dutch policy (particularly foreign policy). The most important feature of Dutch internal politics throughout the seventeenth century was the frequently turbulent and bloody struggle between the States-General (dominated by regents of Holland) and the House of Orange.

Between 1650 and 1672 the United Provinces was a republic, officially anti-Orangist in its ideology, and within which the young William was excluded even from the customary office of stadtholder.[11] Following his recovery of this office in 1672 amid the military crisis caused by the French invasion he had struggled unsuccessfully to acquire with it power over foreign policy. His greatest frustration in this respect had occurred following the marriage alliance with Mary Stuart in November 1677. This had apparently been accompanied by the prospect of Anglo-Dutch military action against France. It was not simply that Charles II's real relationship with Louis XIV might never have made that possible. In addition the Stuart–Orange match reignited republican fears in the Netherlands of an Orange plot to usurp monarchical power.[12]

One result was the Treaty of Nimuegen (1678), by which the States-General accepted the offer of a commercially beneficial peace with France. A clear implication of this treaty, concluded against the implacable opposition, and 'almost over the dead body', of the prince himself, was that under present circumstances the States-General considered Louis XIV less of a danger to their liberties than the stadtholder.[13] In the words of an English observer, the Stuart–Orange match had reignited 'the suspicion of the states party in Holland that there was a plot against their liberties . . . they had therefore foresaken the coalition against France'.[14] As Ranke concluded: '[The object of Charles II and the Prince of Orange] had been to take into their own hands the decision of European affairs. As matters turned out,

---

10 Sidney, *Letters to Henry Savile*, pp. 50–1.
11 Israel, *Dutch Republic*, ch. 32; P. Geyl, *The Netherlands in the Seventeenth Century, Part Two, 1648–1715* (London 1964); 'de Witt' [de la Court], *True Interest*.
12 Scott, *Restoration Crisis*, ch. 6.
13 J. P. Kenyon, *Robert Spencer, Earl of Sunderland 1641–1703* (Cambridge 1958), pp. 37–8; Scott, *Restoration Crisis*, pp. 108–9.
14 Quoted in J. Ralph, *The History of England* (2 vols., London 1744), vol. I, p. 488; Haley, *Shaftesbury*, p. 502.

their decision was far more dependent on the union of Louis XIV with the aristocracy in Holland and the opposition . . . in England.'[15]

Ten years later William's first military decision from England, over a month before he was made king, was to send 8,000 English troops to the Netherlands to 'act against France' as England was obliged to under the terms of the Treaty of Nimuegen 'according to mutual stipulation, against the violater of that treaty'.[16] For by 1688 the Franco-Dutch alliance at Nimuegen was a thing of the past. Under these circumstances it was only by this exceptionally risky military expedition that William finally reclaimed for the Anglo-Dutch marriage alliance what had been for him its original military purposes. This he did by abandoning its dynastic basis, not only by jettisoning its obstructive Stuart component and cementing a military alliance with the anti-French English parliamentary elite instead, but also by leading what was an invasion by the Dutch republic.

Most remarkable about this was its basis in a unity of Dutch domestic vision with no recent precedent. It was only this which made possible the equipment of such an expedition so quickly. The Dutch republic was the only state in Europe capable of such an achievement at this time. And at the core of the expeditionary force were the republic's best troops. Not only the expedition itself but 'William III's entire military and diplomatic stance on the continent was crucially dependent on a continuing close collaboration with the states of Holland, including Amsterdam, and this alone accorded the regents a far from negligible weight in British affairs down to the end of the Nine Years War, in 1697.'[17]

While the invasion was occurring great efforts were made to insist not only in England, but also to the continental allies of the Dutch, that the expedition had no dynastic basis. Its aim was not to dethrone England's legitimate monarch, or alter the legitimate succession, 'et moins encore pour exterminer la religion catholique, ou pour la persécuter'. It was, rather, simply to overthrow James' arbitrary government and establish 'un Parlement libre et legitime'. This would give 'au peuple une entière assurance que les loix, droits et privilèges de leur royaume, ne seront pas violez ny revoquez à l'avenir'.[18] More importantly, from the point of view of the invasion's military objectives, it would give free expression to that anti-

15 Ranke, *History of England*, vol. IV, p. 561.   16 Israel, 'Dutch Role', p. 134.
17 Israel, 'General Introduction', p. 21.   18 Quoted *ibid.*, p. 22; Israel, 'Dutch Role', pp. 121–2.

French military fervour that William had observed dominating the English House of Commons since 1672.[19]

Thus, if the invasion can no longer credibly be regarded as the response to an invitation by seven English people, it is no more credible to consider it an expedition by William to take the crown. This was not simply because of the weakness of William's dynastic claim, which the appropriate military circumstances could (and did) render irrelevant. More importantly the co-operation of the States-General that made the expedition possible would not have been forthcoming for an act of dynastic aggression which would have endangered Dutch liberties. Above all, in the circumstances of the invasion itself a specifically dynastic ambition did not make strategic sense. James' flight was unpredictable. What was strategically necessary was the summoning of an English parliament.

Previous co-operation between the princes of Orange and the States-General had occurred in circumstances of military emergency in which the importance of the stadtholder's role was not in question. Such circumstances had played a key role in the life of the republic, particularly during the war of independence against Spain. It was following the end of this war in 1648 that periodic co-operation had given way to sustained rivalry. In the period to 1688 the new military danger to the republic had become France. From the 1660s France's successful policy of appeasement of the regents of Holland (including Amsterdam and Leiden) had appealed to the declared republican conception of public interest in offering the peace necessary for prosperous trade. It was the pursuit of this interest, against the prince of Orange's desire for military confrontation, which was held to have left the republic open to the catastrophic French invasion of 1672. It was the revival of the same policy, thanks to the assiduous work of the ambassador, d'Avaux, which had been responsible for the acceptance by the States-General of the Treaty of Nimuegen in 1678.[20]

For the Dutch state the circumstances of 1687–8 constituted a new military emergency. This is the explanation for a naval descent upon England without European precedent in terms of scale and risk.[21] From the beginning of the history of the independent United Provinces (founded by the Treaty of Utrecht in 1584), absolute necessity had been the mother of invention. The background to this emergency lay in the collapse, from 1687, of

19 K. D. H. Haley, *William of Orange and the English Opposition 1672–1674* (London 1953); Stephen Baxter, *William III.*   20 D'Avaux, *Negotiations*, vol. I.

21 Israel and Parker, 'Of Providence and Protestant Winds'.

the political alliance between France and the Dutch regents. By this year the trade concessions granted by the Treaty of Nimuegen, with other developments (including the flight of Huguenots to the Netherlands), had become intolerable to the French state.

The result was a series of punitive French measures against Dutch commerce which had a devastating impact and provoked calls for retaliation. The result of this was an alteration of political perceptions within the republic. It was within this context that in early 1688 preparations for the invasion of England began. 'Again and again d'Avaux warned his master that the sole means of mobilizing the regents to stop the sending of the invasion armada to England was "en retablissant le commerce sur le pied du traite de Nimegue".'[22] It was in September that William finally secured the agreement of the town councils, provincial assemblies and the States of Holland 'that France had gravely damaged Dutch commerce and navigation, and the Republic's fisheries, that Louis XIV maintained close links with James II, [and] that the Dutch forces should now be fully mobilized for war'.[23]

Time and again republican publications had reiterated that these commercial considerations were the lifeblood of the Dutch state. France had now transformed itself from being the ally of this entity into its mortal enemy. Moreover, in his emphasis upon Anglo-French collusion, William played heavily upon memories of 1672, to which the regents remained particularly sensitive. Louis XIV's response to these developments, in late September 1688, was to order the arrest of all Dutch shipping in French ports. On 29 September Caspar Fagel laid before a secret session of the States of Holland 'the full plan, and the strategic logic behind it':

France had grievously damaged Dutch trade, shipping and fisheries; war with France was now unavoidable; if the Republic remained in a defensive posture, France, in alliance with England . . . would overwhelm [it]; the only way, in these circumstances, in which the Dutch state could be made secure was to break the 'absolute power' of James II quickly, suppress the Catholic pro-French influence in England, convene Parliament and restore its authority, and turn England round against France . . .

This was the objective and a breathtakingly grand and ambitious one it was too. It could not conceivably have succeeded without the concerted, unified, support of all

22 D'Avaux, *Negotiations*, vol. VI, pp. 175, 208, 229, 255, quoted in Israel, 'Dutch Role', p. 116.   23 Israel, 'Dutch Role', p. 118.

sections of the Dutch state – something exceedingly rare in seventeenth-century Dutch history – but this was now assured thanks to the actions of Louis XIV.[24]

Thus the Dutch invasion was, unsurprisingly, a response to Dutch circumstances. That this response should have taken this remarkable form, however, owed a significant amount to the fact and history of England's troubles. This continuing instability, political and religious disaffection, and military vulnerability created one of the great *occasioni* of history. In the words of Sidney in the *Court Maxims*:

Certainly England is worth conquering, and whenever there is a probability of getting it, it will surely be attempted. When the people are strong, numerous, valiant, wise . . . well content with their condition, a conquest is difficult. If weak, cowardly, without discipline, poor, discontented, they are easily subdued; and this is our condition . . . nothing can be added to render them an easy prey to a foreigner, unless the sense of their misery and hate of them that cause it make them look on any invader as a deliverer, and rather submit to him than fight for . . . cruel masters at home.[25]

RESTORATION PRINCIPLES

Institutional restoration entailed that of monarchy, parliaments and the church. That the Dutch invasion should seek the summoning of a 'free and legal parliament' is not surprising. Since the shocking Anglo-French alliance of 1670–3, English parliaments had shown themselves to be overwhelmingly in favour of war with France. It was this alliance which had established the context for the subsequent crisis of parliaments. In the words of the Commons' *Declaration* of 1680:

Ministers of England were made Instruments . . . to make War upon a Protestant State . . . to advance and augment the dreadful power of the French King . . . and to press upon that State the public exercise of the Roman Catholic religion . . . [and] When in the next Parliament the house of Commons were prepared to bring to a legal Tryal the principal Conspirators in this Plot, that Parliament was first Prorogued, and then Dissolved.[26]

Now William's *Declaration* focused upon the activities of 'Those evil counsellors' who, in prosecution of the same 'execrable' design, had once

24 *Ibid.*, pp. 119–20.   25 Sidney, *Court Maxims*, p. 78.
26 *Humble Address of the Commons*, pp. 77–82.

again attempted to set aside both parliaments and the laws. This helps to explain why William's first move, the day after the *Declaration* was read, should have been the summoning of an Assembly of Commoners composed of members of that same 1680 House of Commons (elected in September 1679, and re-elected in early 1681) together with their allies in the city of London. It was this body which petitioned him to assume the *de facto* government of the kingdom and advised the election of the Convention. It was subsequently that Convention, containing many of the same members, that voted to support William's declaration of war against France. The result was not only the achievement of the invasion's military objective but also the securing, as a means to this end, of the future of English parliaments. One necessary means for making Anglo-Dutch military co-operation effective was the securing of the Dutch-style government of estates in England.

No less important to the achievement of Dutch objectives was the preservation of the English monarchy. William in particular intervened in the third and final crisis of the Stuart monarchy partly to rescue it from the Dutch-style republicanism he imagined, and the English-style republicanism the nation remembered, to have been the consequence of the first. In this he had a personal dynastic interest. But this was equally the interest of the Dutch state, as Anglo-Dutch military history showed. As Pensionary de Witt had asked in 1665: 'what would the effect be of turning England [back] into a Commonwealth, if it could possibly be brought about, but the ruin of Holland?'[27] Thus William's biographer concluded similarly: 'The worst of all English governments, from the Dutch point of view, would be a republic. The history of the Commonwealth and Protectorate made that all too clear.'[28]

English fear of a republican outcome to this crisis was highly evident, both in and outside the Convention. It was also entirely understandable, given how few years had passed since that last such scare. It was given further credence by radical talk, speeches and publications calling for a republic.[29] This was partly why the Earl of Halifax noted William's view at the end of December 1688

that the Commonwealth party was the strongest in England; he had then that impression given. They made haste to give him that opinion . . . Said that at best they

---

27 British Library Add MS 63,057, vol. I, p. 393.   28 Stephen Baxter, *William III*, p. 167.
29 Kenyon, *Revolution Principles*, pp. 8–9.

would have a Duke of Venice; in that perhaps he was not so much mistaken. Said he did not come over to establish a commonwealth . . . He said with the strongest asseverations that he would go if they went about to make him a regent.[30]

The survival of England's militarily ineffectual monarchy was no more to be taken for granted in 1689 than the survival of parliaments. This was a potentially dangerous moment, when the country had just been invaded by a republican state. Yet an intact English monarchy was important to the speedy realisation of Dutch military objectives. While the financial support of parliament was essential to its realisation in practice, the government of war and peace lay with the crown. Given his own struggles to influence foreign policy since 1672, this is not a consideration likely to have escaped William's attention.

This is not to say that a specific objective of the invasion was the crown itself. It was essential to its prospects for success that the invasion had general military rather than specific political objectives. What was minimally necessary was a sufficient alteration of the English domestic situation to produce a change in foreign policy. In the context of a Dutch occupation there was more than one way in which this could be achieved. The suggestion of some flexibility in this area is reinforced by William's agreeing to treat with James on November 27th. This intention was overtaken by the king's flight from the capital in the face of anti-catholic rioting on December 11th. This reinforces the suggestion that in the events leading to James' actual deposition by William on December 18th we see the ruthless exploitation of circumstances rather than the masterful execution of a plan.

Restoration was, finally, restoration of the church. It may be, as Mark Goldie has argued, that before the Dutch invasion the church was in the process of rescuing itself.[31] But it was doing so amid circumstances not only of legal assault from its own governor but also of simultaneous inundation from fanaticism and popery. Whether without external intervention these floodgates might have been closed we cannot know. Nor were they subsequently closed entirely, at least on the protestant side. It was such conservative moderation, however, learning from the failures of the 1660s, that allowed the settlement of 1689 to provide for the final security not only of parliaments and monarchy but the church. In its immediate context the

---

30 J. Western, *Monarchy and Revolution: The English State in the 1680s* (London 1972), p. 302.
31 Goldie, 'Political Thought of the Anglican Revolution'.

most important effect of the act of 1 William and Mary c. 18 was to restore
the legal limits to religious worship which had been suspended, and so the
church to its position of legally protected privilege.[32]

More generally the declared objective of the invasion, at least within
England, was the defence not simply of the church but of protestantism.
In hindsight historians of seventeenth-century England have underesti-
mated the fragility of this, as of parliaments and monarchy. Neither Dutch
nor English pronouncements in 1688–9 leave us in any doubt that the survival of protestantism was one of the key matters considered to be at stake
in the military contest against France. Nor do Louis XIV's confessional
policies give us much reason to question this judgement. As in 1640,
therefore, there seems little reason to dispute the contemporary view that
upon the outcome of these events and the subsequent military conflict
may have depended the future not simply of English but European protestantism.

There is reason to believe, therefore, that in the restoration of English
parliaments, monarchy and church the Dutch invasion was a, and perhaps
the, decisive factor. Its efficacy in this respect was, however, greatly assisted
not only by English support but also by English experience in the attempted
realisation of these objectives.

RESTORATION PRACTICE

The principal stages of this restoration followed an established English
pattern. From the beginning restoration had, like the troubles, depended
upon external intervention. The first of these was Monck's invasion from
Scotland in 1659, followed by the importation of Charles II from the
Netherlands. The second was Louis XIV's rapprochement with Charles II in
January 1681. William's military occupation of London from December
1688 was, as we have seen, comparable to Monck's. Like Monck, William
made sure – amid some grumbling – to send remaining local troops out of
the city. During the remainder of the occupation he busied himself with
quasi-constitutional arrangements for the replacement of the existing
government.

---

32 *An Act for exempting their Majestyes Protestant Subjects dissenting from the Church of
England from the penalties of certain laws* (London 1689). See Horwitz, *Revolution Politicks*
(Cambridge 1968), pp. 87–94; John Morrill, 'The Sensible Revolution', in Israel, *Anglo-
Dutch Moment*, p. 96.

The most important instrument for this purpose was a Convention. The context for this, in 1689 as in 1660, was an interregnum that had been created by military means. The device of a Convention summoned during an interregnum to settle the realm in a religious or dynastic emergency had been contemplated by William Cecil over a century earlier.[33] Debate about the existence, cause and status of the interregnum greatly preoccupied both Conventions.[34] In general, however, contemporaries in 1689 showed a greater capacity than their less experienced mid-century predecessors to recognise and make use of facts on the ground. Thus when Sir Joseph Tredenham protested 'I cannot agree . . . we have no such thing in our Government as an interregnum' and was told, '[N]ow that the House has resolved that the Throne is vacant, no man can speak against the foundation of your Vote', he responded: 'I must acquiesce.'[35] Still more importantly the Convention of 1660 was a precedent, for good and ill, of which the members of the 1689 body were keenly aware. As in relation to the troubles, therefore, it was this context of repetition – of a sequence of attempts at restoration anchored in precedent – which established the basis for contemporary perceptions.

In addition there were longer-term English contexts for these events. The arrival of a prince with a weak hereditary claim to the throne vindicated by a strong army was anything but unprecedented in English history. At the Conference held between the Commons and the Lords to discuss what the former had declared to be the 'Vacancy of the Throne', this precedent was cited:

If your Lordships please to look into the Record in that case, there was first a Resignation of the Crown and Government made and subscribed by King Richard the Second, and this is brought into the Parliament, and there they take notice, that the *Sedes Regalis* (those are the words) *suit vacua*; and the Resignation being read both in *Latin* and *English* . . . it was accepted by the Lords and Commons.

To this it was responded (by the Earl of Clarendon) that Henry IV's hereditary claim was so poor that what followed was in fact an election, and not a

33 Collinson, 'Elizabethan Exclusion Crisis', 'Appendix: the Interregnum Scheme of 1584–1585', pp. 87–92.
34 See in particular *The Debate at Large between the Lords and Commons . . . Anno 1688 . . . Relating to the Word* ABDICATED, *and the Vacancy of the* THRONE (2nd edn, London 1705).   35 Grey, *Debates 1667–1694*, vol. IX, p. 50.

precedent to encourage emulation, since 'All the Kings that were thus taken in . . . scarce passed any one Year in any of their Reigns, without being disturbed in the Possession.'[36]

Alongside this method of determining the succession there was, as we have seen, a newer factor which had developed since the sixteenth century. This was the claim by parliament, and in particular the House of Commons, to the right to do so on confessional grounds. Originating in the use of parliament to attend to the dynastic needs of a prince (in 1529–33), and consistently denied by Elizabeth and the Stuarts from 1558 to 1688, this was over the same period an equally consistent feature of parliamentary self-understanding. It was claimed, and assumed, throughout the Elizabethan succession crises; it was arguably on display in practice in the reconstruction of the monarchy from 1660; it was reasserted with undiminished tenacity between 1678 and 1681. In 1688–9, however, in place of the earlier stout resistance of Charles II there was the military assistance for this claim of William of Orange. It was accordingly secured (and, more importantly, imposed upon the Lords) after a relatively brief debate. In the course of this the Earl of Nottingham put the concern:

Gentlemen, you of the Committee of the Commons, we differ from you indeed about the Words Abdicated and Deserted . . . upon the Account of the Consequence drawn in the Conclusion of your vote, *That the Throne is thereby Vacant*: that is, What the Commons mean by this Expression? Whether you mean it is so Vacant as to null the Succession in the Hereditary Line, and so all the Heirs to be cut off, which we say will make the Crown *Elective*?[37]

This implication was denied by Serjeant Maynard, who had earlier made the claim in the Commons, supported by Colonel Birch: 'In Queen Elizabeth's time, an Act passed: "That it was a crime, to maintain, that the Parliament could not dispose of the Crown in the Queen of Scots case".'[38]

His acceptance of the *de facto* government of the kingdom from December 1688 had given William control of the English army as well as of finance and administration. As we will see, this was a mixed blessing: where the New Model Army had been disbanded in 1660 James II's army disintegrated.[39] In the first months of 1689 English troops were sent to the Netherlands (and Ireland) and Dutch reinforcements brought to England

---

36 *Debate at Large*, pp. 39–40.   37 *Ibid.*, p. 13.   38 *Ibid.*, p. 58.
39 Childs, *British Army*, pp. 4–5.

so that by May Dutch troops in England outnumbered English by over 5,000.[40] This military context was, finally, crucially important in relation to the major constitutional instrument of restoration: the Convention itself. As Israel has pointed out:

Contemporary Jacobite and French critics contended that the Convention was in no sense a 'free parliament' because it convened at the bidding of a foreign prince who had already assumed control of the country's army, finances, and interim administration in a London occupied by a foreign army. No doubt one might object that such claims were biased and exaggerated; but one might also wonder whether the modern historian is being objective in ignoring these allegations.[41]

In relation to the pressure effectively applied to the House of Lords in particular these political and military circumstances were by no means unimportant. It seems indisputable more generally that without them the proceedings of the Convention, had they taken place at all, could hardly have come to such a decisive and speedy conclusion. In the words of the Earl of Nottingham: 'Gentlemen, I would not protract Time, which is now so necessary to be husbanded; noe perplex Debates about any Affair like that which now lies before us: It is not a Question barely about Words, but Things.'[42] Viewed against the background of previous parliamentary deliberations across the century, particularly in times of crisis, the most obvious sign of the Dutch military presence is surely the fact that from the meeting of the Convention to the offer of the crown was a period of little over three weeks. The most important 'Thing' limiting the efficacy of 'Words' by James' supporters was the militarily induced absence of the king himself. This was so despite the fact that 'a large part of the nation never regarded William as their legitimate monarch'.[43]

As several contemporaries noted, the prince's acceptance of the crown shocked many of his former Tory supporters, including Danby, and intensified the growing reaction against the revolution which was evident as early as February 1689. Radical Whig nobles such as Lord Mordaunt (said to have been the first English nobleman to have proposed to William that he should invade England) were similarly deeply alienated.[44] Nevertheless in the Convention the invasion supplied the instrument through which England's

40 Israel, 'Dutch Role', pp. 134, 146.   41 *Ibid.*, p. 130.
42 *Debate at Large*, p. 19.   43 Israel, 'Dutch Role', p. 132.
44 *Debate at Large*, p. 132.

political elite might once more attempt restoration. As in 1680–1 the wish of a whig-led majority in the Commons to exclude James – to privilege confessional over dynastic continuity – was to divide the elite and particularly the Commons from the Lords. What inspired agreement was the broader agenda of restoration: the securing of parliaments, the monarchy and church. In the words of Sir George Treby: 'Tis no less a Question then, whether we shall be governed by Popery and Arbitrary Government, or . . . be rid of both.'[45]

SECOND CONVENTION

This second attempt at a restoration settlement was a highly self-conscious one. Members of the Convention Commons showed themselves particularly mindful of the precedent set by the previous Convention. One occasion upon which this manifested itself was in the Grand Committee on the king's speech on 19–20 February 1689 which became a debate on the assembly's own constitutional status. One member hoped that the authority of a Convention would be sufficient to transact the king's business:

To prepare ourselves against any foreign Invasion, or intestine Troubles at home, there will be a necessity of raising Money, which must be done in a parliamentary way. And if we stay to call a new Parliament, it will be too late; therefore I move to turn this Convention into a Parliament.

The speaker went on to allege precedents for such a proceeding, including the fact that 'In the 12th of King Charles II, a Convention was called at that King's instance when beyond sea: 'Twas called by desire of the King, when at *Breda*, and after 'twas convened several Acts passed; some were confirmed by the subsequent Parliament, and some not; and those not confirmed were thought valid by the Judges.'[46] This was disputed, and there followed a long argument about the parliamentary status of a Convention, in relation both to medieval and restoration precedent. The following morning a message from the king arrived urging the House to come to the matter in hand, following which there was 'a long silence'. Then the argument resumed, beginning with Maynard's assertion that they need not doubt their legal status when in the face of the danger from France 'not only to the safety of the Nation, but the Protestant Religion abroad . . . *Salus*

---

45 Grey, *Debates 1667–1694*, vol. IX, p. 13.   46 *Ibid.*, pp. 84–5.

populi suprema lex esto . . . you are moved to make this Convention a Parliament; but I think we are one already. What is a Parliament, but King, Lords and Commons?'[47] This view was opposed by several members but supported, predictably, by Colonel Birch:

I have heard a Debate of this nature forty years ago, and I stand amazed at it: I will not bring the Precedents of *Edward II*, and *Henry IV*, to justify our proceedings, but what I remember of my Knowledge. I hope we shall not fall under this Debate now, and not forty years ago, when we were under much harder circumstances, when any little words dropt then, about the validity of that Parliament, they were smiled at, and not worth an answer . . . from the best of Precedents, that of 1660, you are a Parliament . . . [indeed] that of 1660 Parliament was not so clearly called as this. Cavaliers were excluded by those that had power to do it, and they did it.[48]

This suggestion provoked agreement from many members: 'I think we are a much better Parliament than that of 1660' (Sir Thomas Lee); 'your Elections were as free as ever . . . In the Parliament of 1660, there were Qualifications for the Members, and the Lords were not called by Writ, and (a greater thing) a Commonwealth called it, which was quite another Government' (Sir Richard Temple).[49] In due course it was resolved 'That the Lords Spiritual and Temporal, and the Commons, now sitting at Westminster, are a Parliament'.[50]

Another return to this precedent occurred a month later when the king offered that important restoration device of 'an Act of general Oblivion and Indemnity'. As in 1660 the Commons began to debate exceptions to this: 'If there be not some examples made . . . you will never want those to overturn your Government.' For the appropriate procedure the House was referred by Sir Henry Capel to the 'Precedent of the Convention . . . in that Parliament, were men of great understanding and worth, and you cannot do better than search those precedents out of the Journals'. There followed a debate about the general appropriateness of this model. 'We owe much of our misfortunes to that Convention; therefore I would not have that made a Precedent.' 'I am of opinion that was a happy Parliament. I remember the perplexity the Nation was in, and the settlement they made.'[51]

It was a consequence of recent events that most members were mindful of the shortcomings of previous attempts at settlement. In the words of Sir William Williams, Speaker of the parliaments of 1679–81, 'Because King

---

47 *Ibid.*, pp. 92–3.   48 *Ibid.*, pp. 101–2.   49 *Ibid.*, pp. 101, 104.
50 *Ibid.*, p. 106.   51 *Ibid.*, pp. 186–7.

Charles was called home by the Convention, and nothing settled, you found the consequence. Charles II was a young man, in the strength of his youth, and, you know, much Money Was given him, and what became of it?'[52] Mr Sacheverell agreed: 'In the great joy of the King's Return, the Parliament overshot themselves so much, and to redress a few Grievances they got so much Money, that they could live without you.'[53] Accordingly this settlement was achieved by learning from the earlier stages of the process. The restoration of parliament was secured, and the century-long struggle for parliaments won, by making annual parliaments financially indispensable. Monarchy was restored, and the prospect of future troubles greatly reduced, by the resolution 'That no Popish successor shall be capable to inherit the Crown of England, and no Papist capable of succeeding to the Crown'.[54] Restoration of the church was achieved without the destabilising reaction of the 1662–5 settlement. Here too Birch argued from experience, in favour of the limited toleration of protestant dissent:

let me remind you what ill success we have had with the Scots, (which put them in Rebellion) when Archbishop Laud would not have a hair bated of the Discipline of the Church . . . That brought on the War in England, and was mostly the cause of it. But what success have we had these twenty years, since the severe Act of Uniformity and prosecution of Dissenters? None but abatement of rents, and loss of trade.[55]

Even in relation to the necessary severity against popery Maynard was keen to stress that this need not entail the persecution of catholics. 'I would not imitate their Cruelty; I am far from it. I would let tham have their Religion in their private Houses, but no harbouring Priests and Jesuits.'[56]

RESTORATION AND WAR

These were early steps in a process of restoration that made other pragmatic adjustments. The institutional attempt to restore unity of political as of religious ideology was moderated or abandoned. Eventually ideological plurality became the new norm, under structured circumstances. In 1695 press licensing was allowed to lapse permanently, as it had been temporarily in 1679. Yet the biggest difference between this settlement and that in 1660–5 was a general one, determined by its context. In 1660–5 domestic

---

52 *Ibid.*, p. 30.   53 *Ibid.*, p. 33.   54 *Ibid.*, p. 72.   55 *Ibid.*, pp. 169, 195.
56 *Ibid.*, p. 169.

settlement and reconstruction was the end. In 1689–1701 it was the means to a greater and more urgent military end. In this, from the standpoint both of king and parliaments, lay the key to its pragmatism. During the 1690s there could be no actual security from popery and arbitrary government except through successful war with France.

Thus all the constitutional debates of the Convention were comparatively brief (the first parliament of 1679 had spent nine days debating the choice of its Speaker) because the urgent business was 'against that great Monster the French King, who invades the Hollanders'.[57] William had opened the Convention on 22 January by stating that the urgent priority was large-scale military assistance to the United Provinces; the point was repeated in his speech of February 18th.[58] Whatever hesitations there may have been at the financial implications of this demand were removed by James' landing in Ireland in April (war was declared against France in May). Indeed, as we will see, the single most remarkable feature of the politics of the 1690s in its English context was the ongoing scale of parliamentary funding for war.

The same pragmatism was evident from the king. This was seen most dramatically in the Triennial Act of late 1694. Against the background of the troubles this was a spectacular constitutional development: a monarch whose priorities were so overwhelmingly military that he was prepared reluctantly to trade his most important domestic prerogative for the where-withal to make war.[59] This was a reversal of Stuart strategy. In the European context its effect was to make both parliaments and crown more powerful. In domestic terms, however, it signalled an alteration of their relationship in favour of the former.

One historian indeed has discerned a 'relentless' campaign by parliamentarians of all political hues between 1691 and 1697 to 'subordinate the king and court to parliament':

This crucial transition in English history was powered by the extraction of resources from the English people on an unprecedented scale for continental war and the great wave of resentment and xenophobia which accompanied that process ... ultimately, what is perhaps most important about the dominance of 'Dutch counsels and Dutch measures of acting' in Britain in the years 1688–91 is that it achieved, as nothing else possibly could have done, the mobilizing of every English political strand and faction behind th[is] drive.[60]

---

57 *Ibid.*, p. 68.   58 Israel, 'Dutch Role', p. 132.
59 Henry Horwitz, *Parliament, Policy and Politics in the Reign of William III* (Manchester 1977).   60 Israel, 'Dutch Role', p. 160.

In fact as the history of the troubles has reminded us, there was an equally major English stake in this war. Had this not been the case then resources on such an astonishing scale could not have been extracted. But this process was indeed accompanied by a series of measures for the continued consolidation of parliaments and protestantism that culminated in the provisions of the Act of Settlement (1701). Thus the struggles against popery and arbitrary government outside and within the country proceeded simultaneously. The result was restoration by political as well as fiscal transformation.[61]

To the extent that success in this struggle hinged upon the military outcome, the settlement of 1689 marked its beginning, not its end. Its most important aspect would be Dutch-supervised reconstruction of English military capacity. Thus the principal determinant of the shape of the third restoration settlement was ultimately neither the initial invasion nor the Convention but the military process that they set in train. It was thus only at the end of a precarious and unprecedentedly expensive military struggle that restoration came to be secure. This struggle cost blood: in no respect is the myth of this 'peaceful revolution' more obviously exposed. Even in England, as we have seen, the initial invasion and its aftermath had not been entirely peaceful. In Scotland settlement was secured by a military process entailing many casualties and lasting almost a year; in Ireland tens of thousands were to be killed.[62] These in turn were early and local theatres in a much larger-scale military conflict intrinsic to the settlement. This continued with enormous loss of life until 1713.

In this sense the process of restoration in England was little more peaceful than the troubles. This is because it was the troubles transposed to the European theatre. Between 1689 and 1713 monarch and parliaments were finally united in the military struggle against popery and arbitrary government. English parliaments had, that is to say, found a monarch (and a succession) who would assist them in this struggle. This left a monarchical 'Pretender' helplessly outside the country, as it had in the 1650s.

The struggle for protestantism and parliaments had never been achievable in England alone. Now after a century of danger there came the opportunity to confront these menaces directly. Civil war subsided in England only in the context of successful war abroad. In the words of Linda Colley, 'A

---

61 Geoffrey Holmes, *The Making of a Great Power: Late Stuart and Early Georgian Britain 1660–1722* (London 1993), pp. 33–4; Hoak and Feingold, 'Introduction', pp. 6, 13; Horwitz, *Parliament*, pp. 281–3.   62 Glassey, 'Introduction', p. 6.

fundamental reason why Britain was not torn apart by civil war after 1688 was that its inhabitants' aggression was channelled so regularly and so remorselessly into war and imperial expansion abroad.'[63] This military process, by which the settlement was defended and the state transformed, is the subject of the final chapter.

It was the final effect of Dutch military intervention in England that the constitutional outcome of English statebuilding would be relatively unusual in European terms. There the modernisation of the unreformed polity did not occur at the expense either of representative assemblies or of monarchy. Instead it relied upon their co-operation, alongside that of other bodies like the government of the city of London. Above all it relied upon Dutch experience and priorities, and upon the peculiar circumstances pertaining to Anglo-Dutch alliance and government. In the words of Charles Davenant:

While our fears of France and Popery continue, the side that is for keeping the government within its ancient limits, will always have sufficient strength and credit . . . there seems the less reason to fear any breach upon our constitution, because it is as much the interest of the prince, as our own, to preserve it.[64]

63 Colley, *Britons*, p. 53.
64 Charles Davenant, *An Essay Upon Ways and Means* (1695), p. 77, quoted in Kustaa Multamaki, *Towards Great Britain: Commerce and Conquest in the Thought of Algernon Sidney and Charles Davenant* (Helsinki 1999), p. 160.

21

Anglo-Dutch statebuilding

[W]e took this war in hand to assert the liberties of Europe and, to encourage us to carry it on, we have examples, ancient and modern, of nations that have resisted great monarchies, and who have worked out their freedom by patience, wisdom and courage.

Charles Davenant, *An Essay Upon Ways and Means* (1695)[1]

CONTINUITY AND CHANGE

With the recovery of its international context the complexity of the 'glorious revolution' and its consequences is increasingly remarked upon. There is something revealing, in this respect, about the domination of recent publication on this subject by collections of essays. As the introduction to one has remarked, 'no new narrative' has yet emerged.[2]

This complexity follows not only from the internationality of these circumstances but from the resulting relationship between continuity and change. Between 1688 and 1714 the fortunes of the United Provinces, England, Scotland, Ireland, France, the Habsburg monarchy and Spain were more than ever dependent upon the outcome of the military struggle between them. Like the Thirty Years War in its time this committed resources on a scale unprecedented in European history. The result was to transform not only this European relationship but the internal political and economic landscape of England. This latter transformation was so rapid and spectacular that the word 'revolution' is now back in fashion to describe it. Indeed it has been argued that, 'revisionism' having cut all other seventeenth-century revolutions down to size, 'the financial revolution' survives

1 Davenant, *An Essay Upon Ways and Means*, in *Political and Commercial Works*, vol. I, p. 10.
2 Hoak and Feingold, *World of William and Mary*, 'Preface', pp. viii–ix.

pre-eminent.[3] By comparison, the revolutionary status of the events of 1688–9 themselves has become unclear. What is unquestionable is the profundity of the transformation, economic, political and fiscal, visited upon England by its participation in the European military process which those events, and that invasion, unleashed.

In England, as earlier in the Netherlands, military necessity provided the cutting edge for change. It is for this reason that some historians have argued that

the true revolution of the seventeenth century occurred neither in the 1640s . . . nor in the 1650s . . . but in the 1690s. This revolution marked the origins of the modern British state – the financial, military, and bureaucratic product of England's costly and incessant warfare against Louis XIV. The centrepiece of this settlement was the founding of the Bank of England.[4]

Nevertheless the question of what was actually 'revolutionary' about these developments is not one currently being addressed with a great deal of conceptual clarity. Geoffrey Holmes saw this as the outcome of

a revolution whose rationale had been to *preserve* everything that, by general consent was best in the restored constitution of 1660 and whose supporters saw James . . . as the dangerous innovator . . . the tiny republican fringe . . . [never attempted any serious challenge] to the central constitutional dogma of 1660 – that the government of England 'is and ought to be by King, Lords and Commons'.[5]

This 'revolution' achieved its objectives by 'steady and organic' rather than radical change. While incorporating vital adaptation and modernisation, Holmes' 'revolution' in fact appears to have been the successful restoration at last.[6]

This was by no means unprecedented in European history. A century earlier the Dutch revolt, in defence of similar conservative religious and political objectives, had unleashed a process of innovative statebuilding with no less far-reaching consequences.[7] It is a key argument of this chapter

3 David Armitage, 'The Projecting Age: William Paterson and the Bank of England', *History Today*, June 1994, p. 5.   4 Hoak and Feingold, 'Introduction', p. 10.

5 Holmes, *Making of a Great Power*, pp. 220–1.

6 John Pocock has spoken of 'three revolutions' of these years, corresponding approximately to this study's three processes: Pocock, 'Standing Army and Public Credit', pp. 87–8.

7 J. H. Shennan, *The Origins of the Modern European State 1450–1725* (London 1974), pp. 83–4.

that the English process benefited directly from this Dutch experience. Meanwhile the ultimate success of English statebuilding, and with it of restoration, does not mean that either the troubles or the real revolution ended in 1689. Restoration history is the struggle between these three processes. Yet it was between 1689 and 1720 that the outcome of this struggle was decided. Our focus here is upon four early aspects of this situation. The first, after the externalisation of popery and arbitrary government, was the military mobilisation against it. From this there followed the completion of institutional restoration internally as well as militarily; the development of new structures for the containment of the internal ideological legacy of the troubles; and the wider development of the modern structures of the military-fiscal state. The eventual result was the English acquisition of relative mastery of its European situation. If these developments owed much to their international, and particularly Anglo-Dutch context, they owed as much to the investment of the present with the experience, and perspectives, of England's troubles.

Characteristically, modern historical analysis of the 1690s has been preoccupied by the question of change. 'What changes were occurring?', historians have asked, and 'were they the consequence of the "revolution" or of the subsequent war'? Contemporaries became, in this decade, more than usually aware themselves of the fact of change. As Charles Davenant put it: 'We shall hardly be permitted to live in the way our ancestors did, though inclined to.'[8] However, the context for contemporary perceptions was not the future but the past. From this point of view the key question was a different one. To what extent did the 'revolution' and its military consequences attend to the anxieties behind the troubles, thus achieving restoration?

ANGLO-SAXON ATTITUDES

Among other changes in the 1690s historians have posited a change in contemporary attitudes. How else are we explain the single most important transformation of the decade: parliament's willingness and capacity to fund war on an unprecedented scale? It is indeed the most striking feature of the parliamentary history of the decade: the persistent support for a continen-

---

8 Quoted in Istvan Hont, 'Free Trade and the Economic Limits to National Politics: Neo-Machiavellian Political Economy Reconsidered', in John Dunn (ed.), *The Economic Limits to Modern Politics* (Cambridge 1990), p. 67.

tal land-based military strategy, despite its unpopularity and its indifferent success; the annual votes of several million pounds almost regardless of recent success or failure. As Burnet remarked in May 1690: 'I was never more surprised in my whole life than I am to see the House of Commons in such a temper. All that I know say plainly, they dare not go back into their country if they do not give money liberally.'[9]

Historians have spoken in this context of the modification of previously insular English political attitudes under the pressure of war and the government of a foreign king.[10] Geoffrey Holmes has spoken of a 'revolution in English attitudes to Europe'. This was provoked not only by new political and military but also cultural circumstances. These included the news and print culture freed from restraint after the expiry of the licensing act in 1695, and 'a degree of political education which had simply not existed for most of the seventeenth century':

Events abroad, which for much of the seventeenth century had never evoked more than a spasmodic response from English governments, and rarely an effective one had, well before 1714, become for informed Britons a regular source of interest and concern.

The result was that by the beginning of the eighteenth century

a substantial body of English opinion, much of it concentrated in the Whig party, had at length come to accept the 'Williamist' view of the kingdom's destiny . . . the outward-looking view that the only real safety for the English nation and for her Protestant religion lay not in disengagement from the continent but in her involvement.[11]

Yet, as we have seen, the view that this attitude itself was either new or Williamite has no basis in seventeenth-century history. It was precisely the effect of European events on English 'passions' that established the context for the first episode of the troubles between 1618 and 1648. The accompanying opinion that the only real safety for protestantism and the kingdom lay in military engagement in Europe, alongside the United Provinces, was over a century old. It had resulted in military intervention against Spain and

---

9 Quoted in Horwitz, *Parliament*, pp. 62–3.
10 This is one theme of Stephen Baxter's still indispensable *William III*. See also Horwitz, *Parliament*, p. 20; J. R. Jones (ed.), *Liberty Secured? Britain Before and After 1688* (Stanford 1992), 'Introduction'; Holmes, *Making of a Great Power*, pp. 245–6.
11 Holmes, *Making of a Great Power*, pp. 245–6.

the Habsburgs in the 1580s and 1620s. The resulting public hunger for European news is one of the most consistent features of English history from 1620. The resulting combination of confessional military struggle, widely informed public opinion and anxiety, and the resulting rapid development of print culture had been of the essence of the seventeenth-century experience.

The same confessional anxieties, redirected against France, had driven the parliamentary politics of 1670–81, before being reignited between 1688 and 1714. It was the objective of the Dutch invasion, requiring the summoning of a 'free' parliament, to unleash that demonstrated animosity against France. Accordingly, the unanimous resolution of the Commons, on 27 February 1689, to 'stand by and assist the King with their lives and fortunes, in supporting his alliances abroad, in reducing of Ireland, and in defence of the Protestant religion, and laws of the Kingdom'[12] was not the result of a 'Williamite' transformation. This parliamentary perspective was not a consequence of William's invasion, but one of its causes. It was crucial, in London and the Commons, to the speed and completeness of the expedition's initial success.

Most importantly it was the same perspective that underwrote the achievement of the government's longer-term military objectives. That is why it was to this confessional perception that all the court's own military propaganda for domestic consumption was directed between 1689 and 1697.[13] This set the present military struggle within the context of the English parliamentary struggle for the defence of English and European protestantism since the 1550s. In his study of this campaign Tony Claydon has remarked upon 'the relative neglect of "balance of power" and commercial rhetorics to sell the war'. The focus was squarely upon that 'general interest of the Reformed Church and Religion' which had been the focus of parliamentary concern since the 1580s.[14] As Sir Charles Sedley put it in December 1693, echoing countless Elizabethan and Stuart ancestors: in the war 'to defend us from France and popery . . . If Holland be destroyed it is our turn next.'[15]

It was thus not the parliamentary anxiety for military action against the European popish menace that was new. What was new was a monarch whose own priority was to give this practical expression. It was this which

---

12 Quoted in Horwitz, *Parliament*, p. 27.   13 Claydon, *William III*.
14 Quoted *ibid.*, pp. 136–41, 146.   15 *Ibid.*, pp. 125–9.

unlocked the door to political and military transformation. This could not, on its own, have been enough. In the words of Davenant: 'whenever this war cease, it will not be for want of mutual hatred in the opposite parties, nor for want of men to fight the quarrel, but that side must first give out where money is first failing'.[16] Yet as the national debt attested, during the early 1690s parliamentary military supply greatly exceeded actual income available. It is therefore impossible to understand the scale of parliamentary commitment to the Nine Years War without understanding it as an ideological war drawing upon a century of English anxiety. The precedent for this, of course, lay in the 1640s, a period that had set in train its own process of fiscal innovation.

Thus, ironically, it was partly this thing that had not changed – public belief – which provided the ideological context for administrative and fiscal transformation. It was when the anxieties informing the troubles became effectively militarily directed outside the country that the potential for restoration as statebuilding emerged. To this context sheer military necessity was crucial. The early 1690s were not, however, the first time an English parliament had faced the appearance of an imminent popish invasion. In the 1580s, 1620s and 1670s, it had been lucky. In the 1640s and early 1650s it had secured itself by military force. It was in the 1690s, however, that there emerged for the first time the political context within which this security could be made permanent.

The first necessity, in 1689, if these English perspectives were to be given military expression, was military reconstruction. 'Instead of finding a country ready to engage in a major foreign war, William was faced with political confusion, divided loyalties and a military muddle. The army required reorganisation from top to bottom.' The shattered remnants of the English army were militarily useless, or worse. Their commanders were divided in their political loyalties. The state and discipline of the rank and file was 'deplorable'. There was a dire lack of experience and competence at every level. We are reminded irresistibly of the Mansfeldt fiasco of 1624–5 when nearly half the English troops sent to Ireland in 1689 died because, unlike their Dutch and Huguenot counterparts, their commanders failed to take elementary health measures.[17] The recovery of Ireland, like the outcome of this war more generally, was to be crucially dependent upon the

16 Davenant, *Ways and Means*, in *Political and Commercial Works*, vol. I, pp. 15, 19.
17 Stephen Baxter, *William III*, pp. 281, 285; Childs, *British Army*, pp. 8–9.

military experience of the allies and the personal leadership and experience of William. When English commanders like Marlborough demanded posts for which they were still inadequately qualified, complaining about the seniority over them of 'foreigners' like Solms, Leinster, Schomberg jnr and Ginckel, William refused. In this European war, he appointed men according to experience, not national origin.[18]

It is small wonder that William, like his commander Schomberg, took a dim view of the treasonous English military rabble. He 'initially trusted no one who was not Dutch or demonstrably not English'. Having sent what English troops there were out of London, to be replaced by Dutch and German guards, another early transfer was that of 3,000 English with 6,000 Dutch troops to the Netherlands, leaving 3,000 Dutch behind.[19] By May 1689 there were 10,000 English troops in the Netherlands receiving arduous on-the-job training among the Dutch infantry, the best (and best-disciplined) in Europe at this time. Meanwhile the king was careful to appoint Dutchmen 'not only to the highest commands' in the English army 'but also as provost marshals and ordnance officials'. There was little material military infrastructure left in England: no transport trains, few arms. In the words of a correspondent of John Locke, the new English regiments of 1689 'wanted nothing to be complete but clothes, boots, arms, horses, men and officers'.[20] Rearmament of the English army took place from Holland; a Dutchman was appointed controller-general of the artillery; supply was delegated to Dutch contractors; when the English secretaries at war proved incompetent, William took over personally.[21]

Thus the first contribution of the new Anglo-Dutch government to the deferred process of English statebuilding was the construction of a functional English army. This was a prolonged process, drawing upon experience, blood and treasure. That its eventual result would be one of the finest armies in Europe became clear first in 1696, and more decisively in 1702–14. Here, as elsewhere, restoration hinged upon the construction, or reconstruction, of effective public or administrative structures in relation to the practical problems at hand. Properly directed, these had the capacity to lay English religious and political fears to rest. In the words of the House of Commons on 1 February 1689, so reminiscent of those of the 1640s:

18 Stephen Baxter, *William III*, pp. 298–9.   19 Childs, *British Army*, p. 19.
20 *Ibid.*, p. 29; Stephen Baxter, *William III*, p. 285.   21 Stephen Baxter, *William III*, p. 285.

the thanks of this House be given to the officers, soldiers and marines in the army and the fleet for having testified their steady adherence to the protestant religion and been instrumental in delivering their kingdom from popery and slavery; and also to all such who have appeared in arms for that purpose.[22]

The wars of these years were therefore the last phase of the troubles. The struggle against popery and arbitrary government had always been a military one and here as earlier it was force of arms that would determine its outcome. By 1713 the destabilising consequences of the military weakness of the 1620s had finally been overcome.

NEW PARLIAMENTS, NEW PRINCE

In 1625 the House of Commons had also supported war in theory, while failing to do so in practice. What had changed? The most important answer is the gradual removal of parliament's internal religious and political fears. The crucial problem in 1625 had been not parliamentary poverty, but disobedience. In the 1690s this changed.

The first parliament of Charles I's reign had opened in the shadow of military failure. The Nine Years War, though conducted with vastly greater professionalism, was also hard, and casualties heavy, and still it attracted parliamentary financial support.[23] This may say something about the extent of perceived military necessity: the danger of a French invasion. It may reflect the experience of 1642–53, when elements of the Commons had learned how to run a war successfully. These factors could not, however, have transformed the political situation in practice, had the Commons continued to fear, as they did in 1625–9, for both their religion and their 'liberties'. As a loyalist MP said in March 1690 in favour of granting the king a permanent revenue: 'If we had a Popish King, I should be more careful than under the King I am . . . In King Charles I's time, the not settling the Revenue upon him for Life drew on us all the mischiefs which followed.'[24]

22 Quoted in Childs, *British Army*, p. 19.
23 The single most striking example was probably the voting of £4,017,000, only £188,000 less than requested, in November 1692 following the heavy casualties at Steenkirk and the loss of Namur; see Horwitz, *Parliament*, ch. 5, esp. p. 106. Other aspects of the Commons' responses, such as the motion that the Admiralty be entrusted to 'such persons as have known experience in maritime affairs and that all orders to the fleet may pass through the said Commissioners' (*ibid.*), will ring a bell with any historian of the 1620s.
24 Grey, *Debates 1667–1694*, vol. X, p. 16.

Members did not, in the 1690s, as they did from 1625, have to fear for threats to protestantism and parliaments from the court itself. In addition to having delivered them from this immediate danger, and their own impeccable religious credentials, William and Mary had consented to the future confessional binding of the crown. The securing of parliaments, which was the single most important political precondition for adequate military supply, was both a longer and tenser process. The objective was achieved, firstly, by resisting the continuing pressure from the court to provide a permanent royal revenue. This resistance was maintained with full historical consciousness of its significance. 'You have an infallible security for the administration of government', explained William Harbord, 'all the revenue is in your hands, which fell with the last King, and you may keep that back.' 'We have had such violation of our Liberties in the last reigns', agreed William Garraway, 'that the Prince of Orange cannot take it ill, if we make conditions, to secure ourselves for the future.'[25] In fact the king did take it very ill. Yet by necessitating annual parliamentary sessions this did more than any other single thing to redirect the anxieties behind the troubles from political dysfunction to military function.

The second important step in this direction was the Triennial Act. Once again this was resisted by the court, the first such bill being refused in March 1693, with William 'in some anger answer[ing] that he would never pass it'. This disappointment contributed to the Commons' protest the following January

how few the instances have been, in former reigns, of denying the royal assent to bills for redress of grievances, and the great grief of the Commons for his having given the royal assent to several public bills . . . *after their having so freely voted to supply the public occasions.*[26]

By December, with an upturn in English military fortunes and a further astonishing supply of £4,883,000 secured for the coming season, the bill received the royal assent.[27] In the 1620s, as we have seen, its religious and political anxieties had led the Commons to trespass upon royal prerogatives in both 1621 and 1625–9. The reaction of both kings had been to give priority to the defence of those prerogatives: to the defence of the substance of kingship in England. Ultimately that had meant abandonment of the European military effort, though Charles had initially taken the defence of

25 Both quoted in Brewer, *Sinews of Power*, p. 143.
26 Quoted in Horwitz, *Parliament*, pp. 118, 121 (my emphasis).   27 *Ibid.*, pp. 134–8.

his prerogatives to be essential, rather than alternative, to the prosecution of war.

William III was not less tenacious of the substance of kingship. Though 'some wished to make him', he reiterated in March 1690, 'a Doge of Venice, he would, since he had been called to the throne by God, maintain the authority reposed in him . . . he would not be dealt with as Charles II'.[28] William had, however, a different sense of what the substance of kingship was. Unlike the Stuarts he had not, after all, been 'called to the throne' by heredity but by military force. He was in Machiavelli's terms a new prince, who had secured a principality 'by his own arms . . . his own personal courage and talents'.[29] If Charles II was the symbol in his mind of political impotence, it was above all because of that *military* ineffectuality which William had observed in disgust throughout the 1670s. By this Charles had accepted political obedience to France rather than submit to parliamentary determination of his own foreign policy. If the Stuart monarchy was militarily useless, as the seventeenth-century record seemed to suggest, its substance would not be enhanced by sacrificing everything to the defence of internal prerogatives.

William would guard, first and foremost, against the re-establishment of an English republic. Thereafter he 'cared very much less for the preservation of the prerogative than his uncles . . . what he wanted was the real exercise of power . . . no English [foreign policy was] worth anything without parliamentary confirmation'.[30] For Charles I war, the sport of princes, was essential to monarchical power. For William monarchical power was essential to war. Accordingly the constitutional changes of 1689–1701, while securing parliaments, also recovered, after a century of disaster, the military substance of English monarchy. This parliamentary monarchy was the centrepiece of the newly constructed English state.

It was thus in the context of this military struggle that there occurred all those constitutional alterations which amounted to the creation of a strong parliamentary monarchy. In addition to the new financial settlement, these included the *Declaration of Rights* (taking the *Petition of Right* as its precedent); the regulation by statute of the succession; and the surrender of the sole monarchical government of parliament's being. They included the new

28 Quoted *ibid.*, p. 42.
29 Machiavelli, *The Prince*, in Machiavelli, *The History of Florence, and of the Affairs of Italy . . . together with The Prince* (London 1847), ch. 1: 'Of the different kinds of principalities, and the means by which they are acquired'.   30 Stephen Baxter, *William III*, p. 167.

coronation oath in which the monarch undertook to govern not only 'for the maintaining of the Protestant religion and the laws and liberties of this nation', but 'according to the statutes in Parliament agreed on, and the laws and customs of the same'.[31] They included parliamentary control of the army, demonstrated to William's disgust in 1698;[32] and the Act of Succession of 1701, which removed the power of royal pardon in relationship to parliamentary impeachments, and subjected aspects of foreign policy, the king's dispensation of patronage, his relationship with his Privy Council and the whereabouts of his person to parliamentary approval.[33]

The background to all these measures in the experience of the troubles requires no emphasis. Their effect was, said John Somers, to settle in security after a century of strife that government first described by Fortescue as 'legal, not arbitrary, and political, not absolute'.[34] In fact it achieved that security, external as well as internal, by drawing upon hard-won experience to subject that constitution to systematic modern reform. It is time to turn now from the political to the fiscal and administrative elements of that reform which resulted in the attainment, between 1688 and 1714, of what John Brewer has called 'all the acquirements of a powerful fiscal-military state': high taxes, a growing and well-organised civil administration, a greatly increased military establishment and all other features becoming a European great power.[35]

ANGLO-DUTCH STATEBUILDING

It was these broader developments that have rightly been seen as both the most striking in themselves, and the most significant in terms of their longer-term effects. They included an increase in annual English military expenditure from £169,335 in 1688–9, to £788,420 in 1692, to £1,174,717 in 1696, to £2,546,358 in 1711.[36] They included the enormous expansion of those executive departments of state concerned with war (the Admiralty, the War Office and the Treasury, including the Exchequer,

---

31 Holmes, *Making of a Great Power*, p. 216; J. R. Jones, *Liberty Secured?*, p. 30.

32 *Ibid.*, pp. 33–4; Hoak and Feingold, 'Introduction', pp. 6, 13.

33 Horwitz, *Parliament*, pp. 281–3.   34 J. R. Jones, *Liberty Secured?*, p. 35.

35 Brewer, *Sinews of Power*, p. 140.

36 D. W. Jones, 'Defending the Revolution: The Economics, Logistics and Finance of England's War Effort 1688–1712', in Hoak and Feingold, *William and Mary*, p. 65; see also Brewer, *Sinews of Power*, fig. 4.2.

Customs, and Excise). By the early eighteenth century these, to say nothing of the industries and subdepartments to which they gave rise (by 1714 the British Navy, the largest in Europe, employed more workers than any other industry in the country), dwarfed the court.[37] By 1711 England was paying for 171,000 troops (58,000 subject and 113,750 foreign). In the longer term the annual tax revenues of the state increased from about £2 million in 1690 to just under £20 million in 1790.[38] The consequences included European great-power status, the massive development of England's fiscal structures and its global trading economy, and (in 1707) the transformation of the English into a British state.[39] As every visitation of the troubles had involved all three Stuart kingdoms, so to secure itself restoration had to become not simply Anglo-Dutch but British.

Historians examining these developments have rightly been concerned to answer two questions. Were they really so sudden; that is to say, what was their pre-history? Secondly, how much did they owe to the European and specifically Dutch example? The answer to the first of these questions has already been touched upon in chapter 17. Their principal practical pre-history within England belongs both to the periods 1642–59 and 1660–88.[40] During the first, under similar pressure of war, there were innovations both in taxation and in fiscal administration which were to become important in the 1690s. After the restoration, which did nothing to arrest the transition from a demesne to a tax state, there were further developments in both areas.[41] These early measures were themselves indebted to Dutch example. The United Provinces, where excise was the main tax, was the model for its introduction to England by Pym in 1643. Downing, moderniser of the Treasury and described by Pepys as 'an inventor of taxes', was as we have seen a shrewd and envious student of Dutch success.[42] 'Downing's lasting contribution', concluded Charles Wilson, 'was that he brought to bear his observation of Dutch economic practice on English economic theory and policy.'[43]

37 Plumb, *Stability*, ch. 4, esp. p. 119.   38 Brewer, *Sinews of Power*, p. 90.

39 Colley, *Britons*.

40 For aspects of their longer-term intellectual pre-history, see Multamaki, *Towards Great Britain*.

41 Braddick, *Parliamentary Taxation*, pp. 1–13; Bonney, *European Dynastic States*, p. 352.

42 'T Hart, '"The Devil or the Dutch"', pp. 43–4; Pepys, *Diary*, vol. VIII, p. 30; Roseveare, *Treasury 1660–1870*, pp. 23–5.   43 Wilson, *Profit and Power*, pp. 94–103.

Important though it was, this pre-history of the military-fiscal state does not detract from either the speed or scale of the transformation from 1689. The engine of this was of course the war. The key to the resulting 'financial revolution' was not just the adaptation and enormous extension of existing modes of taxation, in particular customs, excise and the land tax. It was the development of a new system of deficit financing, which grew into the national debt. This depended crucially not simply upon sound credit backed by parliamentary finance and its integration with the London stock market, but also upon new financial institutions, most importantly the Bank of England (1694). From this followed, in due course, other banks, an insurance sector and an entire infrastructure of credit crucial to the increasingly interdependent conduct both of war and trade.[44]

That the Bank of England drew upon Dutch example (the Bank of Amsterdam, 'the great Sinews of Trade') is not in doubt. It also drew crucially upon Dutch finance. When Downing had argued for 'the Establishment of [a] Bank' on the Dutch model in 1665 he was attacked by Clarendon for attempting to introduce republican fiscal institutions incompatible with a monarchy.[45] When the proposal for the Bank of England was debated in the Lords in January 1694, this same objection was raised, among others ('that it would undermine royal authority for banks were only fit for republics').[46] Yet the measure passed, not only because the king supported it, but because to prolong an argument with the Commons about it would delay supply for the war.

It was not simply the case, therefore, that during the 1690s taxation was unprecedentedly heavy in English terms. The core of the fiscal and military achievement of the 1690s was the development of a system of public credit which 'enabled England to spend on war out of all proportion to its tax revenue'.[47] The new relationship between loans and taxes worked as a whole on a Dutch model in that it 'used a public bank to handle the loans, based the debt on long-term redeemable annuities, and spread the debt amongst a substantial number of borrowers'.[48] In 1985 James Tracy argued that this development had first occurred in the Habsburg Netherlands in the middle of the sixteenth century before later being transferred to England in the

44 Dickson, *Financial Revolution*, pp. 5–7.
45 John Beresford, *The Godfather of Downing Street* (London 1925), pp. 210–11.
46 Quoted in Horwitz, *Parliament*, p. 131.   47 Dickson, *Financial Revolution*, p. 9.
48 Brewer, *Sinews of Power*, p. 133.

context of Anglo-Dutch partnership in the 1690s.[49] Recent scholars have gone on to make the (perhaps obvious) point that all such borrowings entailed adaptation, so that the British result was also the unique outcome of local circumstances.[50] In the summary of John Brewer, although precise links between the English financial revolution and the Dutch system with its origins in the sixteenth-century Habsburg Netherlands have not been securely established,

the similarities are so great, the obsession of English ministers with Dutch methods so well known, and the arrival of William III with his Dutch advisers so timely, that it is hard to believe that contemporaries were wrong when they described the new fiscal arrangements as 'Dutch finance'.[51]

Crucial was the participation, alongside parliaments, of London. Like parliaments, the city was just as important to the ending of the troubles, by means of successful statebuilding, as it had been to their progress. Essential to this were not only its fiscal resources and expertise but also its position at the heart of a rapidly developing global trading economy. In relation to trade, as to taxes, steady development had been occurring throughout the century, and particularly since 1660. The international status of England as a mercantile economy was, however, transformed between 1689 and 1720. In 1690 the Netherlands remained the dominant global trading economy; by 1720 that supremacy had passed to Britain. As contemporaries rapidly recognised, military capacity itself became crucially dependent upon trade. 'Trade is now becoming', wrote Andrew Fletcher of Saltoun, 'the golden ball, for which all nations of the world are contending, and the occasion of so great partialities, that not only every nation is endeavouring to possess the trade of the whole world, but every city to draw all to itself.'[52] In the words of William Paterson, founder of the Bank of England: 'the Wars of these times are rather to be Waged with gold than with Iron'.[53] It was fortunate that this was not entirely the case, since the short-term impact of the Nine Years War upon trade in England and Scotland was disastrous, resulting in a collapse of the money supply and (for one season, in 1695–6) of allied military activity. This was, however, part of a steep military-fiscal learning curve. In the longer term, more experienced war management,

---

49 James Tracy, *A Financial Revolution in the Habsburg Netherlands* (Cambridge 1985).
50 'T Hart, '"The Devil or the Dutch"', conclusion.   51 Brewer, *Sinews of Power*, p. 133.
52 Quoted in Hont, 'Free Trade', p. 41.
53 Quoted in Armitage, 'The Projecting Age', p. 7; Roseveare, *Financial Revolution*, p. 1.

combined with buoyant mercantile activity, particularly the India trade, was crucial to British success in the more decisive contest of 1701–13.[54]

The 'financial revolution' has accordingly rightly been described as a system of public credit whereby trading wealth could underwrite government security and military expenditure.[55] To the English economic developments underlying these military achievements – and they included the rapid growth of manufacturing as well as trade – direct Dutch participation was crucial. From 1689 the migration of Dutch financiers to London had enabled it to develop an Amsterdam-style stock market. By 1723–4 total foreign, mainly Dutch holdings of stock in the Bank of England, the East India Company and the South Sea Company were 9.2 per cent; by 1750 it was 19.2 per cent. This has led one recent historian to conclude that the eclipse of the Netherlands by Britain as a manufacturing and trading power during the early eighteenth century was 'in considerable part financed by the Dutch themselves'.[56] More important than direct investment, however, was Dutch expertise: this was the period when 'England's apprenticeship' bore rapid fruit.

Throughout the restoration period English observers of the United Provinces like Bethel and Sidney had been making the point that, given how 'rich powerful and prosperous' that country had become by 'good government and liberty of traffick . . . England, if so governed may promise itself incomparibly more; abounding in all they want; and being free from all the inconveniencies they suffer'd or fear'd, apprehending no opposition but that of ye Stuart family'.[57] If the government of the country remained monarchical from the 1690s, and would not therefore have satisfied Sidney, it was also parliamentary. It was not the government of 'ye Stuart family' as that had been. In the words of William Penn: "tis the great interest of a Prince, that the People should have a share in the making of their own Laws . . . [because] it makes Men Diligent, and increaseth Trade, which advances the Revenue: for where Men are not Free, they will never seek to improve, because they are not sure of what they have, and less of what they get'.[58]

54 D. W. Jones, 'Defending the Revolution', pp. 61, 66–7, 71; D. W. Jones, *War and Economy in the Age of William III and Marlborough* (London 1988).
55 'T Hart, '"The Devil or the Dutch"', p. 40.
56 Peter Spufford, 'Access to Credit and Capital in the Commercial Centres of Europe', in Davids and Lucassen, *Miracle Mirrored*, p. 328.
57 Sidney, *Court Maxims*, p. 162; Scott, *English Republic*, p. 205.
58 Penn, *England's Present Interest Considered*, in *Works*, vol. I, pp. 678–9.

Charles Davenant, having explained that 'trade, as it is now become the strength of the kingdom . . . so it is the living fountain from whence we draw all our nourishment', argued:

nothing can more contribute to the rendering England populous and strong, than to have liberty upon a right foot, and our legal constitution firmly preserved . . . great monarchies do easily overrun and swallow up the lesser tyrannies and principalities . . . but they find much harder work, and another sort of opposition, when they come to invade commonwealths, or mixed governments, where people have an interest in the laws.[59]

This last point had been a central one in Sidney's *Discourses*, first published, and widely read, by Davenant among others, in 1698.

Both England and the United Provinces had emerged victorious from their troubles, their protestantism and representative assemblies intact. Both had, in the process, become fiscal, mercantile and military great powers. In the 1580s the United Provinces had received limited but important assistance from England. In the 1690s Dutch intervention and subsequent involvement in the opposite direction had been more important. These fiscal developments could have occurred only during the 1690s, alongside certain political as well as military developments. In the context of European statebuilding it is certainly no coincidence that Britain became the only major eighteenth-century power 'apart from the Dutch Republic . . . in which the strength and funding of the army and navy were determined by "the estates"'.[60]

Yet, as we have seen, these constitutional developments were equally the direct result of English experience. We should accordingly see the 'Anglo-Dutch decade' not simply as bringing Dutch experience to England, but also as helping to give structural form to English experience and perspectives which were specifically protestant and parliamentary. It is certainly the case, however, that in so far as English statebuilding had a European fiscal and political model, that model was Dutch.[61]

The broadest context in which the developments we have been discussing have so far been placed is neither English nor Anglo-Dutch. It relates the experiences of both countries to their position within an 'entire trade-route

---

59 Davenant, *Essay Upon the Probable Means*, in *Political and Commercial Works*, vol. II, pp. 185–6; Davenant, *Ways and Means*, in *Political and Commercial Works*, pp. 4–5.
60 Brewer, *Sinews of Power*, p. 43.
61 *Ibid.*, pp. 43, 133; Speck, 'Britain and the Dutch Republic'.

belt stretching from Northern Italy to the British Isles'. This coincided with a 'blue banana' of European urbanisation.[62] Such an analysis has the virtue of uncovering not only certain important features of supra-national historical geography. By showing England's participation in a long-term westward movement of wealth and power within this crescent, it also reminds us of a further important feature of the relevant historical context.

The relative speed of English statebuilding, of Britain's subsequent rise to great power status, may owe a good deal to its lateness in European terms. Accordingly, it benefited not only from the experience of its own earlier failures and deferral but from Dutch experience as well.[63] One historian has spoken of the 'half-truth' that the transformation of public structures in the 1690s was the consequence of the arrival of 'Dutch William, with Dutch banking, Dutch stock-jobbing, Dutch taxes' and all the other paraphernalia of 'Dutch finance'.[64] Students of the history of England's troubles are in the best position to understand the ways in which the national experience was crucial to the eventual outcome.

PARTY

Restoration in England was, first and foremost, the (re-)establishment of public institutional structures. Their purpose was not only the efficient conduct of business – political, mercantile or financial – but the recontainment of public belief. Some attention has already been given to the adaptation of religious and political institutions in a way that helped to redirect belief from the destabilisation to the service of the state. There is one further development in this area that remains to be mentioned.

For while the spectres behind the troubles were being confronted militarily, their ideological legacy remained potent at home. That ideological polarisation which was the first manifestation of the troubles did not simply fade away. The structures which were developed for this purpose were of course those of party. In this most crucial area the ideological legacy of the civil wars was not buried but eventually recognised and effectively contained.

The institutionalisation of ideological division was, in contemporary terms, not a victory but a defeat. Few involved accepted party as a system,

---

62 Davids and Lucassen, 'Conclusion', in Davids and Lucassen, *Miracle Mirrored*, pp. 453–4. It is not clear whether the term 'blue banana' will catch on.
63 Speck, 'Britain and the Dutch Republic', p. 183.   64 Roseveare, *Financial Revolution*, p. 3.

for to do so would have involved the abandonment of the fundamental restoration objective of unity. Parties were, in the formulation of Jean Bodin, 'dangerous and pernicious in every sort of Commonweal'.[65] They were manifestations of 'faction', one part of that 'Rebellion and Faction' which it was the purpose of monarchical restoration to heal. The 'first age of party' was accordingly punctuated, from every side, by self-denunciation, particularly in relation to the perceived need for protestant and national unity in time of war. The accusation of being a 'factious party' and of 'perpetually raising factions in the state' became the standard on both sides.[66] Like so much else about the period this was also reminiscent of the rhetoric that had accompanied the previous military struggles of the 1620s as well as the 1640s. In the former the increasingly obvious disunity at home had been lamented as a victory for the popish enemy.[67] During the 1640s contemporaries had similarly denounced name-calling and division while participating in it at the same time.[68]

What historians have called 'the rage of party' developed most particularly within the period between the passage of the Triennial Act (December 1694) and its replacement by the Septennial Act (1716).[69] It coincided, that is to say, with the regular elections which were the single most important factor in the establishment, by 1708–17, of something close to a two-party system. Other factors included the lapse of the Licensing Act, and the permanent establishment of parliament as the focal point of national political life. Most important, as we have seen, alongside the increasing security of protestantism and parliamentary monarchy at home, was the effective confrontation of popery and arbitrary government abroad. A pamphleteer in early 1642 had wished in vain 'That inke, rather then Bloud may be spilt; that Paper rather than Soules may perish'.[70] In the period 1689–1714 blood was still being spilled, but outside England.

This is not to deny the real ferocity of party dispute in this period. That it

---

65 Quoted in Bonney, *European Dynastic States*, p. 330.

66 Kenyon, *Revolution Principles*, p. 46.   67 Cust, 'News and Politics', p. 85.

68 *Ibid.*, p. 86; John Rous (1642): 'Some yet call the Parliament side Roundheads, who be themselves, in requittal, called Malignants . . . but what title they deserve let themselves judge, who hate reformation and would bring in tyrannie' (*ibid.*, p. 85).

69 Geoffrey Holmes, *British Politics in the Reign of Anne* (revised edn, London 1987); see also Holmes, *Making of a Great Power*, pp. 325–50; Kenyon, *Revolution Principles*; C. Jones, *Britain in the First Age of Party* (London 1987).

70 *Proquiritatio . . . Or, A Petition to the People* (London 1642). I am grateful to Geoff Kemp for this reference.

kept the country ideologically within the seventeenth century is evident on all hands. The secure location of party rhetoric within the history of the troubles is one of the hallmarks of the period. Whigs remained 'Phanatiques . . . the dregs of the populace, the creatures of a sectarian army, the worst part of a body, that was bad enough in its best . . . atheists, Hobbists, commonwealthsmen':

if we were to consider its progress, in all the series of rebellions, from the odious and never-to-be forgotten era of transcendent villainy in the year forty-one, we shall find the same Jesuitical principles, like a plotter in masquerade, only changing their name, but carrying on the same machinations and wicked practices in church and state, to the subversion of our constitution in both down to the present day.[71]

Tories exhibited

the sense of a party that cannot be matched but in France and Turkey: they are Capuchins, Mendicants, Cordeliers, Carthusians, Regulars, Irregulars, High Flyers, Tantivies, Bellswaggerists, Mufti and Priests . . . The followers of this party build their faith upon the tenets of Ignatius Loyola, and those in England take their opinions from Laud, Parker and Old Towser.[72]

In this respect, Geoffrey Holmes has remarked, the period was 'as much the end of an old era as the beginning of a new one . . . It saw the climax and final subsidence of that sustained religious conflict' that had been going on since 1529. In particular 'Religious controversy . . . meat and drink to post-Revolution Englishmen . . . reached a peak in Anne's reign', to decline only from 1725.[73] Rhetorically then, even within the country, the troubles continued.

Accordingly, for J. H. Plumb, far from being a step beyond the troubles, party politics was of their essence. 'Party division' both 'created instability', and was 'the true reflection of it'.[74] This is, however, a matter of perspective. From the standpoint of Sir Robert Walpole, the architect of what Plumb took to be stability, this was the case. Had Walpole lived through the actual troubles he might have noted a considerable difference between the rage of party and the clash of steel.

This institutionalisation of party was, then, the result of fundamental

---

71 Quoted in Kenyon, *Revolution Principles*, pp. 76–7, 95.   72 Quoted *ibid.*, p. 94.
73 Holmes, *Making of a Great Power*, p. 350.
74 Plumb, *Stability*, p. 157. The continuation of conflict is also a theme of Tim Harris, *Politics Under the Later Stuarts: Party Conflict in a Divided Society, 1660–1715* (London 1993).

political changes that did not occur until after 1688. It is for this reason that attempts by historians of the 'long eighteenth century' to pre-date the phenomenon have been misconceived. This is not to say that the *ideological* polarisation which eventually informed the party system had not existed earlier in the seventeenth century. Party politics was nothing other than the institutionalisation of that polarity of belief that had been both cause and consequence of the troubles. As John Tutchin put it, with the inflection of hindsight in 1702:

Now, as this too much divided Nation has always been compos'd of two contending Parties, those Parties have been distinguish'd, as in like cases, by Names of Contempt; and tho' they have often chang'd them on either side, as Cavalier and Roundhead, Royalists and Rebels, Malignants and Phanaticks, Tories and Whigs, yet the Division has always been barely the Church and the Dissenters, and there it continues to this day.[75]

This is why it is no more appropriate to speak of the birth of party in 1678–83 than during the 1620s or 1640s. When during the 1620s this polarity of belief took up residence behind the names of arminian and puritan the eventual result was civil war. When in the late 1670s the same phenomenon occurred civil war was averted by the operation of public memory. It was during the 1690s and 1700s, however, under new and evolving institutional circumstances, that a system developed, for the first time, which made the simultaneous existence of these polarities possible, and part of the normal operation of electoral politics.

THE END OF THE ENGLISH REVOLUTION

This completion of restoration did not mean that the troubles and revolution left no legacy. It meant that they gradually ceased to be competitors for the government of the country. In relation to the troubles, as we have seen, this process of transition took time. The same is true in relation to the revolution.

In 1689 this had made a limited impact in institutional terms, most obviously upon the religious settlement. From its inception, however, the substance of the revolution had lain not in institutional but in (protestant and republican) moral aspirations. In these terms, throughout the 1690s and beyond a continuing impact was visible.

---

75 Quoted in Keeble, *Literary Culture of Nonconformity*, p. 44.

Much attention has been paid, on the one hand, to the protestant 'moral revolution' of the 1690s.[76] The accompanying atmosphere of providentialism, biblical piety and fast days, in conjunction with the military struggle against popery, were all reminiscent of the 1640s and 1650s. Accordingly, more than one historian has warned us against 'the fashionable notion that 1688 marks the beginning of a "long eighteenth century" . . . [since] the continuities between the Cromwellian and the Williamite eras are very striking'.[77]

Similar claims might be made for republicanism in the 1690s. It is true that republican aspirations for the settlement of 1689 were quickly disappointed by the combination of parliamentary opinion and armed force.[78] This did not, of course, dispose of republican opinion itself, which survived to inform the debate concerning military disbandment in 1698; to support a surge of republican publication between 1698 and 1700 including the classic works of Sidney, Milton and Harrington, as well as the ersatz Ludlow.[79] In the longer term, in work like Trenchard and Gordon's *Cato's Letters*, the literary and intellectual legacy of English republicanism remained alive to inform radical whiggism in England, Scotland and, most successfully, America.[80]

Yet all historians have agreed in seeing in the same period a loss of radical vigour. It was not simply that 'Republican publication consisted more and more of republication.' In the words of Blair Worden

As the eighteenth century progressed the teaching of republicanism became ever less precise . . . The movement became ever more a language, ever less a programme. It spoke less and less of particular constitutional defects, more and more of 'public spirit' and of 'the spirit of liberty'. Political health seemed more a matter of a nation's manners and morals than of its constitution.

---

76 John Spurr, 'The Church, the Societies, and the Moral Revolution of 1688', in John Walsh, Colin Haydon and Stephen Taylor (eds.), *The Church of England c. 1689–c. 1833: From Toleration to Tractarianism* (Cambridge 1993); Bahlman, *Moral Revolution.*

77 Rose, 'Providence', p. 169; Claydon, *William III.*

78 Kenyon, *Revolution Principles*, esp. pp. 1–10; Holmes, *Making of a Great Power*, pp. 278–9.

79 Goldie, 'True Whiggism'; Pocock, *Machiavellian Moment*, chs. 12–13; Blair Worden, 'The Revolution and the English Republican Tradition', in Israel, *Anglo-Dutch Moment.*

80 Robbins, *Eighteenth-Century Commonwealthsman*; Pocock, *Machiavellian Moment*, pt 3; John Robertson, *The Militia Issue and the Scottish Enlightenment* (Edinburgh 1985); Bailyn, *Ideological Origins*; Scott, *English Republic*, pp. 5–6.

This book has argued that the English revolution was always 'more a matter of a nation's manners and morals than of its constitution'.[81] This was as true of its republican as its protestant dimension, and helps to account for the close relationship between the two. Yet what Worden accurately records here is a retreat from political centre stage, a retreat from the struggle to run the country. For this there were two principal reasons.

One was that the revolution was the product of a specific and spectacular political upheaval. Its anti-formalism had developed within the chasm created by the destruction of traditional religious and political institutions. It was not simply that in 1688–9 no such chasm was allowed to develop. Thereafter institutional construction was the essence of the statebuilding process.

Thereafter radical protestantism and republicanism remained dependent upon the writings of the generation that had experienced that unique earlier upheaval. It is true that a new generation of admirers grew up devoted to the reapplication of these ideas. But this involved a process of adaptation – sometimes outright fabrication – within a very different political world. In particular it involved adaptation to the existence of the church, of an all-powerful parliament and of the monarchy. In its *political* aspirations English radicalism had opposed all of these. It had sought not only the permanent abolition of the church, and of the monarchy, but also the severe truncation of parliamentary power. In the era of statebuilding, this revolution increasingly slipped from view.

The institutional destruction of the 1640s had been the product of a military struggle against popery and arbitrary power. The reconstruction of 1689–1714 was the product of a similar process. Because the latter united parliament, the city of London and the monarchy, it was one of which the political elite kept control. John Brewer remarked upon the apparent paradox, against the background of England's troubles, that the opponent of state power, parliament, became the principal instrument in its creation.[82] Yet of course parliaments had never opposed state power. What they opposed was their own elimination in the course of its construction. The struggle was against arbitrary government, not absolutism; for participation in government, not its abolition. In the 1690s parliaments were to

81 Worden, 'The Revolution and the English Republican Tradition', p. 269.
82 Brewer, *Sinews of Power*, p. 159.

show, as they had in the 1640s, that it was they who had the capacity to build the state. 'Our dear bought experience has taught us what Vast Taxes are necessary to maintain the armies and Fleet, which are requisite; and for the defence of our religious and civil rights.'[83] This was a fiscal and military process of which the weak English monarchy had been incapable alone.

The result was a paradoxical radical legacy. On the one hand the first militarily effective early modern English (and British) government was republican. The course of English statebuilding was dependent upon the Dutch and English republican fiscal, administrative and military achievement. The result, on the other hand, was not simply the end of the English revolution. It was the Levellers' nightmare.

Parliaments might have won the religious and political struggle of the troubles, and with it the capacity to enshrine certain 'liberties' in law, but against their power there was now no protection. This state, which was one not of citizenship but subjection, was one from which the American colonies took care to constitutionally dissociate themselves.

That the essentials of this British state remain with us today owes most to its remarkable capacity in the intervening three hundred years to defend itself by war. The result is one of the oldest complexes of public institutions in present-day Europe. How long radical reform can continue to be successfully resisted by an overmighty parliamentary political establishment is impossible to predict. The importance of this resistance was, in 1997, the one thing upon which Tony Benn and Enoch Powell could agree.

We still live in restoration times. What the restoration process made possible finally was 'That the memory of what is passed may be buried to the World'.[84] If it is impossible for historians to predict the future, and inappropriate for them to prescribe it, it is this legacy which they may challenge.

83 Quoted *ibid.*, p. 142.   84 Charles II, *Preface to the Declaration of Breda*, p. 9.

Sources cited

Place of publication London unless otherwise specified.

PRIMARY SOURCES

Manuscripts

Bodleian Library, Oxford, Clarendon MSS, vols. 104, 105
  MS Eng. hist c. 487, Edmund Ludlow, 'A Voyce from the Watchtower'
British Library, Add MS 4181, 'The Relation of sr Balthazar Gerbier kyt', 26 June 1648
  Add MS 38,847, 'The Rye House Plot: Robert West's full Confession to the King'
  Add MS 44,729
  Add MS 63,057, vols. I–II, Transcript of Burnet's *History of His Own Time*
  Egerton MS 2538, Letters of Sir George Downing
  Egerton MS 2618
  Sloane MS 2723
Cambridge University Library, marginal note on *An Impartial Account of the Proceedings of the Common Hall of the City of London at Guildhal* (24 June 1682), probably by Ralph Verney, in Sel.2.118
Downing College, Cambridge Library, Archive Box 198
  Sir George Downing Letter Book 1658
  MS Z.4.17/16, 'Transcript of my Ld Shaftsburyes Letter to ye Ea. of Carlisle, Feb 3d 1674 [1675]'
  MS Z.4.17/22, 'Transcripts out of ye Journall books of ye Lords' house'
East Sussex Record Office, Lewes, Glynde Place Archives, no. 794, Letters from Algernon Sidney to John Hampden (and one other), 1683
Hartlib Papers, electronic edn: de Hohenlohe, Ludovicus Gustavus, Address to Cromwell, January 1657, 54/63A–64B
  Dury, John, 'Concerning the Question Whether it be lawfull to admit Iewes'. 68/8/1B
  Dury, John, 'Memo on an English College in Heildeburg' [undated], 67/19/1A–2B

Dury, John, Tract on Church Government, 27 December 1641 68/9/2B

Hall, Joseph to Samuel Hartlib, [1638?], 45/3/43A

Hartlib correspondence, 54/63A–64B; 46/14/6A–7B; 46/14/3A–3B; 67/19/1A–2B

Worsley, Benjamin, 27 September 1654, 65/15/1A–4B

Hartlib Papers, University of Sheffield, Samuel Hartlib, 'Ephemerides' (1656)

Kent Archives Office, Maidstone, De Lisle MS, U1475 Z1/9

Longleat, Bath, MSS, Whitelocke Papers, vol. XIX

Public Record Office, London, Baschet transcripts, 31/3, nos. 125 (1670); nos. 140–56 (1678–83)

State Papers 21/81/94

State Papers 29 no. 428; 44 nos. 81–2

Warwickshire Record Office MS, CR1886, Algernon Sidney, 'Court Maxims'

Westminster, House of Lords MSS, Committee Book, HL vol. IV, 1688–9

Newspapers and pamphlets

An Account of the Reasons which induced Charles II . . . to declare War against the States General . . . in 1672 (1689)

An Act for exempting their Majestyes Protestant Subjects dissenting from the Church of England from the penalties of certain laws (1689)

Act for the Relief and Employment of the Poor (1649)

An Address agreed upon at the Committee for the French War, and read in the House of Commons, April the 19th, 1689, in *Harleian Miscellany*, vol. I

An Advertisement to the whole Kingdome of England (1642)

Advice to the Men of Shaftesbury (1681)

An Answer to Blundell the Jesuits Letter (1679)

An Attempt Towards a Coalition of English Protestants (1715)

Auxilium Patris [Abiezer Coppe], *A Fiery Flying Roll*, with *A Second Fiery Flying Roule* (4 January 1650; repr. Exeter 1973)

Ball, William, *The Rule of a Free-Born People* (1646)

Barrow, Humphrey, *The Relief of the Poor, and Advancement of Learning Proposed* (1656)

Bedloe, William, *A Narrative and Impartial Discovery of the Horrid Popish Plot* (1679)

Bethel, Slingsby, *The Interest of Princes and States* (1680)

   The Present Interest of England Stated (1671)

   The Vindication of Slingsby Bethel Esq (1681)

   The World's Mistake in Oliver Cromwell (1668)

[Bethel, Slingsby], *The Right of Chusing Sheriffs* (1689)

Bolron, Robert, *The Narrative of Robert Bolron . . . Concerning the Late Horrid Popish Plot* (1680)

Burton, Henry, *A Vindication of Churches, commonly called Independent* (1644)

Capel, Arthur, Earl of Essex, *The Earl of Essex his Speech . . . [and] Petition* (25 January 1681), in Scott, *Somers Tracts*, vol. III

The Character of a Good Man, neither Whig or Tory (1681)

The Character of a Modern Whig (1681)

The Character of a Rebellion, and What England May Expect From One (1681)

The Character of a Tory (1681)

Charles II, *His Majesties Declaration to All His loving Subjects* (26 December 1662)

   His Majesties Declaration to all His Loving Subjects, concerning the Treasonable Conspiracy against his Sacred Person and Government, Lately Discovered (28 July 1683)

   His Majesties Declaration to all his Loving Subjects touching the Causes and Reasons that Moved Him to Dissolve the Two Last Parliaments (April 1681)

   His Majesties Gracious Answer to The Earl of Manchester's Speech (29 May 1660)

   His Majesties Gracious Message To the House of Commons (20 June 1660)

   His Majesties Gracious Speech to both Houses of Parliament Jan 7 1674 [1675]

   His Majesties Gracious Speech to the House of Peers, The 27th of July 1660, Concerning the speedy passing of the Bill of Indemnity and Oblivion

   His Majesties Gracious Speech To The Lords and Commons (8 May 1661)

   His Majesties Gracious Speech Together with the Lord Chancellors . . . on Saturday the 29th day of September 1660

   His Majesties Letter to His Excellency The Lord General Monck (24 May 1660)

   His Majesties most Gracious Speech . . . to Parliament (21 October 1678)

   His Majesties Most Gracious Speech, Together with the Lord Chancellors (13 September 1660)

   His Majesty's Gracious Speech (March 1679)

   King Charls II His Declaration To all His Loving Subjects . . . Dated from his Court at Breda in Holland The 4/14 of Aprill 1660

   Preface to the Declaration of Breda, in *Two Letters From His Majesty*

   Two Letters from His Majesty. The One To the Speaker of the Commons Assembled in Parliament. The other to His Excellencie The Lord Generall Monck . . . Read in the House of Commons assembled in Parliament, Tuesday May 1 1660

The continuation of our Weekely Newes, no. 17, 14 April 1625

A Continuation of the Newes of this Present Weeke, no. 5, 5 November 1622

Cooke, Edward, *Memorabilia; Or the Most Remarkable Passages and Counsels Collected out of the Several Declarations and Speeches . . . Made by the King* (1681)

Coppe, Abiezer, *Some Sweet Sips, of Some Sprituall Wine* (1649), in Nigel Smith, *A Collection of Ranter Writings*

The Debate at Large between the Lords and Commons . . . Anno 1688 . . . Relating to the Word ABDICATED, and the Vacancy of the THRONE (2nd edn, 1705)

The Declaration and Petition of the Prince Palsgrave of the Rhyne, and the Queene his Mother, disclaiming and discountenancing Prince Robert, in all his uncivill actions (1642)

A Declaration of the Causes moving the queene of England to give aid to the defence of the Low Countries (October 1584), in Scott, *Somers Tracts*, vol. I

The Declaration of the Rebels Now in Arms in the West of Scotland (1679)

A Dialogue at Oxford (1681)

A Dialogue between the Ghosts of the two last Parliaments (1681)

Dugdale, Richard, *A Most Serious Expostulation With Severall of my Fellow Citizens* (1680)

Elizabeth I, *The Last Speech and Thanks of Queen Elizabeth of Ever Blessed Memory, to her Last Parliament, after her Delivery from the Popish Plots etc [2 October 1601]* (1679)

England's Concern in the Case of HRH James Duke of York . . . to be read by all subjects, whether of Royal or Republican Opinions (1680), in Scott, *Somers Tracts*, vol. VIII

England's Memorable Accidents, 26 September–2 October 1642; 3–10 October 1642; 24–31 October 1642; 15 December 1642

An Essay upon the Change of Manners. Being a second Part of the true Protestant's Appeal to the City and Country (1681)

Everard, Edmund, *Discourses of the Present State of the Protestant Princes of Europe* (1679)

An Exact and most Impartial Accompt of the Indictment, Arraignment, Trial, and Judgement (according to Law) of Twenty nine Regicides (1660)

An Examination of the Impartial State of the Case of the Earl of Danby (1680)

An Explanation of the Lord Treasurers Letter to Mr Montague . . . March 25th (1679)

Fair Warning, or the Burnt Child Dreads the Fire [1680]

Filmer, Sir Robert, *Observations concerning the Originall of Government* (1652)
Reflections concerning the Originall of Government (1679)

The French Intrigues Discovered. With the Methods and Arts to Retrench the Potency of France by Land and Sea (1681)

G. L. V., *British Lightning: or, Suddaine Tumults in England, Scotland, and Ireland, to warne the United Provinces to understand the Dangers and the Causes thereof* (1643), in Scott, *Somers Tracts*, vol. V

Goodman Country: To His Worship the City of London (1680)

Hall, John, *The Grounds and Reasons of Monarchy Considered* (1651)

Hickes, George, *A Sermon Preached before the Lord Mayor, Aldermen and Citizens . . . at Bow-Church on the 30th of January 1681/2*

The History of Whiggism, or, The Whiggish Plots in the Reign of King Charles the First (1682)

Holles, Denzil, Lord, *A Letter to Mons Van B de M—* (1676)

The Humble Address of the Commons in Parliament Assembled, Presented to His Majesty, Monday 28th day of November 1680 (1680)

The Humble Petition and Address of the . . . Lord Mayor, Aldermen and Commons of the city of London (1681)

The Humble Petition of the City of London for the Sitting of this present Parliament Prorogu'd to the Twentieth Instant (13 January 1680 [1681])

The Humble Representation and Petition of the Lords and the Commons concerning Romish Priests and Jesuits (1663)

An Impartial Account of the Arraignment, Trial and Condemnation of Thomas Late Earl of Stafford 1641 (1679)

An Impartial Account of the Proceedings of the Common Hall of the City of London at Guildhal (24 June 1682)

The Interest of England Maintained (1646)

[Ireton, Henry], *The Humble Remonstrance of his Excellency the Lord General Fairfax* (16 November 1648)

James II, 'Life of James II 1660–1698, Written by Himself', in J. MacPherson (ed.), *Original Papers* (2 vols., 1775), vol. I

Laud, William, *The History of the Troubles and Tryal of William Laud . . . Wrote by Himself, during his Imprisonment in the Tower* (1654)

Laurence, Thomas, *Some Pitty on the Poor* [n.d.]

A Letter from a Person of Quality to His Friend in the Country (1675)

A Letter to a Friend in the Country, Touching the Present Fears and Jealousie of the Nation (29 February 1680 [1681])

A Letter to a Noble Peer [Essex] about his late Speech and Petition (1681)

A Letter to the Kings most Excellent Majesty from The Commons of England (14 May 1660)

A Letter Written from the Tower by Mr Stephen Colledge . . . to Dick Janeway's wife (July 1681)

Lilburne, John, *England's New Chains Discovered* (1649)

   A Postscript to London's Liberty

London's New Recorder: Or, certain Queres to be resolved by the old Recorder, for London's further welfare (1647)

The Loyal Protestant's Vindication . . . By a Queen Elizabeth Protestant (1681)

Manchester, Earl of, *The Earl of Manchester's Speech to His Majesty* (1660)

March, John, *The False Prophet Unmaskt, or the Wolfe Stript of his SHEEPS-CLOTH-ING, in a Sermon* (1683)

Marvell, Andrew, *An Account of the Growth of Popery and Arbitrary Government in England. More particularly, from the long Prorogation of November 1675* (Amsterdam 1677)

A Memorial from the English Protestants, for their Highnesses the Prince and Princess of Orange (1688)

Mercurius Politicus, no. 1, 6–13 June 1650; no. 26, 28 November–5 December 1650; no. 35, 6 February 1651; no. 51, 22–9 May 1651; no. 52, 29 May–5 June 1651; no. 68, 18–25 September 1651; no. 70, 2–9 October 1651; no. 85, 18–25 January 1652; no. 87, 3–10 February 1652; no. 101, 6–13 May 1652; no. 103, 20–7 May 1652; no. 104, 27 May–3 June 1652; no. 354, 19–26 March 1657

The Moderate Intelligencer: Impartially communicating Martial Affaires to the Kingdome of England, no. 169, 8–15 June 1648; no. 179 (17 August 1648)

Monck, G., *A Letter from His Excellencie the Lord General Monck, And the Officers under his Command, To The Parliament* (11 February 1659)

Mowbray, Lawrence, *The Narrative of Lawrence Mowbray of Leeds* (1680)

The Parallel: or, The New Specious Association an old Rebellious Covenant (1682)

The Parliament Scout Communicating His Intelligence to the Kingdome, no. 23 (24 November–1 December 1643)

Penn, William, *England's Present Interest* (1675)

The People's Right Briefly Asserted, Printed for the Information of the Commonality of England, France, and all other Neighbour Nations, that groan under the oppression of Tyrannical Government (1649)

Perfect Occurrences of Parliament, 13–20 September 1644; 22–9 August 1645

Philanglus [William Penn], *England's Great Interest in the Choice of This New Parliament* (1679)

Philolaus, *A Character of Popery and Arbitrary Government . . . [and] how [to] prevent the same, by Choosing Good Members to serve in this New Parliament* (1679)

Philo-Patris, *A Seasonable Address to the . . . City of London* (1680)

The Plot Reviv'd: or a Memorial of the late and present Popish Plots (April 1680)

The Popish Plot, Taken from Several Depositions Made before the Parliament (1678), in Scott, *Somers Tracts*, vol. VIII

The Popish Wonder, being Truth Confest by Papists (1680)

The Presbyterian's Prophecie, concerning the King, Parliament, City, Army and Kingdome (1648)

The Present Case of England, and the Protestant Interest (1690), in *Harleian Miscellany*, vol. I

Proquiritatio . . . Or, A Petition to the People (1642)

R. B., *The Poor Mans Friend or a Narrative of what progress many worthy Citizens of London have made in that Godly work of providing for the* POOR (16 March 1649)

Rationalis, Theophilus, *Multum in Parvo aut Vox Veritatis: Wherein the . . . Transactions of . . . Parliament Ad 1640, 1641. As also 1680, 1681. are most faithfully and impartially Examined, Collected, and Compared* (1681)

Reasons Offered by a Well-Wisher to the King and Kingdom (1681)

Reflections upon some passages of Mr LeClerc's Life of John Locke (1711)

A Remonstrance of His Excellency Thomas Lord Fairfax . . . and of the Generall Councell of Officers Held at St Albans the 16 of November 1648 (1648)

Sedgewick, William, *The Parliament Under the power of the Sword. With a briefe Answer thereunto By some of the Army* (1648)

The Spiritual Madman, Or A Prophesie (1648)

A Speech Made by a True Protestant English Gentleman To Incourage the City of London to Petition for the Sitting of the Parliment [1680]

The Speeches, Discourses and Prayers, of Colonel John Barkstead, Col. John Okey, and Mr Miles Corbet, Upon the 19th of April, being the Day of their suffering at Tyburn. Together with an Account of the Occasion and Manner of their Taking in Holland (1662)

A True and Just Account of a Most Horrid and Bloody Plot conspired against His Most Sacred Majesty (1683)

The True Protestant's Appeal to the City and Country (1681)

The Tryal of George Busby (1681)

The Tryal of John Hambden 6 February 1684 (1684)

The Tryal of William Viscount Stafford for High Treason (1681)

The Tryals of William Ireland, Thomas Pickering, and John Grove (December 1678)

Turner, Sir Edward, *The Speech of Sir Edward Turner KT, Speaker of the House of Commons, to the Kings most Excellent Majesty* (1666)

The Speech of Sr Edward Turner (20 December 1661)

The Speeches of Sir Edward Turner KT, Before the King, Lords and Commons (10 May 1661)

The Two Associations. One Subscribed by CLVI Members of the House of Commons In the Year 1643. The other seized in the Closet of the Earl of Shaftsbury (1681)

The Votes and Orders of the Honourable House of Commons Passed February 25, and 26 1662, Upon Reading His Majesties Gracious Declaration and Speech (1662)

Vox Populi: or the People's Claim to their Parliament's Sitting (1681)

Wee have brought our Hogges to a Faire Market (1648)

William III [Caspar Fagel], *The Declaration of His Highness . . . for restoring the laws and liberties of England, Scotland, and Ireland* (1688), in Beddard, *Kingdom Without a King*

Williams, William, *The Speech of the Hon. William Williams . . . upon the Electing of him Speaker* (21 March 1680)

A Winter Dream (1648)

Books

Ailesbury, Thomas, Earl of, *Ailesbury Memoirs* (2 vols., 1890)

Aristotle, *The Politics*, ed. Stephen Everson (Cambridge 1988)

Ashton, Robert (ed.), *James I by His Contemporaries* (1969)

Aubrey, John, *Aubrey's Brief Lives*, ed. O. L. Dick (1958)

Aylmer, Gerald (ed.), *The Levellers in the English Revolution* (1975)

Bacon, Francis, *Bacon's Essays*, ed. E. A. Abbott (2 vols., 1889)

Bacon, Nathaniel, *A Historical and Political Discourse of the Laws and Government of England* (1649)

Barbour, H. and Roberts, A. O. (eds.), *Early Quaker Writings 1650–1700* (Grand Rapids, Mich. 1973)

Baxter, Richard, *Reliquiae Baxterianae: or Mr Richard Baxter's Narrative of the most Memorable Passages of his Life and Times* (1696)

Baylor, Michael (ed.), *The Radical Reformation* (Cambridge 1991)

Beddard, Robert (ed.), *A Kingdom Without a King* (Oxford 1988)

Berry, B. E., *Life and Letters of Rachel Wriothesley, Lady Russell* (2 vols., 1819)

Bodin, Jean, *Six Bookes of a Commonweale* (1606), ed. K. D. McRae (Cambridge, Mass. 1962)

Booth, Henry, 1st Earl of Warrington, *The Works of Henry late L. Delamer and Earl of Warrington* (1694)

Buchanan, George, *De Jure Regni apud Scotos*, trans. 'Philalethes' (1680)

Bunyan, John, *The Pilgrim's Progress* (1st pub. 1678)

Burnet, Gilbert, *History of my Own Time* (2 vols., Oxford 1823)

Burton, Thomas, *Burton's Diary*, ed. J. T. Rutt (4 vols., 1828)

Calendar of State Papers Domestic, July–December 1682; January–June 1683

Clarke, J., *The Life of James II* (2 vols., 1816)

Cobbett, William, *The Parliamentary History of England from the Earliest Period to 1803* (36 vols., 1806–20)

A Collection of State Tracts published during the Reign of King William III (1706), vol. II

Cromwell, Oliver, *Oliver Cromwell's Letters and Speeches*, ed. Thomas Carlyle (3 vols., 1857)

Dalrymple, J., *Memoirs of Great Britain and Ireland* (2 vols., 1773)

Dancer, Thomas, *Metamorphosis Anglorum* [1659]

D'Avaux, *Negotiations of Count d'Avaux* (4 vols., 1756)

Davenant, Charles, *The Political and Commercial Works of . . . Charles D'Avenant*, ed. Sir Charles Whitworth (5 vols., 1771)

'De Witt and other Great Men in Holland' [Pieter de la Court], *The True Interest and Political Maxims of the Republic of Holland* (1702)

Democritus Junior [Robert Burton], *The Anatomy of Melancholy: What it is* (Oxford 1624)

D'Ewes, Simonds, *The Autobiography and Correspondence of Sir Simonds D'Ewes*, ed. J. O. Halliwell (1845)

Donne, John, *John Donne: The Complete English Poems*, ed. A. J. Smith (1986)

Dryden, John, *Absalom and Achitophel*, 5th edn, rev. (1682)

The Medall: A Satyre against Sedition (1682)

Prologue to the Duke of Guise (1682)

Dugdale, William, *A Short View of the Late Troubles in England* (1681)

Edwards, Thomas, *Gangraena* (1646; repr. Exeter 1977)

Evelyn, John, *The Diary of John Evelyn*, ed. Esmond de Beer (Oxford 1955)

Memoirs, ed. W. Bray (2 vols., 1818)

Filmer, Sir Robert, *Patriarcha* (1680)

Patriarcha and Other Writings, ed. Johann Sommerville (Cambridge 1991)

Firth, C. H. (ed.), *The Clarke Papers* (4 vols., 1899–1965)

Fletcher, Andrew, *The Political Works of Andrew Fletcher of Saltoun* (1737)

Fox, George, *Journal*, in *George Fox and the Children of Light*, ed. Jonathan Fryer (1991)

Franklin, J. H. (ed.), *Constitutionalism and Resistance in the Sixteenth Century* (New York 1969)

Gardiner, S. R. (ed.), *The Constitutional Documents of the Puritan Revolution 1625–1660* (Oxford 1979)

Debates in the House of Commons in 1625 (1873)

Parliamentary Debates in 1610 (1862)

Grey, A., *Debates of the House of Commons, from the Year 1667 to the Year 1694* (10 vols., 1763)

Grey, Ford, Lord, *The Secret History of the Rye House Plot* (1754)

Grotius, Hugo, *De Jure Belli ac Pacis Libri Tres*, trans. F. W. Kelsey (Oxford 1925), vol. II, *The Translation Book I*

Hale, J. R. (ed.), *The Evolution of British Historiography from Bacon to Namier* (1967)

Haller, W. and Davies, G. (eds.), *The Leveller Tracts 1647–1653* (Gloucester, Mass. 1964)

The Harleian Miscellany: Or, a Collection of Scarce, Curious, and Entertaining Pamphlets and Tracts, vol. I (1744)

Harrington, James, *Oceana*, in *Political Works*

The Political Works of James Harrington, ed. J. G. A. Pocock (Cambridge 1977)

Heylyn, Peter, *A Briefe and Moderate Answer, to the seditious and scandalous challenges of Henry Burton* (1637)

Historical Manuscripts Commission report, House of Lords MSS 13th Rep 17.3

Hobbes, Thomas, *Leviathan*, ed. C. B. MacPherson (1984)

Leviathan, ed. Richard Tuck (Cambridge 1991)

Of Liberty and Necessity: A Treatise (1654), in *The English Works of Thomas Hobbes*, ed. Sir William Molesworth, vol. VI (1840)

Of the Life and History of Thucydides (1628), in *Hobbes' Thucydides*, ed. R. B. Schlatter (New Brunswick, N.J. 1975)

Hume, David, *The History of England from the Invasion of Julius Caesar to The Revolution in 1688* (2 vols., 1754–7; 6 vols., Indianapolis 1983)

Hutchinson, Lucy, *Memoirs of Colonel Hutchinson*, ed. J. Hutchinson (repr. 1965)
   Memoirs of the Life of Colonel Hutchinson, ed. N. H. Keeble (1995)
Hyde, Edward, Earl of Clarendon, *The Continuation of the Life of Edward Earl of Clarendon . . . Written by Himself*, vol. II (Oxford 1760)
   The History of the Rebellion and Civil Wars in England, ed. W. D. Macray (6 vols., Oxford 1888)
   The Life of Edward Earl of Clarendon . . . Written by Himself, vol. I (Oxford 1760)
Jones, D. L. (ed.), *A Parliamentary History of the Glorious Revolution* (1988)
Jusserand, J. J., *Recueil des instructions données aux ambassadeurs et ministres de France*, vol. XXV, *Angleterre* (Paris 1929)
Kenyon, J. P. (ed.), *The Stuart Constitution 1603–1688* (Cambridge 1986)
Knowles, W. (ed.), *The Earl of Strafforde's Letters and Dispatches* (2 vols., 1739)
Larkin, James and Hughes, Paul (eds.), *Stuart Royal Proclamations* (2 vols., Oxford 1973–83)
Locke, John, *The Correspondence of John Locke*, ed. E. S. de Beer (8 vols., Oxford 1976–89)
   Locke's Two Treatises of Government, ed. Peter Laslett (2nd edn, Cambridge 1967)
   Two Tracts, ed. Philip Abrams (Cambridge 1967)
Lords, House of, *Journal of the House of Lords*
Ludlow, Edmund, *A Voyce From the Watchtower*, ed. A. B. Worden (1978)
Luttrell, N., *A Brief Historical Relation of State Affairs* (Oxford 1857)
Machiavelli, N., *The Discourses*, ed. Bernard Crick (Harmondsworth 1985)
   The Prince, in Machiavelli, *The History of Florence, and of the Affairs of Italy . . . together with The Prince* (1847)
May, Thomas, *The History of the Parliament of England: which began November the third 1640* (1647)
Milton, John, *Areopagitica; a Speech of Mr John Milton for the Liberty of Unlicenc'd Printing* (1644), ed. J. C. Suffolk (1968)
   Complete Prose Works, ed. D. M. Wolfe et al. (8 vols., New Haven 1953–82)
   Eikonoklastes, in *Complete Prose Works*, vol. III
   Milton's Areopagitica, ed. H. B. Cotterill (1949)
   Paradise Lost, in *Poetical Works*
   The Poetical Works of John Milton, ed. H. C. Beeching (Oxford 1922)
   Political Writings, ed. Martin Dzelzainis (Cambridge 1991)
   The Prose Works of J. Milton, ed. J. A. St John (5 vols., 1848–53)
   The Readie and Easye Way (2nd edn 1660), ed. Howard Erskine-Hill and Graham Storey (Cambridge 1983)
More, Thomas, *Utopia* (Harmondsworth 1977)
   Utopia: The Best State of a Commonwealth and the New Island of Utopia, ed. E. Surtz (New Haven 1964)
Nedham, Marchamont, *The Case of the Commonwealth of England, Stated*, ed. Philip A. Knachel (Charlottesville 1969)

Neville, Henry, *Plato Redivivus* (1680), in C. Robbins (ed.), *Two English Republican Tracts* (Cambridge 1969)

North, Roger, *Examen* (1740)

Notestein, W. and Relf, F. H. (eds.), *The Commons Debates for 1629* (Minneapolis 1921)

Nuttall, Geoffrey (ed.), *Early Quaker Letters from the Swarthmore MSS to 1660* (1952)

Penn, William, *The Works of William Penn* (2 vols., 1756)

Pepys, Samuel, *The Diary of Samuel Pepys*, ed. Robert Latham and William Matthews (11 vols., 1970)

Petty, Sir William, *Political Arithmetic* (1690), in G. A. Aitken (ed.), *Later Stuart Tracts* (1903)

Philalethes [Tyrrell, James], *Patriarcha Non Monarcha* (1681)

Plato, *The Portable Plato*, ed. Scott Buchanan (Harmondsworth 1976)
  The Republic, trans. H. D. P. Lee (Harmondsworth 1959)

Puffendorf, Samuel von, *The Law of Nature and Nations* (1749)

Ralph, J., *The History of England* (2 vols., 1744)

Reresby, John, *Memoirs of Sir John Reresby*, ed. Andrew Browning (Glasgow 1936)

Rous, John, *Diary of John Rous . . . from 1625 to 1642*, ed. M. A. Everett Green (1856)

Rousseau, Jean-Jacques, *Political Writings*, ed. C. E. Vaughan (2 vols., Oxford 1962)

Rushworth, John, *Historical Collections . . . beginning the Sixteenth Year of King James, Anno 1618. And ending the Fifth Year of King Charls, Anno 1629* (3 vols., 1659–82)

Savile, George, Marquis of Halifax, *The Works of George Savile Marquis of Halifax*, ed. Mark N. Brown (3 vols., Oxford 1989)

Scott, Sir Walter (ed.), *A Collection of Scarce and Valuable Tracts . . . of the Late Lord Somers* (13 vols., 1808–15)

Shakespeare, William, *The Tragedie of King Lear*, in *Mr William Shakespeare's Comedies, Histories and Tragedies* (1623)

Sharp, Andrew (ed.), *Political Ideas of the English Civil Wars 1641–1649* (1983)

Sidney, Algernon, *The Apology of A. Sydney, in the Day of his Death*, in *Sydney on Government*
  Court Maxims, ed. Hans Blom, Eco Haitsma Mulier and Ronald Janse (Cambridge 1996)
  Discourses Concerning Government, in *Sydney on Government*
  Discourses Concerning Government, ed. T. West (Indianapolis 1990)
  Letters of A. Sydney to Henry Savile Ambassador in France, in *Sydney on Government*
  Sydney on Government: The Works of Algernon Sydney, ed. J. Robertson (1772)
  The Tryal of Algernon Sydney, in *Sydney on Government*

[Sidney, Algernon and Jones, Sir William], *A Just and Modest Vindication of the Proceedings of the Two Last Parliaments* (1681), in *State Tracts of the Reign of Charles II* (1689), vol. IV, Appendix 15

Sidney, Henry, *Diary of the Times of Charles II*, ed. R. W. Blencowe (2 vols., 1843)

Smith, Nigel (ed.), *A Collection of Ranter Writings* (1983)

Spinoza, Benedict de, *The Political Works*, ed. A. G. Wernham (Oxford 1958)

Stubbe, Henry, *An Essay in Defence of the Good Old Cause* (1659)

Temple, Sir William, *The Works of Sir William Temple* (2 vols., 1720)

Thurloe, John, *A Collection of the State Papers of John Thurloe* (7 vols., 1742)

van Gelderen, Martin (ed.), *The Dutch Revolt* (Cambridge 1993)

Vane, Sir Henry jun., *The Retired Man's Meditations* (1655)

Walwyn, William, *The Writings of William Walwyn*, ed. J. R. McMichael and B. Taft (Athens, Ga. 1989)

Winstanley, Gerrard, *Winstanley: The Law of Freedom and Other Writings*, ed. Christopher Hill (1973)

The Works, with an Appendix of Documents Relating to the Digger Movement, ed. G. H. Sabine (Ithaca, N.Y. 1951)

W[ither], G[eorge], *Respublica Anglicana or the Historie of the Parliament* (1650)

Wolfe, D. M. (ed.), *Leveller Manifestoes of the Puritan Revolution* (New York 1967)

Woodhouse, A. S. P. (ed.), *Puritanism and Liberty: Being the Army Debates (1647–1649) from the Clarke Manuscripts with Supplementary Documents* (1951)

Wren, Matthew, *Considerations upon Mr Harrington's Oceana* (1657)

SECONDARY SOURCES

Books and articles

Acheson, R. J., *Radical Puritans in England 1550–1660* (1990)

Adams, S. L., 'Foreign Policy and the Parliaments of 1621 and 1624', in K. Sharpe (ed.), *Faction and Parliament* (Oxford 1978)

review of Cogswell, *Blessed Revolution*, in *Parliamentary History* 2, 2, 1992

Adamson, J. S. A., 'The Baronial Context of the English Civil War', *Transactions of the Royal Historical Society* 5th ser., 40, 1990

Alford, Stephen, *The Early Elizabethan Polity: William Cecil and the British Succession Crisis 1558–1569* (Cambridge 1998)

Archer, Ian, *The Pursuit of Stability: Social Relations in Elizabethan London* (Cambridge 1991)

Armitage, David, 'The Projecting Age: William Paterson and the Bank of England', *History Today*, June 1994

Armitage, David, Himy, Armand and Skinner, Quentin (eds.), *Milton and Republicanism* (Cambridge 1995)

Ashcraft, Richard, *Revolutionary Politics and John Locke's Two Treatises of Government* (Princeton 1987)

Ashley, Maurice, *John Wildman: Plotter and Postmaster* (1947)

Ashton, Robert, *Counter-Revolution: The Second Civil War and Its Origins 1646–1648* (1994)

Aylmer, G. E., 'Centre and Locality: The Nature of Power Elites', in Reinhard, *Power Elites and State Building*

  The State's Servants: The Civil Service of the English Republic 1649–1660 (1973)

Bahlman, Dudley, *The Moral Revolution of 1688* (New Haven 1957)

Bailyn, Bernard, *The Ideological Origins of the American Revolution* (Cambridge, Mass. 1971)

Ball, Terence, Farr, James and Hanson, Russell (eds.), *Political Innovation and Conceptual Change* (Cambridge 1989)

Barber, Sarah, *Regicide and Republicanism: Politics and Ethics in the English Revolution* (Edinburgh 1998)

Baxter, Stephen, *William III and the Defense of European Liberty 1650–1702* (New York 1966)

Beddard, Robert, 'The Unexpected Whig Revolution of 1688', in Beddard, *Revolutions of 1688*

Beddard, Robert (ed.), *The Revolutions of 1688* (Oxford 1991)

Behrens, Betty, 'The Whig Theory of the Constitution in the Reign of Charles II', *Cambridge Historical Journal* 7, 1941–3

Beier, A. L. and Finlay, Roger, *London 1500–1700: The Making of the Metropolis* (1986)

Beresford, John, *The Godfather of Downing Street* (1925)

Bird, R., *The Turbulent London of Richard II* (1949)

Bliss, Robert, *Revolution and Empire: English Politics and the American Colonies in the Seventeenth Century* (Manchester 1990)

Bock, Gisela, Skinner, Quentin and Viroli, Maurizio (eds.), *Machiavelli and Republicanism* (Cambridge 1990)

Bonney, Richard, *The European Dynastic States 1494–1660* (Oxford 1991)

Bosher, J. F., 'The Franco-Catholic Danger 1660–1715', *History* 79, 255, February 1994

Braddick, Michael, *The Nerves of State: Taxation and the Financing of the English State, 1558–1714* (Manchester 1996)

  Parliamentary Taxation in Seventeenth-Century England: Local Administration and Response (1994)

Bradshaw, Brendan and Morrill, John (eds.), *The British Problem, c. 1534–1707: State Formation in the Atlantic Archipelago* (1996)

Braun, Rudolf, 'Taxation, Sociopolitical Structure and Statebuilding: Great Britain and Brandenburg-Prussia', in Tilly, *Formation of Nation States*

Brett-James, Norman G., *The Growth of Stuart London* (1935)

Brewer, John, *Sinews of Power: War, Money and the English State 1688–1783* (1989)

Bridgen, Susan, *Reformation London* (Oxford 1989)

Briggs, Robin, *Early Modern France 1560–1715* (Oxford 1977)

Brown, A. L., *The Governance of Late Medieval England 1272–1461* (1989)

Browning, Andrew, *Thomas Osborne, Earl of Danby* (3 vols., 1944–51)

Burgess, Glenn, *Absolute Monarchy and the Stuart Constitution* (New Haven 1996)
   'The Impact on Political Thought: Rhetorics for Troubled Times', in John Morrill
      (ed.), *The Impact of the English Civil War* (1991)
   'Introduction: The New British History', in Burgess, *The New British History*
   The Politics of the Ancient Constitution (1992)
   'Protestant Polemic: The Leveller Pamphlets', *Parergon* n.s. 11, 2, December 1993
   'Scottish or British?: Politics and Political Thought in Scotland, c. 1500–1707',
      Historical Journal 41, 2, 1998

Burgess, Glenn (ed.), *The New British History* (1999)

Burns, J. H., with Mark Goldie (eds.), *The Cambridge History of Political Thought
      1450–1700* (Cambridge 1991)

Butler, Martin, *Theatre and Crisis 1632–1642* (Cambridge 1984)

Calder, Angus, *The Myth of the Blitz* (1991)

Cannadine, David, 'British History: Past, Present – and Future?', *Past and Present*
      116, August 1987

Canny, N. (ed.), *The Oxford History of the British Empire Volume 1, The Origins of
      Empire: British Overseas Enterprise to the close of the Seventeenth Century*
      (Oxford 1998)

Capern, Amanda, 'The Caroline Church: James Ussher and the Irish Dimension',
      Historical Journal 39, 1, 1996

Carlton, Charles, *Charles I: The Personal Monarch* (1983)
   Going to the Wars: The Experience of the British Civil Wars 1638–1651 (1992)

Carsten, F. L. (ed.), *The New Cambridge Modern History*, vol. V, *The Ascendancy of
      France* (Cambridge 1961)

Carswell, John, *The Descent on England: A Study of the English Revolution of 1688
      and Its European Background* (1969)

Cartwright, Julia, *Sacharissa* (1901)

Chandaman, C. D., *The English Public Revenue 1660–1688* (Oxford 1975)

Childs, John, *The British Army of William III 1689–1702* (Manchester 1987)

Clark, J. C. D., *English Society 1688–1832* (Cambridge 1986)
   *Revolution and Rebellion: State and Society in England in the Seventeenth and
      Eighteenth Centuries* (Cambridge 1986)

Claydon, Tony, 'Problems with the British Problem', *Parliamentary History* 16, 2,
      1997
   William III and the Godly Revolution (Cambridge 1996)

Clifton, Robin, *The Last Popular Rebellion: The Western Rising of 1685* (1984)

Coffey, John, *Politics, Religion and the British Revolutions: The Mind of Samuel Rutherford* (Cambridge 1997)

Cogswell, Thomas, *The Blessed Revolution: English Politics and the Coming of War* (Cambridge 1989)

Coleman, Christopher and Starkey, David (eds.), *Revolution Reassessed: Revisions in the History of Tudor Government and Administration* (1986)

Colie, Rosalie, 'John Locke in the Republic of Letters', in E. H. Kossman (ed.), *Britain and the Netherlands* (1960), vol. I

Colley, Linda, *Britons: Forging the Nation 1707–1837* (New Haven 1992)

Collinson, Patrick, *Archbishop Grindal 1519–1583: The Struggle for a Reformed Church* (1979)

'Comment on Eamon Duffy's Neale Lecture and the Colloquium', in Tyacke, *England's Long Reformation*

De Republica Anglorum: Or, History with the Politics Put Back (Cambridge 1990)

'The Elizabethan Exclusion Crisis and the Elizabethan Polity', *Proceedings of the British Academy* 84, 1994

Godly People (1983)

'The Monarchical Republic of Elizabeth I', *Bulletin of the John Rylands Library* 69, 1987

The Religion of Protestants 1559–1625 (Oxford 1982)

Condren, Conal, *The Language of Politics in Seventeenth-Century England* (1994)

'On the Rhetorical Foundations of *Leviathan*', *History of Political Thought* 11, 4, Winter 1990

'Radicals, Conservatives and Moderates in Early Modern Political Thought: A Case of Sandwich Islands Syndrome?', *History of Political Thought* 10, 3, 1989

Connerton, Paul, *How Societies Remember* (Cambridge 1994)

Connif, J., 'Reason and History in Early Whig Thought: The Case of Algernon Sidney', *Journal of the History of Ideas* 43, 3, 1982

Cooper, J. M., 'Aristotle and the Goods of Fortune', *Philosophical Review* 94, 1985

Cooper, J. P. (ed.), *The New Cambridge Modern History of Europe*, vol. IV, *1609–1658/9* (Cambridge 1970)

Cornford, F. M., *Thucydides Mythhistoricus* (1907)

Coward, Barry, *Oliver Cromwell: A Profile* (1991)

The Stuart Age: England 1603–1714 (2nd edn, 1994)

Cranston, Maurice, *John Locke* (New York 1979)

Crawford, Patricia, 'Charles Stuart, That Man of Blood', *Journal of British Studies* 16, 2, 1977

Cressy, David, *Bonfires and Bells: National Memory and the Protestant Calendar in Elizabethan and Stuart England* (1989)

Cust, Richard, *The Forced Loan and English Politics 1626–1628* (Oxford 1987)

'News and Politics in Early Seventeenth-Century England', *Past and Present* 112, August 1986

Davids, Karel, and Lucassen, Jan, 'Conclusion', in Davids and Lucassen, *Miracle Mirrored*

Davids, Karel, and Lucassen, Jan (eds.), *A Miracle Mirrored: The Dutch Republic in European Perspective* (Cambridge 1995)

Davies, Julian, *The Caroline Captivity of the Church* (Oxford 1992)

Davis, J. C., 'Against Formality: One Aspect of the English Revolution', *Transactions of the Royal Historical Society*, 6th ser., 3, 1993

'Cromwell's Religion', in Morrill, *Oliver Cromwell and the English Revolution*

Fear Myth and History: The Ranters and the Historians (Cambridge 1987)

'Gerrard Winstanley and the Restoration of True Magistracy', *Past and Present* 70, February 1976

'The Levellers and Christianity', in Brian Manning (ed.), *Politics, Religion and the English Civil War* (1973)

'The Levellers and Democracy', *Past and Present* 40, July 1968

'Pocock's Harrington: Grace, Nature and Art in the Classical Republicanism of James Harrington', *Historical Journal* 24, 3, 1981

'Puritanism and Revolution: Themes, Categories, Methods and Conclusions', *Historical Journal* 34, 2, 1991

'Radicalism in a Traditional Society: The Evaluation of Radical Thought in the English Commonwealth 1649–1660', *History of Political Thought* 3, 2, 1982

'Religion and the Struggle for Freedom in the English Revolution', *Historical Journal* 35, 3, 1992

review of Greaves and Zaller, *Biographical Dictionary*, in *Political Science* 37, 1985

review of R. A. Mason (ed.), *Scots and Britons: Scottish Political Thought and the Union of 1603* (Cambridge 1994), in *Journal of Ecclesiastical History* 46, 4, October 1995

Utopia and the Ideal Society: A Study of English Utopian Writing 1516–1700 (Cambridge 1981)

De Krey, Gary, 'The First Restoration Crisis: Conscience and Coercion in London 1667–1673', *Albion* 25, 4, Winter 1993

A Fractured Society 1688–1715 (Oxford 1985)

'The London Whigs and the Exclusion Crisis Reconsidered', in A. L. Beier, David Cannadine and James Rosenheim (eds.), *The First Modern Society* (Cambridge 1989)

'Party Lines: A Reply', *Albion* 25, 4, Winter 1993

'Rethinking the Restoration: Dissenting Cases for Conscience 1667–1672', *Historical Journal* 38, 1, 1995

'Revolution *Redivivus*: 1688–1689 and the Radical Tradition in Seventeenth-Century London Politics', in Schwoerer, *Revolution of 1688–1689*

D'Entreves, A. P., *Natural Law* (2nd edn, 1970)

Dickson, P. G. M., *The Financial Revolution in England 1688–1756* (1967)

Donagan, Barbara, 'Codes and Conduct in the English Civil War', *Past and Present* 118, February 1988

Downs, Michael, *James Harrington* (Boston 1977)

Duffy, Eamon, 'The Long Reformation: Catholicism, Protestantism and the Multitude', in Tyacke, *England's Long Reformation*

Dunn, John, 'Revolution', in Ball, Farr and Hanson, *Political Innovation and Conceptual Change*

Dzelzainis, Martin, 'Milton's Classical Republicanism', in Armitage, Himy and Skinner, *Milton and Republicanism*

Elliott, J. H., *National and Comparative History* (Oxford 1991)
    Richelieu and Olivares (Cambridge 1984)

Elton, G. R., 'A High Road to Civil War?', in C. H. Carter (ed.), *From the Renaissance to the Counter-Reformation* (1966)
    Policy and Police: The Enforcement of the Reformation (Cambridge 1972)
    'The Stuart Century', in Elton, *Studies in Tudor and Stuart Politics and Government*, vol. II (Cambridge 1974)
    'Tudor Government', *Historical Journal* 31, 2, 1988
    The Tudor Revolution in Government (Cambridge 1953)

Evans, R. J. W., *The Making of the Habsburg Monarchy 1550–1700* (Oxford 1979)

Fairburn, Miles, *Nearly out of Heart and Hope: The Puzzle of a Colonial Labourer's Diary* (Auckland 1995)

Feiling, K., *A History of the Tory Party 1640–1714* (Oxford 1924)

Ferro, Marc, *The Use and Abuse of History: Or How the Past Is Taught* (1981)

Fincham, Ken, 'Prelacy and Politics: Archbishop Abbot's Defence of Protestant Orthodoxy', *Historical Research* 61, 144, 1988

Fink, Zera, *The Classical Republicans* (Evanston, Ill. 1945)

Firth, Sir Charles, 'Sir George Downing', *Dictionary of National Biography*, vol. XV

Fissel, Mark, *The Bishops' Wars: Charles I's Campaigns in Scotland 1638–1640* (Cambridge 1994)

Fitzmaurice, Andrew, 'The Civic Solution to the Crisis of English Colonization, 1609–1625', *Historical Journal* 42, 1, March 1999

Fletcher, Anthony, *The Outbreak of the English Civil War* (1981)
    review of Russell, *Causes of the English Civil War, Unrevolutionary England*, and *Fall of the British Monarchies*, in *Historical Journal* 36, 1, 1993

Frank, J., *The Levellers* (1957)

Freist, Dagmar, *Governed by Opinion: Politics, Religion and the Dynamics of Communication in Stuart London 1637–1645* (1997)

Fukuda, Arihiro, *Sovereignty and the Sword: Harrington, Hobbes, and Mixed Government in the English Civil Wars* (Oxford 1997)

Gardiner, S. R., *History of England from the Accession of James I to the Outbreak of the Civil War 1603–1642* (10 vols., 1895)

The Thirty Years War 1618–1648 (1874)

Gentles, Ian, *The New Model Army in England, Ireland and Scotland 1645–1653* (1992)

Geyl, P., *The Netherlands in the Seventeenth Century Part Two 1648–1715* (1964)

Glassey, Lionel, 'Introduction', in Glassey, *Reigns of Charles II and James VII and II*

Glassey, Lionel (ed.), *The Reigns of Charles II and James VII and II* (1997)

Goldie, Mark, 'The Civil Religion of James Harrington', in Pagden, *Languages of Political Theory*

'Divergence and Union: Scotland and England 1660–1707', in Bradshaw and Morrill, *The British Problem*

'The Hilton Gang and the Purge of London in the 1680s', in Howard Nenner (ed.), *Politics and the Political Imagination in Later Stuart Britain* (Rochester, N.Y. 1997)

'The Political Thought of the Anglican Revolution', in Beddard, *Revolutions of 1688*

'Restoration Political Thought', in Glassey, *Reigns of Charles II and James VII and II*

'The Revolution of 1689 and the Structure of Political Argument', *Bulletin of Research in the Humanities* 83, 1980

'The Roots of True Whiggism 1688–1694', *History of Political Thought* 1, 2, 1980

Greaves, Richard, *Deliver Us from Evil: The Radical Underground in Britain, 1660–1663* (Oxford 1986)

Enemies Under His Feet: Radicals and Nonconformists in Britain, 1664–1667 (Stanford 1990)

'Great Scott!: The Restoration in Turmoil, or, Restoration Crises and the Emergence of Party', *Albion* 25, 4, Winter 1993

'"Let Truth Be Free": John Bunyan and the Restoration Crisis of 1667–1673', *Albion* 28, 4, Winter 1996

Secrets of the Kingdom: British Radicals from the Popish Plot to the Revolution of 1688–1689 (Stanford 1992)

Greaves, Richard and Zaller, Robert (eds.), *A Biographical Dictionary of British Radicals* (3 vols., Brighton 1982)

Green, Ian, *The Re-establishment of the Church of England* (1978)

Greengrass, Mark, *Governing Passions: The Reformation of the Kingdom in the French Civil Wars 1576–1586* (forthcoming)

Greengrass, Mark, Leslie, Michael and Raylor, Timothy, 'Introduction', in Greengrass, Leslie and Raylor, *Samuel Hartlib and Universal Reformation*

Greengrass, Mark, Leslie, Michael and Raylor, Timothy (eds.), *Samuel Hartlib and Universal Reformation: Studies in Intellectual Communication* (Cambridge 1994)

Gregg, Pauline, *Free-Born John: A Biography of John Lilburne* (1961)

Grell, O., Israel, J. and Tyacke, N. (eds.), *From Persecution to Toleration: The Glorious Revolution and Religion in England* (1991)

Guy, John, 'The Origins of the Petition of Right Reconsidered', *Historical Journal* 25, 2, 1982

Tudor England (1988)

Haakonssen, K., *Natural Law and Moral Philosophy* (Cambridge 1996)

Haley, K. D. H., *The First Earl of Shaftesbury* (Oxford 1968)

William of Orange and the English Opposition 1672–1674 (1953)

Haller, William, *Liberty and Reformation in the Puritan Revolution* (New York 1955)

The Rise of Puritanism (New York 1938)

Hampsher-Monk, Iain, 'Putney, Property, and Professor MacPherson', *Political Studies* 24, 1976

Harris, R. W., *Clarendon and the English Revolution* (1983)

Harris, Tim, '"Lives, Liberties and Estates": Rhetorics of Liberty in the Reign of Charles II', in Harris, Seaward and Goldie, *Politics of Religion in Restoration England*

London Crowds in the Reign of Charles II (Cambridge 1987)

Politics Under the Later Stuarts: Party Conflict in a Divided Society, 1660–1715 (1993)

Harris, Tim, Seaward, Paul and Goldie, Mark (eds.), *The Politics of Religion in Restoration England* (Oxford 1990)

Harth, Philip, *Pen for a Party: Dryden's Tory Propaganda in Its Contexts* (Princeton 1993)

Havran, Martin J., *The Catholics in Caroline England* (Stanford 1962)

Henning, Basil D. (ed.), *The House of Commons 1660–1690* (3 vols., 1983)

Hexter, J. H., 'The Early Stuarts and Parliament: Old Hat and the *Nouvelle Vague*', *Parliamentary History* 1, 1, 1982

Hexter, J. H. (ed.), *Parliament and Liberty from the Reign of Elizabeth to the English Civil War* (Stanford 1992)

Hibbard, Caroline, *Charles I and the Popish Plot* (Chapel Hill 1983)

Hill, Christopher, *The Century of Revolution 1603–1714* (1969)

Economic Problems of the Church from Archbishop Whitgift to the Long Parliament (Oxford 1956)

The English Bible and the Seventeenth-Century Revolution (1993)

The Experience of Defeat: Milton and Some Contemporaries (1984)

'Irreligion in the "Puritan" Revolution', in J. F. McGregor and B. Reay (eds.), *Radical Religion in the English Revolution* (Oxford 1984)

Puritanism and Revolution (1958)

The World Turned Upside Down: Radical Ideas During the English Revolution (1972)

Himy, Armand, '*Paradise Lost* as a Republican "Tractatus Theologico-Politicus"', in Armitage, Himy and Skinner, *Milton and Republicanism*

Hirst, Derek, *Authority and Conflict: England 1603–1658* (1986)

'The English Republic and the Meaning of Britain', in Bradshaw and Morrill, *The British Problem*

'Locating the 1650s in England's Seventeenth Century', *History* 81, 3, 1996

'The Lord Protector 1653–1658', in Morrill, *Oliver Cromwell and the English Revolution*

'Parliament, Law and War in the 1620s', *Historical Journal* 23, 2, 1980

The Representative of the People?: Voters and Voting in England Under the Early Stuarts (Cambridge 1975)

Hoak, Dale and Feingold, Mordechai, 'Introduction', in Hoak and Feingold, *World of William and Mary*

Hoak, Dale and Feingold, Mordechai (eds.), *The World of William and Mary: Anglo-Dutch Perspectives on the Revolution of 1688–1689* (Stanford 1996)

Holmes, Geoffrey, *British Politics in the Reign of Anne* (revised edn, 1987)

The Making of a Great Power: Late Stuart and Early Georgian Britain 1660–1722 (1993)

Hont, Istvan, 'Free Trade and the Economic Limits to National Politics: Neo-Machiavellian Political Economy Reconsidered', in John Dunn (ed.), *The Economic Limits to Modern Politics* (Cambridge 1990)

Horst, Irvin B., *The Radical Brethren: Anabaptism and the English Reformation to 1558* (Nieuwkoop 1972)

Horwitz, Henry, *Parliament, Policy and Politics in the Reign of William III* (Manchester 1977)

Revolution Politicks (Cambridge 1968)

Hughes, Ann, *The Causes of the English Civil War* (2nd edn, 1998)

Hutton, Ronald, *Charles II* (Oxford 1991)

'The Making of the Secret Treaty of Dover', *Historical Journal* 29, 2, 1986

'The Religion of Charles II', in Smuts, *The Stuart Court and Europe*

The Royalist War Effort 1642–1646 (1982)

Ingrao, C. W., *The Habsburg Monarchy 1618–1815* (Cambridge 1994)

Israel, Jonathan, *The Dutch Republic: Its Rise, Greatness, and Fall 1477–1806* (Oxford 1995)

'The Dutch Role in the Glorious Revolution', in Israel, *Anglo-Dutch Moment*

'England, the Dutch Republic and Europe in the Seventeenth Century', *Historical Journal* 40, 4, 1997

'General Introduction', in Israel, *Anglo-Dutch Moment*

Israel, Jonathan (ed.), *The Anglo-Dutch Moment: Essays on the Glorious Revolution and Its World Impact* (Cambridge 1991)

Israel, Jonathan and Parker, Geoffrey, 'Of Providence and Protestant Winds: The Spanish Armada of 1588 and the Dutch Armada of 1688', in Israel, *Anglo-Dutch Moment*

James, Susan, *Passion and Action: The Emotions in Seventeenth-Century Philosophy*

(Oxford 1997)

Johns, Adrian, *The Nature of the Book: Print and Knowledge in the Making* (Chicago 1998)

Johnston, David, *The Rhetoric of Leviathan* (Princeton 1986)

Jones, C., *Britain in the First Age of Party* (1987)

Jones, D. W., 'Defending the Revolution: The Economics, Logistics and Finance of England's War Effort 1688–1712', in Hoak and Feingold, *William and Mary War and Economy in the Age of William III and Marlborough* (1988)

Jones, Edwin, *The English Nation: The Great Myth* (Stroud 1998)

Jones, G. H., 'The Irish Fright of 1688: Real Violent and Imagined Massacre', *Bulletin of the Institute of Historical Research* 55, 1982

Jones, J. R., *Country and Court: England 1658–1714* (1978)

The First Whigs (1961)

The Revolution of 1688 in England (1972)

Jones, J. R. (ed.), *Liberty Secured?: Britain Before and After 1688* (Stanford 1992)

Judson, M. A., *The Crisis of the Constitution* (New Brunswick, N.J. 1949)

The Political Thought of Sir Henry Vane the Younger (Philadelphia 1969)

Karsten, P., *Patriot Heroes in England and America* (Madison 1978)

Keeble, N. H., *The Literary Culture of Nonconformity in Later Seventeenth-Century England* (Athens, Ga. 1987)

Kenyon, J. P., 'The Earl of Sunderland and the Revolution of 1688', *Cambridge Historical Journal* 11, 3, 1955

The Nobility in the Revolution of 1688 (Hull 1963)

The Popish Plot (Harmondsworth 1972)

Revolution Principles: The Politics of Party 1689–1720 (Cambridge 1977)

Robert Spencer, Earl of Sunderland 1641–1703 (Cambridge 1958)

Kerrigan, John, 'Birth of a Naison', *London Review of Books*, 5 June 1997

Kishlansky, Mark, 'The Army and the Levellers: The Roads to Putney', *Historical Journal* 22, 4, 1979

A Monarchy Transformed: Britain 1603–1714 (1996)

The Rise of the New Model Army (Cambridge 1979)

'Tyranny Denied: Charles I, Attorney General Heath, and the Five Knights Case', *Historical Journal* 42, 1, March 1999

Klassen, P. J., *The Economics of Anabaptism 1525–1560* (The Hague 1964)

Knights, Mark, 'London's "Monster" Petition of 1680', *Historical Journal* 36, 1, 1993

Politics and Opinion in Crisis 1678–1681 (Cambridge 1994)

Koenigsberger, H. G., 'The Crisis of the Seventeenth Century: A Farewell?', in Koenigsberger, *Politicians and Virtuosi*

'Dominium Regale or Dominium Politicum et Regale', in Koenigsberger, *Politicians and Virtuosi*

Politicians and Virtuosi (1986)

Lake, P. G., 'Calvinism and the English Church 1570–1635', *Past and Present* 114, February 1987

'Constitutional Consensus and Puritan Opposition in the 1620s: Thomas Scott and the Spanish Match', *Historical Journal* 25, 4, 1982

Lamont, William, *Richard Baxter and the Millennium* (1979)

Lee, Maurice, *The Cabal* (1965)

Lenman, Bruce, 'English Thought in the Era of the Revolution', in Hoak and Feingold, *William and Mary*

Levi, A., *French Moralists: The Theory of the Passions* (1964)

Levine, Mortimer, *The Early Elizabethan Succession Question 1558–1568* (Stanford 1966)

Lindley, Keith, *Popular Politics and Religion in Civil War London* (1997)

Lipson, E., 'The Elections to the Exclusion Parliaments 1679–1681', *English Historical Review* 28, 1913

Liu, Tai, *Discord in Zion* (The Hague 1973)

Loach, Jennifer, *Parliament Under the Tudors* (Oxford 1991)

MacCaffrey, W. T., *Elizabeth I: War and Politics 1588–1603* (Princeton 1992)

Queen Elizabeth and the Making of Policy 1572–1588 (Princeton 1981)

McDowell, Nicholas, 'A Ranter Reconsidered: Abiezer Coppe and Civil War Stereotypes', *The Seventeenth Century* 12, 2, 1997

McGee, J. Sears, 'William Laud and the Outward Face of Religion', in R. DeMolen (ed.), *Leaders of the Reformation* (1984)

MacGillivray, R., *Restoration Historians and the English Civil War* (The Hague 1974)

MacInnes, Allan, *Charles I and the Making of the Covenanting Movement* (Edinburgh 1991)

McKeon, Michael, 'Politics of Discourses and the Rise of the Aesthetic', in K. Sharpe and S. Zwicker (eds.), *Politics of Discourse* (Los Angeles 1987)

MacLachlan, A., *The Rise and Fall of Revolutionary England: An Essay on the Fabrication of Seventeenth-Century History* (1996)

MacPherson, C. B., *The Political Theory of Possessive Individualism: Hobbes to Locke* (Oxford 1962)

Maguire, Nancy Klein, 'The Duchess of Portsmouth: English Royal Consort and French Politician, 1670–1685', in Smuts, *The Stuart Court and Europe*

Regicide and Restoration: English Tragicomedy 1660–1671 (Cambridge 1992)

Malcolm, Noel, 'Hobbes and Spinoza', in Burns with Goldie, *Cambridge History of Political Thought*

Malekin, Peter, *Liberty and Love: English Literature and Society 1640–1688* (1981)

Marshall, John, *John Locke: Resistance, Religion and Responsibility* (1994)

Marshall, P.J. (ed.), *The Oxford History of the British Empire Volume II, The Eighteenth Century* (Oxford 1998)

Mendle, Michael, *Henry Parker and the English Civil War* (Cambridge 1995)

Miller, John, *Charles II: A Study in Kingship* (1991)

James II (1978)

Popery and Politics in England 1660–1688 (Cambridge 1973)

'The Potential for Absolutism in Later Stuart England', *History* 69, 1984

Milne, Dorothy, 'The Results of the Rye House Plot', *Transactions of the Royal Historical Society* 5th ser., 1, 1951

Milton, Anthony, *Catholic and Reformed: The Roman and Protestant Churches in English Protestant Thought 1600–1640* (Cambridge 1995)

Morrill, John, 'The Army Revolt of 1647', in Morrill, *Oliver Cromwell and the English Revolution*

'The British Problem', in Bradshaw and Morrill, *The British Problem*

'The Church in England 1642–1649', in Morrill, *The Nature of the English Revolution*

The Nature of the English Revolution (1993)

'The Religious Context of the English Civil War', in Morrill, *The Nature of the English Revolution*

Revolt in the Provinces: The English People and the Tragedies of War (1999)

The Revolt of the Provinces: Conservatives and Radicals in the English Civil War 1630–1650 (1976)

'The Sensible Revolution', in Israel, *Anglo-Dutch Moment*

'Three Kingdoms and One Commonwealth?: The Enigma of Mid-Seventeenth-Century Britain and Ireland', in A. Grant and K. Stringer (eds.), *Uniting the Kingdom: The Making of British History* (1995)

Morrill, John (ed.), *Oliver Cromwell and the English Revolution* (1990)

Revolution and Restoration: England in the 1650s (1992)

The Scottish National Covenant in Its British Context 1637–1651 (1990)

Mulgan, John, *Report on Experience* (Oxford 1947)

Mullett, Michael, *Radical Religious Movements in Early Modern Europe* (1980)

Multamaki, Kustaa, *Towards Great Britain: Commerce and Conquest in the Thought of Algernon Sidney and Charles Davenant* (Helsinki 1999)

Munz, Peter, *The Shapes of Time: A New Look at the Philosophy of History* (Middletown, Conn. 1977)

Norbrook, David, *Poetry and Politics in the English Renaissance* (1984)

Writing the English Republic: Poetry, Rhetoric and Politics 1627–1660 (Cambridge 1999)

Nuttall, Geoffrey, *Christian Pacifism in History* (Oxford 1958)

'Order and Authority: Creating Party in Restoration England', special issue of *Albion* 25, 4, Winter 1993

Pagden, A., *Lords of All the World: Ideologies of Empire in Spain, Britain and France c.1500–1800* (New Haven 1995)

Pagden, A. (ed.), *The Languages of Political Theory in Early Modern Europe* (Cambridge 1988)

Parker, Geoffrey, *Europe in Crisis 1598–1648* (1979)

The Military Revolution: Military Innovation and the Rise of the West 1500–1800 (Cambridge 1996)

The Thirty Years War (1987)

Parker, Geoffrey and Israel, Jonathan, 'Of Providence and Protestant Winds: The Spanish Armada of 1588 and the Dutch Armada of 1688', in Israel, *Anglo-Dutch Moment*

Patterson, Annabel, *Early Modern Liberalism* (Cambridge 1997)

Patterson, W. B., *King James VI and I and the Reunion of Christendom* (Cambridge 1997)

Pearl, Valerie, *London and the Outbreak of the Puritan Revolution* (1961)

Peck, Linda Levy (ed.), *The Mental World of the Jacobean Court* (Cambridge 1991)

Peltonen, Markku, 'Citizenship and Republicanism in Elizabethan England', in Skinner and van Gelderen, *Republicanism and Constitutionalism*

Classical Humanism and Republicanism in English Political Thought 1570–1640 (Cambridge 1995)

Phillipson, N. and Skinner, Q. (eds.), *Political Discourse in Early Modern Britain* (Cambridge 1993)

Pincus, Steven, 'The English Debate over Universal Monarchy', in J. Robertson (ed.), *A Union for Empire: Political Thought and the British Union of 1707* (Cambridge 1995)

'Neither Machiavellian Moment nor Possessive Individualism: Commercial Society and the Defenders of the English Commonwealth', *American Historical Review*, June 1998

Protestantism and Patriotism (Cambridge 1996)

Plumb, J. H., *The Growth of Political Stability in England 1675–1725* (1967)

Pocock, J. G. A., *The Ancient Constitution and the Feudal Law: A Reissue with Retrospect* (Cambridge 1987)

'The Atlantic Archipelago and the War of the Three Kingdoms', in Bradshaw and Morrill, *The British Problem*

'British History: A Plea for a New Subject', *Journal of Modern History* 47, December 1975

'A Discourse of Sovereignty: Observations on the Work in Progress', in Phillipson and Skinner, *Political Discourse in Early Modern Britain*

'England's Cato: The Virtues and Fortunes of Algernon Sidney', *Historical Journal* 37, 4, 1994

'The Fourth English Civil War: Dissolution, Desertion, and Alternative Histories in the Glorious Revolution', in Schwoerer, *Revolution of 1688–1689*

'Historical Introduction', in Harrington, *Political Works*

'The Limits and Divisions of British History: In Search of the Unknown Subject', *American Historical Review* 87, 2, April 1987

The Machiavellian Moment: Florentine Political Thought and the Atlantic Republican Tradition (Princeton 1975)

Politics, Language and Time: Essays on Political Thought and Theory (New York 1971)

'Spinoza and Harrington: An Exercise in Comparison', *Bijdragen en Mededelingen Betreffende de Geschiedenis der Nederlanden* 102, 3, 1987

'Standing Army and Public Credit: The Institutions of Leviathan', in Hoak and Feingold, *William and Mary*

Virtue, Commerce and History (Cambridge 1985)

Powicke, F. M., *The Reformation in England* (Oxford 1941)

Raab, Felix, *The English Face of Machiavelli* (1964)

Rahe, Paul, 'Antiquity Surpassed: The Repudiation of Classical Republicanism', in Wootton, *Republicanism, Liberty, and Commercial Society*

Republics Ancient and Modern (3 vols., Chapel Hill 1994)

Ranke, Leopold von, *A History of England Principally in the Seventeenth Century* (6 vols., Oxford 1875)

Raymond, Joad (ed.), *Making the News: An Anthology of the Newsbooks of Revolutionary England 1641–1660* (Moreton-in-Marsh 1993)

Reay, Barry, *The Quakers and the English Revolution* (1985)

Reeve, John, 'Britain or Europe? The Context of Early Modern English History: Political and Cultural, Economic and Social, Naval and Military', in Burgess, *The New British History*

Charles I and the Road to Personal Rule (Cambridge 1989)

'The Politics of War Finance in an Age of Confessional Strife: A Comparative Anglo-European View', *Parergon* n.s., 14, 1, 1996

Reik, Miriam, *The Golden Lands of Thomas Hobbes* (Detroit 1977)

Reinhard, Wolfgang, 'Power Elites, State Servants, Ruling Classes, and the Growth of State Power', in Reinhard, *Power Elites and State Building*

Reinhard, Wolfgang (ed.), *Power Elites and State Building* (Oxford 1996)

Robbins, Caroline, *The Eighteenth-Century Commonwealthsman* (Cambridge, Mass. 1959)

Roberts, Clayton, 'The Impeachment of the Earl of Clarendon', *Cambridge Historical Journal* 13, 1, 1957

Roberts, Stephen, *Recovery and Restoration in an English County: Devon Local Administration 1646–1670* (Exeter 1985)

Robertson, John, *The Militia Issue and the Scottish Enlightenment* (Edinburgh 1985)

Ronalds, F. S., *The Attempted Whig Revolution of 1678–1681* (Urbana, Ill. 1937)

Rose, Craig, 'Providence, Protestant Union and Godly Reformation in the 1690s', *Transactions of the Royal Historical Society* 6th ser., 3, 1993

Roseveare, Henry, *The Financial Revolution 1660–1760* (1991)

'Prejudice and Policy: Sir George Downing as Parliamentary Entrepreneur', in D.

C. Coleman and Peter Mathias (eds.), *Enterprise and History: Essays in Honour of Charles Wilson* (Cambridge 1986)

The Treasury 1660–1870: The Foundations of Control (1973)

Roy, Ian, '"England Turned Germany": The Aftermath of the Civil War in Its European Context', *Transactions of the Royal Historical Society* 5th ser., 28, 1978

Russell, Conrad, *The Causes of the English Civil War* (Oxford 1990)

The Fall of the British Monarchies 1637–1642 (Oxford 1991)

'The Irish Rebellion of 1641', in Russell, *Unrevolutionary England*

'Monarchies, Wars and Estates in England, France and Spain 1580–1640', in Russell, *Unrevolutionary England*

'Parliamentary History in Perspective 1604–1629', in Russell, *Unrevolutionary England*

Parliaments and English Politics 1621–1629 (Oxford 1979)

review of Hexter, *Parliament and Liberty*, in *History* 78, June 1993

Unrevolutionary England (1990)

Salmon, J. H., *The French Religious Wars in English Political Thought* (Cambridge 1959)

Renaissance and Revolt (Cambridge 1987)

Salt, Peter, 'Sir Simonds D'Ewes and the Levying of Ship Money, 1635–1640', *Historical Journal* 37, 2, 1984

Sanderson, John, *'But the People's Creatures': The Philosophical Basis of the English Civil War* (Manchester 1989)

Schenck, W., *The Concern for Social Justice in the Puritan Revolution* (1948)

Schwoerer, Lois, *The Declaration of Rights, 1689* (Baltimore and London 1981)

'Introduction', in Schwoerer, *Revolution of 1688–1689*

Schwoerer, Lois (ed.), *The Revolution of 1688–1689* (Cambridge 1992)

Scott, Jonathan, *Algernon Sidney and the English Republic 1623–1677* (Cambridge 1988)

Algernon Sidney and the Restoration Crisis 1677–1683 (Cambridge 1991)

'Classical Republicanism in Seventeenth-Century England and the Netherlands', in Skinner and van Gelderen, *Republicanism and Constitutionalism*

'England's Troubles: Exhuming the Popish Plot', in Harris, Seaward and Goldie, *Politics of Religion in Restoration England*

'England's Troubles 1603–1702', in Smuts, *The Stuart Court and Europe*

'The English Republican Imagination', in Morrill, *Revolution and Restoration*

Harry's Absence: Looking for My Father on the Mountain (Wellington 1997)

'The Law of War: Grotius, Sidney, Locke and the Political Theory of Rebellion', *History of Political Thought* 13, 4, Winter 1992

'The Peace of Silence: Thucydides and the English Civil War', in Miles Fairburn and W. H. Oliver (eds.), *The Certainty of Doubt: Essays in Honour of Peter Munz* (Wellington 1996)

'The Pragmatic Republicanism of Sir George Downing 1623–1683', in Paul

Millett (ed.), *Essays on the History of Downing College* (forthcoming)

'Radicalism and Restoration: The Shape of the Stuart Experience', *Historical Journal* 31, 2, 1988

'The Rapture of Motion: James Harrington's Republicanism', in Phillipson and Skinner, *Political Discourse in Early Modern Britain*

'Restoration Process: Or, If This Isn't a Party We're Not Having a Good Time', *Albion* 25, 4, Winter 1993

review of Peltonen, *Classical Humanism and Republicanism*, Armitage, Himy and Skinner, *Milton and Republicanism*, and Sidney, *Court Maxims*, ed. Blom, Haitsma Mulier and Janse, in *English Historical Review*, September 1997

review of Wootton, *Republicanism, Liberty, and Commercial Society*, in *Parliamentary History* 16, 2, 1997

Seaver, Paul, *Wallington's World: A Puritan Artisan in Seventeenth-Century London* (Stanford 1985)

Seaward, Paul, *The Cavalier Parliament and the Reconstruction of the Old Regime* (Cambridge 1989)

Shackleton, R., 'Montesquieu and Machiavelli: A Reappraisal', *Comparative Literature Studies* 1, 1, 1964

Sharpe, Kevin, *Criticism and Compliment: The Politics of Literature in the England of Charles I* (Cambridge 1987)

The Personal Rule of Charles I (New Haven 1992)

Sharpe, Kevin and Lake, Peter, 'Introduction', in Lake and Sharpe (eds.), *Culture and Politics in Early Stuart England* (1994)

Shaw, H., *The Levellers* (1968)

Shennan, J. H., *The Origins of the Modern European State 1450–1725* (1974)

Skinner, Quentin, *The Foundations of Modern Political Thought* (2 vols., Cambridge 1978)

Liberty Before Liberalism (Cambridge 1997)

Machiavelli (Oxford 1981)

Reason and Rhetoric in the Philosophy of Hobbes (Cambridge 1996)

'A Reply to My Critics', in James Tully (ed.), *Meaning and Context: Quentin Skinner and His Critics* (Princeton 1988)

'The Republican Ideal of Political Liberty', in Bock, Skinner and Viroli, *Machiavelli and Republicanism*

'The State', in Ball, Farr and Hanson, *Political Innovation and Conceptual Change*

'Thomas Hobbes on the Proper Signification of Liberty', *Transactions of the Royal Historical Society* 5th ser., 40, 1990

Skinner, Quentin and van Gelderen, Martin (eds.), *Republicanism and Constitutionalism in Early Modern Europe* (Cambridge, forthcoming)

Smith, David, *A History of the Modern British Isles 1603–1707: The Double Crown* (Oxford 1998)

'The Struggle for New Constitutional and Institutional Forms', in Morrill, *Revolution and Restoration*

Smith, Nigel, *Literature and Revolution in England 1640–1660* (New Haven 1994)

Perfection Proclaimed: Language and Literature in English Radical Religion 1640–1660 (Oxford 1989)

'Popular Republicanism in the 1650s', in Armitage, Himy and Skinner, *Milton and Republicanism*

Smuts, R. Malcolm (ed.), *The Stuart Court and Europe* (Cambridge 1996)

Solt, Leo, *Saints in Arms* (Stanford 1959)

Sommerville, J. P., 'James I and the Divine Right of Kings: English Politics and Continental Theory', in Peck, *Mental World of the Jacobean Court*

Politics and Ideology in England 1603–1640 (1986)

Thomas Hobbes: Political Ideas in Historical Context (1992)

Speck, William, 'Britain and the Dutch Republic', in Davids and Lucassen, *A Miracle Mirrored*

Reluctant Revolutionaries (Oxford 1989)

Spellman, W., *John Locke* (1997)

Spufford, Peter, 'Access to Credit and Capital in the Commercial Centres of Europe', in Davids and Lucassen, *A Miracle Mirrored*

Spurr, John, 'The Church, the Societies, and the Moral Revolution of 1688', in John Walsh, Colin Haydon and Stephen Taylor (eds.), *The Church of England c. 1689–c. 1833: From Toleration to Tractarianism* (Cambridge 1993)

'Religion in Restoration England', in Glassey, *Reigns of Charles II and James VII and II*

The Restoration Church of England 1646–1689 (New Haven 1991)

Starkey, David, 'A Reply. Tudor Government: The Facts?', *Historical Journal* 31, 4, 1988

Stayer, James, *The German Peasants War and Anabaptist Community of Goods* (Montreal 1991)

Stevenson, David, *The Scottish Revolution 1637–1644* (1973)

Stone, L., 'Literacy and Education in England 1600–1900', *Past and Present* 42, February 1969

Strachan, Michael, *Sir Thomas Roe: A Life 1581–1644* (Salisbury 1989)

Strauss, Leo, *The Political Philosophy of Hobbes* (Chicago 1952)

Sullivan, Vickie, 'The Civic Humanist Portrait of Machiavelli's English Successors', *History of Political Thought* 15, Spring 1994

'T Hart, Marjolein, '"The Devil or the Dutch": Holland's Impact on the Financial Revolution in England, 1643–1694', *Parliaments, Estates and Representation* 11, 1, June 1991

Taylor, A. J. P., 'Reply', *Journal of Modern History* 47, December 1975

Thomas, Keith, 'The Levellers and the Franchise', in G. E. Aylmer (ed.), *The Interregnum: The Quest for Settlement 1646–1660* (1972)

   'The Meaning of Literacy in Early Modern England', in G. Baumann (ed.), *The Written Word: Literacy in Transition* (1986)

Tilly, Charles, 'Reflections on the History of European State-Making', in Tilly, *Formation of Nation States*

Tilly, Charles (ed.), *The Formation of Nation States in Western Europe* (Princeton 1975)

Todd, Margo, *Christian Humanism and the Puritan Social Order* (Cambridge 1987)

Tolmie, Murray, *The Triumph of the Saints* (Cambridge 1977)

Tracy, James, *A Financial Revolution in the Habsburg Netherlands* (Cambridge 1985)

Trevelyan, G. M., *England Under the Stuarts* (1904)

   History of England (2nd edn, 1937)

Trevor-Roper, H. R., Lord Dacre, *Catholics, Anglicans and Puritans: Seventeenth-Century Essays* (1989)

   'The Continuity of the English Revolution', *Transactions of the Royal Historical Society* 6th ser., 1, 1991

   Religion, the Reformation and Social Change (1967)

   'Three Foreigners: The Philosophers of the Puritan Revolution', in Trevor-Roper, *Social Change*

Tuck, Richard, 'The "Modern" Theory of Natural Law', in Pagden, *Languages of Political Theory*

   Natural Rights Theories (Cambridge 1979)

   'A New Date for Filmer's *Patriarcha*', *Historical Journal* 29, 1, 1986

   Philosophy and Government 1572–1651 (Cambridge 1993)

Tully, James, *A Discourse on Property* (1980)

Tyacke, Nicholas, 'Anglican Attitudes: Some Recent Writings on English Religious History, from the Reformation to the Civil War', *Journal of British Studies* 35, April 1996

   Anti-Calvinists: The Rise of English Arminianism c. 1590–1640 (Oxford 1987)

   'Introduction: Re-thinking the "English Reformation"', in Tyacke, *England's Long Reformation*

   'Puritanism, Arminianism and Counter-Revolution', in Conrad Russell (ed.), *The Origins of the English Civil War* (1973)

Tyacke, Nicholas (ed.), *England's Long Reformation 1500–1800* (1998)

Underdown, David, *Pride's Purge* (1971)

van Gelderen, Martin, 'The Machiavellian Moment and the Dutch Revolt', in Bock, Skinner and Viroli, *Machiavelli and Republicanism*

   The Political Thought of the Dutch Revolt 1555–1590 (Cambridge 1993)

Viroli, Maurizio, *From Politics to Reason of State: The Acquisition and Transformation of the Language of Politics 1250–1600* (Cambridge 1992)

'Machiavelli and the Republican Idea of Politics', in Bock, Skinner and Viroli, *Machiavelli and Republicanism*

Wallace, J. M., *Destiny His Choice: The Loyalism of Andrew Marvell* (Cambridge 1980)

Walsham, Alexandra, '"The Fatall Vesper": Providentialism and Anti-Popery in Late Jacobean London', *Past and Present* 144, August 1994

Webb, Stephen Saunders, *The Governors-General: The English Army and the Definition of the Empire 1569–1681* (Chapel Hill 1979)

Webster, Charles, *The Great Instauration: Science, Medicine and Reform, 1626–1660* (1975)

Wedgwood, C. V., *The Trial of Charles I* (1966)

Weir, Robert, '"Shaftesbury's Darling": British Settlement in the Carolinas at the Close of the Seventeenth Century', in Canny, *The Origins of Empire*

Western, J., *Monarchy and Revolution: The English State in the 1680s* (1972)

White, P., *Predestination, Policy and Polemic: Conflict and Consensus in the English Church from the Reformation to the Civil War* (Cambridge 1992)

Williams, G. H., *The Radical Reformation* (1962)

Wilson, Charles, *Profit and Power: A Study of England and the Dutch Wars* (1957)

Winter, Jay, *Sites of Memory, Sites of Mourning: The Great War in European Cultural History* (Cambridge 1995)

Woolrych, Austin, 'Putney Revisited', in S. Roberts (ed.), *Politics and People in Revolutionary England* (1986)

Soldiers and Statesmen: The General Council of the Army and Its Debates, 1647–1648 (Oxford 1987)

Wootton, David, 'From Rebellion to Revolution: The Crisis of the Winter of 1642/3 and the Origins of Civil War Radicalism', *English Historical Review*, July 1990

'Leveller Democracy and the Puritan Revolution', in Burns and Goldie, *Cambridge History of Political Thought*

Wootton, David (ed.), *Republicanism, Liberty and Commercial Society 1649–1776* (Stanford 1994)

Worden, Blair, 'Classical Republicanism and the Puritan Revolution', in V. Pearl, H. Lloyd-Jones and B. Worden (eds.), *History and Imagination* (Oxford 1981)

'Conrad Russell's Civil War', *London Review of Books*, 29 August 1991

'Harrington's Oceana: Origins and Aftermath, 1651–1660' in Wootton, *Republicanism, Liberty and Commercial Society*

'James Harrington and "The Commonwealth of Oceana" 1656', in Wootton, *Republicanism, Liberty and Commercial Society*

'Marchamont Nedham and the Beginnings of English Republicanism, 1649–1656', in Wootton, *Republicanism, Liberty and Commercial Society*

'Milton and the Tyranny of Heaven', in Bock, Skinner and Viroli, *Machiavelli and Republicanism*

'Oliver Cromwell and the Sin of Achan', in Derek Beales and Geoffrey Best (eds.), *History, Society and the Churches* (1985)

'The Politics of Marvell's Horatian Ode', *Historical Journal* 27, 3, 1984

'Republicanism and the Restoration 1660–1683', in Wootton, *Republicanism, Liberty and Commercial Society*

'The Revolution and the English Republican Tradition', in Israel, *Anglo-Dutch Moment*

The Rump Parliament (Cambridge 1975)

The Sound of Virtue: Philip Sidney's Arcadia and Elizabethan Politics (New Haven 1996)

Wormald, Jenny, 'James VI and I, *Basilikon Doron* and *The Trew Law of Free Monarchies*', in Peck, *Mental World of the Jacobean Court*

Zagorin, Perez, *A History of Political Thought in the English Revolution* (1954)

Zaller, Robert, 'The Crisis of European Liberty', in Hexter, *Parliament and Liberty*

Zuckert, Michael, *Natural Rights and the New Republicanism* (Princeton 1994)

Unpublished

Alford, Stephen, 'William Cecil and the British Succession Crisis of the 1560s', Ph.D thesis, St Andrews 1996

Allan, Diana, 'John Vicars', undergraduate dissertation, Cambridge 1995

Baldwin, Geoffrey, 'The Self and the State 1580–1660', Ph.D thesis, Cambridge 1998

Birmingham, R., 'Continental Resonances in Mid-Seventeenth-Century English Radical Religious Ideas', MPhil. thesis, Cambridge 1998

Fitzmaurice, Andrew, 'Classical Rhetoric and the Literature of Discovery 1570–1630', Ph.D thesis, Cambridge 1996

Frearson, Michael, 'An Aspect of the Production of the Newsbooks of the 1620s', Cambridge seminar paper, 1993

'The English Corantos of the 1620s', Ph.D thesis, Cambridge 1994

Kishlansky, Mark, 'Charles I: The Man Who Would Be King', paper delivered at Downing College, Cambridge, 28 January 1998

Knights, Mark, 'Politics and Opinion During the Exclusion Crisis 1678–1681', DPhil. thesis, Oxford 1989

Lee, Colin, 'Charles II and the Destruction of the Earl of Clarendon', paper delivered at Cambridge, 10 November 1993

Maloy, Jason, 'Representation in English Political Thought 1660–1678', MPhil. thesis, Cambridge 1997

Morrill, John, 'The Case of the Armie Truly Re-Stated', draft article

Morrill, John and Baker, Philip, 'Oliver Cromwell, the Regicide, and the Sons of Zeruiah', paper given at Downing College, Cambridge, February 1999

Norbrook, David, 'Lucy Hutchinson and the Historiography of the English Revolution', paper given at Keele, 13 March 1999

  'Writing the English Republic: Poetry, Rhetoric and Politics 1627–1660', manuscript submitted to Cambridge University Press, 1997

Parkin, Jon, 'Trespassing on the Territories of Malmesbury: Richard Cumberland's *De Legibus Naturae*', Ph.D thesis, Cambridge 1995

Peekna, Kalev P., 'British Aspects of English Political Culture 1660–1685', MPhil. thesis, Cambridge 1996

Remer, Gary, 'James Harrington's New Deliberative Rhetoric: Reflection of an Anticlassical Republicanism', draft article

Russell, Conrad, 'Parliaments and the English State at the End of the Sixteenth Century', first Trevelyan Lecture, Cambridge 1995

Salt, Peter, 'Charles I: A Bad King?', unpublished paper

Skinner, Quentin, 'The Liberty of the Subject', lecture given at Keele University, 12 March 1999

Smith, Hannah, 'Images of Charles II', MPhil. thesis, Cambridge 1998

Walker, J., 'The Republican Party in England from the Restoration to the Revolution', Ph.D thesis, Manchester 1930

Ward, Ian, 'The English Peerage 1648–1660', Ph.D thesis, Cambridge 1989

Index

English republic, 235–6, 267, 276
  anti-monarchism, 306–13
  Council of State, 298, 326
  difficulties of, 308–9
  military power, 309–10, 312, 397
  see also Protectorate
English republicanism, 6, 37–8, 75–80,
    230, 234, 326, 425, 433, 441, 446
  and classical republicanism, 291–4,
    296, 310, 318
  and education, 310–11
  failure of, 347–8, 411
  historiography of, 230, 232, 290–4,
    295, 346
  and innovation, 235–6
  intellectual origins, 243–4, 294–7
  and Machiavelli, 306–11, 323
  and monarchy, 297, 299–316
  moral philosophy of, 291–2, 296,
    317–24, 334–41, 343, 377, 387
  and political theory, 245–6, 288
  and practice, 295, 296, 297–9
  and radicalism, 354
  and religion, 295
  and statebuilding, 306, 399
  survival of, 346, 494–6
  see also English republic
English revolution, 29, 47, 118, 134
  defeat of, 267–8, 289
  intellectual context, 242–5
  intellectual impact of, 39, 343, 388,
    493–4
  lack of institutional basis, 34–5
  legacy of, 493–6
  modern views of, 22–4, 33–4
  moral aspirations of, 158–9, 230,
    231–2, 243–4, 493, 494
  origins of, 236, 237
  political theory, 245–6
  and radical change, 7, 231, 243
  sectarianisation of, 237–9, 290
  shape of, 239–42
  substance of, 230, 231, 234, 236, 238,
    239, 243
  three phases of, 6
Enlightenment, 6, 38, 343
episcopacy, 144, 236, 374, 408, 420
equality, 276, 282, 343
Essex, earl of, 200, 203, 204, 432, 446

Europe, 6, 23, 38, 56–7, 134, 157, 225,
    371
  attitudes to, 477–9
  counter-reformation, 30, 66, 69, 70,
    99–103, 117, 131, 132
  military growth, 81
  monarchy, 82, 83, 303, 304, 351, 353
  population increase, 81
  religious wars, 11, 28–30, 48, 54–5,
    81, 82, 84, 90, 92–3, 98–101, 137,
    141–2, 393
  statebuilding, 5, 53, 58, 67, 80–4, 114,
    116, 117, 118, 391–2
  towns, 85–6
  see also European context
European context, 4–5, 6, 10–16, 21, 24,
    27–33, 54ff., 58, 65, 66–7, 71, 85,
    112, 204, 428, 477–9
  of British rebellions, 27–8, 136
  of Caroline statebuilding, 114–18
  of civil war radicalism, 37
  of Dutch invasion, 214, 218, 456–61
  of glorious revolution, 206, 207,
    209–11, 213ff., 455
  and religious wars, 28–30, 136–42,
    151
  of restoration, 161, 166–70, 171
Evelyn, John, 210, 215, 220, 392
Exchequer, 402, 484
excise, 401, 402, 404, 414, 485, 486
exclusion crisis, 5, 25, 189, 198, 223
executions, 47, 186, 224, 381, 418, 443
exiles, 204, 221, 298, 351, 365, 366–71,
    417–18
experience, 328, 331

Fagel, Caspar, 456, 460
Fairfax, Thomas, 152
'fanatic plot' (1683), 444, 445–9
fanaticism, 209, 433, 442, 443, 445
  see also 'fanatic plot' (1683)
fears, 30, 55–7, 69, 89, 146, 166, 167
  religious, 89–94
  see also arbitrary government;
    popery
Fell, bishop, 442
Ferdinand II of Hapsburg, 28, 53, 99,
    102, 103, 117, 118, 131
Ferguson, Robert, 379